Visual C++ 6
from the Ground Up

About the Author...

John Mueller is a freelance author and technical editor. He has writing in his blood, having produced 40 books and almost 200 articles to date. The topics range from networking to artificial intelligence and from database management to heads-down programming. Some of his current books include a Visual Studio programmer's guide and a Windows NT Web server handbook. His technical editing skills have helped over 22 authors refine the content of their manuscripts, some of which are certification related. In addition to book projects, John has provided technical editing services to both *Data Based Advisor* and *Coast Compute* magazines. A recognized authority on computer-industry certifications, he's also contributed certification-related articles to magazines like *Certified Professional Magazine*.

When John isn't working at the computer, you can find him in his workshop. He's an avid woodworker and candle maker. On any given afternoon, you can find him working at a lathe or putting the finishing touches on a bookcase. One of his newest craft projects is glycerin-soap making, which comes in pretty handy for gift baskets. You can reach John on the Internet at **jmueller@mwt.net.** John is also setting up a new Web site at: **http://www.mwt.net/~jmueller/**. Feel free to take a look and suggest ways that he can improve it.

Visual C++ 6
from the Ground Up

John Paul Mueller

Osborne/**McGraw-Hill**

Berkeley   New York   St. Louis   San Francisco
Auckland   Bogotá   Hamburg   London   Madrid
Mexico City   Milan   Montreal   New Delhi   Panama City
Paris   São Paulo   Singapore   Sydney
Tokyo   Toronto

Osborne/**McGraw-Hill**
2600 Tenth Street
Berkeley, California 94710
U.S.A.

For information on translations or book distributors outside the U.S.A., or to arrange bulk purchase discounts for sales promotions, premiums, or fund-raisers, please contact Osborne/**McGraw-Hill** at the above address.

Visual C++ 6 from the Ground Up

34567890 AGM AGM 901987654321098

ISBN 0-07-882506-7

Publisher
Brandon A. Nordin

Editor-in-Chief
Scott Rogers

Acquisitions Editor
Wendy Rinaldi

Project Editors
Nancy McLaughlin
Betsy Manini

Editorial Assistant
Debbie Escobedo

Technical Editor
Greg Guntle

Copy Editor
Kathryn Hashimoto

Proofreader
Stefany Otis

Indexer
David Heiret

Computer Designers
Michelle Galicia
Jani Beckwith

Illustrator
Brian Wells

Cover Design
John Nedwidek

Dedication

This book is dedicated to my great-aunt Elise. She's the kind of person that everyone remembers in the kindest way, and she had a significant impact on my life as well. I'll always remember that she thought I would succeed in whatever I set my mind to do.

Contents at a Glance

Contents

Acknowledgments

Thanks to my wife, Rebecca, for working with me to get this book completed. I really don't know what I would have done without her help in researching and compiling some of the information that appears in this book (especially the Glossary). She also did a fine job of proofreading my rough draft and page proofing the final result.

Greg Guntle deserves thanks for his technical edit of this book. He greatly added to the accuracy and depth of the material that you see here.

Matt Wagner, my agent, deserves credit for helping me get the contract in the first place and for taking care of all the details that most authors don't really think about.

The technical support staff at Microsoft deserves credit for answering the questions that helped fill in the blanks and made the Visual C++ learning experience go faster. Likewise, I'd like to thank the people on the various Internet newsgroups that I visited who helped provide insights into C++ programming techniques. Especially important were the tips on how to work with OLE-DB and ADO.

Finally, I would like to thank Wendy Rinaldi, Nancy McLaughlin, Kathryn Hashimoto and the entire Production staff at Osborne for their assistance in bringing this book to print. I especially appreciate Wendy's patience when things didn't go exceptionally well.

Introduction

Anyone who has used Microsoft Visual C++ over the years will attest to the enormous amount of change that has occurred in this product. Microsoft has gone to great lengths to make the latest version of Visual C++ easier to use. However, for the Visual C++ programmer, writing programs is still more art than science. Just about the time that Microsoft creates a new Wizard to take the mystery out of one area of programming (like the updated ATL Wizard in this version of Visual C++), some new technology comes along to put the mystery right back in (like OLE-DB and ADO support).

Change is also the reason that you need yet another C++ book. Microsoft is constantly adding new features to Visual C++. While this book won't tell you much about basic C++ programming from a theoretical perspective, it will tell you how to use the new features that Microsoft has added in. For example, you'll find a lot of ActiveX and other Internet-related features in recent releases of this product. The Internet has played a more predominant role with every release of the product, and the 6.x version isn't any different. It's the quest for speed that's driving use of Visual C++ in certain Internet components. Downloading a large application from the Internet isn't a choice; users want small, fast applications. Sound familiar? We'll be spending a lot of time looking at how you can use Visual C++ to its best advantage within today's Internet-driven programming environment.

ActiveX is just one method of interacting with the user and distributing applications on the Internet. It gives the webmaster a lot more in the way of tools to dazzle potential visitors. In many cases, you get all of these capabilities without writing a single line of script. Obviously, the first question is, "Who cares?" The answer is all those companies that are trying to develop intranet or Internet sites. A recent survey showed that 48 percent of the companies responding are implementing applications on the Internet today. Another 14 percent said they planned to do so within the next six months, and 16 percent planned to do so within a year (for a total of 78 percent). Obviously there's more than a little interest in Internet applications.

This version of Visual C++ also includes support for adding a browser right into your application. You can use this browser support for a variety of purposes including placing help files on your Web server so that people can access them wherever they may be. Just think about the advantages of adding a help desk view into your application. The reduction in support calls alone makes such an addition worth the effort. This same browser support can provide a method for employees on the road to upload information to the company and to download things like the most recent sales statistics and brochures.

Why is the Internet such a hot environment? Another survey asked businesses why they would use the Internet to provide some kind of value-added service or better access to information by employees. Seventy-nine percent of the people surveyed cited ease of use. All you need to access the vast quantity of information on the Internet is an ISP (Internet Service Provider) and a browser. The browser is no more difficult to install than any other Windows application—sometimes even less. In addition, a number of ISPs supply installation programs that are so automatic, the user doesn't have to do much more than supply a name, address, and some billing information like a credit card number. For example, the Pacific Bell installation program that I recently tried automatically created the connection I needed under Windows 95, dialed their local Web site to help me find the best access number, and performed a setup by checking another Web site.

Microsoft is capitalizing on some of these statistical reasons for using the Internet by adding distributed database support to Visual C++. The OLE-DB and ADO coverage in this book will tell you how Microsoft has made it easier to create a connection to your database regardless of where that database might be. You can even create a connection to it over the Internet if the provider for your OLE-DB connection allows you to do so.

Obviously, if ease of use was the only reason to use the Internet, many companies would have more than enough reason to do so. However, there are other reasons that came out of the survey, including ease of availability (69 percent), use of existing infrastructure (65 percent), cost (51 percent), and ease of maintenance (36 percent)—the survey allowed the reader to select more than one answer in this area. The Internet provides a central repository of information and is probably the best way for most companies to give ready access to company databases to distant employees.

Any programmer will tell you that just getting the code to work usually isn't enough to consider the application written. There are many aesthetic considerations as well. For example, you can write code that executes fast or reduces the final size of the executable code. In fact, writing small, tight code is the mark of an expert programmer. It's such an important goal that entire books have been written to show how to get the very most out of every line of code.

The choice of programming language defines the kinds of things a programmer can do within an application and how fast he or she can do them. Visual C++ is known for its outstanding flexibility: you can literally do anything with it without contorting your code into a mass of spaghetti. C++ is also known for creating very fast applications when used correctly. However, this very flexibility and speed often gets the novice programmer into trouble and can create situations where subtle bugs creep in. Many opponents of Visual C++ also point to the long development times when using this language—a fact not lost on users of RAD (rapid application development) languages like Visual Basic.

Some people have been going so far as to say that the days of C++ are numbered. Fast machines don't require code that's as small and fast as before. In addition, as applications become more complex, getting an application completed in a reasonable amount of time is essential. The long development and debug cycles for C++ applications really don't seem to fit into today's application programming environment.

Fortunately for C++ programmers, there are some kinds of programming that RAD languages will never replace. Even if RAD languages have replaced C++ for some types of applications, programmers will still need to write small, tight code when it comes to operating system services or device drivers. Code that gets used over and over again to perform relatively low-level tasks is still the domain of the C++ programmer.

What's in This Book

Now that I've piqued your curiosity a bit, let's look at what this book has to offer. There are four main points of emphasis: general application programming, Internet-related programming, database programming, and application packaging. We'll also spend a little time with the basics. For example, we'll look at what this latest version of Visual C++ has to offer in the way of interface elements and new programming features.

The general programming section of this book will show you how to create some basic applications using the MFC AppWizard. We won't spend a lot of time looking at the details of creating specific kinds of applications, but you will see how to create the various application types that the MFC AppWizard can provide. Obviously, I'm assuming a certain amount of C++ programming experience on your part in this section. Sure, we'll cover all of the details of creating the application itself, but you should have some idea of how to use C++ in general, especially the language elements.

The database programming examples will provide a wealth of information to someone who already knows a few of the basics of working with databases. If you don't understand what tables are and have a fairly firm grasp of relational theory, you might want to spend a little time looking at these topics before delving into the material provided in Part II of the book. We will look at some of the basic skills required to use C++ to work with databases. You'll also gain an understanding of the differences between ODBC (Open Database Connectivity), OLE-DB (object linking and embedding database), ADO (ActiveX Data Objects), and DAO (Data Access Objects). We'll even spend a chapter each on ODBC and ADO database programming.

Internet programming coverage actually begins in Part I of the book. We'll look at how you can create an HTML-based application. In Part II I'll discuss how you can create a connection to your database over the Internet, but we won't look at any actual example code. Part III is where the main Internet coverage appears. We're going to look at ActiveX programming from the intermediate programmer level. If you're a novice programmer, you may find some of the concepts a little too difficult to understand. However, some sections, like Chapter 8 on HTML, will help just about anyone. In addition, Part III will show you how to work with ActiveX Documents, ISAPI Filters, and ISAPI Extensions.

In Part IV we'll talk about everything from security to putting together a help file. In fact, we'll look at two different techniques for using a help file under Visual C++: standard help files and the newer HTML help files that Microsoft is using in its products. You'll also get a chance to learn about getting your application distributed, which can be quite a task even in the corporate environment.

To use this book, you'll have to have an understanding of the C programming language, which doesn't mean that you'll need to be a C programming guru. You won't find much novice-level material in this book, but anyone with a reasonable amount of C programming skill will be able to figure out what's going on. Knowledge of Microsoft Visual C++ is highly recommended as well, since all of the examples use Visual C++ as their basis. Even though we go through a basic control programming example, a knowledge of writing OCXs or DLLs will also come in handy. You'll learn the information in this book a lot faster if you've gotten a little bit of lower-level programming under your belt before you begin. Again, there are some "refresher course"-style examples, but they don't provide a lot of novice-level information.

Of course, this is just an overview. You'll find that this book is packed with all kinds of useful tips and hints about using Visual C++ to its fullest.

What's New in This Edition?

There were three main sources for ideas for new content in this book. First, I spent a good deal of time reading all of the e-mail you sent me. Reader e-mail figures prominently in any book that I write since you're the ones using the material I provide. Second, Visual C++ itself provided some idea. I had to cover all of the new features that this product provides. Finally, I spent a lot of time on the various Visual C++ newsgroups looking at message threads. Some message threads appeared with great regularity, which pointed out areas that people are having trouble with when using Visual C++.

Chapter 1 is new for the most part. I've rewritten it to provide a complete overview of the new features that this version of Visual C++ provides. In addition, some elements in the chapter have been reformatted to present the information in a more readable form. I've tried to make better use of bulleted lists and tables so that you can find the information you need faster.

Some readers complained that I favored new language features in lieu of general programming in the previous edition of the book. You'll notice that I provided a lot more in the way of general application programming material in this edition. There are several new sections of material in Chapters 2 and 3, along with one new example program.

The database section of the book has been updated in a number of ways. Even though DAO is still a viable technology, it's on its way out. I've replaced the DAO sections of the book with the newer OLE-DB and ADO technologies. In addition, the database chapters have a stronger emphasis on how to make connections to your database through a Web server, rather than the more traditional network route.

The Internet section of the book contains information about new and updated technologies as well. For example, you'll find a discussion of COM+ in Chapter 8. I've also provided some information about the Active Template Library (ATL).

Some of the heaviest changes in the Internet section of the book appear in Chapter 13. Many of you expressed interest in finding out more about ISAPI and how you can use it to make your Web server more efficient. This chapter provides a lot more information about ISAPI and two new programming examples, including a second ISAPI Filter example that shows how to add security to your Web server.

Part IV of the book contains numerous changes, the most obvious of which is the inclusion of HTML-based help in Chapter 15. You'll not only learn how to create HTML-based help, but how to add it to your application as well. In addition to better help file information, you'll find updates on security and packaging methods. Overall, the updates in this section should help you provide much more in the way of application support to the people who use your applications.

What You'll Need

If all you're interested in is Parts I, II, and IV of this book, all you really need is a copy of Microsoft Visual C++ 6. You won't be able to use the older versions of the product in most cases because I plan to use new features in every example. (Visual C++ 5 may work marginally for some examples.) Make sure you also have the latest patches and service packs installed for whatever version of Windows you're using. I used the OSR2 version of Windows 95 and Windows NT 4 with service pack 3 installed while testing the examples for this book.

If you plan to work with the Internet Information Server (IIS) examples in Chapter 14, make sure you install Windows NT Server 4 and update it with service pack 3. You'll also need a copy of IIS 4.0 on your server. Some of the example code may not work at all with older versions of IIS. All of the examples in Chapter 14 assume you're using a full-fledged copy of IIS with all features installed, not one of the alternatives that you could potentially use for a Web server.

NOTE: Many of the concepts you'll learn in this book won't appear in your online documentation. Some of it is so new that it only appears on selected Web sites. You'll find either a tip or a note alerting you to the location of such information throughout the book. In addition, Microsoft made some material available only through selected channels like an MSDN subscription. Other pieces of information are simply undocumented, and you won't find them anywhere except within a newsgroup when someone finds the feature accidentally.

You'll also need a computer running Windows 95/98 or Windows NT 4.0 to use as a workstation. Both your Web server and workstation will require enough RAM and other resources to fully support the tools you'll need throughout this book. In most cases that means you'll need a minimum of a 200 MHz Pentium MMX computer with 64MB of RAM and at least 3GB of hard disk space. Even though you could potentially get by with less, you'll find that a lower-end computer will quickly bog down as you try to write code and test it. I did try running Visual C++ on a 166 MHz Pentium with 32MB of RAM and the performance was terrible.

Conventions Used in This Book

In this section we'll cover usage conventions. We'll discuss programming conventions a little later when we look at Hungarian Notation and how to use it. This book uses the following conventions:

[<Filename>]	When you see square brackets around a value, switch, or command, it means that this is an optional component. You don't have to include it as part of the command line or dialog field unless you want the additional functionality that the value, switch, or command provides.
<Filename>	A variable name between angle brackets is a value that you need to replace with something else. The variable name you'll see usually provides a clue as to what kind of information you need to supply. In this case, you'll need to provide a filename. Never type the angle brackets when you type the value.

ALL CAPS	There are three places you'll see ALL CAPS: commands, filenames, and case-sensitive registry entries. Normally you'll type a command at the DOS prompt, within a PIF file field, or within the Run dialog field. If you see all caps somewhere else, it's safe to assume that the item is a case-sensitive registry entry or some other value like a filename.
File | Open	Menus and the selections on them appear with a vertical bar. "File | Open" means "Access the File menu and choose Open."
italic	There are three places you see italic text: new words, multi-value entries, and undefined values. You'll always see a value in italic whenever the actual value of something is unknown. The book also uses italic where more than one value might be correct. For example, you might see FILE*xxxx*0 in text. This means that the value could be anywhere between FILE0000 and FILE9999.
monospace	It's important to differentiate the text that you'll use in a macro or type at the command line from the text that explains it. This book uses monospaced type to make this differentiation. Every time you see monospaced text, you'll know that the information you see will appear in a macro, within a system file like CONFIG.SYS or AUTOEXEC.BAT, or as something you'll type at the command line. You'll even see the switches used with Windows commands in this text. There is another time you'll see monospaced text. Every code listing uses monospaced code to make the text easier to read. Using monospaced text also makes it easier to add things like indentation to the coding example.

Icons

This book contains many icons that help you identify certain types of information. The following paragraphs describe the purpose of each icon.

NOTE: Notes tell you about interesting facts that don't necessarily affect your ability to use the other information in the book. I use note boxes to give you bits of information that I've picked up while using Visual C++, Windows NT, or Windows 95.

 TIP: Everyone likes tips, because they tell you new ways of doing things that you might not have thought about before. Tip boxes also provide an alternative way of doing something that you might like better than the first approach I provided.

 CAUTION: This means watch out! Cautions almost always tell you about some kind of system or data damage that'll occur if you perform a certain action (or fail to perform others). Make sure you understand a caution thoroughly before you follow any instructions that come after it.

 WEB LINK: The Internet contains a wealth of information, but finding it can be difficult, to say the least. Web Links help you find new sources of information on the Internet that you can use to improve your programming or learn new techniques. You'll also find newsgroup Web Links that tell where you can find other people to talk with about Visual C++. Finally, Web Links will help you find utility programs that'll make programming faster and easier than before.

 PORTABILITY: Making sure your code will run in a variety of situations and on a variety of platforms is always a good idea. Whenever you see this icon, you'll learn about an issue that could affect your ability to move code or executable from one machine to another. Make sure you pay special attention to these icons if the ability to use your program on more than one machine type or in more than one operating system environment is important.

IN DEPTH

These boxes will contain additional information that you don't necessarily have to know to write a good program. The In Depth boxes will provide interesting material that an intermediate or advanced programmer will want to use to enhance the applications they create or their own personal productivity.

You'll also find a variety of margin notes in the book. They describe some bit of information you should remember before starting a procedure or performing other kinds of work. Margin notes also contain useful tidbits like the location of a file or something you should look for in an example program. In most cases margin notes are simply helpful nuggets of information you can use to improve your programming as a whole.

An Overview of Hungarian Notation

Secret codes—the stuff of spy movies and a variety of other human endeavors. When you first see Hungarian Notation, you may view it as just another secret code. It contains all the elements of a secret code including an arcane series of letters that you have to decode and an almost indecipherable result when you do. However, it won't take long for you to realize that it is other programmers' code that's secret, not the Hungarian Notation used in this book.

Hungarian Notation can save you a lot of time and effort. Anyone who has spent enough time programming realizes the value of good documentation when you try to understand what you did in a previous coding session or to interpret someone else's code. That's part of what Hungarian Notation will do for you—document your code.

An understanding of Hungarian Notation will also help you gain more insight from the examples in this book and from the Microsoft (and other vendor) manuals in general. Just about every Windows programming language vendor uses some form of Hungarian Notation in their manuals. In addition, these same concepts are equally applicable to other languages like Visual FoxPro, Delphi, and Visual Basic. The codes remain similar across a variety of programming languages, even when the language itself doesn't.

So what precisely is Hungarian Notation? It's a way of telling other people what you intend to do with a variable. Knowing what a variable is supposed to do can often help explain the code itself. For example, if I tell you that a particular variable contains a handle to a window, then you know a lot more about it than the fact that it is simply a variable. You can interpret the code surrounding that variable with the understanding that it's supposed to do something with a window.

The first stage of development for this variable-naming system was started by Charles Simonyi of Microsoft Corporation. He called his system Hungarian Notation, so that's the name we'll use here. There are many places where you can obtain a copy of his work, including BBSs and some of the Microsoft programming Web sites on the Internet. (Many online services like CompuServe also carry copies of Hungarian Notation in its various incarnations.) Simonyi's work was further enhanced by other developers. For example, Xbase programmers use their own special version of Hungarian Notation. It takes into account the different types of variables that Xbase provides. An enhanced Xbase version of Hungarian Notation was published by Robert A. Difalco of Fresh Technologies. You can find his work on a few DBMS-specific BBSs as well as the Computer Associates Clipper forum on CompuServe.

The basis for the ideas presented in this section is found in one form or another in one of the two previously mentioned documents. The purpose in publishing them here is to make you aware of the exact nature of the conventions I employ and how you can best use them in your own code. There are four reasons why you should use these naming conventions in your programs.

◆ *Mnemonic Value*   This allows you to remember the name of a variable more easily, an important consideration for team projects.

◆ *Suggestive Value*   You may not be the only one modifying your code. If you're working on a team project, others in the team will most likely at least look at the code you have written. Using these conventions will help others understand what you mean when using a specific convention.

◆ *Consistency*   A programmer's work is often viewed not only in terms of efficiency or functionality but also for ease of readability by other programmers. Using these conventions will help you maintain uniform code from one project to another. Other programmers will be able to anticipate the value or function of a section of code simply by the conventions you use.

◆ *Speed of Decision*   In the business world, the speed at which you can create and modify code will often determine how successful a particular venture will be. Using consistent code will reduce the time you spend trying to decide what someone meant when creating a variable or function. This reduction in decision time will increase the amount of time you have available for productive work.

Now that I've told you why you should use Hungarian Notation, let's look at how I plan to implement it in this book. I'll use the rules in the following section when naming variables. You'll also see me use them when naming database fields or other value-related constructs. Some functions and procedures will use them as well, but only if Hungarian Notation will make the meaning of the function or procedure clearer.

Rule 1: Prefixing a Variable

Always prefix a variable with one or more lowercase letters indicating its type. In most cases this is the first letter of the variable type, so it's easy to remember what letter to use. The following examples show the most common prefixes for Visual Basic, Delphi, and C. (There are literally hundreds of combinations used in Windows that don't appear here.) You'll also see a few database-specific identifiers provided here:

a	Array
c	Character
d	Date
dbl	Double
dc	Device Context
dw	Double Word
f	Flag, Boolean, or Logical
h	Handle
i	Integer
inst	Instance
l	Long
li	Long Integer
lp	Long Pointer
msg	Message
n	Numeric
o	Object
pal	Palette
psz	Pointer to a Zero Terminated String
ptr	Pointer (or P when used with other variables like psz)
r	Real

rc	Rectangle
rgb	Red, Green, Blue (color variable)
rsrc	Resource
sgl	Single
si	Short Integer
sz	Zero Terminated String
u	Unsigned
ui	Unsigned Integer or Byte
w	Word
wnd	Window

Rule 2: Identifying State Variables

Some variables represent the state of an object like a database, a field, or a control. They might even store the state of another variable. Telling other programmers that a variable monitors the current state of an object can help them see its significance within the program. You can identify state variables using one of the following three-character qualifiers:

New	A New state
Sav	A Saved state
Tem	A Temporary state

Rule 3: Using a Standard Qualifier

A standard qualifier can help someone see the purpose of a variable almost instantly. This isn't the type of information that the variable contains, but how it reacts with other variables. For example, using the Clr qualifier tells the viewer that this variable is used in some way with color. You can even combine the qualifiers to amplify their effect and describe how the variable is used. For example, cClrCrs is a character variable that determines the color of the cursor on the display. Using one to three of these qualifiers is usually sufficient to describe the purpose of a variable. The following standard qualifiers are examples of the more common types:

Ar	Array
Attr	Attribute
B	Bottom

Clr	Color
Col	Column
Crs	Cursor
Dbf	Database File
F	First
File	File
Fld	Field
L	Last/Left
Msg	Message
Name	Name
Ntx	Index File
R	Right
Rec	Record Number
Ret	Return Value
Scr	Screen
Str	String
T	Top
X	Row
Y	Column

Rule 4: Adding Descriptive Text

Once you clearly define the variable's contents and purpose, you can refine the definition with some descriptive text. For example, you might have a long pointer to a string containing an employee's name that looks like this: lpszEmpName. The first two letters tell you that this is a long pointer. The second two letters tell you that this is a zero (or null) terminated string. The rest of the letters tell you that this is an employee name. (Notice that I used the standard qualifier, Name, for this example.) Seeing a variable name like this in a piece of code tells you what to expect from it at a glance.

Rule 5: Creating More Than One Variable

There are times when you won't be able to satisfy every need in a particular module using a single variable. In those cases you might want to create more than one of that variable type and simply number them. You could also designate its function using some type of number indicator like those shown here:

1,2,3	State pointer references as in cSavClr1, cSavClr2, etc.
Max	Strict upper limit as in nFldMax, maximum number of Fields
Min	Strict lower limit as in nRecMin, minimum number of Records
Ord	An ordinal number of some type

PART I

Visual C++ Basics

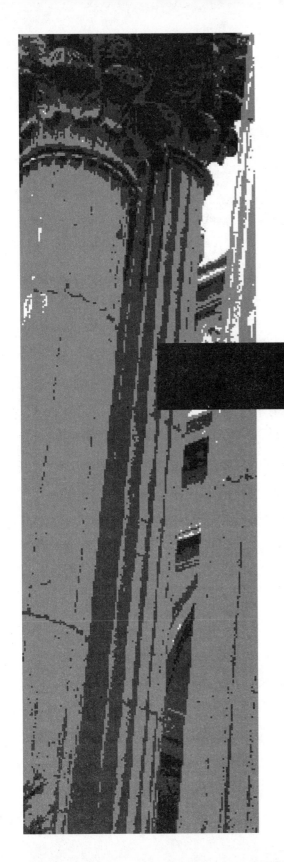

CHAPTER 1

An Introduction to
Visual C++

Only real programmers use Visual C++. Then again, maybe not. It seems that recently a lot of professional programmers have given up totally on this language and moved to the RAD environments provided by other products. Visual C++ is viewed by many as too old, too cumbersome, and simply too difficult to learn.

It's true that Visual C++ does have a more significant learning curve than other languages do. The fact that you can easily introduce subtle bugs that take hours to troubleshoot later on doesn't help programmer productivity one iota.

However, let's put those negatives aside for a moment and look at some of the good things that Visual C++ has to offer. One of the very best reasons to use C++ at all is flexibility. You have total control over your programming environment. Other languages tend to protect the programmer, which can be a very good thing when time is of the essence. Unfortunately, that protection can get in the way, and that's when you need something like C++ to cut through the red tape to get the job done.

Visual C++ has also long enjoyed a reputation for creating small and efficient programs. A program you write using this language can operate at nearly the same speeds as one written in assembler, without all of the problems. C++ represents the halfway point between the vagaries of register-level programming that you'll find in assembler and the protected environments of languages like Pascal.

The fact that C++ is a great language for writing low-level code like operating systems, device drivers, and DLLs probably hasn't escaped your attention either. These three kinds of code still represent the major places where you'll find Visual C++ used. The small, fast code that Visual C++ produces is very much appreciated in the time-critical environment of an operating system.

So far I haven't told you anything that you haven't read a million times in other books. Let's look at something unique to this version of Visual C++. One of the latest features that Microsoft has added is better prototyping capabilities through the use of enhanced wizards. Now, this feature won't place Visual C++ on par with products like Visual Basic, but it does reduce the time required to get an application started—a welcome change. In addition, these enhanced wizards make Visual C++ much friendlier than before. (We'll explore the other new features for Visual C++ throughout the rest of this chapter.)

Visual C++ is also the ideal programming environment for writing ActiveX controls, along with IIS-specific code like ISAPI (Internet Server Application

Programming Interface) extensions and ISAPI filters. Even if other application programming belongs to the RAD programming environments, no one wants to take the time to download a bloated control from the Internet or saddle their Web server with a slow filter. Visual C++ produces the small executable that people really want. In addition, the added flexibility that Visual C++ provides actually makes writing these kinds of application easier. We'll spend some time looking at ActiveX controls in this book, so I won't go into much more detail now. I've also included examples of ISAPI extensions and ISAPI filters for those of you who work with Web servers.

Another area where Visual C++ excels is database programming. I'm not necessarily talking about writing a full-fledged inventory control system using Visual C++—that would really take a long time. However, Internet users do require access to the data contained in database managers. Visual C++ can provide the speed needed to get that information quickly without too much more programming than a RAD language would require.

Why Visual C++?

We've already looked at the general question of why you'd use C++ as a programming language. However, that doesn't tell you too much about why Visual C++ is the product you should use if you want to produce programs for Windows. The most basic reason is easy to understand: Since Microsoft is the maker of Windows, the people there have the best idea of how things work inside the operating system. You'll find this inside knowledge at work in the Windows API hooks found in the MFC (Microsoft Foundation Classes).

Visual C++ also offers many features that you may not find in other products. Even though you could get around any deficiencies in another product by building your own tools, why reinvent the wheel? The two features that we'll cover most in this book are database programming and ActiveX technologies including both controls and documents. We'll also treat other Internet-related topics like ISAPI and new application types like DHTML-based applications. Visual C++ enables you to access all of these technologies right out of the box without the need to purchase third-party products.

Longevity is another reason to use Visual C++. Some developers that I've talked with are concerned about the future of some companies in the computer industry. They worry that these companies may not be around later on to support the products they've created. A developer needs great support today and tomorrow. Since every implementation of C++ has small differences, especially if you use vendor-specific bells and whistles, it really pays to go with a product that you can depend on. Suffice it to say that Microsoft won't be going anywhere in the near future—so using its product means that you should always have an upgrade route to better products as they are released.

What's New in This Version?

The big word in programming these days is the Internet. Just about every product you'll pick up now has some new Internet-related widget, and Visual C++ is no exception. We'll examine the new (and updated) Internet-related features throughout the book. Table 1-1 contains a complete list of new features for Visual C++ and tells which editions contain these features (obviously, the Enterprise edition is the most complete). You'll also find an overview of Internet-specific features in paragraphs that follow so you can determine how Visual C++ will best serve your Internet, desktop, and database programming needs.

Feature	Learning (Standard) Edition	Professional Edition	Enterprise Edition
Active Template Library (ATL)	X[1]	X	X
Application distribution license	X	X	X
AppWizard and data sources	X	X	X
ASA400 database access through OLE-DB			X
AutoCompletion (automatic statement completion)	X	X	X
Client-server application development	\[2]	\	X
Code optimization and Profiler		X	X
Custom AppWizard creation		X	X
Data-bound controls (RemoteData)		X	X
Extended stored procedure wizard			X
InstallShield		X	X
Internet Information Server (IIS) 4.0			X

Visual C++ Feature Comparison by Edition

Table 1-1.

Feature	Learning (Standard) Edition	Professional Edition	Enterprise Edition
MFC data binding		X	X
MFC database classes (DAO, ODBC, and file I/O)	X	X	X
MFC database classes (OLE-DB and ADO); also referred to as OLE-DB Templates		X	X
Microsoft Transaction Server (MTS)			X
Proxy Server			X
Remote automation components			X
Remote Data Objects (RDO)		X	X
SNA Server			X
SQL database tools		X	X
SQL editing, debugging, and stored procedures debugging			X
SQL Server 6.5 Developer edition and service pack 3			X
Static linking to the MFC library		X	X
System Management Server (SMS)			X
TSQL debugging			X
Visual database tools		\	X
Visual modeler			X
Visual SourceSafe version control			X
Visual Studio Enterprise Edition (VSEE) solutions book			X

Visual C++
Feature
Comparison
by Edition
(*continued*)

Table 1-1.

[1]X indicates full compliance

[2]\ indicates partial compliance

The /GZ Compiler Option (Catch Release-Build Errors in Debug Build)

Ever run into a bug that's there in your release build (when you can't access the information required to catch it), but totally absent in your debug build? This compiler option is designed to help you around that problem. It allows you to use the /O1, /O2, /Ox, or /Og optimization switches, a source of many release-build problems. However, Visual C++ will ignore any #pragma optimization statements in your code, which means that you may not find all optimization bugs. The /GZ compiler option also performs the following three tasks:

◆ *Automatic initialization of local variables* Visual C++ will automatically initialize local variables to a value of OxCC. This means you'll be able to find uninitialized variables faster. It also allows you to find variables not normally pointed out with the C4700 or C4701 warning messages.

◆ *Function pointer call stack validation* Visual C++ checks each function to make sure it works properly with the stack. The ESP register value is checked on function exit to make sure that it's the same as on function entry. This check allows you to find mismatches between what the called function expects in the way of cleanup and what the calling function provides in the way of cleanup when used to call a function through a function pointer.

◆ *Call stack validation* Visual C++ checks the stack pointer (ESP register) at the end of each call to make sure it hasn't changed. This allows you to find errors in inline assembler routines or mismatches in function calls.

The _ _forceinline Keyword

This is a new version of the _ _inline keyword provided in previous versions of Visual C++. Placing functions inline eliminates function calling overhead by placing the called function directly within the calling function. You use it to enhance application speed. Unfortunately, using inline code also increases code size because the inline function will appear within the calling function each time the inline function is called.

Visual C++ normally performs a cost analysis of the inline function to see if it's actually worth the increase in code size to gain the speed advantage of using inline code. There are two situations where Visual C++ normally creates a separate copy of the inline function and calls it separately instead of using inline code: recursive function calls and functions that are referred to elsewhere in a translation unit.

The _ _forceinline keyword tells Visual C++ not to perform the normal analysis and to always use inline code. In other words, the programmer is taking responsibility for any large increases in code size that may result when using inline code in certain situations like recursive function calls. As a result, you have to use this new keyword with extreme care to ensure your code size remains manageable.

There are still some situations where the compiler still can't force inline code, even if you've used the _ _forceinline keyword. For example, you can't use inline code with the /Ob0 command line switch (the normal switch for debug builds). Another situation when you can't use inline code is if the called function has a variable list of arguments. Whenever the compiler runs into a situation where it can't force inline code, you'll get a level 1 warning message (number 4714).

ADO Data Binding

Microsoft is constantly trying to improve data access for its programming language products. ADO (ActiveX Data Objects) represents a new way to provide database access through the combination of data-bound ActiveX controls and an ADODC (ADO Data Control). The ADODC acts as a data source that defines where the information you want to display is stored and the requirements for accessing that data. You'll need to provide the ADODC with six pieces of information: OLE-DB provider name (like SQL Server), DSN (the data source name as specified in the ODBC applet of the Control Panel), user name, password, record source (usually a SQL query), and connection string. The ActiveX controls are used to display the contents of the data source.

ADO provides several advantages over previous database access methods. The following list will describe them for you.

◆ *Independently created objects* You no longer have to thread your way through a hierarchy of objects. This feature allows you to create only the objects you need, reducing memory requirements and enhancing application speed as a result.

◆ *Batch updating*   Instead of sending one change to the server, you can collect them in local memory and send all of them to the server at once. This results in improved application performance (because the update can be performed in the background) and reduced network load.

◆ *Stored procedures*   These procedures reside on the server as part of the database manager and are used to perform specific tasks on the dataset. ADO allows you to use stored procedures with in/out parameters and return value.

◆ *Multiple cursor types*   Essentially, cursors point to the data that you're currently working with. Theoretically, you can even use back-end-specific cursors.

◆ *Returned row limits*   You only get the amount of data you actually need to meet a user request.

◆ *Multiple recordset objects*   Allows you to work with multiple recordsets returned by stored procedures or batch processing.

◆ *Free threaded objects*   Enhances Web server performance.

There are two data-binding models used for ActiveX controls. The first, simple data binding, allows an ActiveX control like a text box to display a single field of a single record. The second, complex data binding, allows an ActiveX control like a grid to display multiple fields and records at the same time. Complex data binding also requires the ActiveX control to manage which records and fields are displayed, something that the ADODC normally takes care of for simple data binding.

Visual C++ comes with several ActiveX controls that support ADO, including these controls:

◆ DataGrid

◆ DataCombo

◆ DataList

◆ Hierarchical Flex Grid

◆ Date and Time Picker

ATL Composite Control

This feature will allow you to create a new ATL (Active Template Library) based control using other controls at your disposal. What you'll start out with is a dialog box that you can fill with Windows and ActiveX controls. The dialog box takes up the entire client area of your new control. You can create an ATL composite control using one of two wizards: ATL COM AppWizard or ATL Object Wizard.

The reason that most programmers will use this technology is to create a form that they can display as a single ActiveX control. For example, if you're currently forcing the user to download a form's worth of controls to display a Web page, you can reduce the complexity of the task using an ATL composite control. The user will need to download only one control once you make the change. Not only will this make the download quicker, but you'll reduce user frustration as well (the whole control will download or it won't—no more partial form downloads).

AutoCompletion

The AutoCompletion feature helps complete statements in your C++ header and source code files for you. What you'll see is a list box with possible completion lines. For example, consider the following code:

```
CString      oMyString;

oMyString.
```

As soon as you type the period for oMyString, you'll see a list box containing the various methods and properties associated with a CString object. At this point, you could simply scroll down to the method or property you wanted to use and click on it. As an alternative, you could type the first few letters of the method or property that you wanted to use; the list will scroll to show you methods and properties of that name. Once you do select a method or property, Visual C++ will automatically type the name of the method or property you want to use. The result is that you'll spend a whole lot less time tracking down typos and more time coding.

 TIP: If you lose the AutoCompletion list box, right-click next to the place it originally appeared and choose List Members from the context menu. The list box will reappear.

Now, let's say that you're looking through the AutoCompletion list and aren't sure about the limitations of the AnsiToOem() method of the CString object.

If you highlight this item and then position your mouse over it, what you'll see is some balloon help telling you there is a 255 character maximum. This form of balloon help is another new Visual C++ feature, called Doc Comments.

Not only do Doc Comments come as part of the Visual C++ package, you can add them to your functions and variables as well. All you need to do is add a comment either before the function or variable declaration, or on the same line as the declaration. You can use this feature to tell someone all about a function or variable that you've provided. Obviously, you don't want to make this comment too large. Microsoft places a 12-line limit on Doc Comments, which should be sufficient for most purposes.

Doc Comments aren't limited to the AutoCompletion list box. Try positioning your mouse over a variable or function. What you'll see is the same balloon help that Doc Comments provides within the AutoCompletion list box. As you can see, Doc Comments is a very fast way to provide continuous documentation for your application and makes it less likely that someone will have trouble using the code that you've designed.

ClassView and WizardBar Improvements

Microsoft has provided some new features for both ClassView and WizardBar. The following list tells you about them.

◆ *Delete member function*   You now have the ability to remove a member function with a lot less work. All you need to do is place the cursor anywhere within the member function, and choose Delete from the WizardBar Actions drop-down list box or Delete Function on the Message Maps tab of the ClassWizard dialog box. In either case, Visual C++ will remove the function declaration from the header file and comment out the function body from the source code. This allows you to recover the function later if you decide you need it after all.

◆ *Go to Dialog Editor*   This option is available only when you're creating an application with a dialog box. Select the class containing the dialog box, and then choose the Go to Dialog Editor option from the WizardBar Actions drop-down list box.

◆ *New form*   Adds a new form class to your project. What you'll see is a New Form dialog where you'll choose the form name, its base class (the most common being CDaoRecordView, CFormView, CDialog, and CRecordView), and a resource ID. The base class choices that you'll see are partly dependent on the type of application you're creating and any

You can also access the New Form dialog box using the Insert I New Form command.

choices you made when using the application wizard. In some cases, you'll also get to choose the level of automation and provide document template information. Visual C++ will gray these options in the New Form dialog box when they're not available.

◆ *Empty class tracking*   The WizardBar now tracks all classes, even those without member functions. The Members combo box on the WizardBar will display "No Members - Create New Class" if you choose a class without members. The default WizardBar action is to add a new member function to empty classes.

Command-Line Builds

Visual C++ provides a new MSDEV utility that allows you to build projects at the command line without exporting a MAKE file first, and then using the NMAKE utility. The syntax for the MSDEV utility is as follows:

```
MSDEV <Filename> [/MAKE "<Project Name> - <Configuration Name> |
ALL"] [/REBUILD /CLEAN /NORECURSE /OUT <Log File> /USEENV]
```

You must provide a DSP (project) or DSW (workspace) filename. The following list describes the optional command line switches.

◆ */MAKE*   Allows you to define which project and configuration to make. The project name is always the name that you've given the project during the creation process. The configuration name can be either something specific like Win32 Debug or all of the available configurations (using the ALL keyword). Visual C++ allows multiple /MAKE arguments on a single command line, so you can create any number of configurations.

◆ */REBUILD*   Clears all intermediate files before beginning the compile. It then builds the new intermediate files. This ensures that you get a completely clean build.

◆ */CLEAN*   Clears all intermediate files before beginning the compile, but doesn't rebuild them.

◆ */NORECURSE*   Builds the current project but not any dependent projects.

◆ */OUT <Log File>*   Redirects the output from the screen to a log file. The log file allows you to analyze build errors and correct them.

◆ */USEENV*   Ignores the tools.options.directories settings found in the DSW or DSP file and uses the current environment settings in their place. This allows you to override environment settings without reopening Visual C++, but it also means that you may introduce errors.

Compiler Throughput Improvements

Compiling projects with large PCH files will take less time. You'll also notice improvements in smaller projects, but the improvements are most noticeable with projects that use large PCH files.

Delay Load Imports

Normally, there are two choices when working with DLLs: you can automatically load them with the application or you can load and unload them manually as needed. The delay loads feature gives you a third option. It allows an application to load a DLL automatically when needed. This means that if a user doesn't require the services of, say, the spelling checker in your word processing application, then that DLL doesn't get loaded.

Using this feature doesn't require much extra work on your part. All that's required is that you add the /DELAYLOAD command line switch when linking your application and the DELAYIMP.LIB to the list of linked files.

Dynamic HTML

A new MFC class, CHTML, allows you to add a Dynamic HTML (DHTML) view to your application. What this class really gives you is the ability to add a Web browser to your application without a lot of extra programming. Obviously, since this is a Microsoft product, your Web browser will mimic the characteristics of Internet Explorer 4. This feature allows you to mix desktop and Internet applications in a way that's almost transparent to the user.

Dynamic Parsing

ClassView is now automatically updated as you type new class, function, and variable information into your application. This allows you to see changes to your application as you make them rather than waiting until you save the source file. It also means that elements like the WizardBar and ClassWizard are always up to date.

NOTE: There are currently some problems with this feature that Microsoft promises to fix by product release (at least as of this writing). For example, certain types of typos can cause Visual C++ to parse what you're trying to do incorrectly and the IDE will freeze as a result. In all cases, restarting the IDE will clear the problem.

The Edit and Continue Feature

The edit and continue feature will allow you to make small changes to your application while you're debugging it, without rebuilding the project from scratch. Not only will this make debugging faster, but you could perform "what-if" analysis on your application as well.

There are limitations to what you can do with edit and continue. Visual C++ will simply prompt you to rebuild your application if you exceed the bounds of what edit and continue can do for you. The following list provides some general guidelines on places where you can't use edit and continue.

◆ Header files
◆ Global/static data
◆ Class definitions and function prototypes
◆ Introduction of new variable types
◆ Exception handling blocks

The edit and continue feature is on by default, so you don't need to do anything special to use it. If you do want to turn the feature off, use the Tools | Options command to display the Options dialog. Select the Debug tab and uncheck the Debug Commands Invoke Edit and Continue Debugging option. You'll need to completely rebuild your project when turning this feature on or off.

The Extended Stored Procedure Wizard

Stored procedures allow you to manipulate database data in some way and provide a result as an output to the user. Visual C++ provides a new wizard that helps you create stored procedures for SQL Server. These stored procedures use a COM interface with a single function named the *extended stored procedure*. Once you register the extended stored procedure DLL on the

SQL Server, you'll be able to access the data that it retrieves using a standard COM interface.

New Debugger Features

Visual C++ provides a wealth of new debugger features that make it easier to find bugs in your application. Table 1-2 contains a complete list of these new features and provides an overview of each one.

Feature	Description
Auto expansion of VARIANTs and GUIDs	The AUTOEXP.DAT (auto-expand) file contains new rules that allow you to display VARIANTs and GUIDs in more meaningful ways. (The AUTOEXP.DAT file appears in the Program Files\Microsoft Visual Studio\Common\MSDev98\Bin directory on your hard drive.) For example, a VARIANT will now appear as the data type that it actually contains; a string will actually look like a string. In addition, Visual C++ will display the VARIANT type along with its value. GUIDs won't necessarily display as a string of numbers; Visual C++ will attempt to find the GUID name in the registry and display the name instead.
Debugger formatting symbols	Visual C++ sports a whole list of new debugger symbols: **,hr** displays 32-bit result or error codes as common COM return values like S_OK or E_NOTIMPL. If it can't display a precise error value, then Visual C++ will attempt to turn the return value into a comment like "Not enough memory." **,mq** allows you to display memory as four quadwords to compensate for 64-bit registers. **,st** displays strings in Unicode or ANSI format depending on the Unicode Strings setting in the AUTOEXP.DAT file. **,wc** displays numeric values as decoded Windows class flags (WC_ constants). **,wm** displays numeric values as decoded Windows message values (WM_ constants).

New Debugger Feature Overview

Table 1-2.

Feature	Description
Disassembler output	You'll see a lot more information in the disassembled output, including symbolic information when it is available.
Load COFF & Exports	You'll find this option on the Debug tab of the Options dialog (which you can access using the Tools | Options command). It allows you to load additional debugging information used by compilers other than Visual C++ (which uses CodeView format debug information). For example, Visual Basic provides Common Object File Format (COFF) debug information in the MSVBVM50.DBG file. The exports option comes into play when no other debugging information (at least that Visual C++ can recognize) is available. Visual C++ will load the contents of the Exports table of each DLL and attempt to convert it into symbolic information for debugging purposes.
Registers	There are several new registers that will help you to find out more about your application. The Thread Information Blocks (TIBs) pseudo-register that provides information about the current thread. The ERR pseudo-register displays the error code of the last error that occurred in your application. This register performs the same task as the GetLastError() function call. Adding the ,hr modifier to the ERR register tells it to display a 32-bit error code along with a comment like "Not enough memory." The 64-bit MMX register set now appears in both the Watch and Quick Watch windows. You'll see these registers displayed on all x86 machines even if they don't support the MMX instruction set.
Undecorated symbols	What this means in simple terms is that you'll no longer see long lists of meaningless garbage characters with function names hidden somewhere inside. In addition, all function names will include parameter information when it is available.
V-Table and Function Pointer display	Function pointers and virtual table entries are displayed as text entries (symbolically) which, whenever possible, include parameters instead of hex addresses.

New Debugger Feature Overview (*continued*)

Table 1-2.

OLE-DB Provider Templates

The OLE-DB provider templates allow you to develop OLE-DB access interfaces, essentially a remote connection to a database. The templates don't perform any magic; all they do is make accessing OLE-DB technology easier. OLE-DB is Microsoft's latest database technology. It's designed to provide high performance for database management systems (DBMS) that include an OLE-DB provider.

Resource Editor Improvements for Data-Bound Controls

The resource editor allows you to use all the latest ADO and OLE-DB technology to create connections to your database. You'll need to use the new ADODC data source control to create the connection. In addition, you must use the newer ADO compatible data-bound controls to display data. The only exception to this rule is simple bound controls, which you can use interchangeably with both the ADODC and MSRDC (Microsoft Remote Data Control) data source controls.

Wizard Support for DocObject Containment

The MFC AppWizard contains a new option in the third step, Active Document Container. This option is only available if you choose the Container or Both Container and Server compound document feature options.

Using DocObject containment (enabled with the Active Document Container option) allows you to use a single frame for all of the types of documents that your application supports instead of creating a separate frame for each one. To get a good idea of exactly how this technology works, check out the Microsoft Office Binder. Normally, OLE will allow you to interact with a single object within a compound document. The DocObject containment technology allows you to activate an entire document, including menus, toolbars, and other support features, within a single frame.

WizardBar Performance Improvements

Projects with a lot of dialogs and controls (as witnessed by large CLW files) used to slow to a crawl when WizardBar was visible in the dialog editor. Microsoft has taken steps to improve performance and reduce the impact WizardBar has on IDE performance.

A Few Gotchas

Like just about every other product on the market today, Visual C++ has a few gotchas that prevent it from working as it should (or at least as you expected). None of the gotchas (some people might call them bugs or unfortunate changes) I've found so far are so terrible that they prevent you from working, but they're a nuisance just the same. Microsoft is probably going to release one or more patch files for Visual C++ 6.0, so hopefully some of the things I'm going to talk about will be fixed by the time you read this. Even if it's obvious that Microsoft won't provide a workaround for the problem, you'll at least be aware that you have to make changes in your code to accommodate the new feature.

NOTE: This section isn't meant to be a bug list of everything that's wrong with Visual C++. It's more of a catalogue of fit-and-finish problems that'll be obvious to the casual observer and some of the ways you can work around them. Hopefully, Microsoft will get some of those deep, dark, hidden problems fixed as well—even if I don't cover them here.

The first thing that you'll notice is that InfoViewer has been replaced by a non-integrated help based on MSDN (Microsoft Developer Network). You'll still be able to highlight a command and receive help on it, but the non-integrated nature of MSDN means that the help you'll receive will be through an external program, which means that you'll use a lot of extra memory getting help now. In addition, the search capabilities of MSDN are a whole lot less useful than what you used to get with InfoViewer. MSDN doesn't provide all of the options that InfoViewer did. There are a lot of other problems with the MSDN-based help too, most of which are related to its reliance on a good Internet connection. On the whole you'll find that help in Visual C++ 6.0 has taken a giant leap backward—this really is one of the poorer decisions that Microsoft made regarding the product upgrade.

Another problem that you'll encounter is that not all of the programs copied into your Bin folder will appear as shortcuts in the Microsoft Visual C++ 6.0 folder in your Start menu. For example, you'll find that the Help Workshop shortcut is there, but the Hotspot Editor shortcut is not. We'll cover as many of these useful utilities as possible throughout the book so that you at least know they're there. Then you can add them to the Windows 95, Windows 98, or Windows NT Start menu for later use. Again, it's no big deal that some shortcuts are missing from the Start menu, but it makes you wonder how many other things Microsoft failed to mention in passing.

Probably as part of the scare about year 2,000 date problems, you can no longer use two-digit dates with COleDateTime. Even though the class may accept the two-digit date, subsequent calls to member functions like GetMonth or GetMinute will fail. This means that you, as a programmer, will have to rework all of those old programs. Otherwise, you could end up getting mysterious errors even though the program is written correctly.

While the interface itself isn't a bug per se, it's a cause for concern for people who use multiple languages. Microsoft is making a concerted effort to make the interfaces of all its language products the same, which means that except for language details, you could move from one environment to the next with very little training. The exception to this rule is Visual C++, which will retain the look it's had for quite some time now. Even though this means you won't have to learn a new interface right now, it also means that people using other Microsoft products will have to be retrained on the IDE before using Visual C++. Fortunately, Microsoft plans (at least according to the people I spoke with) to change this sometime in the near future.

Looking at the Interface Elements

Before we can do much programming together, I'd like to spend some time showing you the Developer Studio interface. That way, everyone will be using the same terminology. You may also learn about some new features that you haven't gotten to use in the past. For example, we'll take a look at the toolbars and some of the new features they produce. If you're an experienced Visual C++ user and really don't think you have anything new to learn about the interface, feel free to skip this section.

MFC Studio Window Elements

When you're editing a program with Visual C++, you can divide the display into three functional areas: toolbars, views, and editor window. Each area works independently of the others, so that you can move around as needed. Figure 1-1 shows a typical editor display and the locations of these three areas.

NOTE: We're going to talk about the various windows, views, and toolbars in this section. You'll find information about them in the sections that follow.

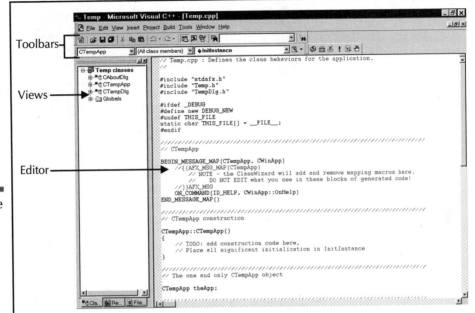

Toolbars

Views

Editor

You can divide the Developer Studio screen into three functional areas.

Figure 1-1.

There are two types of windows that you'll commonly run into: *text windows* and *resource windows*.

Figure 1-1 shows a typical text-editing window. Anytime you need to modify your code or view a text file, you'll see this kind of window.

Visual C++ uses a variety of methods to make your coding experience easier. The first thing you'll notice in the text window is that your code gets highlighted. For example, the default color for keywords is blue, while comments appear in green. Using color coding in this way helps you see the code for what it is.

Along the left edge of the text window you'll see a bar. This is where Visual C++ places various symbols, and you may even see it colored to differentiate between data and control areas of your code. For example, when you set a breakpoint in your code, Visual C++ displays a stop sign here. If the breakpoint is enabled, the stop sign is red; otherwise, it's white.

You can also right-click in various areas of the text window to display a context menu. The context menu contains options for the things you'll do on a regular basis—unlike other aspects of the Developer Studio interface; there isn't any straightforward way to modify it. Here's an example of the context menu you might see if you right-click in the text editor.

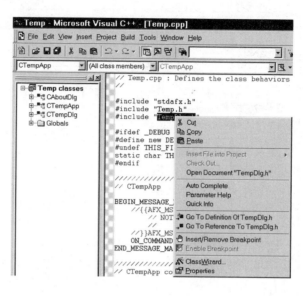

Notice that you can cut, copy, or paste text, just as in any editor. I've also highlighted an #include file entry, so the context menu gives you a chance to open it. If you hadn't already included this file in a project, the Insert File into Project option would give you a chance to do so. The Check Out option is used with team projects and allows you to take control of the file for a while so that you can edit it. The next three entries allow you to find out more about the current entry. For example, the Parameter Help option allows you to learn about the parameters associated with a function call, while Auto Complete helps you finish typing the function call. The next two entries are used for browsing your project. You can find where a particular entry is either referenced or defined. Since these entries rely on the BSC file created during a build of the project, you'll want to make sure you have a recent build available before using them. The next two entries, Insert/Remove Breakpoint and Enable Breakpoint, are for debugging your application. Finally, you can open the ClassWizard to work with the highlighted object some more (we'll do this a lot throughout the book) or view the properties for this document.

Our final window example is one of the ones you'll see when editing resources. Figure 1-2 shows a typical example, though the resource editing windows are far more varied than any other type that we've talked about so far. (Don't worry, we'll cover just about every kind of resource editor window somewhere in the book.)

In this case, we're looking at a dialog box. Notice that there are four controls, two of which are selected (you can see the sizing handles surrounding the

1

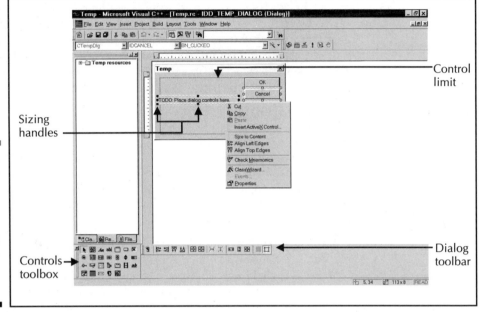

Control
limit

Sizing
handles

Controls
toolbox

Dialog
toolbar

There are a lot
of different
kinds of
resource
editing
windows—this
one shows a
dialog box.

Figure 1-2.

two selected controls). You should also see a faint line around the edge
of the dialog box (it's blue when using the default color settings). This line
determines the outer limit for all the controls you want to place on the
dialog box.

In the lower-left corner of Figure 1-2, you'll see the Controls toolbox. This
contains an assortment of controls you can place on the dialog box. If you
want to add a new control to the toolbox, use the Project I Add to Project I
Components and Controls command. Right next to the toolbox you'll see a
Dialog toolbar. It contains quite a few features that make it easier to line
things up on the dialog. For example, the Make Same Size button makes any
number of controls you've selected the same size as the first control. There's
also a Test pushbutton that allows you to see how the dialog box will look
when it's complete.

Let's talk about the context menu shown in Figure 1-2. Since we've already
talked about the majority of these options, let's look at the three most
important options. The Insert ActiveX Control option allows you to add an
ActiveX control to the dialog without actually adding it to the project. This
allows you to see how the control will work before you generate a lot of code
for it. Remember to add the control to the project later if you do decide to

use it. The Check Mnemonics option tells Visual C++ to look at all of the controls you've added and make sure that none of them have the same name or violate any rules. It's an important check to make once you have the dialog all put together. Finally, the Events option displays a dialog that tells you what events the selected object supports. The same dialog allows you to create a handler for any of the events that you want to monitor. We'll talk about how you can use this feature in Chapter 2.

ClassView

You'll probably spend most of your time with ClassView showing. This view provides a hierarchical listing of all the classes in your project. You can expand them to show what these classes contain. For example, your classes will contain member functions that you'll want to edit. Figure 1-3 shows a typical ClassView.

Notice that a special icon precedes each of the entries in the hierarchy. For example, each of the classes has a special class icon that looks like three boxes connected with lines. There are three kinds of member functions that ClassView will display. The first is the public member function, which uses a single purple box as an icon. The second is the private member function,

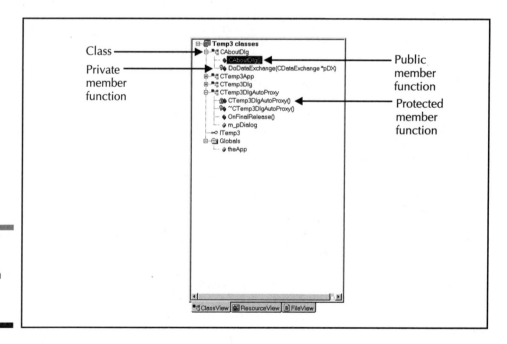

ClassView
shows all of
the classes in
your project.

Figure 1-3.

which uses the same purple box, but adds a key to the icon. The third is the protected member function, which has a purple box and lock icon. Likewise, there are three kinds of variables, all of which use turquoise icons. If you see a green box, you know that you're looking at a method for a COM object. There are a few other icon types, but these are the six that you really have to know in order to create most projects.

TIP: You can hide ClassView (or any of the other views, for that matter) by right-clicking in the ClassView window and then selecting Hide from the context menu. Use the View | Workspace command to display the ClassView window again.

ResourceView

ResourceView contains a hierarchical listing of all the resources in your project. Any graphic image, string value, toolbar, or other noncode element needed for the program to work could be considered a resource. Figure 1-4 shows a typical ResourceView window.

ResourceView provides a complete listing of all the resources required by your application.

Figure 1-4.

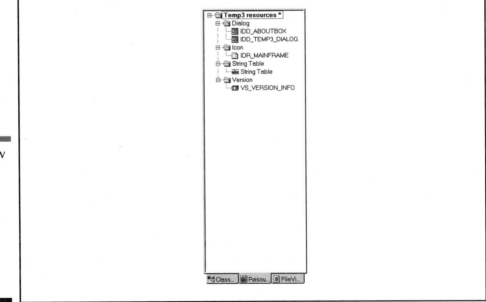

Each kind of resource you can create in Visual C++ has its own folder. If you don't use a particular resource, you won't see a folder for it. Within each folder you'll find the resources for your project. For example, the Dialog folder would contain all of the dialogs in your project, including the About box. Every resource also uses its own kind of icon.

T IP: Right-click the topmost folder in ResourceView and you'll see a context menu that gives you access to the two resource-specific dialogs: Resource Includes and Resource Symbols. Right-click on a specific resource folder and you'll get a context menu that includes special options for adding new resources of that type.

FileView

FileView contains a complete list of all of the files in your project, whether they include code or not. Figure 1-5 shows a typical example of what you'll

FileView contains a complete list of all the files in your projects—even if they don't contain any code or resources.

Figure 1-5.

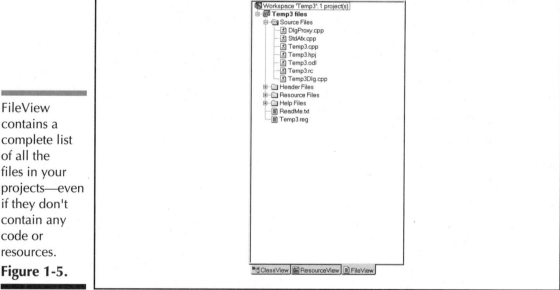

see in this window. Notice that it includes everything from source code files to the ReadMe.txt file that Visual C++ generates automatically for you.

Each file type normally has its own folder. For example, all of the source code files appear in the Source Files folder. Not only can you move files from folder to folder, you can also create new folders to hold specific types of files based on their extension. I often create a Text File folder to hold all of my TXT extension files. All you need to do to create a new folder is right-click on the folder or project entry where you want to add the folder, and then select New Folder from the context menu. You'll see a New Folder dialog like the one shown here. Just type the name of the folder and associated file extension, and then click on OK to complete the process.

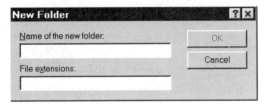

Toolbars

Toolbars are the final topic that we need to talk about when it comes to the Developer Studio interface. The first thing you should know is that Visual

C++ comes with a lot more toolbars than you'll see when you first start it up. Right-click anywhere in the toolbar area and you'll see a context menu like this one.

What you're seeing is a list of all the standard toolbars that Visual C++ provides. Any menu entries with a check mark next to them are currently displayed in the toolbar area. If you want to add a toolbar to the toolbar area, just click on its entry in the context menu. Likewise, to remove a toolbar, click on its entry again to remove the check mark.

Notice the Customize option on the context menu. Choose this option and you'll see a dialog like this one.

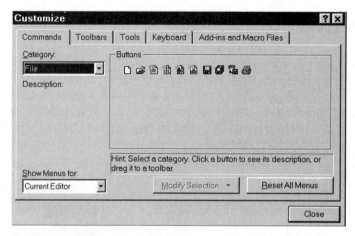

The Customize dialog contains pages that allow you to reconfigure most of the Developer Studio interface. However, we're most interested in the Commands tab. It contains a series of icons (which represent commands) or text commands for every menu and toolbar. If you want to add a command to one of the existing toolbars, just grab one of the icons (or text commands) and drag it over to the toolbar. The command you've selected will appear on the toolbar, making it a lot faster to access. If you select a command that doesn't already have an icon associated with it, you'll see a Button Appearance dialog that will allow you to select an icon for the command.

This same feature works with menus too. All you need to do is open the drop-down menu you want to change, grab the command you want to add from the Commands tab, and then drag it over to the position where you want to see it on the menu. In this case, you'll always see the text version of the command rather than an icon.

Removing unneeded commands from a toolbar or menu is just as easy. Simply grab the command you no longer want and drag it over to the Customize dialog. The command will disappear from the menu or toolbar, though it'll still be accessible anytime you want to add it back in.

You can also move toolbars around as needed to make space. Just click on what looks like a set of double bars at the left edge of the toolbar, and then drag it where you want it. Likewise, if you don't like the current position of a menu, just grab it (with the Customize dialog open) and move it where you want it.

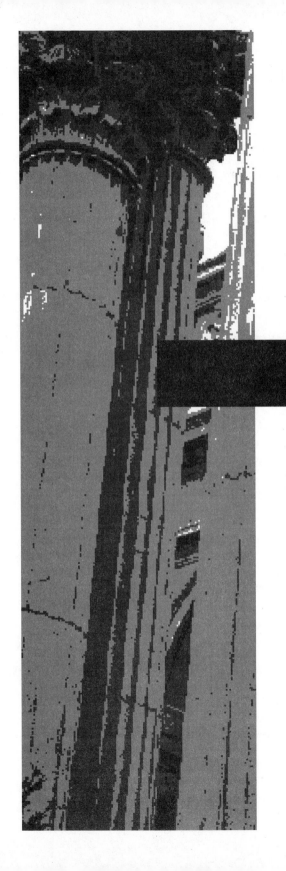

CHAPTER 2

Building a Basic Application

Learning a new language, or even updating your knowledge of a language you've used for a while, is almost never a picnic. The old language is comfortable and the new language will likely contain unfamiliar twists and turns that make using it uncomfortable at best. Yet, if you want to stay current in this business, you're going to have to learn that new language (or at least update your knowledge of the old one).

So, how do you get over the learning curve with the least amount of discomfort? Many programmers I know have a basic application they build to learn the language. In fact, really good programmers have several basic applications they call a "test suite," whose whole purpose in life is to teach and examine. The application may not be all that functional, though some form of functionality is a plus. Otherwise, you really don't know if you've succeeded in learning about the language after all.

This chapter is going to be your first exposure to programming in Visual C++ 6.0, since the last chapter looked at what you could expect from the product. Even if you're a C++ guru, you owe it to yourself to spend a little time "playing" with this new version of the product in order to understand how it can help you. Building this "test suite" will help you learn how to use Visual C++ and see what it can do for you.

Of course, we'll also spend some time making these sample programs at least marginally functional. In most cases, for simplicity, I'll leave the implementation of the full capabilities of the program to you. However, don't lose sight of the fact that the entire purpose of this chapter is play—when working with the samples starts to look too much like work, perhaps it's time to put them aside and get something really useful done.

WEB LINK: Any serious Visual C++ programmer will spend some time on the Internet learning about new programming techniques. Microsoft hosts a variety of Visual C++ newsgroups, some of which are quite specific. The most generic newsgroup is **microsoft.public.vc.language**. If you want to learn what's going on with ActiveX technology, you might want to look at **microsoft.public.vc.activextemplatelib**. A good place to look for database specifics is **microsoft.public.vc.database**. One of the most active newsgroups is **microsoft.public.vc.mfc**, which is devoted to working with the Microsoft Foundation Classes (MFC). However, there are two other MFC-related newsgroups: **microsoft.public.vc.mfc.docview** and **microsoft.public. vc.mfc.macintosh**. Finally, don't forget to check out the general windows programming groups located under the **microsoft.public.win32. programmer** folder (there is a whole list of programmer-related newsgroups, so you'll need to choose the ones that best suit your needs).

Understanding the Application Types

Visual C++ is quite capable of creating any application you can imagine (and perhaps a few that you can't). However, there are five application types that exemplify applications as a whole, and that's what we'll concentrate on first.

2

◆ Console applications represent those situations where you really need to maintain some type of compatibility with legacy systems or don't need a full-fledged interface for the user to work with.

◆ Dialog-based applications are normally reserved for utilities or an application that's too small to require a complete menuing system.

◆ Single-document applications are representative of simple applications that work with their own data like note takers or small database front ends. These applications also require a menuing system of some type.

◆ Multiple-document applications include full-fledged applications like word processors and spreadsheets. When you think about it, they represent that fringe area of C++ programming where you need to weigh the flexibility of C++ against the development speed offered by RAD programming environments like Visual Basic.

◆ HTML-based applications are new to Visual C++ 6.0. They're applications that work with data of some type (like single-document or multiple-document applications) but with an Internet twist. Instead of a standard editor, your user will see what amounts to a Web browser front end.

NOTE: Remember that we're talking about applications in this chapter. Visual C++ is capable of creating all kinds of different code. You can use it to create DLLs, ActiveX controls, ISAPI extensions, device drivers, background executing programs like screen savers, and even extensions to Visual C++ itself. We're only talking about general applications in this chapter, but we'll cover many of these other possibilities as the book progresses.

Console

I made some statements previously that gave you an overall sense of what a console application is, but they were too sweeping to really tell you what a console application is all about. A console application has a DOS window look rather than the more familiar Windows-style appearance. It uses a monospaced font, just like you would see in a DOS window, and you can use standard C functions for output like printf() and scanf(). However, internally, the program is a Windows application. Here's a typical example of a console application (we'll actually build this one later in the chapter).

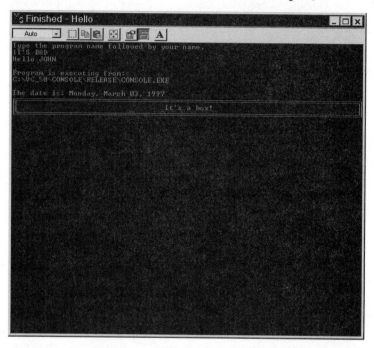

So, why would you want to create a crossbreed monstrosity like this? Say you have some old legacy code that works just fine, but it's built into a DOS application. You want to move the program to Windows but don't have the time to convert everything over to standard Windows calls. A console application provides a sort of middle ground. You can use that old code (at least part of it) but still execute the program within Windows.

There's another benefit to working with console applications. If you move your application from DOS to Windows, it's going to look different. There isn't any way around it; from a user perspective you may just as well introduce a totally different application. You're going to have to plan on retraining everyone and everything that entails. On the other hand, a console application will look enough like the DOS application everyone is used to using that you probably won't have much, if any, retraining. About the only thing you'll need to worry about is getting everyone used to running the application in a different way.

Don't get the idea, though, that a console application is the ideal setup for every DOS application you need to move to Windows. The bottom line is that you're going to create a new application either way. The only difference is the amount of code reuse and hence the amount of time it'll take to create the new application. In fact, when you think about it, if you decide to go the console application route, you'll eventually write two applications. Most companies find out that they eventually have to bear the cost of converting their DOS applications to Windows anyway.

Of course, you also have to ask yourself about the advisability of writing a console application when the DOS application will work just fine within a DOS window. Sure, a console application can use some Windows services, but you probably have all the services you need already built into the DOS application. (You'll have access to some MFC functions that could augment your application and make it easier to use.) The more you deviate from your original DOS application to add Windows-style bells and whistles, the less viable a console application becomes.

PORTABILITY: It's safe to assume that you'll be able to move the "business logic" of your DOS application to Windows using a console application. You may also be able to move some of the display and printing elements. However, it's never safe to assume that you'll be able to maintain one set of code for both DOS and Windows by using a console application— the two environments are different enough that you'll always have to make changes in the move from DOS to Windows.

Dialog Based

Many people associate dialogs with configuration screens, About boxes, and other adjuncts to a full-fledged application. Dialog-based applications have a place too. They're extremely useful for utility-type applications where you need to display a fairly minimal amount of data and require minimal user input. Here's an example of a dialog-based application that we'll build later in the chapter.

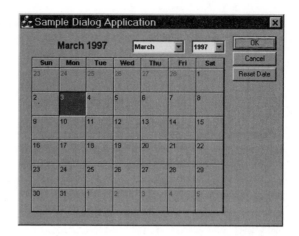

 TIP: When deciding whether to build a dialog-based or window-based application, think utility. If your application fits into the utility category, it's probably a good candidate for a dialog-based interface. On the other hand, if you're thinking about adding a lot of features or allowing the user to interact with the application heavily, you may want to look at a window-based interface. Make sure you take future expansion into account when making your decision—a bad choice today could cost you a lot in rework time tomorrow.

So, what makes a dialog-based application better than a full-fledged window-based application? One of the more important factors is size. You can create two versions of the same application, one that uses a dialog front end and another that depends on a window. The dialog version will be smaller every time. In addition to conserving resources, you may find that the dialog version loads faster. A dialog-based application is simply more efficient than its window-based counterpart.

You may find that building a dialog-based application is faster as well. Dialog-based applications are meant to be small and efficient. If you find that you're adding a lot of bells and whistles to this kind of application, perhaps you've used the wrong kind of application to start with. Dialog-based applications normally eschew menus and other paraphernalia that a window-based application requires to provide a user-friendly front end. Fewer bells and whistles spell reduced development and debugging time for the

Cramming your dialog-based application with excess controls only makes it look tacky and hard to use.

programmer. Obviously, anything that speeds the programmer along is worth looking at.

Dialog-based applications don't have to suffer from lack of essential features either. For example, you can create a perfectly acceptable OLE server out of a dialog-based application. The wizards in Visual C++ will even help you out in this area, so adding OLE support requires a minimal effort on your part.

The only real problem with dialog-based applications is that some programmers feel they can stuff them to the point of breaking. I've seen some dialog-based applications that are so filled with gizmos that you really can't tell what they're supposed to do. While a dialog-based application may look a little more cramped than its window-based counterpart, you should not have it so crammed that no one can use it.

T IP: You can reduce clutter on a dialog-based application by using tabbed pages, just like a property dialog used by Windows for configuration purposes.

Single Document

A single-document application is one like Notepad or Microsoft Paint. It's designed to handle one document at a time, which reduces programming complexity and the amount of resources required to run the application. You'd use this kind of windowed application for something small, like a text editor or perhaps a small graphics editor. A single-document application allows users to interact fully with the document that you want them to create, but it's usually less robust than an application designed to work with multiple documents. In addition, the single-document application usually has a minimum of one less menu than a multiple-document application would—the Window menu that is used to select the document you want to edit.

Use a single-document, window-based interface for smaller applications that require a significant amount of user interaction.

Like the dialog-based application, your single-document application can act as an OLE server. In fact, you'll find that this kind of application can also act as an OLE client, even though very few programmers add this capability into their program. Here's an example of a single-document application we'll create later in the chapter. Notice that it's acting as an OLE client in this case.

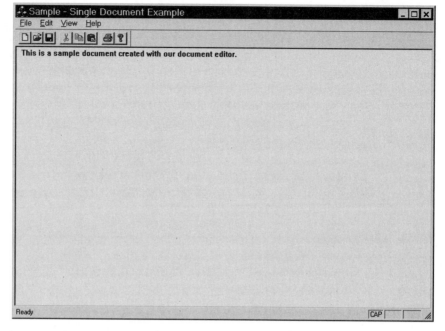

Unfortunately, single-document, window-based applications can suffer from the same problem as a dialog-based application—too much complexity. I still remember problems trying to use older versions of CorelDRAW. Every time I wanted to look at a drawing, I had to close the currently open document before doing so. This limitation made CorelDRAW a little harder to use than it needed to be. For example, I wasted a lot of time trying to compare one drawing against another. (Fortunately, Corel Systems has corrected this oversight in current versions of CorelDRAW.)

TIP: The single-document, window-based application works surprisingly well when it comes to database management systems. The reason is fairly simple. Very few (if any) of your users will need to open more than one database at a time. Even if they do, the rules for working with databases would make it less desirable to allow the user to access multiple databases by themselves. You'll normally want to control all access to the various database elements programmatically and display the results to the user.

Multiple Document

Now we come to the multiple-document application. You'd use this kind of window-based application to create something like a word processor or spreadsheet application. For example, both Microsoft Word and Microsoft Excel are examples of multiple-document applications. If you think about it for a second, a text editor has a limited appeal simply because it can only open one document at a time. People need to be able to compare one document to another; that's why multiple-document applications are not only nice but required in so many situations.

You can convert your multiple-document application to a simple Web browser by using the CHtmlView as your base view class.

Multiple-document applications also tend to be feature rich. (You can still go overboard; just look at all the people complaining about the bloated feature sets of major products produced by vendors today.) A text editor may provide a very simple find function and not offer any means for replacing occurrences of text. A full-fledged word processor provides both search and replace as standard features.

The failings of a multiple-document application begin with the fact that it can handle multiple documents. The capability of handling more than one document at a time means a lot of additional programming. You don't just have to keep track of all the open documents. There's the Window menu to manage and special program features like split screen to consider as well. You'll also need to decide whether the user will be allowed to display more than one document at once. Things like minimizing one document while keeping another maximized require additional code as well. In sum, you'll need to be prepared for some major programming time before you even start a multiple-document application.

Of course, multiple-document applications have plenty of other disadvantages as well. For example, if you've ever tried to use Word for an OLE server, you know all about the frustration of waiting for this behemoth application to open every time you click on a link in another application. You've probably experienced the serious consequences of running out of memory as well. Until recently, every time you wanted to use OLE, you had to have enough memory to run both applications (the client and the server). Fortunately, Microsoft has reduced this requirement somewhat by allowing the server to take over the client's window; now the server only has to worry about working with the document itself. The client window provides a framework for the server's menus and toolbar, so there isn't any extra memory wasted.

HTML-Based Document

Visual C++ 6.0 includes a new category of application, but you won't find it on the Projects tab of the New dialog. You'll create an HTML-based document application on the MFC AppWizard, Step 6 of 6 dialog, which we'll cover in several sections of this chapter. The Base Class combo box contains a CHtmlView entry, which is used to create this new type of application.

So, what good is an HTML-based document application? Think about the advantages of creating your own custom Web browser. You could set it to view the company Web site automatically and restrict the user from viewing non-business-oriented sites on the Web. Since a custom browser need not carry all of the generic features of a full-fledged browser, it would consume less memory and less disk space as well. In other words, you could create an environment that provides all of the functionality of a browser with none of the problems (at least from a company Web site access perspective). Here's a typical example of an HTML-based document application used to access a Web site (the default Web site provided with the CHtmlView class).

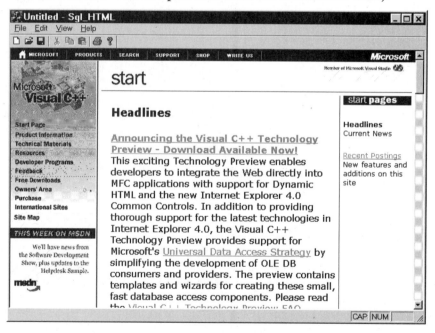

However, this new application type is more valuable than you may initially think. For example, you could add a CHtmlView class to an existing application to allow it to access a Web server-based help desk. (I'll cover

HTML-based help in the "Adding HTML-Based Help to Your Application" section of Chapter 15.) Instead of creating a standard help file and adding it to your application, what you'd do is create a very specialized Web browser and add it instead.

The advantages of HTML-based help are clear. Using the older help files meant that you couldn't easily update the help files for your application once you sent the application to a customer or distributed it throughout the company. Updating HTML help is as easy as changing a file on your Web server. In addition, working with Microsoft Help Workshop left a little to be desired in the ease of use category. HTML-based help requires no compiler or special tools, just a text editor. (Theoretically, you'll want an editor designed to work with HTML before writing a huge help file.)

There are disadvantages to HTML help as well. For one thing, it's a lot more difficult to build adequate search capability into HTML-based help. Since finding the information the user wants is just as important as creating it in the first place, HTML-based help may not be the answer of choice for novice users. In addition, HTML-based help necessitates an Internet (or at least an intranet) connection. If your company has a lot of users on the road, trying to find an Internet connection may not be practical. Of course, you could always create a local copy of the required HTML files, but that would create the same problem as you had before: out-of-date help files.

There are a lot of other uses for this new application type—too many to list here. The important thing to remember is that any application that would benefit from Internet access will benefit from the use of the CHtmlView class. You could use this feature for everything from remote updates of the company database by sales representatives to making it easier for new users to register their product. In other words, the CHtmlView class opens an entirely new world for both you and your users.

Writing a Console Application

A console application, as previously stated, allows you to move the business logic of your application from DOS to Windows. You may also be able to move some (or even most) of the display logic, but you'll likely want to dress it up with features that MFC can provide. In essence, a console application can look just like your old DOS application with a few added features. You need to completely test the application once you get it coded to make sure any features you move from DOS to Windows still work as anticipated.

Let's look at a fairly simple example of what you can do with a console application. In this case, we're not looking at functionality as much as at what you can do overall. The first step, of course, is to create the program shell. The following procedure will take you through the steps required to get that part of the job done.

1. Open Visual C++ if you haven't done so already.

2. Use the File | New command to display a New dialog like the one shown here. Notice that I've already chosen the Projects tab and highlighted the project type that we'll use in this case.

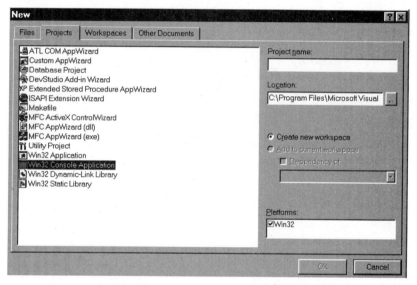

3. Once you choose Win32 Console Application, type a name for your program in the Project Name field. The sample program uses the name Console. You may need to change the contents of the Location field as well. Just click the browse button next to the field and you'll see a Choose Directory dialog, where you can choose a destination directory for your application.

4. Click on OK. You'll see the Win32 Console Application - Step 1 of 1 dialog shown here. Notice that you have a choice of several application types to get you started. This is a new feature of Visual C++ 6.0. Previous versions of Visual C++ would simply create an empty project. You now have a choice of what type of project you want to create (even an empty one).

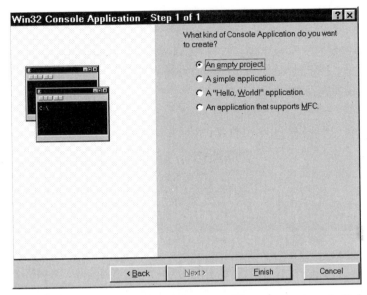

5. Choose the option called An Empty Project (if necessary) and click Finish. You'll see a New Project Information dialog box that tells which options you selected.

6. Click OK to create the example.

There's one more step that you need to perform before this project will be ready to go. It needs to use MFC classes. While you could have added this support as part of the wizard setup, converting DOS applications to Windows use requires less code rewriting if you go this route. Use the Project | Settings command to display the Project Settings dialog. Choose the General tab of the dialog and All Configurations in the Settings For combo box. Choose the Use MFC in a Shared DLL option in the Microsoft Foundation Classes combo box. Click OK to complete the action.

Now it's time to add some code to our example. The first thing you'll need to do is add a file to the project. Let's look at the process for doing that.

1. Use the File | New command to open the New dialog. Choose the Files tab. You'll see a whole list of file types including Resource Template and various graphics files like Icon File.

2. Highlight the C++ Source File option. We need a C++ source file because we'll be adding classes to the sample code.

3. Type **Console** in the File Name field. (Visual C++ will automatically add the correct extension for you.)

4. Click OK. You'll see a blank C++ source file appear.

Now that you've got an empty file to use, it's time to add the code. Listing 2-1 contains the C++ source for our example. Notice that it includes straight C code mixed with the C++ code. I did that on purpose so that you could better see how things work in this environment.

Listing 2-1:

```cpp
#include <afxcoll.h>      // Provides access to MFC functions.

class CDrawBox : public CObject
{
public:

    // Draws the box.
    void DoDraw(char* string);
};

void CDrawBox::DoDraw(char* cValue)
{
    int             iCount;        // Loop counter.
    int             iSpaces;    // Amount of spaces to add for string.

    // Draw the top of the box.
    fprintf(stdout, "\311");
    for (iCount = 1; iCount <= 78; iCount++)
    {
        fprintf(stdout, "\315");
    }
    fprintf(stdout, "\273");

    // Figure out the center of the string, then display it

    // with the box sides.
    iSpaces = (80 - strlen(cValue)) / 2;
    fprintf(stdout, "\272");
    for (iCount = 1; iCount <= iSpaces; iCount++)
    {
        fprintf(stdout, " ");
    }
    fprintf(stdout, "%s", cValue);
```

```
    // Compensate for odd sized strings, then complete the side.
    if ((strlen(cValue) % 2) == 1)
    {
        iSpaces--;
    }
    for (iCount = 1; iCount <= iSpaces; iCount++)
    {
        fprintf(stdout, " ");
    }
    fprintf(stdout, "\272");

    // Draw the bottom of the box.
    fprintf(stdout, "\310");
    for (iCount = 1; iCount <= 78; iCount++)
    {
        fprintf(stdout, "\315");
    }
    fprintf(stdout, "\274\n");
}


int main(int argc, char** argv)
{
    char*       cName;          // Name of person typed at command line.
    char*       cLocale;        // Program execution location.
    CTime       oMyTime;        // A time object.
    CString     cDate;          // String used to hold time and date.
    CDrawBox    oMyDraw;        // Special text display.

    // See if we have enough command line arguments.
    if (argc != 2)
    {

        fprintf(stderr, "Type the program name followed by your name.\n");
        return 1;
    }

    // Get the command line arguments.
    cLocale = argv[0];
    cName = argv[1];

    // Get the current time and put it in a string.
    oMyTime = CTime::GetCurrentTime();
    cDate = oMyTime.Format( "%A, %B %d, %Y" );
```

```
// Display everything we've collected.
fprintf(stdout, "Hello %s\n\n", cName);
fprintf(stdout, "Program is executing from:\n%s\n\n", cLocale);
fprintf(stdout, "The date is: %s\n", cDate);

// Use our class to draw a box around some text.
oMyDraw.DoDraw("It's a box!");

return 0;
}
```

As you can see, I'm showing you four essential techniques in this example. The first thing you'll notice is that the code checks for the proper number of command line arguments. If they aren't there, it displays an error message to the stderr device and then exits with an error code. You can detect this error code from a DOS batch command, but it doesn't affect Windows at all. Once the code establishes that there are enough command line arguments, it places them in a couple of variables for display later.

Up to this point you could have been looking at any DOS application. Notice that the second thing the code does is get the current time. It uses an MFC call to get the job done. So how do you gain access to MFC functions from within a console application? As you see, I included AFXCOLL.H at the very beginning of the code. This file contains all of the defines and class definitions that you'll need to implement a limited number of MFC calls within your console application.

Don't get the idea that you can use MFC calls indiscriminately though. For example, you can't create a CDialog object and then actually expect to use it. Even if you do manage to get the code to compile, either you'll end up with a run-time error or the application will ignore the dialog code altogether.

T IP: A good rule of thumb when deciding which MFC classes to use is to see if the class works with graphical elements. If it does, there's no chance of you using it within a console application. In addition, you'll find that certain system calls are out of reach and that you'll have to exercise care when it comes to security and disk access. If in doubt, stick with the calls listed in AFXCOLL.H (and any associated header files like AFX.H) to the exclusion of everything else. You can safely use all of the calls within AFXCOLL.H in any console application.

Now that we've got some data to display, the code sends it to the stdout device. That's the third technique I wanted to show you. In most cases, stdout will be the display, but you can easily send it elsewhere if so desired.

The point is that you use the same formatting as before. For that matter, you could simply use an fprint() function call in place of the more elaborate fprintf() function call shown in the code.

There's one remaining call in our main() function. We send data to a class called CDrawBox, the fourth technique I wanted to show you. All that this class does is center the text within a text box (using the upper ASCII character set). You've probably seen many DOS applications that do the same thing. The idea here is that we've derived a new class from the MFC CObject class, and then used that class within a console application. Likewise, there isn't anything to stop you from performing similar tricks with the programs you've created. As I said before, the temptation to add a lot of bells and whistles to a DOS application as you move it to Windows certainly is strong. Whether or not an update makes sense depends on how much time you've got for the move and the relative value of the update when viewed within the context of the total application.

Our console application is all ready to go. However, like many of the DOS applications you've written, this one requires a batch file for testing purposes. Listing 2-2 shows the source for the batch file we'll use in this case. All it does is call the program, test for an error value, and then echo a message if the application registered an error. You've already seen the output from this program earlier, so I won't show it again here.

Listing 2-2:
```
@ECHO OFF
CONSOLE
IF ERRORLEVEL==1 ECHO IT'S BAD
CONSOLE JOHN
IF ERRORLEVEL==1 ECHO IT'S BAD
@ECHO ON
```

Writing a Dialog-Based Application

Dialog-based applications are most commonly used for smaller tasks like utility programs, system monitors, or even a wizard. In most cases, they're specifically designed to keep complexity at a minimum. In fact, it's safe to assume that a dialog-based application should always use a minimum of controls.

We're going to look at another simple example. However, in this case, our application is going to use a combination of ActiveX controls and built-in functionality to keep the amount of coding you actually have to do to a minimum. The following procedure will help you get an empty structure together, which we'll fill with code later.

1. Open Visual C++ (if you haven't done so already).

2. Use the File | New command to open the New dialog, then select the Projects tab. In this case, you'll want to choose the MFC AppWizard (EXE) project type from the list.

3. Type a name for your application in the Project Name field. The sample application uses the name Dialog, but you could easily use any name you like. Make sure you change the Location field if necessary (click the browse button next to the Location field).

4. Click on OK. You'll see an MFC AppWizard - Step 1 dialog like the one shown here.

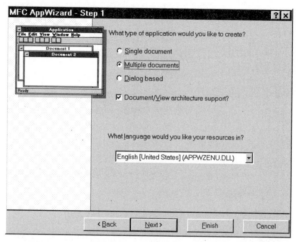

5. Choose the Dialog Based option button, and then click on Next. You'll see an MFC AppWizard - Step 2 of 4 dialog like the one shown here.

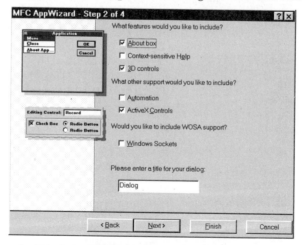

6. Type **Sample Dialog Application** in the Please Enter a Title for Your Dialog field. Notice that this dialog will also allow you to add some

features to your dialog-based application, like context-sensitive help. The Automation checkbox allows you to add OLE automation to your application, which is essentially a form of scripting. You can also add Windows Sockets support to your application on this page—which allows it to communicate over TCP/IP networks.

7. Click Next, and then click Next again. We don't need to change anything on these last two dialogs, but it's handy to know what's available should you need it later. The first page allows you to choose whether to add comments to your code. You also get to choose whether MFC is statically or dynamically linked to your application.

TIP: Statically linking MFC to your application has the benefit of reducing the number of files you have to distribute with your application. In fact, you'll only need to give someone the executable if you want to. It may also improve the chances that your application will run on every machine it's installed on, since your application will always have access to the same version of MFC that you used to design it. The downside to static linking is that your application will be a lot bigger and waste a lot more memory when loaded. In addition, you'll need to relink your application any time you want to add a new feature to it, which can become quite a nuisance after a while.

8. Click Finish. Visual C++ will display a New Project Information dialog like the one shown here. This is your last chance to make sure all of your program settings are correct. A poor choice in settings can actually make your project development time longer rather than shorter.

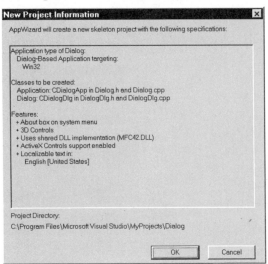

2

9. Click OK. The MFC AppWizard will generate a program shell for you.

Now we've got a basic program shell to work with and it's time to start putting our sample application together. The first thing we'll want to do, since this program uses the Microsoft Calendar control, is to install the ActiveX controls we need. Use the Project | Add to Project | Components and Controls command to display a Components and Controls Gallery dialog like the one shown here.

Make sure you have the OCX controls that come with Visual C++ installed, or you may not have a copy of the Microsoft Calendar control to work with.

Double-click the Registered ActiveX Controls folder and you'll see a list of controls registered on your machine. Find the Calendar Control 8.0 entry (that's the one that shipped with this version of Visual C++), and then click on Insert. Visual C++ will display a dialog asking if you really want to insert this control into your project. Click on OK. Visual C++ will have to add some wrapper classes to your application to accommodate the ActiveX control. It displays the names of those classes in a Confirm Classes dialog like this one.

Click on OK to accept the default ActiveX control class settings. Now you've got a new control to work with. You'll see it added to the toolbox. Click on Close to close the Components and Controls Gallery dialog.

Now it's time to get your dialog box designed. Figure 2-1 shows how I put my dialog together. The current dialog box size is 300×200. I made the Calendar control itself 230×186 in size so that the numbers would be easy to see. Notice that the Calendar control immediately displays the current date, even though the application isn't active right now. That's because the ActiveX control has to activate itself when you place it on the dialog. Even though the application isn't active, the ActiveX control is. This is an important troubleshooting tip when working with ActiveX controls. If you place a control on the dialog and it just sits there, you may not have it installed correctly. Obviously, you'll want to check any documentation to make sure the control is acting as expected.

2

T IP: You'll always see the current control size in the second box of the status bar on the right side of the screen. Directly to the left of this box is another box containing the selected control's position in relation to the upper-right corner of the display area. You can use the contents of these two status bar boxes to very accurately size and position the control on your dialog box.

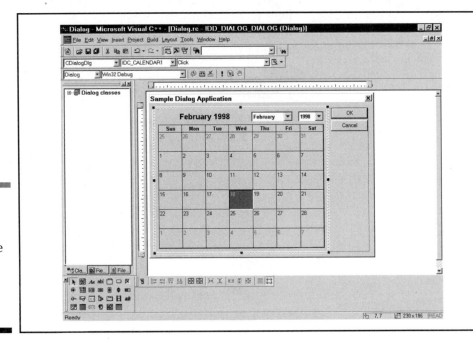

Our sample dialog-based application begins to take shape once the controls are added.

Figure 2-1.

If you compiled and ran the application at this point, you'd find that it was only semifunctional. The calendar would allow you to choose new dates, and you could click on the OK button and see the dialog disappear. Other than that, the program wouldn't do much.

Before we can attach any code to the Calendar control, we have to create a member variable for it. Doing so is relatively easy. CTRL-double-click on the Calendar control and you'll see an Add Member Variable dialog like this one.

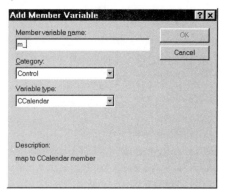

Since this is our first Calendar control, type **Calendar1** after the m_ (don't remove the m_). Click on OK to create the variable.

Detecting a user change to the control is the next thing we need to do. Right-click on the Calendar control and you'll see a context menu. Choose Events from that menu and you'll see a New Windows Message and Event Handlers dialog box like this one.

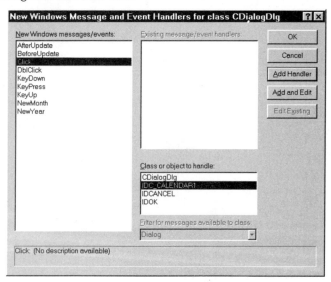

This dialog contains a complete list of all the events that your control can monitor. The programmer set these events up during the design phase of the control. In this case, we'll want to monitor the DblClick event. Highlight the DblClick event entry, and then click on the Add and Edit button. Visual C++ will display an Add Member Function dialog. Click OK to accept the default function name. You'll see a blank function. Now all you need to do is add some code to make it work. Listing 2-3 shows the code you'll need to make this control functional.

Listing 2-3:

```
void CDialogDlg::OnDblClickCalendar1()
{
    CString         cSelectedDate;      // Date selected by user.
    char*        cDay = "  ";     // Selected day.
    char*        cYear = "     ";     // Selected year.

    // Get day from calendar control.
    itoa(m_Calendar1.GetDay(), cDay, 10);
    cSelectedDate = cDay;

    // Get month from calendar control.
    switch (m_Calendar1.GetMonth())
    {
    case 1:
        cSelectedDate = cSelectedDate + " January ";
        break;
    case 2:
        cSelectedDate = cSelectedDate + " February ";
        break;
    case 3:
        cSelectedDate = cSelectedDate + " March ";
        break;
    case 4:
        cSelectedDate = cSelectedDate + " April ";
        break;
    case 5:
        cSelectedDate = cSelectedDate + " May ";
        break;
    case 6:
        cSelectedDate = cSelectedDate + " June ";
        break;
    case 7:
        cSelectedDate = cSelectedDate + " July ";
        break;
```

```
case 8:
    cSelectedDate = cSelectedDate + " August ";
    break;
case 9:
    cSelectedDate = cSelectedDate + " September ";
    break;
case 10:
    cSelectedDate = cSelectedDate + " October ";
    break;
case 11:
    cSelectedDate = cSelectedDate + " November ";
    break;
case 12:
    cSelectedDate = cSelectedDate + " December ";
}

// Get the year.
itoa(m_Calendar1.GetYear(), cYear, 10);
cSelectedDate = cSelectedDate + cYear;

// Display the date.
AfxMessageBox("You double-clicked on: " + cSelectedDate, MB_OK |
MB_ICONINFORMATION, 0);

}
```

At this point, you can run the application and it'll actually do something. Try building and running the application. Double-click on any date and you'll see a dialog similar to the one shown in Figure 2-2. Essentially it displays the date you selected from the Calendar control in an easy-to-read format. While this may not seem very useful at the moment, you could easily expand this utility program in several ways. For example, you could have a little notepad pop up every time you double-clicked on a date. That way you could enter notes for each day as needed. Needless to say, you won't be replacing your contact manager with this utility anytime soon, but it does work very well for short notes—especially on a laptop where space is limited and you don't want a large application using up your battery.

The Calendar control does provide quite a bit of added functionality—most of which we won't look at in this chapter. One thing that would be handy to have is a button for resetting the date back to today's date after you've wandered about during a telephone conversation. Adding such a button is pretty easy. Figure 2-3 shows the button I added to the existing project. It has an ID of IDC_RESET_DATE and a caption of Reset Date. The dialog will look best if you position the control at 243, 39 and make it 50×14 in size.

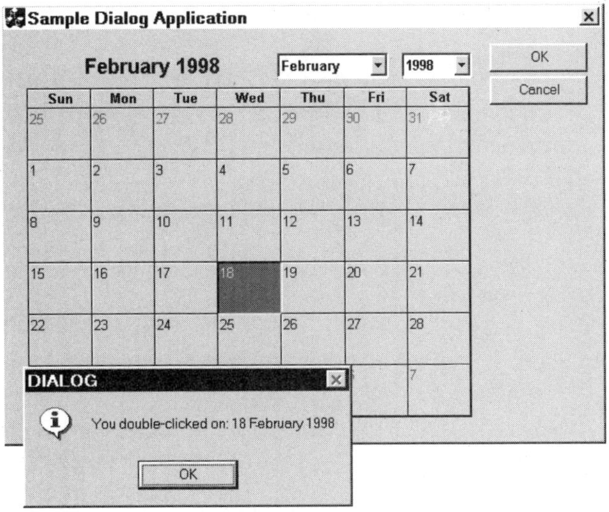

2

The Sample
Dialog
Application
will display a
dialog telling
you the date
you selected.

Figure 2-2.

It's really
handy to have
a button for
resetting the
date to today's
date once
you've looked
at the calendar
for a while.

Figure 2-3.

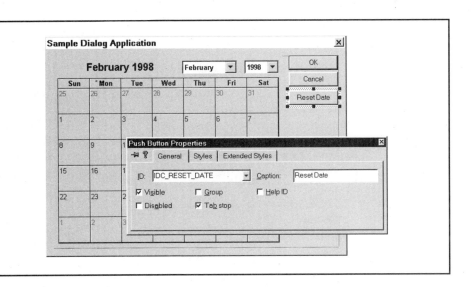

Now that we have a button, let's add some code to it. Right-click on the button and choose Events from the context menu. You'll see a New Windows Message and Event Handlers dialog box. Select the BN_CLICKED event, and then click on Add and Edit. Click OK to accept the default procedure name. You'll see a blank procedure. Listing 2-4 provides the code you'll need to make the procedure work.

Listing 2-4:
```
void CDialogDlg::OnResetDate()
{
    // Reset selected calendar date to today.
    m_Calendar1.Today();

}
```

Now whenever you click on the Reset Date button, the Calendar control will return you to the current month and year. While this code isn't very complicated, it shows you one way that you can add functionality to a dialog-based application without making it too unwieldy to use. Of course, even a few of these buttons could get quite cumbersome after a while.

Writing a Single-Document Application

Every version of Microsoft's Wizards for Visual C++ has gotten a little better. It shouldn't surprise you then that while you can get very close to a working application using one, there are a few things that a less-than-watchful eye might miss when setting up an application in the first place.

This section will look at a single-documentation application—which you could probably use for a small text editor or other lightweight, general-purpose document editor. In this case, we'll create a rich text editor that really doesn't do much more than allow you to edit text right now. Later in the book we'll add functionality to this program and make it something a little more worthwhile.

Begin this project by using the File | New command to display the New dialog. Choose the MFC AppWizard (EXE) project type. Type a name in the Project Name field. The sample application uses Sngl_Doc as an application name, but you can use anything you'd like. Click OK and you'll see the MFC AppWizard - Step 1 dialog. Choose the Single Document option, and then click on Next. You'll see an MFC AppWizard - Step 2 of 6 dialog like the one shown here.

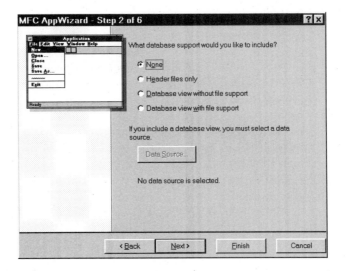

This is the first place you need to make a decision. If you plan on adding database support to your application, you'll also need to decide what level of support to get from the MFC AppWizard. We'll spend quite a bit of time looking at this topic in Part II of the book, so I won't cover it here. Click Next and you'll see the Step 3 dialog shown here.

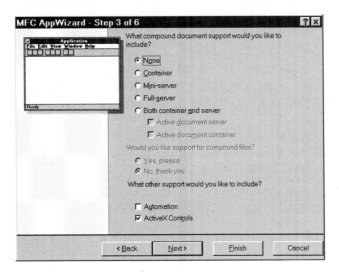

The upper half of this dialog determines what level of OLE support you'll add to your application. The more support you add, the larger your application will be. The very basic level of support is to act as a container. A container can act as a client and store linked and embedded objects. The next level of support, Mini-server, allows you to create compound documents. A mini-server can't work stand-alone. In addition, it can only work with embedded documents. A full server does have the full OLE capability to work as a server, but it can't act as a container. An application like this would work much like Microsoft Paint. You can embed or link a Microsoft Paint document into your application, but Microsoft Paint can't hold objects created by other applications. Finally, the Both Container and Server option gives your application a full array of local OLE support. You can use it as both a server and a client. However, this kind of application won't work with an Internet browser—it's not designed as an ActiveX Document server.

Notice that there are two checkboxes right below the final radio button (Both Container and Server). If you check the first box, Visual C++ will also add the support required to make your application an ActiveX Document Server. An ActiveDocument Server has the ability to create and manage ActiveX documents. The second checkbox, Active Document Container, allows your application to contain ActiveX documents within its frame. In essence, you'll be able to host documents from applications like Microsoft Word or Excel. For right now, choose the Both Container and Server option and check the Active Document Server checkbox. We'll look at the ramifications of this choice in Chapter 11.

There are two other important checkboxes on the Step 3 dialog. The first is Automation. You'll normally want to check this option for larger applications. Automation allows you to manipulate objects created by other applications. It also allows an automation client to manipulate the objects that you expose in your application. For right now, it's safe to think of automation as a sort of scripting capability, though that isn't precisely correct. (The full definition can get rather long and drawn out—we'll cover it later in the book.)

The second option is ActiveX Controls. You have to check this box if you want to use any OCXs in your application—whether they were designed as ActiveX controls or not. Make sure you check both the ActiveX Controls and the Automation checkboxes, and then click Next. You should see a Step 4 dialog like this one.

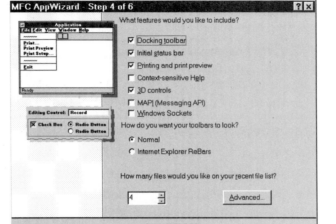

The upper half of this dialog selects the kinds of interface elements you'll include with your application. Normally, you'll want to keep the default settings, since they allow you to create a standard application. Consider checking the Context-Sensitive Help checkbox if you're going to give this application to someone else. We'll look at how you can add context-sensitive help to your application in Chapter 15.

The next two options on this dialog allow you to add communications support. The first option is e-mail-specific. Checking this option will allow you to send and receive e-mail using your application (as long as that e-mail application is MAPI compliant). The second option allows you to communicate across a TCP/IP network. You'll want to check it if you plan to add Internet support to your application.

Visual C++ includes a new feature that allows you to determine your toolbar appearance. You can either choose the Normal (standard C++) appearance or the new look provided by Internet Explorer. There are two advantages to using the Internet Explorer ReBars option: You can add any Windows control to the toolbar (not just menu commands) and you can undock the ReBars, just as you would a command bar.

The only two items left are the recent file list setting and a mysterious button marked Advanced. I normally set my recently used file list setting as high as possible, since I work with a lot of documents. Allowing the user maximum freedom in this area won't impact the size and speed of your application, so setting higher really isn't that big a deal.

Now let's look at that Advanced button. Click this button and you'll see an Advanced Options dialog like the one shown here. This is where you'll set up the document parameters for your application. It's also where you'll choose things like the text that appears in the title bar of your application when people use it. You'll see the name of the current document in the title bar as well.

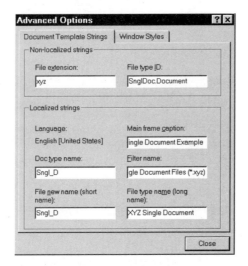

Set up your Advanced Options dialog like the one shown. What you'll end up with is an application that uses the XYZ file extension. The title bar for your application will read "Single Document Example." Every time you see a File Open or File Save dialog, the filter field will read "XYZ Single Document Files (*.xyz)." Finally, when you display the properties dialog for a document you create with this application, it'll inform you that this is an "XYZ Single Document" type of document. Click on Close to make your settings permanent. Click Next twice and you'll see the Step 6 dialog shown here.

This is another one of those tricky areas that I was telling you about. If you didn't really take a good look at what was going on, you'd miss the fact that you could use any base class you'd like for the document view class. Why is that such an important consideration? If you were to keep the default setting, you'd have to write code for just about every action your application performed on the document. That's probably fine if you're creating an entirely new kind of document, but most programs just don't do that. What you really want to do is make an application that acts sort of like another application but offers features that application lacks. In our case, we're creating a text editor, so it doesn't make sense to use CView (the default base class). Using the CEditView or CRichEditView class as a base class will save us a lot of work, because the application will already know how to act as a simple word processor right out of the package. You won't even have to add any code to get this functionality.

To show you just how this works, choose the CRichEditView base class for the CSngl_DocView class in our application. Click on Finish to complete your setup. Click OK when you see the New Project Information dialog, and Visual C++ will create the application for you.

Now build the application and start it. You'll find that you can type text and save it in an XYZ document. This application will read other text and RTF documents with the proper code additions. You can easily expand the application in other ways as well. For example, since it relies on the rich edit control, you can add text formatting and colors. The OLE capabilities that we've added mean that you'll be able to insert graphics as needed. In fact, what you've really ended up with is something that has a lot of potential with very little work.

In case you haven't noticed by now, this particular sample didn't require one ounce of coding on your part. The end result was pretty good and quite unexpected for a C programmer. Figure 2-4 shows the final result for this application so far, but count on seeing this application again as the book progresses.

Our sample application works
pretty well considering we haven't added any code to it.

Figure 2-4.

Writing an HTML-Based Document Application

There isn't any doubt that the Internet is part of many companies' plans for reducing costs and enhancing productivity. In addition, the Internet is a new means for selling products, researching information, and performing a variety of other tasks that many businesses thought impossible just a few years ago. That's why this example is so important. It shows you how to incorporate Internet capability into an application, making it possible to fuse these two diverse media into a coherent whole.

This section will show how to create an HTML-based document shell. Even though the shell you get from the wizard is limited, it can display HTML documents either on or off the Internet. Once you have a basic shell to work with, we'll look at adding some enhancements that most applications will require.

Creating the Basic Shell

2

For this example, we'll be using a variation of the single document application found later in this chapter. Begin this project by using the File | New command to display the New dialog. Choose the MFC AppWizard (EXE) project type. Type a name in the Project Name field. The sample application uses Sgl_HTML as an application name, but you can use anything you'd like. Click OK and you'll see the MFC AppWizard - Step 1 dialog. Choose the Single Document option and then click on Next twice. You should see the MFC AppWizard - Step 3 of 6 dialog.

Normally, you'd want your application to serve as both an OLE server and container. However, it's unlikely that most users will need OLE server features for this type of application, since you'll use it to display Web pages and not create new data. With this in mind, choose the Container option and check the Active Document Container checkbox. Remember that the Active Document Container option allows you to display ActiveX documents produced by applications like Microsoft Word. You'll also want to check the Automation and ActiveX Controls checkboxes. Click Next and you'll see the MFC AppWizard - Step 4 of 6 dialog.

There are a few options that you may want to at least look at on this dialog, the first being the Windows Sockets option. Remember that your application will likely need this support if you're going to use it over the Internet or an intranet. If your application will also support e-mail, you'll need to choose the MAPI option. Finally, since you'll probably need a fairly complex toolbar to allow the user full navigation capabilities, it's important to choose the Internet Explorer ReBars option. For the purposes of this example, I included the Windows Sockets and Internet Explorer ReBars options. I also set the recent file list to hold 16 entries. Click Next twice and you'll see the MFC AppWizard - Step 6 of 6 dialog.

The only change required on this dialog is the Base Class option. You must set it to CHtmlView to get the Internet capability we're looking for. We're done configuring the application. Click Finish to display the New Project Information dialog, and then click OK to complete the shell. If you compile and run your application at this point, you'll see something like this.

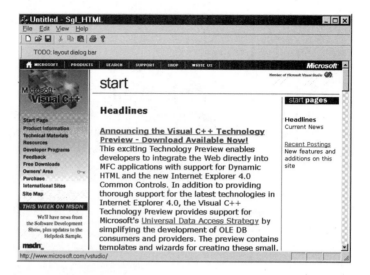

Adding Enhancements

If all you intend to do is display the home page of your Web site, then you might be able to get by with the application shell that we created in the preceding section. In most cases, though, you'll still need to add some basic navigational capability to your application. A user won't be able to get around on your Web site very well using links alone. So, the minimum enhancement you should add is a forward and backward button. Let's look at the process for adding this capability.

The first thing you'll need to do is open the IDR_MAINFRAME dialog. That's right, our Internet Explorer ReBar is actually a dialog, not a standard toolbar. The class for this dialog is CDialogBar instead of the more standard CDialog class that you're used to. As with any other dialog box, you can add standard Windows controls to this one. We'll add two buttons as shown here. Notice that they're labeled Forward and Backward. I've also given them an ID of IDC_FORWARD and IDC_BACKWARD.

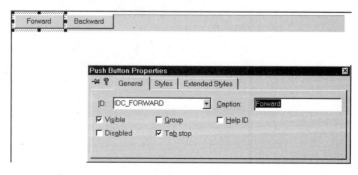

Now we have two buttons sitting on the dialog bar part of the ReBar, but they won't do anything when pressed. In fact, if you compiled the application right now, the two buttons would be grayed out and wouldn't do anything at all. That's because we've told Visual C++ where to draw them but not what to do with them. Making our buttons functional is a three-step process.

1. Define a line between the button and a message handler.
2. Declare the message handler function.
3. Write the message handler code.

Let's begin with the first step, defining a link between the button and the message handler. Since we want these two buttons to affect the contents of the HTML page, we'll want to place that link in the CSgl_HTMLView class using the ON_COMMAND() macro. Listing 2-5 shows the code, in bold type, that you'll need to add to the MESSAGE_MAP section of the CSgl_HTMLView.CPP file. Notice that the ON_COMMAND() macro provides a simple linking function between the buttons (identified by IDC_FORWARD and IDC_BACKWARD) and their associated message handler functions.

Listing 2-5:

```
BEGIN_MESSAGE_MAP(CSgl_HTMLView, CHtmlView)
    //{{AFX_MSG_MAP(CSgl_HTMLView)
            // NOTE - the ClassWizard will add and remove mapping macros here.
        //    DO NOT EDIT what you see in these blocks of generated code!
    ON_WM_DESTROY()
    ON_WM_SETFOCUS()
    ON_WM_SIZE()
    ON_COMMAND(ID_OLE_INSERT_NEW, OnInsertObject)
    ON_COMMAND(ID_CANCEL_EDIT_CNTR, OnCancelEditCntr)
    //}}AFX_MSG_MAP
    // Standard printing commands
    ON_COMMAND(ID_FILE_PRINT, CHtmlView::OnFilePrint)
    ON_COMMAND(ID_FILE_PRINT_DIRECT, CHtmlView::OnFilePrint)
    ON_COMMAND(ID_FILE_PRINT_PREVIEW, CHtmlView::OnFilePrintPreview)

    // Add two macros for our buttons.
    ON_COMMAND(IDC_FORWARD, CSgl_HTMLView::OnForward)
    ON_COMMAND(IDC_BACKWARD, CSgl_HTMLView::OnBackward)
END_MESSAGE_MAP()
```

Now that we've defined a link between the buttons and their associated message handlers, we need to declare the functions in the CSgl_HTMLView.H file. Listing 2-6 shows the method I used for declaring these functions. About the only thing you really need to be sure of is that the functions are declared properly for the kind of message handler you want to create. There are a few things you should note about this declaration. First, I've made the functions public so that they can be accessed outside of the class. Second, I've declared the functions virtual so they can be overridden later if necessary.

Listing 2-6:

```
// Message handlers.
public:

    // Add some movement handlers.
    virtual void OnForward();
    virtual void OnBackward();
```

The message handlers are fairly simple. Listing 2-7 shows the code you'll need to add to the end of the CSgl_HTMLView.CPP file (in the message handler section). All that these message handlers do is call the GoForward() and GoBack() member functions of the CHtmlView class.

Listing 2-7:

```
/////////////////////////////////////////////////////////////////////////
// CSgl_HTMLView message handlers

void CSgl_HTMLView::OnForward()
{
    GoForward();
}

void CSgl_HTMLView::OnBackward()
{
    GoBack();
}
```

If you compile the application now, what you'll see is two buttons added to the ReBar. Click Backward to move back to a previously viewed Web page, or click Forward to see a page that you've just returned from. These two buttons work just as they would in your Web browser. Of course, this is just the beginning. You could add any number of custom buttons or other controls to the dialog bar.

CHAPTER 3

Understanding Visual C++ Resources

R*esources.* The word summons all kinds of images of wealth buried beneath the surface of the earth or sitting right in your backyard. Anything from a tree sitting in a forest to the coal mined from the ground can be a resource in the physical sense. While you won't get precious gems in the physical sense from Visual C++, you can still mine the resources needed to build your program with it.

As in any kind of mine, resources in Visual C++ provide a kind of raw material that you'll combine with program elements to create a finished product. In this case, resources combine with code to create part of an application, like a menu or a toolbar. In fact, most of the elements you can see in your program are derived from a resource of some type. Of course, Visual C++ resources are a bit more than just raw material, but the picture evoked by raw materials is a very useful one. It'll help if you keep it in mind as we discuss the use of resources in the following paragraphs.

Visual C++ supports ten kinds of resources: accelerator, bitmap, cursor, dialog, HTML, icon, menu, string table, toolbar, and version.

So what kinds of things can you dig out of the Visual C++ resource mine? Resources come in various shapes and sizes, including accelerator, bitmap, cursor, dialog, icon, menu, string table, toolbar, and version. We'll eventually work with nine of the ten kinds of resources as the chapter progresses (we'll talk about the HTML resource in Chapter 15). You'll learn that some resources have subtypes and each kind of resource has a specific purpose. In some cases, Visual C++ creates a resource like an About box for you automatically when you design a program using a wizard. Other resources like strings are created as part of designing something else. Finally, you'll design some resources like dialogs manually.

NOTE: We'll use the Sngl_Doc example from Chapter 2 throughout this chapter. All you need to do if you want to keep the two exercises separate is create a copy of the Sngl_Doc project folder. For the purposes of this chapter, all of the Sngl_Doc project files were copied into the Resource project folder.

Fortunately, you can create any resource you need at any time. All you have to do is display the ResourceView, right-click on the Resources folder, and choose Insert from the context menu. What you'll see is an Insert Resource dialog like the one shown here. Notice that it displays all ten of the resource types that we've listed. You should also see that there are three ways to create resources, by using the New, Import, or Custom button on the dialog.

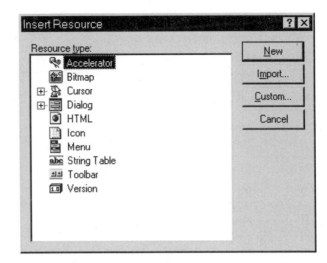

You can use resources from other projects in the current program. For example, you may want to use the same company logo icon in every program you write. All you need to do is right-click on the Resources folder and choose Import rather than Insert from the context menu. You'll see a File Open-type dialog. Just choose the file containing the resource that you want to import. For this reason, you'll want to keep most of your resources separate. Unfortunately, this method only works for icons, cursors, wave files, and Visual Basic form files.

T IP: There are ways to use other kinds of resources, like an About box, from other projects. You simply have to create a separate RC file for the resource you want to share. This works great when it comes to something like an About box. All you need to do is add the RC file to your project, and Visual C++ takes care of the rest. An alternative method to share resources is to copy them to the clipboard, and then paste them into your project once you've created a blank resource of the correct type.

A custom resource is one that you've thought of yourself. In effect, it doesn't manage to fit into the predefined categories that Visual C++ provides. Creating a custom resource entry is easy: just click the Custom button on the Insert Resource dialog. You'll see a New Custom Resource dialog containing a single blank. Simply type the name of your custom resource. At this point, Visual C++ will create a new folder bearing the custom resource name you've provided and a new resource within that folder. You'll have to provide the binary data required to implement the resource.

Customizing the Application Wizard-Supplied Resources

As previously mentioned, Visual C++ will automatically create some types of resources for you when you design your application workspace. For example, unless you tell the MFC AppWizard otherwise, it'll always include an About box in your program. The reason for doing so is simple. It's more than just a little handy; it tells users who designed the program they're using. Some default resources are more fun than utilitarian. Even though you really don't have to have a special program icon, there isn't any way to tell the application wizards that you don't want a custom icon for your program. Again, the reason for including an icon is simple—Windows needs it to display your program in Explorer. Every project you create should have version information. This time the information is for your benefit because it helps you keep track of what version of your product the user has.

The minimum default resources that Visual C++ provides are a custom application icon, an About box, and version information.

As you can see, there are good reasons for having these default resources created automatically for you. In fact, these three kinds of resources represent constants that you should probably consider customizing for every project. This section is going to give you some hints and tips about working with these default resources, though you should come up with a standard customization technique of your own.

Application Icons

Every MFC application program you'll ever create with Visual C++ will have a default application icon. In fact, the icon will always have the same name: IDR_MAINFRAME. You'll find that this icon not only defines how the program icon looks within Explorer (or any other application that displays program icons) but affects the internal representation of your program as well. For example, the About box normally displays this icon as part of its presentation of application information to the user.

The default custom application icon is IDR_ MAINFRAME, though you can add as many icons as needed to your application.

All of the MFC applications you create will also have the same icon to start with. Figure 3-1 shows what it looks like.

If you really don't care what people see when they install your application, they'll see this MFC logo. Personally, I'd rather have something that looks a little more interesting than this, and you should too. After all, this is the icon

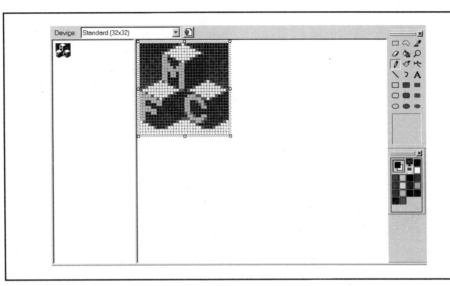

The MFC
AppWizard
provides this
default icon
that you can
use, but you
really should
customize it.
Figure 3-1.

3

that users of your program will see every time they look for it in Explorer or
select it from the Start menu.

T IP: Make sure you change both the 32×32 icon (shown in Figure 3-1)
and the 16×16 icon for your application. The 32×32 icon is the one you see
in Explorer. The 16×16 icon is displayed on the program's control menu and
is used when you see the program on the Windows Taskbar. The Device drop-
down list box (shown in Figure 3-1) is where you choose between the 32×32
and the 16×16 icons.

A second default icon appears when you decide to create a document with
your application, like we did in the Sngl_Doc example in Chapter 2. In that
case you'll see an IDR for each of the document types you've created. In our
example, it's IDR_SNGL_DTYPE. They'll all have the same icon to start with,
though; Figure 3-2 shows the default that the MFC AppWizard provides.
Unlike the application icon, it's almost mandatory to customize your
document icons if your application supports more than one document type.

Besides the ability to draw, you need to know a little about the tools at your
disposal if you want to create effective icons. All the tools you'll require
appear on the right side of the window. They include a set of standard
drawing tools (Graphics toolbar) and a color chart (Colors toolbar), which
you can hide or show just like any other toolbar we've talked about so far.

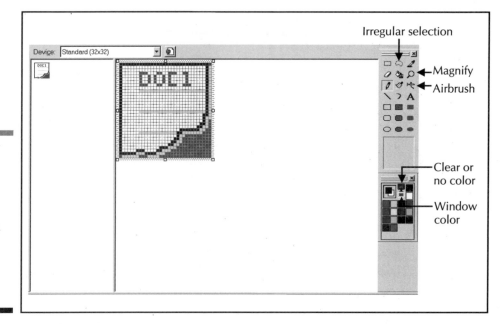

The MFC AppWizard will also supply a document icon like this one if your application needs it.

Figure 3-2.

The tools on the Graphics toolbar, shown in Figure 3-2, shouldn't be all that unfamiliar. You've got the standard selection tools, line drawing tools, and a variety of ellipses and squares. However, Visual C++ also includes an airbrush tool and an irregular selection tool, both of which make drawing a lot easier. You'll also find that the Magnify tool is superior to similar tools in some drawing programs—it can magnify your drawing up to eight times normal size.

The two monitors in the Colors toolbar contain the current window color and a clear color that allows whatever appears below the icon to show through.

There are also two special colors you need to know about on the Colors toolbar, but they're easy to find since they use a monitor symbol in place of a color square.

The upper monitor allows you to create a clear area. In other words, you'll see whatever appears below the area on the desktop or wherever else you place the program icon. The lower monitor allows you to create an area that uses the same color as the user's window foreground color selection. In other words, as you change the window color, the color of this area in your icon will change as well. You'll see the current foreground and background color appears to the left of the two monitors. The foreground color appears in the upper square, while the background color appears in the lower square.

Let's take a look at a sample of what you can do with these two icons. Figure 3-3 shows the sample icons I drew for my version of the program. They may not be very artistic compared to other icons you've seen—a definite argument for having an artist on your staff—but they're better than the default icons

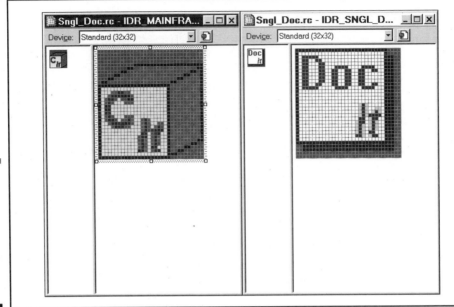

Adding special icons to the program isn't difficult at all; just draw what you want them to look like.

Figure 3-3.

you get with Visual C++. Obviously, you can customize your icons any way you want. Try using a variety of colors. Make sure you experiment with the two custom colors that I mentioned, since they're especially important when creating icons. (A lot of programmers create strange-looking icons that don't really fit in with the rest of the icons on your desktop because they don't know how to use the two special colors effectively.)

WEB LINK: If you need some great inspiration for creating icons, the Internet is literally packed with useful sites you should check out. One of the better sites overall is **http://personal.solutions.net/hillel/ico.htm**. It contains some good examples of cursors, icons, and utilities for creating them. If this site doesn't provide enough ideas, you may want to look at **http://crab.rutgers.edu/icons_new/icons.html**. Even though this site contains mostly GIF icons, the 3,000 examples it provides should give you more than a few ideas. Most of these icons deal with popular topics like *The Simpsons*. Fortunately, the icons are indexed so you don't have to try to dig through all 3,000 at one time. You can also find a good number of topic-specific sites. For example, **http://www.geocities.com/ Area51/8604/xfiles.htm** contains a fairly complete set of *X-Files*-specific icons (in ICO format).

CAUTION: Never assume that you can use any icon (or other graphic for that matter) you find on the Internet in a program you plan to sell or give to other people. Always assume that these resources are good for inspiration and not much else until you've gotten permission in writing from the originator to use them in any other way. Copyright infringement is a serious offense and somewhat easy to commit given the open environment that the Internet provides. The best rule of thumb is to either create your own icons or license them for commercial use from a reliable source.

Notice that I used the clear color on both icons and that I've given them a 3-D look. Again, it's not that they're all that artistic, but they do give the user a specific feel for my program. Obviously, the clear coloring shows up differently inside the editor than it will when the user sees (or actually fails to see) it. Shown here is what the two icons look like when viewed within Explorer.

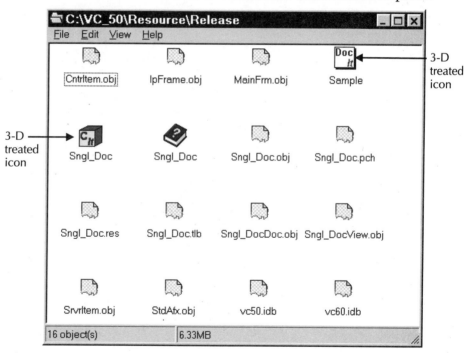

TIP: Make sure you always compile your program again after you've changed the icon, or it won't show up in Explorer. Running the program is a good idea too, since Visual C++ does make registry entries for you when you run the program the first time. Finally, make sure you use the View | Refresh command within Explorer. Otherwise, you'll see the old icons that Explorer stored previously.

3

The About Box

Customizing the About box for your application doesn't have to be a big deal. In fact, you've already started to customize it by modifying the application icon using the information in the previous section. Visual C++ automatically adds the icon you create for your application to the default About box. Here's the default About box for our sample application.

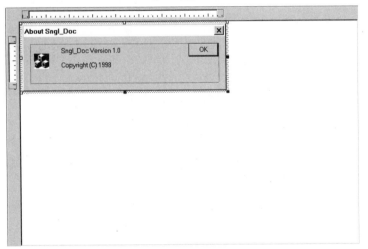

TIP: Since the information that appears in the default About box is always based on the input you provide to the MFC AppWizard, you'll want to give the clearest information possible. Doing so will reduce the amount of work you need to do later. These settings also affect the version information that we'll look at later in the chapter.

So what do you need to provide in a standard About box? The default About box gives you some ideas. Essentially, an About box should provide four pieces of information: your company name, copyright information, the product name, and the version number. If you supply these four essential items, the About box for your application will have everything it absolutely has to have. Notice that the default About box provides three of the four essential pieces of information for you—all you really have to add is a company name if you don't want to do a lot of work.

Of course, you may want to furnish some other essential information to the About box in your application. For example, it's always nice to know where to get technical support. Adding a telephone number and perhaps a few calling instructions is a good idea and doesn't consume too much space. Some companies also add the product registration number as part of the technical support information, but you'll need to begin working with the registry or an INI file to provide this kind of information.

Some useful information includes the current system resources available to support your application. For example, Visual C++ provides a way for you to add the current disk and memory statistics to an About box without too much work on your part. Let's look at how you can add this level of support. The following procedure will help you add disk and memory statistics to any About box (or any other dialog for that matter) that you create.

1. You'll need to resize the About box dialog. It's too small to hold the additional information right now. Obviously, you don't want to make it too large either, since an About box should be small enough to fit in the smallest display area possible. For this example, resize the About box to 250×150. This should give you enough space for the disk and memory statistics and still have room for copyright and other ancillary information.

2. Add two static text controls to the About box. The first will contain memory statistics, the second, disk statistics.

3. Make both controls 150×18 in size. Position the memory statistic static text control at 40, 40. Position the disk statistic static text control at 40, 65. (These positioning figures assume you haven't changed the size of the default static text controls to accommodate more company or product information.)

4. Right-click the memory statistic static control, and then choose Properties from the context menu. Change the ID field for this control to IDC_MEMORY. Do the same thing for the disk statistic static control.

However, in this case change the ID field to IDC_DISK. Uncheck the Group boxes for both controls—we want to work with them as separate static text controls. Now that we have someplace to put the information, it's time to add the code for gathering the information.

5. Use the Project | Add to Project | Components and Controls command to display the Components and Controls Gallery dialog. In the Look In field, double-click on Visual C++ Components and you should see a list of components like the ones shown here.

3

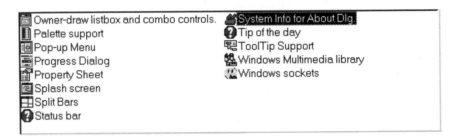

6. Highlight the System Info for About Dlg. component, and then click Insert. Visual C++ will display a dialog asking if you're sure about installing the component.

7. Click OK. Visual C++ will display another dialog telling you that the component you're installing will add information to the About box.

8. Click Yes to continue the installation. Visual C++ will complete the System Info for About Dlg. component installation.

9. Click Close to close the Components and Controls Gallery dialog.

At this point, it doesn't look like anything happened. Visual C++ will just sit there doing nothing at all. Unless you know where to look, you'll never find the code that the System Info for About Dlg. component added. Open the ClassView, and then double-click on the CAboutDlg::OnInitDialog() function. You'll see some new entries in the initialization code, which you'll have to modify as shown in Listing 3-1.

Listing 3-1:

```
BOOL CAboutDlg::OnInitDialog()
{
    CDialog::OnInitDialog();      // CG:  This was added by System Info Component.
```

```
// CG: Following block was added by System Info Component.
{
    CString strFreeDiskSpace;
    CString strFreeMemory;
    CString strFmt;

    // Fill available memory
    MEMORYSTATUS MemStat;
    MemStat.dwLength = sizeof(MEMORYSTATUS);
    GlobalMemoryStatus(&MemStat);
    strFmt.LoadString(CG_IDS_PHYSICAL_MEM);
    strFreeMemory.Format(strFmt, MemStat.dwTotalPhys / 1024L);

    // Display the amount of free memory.
    strFreeMemory = "Free System Memory: " + strFreeMemory;
    SetDlgItemText(IDC_MEMORY, strFreeMemory);

    // Fill disk free information
    struct _diskfree_t diskfree;
    int nDrive = _getdrive(); // use current default drive
    if (_getdiskfree(nDrive, &diskfree) == 0)
    {
        strFmt.LoadString(CG_IDS_DISK_SPACE);
        strFreeDiskSpace.Format(strFmt,
            (DWORD)diskfree.avail_clusters *
            (DWORD)diskfree.sectors_per_cluster *
            (DWORD)diskfree.bytes_per_sector / (DWORD)1024L,
            nDrive-1 + _T('A'));
    }
    else
        strFreeDiskSpace.LoadString(CG_IDS_DISK_SPACE_UNAVAIL);

    // Display the amount of free disk space.
    strFreeDiskSpace = "Free Disk Space: " + strFreeDiskSpace;
    SetDlgItemText(IDC_DISK, strFreeDiskSpace);
}

    return TRUE;     // CG:  This was added by System Info Component.

}
```

Notice that the default code provided by the System Info for About Dlg. component retrieves data for the default drive only. You could easily modify this code to retrieve drive space information for all the drives on the user machine. The memory and disk space strings you'll get also lack any form of prompt like "Free Disk Space" that tells what information is provided by the About box. Unfortunately, this will likely confuse more users than it helps. Make sure you add some kind of a prompt (like the ones shown in Listing 3-1) to cue the user. Finally, notice that the default strings are actually made up of more complex statistics. You could easily add this additional information to your About box should you want to. Here's the final result that this code provides.

3

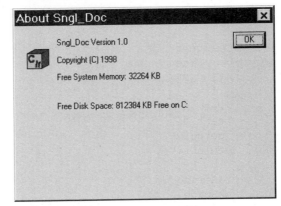

This About box still doesn't provide everything the user will need, but we'll modify it further in the next section of the chapter. For right now, the About box does automatically provide the disk space and memory statistics. It also provides a program name, version, and copyright information. We'll see in the next section, though, that you can automate these three pieces of information as well.

It's time to take one more look at the issue of customization. You can go too far when it comes to customization. Some of the About boxes in applications these days are mini-applications in their own right, which is probably overkill. If you find the need to start adding pushbuttons and a bunch of additional dialogs to the About box, consider putting this information elsewhere, such as in a help file.

Version Information

You might skip the version information resource automatically provided by Visual C++ without really thinking about it. At one time this information was pretty much hidden from everyone but programmers who knew how to retrieve it. The problem is that with the Explorer interface provided by Windows 95 and Windows NT 4 you really can't afford to skip the version information anymore. All you need to do now to display the version information provided by an application is right-click the program icon in Explorer and then choose Properties from the context menu. Select the Version tab of the Properties dialog and here's what you'll see.

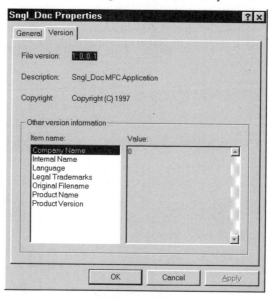

As you can see, the default version information is a lot less than informative. If you leave it in place, users won't even know what company they're dealing with. Since more and more users are becoming aware of what the Properties dialog has to offer, it's becoming more important for programmers to put the right kind of information in here.

TIP: Filling out the version information for your application doesn't have to be a one-way street. You can use this information to fill out other areas of your application as well, which means that you'll only have to change the information in one place to keep it current. We'll look at how you can use this technique for the About box in this section of the chapter, but you'll likely want to use it in other places as well.

IN DEPTH

There are some occasions where you may want to modify the file-specific information in the version information resource. For example, if you double-click the FILEFLAGS entry, you'll see a FILEFLAGS dialog containing two checkboxes. The first checkbox tells whether the version information is for the debug or release version of your program. The second checkbox tells whether this is a prerelease version of your program. You could use the VS_FF_PRERELEASE checkbox for beta versions of your program. Once the program is available for general use, you could remove the check.

The FILEOS entry is another place that offers opportunities for customization. Say your program relies on the special security features that Windows NT provides. You might want to change the FILEOS entry from the default VOS_WINDOWS32 to something like VOS_NT or VOS_NT_WINDOWS32.

It's also important to keep the FILEVERSION and PRODUCTVERSION fields up to date as you modify the application. There are a couple of different ways to use these fields. The best way is simply to ignore the Visual C++ recommended method and type a simple number like 1.0 if this is the first version of your program.

Let's take a look at the version information for our sample application. You'll always find the default information under the Version folder in ResourceView. The default resource name is VS_VERSION_INFO. Figure 3-4 shows what the default version information looks like. The entries above the heavy line normally reflect your application settings. You usually won't need to modify them. It's the entries below the heavy line that begin with Block Header that are of interest

You can modify any of the text entries by double-clicking them. Visual C++ will open an edit box that you can use to change the information. As a minimum you'll want to update the CompanyName, LegalCopyright, and ProductName fields. I normally add some information to the Comments field as well. For example, it's handy to know whom to contact regarding an application or other executable, so I usually add my name and e-mail address. Exactly what you add to this area depends on company policy, legal needs,

Key	Value
FILEVERSION	1, 0, 0, 1
PRODUCTVERSIC	1, 0, 0, 1
FILEFLAGSMASK	0x3fL
FILEFLAGS	0x0L
FILEOS	VOS__WINDOWS32
FILETYPE	VFT_APP
FILESUBTYPE	VFT2_UNKNOWN
Block Header	English (United States) (040904b0)
Comments	
CompanyName	
FileDescription	Sngl_Doc MFC Application
FileVersion	1, 0, 0, 1
InternalName	Sngl_Doc
LegalCopyright	Copyright (C) 1997
LegalTrademarks	
OriginalFilename	Sngl_Doc.EXE
PrivateBuild	
ProductName	Sngl_Doc Application
ProductVersion	1, 0, 0, 1
SpecialBuild	

You'll want to modify the default version information to match the actual information for your company and product.

Figure 3-4.

and personal preference. Here's what my modified version information looks like when viewed in the Properties dialog.

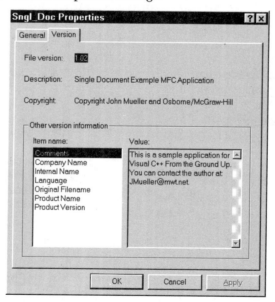

Now that you've spent all the time required to add some version information to your application, it might be nice to get double the use out of it. The same kinds of information that go in your About box normally appear somewhere in the version information as well, so it's a good idea to combine the two. That way you won't have to face the prospect of having an About box that's out of step with the version information. Listing 3-2 shows the code you'd need to add to the CAboutDlg::OnInitDialog() function to add the version information to your About box (we already looked at this function in the About box section of the chapter, so only the new code is shown here— place this code at the very beginning of the function).

Listing 3-2:

```
LPTSTR      lpstrFileName;     // Name of our program.
DWORD       dwHandle;          // A placeholder handle.
DWORD       dwSize;            // Size of the version information block.
LPVOID      lpBuffer;          // Buffer to store version information block.
LPVOID      lpData;            // One version information value.
UINT        uiDataSize;        // Size of the version information value.
CString     strProduct;        // Product name and version.
CString     strCompany;        // Company name and copyright information.

//Initialize our variables and allocate memory.
lpstrFileName = "Sngl_Doc.EXE";
dwHandle = 0;
uiDataSize = 80;
lpData = malloc(uiDataSize);

// Get the version information block size,
// then use it to allocate a storage buffer.
dwSize = GetFileVersionInfoSize(lpstrFileName, &dwHandle);
lpBuffer = malloc(dwSize);

// Get the version information block.
GetFileVersionInfo(lpstrFileName, 0, dwSize, lpBuffer);

// Use the version information block to obtain the product name.
VerQueryValue(lpBuffer,
    TEXT("\\StringFileInfo\\040904B0\\ProductName"),
    &lpData,
    &uiDataSize);
strProduct = LPTSTR(lpData);
strProduct = strProduct + "\n";

// Use the version information block to obtain the product version.
```

```
VerQueryValue(lpBuffer,
    TEXT("\\StringFileInfo\\040904B0\\ProductVersion"),
    &lpData,
    &uiDataSize);
strProduct = strProduct + LPTSTR(lpData);

// Display the product name and version.
SetDlgItemText(IDC_PRODUCT, strProduct);

// Use the version information block to obtain the company name.
VerQueryValue(lpBuffer,
    TEXT("\\StringFileInfo\\040904B0\\CompanyName"),
    &lpData,
    &uiDataSize);
strCompany = LPTSTR(lpData);
strCompany = strCompany + "\n";

// Use the version information block to obtain the copyright information.
VerQueryValue(lpBuffer,
    TEXT("\\StringFileInfo\\040904B0\\LegalCopyright"),
    &lpData,
    &uiDataSize);
strCompany = strCompany + LPTSTR(lpData);

// Display the company name and copyright information.
SetDlgItemText(IDC_COMPANY, strCompany);

// Free the memory we allocated.
free(lpBuffer);
free(lpData);
```

The code is a lot easier to understand than you first might think. You can actually break the whole process down into four simple steps like this:

1. Get the VS_VERSION_INFO structure size using the GetFileVersionInfoSize() function.
2. Use the VS_VERSION_INFO structure size to create a buffer big enough to hold the structure, and then get it using the GetFileVersionInfo() function.
3. Once you have a local copy of the VS_VERSION_INFO structure, use the VerQueryValue() function to get individual strings.
4. Display the strings in your About box.

Now that you've got a better understanding of overall program flow, let's look at some details. The first thing you'll wonder about are the strings that look like this in the VerQueryValue() function calls:

```
TEXT("\\StringFileInfo\\040904b0\\ProductVersion")
```

The first part of the string, StringFileInfo, tells what kind of structure we're referencing within the VS_VERSION_INFO structure. It's a constant when you're dealing with the information below the heavy line in Figure 3-4. The second parameter tells what language version of that information you want to use. Notice that the Block Header entry in Figure 3-4 says that we're using English (United States). If you look right next to that entry, you'll see a series of eight numbers that just happened to match the numbers in our string. That's where you'll get the numbers for your VerQueryValue() call. Finally, the last part of this string is one of the strings in the version information block. In the case of our example string, we're looking for the ProductVersion string. If you look through the example code in Listing 3-2, you'll notice that the only thing that changes from one VerQueryValue() call to the next is the string we're looking for.

There's one last item you'll need to take care of before you can compile the program. Use the Project | Settings command to display the Project Settings dialog. Choose the Link tab of the dialog. We need to add a special library to the program so that we can access version information. Add an entry for VERSION.LIB in the Object/Library Modules field, and then click on OK.

As you can see, for the price of a little boilerplate code (it won't change much, if at all, as you write new applications), you get an About box that automatically updates itself. Here's how our About box looks now. Notice that I did have to reposition the static text controls. I also gave the two default controls new IDs of IDC_PRODUCT and IDC_COMPANY, respectively.

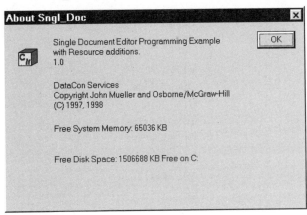

3

Working with Accelerators and Menus

Menus and accelerators go hand in hand. The two resource types are designed to work together to make it easy for the user to get tasks done. You all know what a menu is—it's the physical representation of a hierarchical command structure. An *accelerator* provides the shortcuts in that structure to speed up certain operations. For example, to create a new file you can normally use the File | New command or the accelerator of CTRL-N. Either method produces the same results.

Visual C++ stores menus and accelerators as two different resources. Figure 3-5 shows the main menu and associated accelerator for our sample application. It's interesting to note that both resources use the same name, IDR_MAINFRAME. You'll want to remember this fact since it's the resource name that links the two resources (menu and accelerator) together.

Let's take a look at how menus and accelerators work together. Adding a new entry to an existing accelerator resource is easy. Right-click in the Accelerator window, and then select New Accelerator from the context menu. You'll see an Accel Properties dialog like this one.

The default menu provides the standard functions that you'd expect. An accelerator resource is linked to its associated menu through the name you assign it.

Figure 3-5.

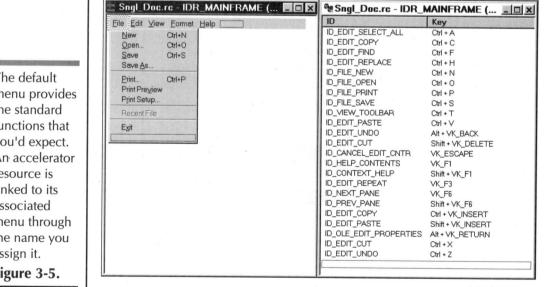

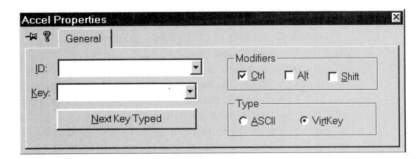

At this point you'll need to choose an ID from the drop-down list box. Menu IDs normally use a combination of the menu levels you need to pass to get to the desired menu entry prefaced by ID. For example, if you want to create an accelerator for the View | Toolbar command (as I did for the example), you'd choose ID_VIEW_TOOLBAR in the ID field. You can also choose between an ASCII and a virtual keystroke (VirtKey). When you're ready to add the keystroke associated with a particular menu command, just click the Next Key Typed button. You'll see a small dialog telling you to press the key combination you want to use as an accelerator. For the purposes of this example, I pressed CTRL-T. What you'll see is a check in the CTRL checkbox and a "T" in the Key field. Click on the Close box to complete adding the accelerator.

If you compiled and ran the program right now, the accelerator you just added would work without a hitch. In fact, you may want to do just that. However, the user wouldn't have any idea that there's an accelerator available for executing a menu command quickly. To add the accelerator keystroke to a menu, you need to modify the current menu.

Adding new text to a menu command is easy. Open the View menu, and then right-click on the Toolbar entry. Select Properties from the context menu and you'll see a Menu Item Properties dialog like this one.

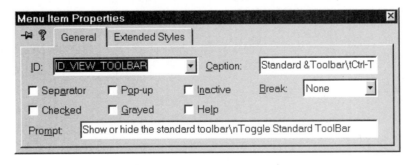

In this case, what we need to do is change the Caption field to take the new accelerator into account. You can use all of the C and Windows formatting characters that you could normally use for text. Changing the Caption field to read "&Toolbar\tCtrl-T" tells Windows that you want to see the word "Toolbar," with the "T" underlined, then a space, and finally CTRL-T to tell the user what accelerator key to use for this menu command.

So what do you do if you want to add new menu entries? Just select a blank spot on either the menu bar or an existing menu and start typing. A Menu Item Properties dialog will automatically appear. For this example, we'll add a Format entry to the menu bar with one option, Font. (Remember to type **&Format** and **&Font** so that the first letter of each entry will be underlined.) Once you have the new menu items added, grab the Format entry and move it to the left of the Help menu. Your menu should look like this.

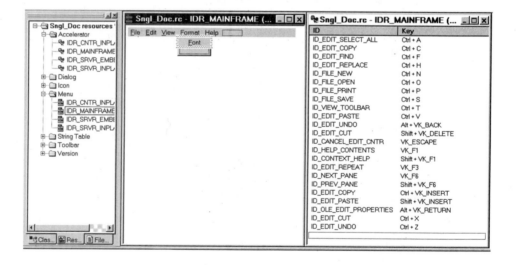

Now we need to add some code to make this new menu entry functional. Right-click the Font entry, and then choose ClassWizard from the context menu. Choose the Message Maps tab. You'll see an MFC ClassWizard dialog like the one shown here.

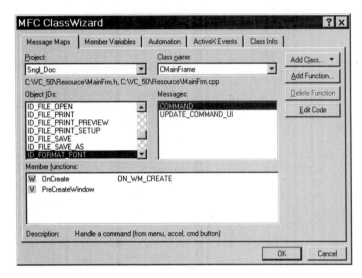

Click on COMMAND in the Messages list. Create the function by clicking on the Add Function button. You'll see an Add Member Function dialog. Click OK to accept the default function name. Edit the new function by clicking on the Edit Code button. Listing 3-3 shows the code required to add font characteristics to our program. Only a rich text editing screen (CRichEdit control) will have this ability in native form, though you could add it to a CEdit control as well.

Listing 3-3:
```
void CMainFrame::OnFormatFont()
{
    CFontDialog    oDialog;    //Create a font dialog.

    //Display the Font common dialog box.
    oDialog.DoModal();
}
```

As you can see, adding the ability to work with fonts in our example is almost too easy. If you compile the example now, you'll be able to change the default font or select text and change the font that way. Here's an example of the ways in which you can change fonts now that we've added this capability to the sample program.

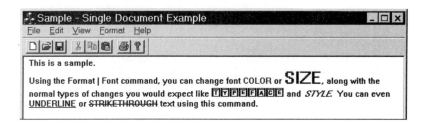

T **IP:** You don't have to work all that hard to display most of the menus you need for an application. All you really need to do is use the right IDs for the various menu options and associated buttons on the toolbars. Unfortunately, many of these special IDs aren't documented right now. For example, if you want to implement a font dialog without doing any programming, make sure that the ID for the menu item is: ID_FORMAT_FONT. Likewise, use the same ID for a toolbar button, if you add one to the application. You can find all of the special IDs, documented or not, in the AFXRES.H file located in the MFC\INCLUDE folder.

Working with Toolbars

If accelerators are the keyboard method for speeding up program access, then toolbars are the mouse counterpart. You'll find that toolbars have become less of an accessory and more of a much-needed part of the user interface. However, toolbars can quickly become too cumbersome to use if you crowd them with a host of buttons that may or may not fit the user's needs. One of the ways around this problem is to create multiple toolbars and then allow the user to decide which ones are needed.

Working with toolbars is just about as easy as working with menus and accelerators. In this case, though, you have to create some linkage between the toolbar and its associated menu command. The default toolbar, IDR_MAINFRAME, includes some of the more common buttons like the ones needed to open files or create new ones.

Let's begin this example by creating a new toolbar—one designed to allow the user to format text. Right-click on the Toolbar folder in ResourceView, and then select Insert Toolbar from the context menu. Visual C++ will automatically create a new toolbar for you. However, the name it gives (IDR_TOOLBAR1) isn't very descriptive. Right-click on the IDR_TOOLBAR1 entry, and then choose Properties from the context menu. You should see a Toolbar Properties dialog like this one.

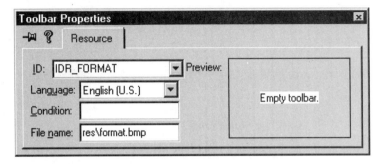

Type **IDR_FORMAT** in the ID field. (Don't worry about changing the File Name field; it changes automatically when you change the ID field.) Click on the Close box to close the Toolbar Properties dialog when you're finished.

Now we need to add some buttons to this toolbar. The buttons will allow the user to perform a variety of tasks without resorting to using the keyboard or moving though the menu system. Figure 3-6 shows the sample toolbar we'll

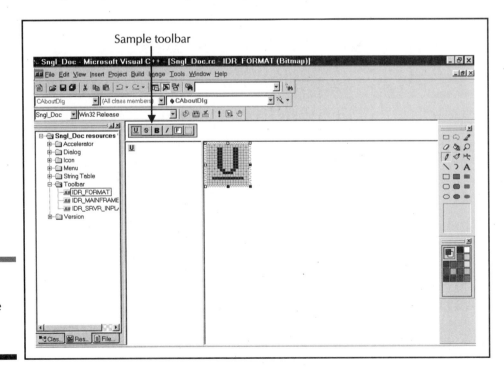

Our sample toolbar includes five buttons.

Figure 3-6.

use for this example. (The buttons represent underline, strikethrough, bold, italic, and font dialog.)

Adding the buttons to the toolbar won't do very much. All you really have is a bitmap of what you want to do in the future. Double-click on the underline button and you'll see a Toolbar Button Properties dialog like the one shown here.

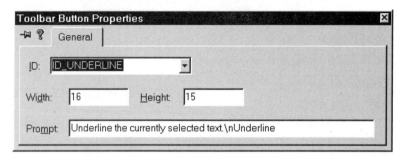

As you can see, I've modified the ID field to read ID_UNDERLINE and the Prompt field to read Underline. Change all of the other buttons in a similar way—ID_STRIKETHROUGH (Strikethrough), ID_BOLD (Bold), ID_ITALIC (Italic), and ID_FORMAT_FONT (Font Dialog). Make sure you type all of the IDs carefully or you'll have problems making the buttons work later. The reason I'm using ID_FORMAT_FONT for the last button is to reduce the amount of coding you'll need to perform. Using this ID means that you don't have to add one line of code to make this button functional. Visual C++ will automatically take care of this button for you through MFC.

Remember to look through the AFXRES.H file located in the MFC\INCLUDE folder for additional standard IDs provided by MFC.

It's time to associate the toolbar with the rest of the application. CTRL-double-click on the underline button. You'll see the MFC ClassWizard, and then an Adding a Class dialog will appear. IDR_FORMAT is a new resource and Visual C++ isn't sure what you want to do with it. You need to associate it with an existing class, so just click OK to accept that default setting. Visual C++ will display a Select Class dialog. Choose the CMainFrame class, and then click on Select. You have now associated the toolbar with the application.

Creating functions to associate with the buttons is easy. Click on a button in the Object IDs list of the MFC ClassWizard, like ID_UNDERLINE, and then click on COMMAND in the Messages list. Create the function by clicking the Add Function button. Visual C++ will display an Add Member Function dialog. Just click OK to accept the default function name. Perform the same set of steps for all of the other buttons. You'll end up with a member functions list like the one shown here.

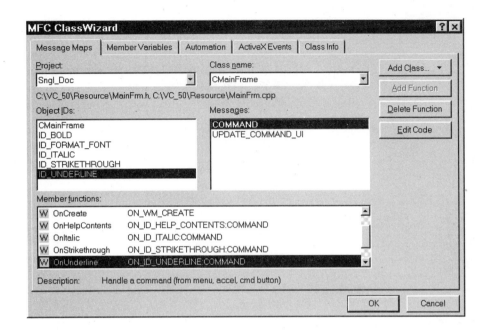

We can add code to the program now to make the buttons functional. Click on any of the member function names (like OnUnderline), and then click the Edit Code button. Visual C++ will display the code editing area. You'll see the function shells that we've just created. Listing 3-4 shows the code you'll need to add.

Listing 3-4:

```
void CMainFrame::OnBold()
{
    CRichEditView*    poView;         // Create a variable to hold our view.

    // Get the active view from the current window. Typecast it as a
    // CRichEditView rather than a CView, the standard return value.
    poView = (CRichEditView*) GetActiveView();

    // Change the font settings as needed.
    poView->OnCharEffect(CFM_BOLD, CFE_BOLD);
}

void CMainFrame::OnItalic()
{
```

```
    CRichEditView*    poView;        // Create a variable to hold our view.
    CHARFORMAT        cfFont;        // Create a structure for the font data.

    // Get the active view from the current window. Typecast it as a
    // CRichEditView rather than a CView, the standard return value.
    poView = (CRichEditView*) GetActiveView();

    // Get the current font settings, then change them to Italic.
    cfFont = poView->GetCharFormatSelection();
    cfFont.dwMask |= CFM_ITALIC;
    cfFont.dwEffects |= CFE_ITALIC;

    // Change the font settings as needed.
    poView->SetCharFormat(cfFont);
}

void CMainFrame::OnStrikethrough()
{
    CRichEditView*    poView;        // Create a variable to hold our view.

    // Get the active view from the current window. Typecast it as a
    // CRichEditView rather than a CView, the standard return value.
    poView = (CRichEditView*) GetActiveView();

    // Change the font settings as needed.
    poView->OnCharEffect(CFM_STRIKEOUT, CFE_STRIKEOUT);
}

void CMainFrame::OnUnderline()
{
    CRichEditView*    poView;        // Create a variable to hold our view.

    // Get the active view from the current window. Typecast it as a
    // CRichEditView rather than a CView, the standard return value.
    poView = (CRichEditView*) GetActiveView();

    // Change the font settings as needed.
    poView->OnCharEffect(CFM_UNDERLINE, CFE_UNDERLINE);
}
```

As you can see from the source code, there are two distinct methods for changing the font attributes you see for a selected group of characters. The first is the easier of the two. All you need to do is get the active view—the part of the window that contains the text that the user is editing. Once you have the view, you can use a special function named OnCharEffect() to change the font attributes. To make this function actually work, you'll need to provide the same font attributes for both arguments. (The CHARFORMAT documentation contains a complete list of attributes and associated defines.)

The second method requires a little more work, but it's also more flexible. In this case you still have to get a copy of the active view. However, this time you use it to fill a CHARFORMAT structure with the current font characteristics. This structure includes everything you need to know like the font name and color, along with font attributes like bold and italic. Once you get the CHARFORMAT structure filled, just change the members you want to change onscreen, and then use the SetCharFormat() function to make the actual change.

In most cases, you'll want to use the first method I showed you for changing font attributes like bold and italic. It's a lot less code and you don't have to fiddle with a structure to get the job done. However, it's nice to know that the CHARFORMAT structure is available in case you need it to make more extensive changes onscreen.

We have a toolbar and some code to make it work. Our sample program is still lacking one important feature. If you run it right now, you won't even see the toolbar. The final step is to add a menu item and some code to make using the toolbar easy. Let's begin with the menu item. All I did was add a new menu item to the View menu using the same procedure we talked about for the Format menu. In the Menu Item Properties dialog, I used ID_VIEW _FORMATTOOLBAR as an ID, &Format Toolbar as a caption, and Show or hide the format toolbar\nToggle Format ToolBar as a prompt. You'll also want to check the Checked checkbox since we'll display the toolbar as a default.

Creating a program shell will be easy. CTRL-double-click on the new Format Toolbar menu entry. You'll see the MFC ClassWizard dialog. Visual C++ should automatically highlight the ID_VIEW_FORMATTOOLBAR entry in the Object IDs list. Highlight the COMMAND option in the Messages list, and then click on Add Function. Finally, click on Edit Code to display the code window.

There are three places you need to add code for the toolbar. The first bit of code appears in the MAINFRAME.H file. You need to add a new variable in the Protected section, right under the initial toolbar variable. The new variable code looks like this:

```
CToolBar m_wndToolBar2;
```

The next bit of code appears in the MAINFRAME.CPP file (see Listing 3-5). This is the code that sets the toolbar characteristics and makes it visible when you start the program. Notice that there are some special coding considerations for making the toolbar dockable (so that you can move it from place to place within the application).

Listing 3-5:

```
int CMainFrame::OnCreate(LPCREATESTRUCT lpCreateStruct)
{
    if (CFrameWnd::OnCreate(lpCreateStruct) == -1)
        return -1;

    if (!m_wndToolBar.Create(this) ||
        !m_wndToolBar.LoadToolBar(IDR_MAINFRAME))
    {
        TRACE0("Failed to create toolbar\n");
        return -1;      // fail to create
    }

    if (!m_wndToolBar2.Create(this) ||
        !m_wndToolBar2.LoadToolBar(IDR_FORMAT))
    {
        TRACE0("Failed to create toolbar\n");
        return -1;      // fail to create
    }

    if (!m_wndStatusBar.Create(this) ||
        !m_wndStatusBar.SetIndicators(indicators,
          sizeof(indicators)/sizeof(UINT)))
    {
        TRACE0("Failed to create status bar\n");
        return -1;      // fail to create
    }

    // TODO: Remove this if you don't want tool tips or a resizeable toolbar
    m_wndToolBar.SetBarStyle(m_wndToolBar.GetBarStyle() |
        CBRS_TOOLTIPS | CBRS_FLYBY | CBRS_SIZE_DYNAMIC);
    m_wndToolBar2.SetBarStyle(m_wndToolBar2.GetBarStyle() |
        CBRS_TOOLTIPS | CBRS_FLYBY | CBRS_SIZE_DYNAMIC);

    // TODO: Delete these three lines if you don't want the toolbar to
    //   be dockable
```

```
    m_wndToolBar.EnableDocking(CBRS_ALIGN_ANY);
    m_wndToolBar2.EnableDocking(CBRS_ALIGN_ANY);
    EnableDocking(CBRS_ALIGN_ANY);
    DockControlBar(&m_wndToolBar);
    DockControlBar(&m_wndToolBar2);

    return 0;
}
```

3

There are three main areas where you need to work with the toolbar code. The first creates the toolbar and then loads the IDR_FORMAT toolbar into it. If this procedure fails, you'll get a "fail to create" message before the application even starts. The second area defines the toolbar style. I used the default settings, which allow the user to resize and move the toolbar around. Tool tips will also appear when the mouse is rested over a button. The final section of code enables toolbar docking, defines where the user can dock the toolbar, and actually docks the toolbar we've created. At this point, your toolbar is visible; the user can move it around and can remove it from sight using the Close box.

Getting the menu command, View | Format Toolbar, to work is fairly easy. Listing 3-6 shows the code you'll need to get this part of the program to work.

Listing 3-6:

```
void CMainFrame::OnViewFormattoolbar()
{
    CMenu*      poMenu;          // Create a pointer to the current menu.

    poMenu = GetMenu();     // Get the menu.

    // Determine if the View | Format Toolbar option is checked. If it
    // is, then hide the format toolbar and uncheck the option. Otherwise,
    // display the toolbar and check the menu item.

    if (poMenu->GetMenuState(ID_VIEW_FORMATTOOLBAR, MF_CHECKED))
    {
        ShowControlBar(&m_wndToolBar2, FALSE, FALSE);
        poMenu->CheckMenuItem(ID_VIEW_FORMATTOOLBAR, MF_UNCHECKED);
    }
    else
    {
        ShowControlBar(&m_wndToolBar2, TRUE, FALSE);
        poMenu->CheckMenuItem(ID_VIEW_FORMATTOOLBAR, MF_CHECKED);
    }
}
```

As you can see, we begin by getting a copy of the CWnd class menu object. Once we have the menu object, it's easy to figure out if the Format Toolbar option is currently checked or not. If the option is checked, the toolbar is visible. You'll use the ShowControlBar() function with the second and third parameters set to false to make the toolbar invisible. The CheckMenuItem() function allows you to remove the check mark from the View | Format Toolbar menu option. Conversely, you use the opposite procedure to make the toolbar visible and check the menu option again.

Go ahead and compile the application one more time so you can check out the various features we've just added. Make sure you try out all of the formatting options and the ability to dock and hide toolbars. Obviously this application isn't as complex as some of the programs you'll see out there right now, but it does make good use of resources. Here's what my version of the program looks like with the toolbars undocked.

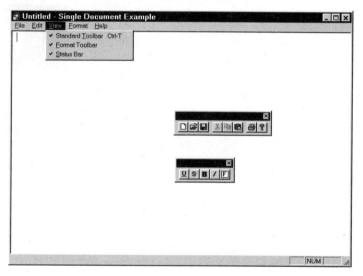

PART II

Visual C++ and Database Management

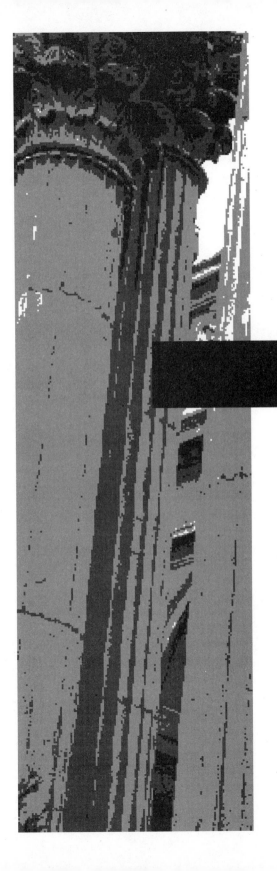

CHAPTER 4

ADO Versus
ODBC

There are a lot of ways to work with databases, and C++ probably isn't the product of choice for most of them. Let's face it, products like dBASE IV, FoxPro, Oracle, and Access have made database management their entire focus. In fact, these products are so good for creating database management programs that they really aren't good for much else. Even if you need something a little more generalized than a dedicated database product to perform some types of work, RAD environments like Visual Basic and Delphi make programming a lot easier than Visual C++ ever thought of being.

Now that I've gotten your attention (and you're probably ready to throw rotten food my way), let me talk about what you'd actually do with Visual C++ when it comes to working with a database management system (DBMS). While all of these other languages do make writing a full-fledged DBMS complete with user interface and high-speed search capability almost child's play, they lack something important that Visual C++ can provide. You can't easily write a utility program for your database using Access. By its very definition, a utility program should be small and portable—Access applications are anything but. Even if the programs created with a product like Access could be small and portable, you'd still need something else: low-level functionality.

Visual C++ is the language of choice for writing database utility programs and drivers.

Just imagine trying to work with real-time data acquisition equipment using something like Visual Basic. RAD environments tend to protect the programmer to the point of total inefficiency when it comes to low-level access. Of course, data acquisition equipment hardly ever relies on a straightforward connection. How are you going to interface Visual Basic to an outside data source that may not even know about Windows, DOS, or a full-fledged operating system for that matter?

It's easy to see that Visual C++ is an indispensable database management tool when it's used for the right purpose. Even though you'll still want to rely on something like Visual Basic for large-scale applications, think of Visual C++ when you're looking at something small, low level, or that provides real-time access. In fact, there's a potential market for Visual C++ database applications you may not have even thought about. Both laptop and palmtop database applications are becoming more common as people use these types of computers out on the road. While you may be able to fit an Access application on today's laptops, older laptops in your company probably won't make the grade when it comes to hard disk size or memory requirements. Palmtops running Windows CE will definitely have trouble running that Access application. Visual C++ provides an invaluable tool when it comes to these new horizons in the database market.

WEB LINK: You don't have to go it alone when it comes to working with Visual C++ and databases. There are database-specific newsgroups like **microsoft.public.access** that can help you with the mechanics of creating a database in the first place. However, these newsgroups provide general information that won't be all that useful when it comes to actually writing an application. The newsgroups you want to look at for Visual C++-specific issues are **microsoft.public.vc.database** and **microsoft.public.vc .mfcdatabase**. If you decide to use ODBC to access your database, you may want to look at the **microsoft.public.odbc.sdk** newsgroup, which talks about a lot more than just the SDK. Programmers interested in the latest technology will want to check out the **microsoft.public.ado** newsgroup, which talks about ADO, or the **microsoft.public.oledb** (object linking and embedding database) newsgroup, which talks about the technology underlying ADO. There is an ADO subgroup at **microsoft.public.ado.rds** that talks about remote data access.

Now that all the smoke has cleared and most people have a better idea of what's going on, there are two main methods for getting your C++ program to access data in a database: ODBC (Open Database Connectivity) and ADO (ActiveX Data Objects). We'll look at both types of access in this chapter, but I think you'll find that ADO is the way to go for new programming situations. It overcomes many of the limitations of older technologies and relies on Microsoft's new low-level access method, OLE-DB (object linking and embedding database). We'll see later in the book just how fast it is to put a database project together using ADO and the various wizards that Visual C++ provides.

ODBC is the method you'll normally use to access data in non-Microsoft databases that don't have an OLE-DB provider; 16-bit ODBC drivers can work very slowly.

ODBC has the reputation of being about the slowest method of accessing data, although unfortunately you'll still need to use it in specific situations where ADO or DAO won't support a database manager but ODBC will. In most cases, this means getting the required drivers from your database vendor, though Visual C++ does come with drivers for some products. (If you're using something really esoteric for a database manager, you'll need to build your own interface—an undertaking not for the faint of heart.) Essentially, you'll always use ODBC to access databases created by DBMS products other than those put out by Microsoft that don't have an OLE-DB provider. ODBC requires some extra work to use as well—the wizards in Visual C++ are tuned for the most part for ADO.

In addition to using ADO and ODBC, you can use older technologies like DAO (Data Access Objects) where a Microsoft product like Access is involved. DAO relies on the Microsoft Jet database engine that you get automatically with Microsoft Access. DAO is also the engine used by older versions of Visual Basic (the latest version of Visual Basic relies on the same ADO/OLE-DB combination that Visual C++ does), so DAO is still a good choice if you need to support older Visual Basic applications.

Even though the Microsoft documentation states that you can use DAO with databases other than those produced by Microsoft products, you'll find that using ADO or ODBC in these situations is much better. Not only will you have fewer compatibility problems, you'll get a speed boost as well because your data requests will go through fewer interface layers. The best rule of thumb to remember is that DAO is designed to work with MDB files.

One of the problems with DAO is that it won't support remote communications. That's one of the reasons that Microsoft came up with RDO (Remote Data Objects). This particular technology saw far more use in Visual Basic applications than it did in Visual C++ applications, so I doubt many of you are using it. However, it's important to remember that RDO is still a viable technology. ADO does have a Remote Data Services (RDS) feature that replaces RDO. In other words, ADO provides the functionality of both DAO and RDO in one package.

What Is ODBC?

Open Database Connectivity (ODBC) is one of the older database interface technologies that Microsoft has introduced. It's actually the predecessor to ADO, which we'll discuss later in this chapter. One of Microsoft's principal reasons for introducing this technology was to give programmers an easy way to access the contents of databases in a very non-language-specific manner. In other words, you won't need to know the Xbase programming language to access a DBF file or Access Basic to grab data in an MDB file. In fact, Visual

4

C++ is one of the programming platforms that Microsoft originally targeted with ODBC.

You'll find that ODBC works much the same as the rest of Windows—it uses drivers contained in DLLs to get the job done. In essence, ODBC provides a set of two drivers: one that speaks the language of the database manager and another that provides a common interface for the programming language. It's the meeting of these two drivers through a common interface that allows Visual C++ to access the contents of the database using a standard set of function calls. Of course, there are other utility-type DLLs associated with ODBC as well. For example, one of these DLLs allows you to administer ODBC data sources. The actual administration interface for ODBC is in a CPL (control panel) file found in the SYSTEM folder—we'll talk more about it later.

ODBC does fulfill its promise to provide access to the contents of a database without too many problems. There are situations where it doesn't provide the best possible data conversion between the database manager and C, but for the most part it works as advertised. The only thing that mars an otherwise great future for ODBC is that it's exceedingly slow—at least the older versions of the product are. When ODBC originally came out, some developers said it would never make much of an impact in the database community because of the speed issues. However, given Microsoft's marketing clout, ODBC has become a qualified success. Just about every database manager worth its salt ships with an ODBC driver of one sort or another today.

Working with ODBC

Before you can do anything with ODBC, you have to have a database—at least in mind. It's usually easier to create the database shell within an application like Access that provides the features needed to do so with the least amount of effort. However, you can create the shell in C++ if you at least have the required ODBC drivers installed. Once you have a database designed, you need to create an ODBC data source for it. That's what we'll look at in this section. The following procedure isn't meant as a rigid course of action; rather, it shows one technique for getting a data source configured.

NOTE: I'll show you how to create an Access database in Chapter 5. For now, just follow along to see part of what we'll do later to access that database.

1. Double-click the 32-bit ODBC applet in the Control Panel. (Some versions of Windows use a simple ODBC applet if there are no 16-bit drivers installed on the current system.) You'll see the ODBC Data Source Administrator dialog similar to the one shown here. Notice that this is the User DSN (data source name) tab. There's also a System DSN tab for system-level databases and a File DSN tab for file-level data sources (which may or may not be a database in the truest sense of the word). You'll also see a default entry for a generic database. That's the entry you would use if you wanted to create a database from within Visual C++.

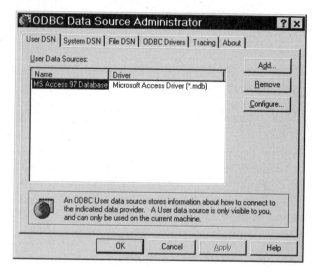

CAUTION: You'll normally need to create an entry on the User DSN tab for local databases and on the System DSN tab for remote databases. Under no circumstances create an entry on both the User DSN and System DSN tabs with the same name. What will normally happen is that you'll attempt to access the database remotely and get really strange and inconsistent error messages from your Web server. In fact, the 32-bit ODBC applet is one of the first places you should look if you get strange error messages during remote database access.

2. Click the Add button. You'll see a Create New Data Source dialog like the one shown here.

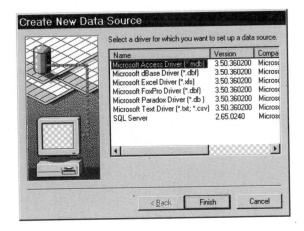

TIP: You can ensure that you're using the most current ODBC drivers available by checking the About tab of the ODBC Data Source Administrator dialog. This tab contains the version numbers of the various ODBC DLLs, the name of the vendor who created them, and the name of the file as it appears in the SYSTEM folder. In most cases you'll be able to use the version number as a method for verifying that your ODBC driver is up-to-date.

3. Choose one of the data sources. For this exercise, I chose an Access data source. Click Finish and you'll see some type of configuration dialog like the ODBC Microsoft Access 97 Setup dialog shown here.

4

NOTE: If you select a data source different from the one I've chosen in this example, the steps required to configure it will differ from the ones shown here—each ODBC driver requires a different type of configuration.

4. Type a data source name in the Data Source Name field. Make sure you choose something descriptive but not overly long. I chose Food Database because I'll eventually create a link to a food inventory-related database.

5. Type a description in the Description field. You'll want to make this entry a bit longer than the previous one since it describes the purpose of your database. On the other hand, you don't want to write a novel the size of *War and Peace*. For this exercise, I typed the following: This database contains inventory information for a food store.

6. Click the Select button. You'll see a File Open-type dialog where you can choose an existing database. The ODBC driver will automatically choose the correct file extension for you.

TIP: You don't absolutely have to design your database in advance. Notice that the Access ODBC driver also includes a button to create a new database. Most, but not all, ODBC drivers provide this feature. Clicking this button will start the database manager application and allow you to design the database. It's interesting to note that the Access ODBC driver will also allow you to compress or repair your database from this dialog.

7. Choose a system database option. In most cases, you'll choose None unless you specifically created a system database for your application. If you do add a system database, it'll appear on the System DSN tab of the ODBC Microsoft Access 97 Setup dialog.

8. Click the Advanced button and you'll see a Set Advanced Options dialog like the one shown here. You won't need to modify many of the entries. However, it almost always pays to add the guest user name to the Login Name field and the guest password to the Password field. This allows a

guest to access your database without really knowing anything about the access at all—not even the name the guest was logged in under.

Set Advanced Options

Default Authorization

Login name:

Password:

OK

Cancel

Options

Type	Value
DefaultDir	c:\VC_50\DB_Samp
Driver	
FIL	MS Access;
ImplicitCommitSync	Yes
MaxBufferSize	512
MaxScanRows	8

Value of   DefaultDir   c:\VC_50\DB_Samp

4

TIP: You may want to look through the list of advanced options provided by your ODBC driver for potential areas of optimization. For example, the Access ODBC driver allows you to change the number of threads that the DBMS uses. The default setting of 3 usually provides good performance, but you may find that more threads in a complex application will speed foreground tasks. Using too many threads does have the overall effect of slowing your application down since Windows uses some processor cycles to manage the thread overhead.

9. Click OK once you've set any advanced options that you need.

10. Click OK again to close the ODBC Microsoft Access 97 Setup dialog. You should see your new entry added to the ODBC Data Source Administrator dialog. If you need to change the settings for the database later, simply highlight it and click on Configure. Getting rid of the database is equally easy. Just highlight the DSN and click on Remove.

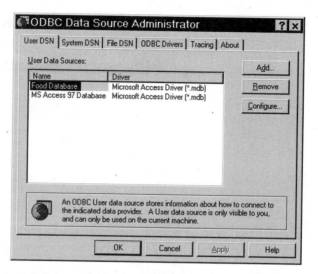

Creating a system DSN is about the same as making a user DSN. The big difference between the two is what they're used for. A system DSN tells your application how to connect with the database and in some cases how to interact with it. A system DSN doesn't contain any of the data for the database—it contains the connection criteria. This could include everything from a user list to the location of important files.

File DSNs

You may have noticed a problem with the example in the previous section. It works fine if you want to configure every machine on your network individually, which probably isn't your idea of a good time. There's another way to store the information needed to create a data source: the file DSN. That's what we'll look at in this section. The following procedure will give you a general idea of how to set up a file DSN.

1. Double-click the 32-bit ODBC applet in the Control Panel. You'll see the ODBC Data Source Administrator dialog. Select the File DSN tab and you'll see a dialog like the one shown here. The first thing you'll need to do is choose a place to store the DSN information.

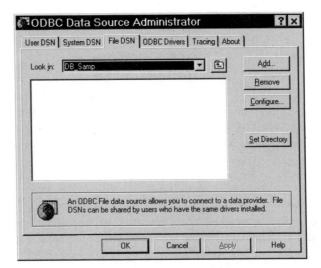

4

2. Click on the Look In drop-down list box. You'll see a list of directories and drives for the current machine. You can use any storage location for the DSN. I normally choose the database storage directory on the network. Using UNC (universal naming convention) directory paths means that everyone will access the DSN file using the same path.

TIP: The Up One Level button (next to the Look In drop-down list box) works just the way it does in Explorer. You can use this button to go up one directory at a time. Eventually you'll end up at My Computer and see a listing of all the drives on your machine.

3. Click Add. You'll see a Create New Data Source dialog.

4. Choose one of the ODBC drivers in the list, and then click Next. For this example, I again chose Access. You'll see the next page of the Create New Data Source dialog shown here. This is where you'll choose a name and storage location for your data source. Click Browse and you'll see a File Open-type dialog box where you can choose a storage location. Type a filename and the ODBC wizard will automatically add DSN as the extension. I chose SAMPLE.DSN as the name for the DSN file in this example.

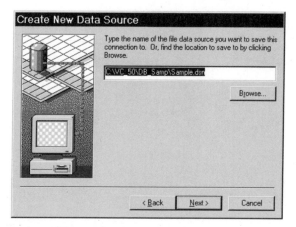

5. Click Next and you'll see a summary dialog like the one shown here. It tells you the parameters for the DSN you're going to create.

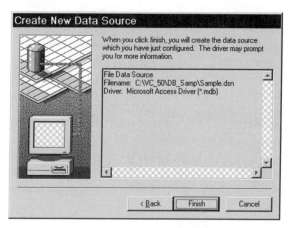

6. Click Finish. At this point you'll see a modified version of the ODBC Microsoft Access 97 Setup dialog. You won't be able to add information in the Data Source Name or Description fields like we did in the previous section. However, everything else will work the same way as before.

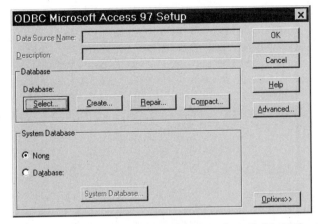

7. Make sure you enter the name of a database by clicking the Select button and then choosing the database you want to use. (You can also click Create if you want to create a new database.)

8. Click OK when you complete the configuration process. You'll see a new DSN file entry in the ODBC Data Source Administrator dialog.

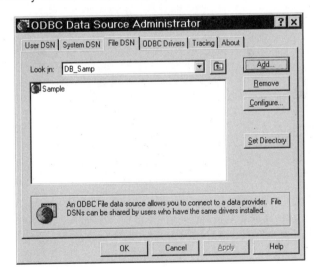

Unlike the previous DSN that we created, this one actually creates a file that you can view and edit with a text editor. Figure 4-1 shows what my file looks like. Notice that it follows a standard INI file format. You can see the [ODBC] heading at the top. All of the settings I chose follow. This file will allow me to choose a data source from Visual C++, yet it's very easy to transfer from machine to machine. I could even change the locations as required during the installation process—this is a real plus when you don't know what kind of setup the user will have.

Logging ODBC Transactions

It's always nice to have a log of whatever you're doing when it comes time to debug an application. The ODBC Data Source Administrator dialog offers this capability as well. You can choose to track the various transactions you make to a database through ODBC. Of course, these logs can get rather large, but you won't be using them all the time.

All you need to do to start logging your transactions is open the ODBC Data Source Administrator dialog by double-clicking the 32-bit ODBC applet in the

The SAMPLE.DSN file contains all of the settings required to use my database from within Visual C++.

Figure 4-1.

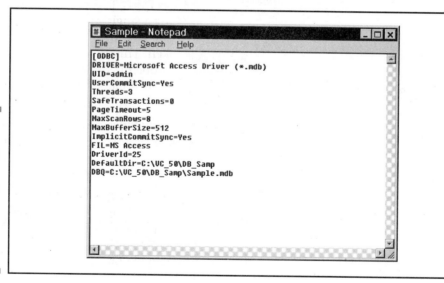

Control Panel. Choose the Tracing tab. You'll see a dialog like the one shown here. (Note that the Windows 98 version of the dialog is slightly different.)

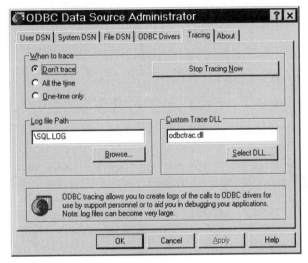

4

As you can see, there are three radio buttons that determine when you'll trace the ODBC calls. The default setting is Don't Trace. You'd select All the Time if you were going to work on debugging a single application. The One-Time Only traces the ODBC calls during the next connection—tracing gets turned off as soon as the connection is broken. This is a good selection to choose when a user calls in with a specific problem. You can monitor the connection during one session and then use that information to help you create a plan for getting rid of the bug.

The trace won't start automatically. You'll need to click on the Start Tracing Now button on the right side of the dialog. The pushbutton caption will change to Stop Tracing Now as soon as tracing starts. Click on the button again to turn tracing off.

The only other setting that you'll need to worry about is the Log File Path. ODBC normally places the transaction information in the SQL.LOG file in your root directory. However, you may want to place that information on a network drive or in a location hidden from the user. The default location normally works fine during the debugging process.

NOTE: Unless you want to create your own logging DLL, don't change the setting in the Custom Trace DLL field. The DLL listed here, ODBCTRAC.DLL, is responsible for maintaining the transaction log.

ADO and OLE-DB—Rungs on the Same Ladder

One of the more confusing things about working with ADO is understanding that it's not the lowest rung on the ladder. OLE-DB is the basis for anything you do with ADO; it provides the basis for communication with the database. ADO is simply a nice wrapper around the services that OLE-DB provides. In fact, you can even bypass ADO and go right to OLE-DB if you want to. However, using ADO will allow you to develop applications much faster. The following sections will help you understand both OLE-DB and ADO.

Understanding OLE-DB

So, what is OLE-DB? As the name implies, it uses OLE (or more specifically, the Component Object Model—COM) to provide a set of interfaces for data access. Just like any other COM object, you can query, create, and destroy an OLE-DB object. The source of an OLE-DB object is called a provider. You'll get a variety of OLE-DB providers as part of the Visual C++ package and more will likely arrive as vendors upgrade their database products. The nice thing about OLE-DB is that the same provider works with any Visual Studio product: Visual C++, Visual Basic, Visual InterDev, and Visual J++.

OLE-DB also relies on events, just as any COM object would. These events tell you when an update of a table is required to show new entries made by other users or when the table you've requested is ready for viewing. You'll also see events used to signal various database errors and other activities that require polling right now.

Microsoft defines four major categories of OLE-DB user. It's important to understand how you fit into the grand scheme of things. The following list breaks the various groups down and tells how they contribute toward the use of OLE-DB as a whole.

◆ *Data provider*   Someone who uses the OLE-DB SDK (software development kit) to create an OLE-DB provider. The provider user interfaces to interact with the database and events to signal special occurrences.

◆ *Data consumer*   An application, system driver, or user that requires access to the information contained in a database.

◆ *Data service provider*   A developer who creates stand-alone utilities (services) that enhance the user's or administrator's ability to use or manage the contents of a database. For example, a developer could create a query engine that allows the user to make natural language requests for information in the database. A service works with the OLE-DB provider and becomes an integral part of it.

◆ *Business component developer*   A developer who creates application modules or components that reduce the amount of coding required to create a database application. A component could be something as generic as a grid control that allows you to display a subset of the records in the database at a glance or something specific to the type of database being accessed.

4

So, how does OLE-DB differ from ODBC? Table 4-1 shows the major differences between the two products. We'll discuss how these differences affect your usage decisions in the "When Should You Use OLE-DB, ADO, or ODBC?" section of this chapter.

Don't get the idea that OLE-DB and ODBC are two completely separate technologies meant to replace each other. There is an ODBC OLE-DB provider that allows you to access all of the functionality that ODBC provides through OLE-DB or ADO. In other words, the two technologies complement each other and are not meant as complete replacements for each other. Can you replace ODBC with ADO or OLE-DB? Yes, but you won't get the very best performance from your applications if you do. The whole idea of OLE-DB is to broaden the range of database types that you can access with your Visual C++ applications. Obviously, if you do need to access both ODBC and tabular data with a single application, OLE-DB provides one of the better solutions for doing so.

Understanding ADO

Now that you've gotten a little better handle on OLE-DB, where does ADO fit in? As previously mentioned, ADO provides an easy method for accessing the

Element	OLE-DB	ODBC	Description
Access type	Component	Direct	OLE-DB provides interfaces that interact with the data, user access to the data is through components designed to interact with OLE-DB.
Data access specialization	Any tabular data	SQL	ODBC has always been designed to use SQL as the basis for data transactions. In some cases, that means the programmer has to make concessions to force the data to fit into the SQL standard.
Driver access method	Component	Native	As mentioned earlier, all access to an OLE-DB provider is through COM interfaces using components of various types. ODBC normally requires direct programming of some type and relies heavily on the level of SQL compatibility enforced by the database vendor.
Programming model	COM	C	OLE-DB relies on COM to provide the programmer with access to the provider. This means that OLE-DB is language independent, while ODBC is language specific.
Technology standard	COM	SQL	OLE-DB adheres to Microsoft's COM standard, which means that it's much more vendor and platform specific than the SQL technology standard used by ODBC.

OLE-DB to
ODBC
Technology
Comparison

Table 4-1.

functionality of an OLE-DB provider. In other words, ADO allows you to create applications quickly and allow Visual C++ to take care of some of the details that you'd normally have to consider when using OLE-DB directly. I've already provided an overview of ADO features in the section on ADO data binding in Chapter 1, so I won't cover them again here.

Like OLE-DB, ADO is based on COM. It provides a dual interface: a program ID of ADODB for local operations and a program ID of ADOR for remote operations. The ADO library itself is free threaded, even though the registry shows it as using the apartment threaded model. The thread safety of ADO depends on the OLE-DB provider that you use. In other words, if you're using Microsoft's ODBC OLE-DB provider you won't have any problems. If you're using a third-party OLE-DB provider, you'll want to check the vendor documentation before assuming that ADO is thread safe (a requirement for using ADO over an Internet or intranet connection).

4

There are seven different objects you'll use to work with ADO. Table 4-2 lists these objects and describes how you'll use them. Most of these object types are replicated in the other technologies that Microsoft has introduced, though the level of ADO object functionality is much greater than that offered by previous technologies. We'll talk more about the ADO classes in the overview section of this chapter.

NOTE: Some ADO objects are represented by interfaces rather than actual classes. Table 4-2 will also tell you about object associations, which will help you understand how to derive the objects not directly represented by Visual C++ classes.

When Should You Use OLE-DB, ADO, or ODBC?

One reason to use ADO in place of ODBC is that ADO offers more objects and methods than ODBC does.

Trying to figure out which technology to use when accessing your data is never an easy job. You may need a common utility to handle more than one database type; part of your data may appear on a local hard drive, part on a network, and still other parts on a mainframe. Even the products that a client normally installs on his or her machine may make the choice more difficult. For example, the level of ODBC support you can expect might rely on which version of Microsoft Office is installed, since this product does provide ODBC support. You'll also find that ADO classes offer more objects and methods

Object	Class	Description
Command	CADOCommand	A command object performs a task using a connection or recordset object. Even though you can execute commands as part of the connection or recordset objects, the command object is much more flexible and allows you to define output parameters.
Connection	CADOConnection	Defines the connection with the OLE-DB provider. You can use this object to perform tasks like beginning, committing, and rolling back transactions. There are also methods for opening or closing the connection and for executing commands.
Error		An error object is created as part of the connection object. It provides additional information about errors raised by the OLE-DB provider. A single error object can contain information about more than one error. Each object is associated with a specific event like committing a transaction.
Field		A field object contains a single column of data contained in a recordset object. In other words, a field could be looked at as a single column in a table and contains one type of data for all of the records associated with a recordset.
Parameter	CADOParameter	Defines a single parameter for a command object. A parameter modifies the result of a stored procedure or query. Parameter objects can provide input, output, or both.

ADO Object
Overview
Table 4-2.

Object	Class	Description
Property		Some OLE-DB providers will need to extend the standard ADO object. Property objects represent one way to perform this task. A property object contains attribute, name, type, and value information.
Recordset	CADORecordset	Contains the result of a query and a cursor for choosing individual elements within the returned table. Visual C++ gives you the option of creating both a connection and a recordset using a single recordset object or of using an existing connection object to support multiple recordset objects.

4

ADO Object
Overview
(*continued*)
Table 4-2.

than ODBC classes do. ADO may offer some features you absolutely have to have in your program—for example, you'll find that both OLE-DB and ADO support DFX_Currency, which has no counterpart in ODBC—but you'll pay a penalty in speed to get them.

There are a few general rules of thumb you can use for making the choice between OLE-DB and ODBC. Since ADO is actually a wrapper for OLE-DB, these same rules apply to it. The following list provides some guidelines you can use to help make the decision between OLE-DB and ODBC.

◆ *Non-OLE environment* If you're trying to access a database that already supports ODBC and that database is on a server that doesn't support OLE, then ODBC is your best choice.

◆ *Non-SQL environment* ODBC is designed to excel at working with SQL. OLE-DB provides some very definite advantages when working with a non-SQL database.

◆ *OLE environment* The choice between OLE-DB and ODBC may be a toss-up when looking at a server that supports OLE. Normally it's a good idea to use ODBC if you have an ODBC driver available; otherwise, OLE-DB may be your only choice.

◆ *Interoperability required* If you need interoperable database components, then OLE-DB is your only choice.

Other issues tend to compound the problem, or at least remove a handy rule that you can use to differentiate the two technologies. For example, there are a few features that both ADO and ODBC have in common. One of these is that Visual C++ allows you to access either technology directly. This means you'll always have full access to every feature that both ADO and ODBC can provide. (Yes, this really is a plus, but it's also a minus since one can't be called definitely superior to the other when it comes to access.)

Some of these technological similarities actually help you move your application from ODBC to ADO or vice versa if you make a wrong decision. Both technologies rely on database objects to manage the underlying DBMS, while recordset objects contain the results of queries made against the DBMS. In addition, both ODBC and ADO use database and recordset objects with similar members. Even though you'll need to make some changes to class and member names, you'll find that the code for both ODBC and ADO programming is remarkably similar.

ODBC and ADO share similar features like recordset and database objects, even though these objects are implemented in a totally different way by MFC.

Both ODBC and ADO rely on external drivers to get the job done. However, with ADO you also get additional help from the Microsoft Jet engine. How can this extra support make programming easier? Consider the case where you need to perform an outer join on two databases that rely on different engines. Under ODBC, you have to perform all the required setups manually. Using ADO means that the Microsoft Jet engine will perform these setups for you. Unfortunately, having ADO do the work means that you'll lose a level of control and some flexibility, which is the reason that you wanted to use C++ to get the data in the first place.

There's one place where you absolutely can't use ADO. If you need 16-bit data access, ADO is out. You'll have to use ODBC whether you want to or not. However, very few people are even working with 16-bit databases anymore. Most of your new projects will use 32-bit interfaces, which means you'll have a choice. Since old projects already have a data access method embedded in the code, you really won't need to make a decision there either.

One area where ODBC falls short is that you can't follow transactions as precisely as you can with ADO. When using ADO with the Microsoft Jet engine, you get workspace-level support for transactions. ODBC only offers transaction support at the database level, which means that you could be tracking transactions from several different workspaces at once. (This makes debugging very difficult and could cause other kinds of problems as well.)

NOTE: ADO provides database-level support when used with an ODBC database; this is the same level of support that ODBC provides. You don't gain the benefit of workspace-level transaction support unless you use the Microsoft Jet engine.

An Overview of Visual C++ ODBC, OLE-DB, and ADO Classes

4

Any discussion of creating database applications in C++ will eventually get to the classes you need to know about in order to actually do something. Each class performs a very specific task, so it's important to know which class to use and where. The overall goal of all the classes is to get specific data from the server and display it on your screen or printer.

It really helps to think of a database object as a pipe that will bring data from the data well to your computer.

The first class you need to know about is CDatabase (ODBC) or CADOConnection (ADO). The objects you create with these classes allow you to gain access to the data within the database. You'll either create a pointer to a particular record or download an entire query; the database object creates the connection that you'll need. What kind of data access you get depends on whether you've created a form view (one-record display of all the data) or a record view (a grid of all records matching a specific criteria).

Once you've got a connection to your database, you'll need some kind of container to hold the information it contains. That's where the CRecordset (ODBC) and CADORecordset (ADO) classes come into play. A recordset holds the data that you'll eventually display onscreen. It helps to think of a *recordset* as a container for holding the data in your database. There are three kinds of recordsets as listed here.

◆ *Table* A table-type recordset represents the data in one table of a database. You can do anything to this single table, including add, remove, or edit records.

◆ *Dynaset* You'll use a dynaset-type recordset when you need to use a query to extract information from one or more tables in a database. As in a table-type recordset, you can add, remove, or edit records in a dynaset-type recordset.

◆ *Snapshot*   This is a static copy of the data contained in one or more tables in a database. As in a dynaset, you'll use a query to extract the information. Unlike in the dynaset, you can't modify the contents of the records. However, you can use a snapshot-type recordset to find data or generate reports.

You may have noticed that I mentioned the term "query" when talking about recordsets. A *query* is simply a question. All you're doing with a query is asking the database to provide you with a set of records that meet specific criteria. When using ODBC, you'll rely on CRecordset class data members to change the query for the records that you want to see. ADO is a little different. You can use the CADOCommand class to create special queries or the CADOConnection to perform standard queries. CADOCommand is a lot more flexible than CADOConnection. You can use it to perform a wide variety of tasks with the database. For example, you can use it to manipulate the structure of the database or perform other administrative tasks.

The final set of classes we'll look at in this chapter are for actually viewing the data once you have it. The CRecordView (ODBC) and CADORecordView (ADO) classes allow you to actually see the data you've collected. Essentially, all this class does is move the data from the recordset object to controls on your dialog or window. You'll also use it to monitor when you've reached the beginning or end of the recordset.

CHAPTER 5

Database Building
Overview

Most applications begin with some kind of recognized need. Suppose you realize that your hard disk requires some type of special maintenance. The next step is a description of the functionality that you need. For example, a utility program may need to access disk resources, determine if there are any problems, and ultimately fix any problems it finds. Once you have some functionality in mind, you start looking at the user interface, and finally you create the code required to make everything work.

Database applications require all of those steps. You still have to see a perceived need for the application, and then decide what that application will do. However, database applications have another step thrown in. The main function of a database application is to access data and conditionally allow a user to manipulate it. (Of course, this is a very simplified view of a much more complex process.) Before you can really do too much with a database application—definitely before any user interface elements are created—you have to design the database itself.

Before you can design a database, you need to know how you'll access it and how the internal database structures work.

Part of the process for deciding how to design your database is figuring out how you plan to access it and how much data you plan to put in it. For example, you wouldn't want to get a server-based DBMS (database management system) if your only goal is to store a few personal names and addresses. You'll also need to know whether the programming language can actually work with the DBMS you have in mind. In Chapter 4, we explored three ways you can access a database from Visual C++: ODBC, OLE-DB, and ADO. I even showed you how to set up a data source name (DSN) for ODBC. Finally, we talked about the kinds of DBMS you could access without getting additional drivers and the process for getting drivers if you need them. Knowing how to access the database, though, doesn't really tell you too much about what a database contains.

In this chapter, we're going to learn what a database is all about on the inside—exploring data as it relates to a DBMS. We'll simply take a look at the basics in layman's terms. For example, by the time you get finished, you'll have some idea of what a table is and how to define it. You'll also learn about queries and indexes. We'll even look at a few interface elements like forms, but only from a very basic level. The most important part is that you'll gain an understanding of how a database functions, which is a prerequisite to accessing them with C++.

There are also a few things we aren't going to cover here because there just isn't space to do so. I'm not going to spend a lot of time talking about relational theory—there are whole books on the market to do that. You won't leave here with a full knowledge of SQL (Structured Query Language) or a complete understanding of user interface design. In sum, you'll know enough to build a simple database that we can use in future chapters—think of this chapter as a database primer and nothing more.

WEB LINK: If you need more information than most books provide or just someone to talk to about your particular database problem, you can always try a newsgroup. For example, you'll find a lot of theoretical information in the **comp.theory.info-retrieval newsgroup**. A whole series of comp.database.<product name> newsgroups like **comp.database. ms-access** are there to help as well. You'll find that these newsgroups can help you discover the theory behind database design. They can also get you over some of the hurdles you'll face when designing a database of your own.

5

An Overview of the Building Blocks

Every database is built of modular pieces. There are pieces that store data, other pieces that organize it, and still others that allow you to find a specific piece of information within the database. A database can also contain interface elements and pieces of code that allow you to manipulate the data it contains. For the most part, though, you'll ignore these last two modular pieces when designing a C++ application. In fact, we won't cover coding in this chapter because you don't need it to write a C++ application. (We'll cover forms simply because they provide a handy way for testing your database structure from within the DBMS before you try to access that structure from Visual C++.)

NOTE: We'll be using Microsoft Access for all of the examples in this chapter. It's not that Access is better than anything out there, but it does provide a wealth of tools you can use to make the database design process easier. Access also comes as part of the Microsoft Office Professional package, so there's a high likelihood that many of you will have a copy to use while reading the book. With that in mind, you should be able to take what you learn here and apply it to other DBMS products.

Figure 5-1 shows an overview of how Visual C++, the database manager, and the database interact. Don't worry if you don't really understand everything that's going on in the figure right now. We'll discuss all of the elements in the following sections. For right now, the figure just provides a general look at how everything fits together.

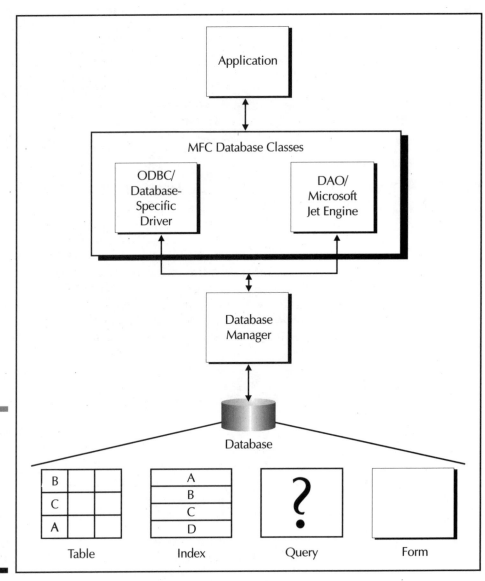

The relationship between Visual C++, the database manager, and the database itself

Figure 5-1.

PORTABILITY: Always ensure that the database and DBMS you choose will actually work with Visual C++ before you begin the design process. The ability to use ADO, OLE-DB, and DAO in addition to ODBC should greatly improve your chances of finding the right solution. In addition, make sure you have a way to use the database with all the platforms you want to write applications for and that the DBMS supports a standard method of file and record locking if you decide to access it from more than one platform. In short, you have to check every computability issue before making a final decision on which DBMS to use—especially if you plan to use it on more than one type of machine.

Database

5

The best way to think about a database is as a container (see Figure 5-1). A database is used to store all of the elements that you'll use to store and manipulate data. Most databases are single files, like the MDB file used by Access. You can also use products that have separate files stored in one location like a directory. In this case, the directory is acting as a database— it's the container that holds all of the other elements together.

NOTE: Ashton-Tate (the originator of dBASE) started using the term "database" to apply to a single Xbase table (DBF file) at one time. In fact, the extension for this file, DBF, actually means "database file." As a result of that marketing decision, some people are still confused about what a table is and what a database is. A database is always the container that holds all of the other data elements together. This includes code, forms, tables, queries, indexes, and reports. No matter what you think right now, throughout this book the term "database" will always refer to the container that holds together all of the data elements for one data set.

A database doesn't just sit there and look pretty. A special application known as a *database manager* can look within the file and extract whatever you need. If you're building the database, you might want to look at the queries or forms you've defined. On the other hand, as a user, your only interest might be some elusive bit of data contained in a table. Whatever your needs, the database manager is the application that looks within the database and gets them for you. In essence, it's like someone looking into a container like a cupboard for a particular piece of glassware or something to eat.

Just like any user, Visual C++ has to ask the data manager to get what it needs out of the database.

When you put a database manager and a database together, you have a database management system (DBMS). In the case of Visual C++, the data manager that's designed to handle the data and the program you write share the role of data manager. In other words, the user will interact with your application to make requests. Your application, in turn, will ask the data manager for the data the user has requested. The data manager will return the data, and your application will display it. This may sound like a lot of work, but it really isn't. Most of it is going to be fairly automatic for you as a C++ programmer (at least if you use the MFC AppWizard to create your application).

Table

A table is the only structure within a database that can hold data. Every other structure is designed to work with the data in some way. A form will display the data, an index orders the data, and a query looks for specific pieces of data. The only structure that actually stores data is a table.

So, how is a table put together? The pictorial representation in Figure 5-1 should give you a good idea. Think for a second about the tables you've created by hand using pen and paper (or those you've seen in books like this one). A table normally contains rows and columns. Likewise, a table in a database contains rows and columns.

Rows (records) always contain one instance of the data you want to store in the database.

The rows are records. Each record represents one occurrence of all the data you want to collect. For example, if you were creating a name and address table, a row (record) would contain all of the information for one person. (At least it would contain all of the information that table was designed to hold—we'll see later that tables are combined in ways that save space on the database server yet allow you to see a fuller picture of whatever data you're looking at.)

Columns (fields) always contain one type of data, like a last name or an address.

Each table column, or field, contains one kind of data. For example, you may have a table column (field) named Last_Name. This field would contain all of the last names for all of the people in your name and address database. Fields always hold one type of data. You can't use a single field to hold address information in one record and age in another. If you need both address and age information, you'll have to construct two fields to hold it.

Getting a particular piece of data or data element from a table is easy. All you need to do is ask for a particular row (record) and column (field). The process of getting data from a database, whether it involves one data element or all of the records that the table has to offer, is called a *query*. Essentially, you ask

Creating a query is like asking the database a question about the contents of a table.

the database manager a question and it responds by giving you the data that matches that question. Visual C++ relies for the most part on a special language for asking questions, called SQL (Structured Query Language). However, you'll find that other mechanisms are available when using ADO, OLE-DB, or DAO. We'll get a kind of bird's-eye view of SQL as the book progresses, but you'll need to spend some additional time learning about it if you want to design complex projects.

Index

A database places data at the end of a table; there's no guarantee in what order you'll find the data in an unindexed table.

If you take another look at Figure 5-1, you'll notice that the entries in the first column of the table are out of order. That's right, a database doesn't have to store the entries you send to a table in any particular order—in fact, it's probably more efficient if it doesn't. If the database manager had to re-sort all of the records in a table every time someone added or removed a record, you probably wouldn't get much work done. Needless to say, you don't always need the data in the same order, so two people could end up fighting over what order the data is in. One person may want an address table sorted by last name; another may need that same table in ZIP code order.

5

So, how do you get the information you need in some kind of order? Indexes are the answer. Figure 5-1 shows two principles that every record takes into account. First, an index never contains all of the entries for the entire table—it only contains a subset. In this case, it only contains the entries in the first field (column). Second, an index is sorted. Even though Figure 5-1 doesn't show it, an index contains pointers to the records in the table. In other words, the data you see when choosing the record is paired with a pointer that the database manager uses to find the entire record. Sorting the index allows you to find the kind of data you want fast. The pointer allows you to find the entire record in the table. Using indexes also allows two people to access the data in one table in two different orders. Since the index, not the table, gets sorted, you can maintain one index for each way that users need the data sorted.

Indexes can span more than one table, as long as those tables are related in some way.

Indexes aren't necessarily limited to a single table. Many database managers will allow you to create indexes that span tables, as long as those tables are related. For example, you could create two tables for keeping track of client purchases. The first table would contain your client list, while the second would contain the details of each purchase. The index could use the customer ID fields plus the purchase number to sort the two tables first by client, then by purchase.

Let's take a look at how this multi-table index concept can work in practice. Figure 5-2 shows an example of a multi-table index. Notice that there's a relationship between the Clients and Purchases tables. A Client ID of 0001 in both tables identifies a client named Ann. However, the Clients table only has one copy of the Client ID, since only one customer can use a Client ID at a time. Since a client can make multiple purchases, the Purchases table contains multiple copies of each Client ID. Notice that Ann has a purchase of $20 in the Purchases table. This purchase is identified with a Purchase ID of 97001. Again, each Purchase ID is unique; otherwise, you couldn't tell one purchase from another. Now take a look at the index. It contains two values, the Client ID and the Purchase ID. It's ordered first by the Client ID, then by the Purchase ID. Even though the tables aren't in order, the index is. The pointers in the index allow you to find information in both tables.

Don't get the idea that indexes are limited to straight entries from a table either. More than a few database programmers have thought up ways to combine table entries or even use special equations to generate non-table index data. Obviously, your choice as to what to put in an index is limited by the rules that the database manager places on you. In other words, you can't decide one day to add some type of numeric calculation to an index if the database manager doesn't permit it. At the same time, it almost always pays to experiment a little if you're having trouble getting the data to the screen in the order that you originally envisioned.

Some DBMSs don't limit you to using field names in an index; you can use complex expressions as well.

Unfortunately, Access doesn't provide any straightforward way of creating complex indexes within the database design view. While you can create an

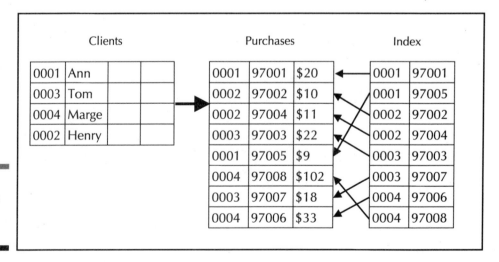

An index can span multiple tables.

Figure 5-2.

index that contains multiple fields and you can control the order in which those fields are sorted separately, you can't use equations or other complex instructions directly. You can create complex indexes using SQL statements in some cases, but that gets to be a complex undertaking of its own. Fortunately, you can provide a complex index as part of a query, which is something we'll look at later in the chapter.

TIP: Even if your DBMS doesn't allow you to add equations or calculated values to an index directly, you may be able to trick it into doing so by adding a special calculated field to the table. The field can contain the calculated value, while the index contains the special field. For example, you could do this using Access. It allows you to assign a default value to a field using the Expression Builder. If the user never sees this field, the result is a special field that you can use for indexing purposes. As you can see, the result is the same, but the method of getting there is a little longer.

5

Query

Always remember that a query is a question that you ask the database about the data it contains.

It's time to look at Figure 5-1 again. The icon I've used to define the query entry says it all from an overview perspective—a query is a question that you've asked the database about the data it contains. Some people may try to convince you that a query is much more by showing you complex SQL statements that really make it difficult to understand what's going on, but the simple truth is that a query is a question.

Every query does have specific components, but this information is only there to help you phrase the question in a way that the DBMS can understand. (Remember that the DBMS is actually responsible for manipulating the contents of the database.) With this in mind, let's look at a fairly simple SQL statement that allows you to view all of the records in two related tables.

```
SELECT Foods.*, Orders.*
FROM Foods INNER JOIN Orders ON Foods.Food_ID = Orders.Food_ID
WHERE ((("Food_ID")<>"VEG-00001-SPL"))
ORDER BY Foods.Food_ID;
```

Let me say first that when using Access, you won't necessarily have to come up with SQL statements like this one unless you really want to. Access will help you create the SQL statement using a Select Query dialog. Now let's look at the statement.

The first thing we do is select two tables and all of the fields within those two tables. The SELECT statement tells the DBMS to select some data. Foods and Orders are the two tables. The asterisks (*) that appear after the table names tell the DBMS to choose all of the fields in those tables. If you had wanted to choose specific fields, you would have typed **\<table name\>.\<field name\>**.

The next line of the SQL statement looks really complex, but all it does is tell the DBMS to relate the two tables. The FROM keyword tells the DBMS that Foods is the master table. INNER JOIN tells how to create a relation to the slave table Orders. The ON keyword tells which fields we're going to relate. In this case, both tables have a field of the same name that we'll use to create the relationship. The criteria for creating a relationship is that you have two fields that contain the same type of information, just like I showed you in Figure 5-2. In that case, the two related fields were Client ID. The slave table normally contains multiple entries for each single entry in the master table, though this isn't absolutely required. (The slave table does have to have at least one entry for each record in the master table.)

You can use SQL to limit the number of records that you actually get. In this case, we tell the DBMS that we don't want to see any records where the Food_ID field equals VEG-00001-SPL. Obviously, you can use any criteria to limit the number of records you get back, and the selection criteria can become quite complicated.

Finally, the ORDER BY keyword tells the DBMS how you want the records sorted. In this case, we want the records sorted in ascending order based on the contents of the Food_ID field. Since SQL allows full use of expressions, you could make the ORDER BY entry as complicated as you like. You can use equations or whatever other criteria you need to get just the data you want in precisely the order you need it.

WEB LINK: If you really want to learn the ins and outs of SQL, look at the Open Group Web site at **http://www.opengroup.org/ot/search.htm**. (The Open Group is a combination of OSF and X/Open.) Type **SQL**, and then click the Search button when asked what you want to look for. You'll find an entire list of the SQL specifications.

Unlike Access, Visual C++ will require you to create these SQL statements by hand in most cases. It doesn't take too much time to figure out that creating

Forms are an onscreen representation of the data you collect from a database using a query.

Reports are a printed representation of the data you collect from a database using a query.

the queries you need in Access (or whatever DBMS you're using) is one way to speed up the development process, especially if you don't know much about writing SQL statements.

Forms and Reports

We've talked about a lot of management and storage issues to this point in the book. It's true that a database requires all of the right internal management structures before you can use it, but there really isn't any reason to go through all this work if you can't use the information you've collected in some way. Forms and reports signify the two most common methods for actually using the information in a database.

Normally, a form represents data you see onscreen, while a report represents the same data sent to a printer. A form usually displays a grid of all the records you've requested or a single record at a time. Reports always display a complete list of the data you've collected, but it's usually not in a grid format. Reports typically provide some kind of structured view of the data you've requested.

A Better Look at Forms

Let's talk about forms a little more. As previously mentioned, there are normally two ways to present data in a form: all the records in a grid or a single record at a time. Figure 5-3 shows a typical grid view, while Figure 5-4

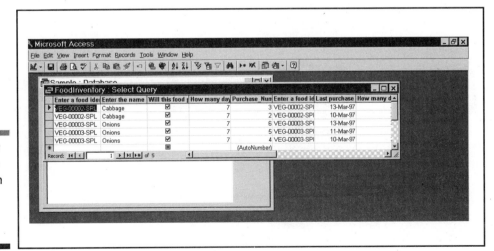

The grid view allows you to see more than one record at a time.

Figure 5-3.

5

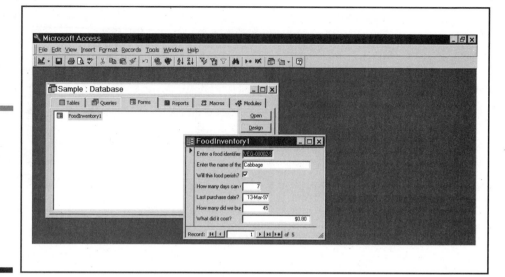

The single-record detail view allows you to see all of the information about one record.

Figure 5-4.

shows a typical single-record detail view. The main advantage to the grid approach is that you can get the big picture. Ordering your data correctly is a definite plus when using this view—you can easily see the relationships between records when the number of records exceeds one screen's worth of information. For example, you may want to order an inventory database by product type before displaying it in a grid. That way you can see how many of like items you have in stock.

The disadvantage to using a grid view of your data is pretty obvious. Not only are all of the fields crushed together, but you very likely won't see all of the fields in the table (or set of tables) without scrolling horizontally. Sure, you can get an overview of a lot of records very quickly, but you won't see the whole picture for an individual record. Some database applications get past this limitation by allowing you to choose a single record from a group of records in grid view and then switch to a single-record detail view.

TIP: Always place the fields you think the user will need most when designing a grid view form. That way, you minimize the amount of horizontal shifting the user will have to do to find important data. Once you have the data sorted by importance, you may want to take the secondary step of grouping like data together. For example, it's very helpful to keep all of the telephone numbers together in an address database. That way, someone can just call one number after another in an attempt to locate a particular person. Always test the arrangement of your grid by either monitoring user usage through events or actually watching them use your application. The less movement that the user has to make in order to find something, the better.

5

Use the grid view to provide users with an overview that they can use to select records, and then use a single-record view to allow users to see all of the details for a record at one glance.

A single-record view has the advantage of precise presentation of one record. You can see everything that the record has to offer. Of course, the disadvantage of this presentation is immediately evident when you look at Figure 5-4. Unlike the grid view, the single-record view doesn't provide any sort of overview. You can't use it to analyze trends or to get a more complete picture of the table contents as a whole. For this reason, a single-record view is normally reserved for detail views of table data. You'll use it to edit or approve a record for deletion once you find what you want using the grid view.

There's a third form view that you may need to use from time to time. It consists of a single-record view form that has a grid added to it. The single record would show the contents of the master table. For example, it might show client information like name, address, and telephone number. The grid contains the records in the slave table that match the master record. For example, the grid might contain a list of all the purchases a client has made during the year.

Always avoid cluttering a form with too much data. Use multiple forms to avoid clutter if necessary.

Unfortunately, trying to come up with a combination-type form that really does the job well is pretty difficult. The grid takes up a lot of screen real estate unless you severely limit the number of fields it shows. As a result, many combination forms end up looking crowded, and the data gets hard to see because there's simply too much to look at. The point is that you want to make data easy to find, which means limiting the amount that the user has to shift through on any given form.

Another form of single-record view uses multiple forms to avoid problems with screen clutter. Say you actually required 50 fields to describe everything you need to know about an item in your inventory. Trying to display that many fields on one screen would produce so much clutter that no one could find anything. What you should do in this case is create a main form that gives an overview of the data in the record, and then use supplementary forms to provide the details. For example, you might want to put inventory notes on one supplementary form, since the notes will tend to take up a lot of space. You might also want to put the vendor data for a particular item on a separate form, since you won't be ordering new quantities of the item on a daily basis in most cases. Of course, adding supplementary forms means adding detail buttons to your main form, which further reduces the amount of available screen space. You need to weigh the problem of screen clutter against the confusion factor of seeing too many buttons on one form. In some cases, the best answer is not to display some piece of information unless you really need it.

A Better Look at Reports

Computers were originally supposed to bring about the paperless office. They appear to have done anything but. You can generate more reports with a computer than any office ever could using typewriters. In fact, it's so easy to create reports that you can start generating paper without really thinking about it.

Traditional reports give you the ability to take information stored in your database and output it in paper form. However, reports don't necessarily appear on paper anymore. For example, if you have a Web site and need to keep employees in a variety of locations up to date about the current company status, you may find yourself publishing that report in a form that can be read in an Internet browser. Electronic mail is playing a larger part in correspondence as well; you might find that a report needs to be in electronic format so that you can mail it to people.

Whatever form a report may take, it has certain characteristics that you need to think about during the creation process: organization, purpose, and audience. The following sections discuss each of these important considerations.

Organization   Before you can organize a report, you need to consider what kind of information you want to see in it and how much of that information is repetitive. Getting rid of unneeded data frees up space for the data that you do want to look at—a very important consideration when using printed media, since you can't scroll the data when using it. Another way to free up space is to keep all repetitive data on one line of the report. This procedure is called *grouping.* Creating groups not only saves space but also helps the report's reader find needed information faster.

Purpose   The purpose of a report determines how much information you should include and whether a summary will work in place of a detailed listing. It's important to give your audience all the information it needs without cluttering the report with information that is not needed. For example, you'd hardly need to tell the people in management every detail of your client database; all they're really interested in is the bottom line. How much did each client purchase or how much was purchased each time?

Let's look again at the Clients and Purchases tables that I introduced in Figure 5-2. If you created a purchases report for this table, you'd definitely want to include all of the summary information in the Purchases table. However, to save space, you'd use all of the client information like the Client ID and Name fields as a heading to group the purchase information. In a report like this, you might not need all of the client information. For example, you could probably get by without adding the address information if the purpose of this report was to generate a call list.

5

What if you wanted to create a general report about the client? In that case, you might include all of the client information in the Clients table and exclude information like the Purchase ID from the Purchases table. In addition, you might simply total each client's purchases and include a single figure in the report rather than create a detailed listing of every purchase.

Audience   Your audience will influence the kind of report you put together. For example, you might find that a report generated for your colleagues can use a very simple and easy-to-read format. You'll probably need such a format because the report will include a lot of detailed information. On the other hand, you'll want to make a report intended for management a little fancier.

T IP: Don't discount your need as the programmer for reports. Sure, you can try to debug every problem encountered with your database setup using forms onscreen. However, reports can help you find more insidious bugs. For example, you might find that your database has a subtle math error that you can only see when you print the contents of the database. The bug may not seem so apparent if you only look at the contents of your database onscreen. Make sure you actually print out the reports you design so that you can see how efficiently they display the contents of the database as well. Even though you're using C++ to design the application, knowing what's possible from within the DBMS itself will help you design better reports from within the Visual C++ environment.

Creating a Database

It's time to look at the process for putting a database together. This isn't going to be the most complex database you've ever seen. In fact, it'll only include two tables to begin with. The whole purpose of this section is to get you started with the basics. Even though we'll be using Access for this example, you can certainly apply the basics you'll learn to other products as well.

NOTE: We'll be using this example database throughout the book, so it's important to understand how it's put together, even if you don't intend to use Access as your DBMS. All of the example code in the database chapters that follow are based on this example table. The principles that you see demonstrated will work with other DBMSs as well. Remember that Visual C++ uses both ODBC and DAO classes that don't depend on specific database implementation.

The first thing you'll need to do is create a new database. The following procedure will help you get started. All of the sample programs assume you named your database Sample and stored it in the DB_Samp directory, but any name and location will do.

1. Start Microsoft Access. You'll see a Microsoft Access dialog like this one that asks what you want to do.

2. Choose the Blank Database option, and then click on OK. You'll see a File New Database dialog that looks similar to a File Save dialog.

3. Type a name for your database (the example uses Sample), choose a directory to store it in (the example uses DB_Samp), and then click Create. At this point, a blank Database dialog like this one will appear.

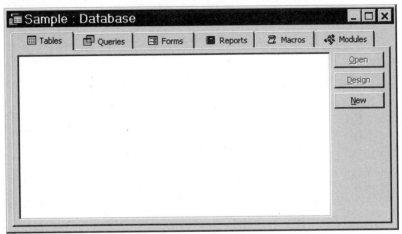

5

Now that you have a blank database at your disposal, you can start filling it with tables, queries, and other paraphernalia that databases hold. The following sections will show you how to create the elements you'll need to use the sample programs in the book. You can, however, add as many elements as you need to experiment with the program. It's always a good idea to keep a sample database that you can use for experimentation purposes.

NOTE: All procedures in the following sections assume that you have the sample database open and ready to use. If you have followed the example in the preceding steps, you should be looking at the Sample: Database dialog.

Adding Tables

We'll need two tables for the example database. The first table, Foods, will contain a list of food inventory items. The second table, Orders, will contain ordering information for the food items. Let's begin by creating the Foods table.

1. Select the Tables tab of the Sample: Database dialog.
2. Click on New. You'll see a New Table dialog like the one shown here.

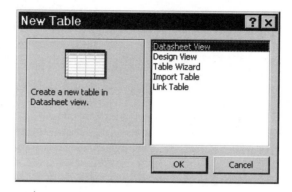

3. Highlight the Design View option, and then click on OK. You'll see a Table design dialog like the one shown in Figure 5-5.

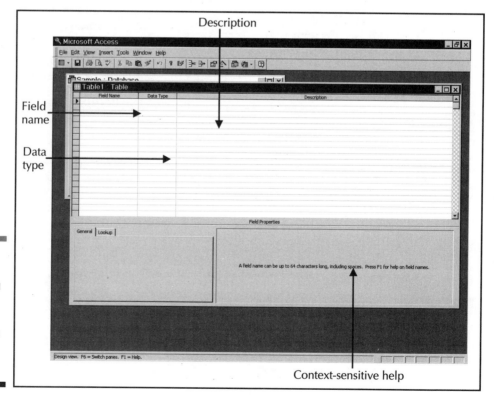

The Table design dialog will allow you to create the tables needed for the sample database.

Figure 5-5.

Let's talk about the Table design dialog for a few minutes. There are three columns in this table. The first column, Field Name, contains the name of the field. All you really need here is a name that describes what kind of information the field will hold. While Access does allow you to use spaces in the field name, you'll want to avoid doing so to make it easier to access the field from within Visual C++. The best way to add space between words in a field name is to use an underscore like this: Field_Name. You'll also want to forego the use of any non-alphanumeric characters like the pound sign (#) or the ampersand (&)—using these characters will definitely cause problems with your C++ program.

The second column, Data Type, defines the kind of data that the field will hold. Access defines a wealth of data types shown in the following list.

5

NOTE: This list of data types reflects all the ones available in the Office 97 version of Access. You may find that an older version of Access provides fewer data types to choose from. We won't use any of the newer data types in our sample database, so older versions of Access should work fine.

◆ *Text*   A short string containing 255 or less characters.

◆ *Memo*   A long string used for storing notes or other large pieces of text.

◆ *Number*   Any kind of numeric value including Byte, Integer, Long Integer, Single, Double, and Replication ID.

NOTE: C++ programmers will know a Replication ID by the term GUID (globally unique identifier). As with C++, a Replica ID is used to identify an Access object.

◆ *Date/Time*   One of several dates and/or time formats available in Access.

◆ *Currency*   A special number format used to store monetary values.

◆ *AutoNumber*   Access can provide a counter as a primary key for your table. The primary key assures that each record has a unique value that you can use to access it, so creating one is essential.

◆ *Yes/No*   C++ programmers will recognize this as a Boolean value. You can format it as Yes/No, On/Off, or True/False in Access. However, the ability to format this value doesn't affect the fact that it's still a Boolean value.

◆ *OLEObject*   Any kind of OLE object supported by the host machine.

◆ *Hyperlink*   This is a fairly recent addition to Access. It allows you to store either a UNC (universal naming convention) path to a resource on the network or a URL (uniform resource locator) to a resource on the Internet. Access even supports the use of anchors on a Web page. For full discussions of URLs and anchors, see Chapter 8.

◆ *Lookup Wizard*   There are some situations where you want the user not to enter just any value into a table but to choose from a specific list of choices. The Lookup Wizard will allow you to create a reference to another table in your database that is used to fill this field. The user will see a list box or combo box onscreen and get to select from a predefined list of choices in the second table.

The third column of the Table design dialog, Description, allows you to add comments to the table in order to document it. You'll find that documenting the exact purpose of each entry in every table of your database becomes essential as the database grows in size. Sometimes you'll find that a field that made sense when you first designed the database is no longer needed. Without proper documentation, you'll find it a lot harder to locate these extra space-consuming fields.

In the lower-left corner of the Table design dialog, you'll see a tabbed dialog called Field Properties. This is where you'll enter Access-specific formatting information for your table. In most cases you'll see a Caption property as a minimum. The Caption property defines how Access refers to the field within forms and reports. You'll also find that setting a caption makes designing your application a bit easier because it forces you to think about the user interface as you design the project.

Right next to the Field Properties dialog in the Table design dialog is a sunken box. This box normally contains helpful tips. For example, if you click on the Field Name column, this box will tell you that a field name can be up to 64 characters in length including spaces.

Now that you've got a better idea of how the Table design dialog works, let's build a couple of tables. Here's what the entries for the Foods table will look like (simply type the entries as shown in the illustration; the illustration also shows which data types you should use).

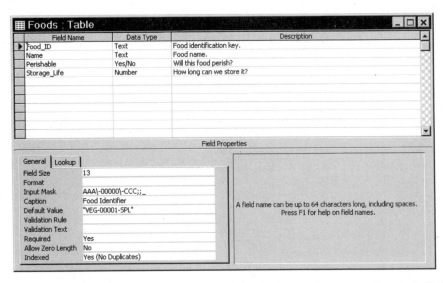

Table 5-1 contains the property values that you'll need to enter for each field.

There are a couple of things we need to look at before this table is complete. The first thing you'll want to do is define a primary key. Since we'll be relating the Foods table to the Orders table using the Food_ID field, we'll make it our primary key. Use the following procedure to assign the primary key to the table.

1. Click the box to the left of the Food_ID field so that the entire field is highlighted as shown here.

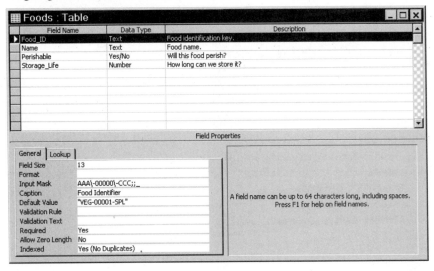

Field	Property Name	Value
Food_ID	Field Size	13
	Input Mask	AAA\-00000\-CCC;;_
	Caption	Food Identifier
	Default Value	"VEG-00001-SPL"
	Required	Yes
	Allow Zero Length	No
	Indexed	Yes (No Duplicates)
Name	Field Size	50
	Caption	Food Name
	Default Value	"Cabbage"
	Required	Yes
	Allow Zero Length	No
	Indexed	Yes (No Duplicates)
Perishable	Caption	Perishable?
	Default Value	True
	Validation Text	You must enter Yes or No
	Required	Yes
	Indexed	Yes (Duplicates OK)
Storage_Life	Caption	Storage Life
	Default Value	7
	Validation Rule	>0
	Validation Text	Value must be greater than 0
	Required	No
	Indexed	No

Property
Values for the
Foods Table
Table 5-1.

2. Use the Edit | Primary Key command to create the primary key. Access will add what looks like a key to the left of the Food_ID field.

Once you've defined a primary key, you'll want to check all of your indexes. Use the View | Indexes command or click the Indexes button on the toolbar to display an Indexes dialog like the one shown here. Notice that Access will allow you to define an index on a single field or a group of fields; you can't create an index using a calculated field or equation. You'll see later that using queries will allow you to get around this limitation.

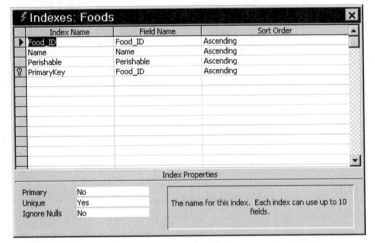

Click the Close box on the Indexes dialog to close it. Now it's time to save our first table. Click the Save button on the toolbar. Access will display a dialog asking you for a table name. Type **Foods**, and then click OK. The table name will appear in the Sample: Database dialog. Click the Close box to close the Table design dialog.

We're going to use the same procedure to create a second table. In this case the name of the table is Orders. Here are all the field entries you'll need for the Orders table (the illustration also contains the data type for each of the fields). Notice that the Purchase_Number and Food_ID fields are both used for the primary key. The Purchase_Number field is the unique field for this table. Table 5-2 contains a complete list of the property values you'll need to define for this table.

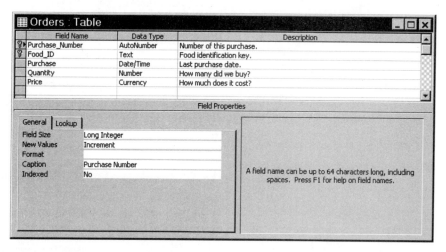

You should notice one major difference in the properties for the Food_ID field in Table 5-1 and the same entry in Table 5-2. Table 5-1 says to index the Food_ID field (see the Indexed property), but not to allow duplicates. That's because we only want one entry for each food item in the database. However, the Indexed property in Table 5-2 says Yes (Duplicates OK), which means that we can have multiple entries there. The reason is simple: You can order the same food item as often as needed, so we have to allow the user to make multiple entries of the same food item in the Orders table.

Let's check out the Indexes dialog again. Click the Indexes button on the toolbar. Here's what you should see. Notice that we defined a multiple field index (PrimaryKey) by typing the name of the index and the name of the first field on one line. The second and subsequent lines contain only a field name.

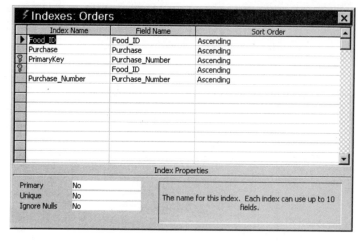

Field	Property Name	Value
Purchase_Number	Field Length	Long Integer
	Caption	Purchase Number
	Indexed	Yes (No Duplicates)
Food_ID	Field Size	13
	Input Mask	AAA\-00000\-CCC;;_
	Caption	Food Identifier
	Default Value	"VEG-00001-SPL"
	Required	Yes
	Allow Zero Length	No
	Indexed	Yes (Duplicates OK)
Purchase	Format	Medium Date
	Caption	Last purchase date?
	Default Value	Now()
	Required	Yes
	Indexed	Yes (Duplicates OK)
Quantity	Field Size	Long Integer
	Caption	How many did we buy?
	Default Value	1
	Validation Rule	>0
	Validation Text	Must be greater than 0
	Required	Yes
	Indexed	No
Price	Format	Currency
	Caption	Price in Dollars
	Default Value	0
	Validation Rule	>0
	Validation Text	Must be greater than 0
	Required	Yes
	Indexed	No

Property
Values for the
Orders Table

Table 5-2.

5

As before, close the Indexes dialog, and then save your new table. Be sure to give it the name Orders.

Now that you've got two tables to use, it's time to fill them with some data. Figure 5-6 shows the data for the Foods table, while Figure 5-7 shows the data for the Orders table. You can add extra data if you like; just make sure that there are one or more entries in the Orders table for each entry you create in the Foods table. Likewise, make sure that you don't enter any records into the Orders table that don't have a corresponding entry in the Foods table.

Using Queries to Order Data

Queries make it incredibly easy to find precisely the data you need. Access makes it even easier to create queries by using a visual query interface. The

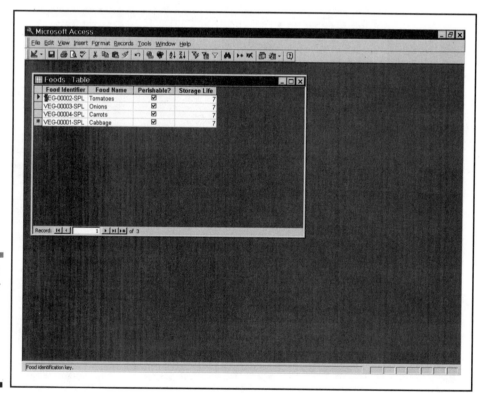

Make sure you have one entry in the Orders table for each entry in the Foods table.

Figure 5-6.

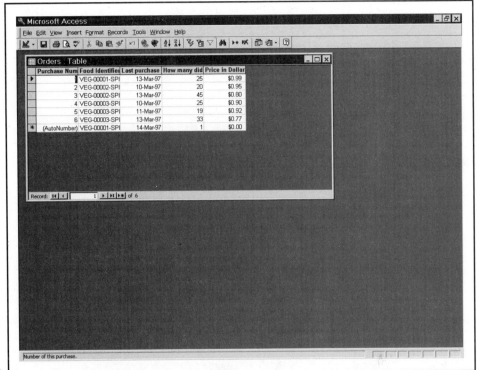

Don't create
any records in
the Orders
table without
a matching
Food_ID in the
Foods table

Figure 5-7.

following procedure will take you through the process of creating a query for
the two tables we just created in the previous section.

1. Click the Queries tab of the Database dialog.
2. Click on New. You'll see a New Query dialog like the one shown here.

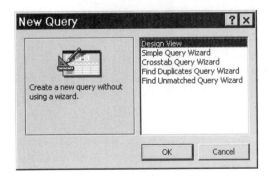

3. Choose Design View, and then click OK. You'll see the Show Table dialog shown here.

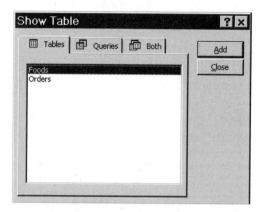

4. Highlight both tables (Foods and Orders), and then click Add. Click Close. The Show Table dialog will disappear and you'll see the Select Query dialog shown here. Notice that Access automatically creates the logical relation between the two tables and that the primary keys are in bold text. Now we need to decide which fields to display in the query.

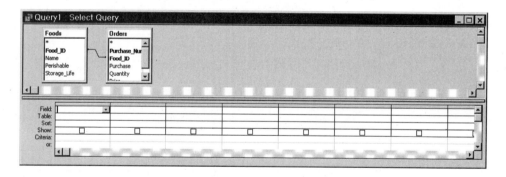

5. Double-click the asterisk in the Foods list. This tells Access that you want to use all the fields in this table for the query.

6. Double-click the Food_ID, Purchase, Quantity, and Price fields in the Orders table. This tells Access that you want to use only three fields from this table. You don't need the Purchase_Number field because Access will update it automatically. So why do we need both Food_ID fields? That's the field that we're using to relate the two tables, so it's important to have both in place. Otherwise, you couldn't add records to the Orders table. Now we need to decide on a display order for the query.

7. Double-click the Food_ID field in the Foods table. In the lower half of the dialog, remove the check mark from the Show property for this field. We don't want to see it twice.

8. Choose Ascending in the Sort property for the Food_ID field. This tells Access how you want to order the information. Sorting by the Food_ID field isn't enough, though, since we can have multiple copies of this field in the Orders table.

9. Double-click the Purchase_Number field in the Orders table and remove the check mark from the Show property. Choose Descending in the Sort property. We now have a means for displaying all of the entries in the Orders table in a particular order. In this case, we'll show the foods in ascending order with the most recent order first. At this point, your Select Query dialog should look like the one shown here.

5

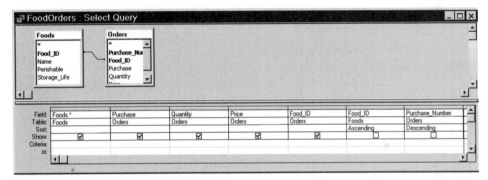

You'll always want to test the queries you create to make sure that they work as intended. One of the easiest ways to do that at this point is to click the Run button on the toolbar. Here's what you should see.

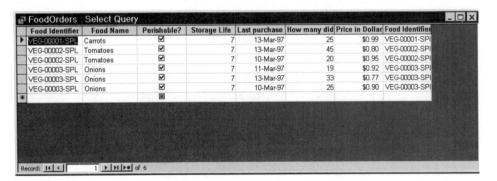

Notice that all six entries from the Orders table appear in the query and that only the fields we selected are present. All of the food identifiers are in alphanumeric order, just as we requested. In addition, the orders appear with the most recent order of each item first, rather than last.

It's time to save our query. Click the Save button, and then type **FoodOrders** in the Save As dialog. Click OK to complete the process. Click the Close button to close the query.

Creating a Test Form

There are two important reasons for you as a Visual C++ programmer to create forms within the DBMS. First, you can test your query one more time in a production-type environment, the same environment you'll test it in under Visual C++. Second, the test form allows you to look at your data without creating a special application. It's really handy to find out if the problem with your Visual C++ program is a result of your program code, the query you've created, the data itself, or some problem with the DBMS. A test form can go a long way toward helping you make this determination.

You don't have to make this form overly complex to allow it to do its job. All you really need is a list of the fields you'll want to look at in the user application. With that in mind, let's create a test form for our sample database using the following procedure.

1. Click the Forms tab of the Database dialog.
2. Click New. You'll see a New Form dialog like the one shown here.

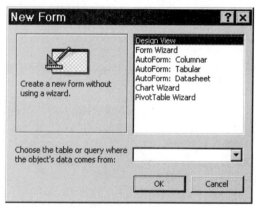

3. Highlight Form Wizard, choose the FoodOrders query in the drop-down list box, and then click OK. You'll see a Form Wizard dialog like the one shown here. Make sure you look at the list of fields. It's important to verify that the Form Wizard has picked up all of the fields that you expected from the query.

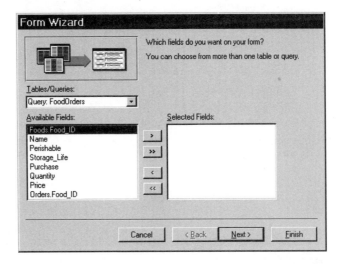

4. Highlight the Orders.Food_ID field, and then click the right arrow button (>). You'll see the field added to the Selected Fields list.

5. Click the double arrow button (>>) to add the remaining fields to the Selected Fields list. Since we really don't need the Foods.Food_ID field, highlight it and then select the left arrow button (<). This will remove it from the Selected Fields list.

6. Click Finish, since we're really not interested in aesthetics here. What you'll see is a single-record view of your data like the one shown here. The first thing you should look for again is the list of fields. Make sure that they're all present. The next thing you should do is verify that the captions you selected are correct. Finally, verify that the data shown onscreen is correct.

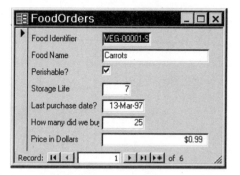

Now that you've got a test form, you can try things like adding new records, deleting records, and looking for specific information. Doing these kinds of tests on an actual form will help you verify that everything actually works as it should before you attempt to use the database in a Visual C++ application.

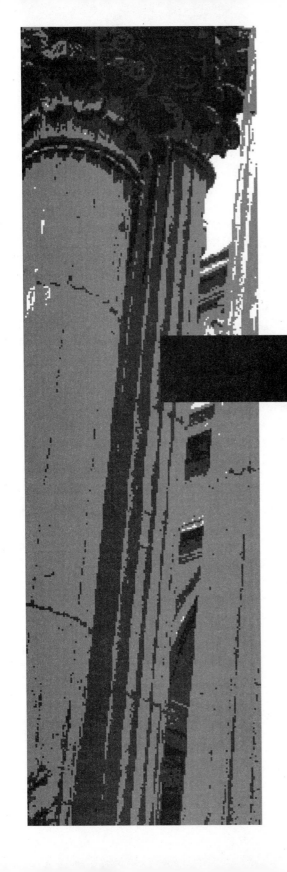

CHAPTER 6

Building a Database Application Using ODBC

In the previous two chapters, I introduced you to some concepts you'll need to actually use in this chapter. The first thing we did was look at some theory behind ADO, OLE-DB, and ODBC. I'm assuming at this point that you've decided to use ODBC instead of ADO or OLE-DB to write your application. If you didn't read Chapter 4, you might want to do so now to make sure that you're actually in the right place.

We spent some time in Chapter 5 looking at how you put a database together. In fact, this chapter assumes that you constructed the sample database in that chapter. I won't spend any time here telling you about the sample database, but you'll need it to make the example code work. All you'll really need are the two tables and the query to make most of this chapter work; you can skip the sample form (the one shown in Chapter 5) if you really want to. (However, the sample form will help you troubleshoot any problems with your tables or query.)

WEB LINK: You'll want to spend some time checking out the newsgroups when it comes to working with ODBC. One of the more popular Microsoft sponsored newsgroups for using ODBC with Access is **microsoft.public.access.odbcclientsvr**. You'll also want to check out the **microsoft.public.sqlserver.odbc** newsgroup if you're working with SQL Server. Of course, there are many other ODBC-specific newsgroups along with the more generic database newsgroups that we talked about in Chapter 5.

There's one last thing you'll need to do before we start looking at some sample ODBC database applications. If you'll remember from Chapter 4, we need an ODBC source before Visual C++ will be able to actually do anything with the sample database. You'll want to use the procedure in the "Working with ODBC" section of Chapter 4 to create a data source name (DSN). Shown here are the parameters I used for creating the DSN for this chapter.

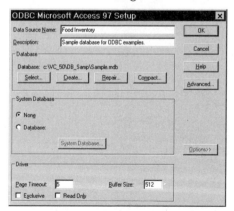

TIP: Always set up all your DSNs before you start writing a Visual C++ program that uses ODBC. Otherwise, you'll have to do some level of code rewriting later. Allow the MFC AppWizard to do as much of the work as possible for you by getting any setups out of the way before you even start Visual C++.

Notice that I set the Data Source Name field to "Food Inventory" and the Description field reads: "Sample database for ODBC examples." Notice also the location and name of the database I'll be using in the examples in this chapter. You may need to modify the settings to fit your system setup; use the Select button as explained in Chapter 4 to select your sample database. Finally, I left the options to their default settings and didn't change any of the settings on the Set Advanced Options dialog. You don't need to add a default user name or password unless you set up security for the database— something we didn't do in Chapter 5.

6

TIP: Make sure you test any ODBC application with the DBMS that you plan to use it with, and then make the client aware of potential application limitations. Some programmers have gotten interesting results when they developed an application using one version of the DBMS and a client tried it in a production environment with a supposedly compatible version of the same DBMS. For example, some users of Office 97 suddenly found that ODBC access times for their applications increased by as much as four times, making the application virtually unusable. (Not everyone runs into this problem, but it does make a good example of what can happen in the right situation.) Even though the application worked as anticipated, updating from the Office 95 version of Access to the Office 97 version had the unanticipated side effect of increasing access times. The developer of this application could have avoided potential problems by making sure that the client understood that his application was only tested to work with Office 95 or by testing it with Office 97 to look for side effects.

Creating a Simple Form View Application

Let's begin by creating the very easiest database application type. We'll use Visual C++ to create a form view of the FoodOrders query we created in Chapter 5. Using queries is the fastest way to get your application up and running, since queries allow you to choose the fields you want to view and order the data without using any code at all. The following procedure takes you through the process of creating the basic application. Since we've already covered the nuances of using Visual C++ to create a basic single-document application in Chapter 2, I won't go into a lot of detail here.

T IP: There's one situation where using tables instead of queries is important. If you want to create a utility for fixing databases damaged in some way by the user, you may need some type of individual table access to do it. Otherwise, the referential integrity rules enforced by Access (or any other good DBMS) may prevent you from actually fixing the problem even if you can see it. Normally you'll want to avoid changing individual tables, though, since the effects can be very unpredictable when the application is running and referential integrity rules are in effect.

1. Start Visual C++.

2. Use the File | New command to display the New dialog. Choose the Projects tab.

3. Type the name of a new application in the Project Name field (the example uses ODBC1), and then highlight MFC AppWizard (EXE) as shown here.

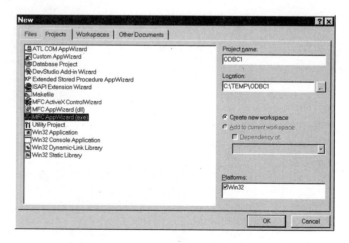

4. Click OK. You'll see the MFC AppWizard - Step 1 dialog shown here.

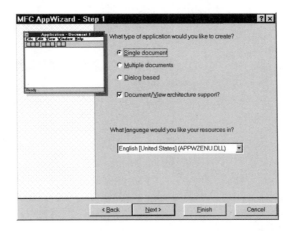

5. Choose Single Document, and then click Next. You'll see the MFC AppWizard - Step 2 of 6 dialog shown here. At this point, we need to choose a database option. (See the In Depth box entitled "Choosing a Database Option" for more details on the database selection choices you have when using Visual C++.)

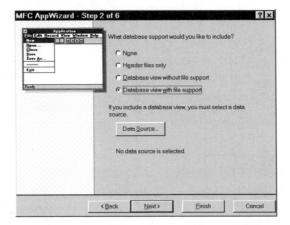

6. Choose the Database View with File Support option. Now we need to choose a data source. Notice that the Data Source button becomes enabled when you choose either the Database View with File Support or Database View without File Support option.

6

7. Click the Data Source button. You'll see a Database Options dialog like this one.

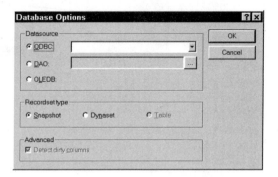

This is another one of those cases where you have to really pay attention to what you're doing when designing an application using the MFC AppWizard. Notice that this dialog allows you to choose not only a data source, but the type of access you want as well. I've already covered the differences between ODBC, DAO, and OLE-DB in Chapter 4. However, notice that you can also choose three kinds of Recordset when you choose either ODBC or DAO. (See the In Depth box entitled "Choosing a Recordset Type" for more details on the recordset option you should choose.) You should also notice the Detect Dirty Columns checkbox in the Advanced section of the dialog. This option, which is only enabled when using DAO, allows you to detect changes to the data you're working with on the server before you write any changes. It makes it possible for you to handle the problem of two users trying to update the data in one record at the same time.

NOTE: At this point, you may be wondering how you would use ADO within a Visual C++ application. You'd need to select OLE-DB as the connection type and then use the ADO classes within your application. While this may seem a bit convoluted, it makes sense when you consider that OLE-DB is the underlying access technology for ADO.

8. Choose the ODBC option, since we'll be using ODBC access in this example. You'll need to choose the Food Inventory entry in the drop-down list box—this is the DSN we created at the beginning of the

chapter. Since you'll probably want to see any changes you make to the database immediately, choose the Dynaset option as well.

9. Click OK. You'll see a Select Database Tables dialog like the one shown here.

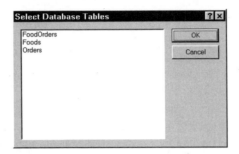

10. Highlight the FoodOrders option. This is the query that we created in Chapter 5. Notice that you could also have chosen one of the two tables, but you'll normally select a query for the reasons that we talked about previously. Always make sure you choose the right entry at this point, because you won't get a second chance later. Trying to code around a bad choice here is almost more work than simply starting the application from scratch, which can lead to costly delays if you're not careful.

6

11. Click OK to return to the MFC AppWizard - Step 2 of 6 dialog. At this point, you've configured your application for use with the sample database we created in Chapter 5.

12. Click Next four times. You should see the MFC AppWizard - Step 6 of 6 dialog shown here.

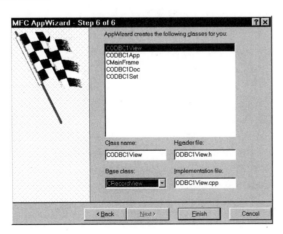

13. Click on CODBC1View. Notice that CRecordView is the base class for our application. You'll find out in the chapters that follow that you don't necessarily have to accept this default, just as we didn't in the single-document application in Chapter 2.

14. Click on Finish. Visual C++ will display a New Project Information dialog like the one shown here.

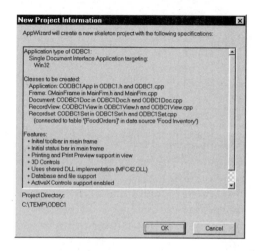

15. Click OK. Visual C++ will generate the application for you.

IN DEPTH

Choosing a Database Option

Visual C++ provides several different options for enabling or disabling database support in your application. The level of database support you choose depends on the kind of application you're creating, though this isn't the only criteria you'll need to consider. For example, you may need a database as part of your application (like a game program), not as something that the user will interact with directly. Likewise, a utility program definitely requires a different level of support than an application you created for secure data entry. However, there are situations where a user may need to access several different versions of the same database, and you'll want to allow the user to open them from within the application. The following list will help you understand the options that are available.

◆ *None*   Selecting this option means that you don't want any database support. Adding it later can be quite a chore, so consider this option carefully if there is any chance your application will need some type of database support. Even non-database applications often make use of databases to store configuration settings or other information. Game programs are well-known for their extensive databases and you'll find that there are few help desk applications that get by without use of a database.

◆ *Header Files Only*   This is the best option to choose if you think you'll need database support but really aren't sure about the details. Visual C++ will add the required header files to your application, but you'll be required to create the database classes yourself. Actually, this is less work than you might think, since the ClassWizard will do the hard part of creating the classes for you. All you'll need to do is add the code required to actually examine the contents of the database.

◆ *Database View without File Support*   There are times when you don't want the user to do anything with files outside the ones that you make available. This option tells Visual C++ to create all the classes required to access the ODBC data source that you've provided but not to make the menu entries required to open other files. Custom database application builders will probably use this option most often. For example, if this application is designed to edit the company's payroll, you don't want the user to open the files individually and circumvent the security measures you've put in place. Eliminating file support may not make your database totally secure but it does eliminate one more potential security hole.

◆ *Database View with File Support*   Utility programs will almost always use this option, since it gives the user the most amount of freedom. Not only will your application have access to the data source you've designed into the application, but you can open external files as well. Of course, the user's ability to actually use this feature depends on the capabilities you've built into the program itself.

6

Choosing a Recordset Type

Visual C++ offers several kinds of recordsets that you can use to customize the way your application works. The fastest way to view these various options involves speed versus features. You'll find that as in most areas of life, if you want added features, you'll have to pay for them with some slower program execution speed. The following list tells you about the recordset options at your disposal. More important than that, it'll tell you whether you're getting better speed or more features from the option.

◆ *Snapshot* The Snapshot option tells Visual C++ to download the entire query in one shot. In other words, you're taking a picture of the contents of the database at one moment in time and using it as the basis for future work. There are three disadvantages to this approach. First, you won't see updates as they're made by other people on the network, which could mean that you're basing a decision on old information. Second, downloading all of these records at one time means that you'll place a heavy burden on the network during the download. Third, the user will end up waiting while the records are downloaded, which will mean an increase in calls about slow network performance. There are two advantages to this approach. First, once the records are downloaded, the network will see little activity from the workstation—freeing bandwidth for other requests. Overall, you'll see an improvement in network throughput. Second, since all of the requested records are on the user's machine, the user will actually see better overall application performance. You'll probably want to restrict the snapshot approach to smaller databases and use it for user information requests rather than data editing sessions.

◆ *Dynaset* When using this option, Visual C++ creates an actual pointer to each record you request. In addition, only the records you actually need to fill the screen get downloaded from the server. The benefits of this approach are obvious. You'll see records onscreen almost immediately. You'll also see changes other users make to the database. Finally, other users will see changes that you make, since the dynaset gets uploaded to the server as you change records. Just as obviously, this approach requires almost constant access to the server, which will reduce overall network throughput and application performance as well. This is the option of choice for creating applications where the user will spend most of his or her time editing data. It's also the best choice for large databases because you'll download only the information that the user actually needs.

◆ *Table*   The other two options we've looked at work at the record level. The table approach (available only when using DAO) places the contents of the query you made into a temporary table. Not only does this reduce the amount of information downloaded from the server, it also means that you as the programmer have more flexibility because you can manipulate the temporary table fields and records directly. How much do you have to pay for this option? If you're not careful, the download process from the server could actually take longer than a recordset does. In addition, you still have the problem of updates—you won't see any of the changes made by other people and they won't see the changes you make. This is probably the best choice when you're using DAO and the user will perform an equal amount of data lookups and data edits.

6

Fixing an MFC AppWizard-Generated Error

Now that you have an application shell, try compiling it. (There really is a point to this exercise, even if you don't see any data.) Run the application and you might get a surprise in the form of this error dialog. (Your dialog may look slightly different than mine, depending on how MFC put the application together for you and the version of Visual C++ that you're using.)

If you didn't see this message, it means that Microsoft fixed a problem with the MFC AppWizard and you can skip the rest of this section. The error message isn't actually coming from your application; it's coming from Access because the MFC AppWizard doesn't handle complex field references correctly. Let's take a look at the problem and the very fast fix for it.

Double-click on the DoFieldExchange() function for the CODBC1Set class. Listing 6-1 shows an example of what you'll see. The RFX_Text() function is transferring data from the database to our Visual C++ application. Notice that the first call is for the Food_ID field. You need to change this field reference from "[Foods.Food_ID]" (which says that there is a field named Foods.Food_ID) to "Foods. [Food_ID]" (which says that there is a field named Food_ID in the Foods table). You'll need to make the same change in the last RFX_Text call. Change the "[Orders.Food_ID]" reference to read "Orders. [Food_ID]".

Listing 6-1:

```
void CODBC1Set::DoFieldExchange(CFieldExchange* pFX)
{
    //{{AFX_FIELD_MAP(CODBC1Set)
    pFX->SetFieldType(CFieldExchange::outputColumn);
    RFX_Text(pFX, _T("[Foods.Food_ID]"), m_Food_ID);
    RFX_Text(pFX, _T("[Name]"), m_Name);
    RFX_Bool(pFX, _T("[Perishable]"), m_Perishable);
    RFX_Int(pFX, _T("[Storage_Life]"), m_Storage_Life);
    RFX_Date(pFX, _T("[Purchase]"), m_Purchase);
    RFX_Long(pFX, _T("[Quantity]"), m_Quantity);
    RFX_Text(pFX, _T("[Price]"), m_Price);
    RFX_Text(pFX, _T("[Orders.Food_ID]"), m_Food_ID2);
    //}}AFX_FIELD_MAP
}
```

Recompile the application. When you run it this time, you won't see any errors. Of course, you won't see any data either—a problem we'll take care of in the next section.

Adding Some Data Display Code

You'll need to perform a few steps before we're ready to add code to this example. The first thing you'll have to do is create the form you'll use to display the data. Figure 6-1 shows the form we'll use in this case. (You can modify it as needed to meet personal tastes; just make sure all of the fields are there.)

I've used the following IDs (from top to bottom) for the various controls—they follow the field values we used for the tables: IDC_FOOD_ID, IDC_NAME, IDC_PERISHABLE, IDC_PRICE, IDC_PURCHASE, IDC_QUANTITY, and IDC_STORAGE_LIFE. The IDC_PRICE control needs its Align Text property set to Right and the Multiline property checked. You'll also want to set the Align Text property to Right and check both the Multiline and Number properties for the other two numeric fields.

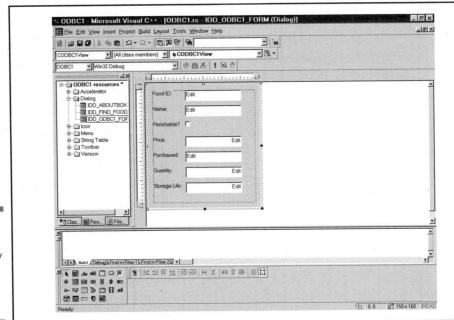

We'll need to construct a form to display the data in our database.

Figure 6-1.

Now I'm going to show you why those control ID values are so important. CTRL-double-click on the IDC_FOOD_ID control. You'll see an Add Member Variable dialog like the one shown here.

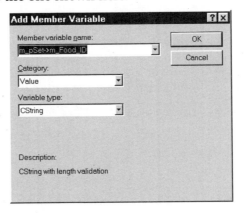

Notice that Visual C++ has already added a value for you in the Member Variable Name field, but that's not the normal procedure for this dialog. Usually all you get is an m_ without anything else. If you were more familiar with the code at this point, you'd know that m_pSet is a pointer to the object containing the current database record. The m_Food_ID variable in that object contains the current value for the Food_ID field in the Foods table. We don't really want that Food_ID field; we want the one in the Orders table. Click on the drop-down list box and you'll see the m_pSet->m_Food_ID2 member variable name, which is attached to the Orders table. Select the Orders table member variable.

If you look through this list, you'll find a pointer to every field in the query we constructed, except the Purchase field in the Orders table. Visual C++ can automatically handle many variable types for you, including most numbers. However, it can't handle times or dates, so you'll have to write some code to retrieve those values. I'll show you how to do that in a few moments. For right now, go ahead and create member variables for the rest of the controls just like we did for the IDC_FOOD_ID control.

Once you get all of the member variables created, it pays to take one more look, just to make sure everything is correct. Use the View | ClassWizard command to display the MFC ClassWizard dialog. Choose the Member Variables tab. Make sure that the CODBC1View class is showing in the Class Name field. (If not, select the CODBC1View class from the drop-down list box.) Your member variable list should match the one shown here.

It's time to compile and run your application. Here's what you should see when you try it out for the first time.

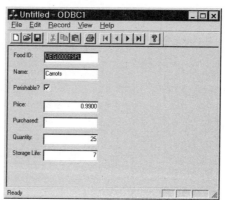

Once you run your application, try moving from record to record in the database. You'll notice that this part of the program appears to work fine. The program will also allow you to change the values of existing records—at least for those fields that contain values. However, you'll also notice a few deficiencies. The first you already know about—we don't have anything showing in the Purchased field. The second problem is that the Price field contains four zero places instead of the two normally associated with monetary values. We'll have to use code to fix both problems.

Before we can make any code changes, we'll need to change some things about the class member variables. Use the View | ClassWizard command to display the MFC ClassWizard dialog. Choose the Member Variables tab and the CODBC1View class like you did the last time. The first thing we'll need to do is delete the variable currently assigned to IDC_PRICE. Highlight it and click the Delete Variable button. Now click the Add Variable button and you'll see an Add Member Variable dialog. Type **m_cPrice** for the member variable name (Visual C++ will supply the m_ automatically). Click OK to add the variable. Do the same thing for IDC_PURCHASE, using a member variable name of **m_cPurchase**. Your MFC ClassWizard dialog should look like the one shown here.

6

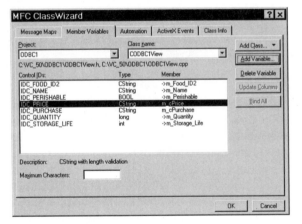

Now that we have some variables, we can add some code. Of course, the first thing we'll want to do is display the information in the database so that we can see changes later. Listing 6-2 shows the code you'll need to add to the DoDataExchange() function of the CODBC1View class. Make absolutely certain that you add the new code at the beginning, not the end, of the function. Otherwise, you'll get strange results.

Listing 6-2:

```
void CODBC1View::DoDataExchange(CDataExchange* pDX)
{
    int     iStrLength;     // Length of the string.

    // Format the price for display by adding a $ and removing the
    // trailing zeroes.
    iStrLength = m_pSet->m_Price.GetLength();
    m_cPrice = "$" + m_pSet->m_Price.Left(iStrLength - 2);

    // Get the date value and convert it to a string.
    m_cPurchase = m_pSet->m_Purchase.Format("%d %B, %Y");

    CRecordView::DoDataExchange(pDX);
    //{{AFX_DATA_MAP(CODBC1View)
    DDX_Text(pDX, IDC_PRICE, m_cPrice);
    DDX_FieldText(pDX, IDC_FOOD_ID2, m_pSet->m_Food_ID2, m_pSet);
    DDX_FieldText(pDX, IDC_NAME, m_pSet->m_Name, m_pSet);
    DDX_FieldCheck(pDX, IDC_PERISHABLE, m_pSet->m_Perishable, m_pSet);
    DDX_FieldText(pDX, IDC_QUANTITY, m_pSet->m_Quantity, m_pSet);
    DDX_FieldText(pDX, IDC_STORAGE_LIFE, m_pSet->m_Storage_Life, m_pSet);
    DDX_Text(pDX, IDC_PURCHASE, m_cPurchase);
    //}}AFX_DATA_MAP
}
```

As you can see, fixing the display problem is relatively easy. All you need to do is grab the values from the m_pSet object manually and then format them as needed. The new code removes the two extra zeroes from the Price field and then adds a dollar sign so you can tell it's a monetary amount. Getting a value for the purchase requires use of the Format() function provided with the CTime class. The funny characters in the string ("%d %B, %Y") determine how the string looks when Format() returns. In this case, I want the day, the month as text, and a four-digit year. Let's look at how the program works now. Compile and run the application and it'll look like this.

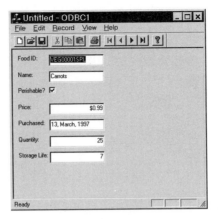

6

Even though we can read the Price and Purchased fields from the database now, we can't update them. (It was important to make sure we could read the fields before we added code to update them; otherwise, you won't know where the code has gone wrong if the application doesn't work as anticipated.) We'll add some code to the end of the DoDataExchange() function this time, since we want to update the database after we've exchanged data with the controls on the form. Listing 6-3 shows the final form of the DoDataExchange() function for now.

Listing 6-3:

```
void CODBC1View::DoDataExchange(CDataExchange* pDX)
{
    int       iStrLength;    // Length of the string.
    int       iDay;          // Purchase day.
    int       iMonth;        // Purchase month.
    int       iYear;         // Purchase year.
    CTime     oTime;         // CTime object;

    // Format the price for display by adding a $ and removing the
    // trailing zeroes.
    iStrLength = m_pSet->m_Price.GetLength();
    m_cPrice = "$" + m_pSet->m_Price.Left(iStrLength - 2);

    // Get the date value and convert it to a string.
    m_cPurchase = m_pSet->m_Purchase.Format("%d %B, %Y");
```

```
CRecordView::DoDataExchange(pDX);
//{{AFX_DATA_MAP(CODBC1View)
DDX_Text(pDX, IDC_PRICE, m_cPrice);
DDX_FieldText(pDX, IDC_FOOD_ID2, m_pSet->m_Food_ID2, m_pSet);
DDX_FieldText(pDX, IDC_NAME, m_pSet->m_Name, m_pSet);
DDX_FieldCheck(pDX, IDC_PERISHABLE, m_pSet->m_Perishable, m_pSet);
DDX_FieldText(pDX, IDC_QUANTITY, m_pSet->m_Quantity, m_pSet);
DDX_FieldText(pDX, IDC_STORAGE_LIFE, m_pSet->m_Storage_Life, m_pSet);
DDX_Text(pDX, IDC_PURCHASE, m_cPurchase);
//}}AFX_DATA_MAP

// Transfer the information to the m_Price variable.
// Remember to remove the dollar sign, if necessary, first.
iStrLength = m_cPrice.GetLength();
if (m_cPrice.Find("$") != -1)
{
    m_pSet->m_Price = m_cPrice.Right(iStrLength - 1);
}
else
{
    m_pSet->m_Price = m_cPrice;
}

// Get the updated year.
iYear = atoi(m_cPurchase.Right(4));

// Get the updated day.
iDay = atoi(m_cPurchase.Left(m_cPurchase.Find(" ") + 1));

// Get the updated month.
if (m_cPurchase.Find("January") != -1)
    iMonth = 1;
if (m_cPurchase.Find("February") != -1)
    iMonth = 2;
if (m_cPurchase.Find("March") != -1)
    iMonth = 3;
if (m_cPurchase.Find("April") != -1)
    iMonth = 4;
if (m_cPurchase.Find("May") != -1)
    iMonth = 5;
if (m_cPurchase.Find("June") != -1)
    iMonth = 6;
if (m_cPurchase.Find("July") != -1)
    iMonth = 7;
```

```
if (m_cPurchase.Find("August") != -1)
    iMonth = 8;
if (m_cPurchase.Find("September") != -1)
    iMonth = 9;
if (m_cPurchase.Find("October") != -1)
    iMonth = 10;
if (m_cPurchase.Find("November") != -1)
    iMonth = 11;
if (m_cPurchase.Find("December") != -1)
    iMonth = 12;

// Transfer the date information to m_Purchase.
oTime = CTime(iYear, iMonth, iDay, 0, 0, 0);
m_pSet->m_Purchase = oTime;

}
```

6

This may look like a lot of additional code, but you can break it down fairly easily. The first thing we need to do is add some new variables to take care of the Purchase field. There are separate variables for day, month, and year. We also need a CTime object that will allow us to create a date to put back into the database.

Taking care of the Price field update requires a simple transfer. However, we can't use the Price field if it contains a dollar sign, so the code uses an IF statement to perform two levels of processing: one with and the other without a dollar sign in the Price field. Notice that this is the first time we use the Find() function of the CString object to determine if there's a dollar sign present. You'll use the Find() function quite a bit in your code, so it's handy to keep this capability in mind as you look for ways to solve problems.

The Purchase field is a CString in our application, which won't easily convert to a CTime object unless we spend a little time parsing it. Our code makes the assumption that the user will always type the date in a format like this: 1 December 1998. Unfortunately, when you create a full-fledged database application, you'll likely need to take more contingencies into account than our example does. The code was purposely kept simple for example purposes. Converting the year and day were very simple using the functions provided with CString and a simple call to the atoi() function. The month represents a little more of a challenge, though, since it's actually written out. The series of IF statements takes care of this need. Finally, we take the three integer representations of the date and convert them into a CTime object. Once we have the CTime object, the database update is a simple transfer.

If you run the application now, you'll be able to retrieve and edit all of the fields in our original query. As you can see, the four- or five-minute process of creating a form in Access turned into a several-hour demonstration in Visual C++. It's important to realize that while Visual C++ gives you a lot of extra flexibility, you're going to pay for it by having to write extra code.

Manipulating the Content of a Database

Our previous example really doesn't go very far when it comes to writing database applications. Even a utility program has to be able to do more with the database than read its contents, which is essentially all we can do right now. For example, we haven't even implemented a method for adding new records or for finding data within the database. You can consider these two features part of any functional database application, even those of the utility variety. In this section of the chapter, we're going to add those two capabilities to our sample database.

Adding Records to a Table

The actual process of adding new records to a table doesn't have to be difficult, as long as you make the right choices during the design stage. In most cases, the DBMS is going to take care of everything for you. All you need to do is provide the right information and in the right way. For example, you may have wondered why I chose to use the Food_ID field from the Orders table rather than the one from the Foods table in the form we designed in the previous section of the chapter. The reason's relatively simple once you think about it. Using the Food_ID field from the Orders table allows the DBMS to make a decision. If you enter an existing Food_ID value after appending a record, the DBMS will simply add a new record to the Orders table. However, if you enter a new Food_ID value, the DBMS adds new records to both the Foods and Orders tables. This decision wouldn't have been possible if you'd used the Food_ID field from the Foods table—the DBMS would have been instructed to add a new record to both tables every time. This would have resulted in duplicated primary key values if the user entered an existing Food_ID value and eventually caused the new record to be rejected.

There are other criteria to consider as well. For example, do you have your application handle data validation, or will the DBMS handle it for you? In most cases, you can provide a friendlier answer if you handle data validation, but doing so means bloating the size of your application. Our application won't perform any data validation for two reasons. First, I want to keep the example simple enough so that you can see what's going on. Second, it's a utility-type program and that means most of the people using this application will be professionals like yourself.

We do have to perform some setup before adding any code to the application. The first thing we need to do is add a menu entry for appending the records. The following procedure will show you how to accomplish this task. (We've done this in Chapter 3, so I won't go through every nuance of the procedure for you.)

1. Choose ResourceView in Visual C++. Double-click on Menu, and then on IDR_MAINFRAME. You'll see a menu bar like this one.

2. Click on the Record menu, and then click on the blank entry at the bottom of the menu. Type **&Append** and you'll see a Menu Item Properties dialog like the one shown here.

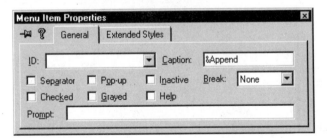

3. Complete the new menu entry by typing **Append a new record to the table.\nAppend Record** in the Prompt field.

4. Click on the Close box in the Menu Item Properties dialog. Visual C++ will automatically assign the new menu item an ID value of ID_RECORD_APPEND (you may want to double-check to see that it actually does).

5. Click the Save All button on the toolbar or use the File | Save All command to ensure all your changes are saved and properly registered for MFC ClassWizard to use.

Now that we have a menu entry to use, we need to add some entries in the ClassWizard to make it functional. Right-click on the menu entry and choose ClassWizard from the context menu. In the MFC ClassWizard dialog, you should see the ID_RECORD_APPEND entry selected in the Object IDs list

6

(select it if it isn't already selected). Choose CODBC1View in the Class Name drop-down list box—this is the class that allows you to view the contents of the database, so it's where you'll need to add any code for appending records as well. Highlight the COMMAND entry in the Messages list, and then click Add Function. You'll see an Add Member Function dialog. Click OK to accept the default function name. Your MFC ClassWizard dialog should look like the one shown here.

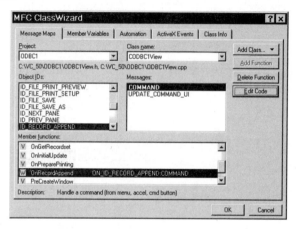

Click OK to close the MFC ClassWizard dialog. Now we need to modify the form we previously created (IDD_ODBC1_FORM). There are more than a few ways to handle appending a new record to the database, but I've chosen to add buttons—in fact, generic buttons, so that they could be used for other purposes if needed. To do this, resize your form to 220×160, and then add two buttons. This is what your form should look like now.

Deselect the Visible property for a control if you want to hide it when the dialog or window is initially displayed.

We don't want the buttons visible (and therefore accessible) all the time, so it's time to change a few properties. Open the Properties dialog for the first button by right-clicking on it and then choosing Properties from the context menu. Clear the check mark from the Visible property and change the ID to IDC_CHOICE1. Do the same thing for the second button, changing its ID to IDC_CHOICE2.

It's also important to add some functions to handle user clicks on the button. All you need to do is right-click on the first button and choose the ClassWizard option from the context menu. Select the Message Maps tab. Select CODBC1View in the Class Name field. Find the IDC_CHOICE1 entry in the Object IDs list and highlight it. Now highlight the BN_CLICKED entry in the Messages field, and then click Add Function to create a function shell to handle user clicks. You'll need to do the same thing for the IDC_CHOICE2 Object ID entry. Here's what your Member Functions list should look like.

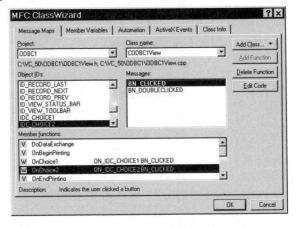

6

Click OK to close the MFC ClassWizard dialog. We had previously added some member variables for each one of the data entry fields on our form. Those member variables allow the program to exchange data with the database. However, now we need to access those data entry fields directly, so it's time to create some more member variables.

Visual C++ allows you to assign more than one member variable to a single object.

CTRL-double-click the IDC_FOOD_ID control on our form. You'll see an Add Member Variable dialog. Type **m_oFood_ID** in the Member Variable Name field, and then choose Control in the Category field. Click OK to complete the process. What you've just done is create a member variable that can access the control on the form directly. Perform the same task for the other data entry controls using the following member variable names: IDC_NAME (m_oName), IDC_PERISHABLE (m_oPerishable), IDC_PRICE (m_oPrice), IDC_PURCHASE (m_oPurchase), IDC_QUANTITY (m_oQuantity), and IDC_STORAGE_LIFE (m_oStorage_Life).

Let's check the results of adding the new variables (always a good idea, since you want to make sure you can actually access them). Right-click anywhere, and then choose ClassWizard from the context menu. Choose the Member Variables tab of the MFC ClassWizard dialog. You should see two variables for every data entry control on the form, as shown here.

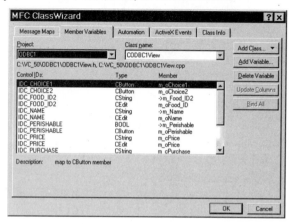

Let's make one more usability change. Wouldn't it be nice if the user could just click a button on the toolbar rather than use the menu each time? Open the Toolbar folder in ResourceView, and then double-click on IDR_MAINFRAME. You'll see a toolbar appear. Add a new button right after the four database movement buttons, and draw a symbol on it like the one shown here. This is the same symbol (or a reasonable facsimile thereof) of the New Record button in Access.

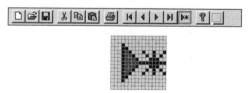

Making this button functional isn't too hard. Double-click on the new Append Record button on the toolbar (not the one that you just drew in the drawing area, but the one on the toolbar itself). You'll see a Toolbar Button Properties dialog. Choose ID_RECORD_APPEND from the ID drop-down list box. This associates your button with the menu command. The Prompt field should automatically fill in with the correct text value, as shown here.

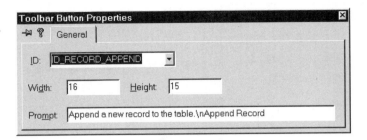

Click the Close box to complete that action. That's all you need to do to add the button to your toolbar and make it functional.

Now it's time to add some code to this part of the example. Listing 6-4 shows the code you'll need to add. Make sure you add each piece of code to the right function. You'll also want to carefully observe the order in which things are done, since some operations have to be done in a specific order. Finally, this code obviously doesn't do any kind of bounds checking, which means that you're going to have to type carefully when testing it out. Make sure that the Food ID field contains enough of the right kind of characters. Use Access to edit the tables by hand if you make a mistake and the program doesn't recover properly.

6

Listing 6-4:
```
void CODBC1View::OnRecordAppend()
{
    // See if the database was opened in read-only mode. If so,
    // display a message, and then exit.
    if (m_pSet->CanAppend() == 0)
        MessageBox("Cannot Append Records",
            "Database Opening Error",
            MB_OK | MB_ICONERROR);
    else
    {
        // Set the option button captions.
        m_oChoice1.SetWindowText("Submit Data");
        m_oChoice2.SetWindowText("Cancel");

        // Display the option buttons.
        m_oChoice1.ShowWindow(SW_SHOW);
        m_oChoice2.ShowWindow(SW_SHOW);
```

```
        // Create a blank record for the user to edit.
        m_oFood_ID.SetWindowText("");
        m_oName.SetWindowText("");
        m_oPerishable.SetCheck(0);
        m_oPrice.SetWindowText("");
        m_oPurchase.SetWindowText("");
        m_oQuantity.SetWindowText("");
        m_oStorage_Life.SetWindowText("");
    }
}

void CODBC1View::OnChoice1()
{
    CString    cValue;        // Current value of edit field.
    int        iCheck;        // Current check value of Perishable field.
    int        iStrLength;    // Length of the string.
    int        iQuantity;     // Value of Quantity field;
    int        iStorage;      // Value of Storage field;
    int        iDay;          // Purchase day.
    int        iMonth;        // Purchase month.
    int        iYear;         // Purchase year.
    CTime      oTime;         // CTime object;
    BOOL       lNew = TRUE;   // New Food ID?

    // Initialize the search value.
    m_oFood_ID.GetWindowText(cValue);

    // Go to the beginning of the query and search
    // for the Food ID entered by the user.
    m_pSet->MoveFirst();
    while (!m_pSet->IsEOF() ^ !lNew)
    {
        // Check if the value is equal.
        if (m_pSet->m_Food_ID == cValue)
            lNew = FALSE;

        // Go to the next record.
        m_pSet->MoveNext();
    }

    // Add a new record.
    m_pSet->AddNew();

    // Save the new data values into the record.
    m_oFood_ID.GetWindowText(cValue);
```

```
m_pSet->m_Food_ID2 = cValue;
m_oFood_ID.GetWindowText(cValue);
m_pSet->m_Name = cValue;

// If this is a new record, place the Food ID in the
// Foods table field as well.
if (lNew)
{
    m_oFood_ID.GetWindowText(cValue);
    m_pSet->m_Food_ID = cValue;
}

// Convert Perishable control value from int to BOOL.
iCheck = m_oPerishable.GetCheck();
if (iCheck == 0)
    m_pSet->m_Perishable = FALSE;
else
    m_pSet->m_Perishable = TRUE;

// Convert and then save the Quantity and Storage fields.
m_oQuantity.GetWindowText(cValue);
iQuantity = atoi(cValue);
m_oStorage_Life.GetWindowText(cValue);
iStorage = atoi(cValue);
m_pSet->m_Quantity = iQuantity;
m_pSet->m_Storage_Life = iStorage;

// Transfer the information to the m_Price variable.
// Remember to remove the dollar sign, if necessary, first.
iStrLength = m_cPrice.GetLength();
if (m_cPrice.Find("$") != -1)
{
    m_pSet->m_Price = m_cPrice.Right(iStrLength - 1);
}
else
{
    m_pSet->m_Price = m_cPrice;
}

// Get the updated year.
iYear = atoi(m_cPurchase.Right(4));

// Get the updated day.
iDay = atoi(m_cPurchase.Left(m_cPurchase.Find(" ") + 1));
```

6

```
    // Get the updated month.
    if (m_cPurchase.Find("January") != -1)
        iMonth = 1;
    if (m_cPurchase.Find("February") != -1)
        iMonth = 2;
    if (m_cPurchase.Find("March") != -1)
        iMonth = 3;
    if (m_cPurchase.Find("April") != -1)
        iMonth = 4;
    if (m_cPurchase.Find("May") != -1)
        iMonth = 5;
    if (m_cPurchase.Find("June") != -1)
        iMonth = 6;
    if (m_cPurchase.Find("July") != -1)
        iMonth = 7;
    if (m_cPurchase.Find("August") != -1)
        iMonth = 8;
    if (m_cPurchase.Find("September") != -1)
        iMonth = 9;
    if (m_cPurchase.Find("October") != -1)
        iMonth = 10;
    if (m_cPurchase.Find("November") != -1)
        iMonth = 11;
    if (m_cPurchase.Find("December") != -1)
        iMonth = 12;

    // Transfer the date information to m_Purchase.
    oTime = CTime(iYear, iMonth, iDay, 0, 0, 0);
    m_pSet->m_Purchase = oTime;

    // Once the user completes the record, update the database.
    m_pSet->Update();

    // Go to the last record so that the user can see the addition.
    m_pSet->MoveLast();

    // Hide the option buttons.
    m_oChoice1.ShowWindow(SW_HIDE);
    m_oChoice2.ShowWindow(SW_HIDE);
}

void CODBC1View::OnChoice2()
{
    int     iStrLength;                   // Length of the string.
    char*   cQuantity = "Empty1";         // Text value of Quantity field.
    char*   cStorage = "Empty2";          // Text value of Storage Life field.
```

```
// Hide the option buttons.
m_oChoice1.ShowWindow(SW_HIDE);
m_oChoice2.ShowWindow(SW_HIDE);

// Restore the display data.
m_oFood_ID.SetWindowText(m_pSet->m_Food_ID2);
m_oName.SetWindowText(m_pSet->m_Name);
m_oPerishable.SetCheck(m_pSet->m_Perishable);

// Process the Quantity and Storage Life fields.
itoa(m_pSet->m_Quantity, cQuantity, 10);
itoa(m_pSet->m_Storage_Life, cStorage, 10);
m_oQuantity.SetWindowText(cQuantity);
m_oStorage_Life.SetWindowText(cStorage);

// Format the price for display by adding a $--the trailing
// zeroes were removed during the data exchange.
iStrLength = m_pSet->m_Price.GetLength();
m_oPrice.SetWindowText("$" + m_pSet->m_Price);

// Get the date value and convert it to a string.
m_oPurchase.SetWindowText(m_pSet->m_Purchase.Format("%d %B, %Y"));
}
```

6

This may look like a lot of code, but it's not too hard to understand if you take it apart. Let's begin with the OnRecordAppend() function. The first thing you should always do is check whether the database will even allow you to append records. You can do this using the CanAppend() function of the CRecordset class. It returns TRUE if you can append the record. If you can't append a record, display an error message and exit as shown in the example code. You could also reopen the database in something other than read-only mode.

The second part of the OnRecordAppend() function does three things. First, we use the SetWindowText() associated with the CWnd class to assign a caption to the two generic buttons we added to the form. It's important to realize that classes always inherit the features of the base class they're derived from. If you look at the CButton class documentation, you'll see that there isn't any way to set the Caption property as you would with a language like Visual Basic, so you need a function like SetWindowText() to do it (even if the function name doesn't appear to match what it's doing). Second, we make the buttons visible using the ShowWindow() function of the CWnd class. Again, this might seem a little counterintuitive, but it works just fine. Third, we need to create blank edit boxes for the user to edit. You could also fill the CEdit controls with suggested values or anything else that seems appropriate.

Let's skip the OnChoice1() function (it gets called if the user clicks on the Submit button) for a second and see what happens if the user clicks on Cancel (which calls the OnChoice2() function). There are two parts to the OnChoice2() function. The first should look familiar. Instead of making the CEdit controls visible, though, we'll hide them this time.

The second part retrieves the current query values and places them back into the CEdit controls on the form. It appears to the user as if you've just restored the record, when all you've really done is restored the values in a form. Notice that we have to use four different techniques to restore the previous values. The first technique is a straight data transfer. The second technique converts the numeric values provided by the database into a string, and then places the string into the form. A third technique recreates what we did in the previous section—it merely formats an existing string so that it actually looks like a currency value. The fourth technique converts a date into a string using the Format() function.

Now let's see what happens if the user fills out the form and clicks the Submit Data button. Remember that this code is simplified for demonstration purposes—you'd want to add some code to verify that each field contained a value that the database could actually use. The first thing that the OnChoice1() function needs to do is see whether we're adding a new entry to an existing Food ID in the Foods table or if we're adding a completely new Food ID. The difference is important, as you'll see in just a few paragraphs. Finding this information out is a four-step process as follows.

1. Get the user-supplied Food ID value. In this case, we use the GetWindowText() function to do it.

2. Go to the beginning of the query using the MoveFirst() function of the CRecordset class.

3. Compare each value in the Food ID field of the query to the user-supplied value. Notice that we move from record to record using the MoveNext() function.

4. If one of the values does match, set lNew to FALSE and exit the search loop.

Once you've determined what kind of record you're going to add, you need to add a blank record to the database using the AddNew() function. This blank record is only in memory at this point. If the user has a power failure, you won't end up with a blank record in the database. The only purpose that the blank record serves at this point is a palette (or blank form, if you prefer) to hold the user-supplied data values.

Now it's time to add the data to our blank record. Notice that the process of getting the data from the form isn't as straightforward as you might initially think. The simplest transfer is from a CEdit control to a string field in the query. We use a two-step process. The first thing you need to do is place the current text in the CEdit control into a temporary variable using the GetWindowText() function. Once you have the temporary variable filled, you can just transfer the information to the database field.

Checkboxes make an interesting case. The checkboxes supported by Visual C++ can contain one of three values: checked, unchecked, or indeterminate. As a result, the GetCheck() function for the CButton class returns an integer, not a Boolean value. You need to convert this integer value to a Boolean value used by Access.

The next conversion is for the Quantity and Storage Life fields. It's a three-step process that mimics the two-step procedure we used for the text fields. However, we need to convert the text value we get with GetWindowText() into the integer value used by the fields—which accounts for the third step. The sample code uses a simple atoi() function to accomplish the task.

You should recognize the next two conversions. They both appear in the DoDataExchange() function in a relatively unchanged form. You still need to take the text value for the Purchased field provided by the control on the form and convert it to a date. Nothing has changed in that regard. Likewise, you'll need to remove the dollar sign from the Price field. Otherwise, Access won't accept the field value.

Now that we have a blank form full of new data values, it's time to update our database with them using the Update() function. This is the only time that the database is truly vulnerable. If you have a power failure during that very short interval of the update, you could get unpredictable results. Suffice it to say that while this approach isn't bulletproof, it does work better than

6

old-technology databases did where the amount of open time for a record was much greater.

The final database-related act of the OnChoice1() function is to move to the last record. You need to do this so that the user can actually see the new record. Otherwise, the user may think that the record didn't get put into the database and attempt to add another one. Notice that the OnChoice1() function ends by hiding the two generic buttons from sight. It's important that the user not be able to access these buttons unless they actually have a new record to edit, so you'll want to keep them hidden whenever possible.

So, what does a blank record look like? Here's our sample program with a blank record in place.

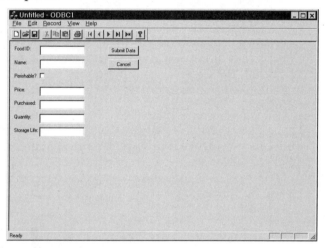

Finding Data in a Database

No matter how nice your application looks, it's not worth much if the user can't find what he or she needs. Figuring out the best way to get the user from one point in the database to another has been the subject of more than a few debates. There are entire chapters of books written on just the topic of finding what you need in the most efficient way possible. We could spend a lot of time looking at search techniques, but that really wouldn't help you much in the long run. When using ODBC, there's one simple way of doing things; it may not be the fastest or most efficient way, but it's very certain to find what you need. That's the technique we'll concentrate on in this section.

Obviously, we're going to spend a little more time with the menu and toolbar before we can go much further. Open the IDR_MAINFRAME menu again. This time we're going to add a Find option under the Record menu. Select the last blank and type **F&ind** (note that the *F* is already underlined for the First Record option). You'll also need to type a prompt like this one in the Prompt field: **Find a record in the database.\nFind Record**. Your Menu Item Properties dialog should look like the one shown here.

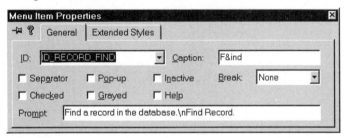

Click on the Close box to make the new menu entry complete. Open the IDR_MAINFRAME toolbar. Here is the new Find button that I added, though you can certainly use any kind of button you want. (Just in case you're wondering—it really is a pair of glasses.)

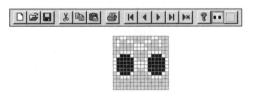

Once you are done with the button, double-click on the toolbar button and you'll see a Toolbar Button Properties dialog. Choose ID_RECORD_FIND from the ID drop-down list box, and then click the Close button.

Now we've got to create a function shell. CTRL-double-click on the ID_RECORD_FIND button and you'll see the MFC ClassWizard. The ID_RECORD_FIND entry should be selected for you. Make sure you choose CODBC1View in the Class Name field. Highlight the COMMAND entry in the Messages list, and then click on Add Function. Click OK to accept the

6

default function name of OnRecordFind in the Add Member Function dialog. (We'll add code to this function later in the section.) At this point, your MFC ClassWizard dialog should look like this.

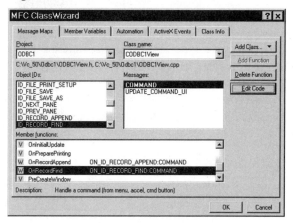

There's still one thing missing. How are you going to ask the user what to find? You'll need a small dialog to get the job done. Close the MFC ClassWizard dialog by clicking OK. Go back to the ResourceView. Right-click on the Dialog folder and choose Insert Dialog from the context menu. Visual C++ will present you with a new dialog. You'll want to change some of the dialog properties before we move on. For one thing, it's a good idea to give your dialog a more recognizable name. Right-click the IDD_DIALOG1 entry in ResourceView, and choose Properties from the context menu. You'll see a Dialog Properties dialog like the one shown here.

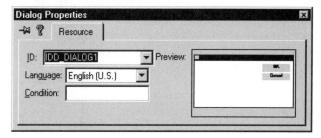

Type **IDD_FIND_FOOD_ID** in the ID field. Click on the Close box to complete the dialog box property changes.

We only need to do two things with the dialog itself. The first thing you'll want to do is give the dialog a more descriptive caption. Right-click on the dialog itself, and choose Properties from the context menu. This time you'll see a Dialog Properties dialog like this one (even though it has the same name as the one we looked at before, this dialog has a different purpose).

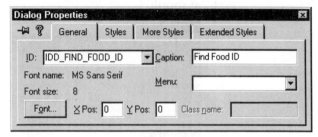

Type **Find Food ID** in the Caption field, and then click on the Close box to complete the change.

Now we need to add a single Static Text and associated Edit Box control to complete the dialog. Here is the completed dialog.

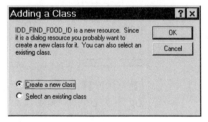

6

The final bit of work for this dialog is to set up the Edit Box control for use. Right-click on the Edit Box control, and choose Properties from the context menu. Change the ID property in the Edit Properties dialog to IDC_FIND_FOOD_ID. Click the Close box to complete the action. Now CTRL-double-click on the Edit Box control. The first thing you're going to see is a somewhat confusing Adding a Class dialog like the one shown here.

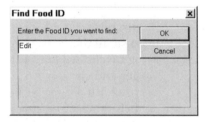

The reason that you're seeing the Adding a Class dialog is that every dialog in your program has to belong somewhere. There are very few cases where you'll want to assign a dialog box to an existing class. Just like the About box in your application, every dialog should have its own class. Click OK to create a new class for our Find Food ID dialog box. Visual C++ will display a New Class dialog like this one.

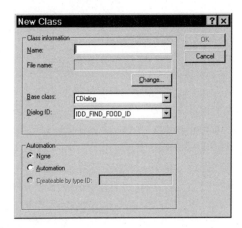

All you really need to do is type in the name of the class in the Name field. You can use any class name you want, but I've chosen FindFoodID for the class name in the example program. Click OK to complete the new class. Click OK to close the MFC ClassWizard. Now, CTRL-double-click the Edit Box control again. This time you'll see the Add Member Variable dialog that you expected to see in the first place. Type **m_FindFoodID** in the Member Variable Name field. Make sure the Category field contains Value and the Variable Type field contains CString. Click on OK to add the member variable.

Remember that OnRecordFind() function skeleton that we created in the CODBC1View class before? It's time to add some code to it. Listing 6-5 shows the code we'll use to find a record in the database.

Listing 6-5:

```
void CODBC1View::OnRecordFind()
{
FindFoodID    oFindIt;                     // Create an instance of our dialog box.
BOOL          lFound = FALSE;              // Did we find a match record?
int           iStrLength;                  // Length of the string.
char*         cQuantity = "Empty1";        // Text value of Quantity field.
char*         cStorage = "Empty2";         // Text value of Storage Life field.
CDBVariant    varBookmark;                 // Positioning bookmark.
```

```
// Display the dialog and determine which button the user pressed to exit.
if (oFindIt.DoModal() == IDOK)
{
    // Save the current position.
    if (m_pSet->CanBookmark())
        m_pSet->GetBookmark(varBookmark);

    // Go to the beginning of the query and search
    // for the Food ID entered by the user.
    m_pSet->MoveFirst();
    while (!m_pSet->IsEOF() ^ lFound)
    {
        // Check if the value is equal.
        if (m_pSet->m_Food_ID == oFindIt.m_FindFoodID)
            lFound = TRUE;

        // Go to the next record.
        else
            m_pSet->MoveNext();
    }

    if (!lFound)
    {
        // Display an error message if we didn't find the record.
        MessageBox("Record not found!",
            "Database Error",
            MB_OK | MB_ICONERROR);

        if (m_pSet->CanBookmark())
            // Restore the current position if
            // the database supports bookmarks.
            m_pSet->SetBookmark(varBookmark);
        else
            // Otherwise, move to the first record.
            m_pSet->MoveFirst();
    }
    else
    {
        // Display the data in the new record.
        m_oFood_ID.SetWindowText(m_pSet->m_Food_ID2);
        m_oName.SetWindowText(m_pSet->m_Name);
        m_oPerishable.SetCheck(m_pSet->m_Perishable);
```

```
                // Process the Quantity and Storage Life fields.
                itoa(m_pSet->m_Quantity, cQuantity, 10);
                itoa(m_pSet->m_Storage_Life, cStorage, 10);
                m_oQuantity.SetWindowText(cQuantity);
                m_oStorage_Life.SetWindowText(cStorage);

                // Format the price for display by adding a $--the trailing
                // zeroes were removed during the data exchange.
                iStrLength = m_pSet->m_Price.GetLength();
                m_oPrice.SetWindowText("$" + m_pSet->m_Price);

                // Get the date value and convert it to a string.
                m_oPurchase.SetWindowText(m_pSet->m_Purchase.Format("%d %B, %Y"));
        }
    }
}
```

Some of the example code should look familiar from other parts of the program. The code does introduce a new function or two. The first thing you should notice is that we check for the current database position. Some kinds of DBMS (Access isn't one of them) support bookmarks. They work just like the bookmarks you use with a book to keep your position as you read it. The first thing you have to ask, though, is whether the DBMS actually supports bookmarks by using the CanBookmark() function. If it does support bookmarks, you can use the GetBookmark() function to save your current position and the SetBookmark() function to restore it.

Notice that our search routine is very simple. If we've found the record the user requested in the dialog, we set a Boolean variable TRUE. Otherwise, we go to the next record. This process continues until we've found either the first record matching the user's criteria or the end of the query. Make sure you test for both items if you set up a similar search routine.

Always reset the record pointer when you complete a search, so that the query is at a known record at the end of the search routine.

There are two courses the program can follow at this point. If we haven't found the requested record, the program displays an error message box. It also tries to return the user to the previous record if the DBMS supports bookmarks. Otherwise, the program returns the user to the first record in the query. It's extremely important to set the record pointer somewhere; otherwise, the DBMS will likely throw an exception, telling you it's lost.

The other course we can follow, if we find the record, is to display the information in the data entry form. That's what the remainder of the code in this section does. You should notice that it looks very similar to the code we used at the end of the OnChoice2() function.

Always use the #include directive to include the header for a dialog box in the module that you intend to use it with.

You'll need to do one additional piece of coding before you can actually compile and run this application. At the top of the ODBCView1.CPP file you'll see a lot of #include directives. If you want to use the Find Food ID dialog box, you'll need to include its header file in the module. Add a new #include directive like the one shown here.

```
// Added for Find Food ID dialog support.
#include "FindFoodID.h"
```

Now that you have all the pieces together, compile and run the program. You'll find that the search routine runs very fast on our small table, but it will bog down as the table gets bigger. In most cases, you'll want to buy one of those heavy books with thousands of search routines if you plan to work on huge databases. This search routine should work fine, though, with a table containing up to about 10,000 records. Of course, all this depends on the complexity of your table relations and the number of fields they contain. Here's what the Find Food ID dialog looks like in action.

6

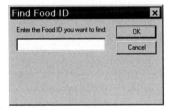

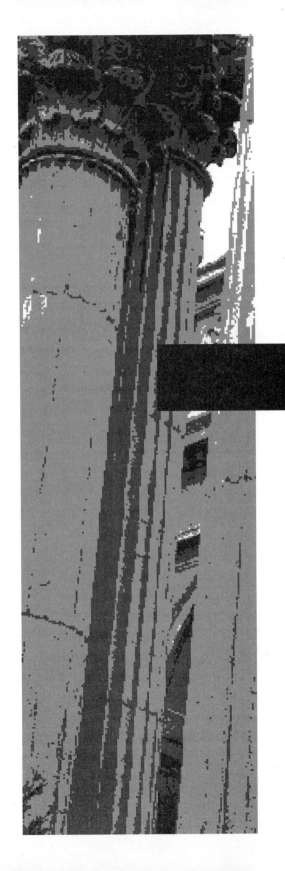

CHAPTER 7

Building a Database Application Using OLE-DB or ADO

OLE-DB (object linking and embedding database) and ADO (ActiveX Data Objects) are the latest addition to Microsoft's line of database access technologies. These two technologies promise to provide a unified interface for accessing all kinds of data, no matter where it may appear on your drive. In addition, they offer the greatest level of flexibility of any Microsoft data access technology to date.

The one thing you'll want to remember when looking at this chapter is that OLE-DB is an underlying data access technology and ADO is a convenient wrapper for it. In addition, OLE-DB is a totally separate product from ODBC. While there are a lot of similarities between building an application with DAO and building one with ODBC, as we did in Chapter 6, building an application with OLE-DB requires entirely different techniques. In fact, it's very easy to look at DAO as an advanced (more capable) form of ODBC with less flexibility (access to fewer database engines). On the other hand, this chapter will show you that OLE-DB represents an entirely new way to access databases.

I'm going to assume that you've already spent some time reading through Chapter 4 learning about the differences between OLE-DB and ODBC before getting to this chapter. You also need to know what ADO is all about. If you haven't looked at Chapter 4, you may want to do so. You'll also want to create the sample database I showed you how to put together in Chapter 5 since we use it in this chapter.

WEB LINK: Make sure you know where to get help from other people when it comes to Visual C++ and the various database access technologies that it supports like DAO, ADO, and OLE-DB. For example, the **microsoft.public.vc.database** newsgroup always has a lot of discussions about these technologies in it. You'll also find some database technology-related discussions in the **microsoft.public.officedev**, **microsoft.public.vc.mfc**, and **microsoft.public.vc.mfcdatabase** newsgroups. There are some non-Microsoft database technology related newsgroups as well: **comp.os.ms-windows.programmer.win32**, **comp.os.ms-windows.programmer.tools.mfc**, and **comp.databases.ms-access**. Interestingly enough, even though discussions about ADO, DAO, and OLE-DB seem to dominate many of the newsgroup discussions on the Internet, there are very few newsgroups that talk about these technologies specifically like the ones you'll find for ODBC. Of course, this means you'll have to spend additional time looking for specific information in the more generic newsgroups (like the ones I just mentioned).

We're going to spend a lot of time talking about both OLE-DB and ADO in this chapter. In fact, we'll begin this chapter in a similar way to Chapter 6—by building a simple application. However, in this case we'll create a grid view in place of the form view we used in the previous chapter. It's important to know how to build more than one kind of simple application. Otherwise, you may not be able to provide clients with all of the views they need to manage their data properly.

NOTE: While we won't explore DAO in this chapter because ADO and OLE-DB have largely replaced it, you can still download DAO-specific versions of the first two samples in this chapter from the Osborne Web site. Just look for the DAO1 and DAO2 examples on the Web site. I've already checked the code to ensure that it works with Visual C++ Version 6.0. All you need to do is look at the code itself to learn how to implement a DAO version of the grid database utility. The comments will help guide you in making the changes required for an MFC AppWizard-generated application. You must have DAO installed on your machine for these examples to work. Use DAO version 3.5 for these examples. You can check your DAO version in one of several ways. First, look in the Program Files\Common Files\Microsoft Shared\DAO folder. If you see a DAO350.DLL file, you have the 3.5 version of DAO installed. You can also look at the Add/Remove Programs applet in the Control Panel. The Install/Uninstall page should have a Data Access Objects (DAO) 3.5 entry if you have DAO version 3.5 installed.

As in the previous chapter, we'll take the sample application and enhance it. In this case we'll add a reporting capability to the sample application. I plan to show you some very OLE-DB-specific ways of doing things. You'll find that at least part of that massive quantity of code we had to use in the previous chapter to do things like search the database are now replaced with simple function calls supported by an OLE-DB or ADO class.

TIP: Unlike ODBC, you won't need a DSN to use OLE-DB or ADO. However, both technologies do rely on knowing a specific location for data on your local drive or network. While you can use UNC (universal naming convention) paths to reduce the chance that users won't be able to find your database, the chance still exists that they won't. Make sure you always check your OLE-DB or ADO application for data access on each machine. Don't assume that a user can access the data simply because you can see the associated database with Explorer.

Creating a Simple Grid View Application

We looked at two different kinds of applications in Chapter 5. Chapter 6 showed you how to create the first of those two types, the form view application. In this section we'll look at the second of the two types, the grid view application. Instead of looking at one record in the query at a time as we did in Chapter 6, we'll look at all the records at once (or at least as many as the screen will hold). Of course, that means using a grid instead of edit boxes to store the various record values.

For the most part you'll find that grids present some special challenges to the programmer when it comes to databases. For example, you now have to keep track of how much of the query is showing if you can't read in the entire query at once. (Some queries may be so large that memory won't allow you to create a grid control that can hold all the values you need to show the user.) You may also find that it takes a little more work to manage all of the fields—especially long text fields like memos. Long or complex fields may require some conditioning or the use of secondary dialogs (a common occurrence with memo fields). We'll forego looking at some of these problem areas in the interest of simplicity in this example. However, it's very important to remember to take them into account if your database tables contain fields with these types of values. (We'll explore some special formatting issues related to date and currency fields, as we did in Chapter 6.)

WEB LINK: You may find that you want some additional training once you get done reading this chapter. There are a lot of places on the Internet that provide training for using Visual C++ with ADO, OLE-DB, DAO, and ODBC. For example, you'll find that Universal Software Solutions at **http://www.unisoftinc.com/courses/** provides in-depth courses on using Visual C++, relational databases, and newer Microsoft object technologies like DCOM and COM+. Another good source is DevelopMentor at **http://www.develop.com/**. It offers a variety of courses on both object technology and Visual C++ in general (including various forms of database access). This company used to offer some DAO-specific classes but have since dropped them.

Creating the ADO1 Project

The process to start an OLE-DB/ADO grid view application will look similar to the one we used in Chapter 6, but there are important differences, so be careful to follow the steps as written. I'll assume that you've already started Visual C++ in the procedure that follows.

1. Use the File | New command to display the New dialog.
2. Choose the MFC AppWizard (EXE) entry on the Projects page.
3. Type **ADO1** (or any other name that suits your needs) in the Project Name field, and then click OK. You'll see the MFC AppWizard - Step 1 dialog shown here.

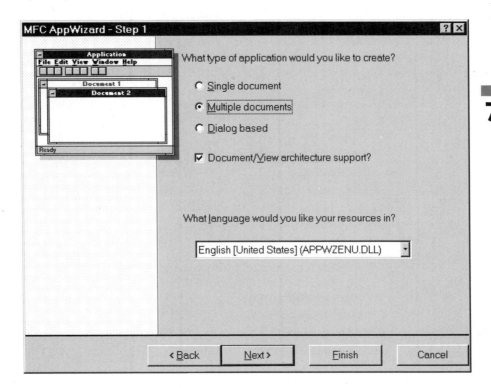

4. Select the Single Document option, and then click Next. You'll see the MFC AppWizard - Step 2 of 6 dialog shown here. The first thing you need to do is choose a level of database support for your application.

7

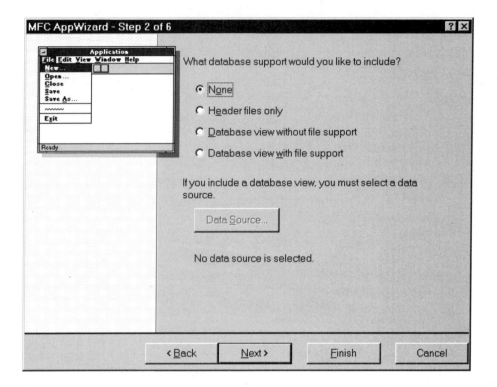

5. Choose Database View Without File Support from the list of options. (For an overview of the various options, see the "Choosing a Database Option" In Depth box in Chapter 6.) Now we need to choose a data source for our application. Remember that OLE-DB uses a provider in place of the mechanism used by ODBC; therefore, we have no need for a DSN.

6. Click the Data Source button. You'll see the Provider tab of the Data Link Properties dialog shown here.

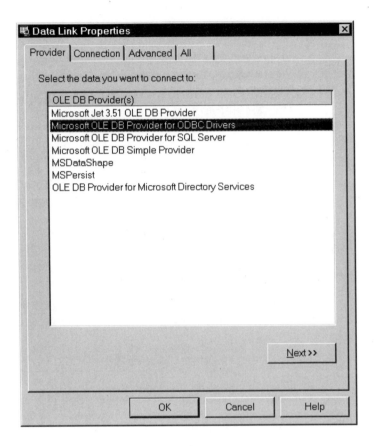

We'll use this dialog to choose the data source and how we'll access it. Since we're using an Access database for this example, we'll work with the Microsoft Jet 3.51 OLE-DB Provider, but working with the other OLE-DB providers is about the same. You will go through the same steps listed here, but the entries that you'll be required to make on the various tabs will vary by provider. For example, SQL Server will require you to enter a server name along with other connection criteria like the type of security that you prefer to use when accessing the server. The Microsoft Jet 3.51 OLE-DB Provider requires the least information for gaining access to the database.

7. Choose the Microsoft Jet 3.51 OLE-DB Provider option, then click Next. You'll see the Connection tab of the Data Link Properties dialog. This is where you specify the location of the database you want to access, along with a user name and password.

8. Type the full path to the database, which is **DBSamp\Sample.MDB** in the case of the example. (You can also use the Browse button to locate the database on your hard drive.)

9. Type a user name and password in the appropriate fields. Neither value should be required for the example database.

10. Click the Test Connection button. You should see a Test Connection Succeeded dialog if you entered the information into the Connection tab properly. If not, make sure you have all of the right values. More often than not, the problem is a mistyped password (something that is easy to do because Visual C++ replaces the password with asterisks).

11. Click OK. You now have a connection to the database that doesn't rely on a DSN.

12. Click OK to close the Database Options dialog. You should see a Select Database Tables dialog like the one shown here.

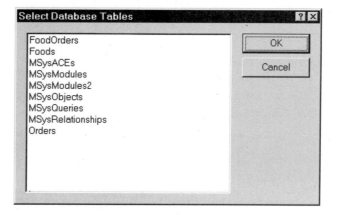

13. Highlight the FoodOrders option. As with the example in Chapter 6, we could have chosen a table if so desired. However, you'll normally use a query to access the contents of a database so that you can get just the data you want and in the order you want it. Click OK. The MFC AppWizard - Step 2 of 6 dialog should now show that you have a data source selected.

14. Click Next four times. You'll see the MFC AppWizard - Step 6 of 6 dialog. There isn't anything to change on this dialog, but you will want to verify that COleDBRecordView has been chosen in the Base Class field. This class will provide you with the functionality needed to make viewing your database easier.

15. Click Finish. You'll see the New Project Information dialog shown here.

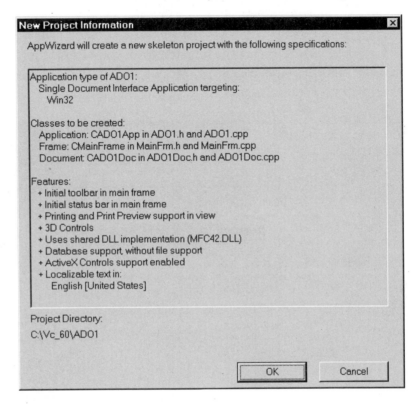

16. Click OK. Visual C++ will create the new project for you.

Designing the Grid View Form

At this point you should be looking at a blank dialog named IDD_ADO1_FORM. You could put anything on this form, including a grid to view all of the records as a table or separate controls for each of the data fields. The choice of how to view the information is up to you. In this case we'll be creating a grid, but it's important to realize that you're not really limited in what type of view you create.

The first thing we'll need to do to create the grid view is to add a grid to our list of controls. Fortunately, there is a special grid that's designed for use with OLE-DB. Obviously, we'll need to do some additional tweaking to get the form right, but adding this particular control will save you a lot of time. The following procedure helps you add it to your Controls toolbar, then add it to the IDD_ADO1_FORM dialog.

1. Use the Project | Add To Project | Components and Controls command to display the Components and Controls Gallery dialog.
2. Double-click the Registered ActiveX Controls folder.
3. Highlight the Microsoft DataGrid Control, Version 6.0 (OLEDB) entry shown here.

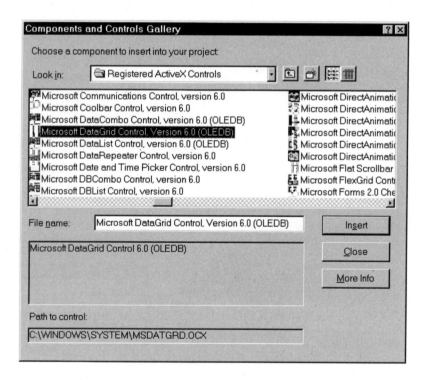

4. Click Insert. Visual C++ will display a dialog asking if you want to insert the component.

5. Click OK. You'll see a Confirm Classes dialog like the one shown here.

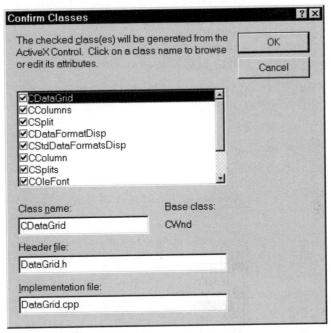

6. Click OK. Visual C++ will add the control to your Controls toolbar.

7. Perform steps 3 through 6 for the Microsoft ADO Data Control, Version 6.0 (OLEDB). The ADO Data Control will make the actual connection to the sample database through the OLE-DB connection we created earlier. You'll need this data source control to activate the grid control that we installed just a few seconds ago.

8. Click Close to close the Components and Controls Gallery dialog.

Now that we've got two controls to use, let's place them on the form and configure them. Don't worry about precise sizing of the controls—we'll change that with code. You will need to place the controls in the corners of the form. Here's the form I'll be using for the example.

7

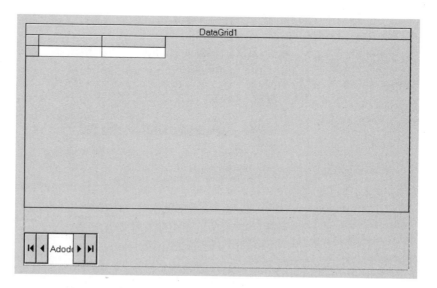

There are several properties that you'll need to change on DataGrid1. Just right-click on the control, then choose Properties from the context menu. Make sure you select the All tab because some properties don't appear on the other property pages. This first property is the most important because it sets the data source for the control. Set the DataSource property to IDC_ADODC1. Since we'll want full control over the database so that we can test the application completely, you'll also want to set the AllowAddNew and AllowDelete properties to True. Normally the Data Grid control is set to allow viewing and modification of records but not adding or deleting records. This represents a halfway point in securing your database. Someone could modify the database contents a little but couldn't do much in the way of real damage without a lot of painstaking work.

Now it's time to configure the data source itself. Right-click on the AdoDC1 control, then choose Properties from the context menu. Select the Control tab. Notice the Use Connection String field on this tab—make sure you select it if it's not already selected. This is where we'll select a data source. (The process for selecting a data source here will look similar to the one we used earlier in the chapter.) The following procedure will take you through the process of building a connection string.

1. Click Build. You'll see the Provider tab of the Data Link Properties dialog.

2. Highlight the Microsoft Jet 3.51 OLE-DB Provider option, then click Next. You'll see the Connection tab of the Data Link Properties dialog.

3. Type the location of your database in the Select or Enter a Database Name field. You can also use the Browse button to locate the database

on either a local or network drive. The example program uses DB_Samp\Sample.MDB for this field.

4. Type a user name and password, if required. (Neither entry is required for the sample database.)

5. Click Test Connection. You'll see a Test Connection Succeeded dialog if the connection information is correct.

6. Click OK twice. The connection is complete.

We have to do one more thing before this setup will become operational. Open the Properties dialog again for the AdoDC1 control. This time choose the RecordSource tab. Near the bottom of this tab you'll see the Command Text (SQL) field. This is where you can enter the command string for getting the data from the database we've just made a connection to. Enter this string to access all the information provided by the FoodOrders query that we set up in Chapter 5.

```
Select * from FoodOrders
```

7

Close the Properties dialog. If you compiled and ran this application right now, you'd be able to see the data in a grid format. Not only that, but you could edit, delete, and add records in the database as well. However, there are some things we do need to code, like the ability of the Data Grid control to resize itself whenever the main window resizes. We'll tackle these tasks in the next section of the chapter.

IN DEPTH

Using Two Database Connections in an Application

You may have noticed that we use two connections for the ADO1 application. We created the first connection during the application design process, while the second connection was created after we added AdoDC1 to the application. AdoDC1 (the second connection) is the active connection when you're viewing the form. If you try to use the first connection (available from the menus and the toolbar until you make changes to them), you won't see any change in the Data Grid contents.

Here's the problem for the developer of a C++ application. There aren't all that many controls like the ADODC control that support OLE-DB natively. If you plan to add single record view forms to your application or reports, you'll probably need that second connection to access the data in the database. In other words, even if you don't use the second connection immediately, always plan to include it in your application, at least until Microsoft makes all of the Visual C++ data-bound controls OLE-DB compatible.

There is a second reason for having two, and perhaps even more, connections. Using two connections allows you more flexibility in creating a high-speed application. You could use one connection for a print window and the other for a data editing window. Having two connections means that you don't have to worry about the status of the connection used with one window when working with a second window. Since the connections are separate, the status of the connection for each window is retained.

Obviously, there is a trade-off when using more than one connection. Sure, you add a little reliability and probably some speed to your application. However, the cost for these features is the use of more memory. If you're writing an application for a memory-constrained system, you may not have the luxury of using two or more data connections. Since a memory-constrained system will already be slower than most machines, the user is unlikely to notice the decrease in speed. You will, however, need to add additional code to ensure that the connection status information for the two windows is maintained properly and that the user doesn't end up corrupting the database inadvertently by doing something like printing and editing the database simultaneously.

Adding Some Form Code to ADO1

The example program isn't complete in a lot of ways, most of which fall into the fit-and-finish category. For example, if you resize the application right now, the form will get bigger, but not the Data Grid control. Another problem that you'll find is that all of the columns in the Data Grid control are set to a general format, which works fine for most of the data we want to display. However, you'll want to set the format to something else for Boolean values, which appear as numbers using the general format.

Before we can cure any of these problems, though, we'll need to create some variables to access the two controls. CTRL-double-click on DataGrid1. You'll see an Add Member Variable dialog like the one shown here.

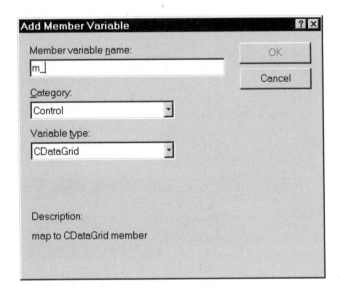

Notice that the Category field has Control selected and that the Variable Type field contains CDataGrid. Type **dataGrid1** in the Member Variable Name field (it should read m_dataGrid1 when you're finished). Click OK to complete the process. Now, do the same thing for AdoDC1. Use m_adoDC1 as the variable name this time.

It's time to add our first function. Open MFC ClassWizard using the View | ClassWizard command. This first bit of code will allow us to reposition and resize the two controls as necessary. Choose CADO1View in the Class Name field and CADO1View in the Object IDs field. Find the WM_SIZE message in the Messages field. Click Add Function. Your MFC AppWizard dialog should look like the one shown here.

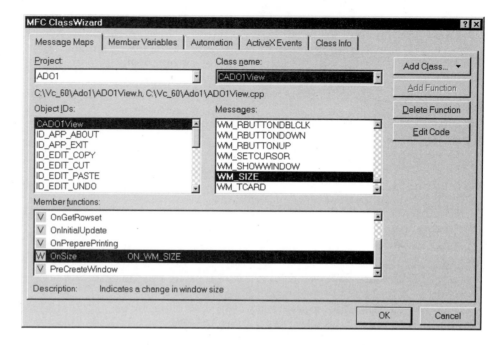

Click Edit Code. You'll be taken to the new function we just created. Listing 7-1 shows the code you'll need to add to make the controls resize properly when we change the application size.

Listing 7-1:

```cpp
void CADO1View::OnSize(UINT nType, int cx, int cy)
{
    int  iHeight, iWidth;     // Control height and width.
    CRect rect;          // Control size.

    // Perform the default action.
    COleDBRecordView::OnSize(nType, cx, cy);

    // Reposition AdoDC1.
    m_adoDC1.GetClientRect(rect);
    iHeight = rect.Height();
    iWidth = rect.Width();
    m_adoDC1.MoveWindow(cx, cy, iWidth, iHeight, TRUE);

    // Resize and reposition DataGrid1
    m_dataGrid1.MoveWindow(0, 0, cx, cy - iHeight, TRUE);
}
```

Fixing the Toolbars and Menus

Toolbars and menus are a part of most applications these days, so the MFC AppWizard creates them for you automatically. Unfortunately, the automatic creation process isn't always perfect, and in some situations no one is to blame for the problem. Our application works just fine if you use the AdoDC1 control to move from record to record, but what if the user wants to use the toolbar or menu instead? The menu and toolbar won't appear to do anything, even though they are moving the record pointer for the first connection. The menu and toolbar currently point at the first connection that we created using the MFC AppWizard. What we need are a menu and toolbar that point to the second connection provided by AdoDC1.

There are two major steps in fixing the menu and toolbar problem. First, we need to give them different IDs so that we'll be able to write code for them. Second, we'll need to provide code for moving the record pointer of the second connection around. The following procedure will help you complete the first step (we'll begin by changing the toolbar).

The First
Record button
looks like this:

7

1. Open the IDR_MAINFRAME toolbar by double-clicking its entry in the Toolbar folder in ResourceView.

2. Double-click the First Record button. You'll see the Toolbar Button Properties dialog shown here. We don't need to change a lot of information in this dialog, just the ID field so that we can add the special code required to access the second database connection.

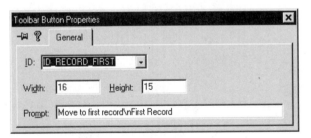

3. Type **ID_RECORD_FIRST2** in the ID field. We'll append the number 2 to any object that accesses the second connection to make the code easier to read.

4. Perform steps 2 and 3 for the Previous Record, Next Record, and Last Record buttons.

5. Open the IDR_MAINFRAME menu by double-clicking its entry in the Menu folder in ResourceView.

6. Right-click the Record | First Record command and choose Properties from the context menu. You'll see the Menu Item Properties dialog shown here. Again, we don't have to change anything but the ID field value.

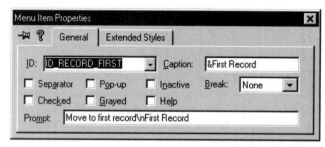

7. Type **ID_RECORD_FIRST2** in the ID field. It's absolutely essential that your entries in this field match the ones for the toolbar precisely. Otherwise, the toolbar and menu won't "track" with each other.

TIP: You can ensure that the toolbar and menu names match by choosing the correct ID value from the drop-down list box rather than typing the value into the ID field. However, in most cases it's just as easy to type in a value if you're adding a number.

8. Repeat steps 6 and 7 for the Record | Previous Record, Record | Next Record, and Record | Last Record commands.

The setup process isn't over quite yet. You'll need to open the MFC ClassWizard using the View | ClassWizard command. Choose CADO1View for the Class Name field. Find ID_RECORD_FIRST2 in the Object IDs field, then choose COMMAND in the Messages field. Click Add Function, then OK when you see the Add Member Function dialog. You've just added a function to handle the First Record menu and toolbar entries. Repeat this process for the ID_RECORD_LAST2, ID_RECORD_NEXT2, and ID_RECORD_PREV2 Object IDs. The MFC AppWizard dialog should look like the one shown here when you finish.

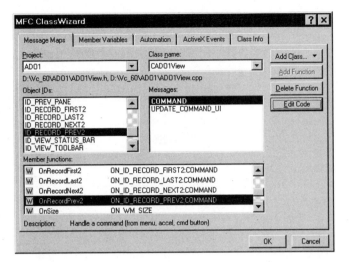

At this point you should have the menu and toolbar setup for accessing the second connection that we created for this program. Now we need to add some code to make the menu and toolbar entries work. Click Edit Code in the MFC AppWizard dialog and Visual C++ will take you to the new functions we just created. Listing 7-2 shows the code you'll need to add. Note that the #include directive needs to appear at the beginning of the code file along with the rest of the #include directives for the file.

Listing 7-2:

```
// Include the C_Recordset class so that we
// can manipulate the recordset directly.
#include "_Recordset.h"

void CADO1View::OnRecordFirst2()
{
    // Move to the first record.
    m_adoDC1.GetRecordset().MoveFirst();
}

void CADO1View::OnRecordLast2()
{
    // Move to the last record.
    m_adoDC1.GetRecordset().MoveLast();
}
```

7

```
void CADO1View::OnRecordNext2()
{
    // Move to the next record.
    m_adoDC1.GetRecordset().MoveNext();
}

void CADO1View::OnRecordPrev2()
{
    // Check to see if we can move the record pointer.
    if (!m_adoDC1.GetRecordset().GetBof())
    {
        // Move to the previous record.
        m_adoDC1.GetRecordset().MovePrevious();

        // Check again for beginning of file.
        if (m_adoDC1.GetRecordset().GetBof())
        {
            // If we are at the beginning of the file,
            // advance the record pointer to the first record.
            m_adoDC1.GetRecordset().MoveNext();
        }
    }
}
```

Most of the code in Listing 7-2 is straightforward. We use the m_adoDC1 memory variable to gain access to the recordset (the records that the user is currently looking at). Once we have access to the recordset, we can move the record pointer to the proper record.

Look at the OnRecordPrev2() function. This function requires a little more code than the other functions because there isn't any default action to perform when we go past the beginning of the file. (If you go past the end of the file, the application automatically adds a new record to the table.) All of this extra code helps you avoid a visual problem that could result in a lot of support calls. If the record pointer ends up at the beginning of the file, the little record pointer indicator on the grid control disappears. To the user this may signify some kind of an error, even though the grid and ADODC are both working properly. Avoiding the problem is simple: just check for the beginning of file indicator and reposition the record pointer appropriately.

7

Avoiding Installation Problems

Database applications are one of the most complex types of applications that you can create. Not only do people expect a lot more in the way of stability and robust functionality from these applications, but the whole scale of the application itself is much larger. For example, most database applications require some type of network support. It's not too difficult to figure out that database applications require more in the way of support than any application, and as a result, you'll find that database applications, even simple ones like the one we just created, require a lot of support files.

The first problem that you'll encounter when creating an installation program is finding all of the files that you need. Normally you'll need to check multiple sources of information before you'll get a complete list. The two file sets that you always have to look for are vendor-specific database access drivers and operating system support files. You may also need configuration utilities and other program files depending on the DBMS you use. The vendor will normally provide you with a complete list of the vendor-specific files hidden in some dark crevice of the documentation; make sure you take the time to seek them out. In some cases the vendor will also be kind enough to provide a list of general operating system files, but be sure you check the Microsoft Web site for a list of the most current drivers before you assume that the vendor's list is accurate or up to date. Table 7-1 provides a complete list of the files you'll need for a database application that relies on the Microsoft Jet Engine. (This table is specifically set up for DAO but will work for other forms of database access as well.)

Purpose	3.0 Version	3.5 Version
Microsoft Jet Engine Library	MSJT3032.DLL	MSJET35.DLL
Microsoft Jet Database Engine Error DLL	MSJTER32.DLL	MSJTER35.DLL
Microsoft Jet Database Engine International DLL	MSJINT32.DLL	MSJINT35.DLL
Visual Basic for Applications Development Environment—Expression Service Loader	VBAJET32.DLL	VBAJET32.DLL
Visual Basic for Applications Runtime—Expression Service	VBAR2232.DLL	VBAR332.DLL
Visual Basic for Applications Object Library	VEN2232.OLB	N/A
Microsoft (R) Red ISAM	MSRD2X32.DLL	MSRD2X35.DLL
*Microsoft Jet xBase ISAM	MSXB3032.DLL	MSXBSE35.DLL
*Microsoft Jet Paradox ISAM	MSPD3032.DLL	MSPDOX35.DLL
*Microsoft Jet Text ISAM	MSTX3032.DLL	MSTEXT35.DLL
*Microsoft Jet Excel ISAM	MSXL3032.DLL	MSEXCL35.DLL
*Microsoft Jet Lotus 1-2-3 ISAM	MSLT3032	MSLTUS35.DLL
*Microsoft Jet Exchange ISAM	N/A	MSEXCH35.DLL
Microsoft Wingman Library	MSWNG300.DLL	MSWNG300.DLL
Microsoft ODBC Desktop Driver Pack	ODBCJT32.DLL	ODBCJT32.DLL
Microsoft ODBC Desktop Driver Pack	ODBCJI32.DLL	ODBCJI32.DLL
ODBC Helper Function DLL	ODBCTL32.DLL	ODBCTL32.DLL
*Microsoft RDO (Remote Data Objects) Engine Control	N/A	MSRDO20.DLL
*Microsoft RDO Client Cursor DLL	N/A	RDOCURS.DLL
*Microsoft Replication Library	N/A	MSREPL35.DLL

Microsoft Jet Engine (DAO) Required Files

Table 7-1.

*An optional file that you may need depending on the database support you plan to provide. (For example, the xBase ISAM DLLs are only needed if you plan to access an xBase database like those created by FoxPro and dBASE.)

Another installation problem is database location. Some programmers assume that the user will require direct network access alone and that the administrator will place the database in a specific location on the server. Avoid making either of these assumptions, especially in today's Internet charged market. Server access may come through an Internet connection or even from a local subset of the records stored on the database. In other words, don't assume anything about where the data will be stored unless you can also assure that you'll personally place that data in the desired location (even so, management may decide that it needs Internet connectivity at any time).

Let's get back to the support files for a moment. Most of you realize that there are problems when an application relies on a specific version of a common support file like the MFC run-time files. The problem greatly increases when you create a database application. For one thing, you still have the MFC runtime to worry about. Added to these support files, though, are the common operating system files for database access along with any vendor-specific files you need. Now you have three product versions to keep track of, and any of them can change at any moment.

The way around this problem is to ensure that you check the versions of each file the users already have installed on their system during installation (now you know why some installation programs grind away for what seems like hours). If the version of a file doesn't match what you've used for the application, then you'll need to ask the user's permission to overwrite the file with the one you need. Now, here's where one of the problems come in. The user is going to assume that newer is automatically better. On the other hand, if your application relies on an older version of the file, it may not run with the newer version. You need to make a special check for a newer version of the file and place some kind of warning in your message that the application may not work with the newer one (unless you know in advance that it will).

T IP: Many database programmers include a routine for checking the file version numbers every time the application starts. In some cases it's overkill to check every file that the application uses. However, it is a good idea to check the version numbers of common or shared files. A user can install another application that overwrites the version of the files required by your application. The only way to ensure that your application has what it needs is to check these files during the program initialization process. It's better to fail gracefully before the application actually starts than to experience a program crash once the application is started and the database is opened.

7

Other installation problems are related to the way that wizards normally design the installation program for you. For example, most installation programs assume that if there is enough space on the user's hard drive to store all of the files for the application, the application will run properly. Unfortunately, with database applications, you also have to take things like a local copy of the recordset into account because the recordset may be too large to store in memory. In other words, you'll need to pad your installation program hard disk requirements to take any processing needs into account, something that you don't really need to do with most application classes.

Adding Reports to an Application

Expect to create at least one, if not more, reports for your database application. Even a small application like the one we've created in this chapter could benefit from multiple report types. For example, you might have an overview report that shows the database contents as a whole by summarizing like data (even the method of summarizing can create multiple reports) and a detail report that shows all of the records. In addition to the data that the report contains and the order in which you present it, there are other things to consider, like the appearance of the report from an aesthetic perspective. You may not want to take the time to print a report using the best-quality type and graphics for a workgroup meeting, but you can bet that such a report will be required for a manager's meeting.

There isn't any way that I can tell you about every nuance there is when creating a report in a section of a chapter. What this chapter will cover are some tips for creating a complex array of reports that include everything you'll need to really view your data and an example of how to accomplish at least some of these goals in a programming example.

Printing Can Be Difficult

Trying to create the reports you need can be difficult, absurdly so in some situations. You might be on a project where five managers all want their own set of reports added to the application, but you know that you really only have time to create one or two of those report sets within the time frame allotted. Don't despair, you probably won't have to write all of those reports anyway if you take a little time to analyze what the managers are looking for and add a little flexibility into the printing process.

Breaking down the reports you need into simple requirements is the first thing you should do when trying to reduce application complexity. It's a good idea to create a table with columns showing simple requirements and then listing the reports along the side. If you can find some method for comparison in the reports, you may be able to combine several of them into a single report and add configuration dialogs as needed. The following list gives you some ideas on what you can do to break down the reports into components parts.

◆ *Sort order*   Every report requires some type of sorting. Otherwise, you'll end up with a list of disorganized data that no one can understand. Remember that one of the main goals for any database is to organize the data it contains into something that is easier to understand. Your reports need to do the same thing. Sort order represents one of the easiest methods for combining two or more reports into a single programming task.

◆ *Groups*   There are times when you want a detail report that groups like items into a single heading. For example, you may create groups by ZIP code in a contact database. The ZIP code would appear as a heading, with all of the contacts in that ZIP code area in order beneath it. Groups aren't much different than sorting when it comes to organizing the data. However, it's very difficult to combine two reports with different groups even if the main part of the printout is the same. The reason is simple: you'd have to add a lot of complexity to the print routine to handle the inclusion of various header types. You can, however, combine two like reports where one includes groups and the other doesn't. All you need to do is include a switch to turn the heading on or off.

◆ *Group totals/summaries*   A lot of reports will provide a footer where the entire report or a related group of numbers is tallied. There are a lot of other statistical uses for footers, but a numeric tally is the most common type. As with group headings, it's difficult, if not impossible, to combine two reports that have different totals or summaries. You can, however, combine a report that doesn't use a footer of any kind with one that does as long as the columns are the same.

◆ *Report appearance*   If you have two reports with similar data but different requirements when it comes to final appearance, try combining them. It doesn't make sense to create two different printing routines if the only difference is the font used for presentation purposes and perhaps a little window dressing like adding the company logo to the top of the report.

◆ *Level of detail*   Some reports are simply an overview of other reports. In other words, there are some reports that only use the parent data in its entirety. The child records are summarized in some way to provide an overview. It's easy to combine an overview report with one that shows

7

the detailed contents of the database. Of course, there is the issue of what the reports contain. For example, if you have one report that shows every invoice for the month in salesperson order and another report that shows the total sales by individual salesperson, you can combine the two reports into one. A simple switch will determine whether the data is summarized or if every record in the child table gets printed as is.

◆ *Filtering* It's very common for someone to ask for some, but not all, of the records in a database. If the only difference between two reports is the filtering used to determine which records get picked, then you can always combine them. Filtering is a function of the query you make to the DBMS, not a function of the code you write. In other words, all you need to do is change one or two lines of code to make the two reports.

At this point you may be wondering why you don't just create a single report with a lot of configuration dialogs that will allow users to generate their own reports. There are several good reasons for not doing so. First, most users are going to be bewildered by the array of dialogs required to create a report. You'll find yourself spending a lot more time trying to get the user up to speed on creating the report than if you designed it yourself. In addition, the second you introduce custom reports, you'll also have to create some method for users to save those reports to disk so that they can create the same report later without a lot of fiddling around.

Another reason to avoid generic reports is the security risk involved. If you give the user too many different methods for creating custom reports, you may find that you've created security holes as well. Management normally wants some assurance that the company's confidential data won't get into the wrong hands. This means adding security and tightly controlling what gets printed out in addition to adding the right security to the database itself.

PORTABILITY: Don't be lulled into a false sense of security when it comes to printer incompatibility problems when working with Windows. Sure, Windows does make things a little easier by providing a consistent programming API for print routines. You also get the distinct advantage of print driver support—at least you won't have to write your own drivers anymore like programmers under DOS did. However, the advantages end there. A vendor can still provide a flaky driver that makes it difficult to get the output from your application looking right. You'll also find that these problems happen more often to the database programmer than anyone else because of the relative complexity of the output you're trying to produce. Just adding text and graphics together and still trying to maintain the alignment of various table elements can be a problem. Suffice it to say that you're going to run into a wealth of printer-related problems when you move your application from the test environment to the outside world. Even the best testing in the world won't help you get around the problems of dealing with poorly designed print drivers or other kinds of compatibility problems.

Adding Print Capabilities to Your Application

Now that we've taken a look at some of the complexities of writing a print routine for your database application, let's look at some ways to solve these programs. Fortunately, you already have three of the function shells you need in the ADO1 application we've been using for example purposes up to this point. Just take a look at the CADO1View class. There are three functions: OnPreparePrinting(), OnBeginPrinting(), and OnEndPrinting(). The first routine allows you to get your printer set up and do any other preparatory tasks like saving the current record number in the query so that you can return there after the print job completes. The second routine, OnBeginPrinting(), allows you to prepare the device context. Think of the device context as an artist's palette—you use it to draw the information you want to send to the printer. We'll run into this particular part of the Windows GDI (Graphics Device Interface) quite often in this example, so you'll have a good idea of what a device context is all about by the time we're done. Finally, the OnEndPrinting() routine allows you to restore global application settings to their preprint condition. For example, this is where you'd return the query pointer to its preprint record.

7

There's one function that's missing. We don't have a print routine to use to send data to the printer. The first thing we'll need to do is add an OnPrint() function to the program using the MFC ClassWizard. The OnPrint() function contains the code required to actually get the printed information out to the printer. This routine also gets called for other print-related tasks like the Print | Preview command provided by most applications. Open the MFC ClassWizard dialog using the View | ClassWizard command. Choose CADO1View in the Class Name field. Highlight CADO1View in the Object IDs list and OnPrint in the Messages list. Click Add Function. The Member Functions list should have a new function added to it as shown here.

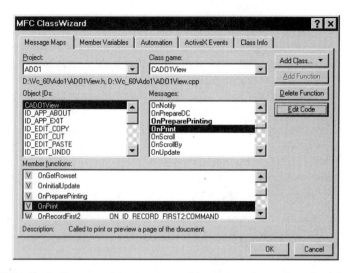

Click the Edit Code button. It's time to add some print-related code to our application. Listing 7-3 contains the code you'll need to add to the OnPrint() function.

Listing 7-3:

```cpp
void CADO1View::OnPrint(CDC* pDC, CPrintInfo* pInfo)
{
    int         iRowCount = 1;          // Current print row count.
    LPSTR       lpstrRow = "EMPTY1";    // Text form of row count.
    CString     cLine;                  // One line of printed output.
    CPen        oPen;                   // Pen for drawing.
    CBrush      oBrush;                 // Brush for shading.
    CFont       oTextFont;              // Font used for displaying text.
    CFont       oHeadFont;              // Font used to display the heading.
    CFont       oColFont;               // Font used to display column headings.
    LOGFONT     lfFont;                 // Font characteristic structure.
    CSize       oFontSize;              // Size of a font.
    COLORREF    clrRef;                 // Color structure.
    int         iRowPos = 120;          // Row position on printed page.
    int         iTextHeight = 0;        // Current text height.
    CRect       oDrawRect;              // Drawing area for printer.
    int         iRecNumPos;             // Record number position.
    int         iFoodIDPos;             // Food ID position.
    int         iNamePos;               // Name position.
    int         iPerishablePos;         // Perishable position.
    int         iPricePos;              // Price position.
    int         iPurchasePos;           // Purchase Date position.
    int         iQuantityPos;           // Quantity position.
```

```
int              iStoragePos;              // Storage Life position.

// Get the drawing area for our print routine.
oDrawRect = pInfo->m_rectDraw;

// Create a pen and select it into our device context.
clrRef = 0x00000000;
oPen.CreatePen(PS_SOLID, 2, clrRef);
pDC->SelectObject(&oPen);

// Create a brush and select it into our device context.
clrRef = 0x00C0C0C0;
oBrush.CreateSolidBrush(clrRef);
pDC->SelectObject(&oBrush);

// Create a heading font and select it into our device context.
oHeadFont.CreatePointFont(240, "Arial", pDC);
pDC->SelectObject(&oHeadFont);

// Display our heading.
oFontSize = pDC->GetOutputTextExtent("The ABC Company");
pDC->Ellipse(500,
    iRowPos - (oFontSize.cy / 2) - 10,
    oDrawRect.Width() - 500,
    iRowPos + (oFontSize.cy / 2) + 10);
pDC->SetBkMode(TRANSPARENT);
pDC->TextOut((oDrawRect.Width() - oFontSize.cx) / 2,
    iRowPos - (oFontSize.cy / 2) - 10,
    "The ABC Company");
pDC->SetBkMode(OPAQUE);

// Create the appropriate space.
oHeadFont.GetLogFont(&lfFont);
iRowPos = abs(lfFont.lfHeight) + 175;

// Create a text font.
oTextFont.CreatePointFont(120, "Arial", pDC);

// Get the current text font height.
oTextFont.GetLogFont(&lfFont);
iTextHeight = abs(lfFont.lfHeight) + 10;

// Create a font for displaying column headings.
lfFont.lfWeight = 700;     // Make it bold, normal is 400.
oColFont.CreateFontIndirect(&lfFont);
```

```
pDC->SelectObject(&oColFont);

// Compute the column spacings.  Set the first column to 1/2 inch.
iRecNumPos = int(oDrawRect.Width() / 17);
iFoodIDPos = iRecNumPos + 50 + pDC->GetOutputTextExtent("##").cx;
iNamePos = iFoodIDPos + 50 + pDC->GetOutputTextExtent("XXX00000XXX").cx;
iPerishablePos = iNamePos + 50 + pDC->GetOutputTextExtent("Xxxxxxxxxxxx").cx;
iPricePos = iPerishablePos + 50 + pDC->GetOutputTextExtent("Perishable").cx;
iPurchasePos = iPricePos + 50 + pDC->GetOutputTextExtent("$00.00").cx;
iQuantityPos = iPurchasePos + 50 + pDC->GetOutputTextExtent("Purchase Date").cx;
iStoragePos = iQuantityPos + 50 + pDC->GetOutputTextExtent("Quantity").cx;

// Display the column headings.
pDC->TextOut(iRecNumPos, iRowPos, "#");
pDC->TextOut(iFoodIDPos, iRowPos, "Food ID");
pDC->TextOut(iNamePos, iRowPos, "Name");
pDC->TextOut(iPerishablePos, iRowPos, "Perishable");
pDC->TextOut(iPricePos, iRowPos, "Price");
pDC->TextOut(iPurchasePos, iRowPos, "Purchase Date");
pDC->TextOut(iQuantityPos, iRowPos, "Quantity");
pDC->TextOut(iStoragePos, iRowPos, "Storage Life");

// Create a space between the column heading and the text.
iRowPos += iTextHeight;
pDC->MoveTo(iRecNumPos, iRowPos);
pDC->LineTo(oDrawRect.Width() - iRecNumPos, iRowPos);
iRowPos += 20;

// Select our text font into the device context.
pDC->SelectObject(&oTextFont);

// Determine the row height.
iTextHeight = 20 + pDC->GetOutputTextExtent("Xy").cy;

// Print the records in a loop.
while (iRowCount < m_dataGrid1.GetVisibleRows())
{

    // Display the current record number.
    itoa(iRowCount, lpstrRow, 10);
    cLine = lpstrRow;
    pDC->TextOut(iRecNumPos, iRowPos, cLine);

    // Print the data.
    m_dataGrid1.SetRow(iRowCount - 1);
```

```
m_dataGrid1.SetCol(0);
pDC->TextOut(iFoodIDPos, iRowPos, m_dataGrid1.GetText());
m_dataGrid1.SetCol(1);
pDC->TextOut(iNamePos, iRowPos, m_dataGrid1.GetText());
m_dataGrid1.SetCol(2);
if (m_dataGrid1.GetText() == "-1")
    pDC->TextOut(iPerishablePos, iRowPos, "Yes");
else
    pDC->TextOut(iPerishablePos, iRowPos, "No");
m_dataGrid1.SetCol(6);
pDC->TextOut(iPricePos, iRowPos, "$" + m_dataGrid1.GetText());
m_dataGrid1.SetCol(4);
pDC->TextOut(iPurchasePos, iRowPos, m_dataGrid1.GetText());
m_dataGrid1.SetCol(5);
pDC->TextOut(iQuantityPos, iRowPos, m_dataGrid1.GetText());
m_dataGrid1.SetCol(3);
pDC->TextOut(iStoragePos, iRowPos, m_dataGrid1.GetText());

    // Advance the row.
    iRowPos += iTextHeight;
    iRowCount ++;
}

//Perform the default action
COleDBRecordView::OnPrint(pDC, pInfo);
}
```

7

This looks like a lot of code and it is. Working with printed output can get fairly complicated without a lot of effort on your part. However, if you divide the task into smaller pieces, it's not too hard to figure out what's going on.

The first thing you need to know about is the mysterious pDC object of class CDC. That's the device context that I mentioned earlier. It helps a lot if you think about pDC as your palette, the area in memory where you'll draw what you want to send to the printer. In fact, Microsoft has done just about everything it can to foster that viewpoint in the naming of functions and structures used with the GDI.

The first thing we do (besides produce what seems like thousands of variables) is create some drawing tools. You can't draw on a palette if you don't have the required drawing tools. In this case, I'll show you how to create the three basic drawing tools that you'll use in most of your programs: a brush, a pen, and a font. Pens can be any color, any one of a range of widths, and you can even choose a drawing pattern like dots. You use a pen for drawing lines, which includes outlines for objects. For example, a square doesn't necessarily need an outline, but most do. You could draw a square using just the fill color. That brings me to a brush. A brush provides fill color for solid objects. Brushes can also have a particular color, and you can choose to create a brush that has a pattern like a crosshatch. Finally, a font is used to write something onscreen. It has a lot of characteristics, most of them too arcane for the typical programmer's tastes. The source code in Listing 7-3 shows you a couple of ways to create fonts that don't require a complete knowledge of desktop publishing to use.

Just because you have a tool to draw with doesn't mean that you can use it. An artist might have a brush hanging from a nail in the wall, but that doesn't mean it's available for use in the current painting. Likewise, when you draw something in Windows, you have to select your tool first. That's what the SelectObject() function does. It allows you to select an object for drawing.

There's one brush, pen, and font object for each device context in Windows. Think of it as having three hands, each one armed with a different tool. Before you can use another tool, you have to put the current one down and then select the new one. Windows takes care of putting a tool down for you automatically. Every time you use the SelectObject() function, you're putting the old tool down and picking up a new one.

Each of your tools is unique in many important ways. If you want an Arial 10 point font, you need a special font tool for that purpose. You'd have to create another font tool if you found that you needed the bold version of that font or if you suddenly wanted to write something in Times New Roman 12. Fortunately, you don't have to create a separate font for each color that you want to use—that feature is controlled by the device context. Another example of how tools are unique is the pen. You need to create a pen for each width and style of line you want. Unlike the font, you'll also need a pen for each color you want to create. The brush is even more unique in some ways. While you can use the same function to create just about any font or pen you want, there is a different function call for each type of brush. For example, if you want to create a crosshatch brush, you need to use the CreateHatchBrush() function in place of the CreateSolidBrush() function shown in the code. It's important to realize the limitations of your existing tools and create new ones as you need them.

NOTE: The drawing commands for this example are optimized for a printer that has a resolution in the range of 300 to 360 dots per inch. If you have a higher resolution printer, you may need to modify the location values to get a clear picture. However, no matter what resolution your printer is, you'll still be able to see how the commands work together to provide some form of output from your database application.

The first thing that we do in the way of drawing for this example is to create an ellipse using the Ellipse() function. Like most solid drawing commands, you need to specify the coordinates of the upper-left and lower-right corners of the graphics primitive. Windows assumes that you want to use the currently selected brush and pen, so you don't need to specify these values.

After drawing the ellipse, the code will place some text within it. The first thing we need to do is set the background drawing mode to transparent so that we don't erase any part of the ellipse. The other mode is opaque, which means that you want to replace the background color as well as add a drawing of some type in the foreground. Look at how the code uses the GetOutputTextExtent() function to determine the length of the text in pixels. This is about the only way to conveniently determine the length of a line of text so that you can center it on the page. The next line uses the TextOut() function to send the text to the printer. The very last line in this section of code resets the background drawing mode to opaque (the default setting) using the SetBkMode() function.

It's time to talk about fonts for a few seconds. There are two convenient methods of creating fonts, and the next section of code shows both. The first method is to use the CreatePointFont() function. All you need is the name of a typeface and the size of the font you want to create in tenths of a point. So, if you wanted to create a 10 point font, you'd need to specify a font size value of 100.

Fonts use a special LOGFONT structure to pass all of the parameters they require. If you use the CreatePointFont() function, Windows creates this structure for you and makes certain assumptions in the process. What if you don't want those defaults? Well, you can create a simple font using

7

CreatePointFont() (like we just did) and then use the GetLogFont() function to fill out the LOGFONT structure for you. Now you have a fully functional structure that you can modify slightly. I emphasize *slightly* because you'll definitely shoot yourself in the foot if you try to make big changes in the structure that Windows just returned. I change the weight of the font from normal to bold, which is an acceptable change as long as you don't make too big a difference in the font weight. Now you can use the CreateFontIndirect() function to create the bold version of the font. Just pass the LOGFONT structure provided by Windows with the lfWeight member change.

Notice that the code creates a bunch of headers using the bold font once it selects that font into the device context. Always remember to create the tool first and then select it as needed to draw on the device context. We also create a group of variables to track the positioning information for the columns. These positioning variables are used for both the headers and the detail information. Note that the method used to derive the positioning information is device independent. In other words, it should look about the same whether you use a 300 dpi printer or one that's capable of 600 dpi. Of course, the random element here is how well Windows can determine the amount of space taken by the text we've provided using the current font. In most cases you'll find that this calculation is accurate, but you may need to play around with it a tad to get a good presentation on all the printers in your company.

Drawing a line under the headings comes next. Notice that drawing a line is a two-step process. First, you use the MoveTo() function to move the pen to a specific point on the page, and then you use the LineTo() function to actually draw the line. Think of MoveTo() as moving with the pen up and LineTo() as moving with the pen down.

The last part of our print routine makes use of the data that's already available in DataGrid1. All that this code does is move from cell to cell in the data grid and print its contents to the printer or screen. So how does the printed output of our application look? Here is an example of what you should see.

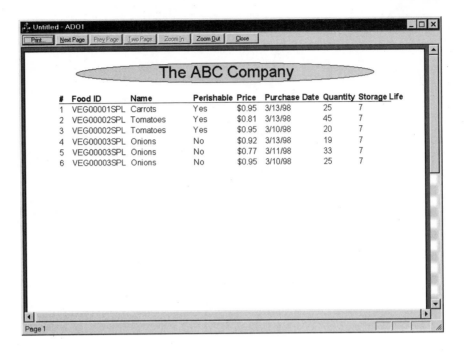

PART III

Visual C++ and the Internet

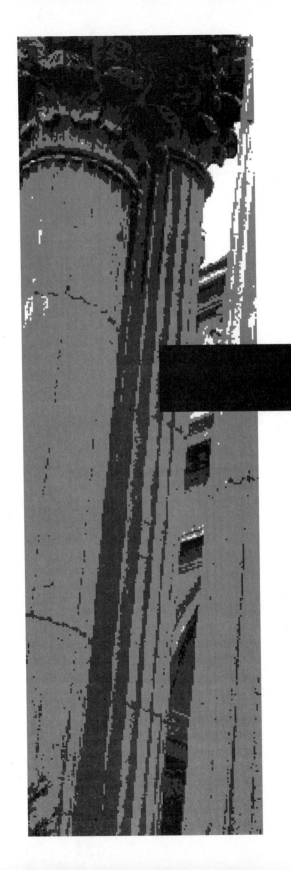

CHAPTER 8

Designing a Web Page

233

No matter how hard you try to avoid it, any type of Internet experience will require some level of HTML (Hypertext Markup Language) knowledge. It seems like a pretty broad statement until you figure out that any kind of normal access to the Internet is going to involve a visit to a Web page. When you type http:, you'll find yourself accessing a Web page that uses HTML through HTTP (Hypertext Transfer Protocol). And there's little you can do in the way of information exchange without typing those letters.

TIP: You can avoid learning about HTML tags for the most part if you want to. Products like Visual InterDev make it easy for you to create Web pages that include ActiveX controls. Of course, this means you'll have to purchase another product in addition to Visual C++ to create and test your ActiveX controls. Obviously, you'll want to weigh the advantages of using a product like Visual InterDev and the disadvantages of buying and learning another product against the number of Web pages you'll actually create. If you're only going to create the occasional Web page, then writing the code by hand may still be the better choice. On the other hand, if creating Web pages consumes a major portion of your time, you'll want to make the investment in a product like Visual InterDev. You can learn more about using Visual C++ with products like Visual InterDev in my upcoming book from Osborne/McGraw-Hill: *Visual Studio: The Complete Reference*. This book shows you how to use the various language products contained in Visual Studio to create applications with greater ease, especially when working in a team environment.

As a Visual C++ programmer who's interested in using ActiveX, you may or may not spend a lot of time creating Web pages. You will, however, need to know how they work so that you can help other people use your controls. Learning HTML might seem a bit daunting at first. There's a wealth of tags (like programming statements) that you can use to create a page. Viewing these tags isn't a problem—just about any browser on the market provides a View | Source command that you can use to look at the underlying HTML for any page on a Web site. Figure 8-1 shows a typical example.

NOTE: As with all the other figures in this book, the ability to configure your browser will change the appearance of the display you see. In addition, Microsoft and Netscape are constantly changing their Web sites and the appearance of their browser. Finally, the addition of plug-ins may change the appearance of your browser slightly. With this in mind, consider all of the figures and illustrations in this chapter as a basis for what you should see. Your actual screen display may vary from the one shown.

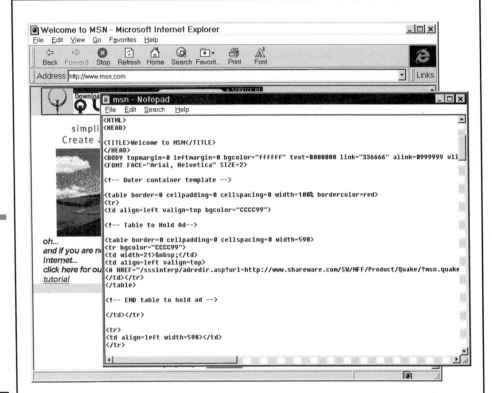

You can view the source for most Web pages—a handy feature when you want to learn something new.

Figure 8-1.

There's a simple way to at least begin the learning process, and that's part of what we'll cover here. You could put together a Web site using a mere 12 HTML tags, and then embellish them using additional tags later. That's what the first section of this chapter will look at. We'll examine the 12 tags that you'll find on any Internet site that provides even a minimal level of functionality.

TIP: You can use the View I Source command to your advantage if you design a lot of Web pages. Simply find a Web site that contains a feature you want to use, then look at the underlying source to see how the programmer accomplished the task. Unlike many programming situations in which the code is hidden, encrypted, or otherwise inaccessible, HTML retains its English-like syntax even when used at an Internet site.

8

Once you have these 12 tags in mind, we'll look at one additional tag that you'll need to make ActiveX work. We'll combine everything you know with an ActiveX control to produce a very simple Web page. (Chapter 11 will show you how to create this ActiveX control.) You'll be able to do something with this page and could even use it as a template for new pages later. The idea is to provide you with a baseline knowledge of HTML, not make you an HTML programming guru.

NOTE: This chapter won't teach you everything you need to know about HTML. Whole books are devoted to this topic, and some people complain that even that isn't enough to do the job. What we're going to do is look at HTML at a very basic level—a level that most of these other books miss. By the time you finish this chapter, you'll have just enough information to make learning additional HTML tags easy.

It may seem strange that an ASCII text file could contain enough information to make ActiveX work. Once you learn about the ActiveX-specific tag, we'll take a look at how the browser interprets this tag and makes ActiveX work. It's not a difficult task once you know the little secrets that Microsoft included with Internet Explorer 3.*x* and 4.*x*.

COM+ will eventually replace ActiveX on the Internet, but ActiveX will remain Microsoft's application component technology.

Microsoft is also introducing a new technology called Component Object Model Plus, or COM+. This is the technology that Microsoft will eventually use to augment programming on the Internet. It's not a replacement for ActiveX, which will remain the technology of choice for creating components, but COM+ eventually will replace ActiveX on the Internet. A section later in this chapter will provide an overview of this exciting new technology and give you some idea of how it'll help you in the future.

Once you've gotten basic HTML and the ActiveX tags down, we'll look at a couple of easy enhancements you can make to simple HTML pages. The two enhancements, sound and animated GIFs, add just enough pizzazz to keep visitors from getting bored. It's important to spice up your Web site without making the pages it contains too large to download in a convenient amount of time.

The final section of this chapter looks at one of the utilities provided with the ActiveX SDK: DIANTZ.EXE. This allows you to compress one or more ActiveX controls and reduce the download time. This same utility will produce the CAB files that Microsoft uses to distribute Windows 95. You'll find that the DIANTZ utility comes in handy for more than just ActiveX development.

A Quick Overview of HTML

You could write a whole book about HTML and not cover all of the variations of all the various tags. Let's take a look at the term "tag" first. Every HTML statement is composed of one or more tags. A tag is like a programming statement. There are tags for beginning and ending the various sections of an HTML document and others that allow various kinds of processing. As companies become more involved with the Internet, the complexion of tags is changing. We'll take a look at a couple of these changes that fall within the scope of this chapter, but there are other changes we won't cover due to space considerations. (The chapter will provide some leads about where you can find some of this additional information.)

The most basic HTML document will likely contain 12 different kinds of tags. Some of these are mandatory; others are only used to provide specific types of functionality. We'll look at the tags in their simplest form—you can add modifiers to most tags to affect the way they work. For example, you could add a font specification or tell the tag to center any text it contains on the page. Table 8-1 provides a quick overview of the 12 basic tags that we'll look at.

8

An Overview of the Twelve Basic HTML Tags

Table 8-1.

Tag	Usage	Description
<HTML> and </HTML>	Mandatory	Every HTML document begins with <HTML> and ends with </HTML>. This is how the browser knows where to start and stop reading.
<HEAD> and </HEAD>	Normally used	When you look at any HTML document, you'll see a heading and a body. The heading normally identifies the Web site and defines the page setup.
<BODY> and </BODY>	Normally used	You'll place the main section of the content of your Web page within these two tags. The body normally contains the information that the user visited your site to find.
<Hx> and </Hx>	Optional	Books and other forms of text normally divide the information they contain into sections using headings. This tag allows you to add headings to your Web site.

Tag	Usage	Description
<P>	Optional	HTML always assumes that all the text you type, whether it appears on the same line or not, is part of the same paragraph. You use this tag to add a carriage return and two line feeds (marking the end of a paragraph).
 	Optional	There are times when you'll want to go to the left margin without adding a new line to the page. That's what this tag is for. It adds a carriage return with a single line feed.
<HR>	Optional	The horizontal rule tag allows you to place a line across the page. It also adds white space between paragraphs.
<A HREF= "*Destination Document*"> and </A>	Optional	Hyperlinks to other documents are the most common component of a Web page.
<A NAME= "*Anchor Name*"> and </A>	Optional	Anchors allow you to move from one point on the page to another. The hyperlink to access this tag looks like this: <A HREF="*Current Document# Anchor Name*">.
<EM> and </EM>	Optional	Different browsers react differently to the emphasis tag. However, the majority simply display text in italic type.
<STRONG> and </STRONG>	Optional	As with the emphasis tag, it's up to the browser to determine how it will react to the <STRONG> tag. Most browsers display text in bold type when they see this tag.
<PRE> and </PRE>	Optional	There are times when you don't want a browser to reformat your text. The preformatted tag tells the browser to leave the text formatting alone.

An Overview
of the Twelve
Basic HTML
Tags
(*continued*)
Table 8-1.

Now that you have the basic idea of what these tags are about, let's look at a few of them in detail. The following sections talk about some of the tags that you'll use on a more or less consistent basis and require more than a modicum of work to use in most cases. Don't worry if you can't quite grasp everything during this discussion; we'll look at actual usage details in the section on creating simple HTML documents. Seeing how the tags work will help you understand how they interact with the browser.

Understanding the <HEAD> Tag

A heading tells the browser what you want to do with the page before it gets displayed—it doesn't provide any form of actual content. For example, look at the source for **http://www.microsoft.com** in Figure 8-2.

Notice that the heading contains a title, some style commands, and a few meta commands. In fact, these three entries represent the only three kinds of tags that you'll normally find in an HTML page heading.

Don't get the idea that the <META> tag is the only form of scripting you'll find in the heading area. For example, if you visit **http://www.netscape.com**, you'll find JavaScript commands in the heading area. It doesn't matter which scripting language the page designer uses; the point is that the script's there to add instructions for certain elements of the page. One way to look at the heading is as a definition area for the rest of the page. It affects the appearance of the page as a whole but doesn't provide any form of content. In fact, you'll normally want to hide the contents of this area from a visitor to your Web site.

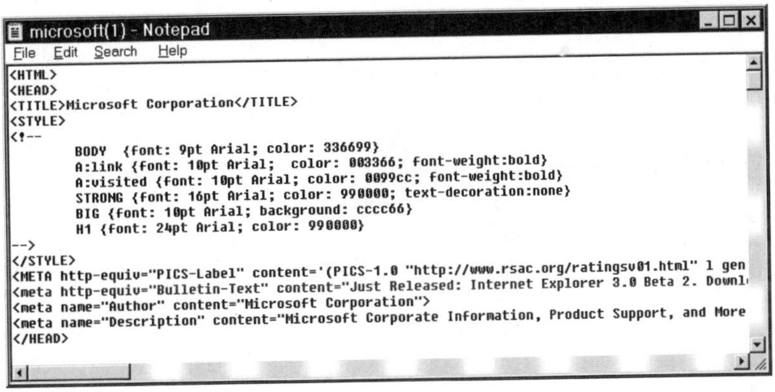

8

The <HEAD> tag won't help much in the content area, but it does define the appearance of the page.

Figure 8-2.

```
microsoft(1) - Notepad                                              _ □ X
File   Edit  Search   Help
<HTML>
<HEAD>
<TITLE>Microsoft Corporation</TITLE>
<STYLE>
<!--
        BODY  {font: 9pt Arial; color: 336699}
        A:link {font: 10pt Arial;  color: 003366; font-weight:bold}
        A:visited {font: 10pt Arial; color: 0099cc; font-weight:bold}
        STRONG {font: 16pt Arial; color: 990000; text-decoration:none}
        BIG {font: 10pt Arial; background: cccc66}
        H1 {font: 24pt Arial; color: 990000}
-->
</STYLE>
<META http-equiv="PICS-Label" content='(PICS-1.0 "http://www.rsac.org/ratingsv01.html" 1 gen
<meta http-equiv="Bulletin-Text" content="Just Released: Internet Explorer 3.0 Beta 2. Downl
<meta name="Author" content="Microsoft Corporation">
<meta name="Description" content="Microsoft Corporate Information, Product Support, and More
</HEAD>
```

Adding Headings Using the <Hx> Tag

Just as a heading in a book separates various sections of text, headings (the <Hx> tag) in an HTML document separate various areas of content. The HTML specification provides six levels of headings. For the most part, the only difference you'll see between heading levels is the size of the font used to display them. The aesthetic appeal of headings is about all you get. There isn't any magic involved when using headings—they won't create a physical separation between sections of text; it's more the way a visitor to your site will perceive the material you have to provide.

T IP: A lower-number heading level uses larger type than a higher number. Users would see a larger font for an <H1> tag than they would for an <H2> tag.

So how do you create a heading? Simply replace the *x* in the <Hx> tag with a number from 1 to 6, type your heading text, and then end the line with an </Hx> tag as follows:

```
<H1>This is a Heading</H1>
```

Another point to remember with headings is that you don't need to add any of the end-of-line tags, such as <P>, <BR>, or <HR>, to the end of the heading. The end tag, </Hx>, automatically adds the required amount of space for you. Of course, this doesn't prevent you from adding extra space if you so desire.

Links and Anchors

Links and anchors provide the special feeling of visiting a Web site. Every time you visit a Web site and see some text underlined, you're probably looking at a link. A *link* connects your current location with some other location. In fact, two common forms of links are used on most Web pages. The first type creates a link to another page (a URL in Internet terminology); it's the one you'll see most often. The second type creates a link to another section of the current page or a specific area of another page. You'll use it to find an anchor (which we'll look at in a few seconds). Here's an example of

Links connect one page to another; anchors create a connection to a specific place on a page.

the two common types of links. Notice that they both use the HREF keyword along with the <A> tag.

```
This is a <A HREF="http://www.microsoft.com">Document</A> link.
This is an <A HREF="http://www.microsoft.com#MyAnchor">Anchor</A> link.
```

In both cases, the text that appears between the <A> and </A> tags is the part of the sentence that appears underlined on the Web site. You should always place some text here, or your link will appear invisible to the user. Notice that the links look exactly alike except for one difference—the anchor link uses a # sign to separate the URL from the anchor name. In this case, we've used MyAnchor as the anchor name. The second link would look for the URL first, and then for a specific anchor location on that page before displaying any content to the user.

T IP: If you want to create an anchor link to an anchor on the current page, you don't need to provide the URL part of the <A> tag. You could abbreviate it as <A HREF="#*Anchor Name*">.

An anchor link also requires you to create an anchor somewhere on the page you specify as part of the <A> tag (unless you want to find a specific location on the current page, in which case you don't need to provide a URL). For example, we looked at an anchor link to MyAnchor on **http://www. microsoft.com**. How would an anchor look for this location?

8

```
This is the <A NAME="MyAnchor">Anchor</A> for this page.
```

As you can see, the big difference between an anchor and a link is the NAME keyword. An anchor always uses NAME in place of HREF. In addition, most browsers won't highlight or underline the text between the <A> and </A> tags since you really can't use them for anything.

Creating a Simple HTML Document

In the previous section, we looked at 12 basic tags for creating HTML pages. These are the tags that just about everyone will use somewhere along the way. Now it's time to look at how you'd actually use those tags to create a page on your Web site. Listing 8-1 shows the source for a sample Web page.

Obviously, you would never create a page like this for actual use. The whole purpose of this page is to see how the 12 tags work.

Listing 8-1:

```
<HTML>
<HEAD>
<TITLE>Sample HTML Page</TITLE>
</HEAD>
<BODY>
<H1>This is a <EM>Level 1</EM> heading.</H1>
Notice that the "Level 1" portion of the heading is emphasized using the
EM tag.<P>
We ended the previous paragraph with a <STRONG>P</STRONG> tag.
This paragraph will end with a <STRONG>BR</STRONG> tag.<BR>
Notice how we used the <STRONG>STRONG</STRONG> tag to add bold
text to the previous paragraph.<HR>
Horizontal rules also have a place on Web sites.  You'll use them most
often to provide separations between major areas of text.  Of course, most
Web sites are starting to use frames because they're more flexible.<HR>
Here are the other five levels of headings.<P>
<H2>Level 2</H2>
<H3>Level 3</H3>
<H4>Level 4</H4>
<H5>Level 5</H5>
<H6>Level 6</H6><HR>
Let's look at some other HTML tags.<P>
Click <A HREF="LISTS.HTM">Here</A> to display the list page.<BR>
Click <A HREF="GRAPH.HTM">Here</A> to display the graphics page.<BR>
Click <A HREF="TABLE.HTM">Here</A> to display a page with tables.<BR>
Click <A HREF="FORM.HTM">Here</A> to display a page with forms.<BR>
Click <A HREF="#MyAnchor">Here</A> to see another
area of this page.<P><P><P><P><P>
This is an <A NAME="MyAnchor">Anchor</A> link area.
</BODY>
</HTML>
```

The <TITLE> tag displays a name for your Web page in the browser title bar.

This source might look a bit daunting at first, but there isn't anything here that we haven't already looked at in the previous section. The first tag, <HTML>, defines the start of the page. You see its counterpart, </HTML>, at the end of the source listing. Next, we divide the document into two sections using the <HEAD> and <BODY> tags (along with their counterparts). The only tag that might mystify you is the <TITLE> tag. It defines the title that you'll see in the browser's title bar. This tag isn't absolutely necessary, but it's nice to give your Web page a title so that other people will know what they're looking at. In addition, the title will help you navigate your own pages as you troubleshoot any problem areas.

The body of the page begins with a level 1 heading, some text with special attributes added, and then a horizontal rule. You'll also find some text that shows the difference between the <P> and <BR> tags here. We'll see what they look like in a few seconds.

The next section of the listing shows you the differences between the five remaining headings. Most browsers will simply use a different type size as you change headings. Unfortunately, most browsers run out of readable font sizes before they run out of heading levels. You'll want to avoid using level 6 headings because they'll be too small for some people to read. Level 5 headings are pretty marginal as well.

The last section of this example page contains some links. We won't look at the linking pages just now; that's an exercise for upcoming sections. However, look at the fifth link, and you'll notice that it's to an anchor on the current page. The last working line of the body area contains this anchor. Make sure you take the time to see how this works with your browsers.

So what does our sample HTML page look like? Figure 8-3 shows how it would look when using Internet Explorer 3.0. You might want to take time to compare the screen shot in the book to the one on your screen if you use another kind of browser. You'll find that not all browsers are the same—there are subtle differences in the way they display things. Differences between machines will only intensify the display differences. Considering that these are common tags, imagine what will happen when you start using some of the more exotic tags that some browsers support but others don't.

8

It's time to expand our HTML horizons just a bit. The next few sections show you how some of the other standard tags work. We won't look at all the details in these sections, but they will provide enough of an overview so that you'll know what you're looking at when you visit other Web sites and view their source codes.

Working with Lists

How many technical books have you seen that don't include any form of bulleted lists or procedures? Putting complex ideas into easily grasped pieces is one of the most basic tasks that any writer can perform. Lists—short bits of text that enumerate ideas—are the answer in most cases. Considering the size limits of most Web pages, lists become even more important. HTML supports three different kinds of lists:

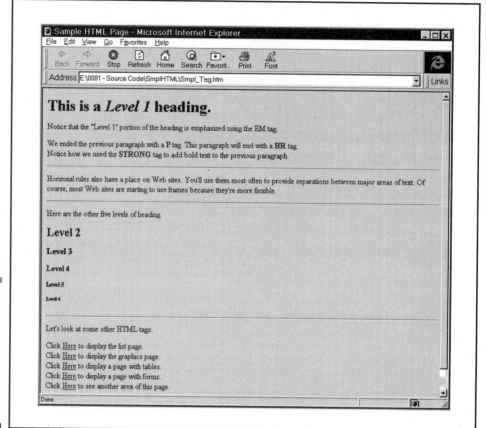

The sample HTML page shows how the 12 basic tags would appear within Internet Explorer 3.0.

Figure 8-3.

◆ *Unordered list* This kind of list uses bullets. You start it with the <UL> tag and end it with the </UL> tag. Items within the list use the <LI> tag.

◆ *Ordered list* Procedures and other numbered forms of text are considered ordered lists. This list format depends on the <OL> and </OL> tags. As with unordered lists, each item begins with the <LI> tag.

◆ *Glossary* This particular list uses two kinds of item entries surrounded by a <DL> and </DL> tag pair. The term that you want to define is preceded by a <DT> tag. The definition gets a <DD> tag.

Even though there are only three list types, you can still get a variety of effects by nesting them just like you would in any other programming

Always add
plenty of
comments to
your HTML
pages since you
may have non-
programmers
editing them
from time to
time.

scenario. You'll see an example of how to do this in Listing 8-2 when we discuss the sample page code.

Of the three list types we've talked about, the glossary list type is the most flexible in some ways. The use of two list element types can provide a little more in the way of aesthetics when you try to display text. The big difference between the <DT> (term) and <DD> (definition) tags is that one of them is indented. You can use this feature to create special effects not related to the display of glossary-type entries. As with some of the other special text tags that we've talked about in this chapter, list tags (<LI>, <DT>, and <DD>) automatically insert a <BR> tag for you at the end of the line. Using a <BR> tag advances the text to the next line but keeps the list together.

It's time to take a look at some examples of list coding. Listing 8-2 shows the first link page from the first page we looked at in Listing 8-1. It contains the three basic list types along with one example showing how to nest them. Make sure you name the resulting file LISTS.HTM so that the link will work as expected. Notice especially that this is the first page to use comments (the <!-Text-> tag).

Listing 8-2:

```
<!-The purpose of this page is to show how to use the list tags.->
<HTML>
<HEAD>
<TITLE>Creating Lists</TITLE>
</HEAD>
<BODY>
<H2>There are three different kinds of Lists:</H2>

<!-Display an unordered list.->
<H3>Unordered</H3>
<UL>
<LI>Item 1
<LI>Item 2
</UL><HR>

<!-Display an ordered list.->
<H3>Ordered</H3>
<OL>
<LI>Item 1
<LI>Item 2
</OL><HR>

<!-Display a glossary list showing the two list entry types.->
<H3>Glossary</H3>
```

8

```
<DL>
<DT>A Term
<DD>This is the definition for it.
<DT>Another Term
<DD>Yet another definition.
</DL><HR>

<!-Show one method of nesting lists.->
<H3>Nested List</H3>
<OL>
<LI>Item 1
     <UL>
     <LI>Subitem 1
     <LI>Subitem 2
     </UL>
<LI>Item 2
</OL>
</BODY>
</HTML>
```

Even though there may be other ways of creating comments, use the <!-*Text*-> tag for consistency.

Now that you have a better idea of how to code the various kinds of list tags, you can see what this page looks like. Figure 8-4 shows a typical example of how you could use lists. Notice that the three list types aren't all that decorative, but they do work.

Adding Graphics

Graphics can really dress up a page of text. Most of us would agree that technical manuals are a lot easier to understand when the author adds enough of the right kind of graphic image. You can add graphics to a Web page as well. However, there are a few limitations in the way that you can add them.

T IP: Some people are overzealous when adding graphics to their Web sites. The result is that most people don't even get to see most of those graphics. Just about any user will press the Stop button on the browser after a minute or so of waiting for graphics to download. In fact, a good rule of thumb is to make the total size of any Web page 60KB or less including graphics and ActiveX controls.

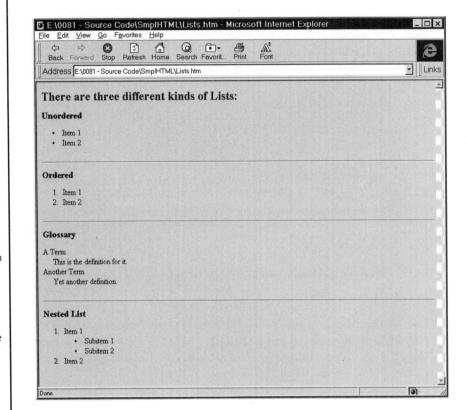

List tags make it easy to enumerate specific points on a Web page or provide glossary-type entries.

Figure 8-4.

Use GIF and JPG images for maximum compatibility; use other image types for maximum pizzazz when you know what browser the visitor will use.

One of the bigger limitations that you'll face is the *kind* of graphics you can display. Many browsers handle only two formats—the ones supported directly by HTML—including GIF (also known as CompuServe format) and JPEG (JPG) images. Any other kind of image you see displayed in your browser is the result of using a plug-in. Both Netscape and Internet Explorer support various kinds of plug-ins. For example, one of the more popular plug-ins will allow you to view AVI (movie) files using your browser. The problem for a Web page designer is that you can't depend on other people owning these plug-ins. As a result, if you plan to create an Internet site with wide appeal, you'll probably need to stick with GIF and JPEG images.

Displaying a graphic image is fairly easy. All you need to do is use the <IMG> tag. This tag accepts a filename as input using the SRC attribute, like this:

```
<IMG SRC="Figure1.Gif">
```

Placing graphics on a page isn't as easy as you might think. As with text, there are very few ways of predetermining the location of a graphic outside of using frames or tables because you can't define an exact position for them. Text usually provides some leeway through the use of tricks like the list tags we looked at in the previous section. Graphics provide no such leeway. You'll probably end up using frames to get the right effect on the majority of browsers if your Web page is very complex in design.

WEB LINK: Microsoft, Netscape, and many other vendors are working on a new HTML standard known as Cascading Style Sheets (CSS). In fact, Internet Explorer 4.*x* already provides partial support for CSS. Part of the purpose for CSS is to provide a consistent method for displaying data without doing a lot of formatting. Another purpose is to make it easier to position screen elements like graphics wherever you want them. Look at **http://www.shadow.net/%7Ebraden/nostyle/** if you want to find out specific information on CSS support in Internet Explorer 3.*x* (the Web site hadn't been updated for Internet Explorer 4.*x* as of this writing). You'll find the specification itself at **http://www.w3.org/pub/WWW/Style/CSS/**. Microsoft also has a CSS gallery at **http://www.microsoft.com/ truetype/css/gallery/entrance.htm**. This particular site won't work with Netscape Communicator since it doesn't support CSS as of this writing. This product does support a competing standard known as JavaScript Style Sheets.

You can define the way text and graphics mix using the <IMG> tag. All you need to do is add the ALIGN attribute. There are three ways to align text:

◆ ALIGN=TOP

◆ ALIGN=MIDDLE

◆ ALIGN=BOTTOM

The ALIGN attribute allows you to change the position in which text is displayed when next to a graphic image.

Let's take a look at some simple code for adding graphics to a Web site. We'll take a deeper look at graphics placement in the "Using Forms" section. All the code in Listing 8-3 does is display a graphic image and show you how to use the ALIGN attribute. (This listing uses a GIF that I drew; you can substitute any GIF file that you have on hand.) This method is suitable for those times when you want to display a company logo or some other simple graphics on a page. Figure 8-5 shows how this code looks in the viewer.

Listing 8-3:

```
<HTML>
<HEAD>
<TITLE>Using Graphics</TITLE>
</HEAD>
<BODY>
<H2>You can align text and graphics in one of three ways.</H2>
<H3>Top</H3>
<IMG SRC="ColorBlk.Gif" ALIGN=TOP>This is at the TOP.<HR>
<H3>Middle</H3>
<IMG SRC="ColorBlk.Gif" ALIGN=MIDDLE>This is in the MIDDLE.<HR>
<H3>Bottom</H3>
<IMG SRC="ColorBlk.Gif" ALIGN=BOTTOM>This is at the BOTTOM.<HR>
</BODY>
</HTML>
```

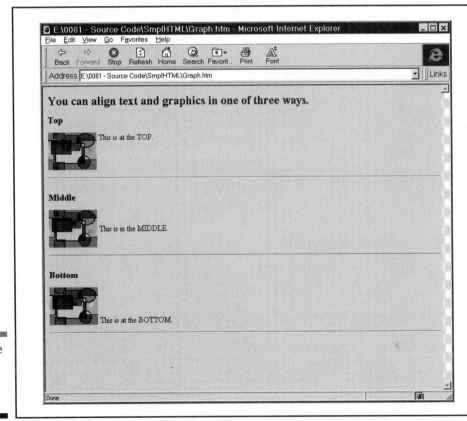

Adding simple graphics is fairly easy.

Figure 8-5.

8

WEB LINK: You may have noticed that some people create links using graphics instead of text (see the "Links and Anchors" section earlier in this chapter for details). This technique is known as *mapping*. Using mapping within your Web page can quickly get complicated if you don't have a utility program to help. You'll find an excellent shareware utility named Map This, which helps you create graphic maps, at: **http://www.ecaetc.ohio-state.edu/tc/mt/**. (You may experience some trouble getting to the Web site since it's often busy; just keep trying—the utility is well worth the effort.)

Creating Tables

Tabular data is part of just about any kind of business display. Spreadsheets are just one example of the accountant's ledger sheet brought to life in the computer. It makes sense then that you can create tables on an HTML page as well. However, you'll need an entire set of tags to make tables work, as shown here.

Tag	Description
<TABLE> and </TABLE>	This set of tags define the beginning and end of the table as a whole.
<TR> and </TR>	Each row is defined with these tags. Normal procedure is to define rows, then columns.
<TD> and </TD>	Every data element, or column, is enclosed within this tag pair.
<CAPTION> and </CAPTION>	These tags define the table's title.
<TH> and </TH>	With this pair of tags, you create headings for each table row or column.

TIP: The <TABLE> tag includes a special BORDER attribute that allows you to enclose the table within lines. The default border size is a width of 1, but you can usually set this value to any width between 1 and 6, depending on the browser.

Let's look at some sample code for two different kinds of tables. Listing 8-4 shows how you can create two different effects using the simple tags we've talked about in this section so far. The first table contains simple text entries; the second mixes text and graphics in complex ways.

T IP: You can center the text in a table using the <CENTER> and </CENTER> tag pair. This same tag pair works with any text you may want to place within a document. It also works with graphics, as shown in Listing 8-4.

Listing 8-4:

```
<HTML>
<HEAD>
<TITLE>Creating Tables</TITLE>
</HEAD>
<BODY>

<!-Create a simple text table.->
<H3>Tables are an important part of Web pages.</H3>
<CAPTION>A Simple Text Table</CAPTION>
<TABLE BORDER>
     <TR>
          <TH></TH>
          <TH>Column A</TH>
          <TH>Column B</TH>
          <TH>Column C</TH>
     </TR>
     <TR>
          <TH>Row 1</TH>
          <TD>Entry A1</TD>
          <TD>Entry B1</TD>
          <TD>Entry C1</TD>
     </TR>
     <TR>
          <TH>Row 2</TH>
          <TD>Entry A2</TD>
          <TD>Entry B2</TD>
          <TD>Entry C2</TD>
     </TR>
     <TR>
          <TH>Row 3</TH>
```

8

```
            <TD>Entry A3</TD>
            <TD>Entry B3</TD>
            <TD>Entry C3</TD>
    </TR>
</TABLE><HR>

<!-Create a complex table with mixed text and graphics->
<H3>You aren't limited to text in a table.</H3>
<TABLE BORDER=3>
    <TR>
            <TD><IMG SRC="ColorBlk.Gif"></TD>
            <TD><IMG SRC="ColorBlk.Gif" ALIGN=MIDDLE> Text and Graphics. </TD>
            <TD>Text Alone</TD>
    </TR>
    <TR>
            <TD>Some more text.</TD>
            <TD><CENTER><IMG SRC="ColorBlk.Gif"></CENTER></TD>
            <TD>Some more text.</TD>
    </TR>
    <TR>
            <TD><IMG SRC="ColorBlk.Gif"></TD>
            <TD><CENTER>Some more text.</CENTER></TD>
            <TD><IMG SRC="ColorBlk.Gif"></TD>
    </TR>
</TABLE>
</BODY>
</HTML>
```

Indenting your code can help you keep rows and columns in a table separate and easy to see.

This looks like a lot of code, and it was a bit tedious to write by hand. (Code like this demonstrates yet another reason why you should invest in some kind of GUI front end for writing your HTML page code if you plan to write a lot of it.) Figure 8-6 shows what it looks like in the browser. The code also illustrates the one basic rule to follow: Always work on the rows first, the columns second. If you follow that simple rule, you won't experience any problems putting tables together. Notice that the second table mixes text and graphics. Even though the table looks a lot more complex, the same pattern of rows, then columns holds true. Notice the difference between the standard one-width border used for the first table and the three-width border used for the second table. The three-width border takes up a lot more space, but it's also more dramatic.

Use the <CENTER> tag to center text anywhere on a Web page—including tables and forms.

The first table also includes the <TH> tag for both rows and columns. There are two main differences between the standard text and header text. Standard text is normally left-justified, while heading text is centered. You can change this behavior using the <CENTER> tag, as shown in Listing 8-4. In addition, the heading text uses a bold font.

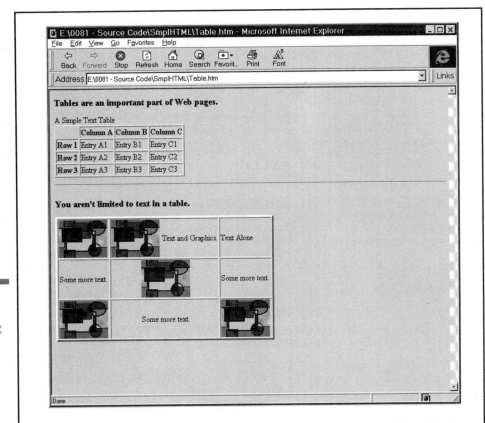

Tables are
easy once
you figure out
that rows
come first,
columns
second.

Figure 8-6.

8

Using Forms

The last fundamental piece of HTML coding we'll look at is forms. You can
use forms in a variety of ways—most of which have to do with data entry
rather than data dissemination. Of all the techniques we've looked at so far,
forms provide the only method for adding items like radio buttons and
checkboxes to your Web site using standard HTML. We won't go into all of
the vagaries of using forms here, since ActiveX largely replaces the need to
use them at all. It's important, though, to know that there are alternatives to
using ActiveX.

Every form begins with a <FORM> tag. You must include two attributes,
METHOD and ACTION, in addition to the tag itself. The METHOD attribute
defines how you intend to work with the data gathered in the form. There
are two standard methods: POST and GET. The POST method is used most

often for data entry forms. It allows you to send data from the client machine to the host. The GET method is used for data query forms. For example, when you go to your favorite Web search page, you're really filling out a form using the GET method. The ACTION attribute tells the Web server where to find a CGI script for handling the input from the form. A typical <FORM> tag looks like this:

```
<FORM METHOD=GET ACTION="/cgi-bin/query">
```

The main tag that you'll use in creating a form is the <INPUT> tag. There are a variety of ways to use this particular tag—more than we'll cover here. In addition to the basic information you'll find here, the <INPUT> tag is usually enhanced by the browser's vendor to provide additional functionality. For example, you may find that one browser supports more kinds of buttons than another one will. With that in mind, let's take a quick look at the various attributes used with this tag:

◆ *TYPE*   The kind of control—button, text box, and so on—is defined with this attribute.

◆ *VALUE*   The impact of this attribute depends on the kind of control. For example, it defines the caption for a button but the contents of a text box.

◆ *NAME*   This attribute references the variable used to hold the output from this particular control.

◆ *SIZE*   The size of the control—usually the width in characters—is defined with this attribute.

◆ *CHECKED*   Use this with radio buttons and other controls that have a checked or unchecked state.

◆ *ROWS*   The number of rows to allocate for a particular control—usually the height of the control—is defined with this attribute.

Besides the <INPUT> tag, you can use the <SELECT> tag to create pop-up lists or menus. It works about the same way as the lists we created previously in this chapter. You end the list with a </SELECT> tag. In between the <SELECT> and </SELECT> tags, you use either <OPTION> or <OPTION SELECTED> tags to create a list of entries for your pop-up list. The <OPTION SELECTED> tag indicates which option you want selected when the user initially views the page.

The final form-specific tags allow you to create a text area. This allows you to display a lot of text in a small area or provide a large area for user notes or comments. A text area uses the <TEXTAREA> and </TEXTAREA> tag pair. You can also add an optional attribute, NAME, to the <TEXTAREA> tag so that you can retrieve its contents later.

Now that you have a basic idea of how these tags work, let's take a look at some actual code. Listing 8-5 shows the example code for a form. (Name the resulting file FORM.HTM so that the link in Listing 8-1 will work properly.) It includes one example of each type of basic control you can use, plus one extended control that we'll look at in more detail near the end of this section. Figure 8-7 shows what this page would look like when viewed from Internet Explorer—your view may vary slightly if you're using a different browser. Notice that the three button types are centered at the bottom of the page using the <CENTER> tag.

Listing 8-5:

```
<!-This is a very simple nonfunctional form.  It won't->
<!-show you how to write the CGI scripts normally required->
<!-to make the form functional.  To see a full form->
<!-implementation, look at a Web site like http://www-msn.lycos.com/.->

<HTML>
<HEAD>
<TITLE>New Page</TITLE>
</HEAD>
<BODY>
<H2>This is our sample form.</H2>

<!-Create a simple form using standard controls.->
<FORM METHOD=GET ACTION="/cgi-bin/query">

<!-Create a text field.->
<STRONG>This is a text field: </STRONG>
<INPUT TYPE="text" VALUE="Some Text" NAME="Text1" SIZE=20><P>

<!-Add some radio buttons.->
<STRONG>These are some radio buttons.</STRONG><P>
<INPUT TYPE="radio" NAME="Radio1" VALUE="Button 1" CHECKED>Button 1<BR>
<INPUT TYPE="radio" NAME="Radio1" VALUE="Button 2">Button 2<BR>
<INPUT TYPE="radio" NAME="Radio1" VALUE="Button 3">Button 3<P>

<!-Add some check boxes.->
<STRONG>These are some check boxes.</STRONG><P>
```

8

```
<INPUT TYPE="checkbox" NAME="Checkbox 1" VALUE="Checkbox 1">Checkbox 1<BR>
<INPUT TYPE="checkbox" NAME="Checkbox 2" VALUE="Checkbox 2">Checkbox 2<BR>
<INPUT TYPE="checkbox" NAME="Checkbox 3" VALUE="Checkbox 3">Checkbox 3<P>

<!-Popup lists and menus require a different format.->
<STRONG>Here's a popup list: </STRONG>
<SELECT NAME="Popup 1">
     <OPTION>
Item One
     <OPTION SELECTED>
Item Two
     <OPTION>
Item Three
</SELECT>
<P>

<!-You can also create areas of text onscreen.->
<STRONG>Adding text areas is easy using the TEXTAREA tag.</STRONG><P>
<TEXTAREA ROWS=3 NAME="Text Area 1">
This is some text that got added to the display to show the effect of the
TEXTAREA tag.  You'll find it quite handy as you create Web pages with
a lot of information to convey.  It's very important to provide the users of
your site with complete information, and this tag helps you do it.
</TEXTAREA><P><P>

<!-Every form requires a Submit button to send data to the server.->
<CENTER>
<INPUT TYPE=submit VALUE="Submit">

<!-This optional Reset button will save the user time.->
<INPUT TYPE=reset VALUE="Reset">

<!-This is a standard button type.  We'll use it to cancel the form.->
<INPUT TYPE=button VALUE="Cancel">

</CENTER>
</FORM>
</BODY>
</HTML>
```

As you can see, the majority of the controls shown use the <INPUT> tag. The main difference between control types is defined by the TYPE attribute. You can select any of the controls if you want to see how they work. The only button that doesn't work correctly is the Submit button, because we haven't

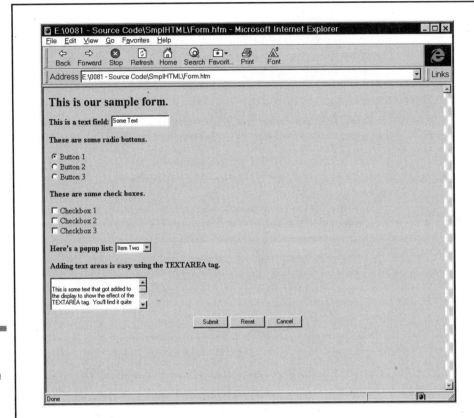

Forms allow
you to get
feedback from
the viewer.
Figure 8-7.

written a CGI script to do something with the information on the form. The
Cancel button is nonfunctional, but we'll fix that in a moment.

Something else you should notice about the source code are the two specific
button types: Submit and Reset. The Submit button always takes the action
listed in the ACTION attribute of the <FORM> tag. You must provide a
Submit button if you intend to process the information in the form using
standard methods. The Reset button always resets the contents of any
controls on a form to their initial state. This allows the user to restart the
form from scratch without leaving the site first and reentering.

The Cancel button in this example is still nonfunctional. You could click it,
but nothing would happen. The Cancel button represents the standard
button type for HTML documents. To make it work, you have to add an

ONCLICK argument that calls a script or performs some other action. ActiveX Control Pad provides an easy method for you to create this script once you create the button itself. The following procedure shows a quick method for assigning just about any default action to a button (or other control, for that matter).

NOTE: You can download your own copy of ActiveX Control Pad from the Microsoft Web site at **http://www.microsoft.com/workshop/author/cpad/**.

1. Once you install ActiveX Control Pad on your machine, use the File | Open command to open the FORM.HTM file. (The code for this file is shown in Listing 8-5.)

2. Use the Tools | Script Wizard command to display the Script Wizard dialog shown in Figure 8-8. What you'll see is three list boxes and some buttons. The first list box contains a list of the controls you've defined; the second contains a list of actions you can associate with events of those controls; the third contains a list of actions currently assigned to a particular event.

3. Click on the plus sign next to the Cancel entry in the first list box, and then click on the onClick event. This tells Script Wizard that you want to assign some action to the onClick event of the Cancel button.

4. Click on the Go To Page action in the second list box. This means that when you click on the Cancel button on the form, you'll go to another page. In this case, you'll go to the previous page of our example Web site.

5. Click on the Insert Action button. You'll see the Go To Page dialog, shown here. This is where you tell Script Wizard where you want to go.

6. Type the name of a page on your Web site in the Enter a Text String field. In this example, you would type **SMPL_TAG.HTM**. Notice that you don't need to include double or single quotes—the Wizard takes care of that for you automatically.

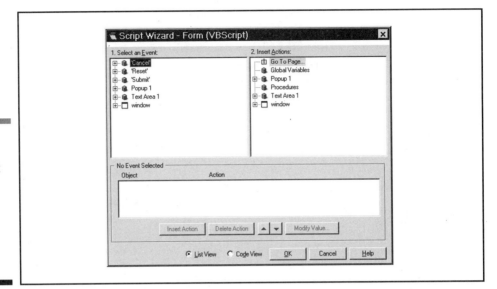

The Script
Wizard
displays a list
of your
controls and
the actions
associated
with them.
Figure 8-8.

7. Click on OK. You should see an action associated with the onClick event of the Cancel button now, as shown in Figure 8-9. If you saved this document back to disk, then looked at the page with a browser, pressing the Cancel button would take you back to the previous page.

The Script Wizard automatically makes any needed changes to your code. In this case, it added an ONCLICK attribute to the Cancel button we defined in Listing 8-5. The code now appears as follows:

```
<!-This is a standard button type.  We'll use it to cancel the form.->
<INPUT LANGUAGE="VBScript" TYPE=button VALUE="Cancel"
     ONCLICK="Window.location.href = 'SMPL_TAG.HTM'">
```

Where Does ActiveX Fit In?

We've spent just about the entire chapter talking about coding techniques that you could use with any browser. These techniques are important to the Visual C++ developer working with ActiveX as well, since it's unlikely that you'll want to write controls for every aspect of your Web site. Even if you did write all of the required controls, it's unlikely that anyone would wait for all of them to download. The coding techniques we've looked at so far are generic. Not only will they work with just about every browser available, but

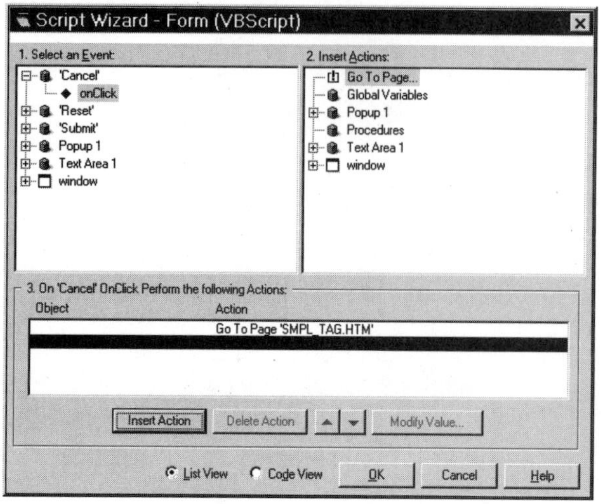

The Script
Wizard
completes the
script you
created by
showing you
the event and
associated
action in the
third list box.
Figure 8-9.

they're also platform independent. ActiveX doesn't provide the same level of support; for the time being it's very much tied to Internet Explorer (or Netscape Navigator with the appropriate plug-in).

You'll be able to build on the knowledge you've gained so far as you work with ActiveX controls. Adding an ActiveX control to your HTML document requires a tag as well, just like all of the other controls we looked at in previous sections. In this case, you'll use the <OBJECT> tag. Let's take a look at a basic <OBJECT> tag. Listing 8-6 contains a typical example of an <OBJECT> tag created using ActiveX Control Pad, but you could just as easily create it by hand. This object tag is set up to work with a control that we'll create in Chapter 10 (in the section, "A Basic MFC-Based Pushbutton Programming Example"). You'll also need to change the CODEBASE property to point to your Web server—we'll talk more about the ActiveX properties in the paragraphs that follow.

Listing 8-6:

```
<HTML>
<HEAD>
<TITLE>This Page Contains an ActiveX Control</TITLE>
</HEAD>
<BODY>

<OBJECT ID="OCXEXMPL1" WIDTH=75 HEIGHT=25
```

```
CLASSID="CLSID:D8D77E03-712A-11CF-8C70-00006E3127B7"
CODEBASE="http://AUX/CONTROLS/OCXEXMPL.OCX">
    <PARAM NAME="_Version" VALUE="65536">
    <PARAM NAME="_ExtentX" VALUE="1976">
    <PARAM NAME="_ExtentY" VALUE="670">
    <PARAM NAME="_StockProps" VALUE="70">
    <PARAM NAME="Caption" VALUE="On">
    <PARAM NAME="OnOff" VALUE="-1">
    <PARAM NAME="ModalResult" VALUE="8">
If you see this message without a corresponding pushbutton, then
your browser doesn't support ActiveX components.
</OBJECT>

</BODY>
</HTML>
```

As with most complex tags, the <OBJECT> tag begins the definition and the </OBJECT> tag ends it.

The <OBJECT> tag recognizes the OCX, CAB, and INF file extensions.

8

Let's begin with the first line of the <OBJECT> tag. The ID attribute tells what kind of control we're dealing with. Notice that no extension is listed—Internet Explorer defaults to an extension of OCX. Internet Explorer currently supports three extensions: OCX, CAB, and INF. We'll discuss the merits of the various types later in this section. You could also specify an URL as part of the ID attribute string. Notice that this first line also includes a WIDTH and HEIGHT attribute to define the size of the control.

Just like every other ActiveX control on your machine, one downloaded from the Internet has a CLASSID attribute. This is the unique number that identifies a particular control to Windows. The number is stored in the Windows registry. We'll see later that this particular feature can help reduce the download time for your controls if you use controls that users are likely to have installed on their machine.

Adding the CODEBASE attribute tells the browser where to find the control on your Internet site if it isn't already installed on the host machine. Think of it as a remote PATH statement like the ones you've placed in AUTOEXEC.BAT. If you don't add a CODEBASE attribute to your <OBJECT> tag, you've effectively disabled download of the control from your Internet site. We'll see how this feature works in the next section.

Now that we've defined an object, a whole string of <PARAM> tags follows. These tags define how you want the control configured when you display it for the user. The <PARAM> tag always includes two attributes: NAME and VALUE. The NAME attribute defines the name of the parameter you want to set. The VALUE attribute assigns a value to the parameter. All values are enclosed in double quotes—even if they're numeric.

The last three parameters in the list are the persistent properties that you could set when using the control in any environment. The Caption property changes the text on the top of the button, just like it would if you were using the control within Visual C++. The OnOff property is special for this control—it allows you to create an On/Off button. We'll see how this works in Chapter 11 when we create an actual control. The ModalResult parameter allows the control to return a value based on its current caption. For example, the control will return a value of 8 when the button caption reads On.

There are also some parameters that you won't normally worry about but are needed when using the control as part of a Web page. The _Version parameter comes into play during the download process. It helps the browser determine when the version of a control on the client machine is out of date with the one on the server. The _ExtentX and _ExtentY properties position the control on the Web page. Finally, the _StockProps property defines the stock properties of a control—you won't normally need to set them.

The next thing you'll see is a string. Someone with an ActiveX-capable browser won't see this string because the browser will ignore it. The string only gets displayed if the client machine doesn't support ActiveX. Essentially, it tells users on the other end that they'd be seeing an ActiveX control right now if their browser provided the right support. You don't have to limit yourself to a string, though; you could always put the HTML equivalent for a control here. For example, this ActiveX control is a pushbutton that you could replace with HTML code, though it wouldn't be nearly as flexible.

Previously we talked about the three kinds of files you can download from the Internet: OCX, CAB, and INF. The OCX file format—also known as the portable executable (PE) format—allows you to send the control to a client in its final format. No additional processing is required at the other side, meaning less support problems for you in the long run. The CAB file format is the same one used by Microsoft for shipping products such as Windows. It has the distinct advantage of letting you ship more than one control in a single package. This format also offers file compression, which will reduce download time for the user. The disadvantage is one of complexity. You have to create several installation files, including an INF file. In addition, users will need to wait for the CAB file to be decompressed and installed once they download it—making this method more likely to frustrate users and cause a lot of problems when they try to cancel the process. The INF format allows you to selectively install one or more controls. It uses an INF file similar in format to the ones that come with Windows. Users will see some type of an installation screen when they visit your site. The downside to this route is that you'll still need to create the INF file. Using an INF file means there is less chance of users getting totally annoyed while they wait for the page to download, and they'll feel that they're at least part of the process. We'll talk about the INF file format later in this chapter (see "Building Component Download (CAB) Files Using DIANTZ.EXE".)

COM+: The Future of the Internet

Any technical discussion of Windows necessarily includes a discussion of the Component Object Model, or COM. COM is the object technology that's used as a basis for all of Windows. It's also the technology that's used as part of Microsoft's move to the Internet. Not only does COM interact with the user, it's the basis of the technology for creating components like pushbuttons used in application programs. In other words, you can't begin to talk about the Windows or Microsoft's vision of the Internet without also talking about COM in some way.

ActiveX was the keyword just a year ago for expressing the new version of COM that Microsoft was promoting for the Internet. However, ActiveX proved too bulky (even though ActiveX controls are much smaller than the OCXs they replaced), too browser dependent, and too much of a security risk for most people's tastes. In addition, the Microsoft marketing department was using ActiveX to describe just about every new technology that Microsoft was coming out with, which only served to confuse the buying public.

8

Now there are two new and exciting terms for you to learn when it comes to the Internet: COM+ and Distributed interNet Applications (DNA). ActiveX is no longer a term that describes every aspect of Microsoft's COM technology; it refers only to the components you create to use with application programs or on an intranet site. Anything to do with the Internet is now addressed as COM+, if you're talking about an enabling technology, or DNA, if you're talking about a specific usage of COM+ technology.

 WEB LINK: You can get an updated view of Microsoft's various COM technologies at **http://www.microsoft.com/com/default.htm**. This site will keep you up to date on the various COM-related technologies that Microsoft is introducing and how they're supposed to work together.

There are, in fact, quite a few COM-based technologies that you need to know about as a C++ programmer. The following sections provide a very quick overview of these technologies and how they fit into the general scheme. Obviously, this discussion will change as Microsoft refines its COM technology.

◆ ***Distributed COM (DCOM)—Network Interface*** This version of COM will allow components and applications to communicate over a network. DCOM is designed to communicate over a broad range of network protocols, including the TCP/IP protocol used by the Internet. What DCOM will do for the developer is allow a client application to communicate directly with a service running on a server using standard COM interface. In essence, this means you could design a control or applet that allows the client application to receive data from the server, then perform local calculations using that data. In addition, DCOM allows for security communication between client and server regardless of the protocol used.

◆ ***COM+—Function*** *Standard COM interface extensions* This is an extension to the existing COM standard. It allows developers to build advanced controls using special COM+ calls. The most important COM extension provided with COM+ is data binding, which allows a component to provide database access. Adding database access means that you can use COM+ to build components for the Internet that can access remote data. COM+ is also the basis for Distributed interNet Applications (DNA) architecture, which is Microsoft's latest vision for the Internet.

Theoretically, DNA will allow COM components to execute on any platform and will allow the developer to use any language to write the component. Part of the ability to work with any language and any platform will come from a new COM+ feature called interceptors. Using interceptors will allow a COM+ component to call a variety of services during run time rather than relying on a specific service. You'll use interceptors to receive and process events related to instance creation, calls and returns, errors, and instance deletion. Interceptors also provide the mechanism to perform transactions and system monitoring.

◆ ***Microsoft Transaction Server (MTS)—Function*** *COM server* Believe it or not, MTS is part of COM. It allows a developer to create "lite" controls that focus on the business logic behind the component rather than all of the interfaces required to implement it. Building lite controls means that you can create them faster and that they'll take little time to download. MTS comes as part of IIS 4.*x*.

◆ ***ActiveX—Function*** *Component building*   Originally introduced as a new technology for the Internet, ActiveX is a component-building technology. It's the third version of Microsoft's component technology. One of the things that sets ActiveX apart from previous versions of OLE Control eXtensions (OCXs) is the fact that you can use them on high latency networks like the Internet. They're also designed to work with Web browsers, though as of the time of writing the only browser that does use them is Internet Explorer. ActiveX controls also feature incremental rendering and code signing, which allows users to identify the authors of controls before they execute.

Downloading ActiveX from the Internet

The inner workings of most of the tags in this chapter are pretty obvious. The browser looks at the tag, then displays what you requested. The whole process is straightforward and easy to understand. The ActiveX <OBJECT> tag isn't quite as simple. What happens when the browser sees an <OBJECT> tag? We know it doesn't simply render the control onscreen—ActiveX controls provide a lot more functionality than that.

Microsoft has included a new Windows API call for browsers to use— CoGetClassObjectFromURL. When a browser sees an <OBJECT> tag, it parses out the CLASSID, CODEBASE, and _Version parameters. It passes these parameters to CoGetClassObjectFromURL, which downloads, verifies, and installs the control if necessary. The first thing this API call does, though, is to check whether the registry currently contains a reference to the CLASSID. You'll find this reference under the HKEY_CLASSES_ROOT I CLSID key of the registry, as shown in Figure 8-10.

8

WEB LINK: The specification for the <OBJECT> tag and associated API calls is in a constant state of flux. If you want to find out the latest information about the <OBJECT> tag, look at **http://www.w3.org/ TR/WD-object.html**.

If CoGetClassObjectFromURL finds an instance of the ActiveX control installed on the client machine, it checks the version number. When the

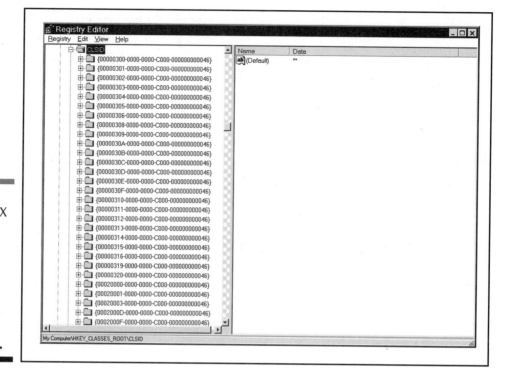

Figure 8-10.

version number of the control installed on the client machine is greater than or equal to the one on the HTML page, CoGetClassObjectFromURL loads the local control instead of downloading the control from the Internet. Once the control is loaded, CoGetClassObjectFromURL creates a class factory for it and passes the class factory back to the browser. (A class factory works just like any other factory would—it produces some item. In this case, it allows the browser to produce an instance of the object.) Otherwise, the API call asks the browser to download the code from the Internet site.

Downloading is an asynchronous process—Windows can perform other ActiveX-related tasks while it waits for a download to complete. Once the browser completes the download and decompresses the file if needed, the Windows Trust Provider Service function WinVerifyTrust is called. This service looks inside the ActiveX control and determines whether there is a signature block. The *signature block* contains the author's name, a public key, and the encrypted digest of the control's contents. Think of an ActiveX control signature block just as you would the signature field on a check, a driver's license, or a contract—it not only tells who you are but also verifies

A **public key** works like the security gate key for a condominium or apartment—it lets you into the main building. A **private key** is like the door key for the condominium or apartment—it lets you into your living quarters.

that you are who you say you are. If the WinVerifyTrust call finds a signature block (also called a *certificate*), it validates the certificate. Each certificate can contain the name of a parent certificate. WinVerifyTrust travels the hierarchical tree of certificates until it comes to the root certificate. It then verifies that this root certificate appears in the list of trusted root certificates. If the certificate does appear, CoGetClassObjectFromURL automatically loads the control and creates a class factory for it. Otherwise, the user gets a message saying that the control isn't trusted. (You'll get to see this message in Chapter 10 when we create an ActiveX control and use it on a Web page.)

Users still have a choice of whether to install an ActiveX control or not, even if it doesn't appear on the trusted list. If users choose to install the control, they also are asked whether they want to add the control's author to their trusted list. Adding the author's name to the list means that any new controls from that same author will be accepted immediately. We'll look at the security issues in more detail in Chapter 14.

So where do these controls get installed? Theoretically, a control designer could put the control anywhere. However, most ActiveX controls downloaded from the Internet don't automatically appear in a location like the user's System folder. They're added to a special folder named OCCACHE that could literally appear anywhere on the user's machine. Normally you'll find this folder located in the main Windows folder, the /SYSTEM folder, or the user's Internet folder. (Some browsers also use the ActiveX Control Cache folder, which is located in the main Windows folder for storing ActiveX controls.)

The most common place to look for ActiveX controls you download from the Internet is the OCCACHE folder.

Loading the control isn't all that involved. The control has to register itself during the installation process. In most cases this means calling the DllRegisterServer API function. Once installed and registered, the CoGetClassObjectFromURL function passes the class factory associated with the control back to the browser. The browser uses the class factory to create an instance of the object. It initializes any parameters passed with the <OBJECT> tag and displays the control onscreen (if necessary).

8

ActiveX and Netscape Navigator

If you're running an intranet site, you always have full control over who visits your site and what browser they use. If you want to use ActiveX, you can simply ask everyone to use Internet Explorer. Internet sites don't have this luxury, so you have to make sure that your site works with the largest number of browsers possible. While Internet Explorer supports ActiveX directly, Netscape Navigator does not. Fortunately, there's an alternative method of making ActiveX work in this environment.

NCompass Labs, Inc. produces a plug-in called ScriptActive, which allows you to view HTML pages containing ActiveX controls using Netscape Navigator 3.0. At the time of this writing, the NCompass plug-in and Internet Explorer 3.0 ActiveX control capabilities are similar, but not exactly the same. You'll probably want to spend a little time researching the plug-in before you use it. NCompass provides support for ScriptActive (and several other products) at **http://www.ncompasslabs.com/**.

Unfortunately, using the current version of ScriptActive isn't straightforward. You have to perform some special formatting of the <OBJECT> tag to get it to work. It's fortunate that the plug-in also includes the HTML Conversion utility named NConvert for performing most of the work for you. The results of using the utility on the standard ActiveMovie control appear in Listing 8-7.

Listing 8-7:

```
<!-Insert an ActiveMovie control.->
<OBJECT ID="ActiveMovie1" WIDTH=267 HEIGHT=73
    CLASSID="CLSID:05589FA1-C356-11CE-BF01-00AA0055595A"
    CODEBASE="http://aux/controls">
  <PARAM NAME="_ExtentX" VALUE="7038">
  <PARAM NAME="_ExtentY" VALUE="1931">
<EMBED NAME="ActiveMovie1" WIDTH=267 HEIGHT=73
    CLASSID="CLSID:05589FA1-C356-11CE-BF01-00AA0055595A"
    CODEBASE="http://aux/controls"
    TYPE="application/oleobject"
   PARAM__ExtentX="7038"
   PARAM__ExtentY="1931"
></OBJECT>
```

CAUTION: Don't edit the ActiveX control by clicking the <OBJECT> tag next to the entry on the HTML page once you make the transition from an <OBJECT> tag specific to an <OBJECT> tag, <EMBED> tag combination. In some situations, the editor will change the <EMBED> tag in such a way that it won't work properly anymore. The best idea is to create your Web page, test it with Internet Explorer, and then add the <EMBED> tags needed to make it work with the NCompass ScriptActive plug-in.

Notice that NConvert takes the <OBJECT> tag information and adds an <EMBED> tag with basically the same information. Navigator recognizes the <EMBED> tag as something it should pass on to a plug-in, which allows ScriptActive to do its work. Since Internet Explorer doesn't understand the <EMBED> tag in this context, the additional information doesn't cause any problems. The reason for this extra bit of code is pretty obvious. The ScriptActive plug-in requires a special TYPE attribute to specify the Internet MIME type for the object. According to the vendor, future versions of ScriptActive won't require this additional information, and you'll be able to use the <OBJECT> tag without modification.

TIP: Once you install the NCompass ScriptActive plug-in, you'll find a new NConvert context menu entry when you right-click on a file. The entry contains two options: Convert and Set Destination Folder. Use the Set Destination Folder option to tell the utility where you want converted files placed. Specify a special directory if you don't want your original file overwritten by the converted file. The Convert option inserts all of the <EMBED> tags required by the current version of the product.

ScriptActive also provides support for VBScript. However, it does so by adding an external AXS file. You'll need to make sure that the AXS file is always in the same directory as the HTML file containing the VBScript. NConvert adds some lines of JavaScript to make the connection between Navigator and ScriptActive. Once ScriptActive gets the request, it looks for the appropriate VBScript code in the AXS file. Unfortunately, the VBScript support provided by ScriptActive is pretty poor. Plan on doing some rework on that VBScript code in the AXS file before you get it to work. The best bet is to use JavaScript and avoid VBScript in the first place if you plan to use one site with both Internet Explorer and Navigator.

Another problem with using ScriptActive is that it doesn't always allow you to access the properties associated with an object. In fact, the level of support even varies by machine—two machines with the same configuration and using the same hardware may show different results on a specific Web page. Different controls seem to provide varying levels of access as well—a more complex control usually presents more problems than a simple one. All of these problems aren't too surprising, considering the constant state of flux that the Internet is in and the relative newness of ActiveX technology. About the best you can hope to achieve is to display the control onscreen. Whether it will actually work or not is another matter.

8

Despite these problems, though, the promise of using ActiveX controls is too great to ignore. A third-party plug-in like ScriptActive is about the only way you can use ActiveX on a Web site and still guarantee that the majority of people visiting it will be able to actually see the content you've provided. There are rumors that the next version of Netscape Navigator will support ActiveX directly, but ScriptActive is your best solution for today.

HTML Enhancements

There are a lot of enhancements you can make to a Web site. In fact, I could probably fill this entire book with various enhancements you'll see on the Internet. The problems with using enhancements to your Web page are twofold. First, most require some commitment in the form of data. You have to consider whether a visitor will actually want to download that data to get a desired effect. Second, you'll find that some enhancements work fine with one browser but not with another. We'll run into some of these incompatibilities as the section progresses, so I won't belabor the point right now.

The two most popular enhancements you can make to a Web site are sound and animation. By far, sound appears to be the more popular of the two. We're not looking at a full-fledged CD here or even a reasonable facsimile. Sounds come in the form of sound bytes—short sounds that add to the effect you're trying to achieve with your Web site. In most cases, you'll use a WAV file to add sound to your site, though some people add music using MIDI files. Whichever form of sound support you use, exercise caution when deciding how much sound to add. Small is better. You'll also want to give people the option of turning the sound off so that they can view your site when working in an office.

Using a marquee is one way to add a form of animation to your Web page. All a marquee does is display a scrolling message or graphic image. The text capabilities you get with this tag are a little limited. Any "fancy" text that you add within the <MARQUEE> tag won't appear onscreen. The text that you start with is the text you keep throughout. This means doing any formatting you want before you actually display the marquee (it also explains why so many programmers prefer to use an image). Microsoft also provides an ActiveX version of the marquee as part of the ActiveX Control Pad utility.

CAUTION: Always use the LOOP attribute whenever you use the <MARQUEE> tag, because some browsers that do support it react strangely if you don't. It's important to get user feedback when you first implement this particular tag, since it is so prone to causing problems with older browsers. A little tweak here or there could make the tag work for everyone's browser that does support it at your site.

Animation can really enhance a site without adding too much overhead (although it does add some). The problem, of course, is spending the time to create some kind of animation routine. Some of you may be tempted to write a script or create an ActiveX control to get the job done, but there's a better way. You don't have to create fancy animation schemes if you don't want to; just use an animated GIF. If you're like me, you're probably asking what an animated GIF is by now, since most programmers have never seen such a thing. In reality, if you've spent much time on the Internet, you probably have seen one or two of these files. All an animated GIF consists of is a series of images that are displayed one at a time on your Web site. If you're very careful, you can use an animated GIF to create an animated effect that both entertains and conserves resources. The best news is that most major browsers provide full support for animated GIFs.

WEB LINK: You can see animated GIFs in action on many Internet sites. One of the more interesting places to look is **http://www.wanderers2.com/rose/animate.html**. This site offers an index of sites you can visit to see various kinds of animated GIFs. Looking at a variety of sites will help you understand what works and what doesn't. You can also download an animated GIF Wizard, make your own animated GIF online, and learn all about how to make animated GIFs.

Using Sounds and Other Effects to Make a Web Page Attractive

Sound bites (in the form of WAV files) go a long way toward dressing up a Web site. However, some users will find them distracting if you continuously

8

play sound bites every time they perform the smallest task. Make your sound bites short and to the point. Add them like a cook would add a spice: A little spice goes a long way toward making a tasty dish. Using too much spice will ruin whatever it is you're trying to create.

Small is better when it comes to Web sites. A recent visit to some Web sites showed that some of them were remarkably colorful and interesting yet proved remarkably fast to download. Looking at the code showed one common element. All of these authors used tables and frames to divide the page into smaller areas. Each area used small icons and graphics to make the page look nice. In addition, the author usually used some kind of coordinating color scheme to allow each frame an individual appearance without making the page look gaudy.

Let's take a look at an example page that demonstrates the concepts we've talked about so far in the chapter. Listings 8-8 through 8-12 show how this page is put together. Notice that it includes some small graphics and frames to organize the information. You'll also see many of the other tricks you've learned in this chapter (and a few new ones as well). Figure 8-11 shows how this page would look—at least in shades of gray. You'll need to construct the page to appreciate the use of color in this case.

Listing 8-8:

```
<!-FRAME.HTM->
<HTML>
<HEAD>
<TITLE>Sample Web Page</TITLE>
</HEAD>

<!-Set the frame parameters.->
<FRAMESET COLS="15%, *" ROWS="20%, 80%">

<!-Add an icon->
<FRAME SCROLLING=NO SRC=Icon.HTM>

<!-Create a heading.->
<FRAME SCROLLING=NO SRC=Heading.HTM>

<!-List some other sites that may be of interest.->
<FRAME SRC=OthrSite.HTM>

<!-Display the main content for our page.->
<FRAME SRC=Main.HTM>

</BODY>
```

Listing 8-9:

```
<!-HEADING.HTM->
<HTML>
<HEAD>
<TITLE>New Page</TITLE>
</HEAD>
<BODY BGCOLOR=WHITE>

<!-Define a heading and marquee for our site.->
<CENTER><H1> Welcome to The TIME Site</H1>
<H3><FONT COLOR=WHITE>
<MARQUEE BGCOLOR=BLUE BEHAVIOR=ALTERNATE WIDTH="75%" LOOP=INFINITE>
    One of the best places on earth to learn that time is money!
</MARQUEE>
</H3><FONT COLOR=BLACK>
</CENTER>

</BODY>
</HTML>
```

Listing 8-10:

```
<!-ICON.HTM->
<HTML>
<HEAD>
<TITLE>New Page</TITLE>
</HEAD>
<BODY BGCOLOR=YELLOW>

<!-Display our icon.->
<IMG SRC=TimeIt.GIF ALT="From 9 to 5">

</BODY>
</HTML>
```

Listing 8-11:

```
<!-OTHRSITE.HTM->
<HTML>
<HEAD>
<TITLE>New Page</TITLE>
</HEAD>
<BODY BGCOLOR=YELLOW>

<!-Display a heading.->
<CENTER><FONT COLOR=BLUE>
<H2>Other Interesting Sites</H2>
</CENTER><FONT COLOR=BLACK>
```

8

```
<!-Display the time management links.->
<P><P><CENTER><H3>Time Management</H3></CENTER>
<A HREF="http://www.time101.com">Time Management 101</A><P>
<A HREF="http://www.businesstime.com">Time Management for Business</A><P>
<A HREF="http://www.killerhelp.com">Killer Time Management Techniques</A><P>

<!-Display the added help links.->
<P><P><CENTER><H3>Getting Help</H3></CENTER>
<A HREF="http://www.superserve.com">Super Services</A><P>
<A HREF="http://www.irons.com">Too Many Irons in Fire</A><P>
<A HREF="http://www.business.com">Business Help to Go</A><P>

</BODY>
</HTML>
```

Listing 8-12:

```
<!-MAIN.HTM->
<HTML>
<HEAD>
<TITLE>New Page</TITLE>
</HEAD>
<BODY BGCOLOR=BLUE LINK=YELLOW VLINK=SILVER>

<!-Play a sound for those entering the Web site.->
<!-Internet Explorer Tag.->
<BGSOUND SRC="TwilZone.WAV" LOOP=1>
<!-Navigator Tag.->
<EMBED SRC="TwilZone.WAV" HIDDEN=TRUE LOOP=1>

<!-Display a heading.->
<CENTER><FONT  COLOR=YELLOW>
<H2>What's Happening This Week?</H2>
</CENTER><FONT COLOR=WHITE>

<!-Display a list of current events.->
<UL>
<LI>Learn how to create time in a bottle--get your own genie.  Demonstrations of how
    to work with a genie every Tuesday and Friday.  Call (555)555-1212 or send email
    care of this site for more details.
<LI>Tired of working too hard for too little time off?  Learn the secrets of cloning
    yourself.  There should be more of you.  Click <A HREF="Clone">HERE</A> for more
    details.
```

```
<LI>Be the envy of every salesperson out there.  Hire an inflatable dummy to
    sit in for you at the office while you go out and make a killing in new
    sales. We'll show you how at <A HREF="http://www.dummy.com">Dummies
    Unlimited</A>.
</UL>

<!-Present an ad for potential future sales.->
<CENTER><HR WIDTH=75%></CENTER>
<STRONG><H3><CENTER><PRE>
Get your ad on this site.  We'll run just about any ad at any time
since we really need the money.  If you want to line our pockets
with your extra cash, give us a call at (555)555-1212.  You can
also send us email which we'll gladly answer Tuesday for some
money today.
</PRE></CENTER></H3></STRONG>

<!-Send us email.->
<CENTER><HR WIDTH=75%></CENTER>
<FONT COLOR=YELLOW SIZE=-1>
&#169;1996 MyCompany and Associates, All Rights Reserved.   Send us some
email: <A HREF="mailto:admin@mycompany.com">&lt;Admin@MyCompany.com&gt;</A>

</BODY>
</HTML>
```

8

NOTE: This example doesn't cover everything you can do. In the next
section, we'll look at animated GIFs.

As you can see, this site presentation isn't overly fancy, but it's more
interesting than some of the places you've probably visited in the past. Let's
take some time to break down the more intriguing sections of the code. The
first thing you'll notice is that the site is broken into five files. You'll find it
easier to maintain sites with frames if you use separate files. In addition, you
could use the same heading and icon file for all of the pages on your site—
saving download time for the user. All that the code in Listing 8-8 does is
divide the browser area into frames, and then define what belongs in each
cell. Notice that you can specifically define the area for each frame as a
percentage or use an asterisk (*). The browser will give defined areas their

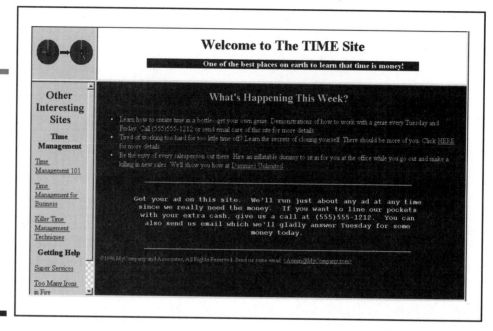

Our example
Web page
shows how
you can
combine
simple tags to
create an
interesting
Web page
without using
a lot of
resources to
do it.

Figure 8-11.

Use an asterisk
(*) to define a
frame that
takes whatever
space is left
over in a window
after the
browser allots
the space
you've
designated to
the other
frames.

percentage of the viewable screen first, and then divide the remaining area
equally among the other cells. You could use this feature to force a certain
aspect ratio on your Web pages.

Listing 8-9 contains the heading for our Web site. About the only interesting
bit of coding here is the use of color to set off the marquee area. Using
coordinating colors throughout your Web site will dress things up, yet it
won't cost the user much in download time. Also notice that this marquee
bounces back and forth instead of going around in circles. The BEHAVIOR
attribute is responsible for this change. Using a variety of attributes to
provide special effects can make your site more appealing. You'll also notice
that this is the only use of animation right now on the site—anything more
might prove distracting.

PORTABILITY: The <MARQUEE> tag works only with Internet
Explorer. If you use Navigator, you'll still see a heading area, but it won't have
the scrolling marquee. One of the better solutions to this problem is to create
a Java applet that simulates the behavior of the <MARQUEE> tag. You could
also create an ActiveX control to do the job, but then you'd have to use
something like NCompass ScriptActive to make the control compatible
with Navigator.

All you'll find in Listing 8-10 is an <IMG> tag for our icon. Notice that the <BODY> tag does contain a BGCOLOR attribute so that the background of the page will match that of the icon. That way, if users resize the display area, they won't see the page color peeking out from underneath the icon.

A lot of Web sites include links to other sites but in a way that doesn't interfere with the Web site as a whole. That's the purpose of the code in Listing 8-11. It organizes the links from the current site to other sites on the Internet without taking up space on the Web page itself. Not only does this tend to make the information easier to find, but you could use it as an index of sorts for your own site.

You'll find some interesting coding techniques in Listing 8-12. The first thing you'll want to look at is how tag attributes are used throughout this page to obtain special effects. For example, notice how the <PRE> tag is used to present special formatting for the note in the middle of the page. You'll also notice that this page uses reverse colors (light text on a dark background instead of the normal arrangement). This special effect sets off the main section of your page from the ancillary areas surrounding it. Several sites on the Internet use this same effect. For example, look at **http://www.pacbell.com**.

This page also uses a new tag, <BGSOUND>. This allows you to play a sound bite when the user enters your Web site. A special LOOP attribute allows you to define how many times the sound bite gets played. Using the <BGSOUND> tag by itself plays the sound one time, though it's normally better to include the LOOP attribute to prevent compatibility problems. Microsoft may decide at a later date that you have to specifically tell the <BGSOUND> tag how many times to play the sound.

8

PORTABILITY: Notice that the <BGSOUND> tag is Internet Explorer specific. We have to use an <EMBED> tag to get Navigator to play the sound. There are a lot of tags like this—Internet Explorer won't recognize the Navigator tag and Navigator won't acknowledge the Internet Explorer tag. As a programmer you'll need to compensate for these problems by adding dual code as needed.

At the bottom of Listing 8-12, you'll see two new ways of doing things as well. The first new technique is the use of &#<number> for special characters. For example, you can produce a copyright symbol using &#169. If you want one of these special characters to appear right beside a normal character, separate the two with a semicolon, like this: ©1996. The second new technique shows one way to allow someone to send you mail about your Web site. All you need to do is provide an HREF like this:

```
<A HREF="mailto:admin@mycompany.com">&lt;Admin@MyCompany.com&gt;</A>
```

The secret here is the "mailto" part of the link. Notice that the link text also uses another form of special character. In this case, &lt and &gt provide less-than and greater-than symbols around the link text.

TIP: The HTML reference provided with the ActiveX Control Pad may be a little incomplete in some areas, but it does provide a full listing of these special characters. Just look at the Character Set category found in the main index.

Adding Animated GIFs

If the previous section didn't show you enough techniques to make your Web site sparkle, there are a host of other ideas you can use. A favorite idea of webmasters the world over is the use of animated GIFs. All that an animated GIF does is pack several pictures into one file. The browser plays these pictures back one at a time—allowing you to create the illusion of continuous animation. You can also use special effects to create a slide show using a GIF. The only problem with this approach is the download time—a slide show tends to put quite a strain on the user's download capability.

NOTE: This section will show you how to create a GIF using the GIF Construction Set from Alchemy Mind Works. You can download it from several places. The best place is straight from the vendor at **http://www.mindworkshop.com/alchemy/gifcon.html**. You can also download it from the animated GIF viewing site mentioned earlier in the chapter: **http://www.wanderers2.com/rose/animate.html**.

We'll use the GIF Construction Set in this example for two reasons. First, since it's shareware, all of you can download it from the Internet and follow along with the examples. Second, it's a really great program, and most people find that it works just fine for creating animated GIFs. At most, you'll notice the lack of an actual drawing program with this program, but Windows already supplies that in the form of Paintbrush or MS Paint.

You'll also need a graphics conversion utility if your drawing program doesn't support the GIF file format directly (neither Paintbrush nor MS Paint do). Both Graphics Workshop from Alchemy Mind Works and Paint Shop Pro by JASC, Inc. are excellent graphics conversion programs. Both vendors provide shareware versions of their product. You can find Alchemy Mind Works at the Internet site provided in the previous note. The JASC product appears on various BBS and CompuServe forums (they may also have an Internet site by the time you read this).

The first thing you'll see when you open GIF Construction Set is a File | Open dialog like the one shown here.

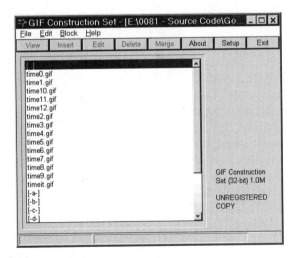

8

NOTE: As with all the other source code materials in this book, you can download TIME.GIF from the Osborne Web site at: **http://www.osborne.com**.

Notice that the directory has several GIF files in it already. TimeIt.GIF is the static file you saw in Figure 8-11. Time0.GIF is a base file—a blank used to create the animation effect. You can save a substantial amount of time by creating such a blank whenever you create an animation. In fact, cartoonists use this very technique. They draw the common elements of an animation once on separate sheets, and then combine them to create the animation. Only unique items are drawn one at a time. Time1.GIF through Time12.GIF are the actual animation files—think of each one as an animation cel.

Let's create an animated GIF using these "cel" files. The following procedure isn't meant to lock you into a particular regimen, but it does show one way to use the GIF Construction Set to create one.

1. Use the File | New command to create a new GIF. You'll see a blank GIF dialog like the one shown here. GIF Construction Set always assumes a standard display size of 640×480 pixels. We'll need to change that value.

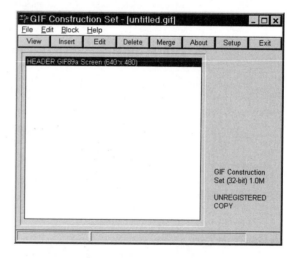

2. Double-click on the Header entry. You'll see the Edit Header dialog, shown here. It allows you to change characteristics associated with the GIF—for example, its size.

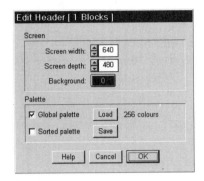

3. Type a new size in both the width and height fields to match the size of your image. For this example, you'd type **90** in the width and height fields. Click on OK to make the change permanent.

4. Click on the Merge button (or use the Block | Merge command). This allows you to add an image to the GIF. You'll see a standard File | Open dialog.

5. Double-click on the first file you want to use in the animation. In this case, you'd double-click Time1.GIF. You'll see the Palette dialog, shown here. The palette for this graphic doesn't match the standard palette used by GIF Construction Set.

8

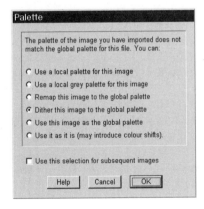

6. Since all of the images in this animation use the same palette, you'll want to select the Use This Image as the Global Palette setting. Click on OK to complete the process. GIF Construction Set will insert a new graphic into the GIF, as shown here.

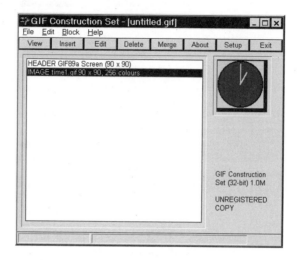

If you click on the Image entry, you'll see an actual copy of the image. Don't worry about this capability right now; however, it does come in handy if you want to make sure you have your animated files in the right sequence.

7. Click on the Merge button. You'll see the same File | Open dialog as before.

NOTE: Some versions of the GIF Construction Set have a Manage button in place of the Merge button. You can still find the Merge option under the Block menu. Use the Block | Merge command in place of the Merge button as required.

8. Select the next image in the series and click OK. Click OK again if GIF Construction Set asks you about the palette setting. GIF Construction Set will automatically insert the image in the next position of the animation sequence.

9. Repeat steps 7 and 8 for the remaining GIFs in this animation (Time2.GIF, Time3.GIF, and so on). Once you complete this step, your

dialog should look like the one shown here. Notice that all 12 images are in order. Now we have to insert some controls to make this image work properly.

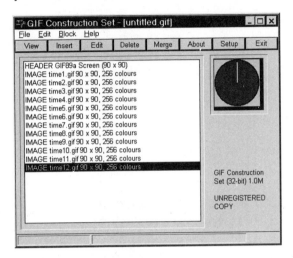

10. Click on the Insert button. You'll see the Insert Object menu, shown here.

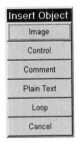

This menu contains every kind of object you can insert into an animated GIF. The two you'll use most often are Loop and Control.

◆ A Loop allows you to define how long the animation continues to go through a sequence of pictures. Wise use of Loop objects can create some pretty interesting effects. Unfortunately, many browsers ignore this particular entry, so you may want to use it sparingly. (If a browser ignores the Loop object, it simply keeps the animated GIF looping forever.)

8

◆ Controls allow you to modify the behavior of the animated GIF. For example, you can use a control to set the time between pictures.

◆ The Image entry is pretty obvious; every picture you want to add to the animated GIF is an Image. You'll use comments to document the behavior of your animated GIF, which is especially important if you plan to allow other people to use it.

◆ Plain Text is simply that—text that gets displayed as part of the animation.

11. Select the Loop entry in the Insert Object menu. GIF Construction Set will automatically place it under the Header entry. Now we need to place Control objects between each picture to time the animation sequence.

12. Click on the first Image entry. GIF Construction Set normally places the next entry right below the one you click.

13. Click on the Insert button and select Control from the Insert Object menu. You'll see a Control entry added to the list, as shown here.

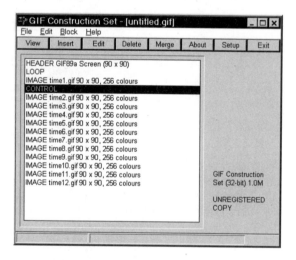

14. Click on the next Image entry.

15. Repeat steps 13 and 14 for each of the images. You'll end up with a series of Image and Control objects, as shown here. (Make sure you add a Control object after the last image, since the animated GIF will automatically loop back to the first image.)

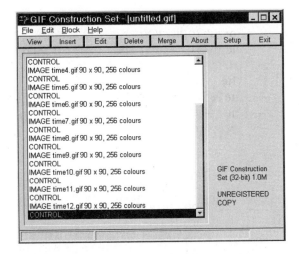

16. Normally you'll find that the default time period between pictures works pretty well. However, let's take a look at what you'd need to do to change the setting. Double-click on the last Control object entry. You'll see the Edit Control Block dialog, shown here.

8

◆ The most commonly used entry is the Delay field. You can use it to control the speed of the animation.

◆ The Transparent Color checkbox will allow whatever appears below the GIF to show through in the areas that are displayed with a certain color. Clicking the pushbutton allows you to select the transparent color.

◆ The Wait for User Input checkbox tells the animation to pause at this point in the animation and wait for the user to provide some kind of input. Normally the user will press a key.

◆ Finally, the Remove By field allows you to determine what to do with this animation cel once the browser displays it. Make sure you leave this entry alone, because you'll get very unpredictable results from some browsers otherwise.

17. Click Cancel to close the dialog.

18. To view the completed animation, click on the View button. Press ESC to exit the viewing area.

19. The only thing left to do is save your animated GIF file. Use the File | Save As command to do that. You could use any filename, but for the purposes of this example, save the file as TimeIt.GIF. That's how we'll access the file later within an HTML page.

If you look at the size of even the modest animation created for this example, you'll find that it consumes about 16.7KB of memory. That's almost one third of your memory budget for this page. What you've got to consider at this point is whether the animation is worth the added memory burden.

Fortunately, there's another way to deal with the problem. Double-click on any of the Image object entries, and you'll see an Edit Image dialog like the one shown here.

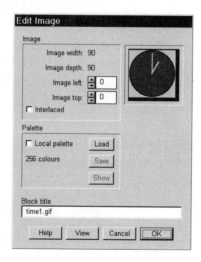

Notice the Image Left and Image Top fields. These fields allow you to choose a starting point for each image in the animation. You really don't need to redisplay the entire clock every time the animation cel changes. All you need to do is overwrite the previous hour-hand position and replace it with the next one in the series. Cropping each image so that the previous hour hand gets covered and the new one displayed could reduce the size of your animated GIF by 75 percent. In other words, that 16.7KB file would be reduced to about 4.7KB. The only thing you need to do is crop the image with your paint program, reinsert it into the animated GIF file using the procedure we just covered, and then use the Image Top and Image Left fields to place the cropped image correctly on the display. This dialog also allows you to choose a new palette for the picture and assign it a different name.

TIP: Unless your animated GIF is very large or your download budget very small, you won't want to take the time to crop every image individually. For example, our sample GIF would probably work fine if it were the only image on the page.

The Interlaced checkbox is pretty interesting too. If this GIF were designed as a static image, you'd want to check this box. Interlaced images are displayed one line at a time. It's the effect you see on most Web sites when downloading a large graphic. Using an interlaced graphic gives users some visual feedback during the download process—it lets them know that the machine hasn't frozen. You'll want to leave this box unchecked for animated GIFs, though, because it takes more time to display an interlaced image. Checking the Interlaced checkbox could actually make the animation look pretty jumpy in this case.

8

Building Component Download (CAB) Files Using DIANTZ.EXE

You learned earlier that you could save the user some time by placing your ActiveX controls in a CAB file. This file format offers the ability to transfer more than one file in a single download and file compression as well. Creating a CAB file doesn't have to be difficult, but you will want to test it thoroughly before using it in a production environment.

NOTE: You may see the DIANTZ.EXE file referred to by one of two other names, depending on what resource you look at. Visual Basic users will know this utility as MAKECAB.EXE. Some versions of the ActiveX SDK shipped with a version of the utility named DIAMOND.EXE. Whatever the name of the utility you use, its purpose is to create CAB files you can use to distribute your application.

The first step is to figure out which files to send to users. For example, users will probably have a copy of all the MFC (Microsoft Foundation Classes) files from using other programs. You don't want them to waste time downloading these files over and over again if they don't need to. In most cases, you'll want to limit yourself to the files that are unique to your Web site.

The second step is to create an INF file. There are several reasons for including this file. For one thing, it can include installation instructions that will make the user's life a lot easier and reduce your support calls. Another good reason for including an INF file is that it contains those common files that your ActiveX control needs but didn't get downloaded as part of the CAB file. You can include instructions for downloading those files from your Internet site if the user really does need them. The Internet Component Download service portion of your browser doesn't understand the full-fledged INF file specification—it can only use a subset of the standard entries. Table 8-2 shows the entries you can use and the order you should use for including them.

Creating an INF file is fairly easy. All you really need to do is think about what you need to include and where it's located. Listing 8-13 shows a typical INF file for a two-file installation. The first file, OCXEXMPL.OCX, is actually located in the CAB. The user will also need MFC40.DLL, but there's a good chance it's already installed on the client machine. The example includes a site to find the file on the Internet server, just in case the client machine doesn't have the required file. Once you have a list of files and an INF file, you can create the Diamond Directive File (DDF) needed by DIANTZ.EXE to create the CAB file. The format of this file is not difficult to understand. Listing 8-14 shows a typical example that you can use to create your own DDF.

Entry	Description
[Add.Code]	
<Filename1>= <Section-Name1> <Filename2>= <Section-Name2> <Filename n>= <Section-Name n>	The [Add.Code] section provides a complete list of all the files that you want to install. This won't include all of the files in the INF file, since you won't want to install the INF file as a minimum. The <Section-Name> part of the entry tells Internet Component Download service where to find the installation instructions for a particular file. (See the next section.)
[Section-Name1]	
Key1=Value1 Key2=Value2 Key n=Value n	Each file-specific section contains one or more keys, just like the keys you've used before with INI files. The following entries explain the key values that Internet Component Download will understand.
File=[<URL> I ThisCAB]	This key tells whether you can download the file from a specific location on the Internet or from this cabinet. Using this key allows you to define locations for files needed by the ActiveX control but not included in the CAB file. Normally these additional support files are located on the Internet server.
File Version= <a>,<b>,<c>,<d>	This key specifies the minimum acceptable version number for a file. If you don't specify a value, Internet Component Download assumes any version is fine. Each letter designates a level of revision. So if your control's version is 1.0, you'd use Version=1,0,0,0.
File-[Mac I Win32]-[x86 I PPC I Mips I Alpha]=[<URL> I IGNORE]	This key allows you to differentiate required support for various platforms. First you define an operating system, then the CPU type. The <URL> parameter allows you to specify a location for the file. The IGNORE argument tells Internet Component Download that the file isn't needed on the specified platform.

INF File Format for Internet Component Download Service

Table 8-2.

8

Entry	Description
CLSID=[<Class ID>]	This key allows you to define a class identification for the file. You won't actually create the CLSID—Visual C++ does this step for you automatically, based on a complex equation developed by Microsoft. There are two places to get this value: your C++ source code and the Windows registry. To find it in the Windows registry, just open the registry editor and use the Edit | Find command to find the name of your OCX under the HKEY_CLASSES_ROOT | CLSID key. The registry form of the CLSID for the example in Chapter 2 is {D8D77E03-712A-11CF- 8C70-00006E3127B7}. The C++ source location is in the control file. For example, the Chapter 2 source code file to look in is OCXEXMPLCTL.CPP. You'll find the identifier in this call: /// Initialize class factory and guide IMPLEMENT_OLECREATE_EX(COCXEXMPLCtrl, "OCXEXMPL.OCXEXMPLCtrl.1", 0xd8d77e03, 0x712a, 0x11cf, 0x8c, 0x70, 0, 0, 0x6e, 0x31, 0x27, 0xb7) /// The CLSID value for an ActiveX control never changes (unless you change something very basic like the name—code changes have no effect), so you only need to find this value once.

INF File Format for Internet Component Download Service (*continued*)

Table 8-2.

Listing 8-13:

```
;INF File for OCXEXMPL.OCX
[Add.Code]
OCXEXMPL.OCX=OCXEXMPL.OCX
MFC40.DLL=MFC40.DLL

[OCXEXMPLE.OCX]
File=thiscab
Clsid=[D8D77E03-712A-11CF-8C70-00006E3127B7]
FileVersion=1,0,0,0
```

```
[MFC40.DLL]
File=http://aux/files/MFC40.DLL
FileVersion=4,0,0,5
```

Listing 8-14:
```
;Diamond Directive File
;Generate a complete error listing for any variable typos.
.OPTION EXPLICIT
;Define the name of the CAB file.
.SET CABINETNAMETEMPLATE=ActiveX.CAB
;Create a cabinet.
.SET CABINET=ON
;Compress the files.
.SET COMPRESS=ON
;List the files.
Install.INF
File1.OCX
File2.OCX
Ù
```

Once you get to this point, creating the CAB file isn't hard. Just use the command line shown here:

```
DIANTZ /F MY.DDF
```

8

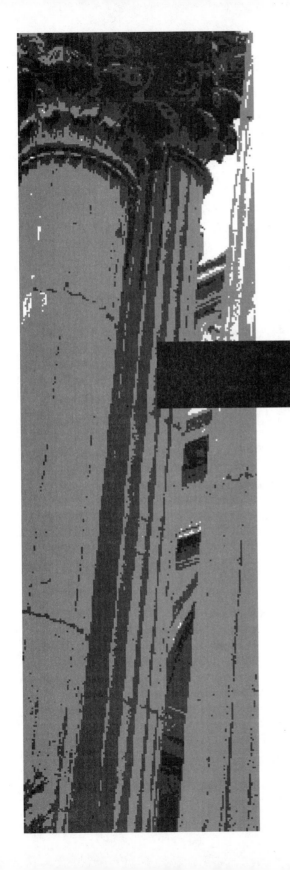

CHAPTER 9

An Overview
of JavaScript

293

If you thought you'd get rid of scripting by using ActiveX controls on your Web site, forget it. ActiveX controls are actually more reliant on scripting than other kinds of Web interface elements. Theoretically, you could place an ActiveX control on a page and allow it to just sit there looking pretty without any scripting, but that's about it. In fact, we'll see in Chapter 10 that while an ActiveX control will perform some function even if you haven't written a script for it, that function is limited to what you designed the control to do when writing it in Visual C++. In other words, the control is internally active without scripting, but scripting allows it to interact with the outside world.

Using scripting lets you save network bandwidth and allows any ActiveX controls on the page to interact with the outside world.

Fortunately, there are some positive features to using scripting languages other than the fact that you need them to use ActiveX controls. Have you ever sat waiting for a CGI script to complete on the host (Internet server) only to find out that the data you entered was incomplete or wrong in some way? A lot of people have had that experience. Since VBScript and JavaScript both execute on the host (in this case the user's machine), you'll find that you can validate information as soon as the user enters it. This saves network bandwidth and makes user feedback instantaneous. Anything that keeps the user happy is bound to save you some time as well.

Obviously, if you're going to spend some time working with a scripting language, it pays to know the players. Some scripting languages are more popular than others, and right now, VBScript and JavaScript seem to be the two getting the most media attention. (Microsoft's version of JavaScript is named JScript; I'll use JavaScript throughout the book to refer to any form of the scripting language.) JavaScript works with both Internet Explorer and Netscape Navigator, while VBScript is an Internet Explorer-only solution. (The NCompass ScriptActive plug-in for Netscape Navigator only does a fair job in allowing you to support VBScript with this browser.) ActiveX Control Pad currently supports both VBScript and JavaScript. You'll find that most of the other tools you see on the market right now support them as well.

The Microsoft name for JavaScript is JScript.

NOTE: Even though you have a choice of using VBScript or JavaScript with ActiveX controls, we'll concentrate on JavaScript in this chapter. There are three good reasons for making this choice. First, JavaScript is much closer in syntax to Visual C++ than VBScript is, so your learning curve will be less steep. Second, JavaScript is supported natively by both major browsers: Internet Explorer and Netscape Navigator. Third, recent Microsoft press releases and other sources like trade press magazines appear to indicate that VBScript is losing popularity in favor of JavaScript.

We'll also take a look at ActiveX Scripting, which is an OLE communication technology rather than a scripting language. You'll get an overview of what the technology involves so you can be prepared to use ActiveX Scripting once it does become available. For the most part, you'll find that ActiveX Scripting relies on current OLE technology with some new interface elements added and a couple of new bells and whistles borrowed from other places. The actual technology is a little more complicated. (We'll definitely look at those new interface elements.)

TIP: If you plan on spending a lot of time developing Web pages using ActiveX controls or any of the scripting technology we discuss in this chapter, you'll definitely want to get something more robust than ActiveX Control Pad. Products like Microsoft Visual InterDev allow you to create Web pages with ease and without knowing too much about the underlying HTML tags. Visual InterDev also allows you to use ActiveX controls within your Web page. ActiveX Control Pad is most useful for experimentation purposes. It allows you to create small test Web pages that include scripts.

This chapter spends most of its time looking at how scripting and ActiveX controls work together. We'll begin with a simple example using some of the controls provided with ActiveX Control Pad. For example, you may have noticed that you can't define any of the entries for a drop-down list box by sticking it on the page and accessing the Properties dialog. The reason is simple: you need a script to add those entries at run time. All sections of this chapter will look at JavaScript, but you can perform similar tasks using VBScript.

Once we get past the basics, we'll spend a little time looking at some intermediate scripting examples. For example, we'll take a look at how you can use scripting to interact with controls you've created. There's a real lack of complex controls available to demonstrate, but we'll view enough of them to give you the general idea of how to use scripts in complex situations.

9

Overview of ActiveX Scripting

At present, ActiveX Scripting isn't a language (macro or otherwise) like the VBScript or JavaScript languages we've talked about so far (we'll look at the JavaScript language in the next section of this chapter). It's better defined as a communication method between a client and server. In essence, it's Microsoft's new name for OLE automation. Saying that OLE automation and ActiveX Scripting are precisely the same wouldn't be correct, since Microsoft hasn't left the capabilities of ActiveX Scripting at the application level. (Most Microsoft products and a few other products such as CorelDRAW! support OLE automation at the application level.) ActiveX Scripting also takes the Internet into account.

PORTABILITY: You may have noticed the OLE Automation checkbox provided by the MFC AppWizard during previous examples in the book. This checkbox will add the same kind of scripting capability to your application as you see in products like CorelDRAW! In other words, you can use the scripting capability on a local machine or network. However, this capability still isn't ActiveX Scripting, since it doesn't take the Internet into account. You still need to add this capability manually to a Visual C++ application. And since the standard for ActiveX Scripting isn't finalized, you'll also be shooting at a moving target by doing so.

Since ActiveX Scripting isn't a language but a communication specification, the scripting language, including syntax, is left to the scripting vendor. The purpose of this standard is to define a method for a scripting host to call on various scripting engines and allow communication between objects within an OLE container. In essence, the script is more a blob of executable code than anything else. It could consist of text, pcode, or even executable code in native binary format. The essence of ActiveX Scripting is that it's an OLE-based communication medium designed for both application and Internet use.

WEB LINK: The ActiveX Scripting specification is a moving target as of this writing. You'll want to spend time looking at the latest news if you intend to use ActiveX Scripting in place of or as an addition to other technologies. Furthermore, this section doesn't provide complete coverage of the calling syntax for all the interface methods required by the OLE host and scripting engine. Look at **http://www.microsoft.com/intdev/sdk/ docs/olescrpt/** for more information about the current ActiveX Scripting specification. There are a couple of good places to look for information about the ActiveX Scripting host, including **http://www.microsoft.com/ msdn/sdk/inetsdk/help/wsh/wobj_2.htm** and **http://www.microsoft. com/msdn/sdk/inetsdk/help/compdev/scripting/hosts.htm**. If you want to learn more about the requirements for building an ActiveX Scripting engine, look at http://**www.microsoft.com/msdn/sdk/ inetsdk/help/compdev/engines/engines.htm.**

Let's take a few moments to define some terms here. First, what precisely is a scripting host? It's an application that supports a scripting engine. When you define a script, it's the host that accepts it and then sends the commands to the engine. The most common example of an ActiveX Scripting host right now is Internet Explorer 3.0. You can also add this capability to Netscape

Navigator using a plug-in. We discuss one of these plug-ins, NCompass ScriptActive, in Chapter 8. A scripting engine isn't limited to either of these products, of course. You could build it into a custom browser application or find it in any number of applications. For example, it's likely that Microsoft will bring all of its application products (such as Microsoft Word) up to this standard in the near future.

An ActiveX scripting engine is the object that actually interprets the script. There are no limitations on the precise language syntax or even the form of the script. You could theoretically write an ActiveX scripting engine for any language, including VBScript, Java, and JavaScript. An ActiveX scripting engine will provide special interfaces, just like any other OLE object that we'll discuss later in this section. In addition, you can write to an ActiveX scripting engine using an OLE automation wrapper (Microsoft plans to provide a special form of OLE automation wrapper for ActiveX Scripting). The advantage to using the wrapper format is that it keeps the code small and lightweight—ideal for browsers and online scripting engines. The disadvantage is that you lose control over the run-time namespace, persistence model, and other authoring elements that you would have if you wrote to the ActiveX Scripting interface directly.

There are four new interface elements required for ActiveX Scripting. The optional IActiveScriptSite and optional IActiveScriptSiteWindow interfaces are host-specific. The IActiveScript and optional IActiveScriptParse interfaces are scripting-engine specific. (If you don't implement IActiveScriptParse, then you need to implement some form of IPersist interface.) Each interface element performs a specific function, as described in the following list.

9

◆ *IActiveScriptSite*   The main purpose of this interface is to create a site for the ActiveX Scripting engine. This corresponds to the idea of a container in other OLE implementations—it's where everything else, such as ActiveX controls, is placed. Since this is a container interface, it monitors events such as the starting and stopping of scripts and when a script error occurs.

◆ *IActiveScriptSiteWindow*   Any ActiveX Scripting host that provides a user interface also needs to provide this interface (servers need not apply). In essence, if you need a window for scripting purposes, you need to implement this interface. IActiveScriptSiteWindow provides two essential methods (though you can provide others as needed): GetWindow(), which creates a window, and EnableModeless(), which allows you to set the modal condition of the window. GetWindow() is similar in functionality to the OLE automation-specific IOleWindow::GetWindow() function, while EnableModeless() is similar in functionality to IOleInPlaceFrame::EnableModeless().

◆ *IActiveScript* This interface allows you to work with the script itself. You can use it to get the scripting site, start or stop the script, work with script items, close the script, or establish thread state and parameters.

◆ *IActiveScriptParse* This interface accepts scripts from the scripting host. It allows you to create a new script, add scriptlets (pieces of raw script text) to an existing script, or parse an existing script.

Visual C++ provides a handy utility, named OLE/COM Object Viewer, which you can use to see these interfaces in more detail (Microsoft shortened the name to OLE View in recent versions of Visual C++). We'll use this utility several times in the book, so you may want to install it if you haven't done so already. Let's take a look at the host side of the ActiveX Scripting issue first. As previously mentioned, Visual C++ still provides an OLE automation interface, which doesn't provide an Internet capability. Go ahead and open the OLE/COM Object Viewer. You'll see a set of folders. Open the Document Objects folder, and then open the XYZ Single Document folder. You'll see a list of interfaces, similar to the list in Figure 9-1, that MFC implemented for you as you built the application.

Notice that I've highlighted the IOleWindow interface in the left pane. If you look in the right pane, you'll see that this interface has five methods. Further research would show that one of those methods is GetWindow(). As previously mentioned, the presence of an IOleWindow interface without the IActiveScriptSiteWindow interface means that your application supports OLE automation, not ActiveX Scripting. Now, if you look at every other application in this list, including Office 97 if you have it, you won't find a single application that supports ActiveX Scripting—yet.

CAUTION: Strange things can happen if you create an instance of an application or control in the OLE/COM Object Viewer and then don't release it. For example, your machine might freeze unexpectedly. Every time you view the interfaces supported by an application or control, you have to create an instance to do it. You can tell if there is an instance of an object by looking at the application name. The OLE/COM Object Viewer displays any open objects with bold type. To release the instance of the object you created, right-click on the object name (like XYZ Single Document), and then choose Release Instance from the context menu. Fortunately, the OLE/COM Object Viewer is good about closing instances of objects before you leave, but you may need to do this during a viewing session if your machine begins to run out of memory. Remember that every instance you create also uses some memory.

The client-side support for ActiveX Scripting is available—at least in a preliminary form. Release the instance of the XYZ Single Document, and

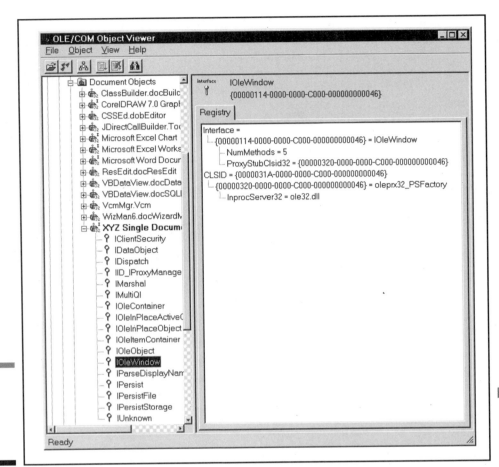

Viewing
ActiveX
interfaces in
OLE View

Figure 9-1.

9

then close the Document Object folder. Now open the ActiveX Scripting Engine folder. You'll see two entries, one for JavaScript and another for VBScript. Both of these entries are for Internet Explorer, but expect to see Netscape Navigator to implement them as well. Open the JScript Language (JavaScript) entry and you'll see a typical list of interfaces like the ones shown in Figure 9-2 (your list may vary slightly from the one shown).

Notice that the highlighted entry, IActiveScript, is the first client-side interface that I described earlier. Right below it you'll see the IActiveScript-Parse interface entry, which is the second client-side interface that I described. Having both of these entries means that Internet Explorer currently supports ActiveX Scripting as a client, but you won't find any associated server entries in this section of the OLE/COM Object Viewer either.

Let's talk a little more about the relationship between an ActiveX Scripting host and client. Three different elements are involved in an ActiveX Scripting

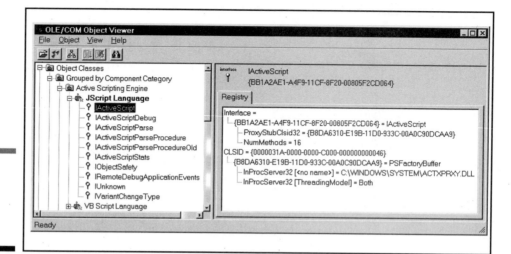

session: the host, an engine, and the window (page) containing the code and controls. Establishing communication between the three elements is an eight-step process, as described here:

1. The host loads a document or project as needed. This isn't an ActiveX Scripting-specific task, since any environment needs to perform this step.

2. The host creates a scripting engine. Normally, it uses the PROGID attribute of the <OBJECT> tag to do this. A call to CoCreateInstance() completes the task.

3. Loading the script comes next, and the host can follow several routes to accomplish it. If the script is stored as persisted data, the host uses the engine's IPersist::Load() to reload it into memory. If the host needs to load a new script, it calls IActiveScriptParse::InitNew() or IPersist::InitNew() to create an empty script. Hosts that maintain scripts as text can then call IActiveScriptParse::ParseScriptText() to load the script into the engine. (Hosts that use other formats to maintain the script will have to devise their own loading method.)

4. Once the host has loaded the script in some way, it has to populate the engine's namespace with entities. An *entity* is a form, page, or other document. The host uses the IActiveScript::AddNamedItem() method to accomplish this task. Obviously, it doesn't need to load any entities stored as part of the script's persistent storage. Lower-level items such as ActiveX controls require a different loading technique. The host uses the ITypeInfo and IDispatch interfaces to get the job done.

5. Now that the ActiveX scripting engine has everything it needs to run the script, the host issues an IActiveScript::SetScriptState(SCRIPTSTATE_CONNECTED) call. This tells the scripting engine to start the script—it's equivalent to calling the Main() function in a standard C program.

6. Before the scripting engine actually starts running the script, it needs to take care of a few housekeeping tasks. For example, it needs to associate a symbol with every top-level item. The scripting engine does this using the IActiveScriptSite::GetItemInfo() method.

7. One of the final steps before the scripting engine actually runs the script is to make the proper connections between script elements and events associated with objects. For example, if there's a script item that deals with the onClick event for a pushbutton, the scripting engine needs to make the connection before it runs the script. The scripting engine uses the IConnectionPoint interface to perform this work.

8. The scripting engine can finally run the script. As it runs the script, the scripting engine will need to access the methods and properties associated with the objects on your HTML page or other document. It does this using the IDispatch::Invoke() or other standard OLE binding methods.

Now that you have a pretty good idea of how a script works, let's take a very quick look at some of the ways a scripting engine reacts when running. The scripting engine doesn't simply have two operating states, on and off. It provides several states that you can use to determine what needs to be done to get it running. (You obtain the current state using the IActiveScript::GetScriptState() method.) The following list tells you about the various scripting engine states.

9

◆ *Uninitialized*   This means that the scripting engine isn't ready to do anything. Normally, the host will have to load a script and any entities required for the script to run before the scripting engine will leave this state.

◆ *Initialized*   The script is loaded (usually with IPersist) and the site for running it is set (using IActiveScriptSite), but the scripting engine isn't actually associated with a host yet. You can't run any code while the scripting engine is in this state. Any code executed with IActiveScriptParse::ParseScriptText() will run once the scripting engine enters the started state.

◆ *Started*   This is a transition state from which you can run code using IDispatch. All the code is loaded along with the objects. However, the scripting engine hasn't created connections between script elements and the object events yet. If the script runs into a situation where it needs to perform event processing, it'll become blocked (stopped) until the scripting engine completes the required initialization.

◆ *Connected*   You'll only get this state when the scripting engine is ready to perform every task required of it.

◆ *Disconnected*   The script essentially pauses when the scripting engine enters this state. The script is still loaded and all the connections are made, but the scripting engine isn't prepared to answer requests from the host. The scripting engine can go from this state back to the connected state without losing the current script running position.

◆ *Closed*   The scripting engine will no longer answer calls when in this state. It enters this state after you send an IActiveScript::Close() call.

Java Scripting Basics

Before we go any further, let's get one thing out of the way. Java and JavaScript are two entirely different entities. If you're looking for a full-fledged programming environment, then Java (or Microsoft's version, named J++), not JavaScript, is the language you're looking for. On the other hand, if you're looking for a macro language of the same caliber (although not the same functionality) as VBScript but with a C orientation, you're looking for JavaScript. Also, Java is a Sun innovation, while JavaScript comes to you from Netscape. Some marketing person at Netscape must have come up with this rather confusing idea of giving both products essentially the same name—the original name for JavaScript was LiveScript.

PORTABILITY: JavaScript has been one of the casualties of the browser wars. Internet Explorer and Netscape Navigator use similar, but not totally compatible, versions of JavaScript in their browsers. Without getting into a lot of politics, the short story is that Microsoft designed its own version of JavaScript after Netscape was slow in delivering a public specification for its version. The rumors right now are that both companies are working on a combined version of the JavaScript standard—I wouldn't hold my breath waiting for it. In the meantime, you'll have to contend with some compatibility problems when using JavaScript. The good news is that with a little effort, you can get one version of your script to work with both browsers. Of course, you'll definitely want to test your scripts under both products to make sure that they'll perform as intended.

Now that we've gotten the distinction between Java and JavaScript out of the way, let's look at the language itself. For the most part you'll find JavaScript used for the same purposes as VBScript—as a means for working with ActiveX

JavaScript and Java are two completely different programming environments, despite the similarity in names.

controls and Java applets on an HTML page. In fact, you can work with any kind of object with JavaScript—sometimes the only limiting factor is figuring out how to do so. JavaScript also comes in handy for a variety of other purposes, most of which we'll see in the next few sections of the chapter. For right now it's important to know only that JavaScript provides a distinctly different feature set from VBScript that allows you to enhance your Web site.

Unlike VBScript, there aren't any directly compatible versions of anything to compare JavaScript to. Comparing it to C (or even Java) wouldn't give you much information because JavaScript was designed as a separate product with a feature set oriented toward Internet use. JavaScript's main claim to fame when it comes to the Internet is compatibility. Sure, you can't move that JavaScript application to your C compiler and expect it to do anything, but you can rely on it to work with more native browser environments than VBScript will. What we'll do in the rest of this section is give a quick overview of what JavaScript does provide, and then we'll look at it in action for the rest of the chapter.

PORTABILITY: Remember that JavaScript uses a C-like syntax. This means that JavaScript will look like C in some situations, while in others JavaScript will use a new construct that you couldn't normally use with C. While you'll be able to use some of the application logic from your C applications in the JavaScript environment, don't plan on doing so without making some level of modifications. JavaScript is in no way directly compatible with Visual C++.

9

JavaScript takes an object map approach to working with HTML documents. It builds a hierarchy of objects starting with the window, the documents within the window, forms within the document, and finally, any objects within the form. Using JavaScript allows you to communicate with each object by defining a path to it. For example, if you wanted to do something to a form, you'd separate the form name from the window name like this: Window1.Form1. Notice that the window name is separated from the form name by a period—many programmers refer to this as a *dot syntax reference*.

There are a few very non-C-like things to know about JavaScript. First, JavaScript is a loosely typed language. That means you don't have to declare your variables. Second, there are objects in JavaScript, but there aren't any classes or inheritance. This means that you can't create new object types. You can, however, extend existing object types to a certain extent. The objects you get to use are the ones contained within an HTML document or form.

For example, even the most basic JavaScript application can access the Window object—every HTML document has to have one of these. Within the Window object, you'll find default objects like Document, Frames, History, and Location.

You can also extend the number of objects available to you, but not using the normal method of creating a new class. The method that we'll cover in this chapter is to use ActiveX controls. The method of extension when using an ActiveX control depends on what properties and methods the control author exposed for you to use. In essence, for an ActiveX control, the properties would appear on the Properties page and the methods would be events that you exposed. (Look at the example in Chapter 10 if you need to know more about building a basic control.) It's important to remember that JavaScript is object based, not object oriented. Finally, JavaScript is dynamically bound. This means it checks for objects at run time. C and Java are both statically bound; they check for objects during compile time.

WEB LINK: There are a lot of places to learn about JavaScript. One of the things you should get first is a language guide. The best place to view the language guide is **http://home.netscape.com/eng/mozilla/Gold/ handbook/javascript/index.html**. You'll find not only a language guide there but also good discussions on various language elements. Fortunately, you can get a tutorial-sized version of the JavaScript documentation in Windows help format from **http://www.jchelp.com/javahelp/ javahelp.htm**.

The most important thing to remember about JavaScript is that, like Java, you're extremely restricted as to what you can do with the system hardware. The reason for this is to prevent (as much as possible) security breaches. Unfortunately, the amount of protection you'll actually get from JavaScript is limited (see the "Three Common JavaScript Security Holes" In Depth box for details). Some people view these restrictions as a real problem, but you can get around most of them using ActiveX controls. Since a user will have to request the ActiveX control before downloading it, security is enhanced. The fact that the ActiveX control has to be signed also helps to improve security. However, no matter what strategy you use, anyone who really wants to damage your machine right now will find a way to do it.

One of the hardware access restrictions you'll run into is that you can't write to files. The only exception to this rule is that you can write to cookies. A *cookie* is a bit of data that you can store to the browser's cache directory. The purpose of a cookie is to store configuration information from one session to the next. Some programmers use the cookie for other small storage purposes as well. For example, you could use it to store the URL of the last site explored by the user so that you can return the user to that site during the next session.

JavaScript supports four different variable types: numbers, strings, Boolean, and a special null value. You can use function calls to convert one variable type to another. However, you can just as easily mix variable types. For example, you could create a variable named nANumber and assign it a numeric value. In the very next line of code you could assign the same variable a string value, and JavaScript won't complain. You can also mix variable types in one line of code. For example, nANumber = "Some Answer Equals " + 42 is perfectly legal in JavaScript. This is one of the reasons you'll want to enforce some kind of variable typing yourself through the use of a notation like Hungarian Notation (explained in the Introduction).

WEB LINK: Like any other aspect of programming, getting feedback from fellow JavaScript programmers is important. One of the best places to get a fairly unbiased opinion of JavaScript programming techniques is at **Comp.Lang.JavaScript**. If you want the Microsoft view, make sure you take a look at **microsoft.public.frontpage.client** or **microsoft.public. activex.programming.scripting.jscript**. (There are other Microsoft newsgroups that get an occasional JavaScript message, but these two newsgroups get the most messages of any of them.) You may also find an occasional mention of JavaScript at **comp.infosystems.www.authoring.html**.

9

Functions are the only form of modular coding you can use within JavaScript. In fact, this is one of the first places where JavaScript actually takes on a C-like look. As with most programming languages, you can accept parameters as part of the function call and provide a return value. The following example shows a typical JavaScript function. Notice that it uses Document.Write()—one of the methods you'll use most often in beginning scripts. You can use it not only to display text but, as we see here, to write HTML code as well.

```
function MyFunction(nSomeValue)
{
    Document.Write("The value received was: ",nSomeValue,".","<BR>")
    Return nSomeValue + 1
}
```

Most languages support some kind of conditional statement, and JavaScript is no exception. The easiest conditional to use is in this form: (<Condition>) ? <Value1> : <Value2>. You'd use it to assign one of two values to a variable. For example, lIsGreater = (Value1 > Value2) ? true : false. If Value1 is greater than Value2, the lIsGreater will equal TRUE. You can use the If...Else conditional statement like this. JavaScript doesn't currently support any form of case (or switch) statement—making it much more difficult to write code that checks a lot of different values.

```
if (Value1 > Value2)
{
    Document.Write("Value 1 is greater than Value 2.")
    Return true
}
else
{
    Document.Write("Value 2 is greater than Value 1.")
    Return false
}
```

Looping is another operation that all programming languages support. You'll find that JavaScript supports two different looping constructs: for and while. Here's an example of each type. You'll notice that they look almost exactly like the equivalent structure in C.

```
for (nCounter = 0, nCounter < 10, nCounter++)
{
    Document.Write(nCounter)
}

while (nCounter < 10)
{
    Document.Write(nCounter)
    nCounter++
}
```

This gives you a very basic overview of JavaScript. You'll get to see a lot of JavaScript code throughout this chapter, so don't worry right now about what you don't know. The main thing you need to remember is that JavaScript is C-*like*—it's not C by any stretch of the imagination (you should have noticed quite a few differences by now).

Three Common JavaScript Security Holes

Lest you think that scripts are easily monitored, there have been more than a few script-related security problems that I've noted in the trade press and newsgroups in recent months. The short version is that neither VBScript nor JavaScript are even close to safe (though more work has been done finding the security holes in JavaScript). You can find out about the currently known security problems with JavaScript at **http://www.osf.org/~loverso/javascript/**. The following list presents three of the most common problems.

◆ *Tricking the user into uploading a file*   Even though JavaScript has to ask the user's permission to upload a file, a hacker could hide this request in a variety of ways. All a hacker really needs is a button with an interesting caption. Uploaded password files like those used for Windows 95 are easily broken—making the hacker's job of breaking into your system easy.

◆ *Obtaining file directories*   A JavaScript application doesn't have to ask anyone's permission to upload a directory of your machine. In fact, it can upload the directories of any network machines you have access to as well. A hacker who knows the organization of your hard drive can break into your system that much more easily.

◆ *Tracking sites visited*   Hackers can learn a lot about you by keeping track of the Web sites you visit. A JavaScript application makes this easy to do. It can track every URL you visit and send the addresses to the hacker's machine. As with the file upload problem, the user has to give permission to do this, but the hacker can disguise this permission as just about anything.

9

Working with Stand-Alone Scripts

JavaScript is pretty straightforward to learn if you know C. Since we've already taken a preliminary look at JavaScript's syntax in the previous sections of this chapter, let's examine a sample script. In this case, we'll look at a very typical application for JavaScript, calculating the results of a user's entries on an order form so that the server doesn't have to keep passing data back and forth over the Internet.

WEB LINK: At the time of this writing, Microsoft hasn't included the ActiveX Control Pad utility with any of its programming products. There are several places to get this utility. You'll find it supplied with your MSDN (Microsoft Developer Network) subscription or download a copy of this at **http://www.microsoft.com/workshop/author/cpad/**. Make sure you look at the rest of the tools in the SiteBuilder Workshop arsenal as well. You'll find all the details at **http://www.microsoft.com/workshop/default.asp**. You'll need to have a copy of this utility before you proceed with the rest of the examples in this chapter, since they all assume you have the ActiveX Control Pad available. (We begin discussing this utility in Chapter 8, so you'll want to read the section in Chapter 8 entitled "Where Does ActiveX Fit In?" if you haven't done so already.)

Listing 9-1 shows a fairly simple JavaScript (and associated HTML) that allows us to display the order form and automatically calculate the amount that the user owes. Take a close look at the listing and you'll see a tag or two that you haven't seen before, along with some unique uses for ones you've already seen. Figure 9-3 shows what this form looks like. Notice that the table is in full view this time. This particular form doesn't include a Submit button yet. The important information here is how to process data contained in a form locally.

Listing 9-1:

```
<HTML>
<HEAD>
<TITLE>Typical Entry Form</TITLE>

<SCRIPT LANGUAGE="JavaScript">
<!--
function CalculateItem1(nAmount)
{
    window.document.DataEntry.Item1Ex.value = nAmount * window.document.
      DataEntry.Item1.value
    CalculateTotals()
}

function CalculateItem2(nAmount)
{
```

```
    window.document.DataEntry.Item2Ex.value = nAmount * window.document.
      DataEntry.Item2.value
    CalculateTotals()
}

function CalculateItem3(nAmount)
{
    window.document.DataEntry.Item3Ex.value = nAmount * window.document.
      DataEntry.Item3.value
     CalculateTotals()
}

function CalculateTotals()
{
    with (window.document.DataEntry)
    {
    // Calculate the item subtotals.
    nTotalItems = parseInt(Item1.value) + parseInt(Item2.value) +
      parseInt(Item3.value)
    nTotalAmount = parseFloat(Item1Ex.value) + parseFloat(Item2Ex.value) +
      parseFloat(Item3Ex.value)

    // Calculate the total amounts.
    nHandling = nTotalItems * 5
    nTax = nTotalAmount * .05
    nTotal = parseFloat(nTotalAmount) + parseFloat(nHandling) + parseFloat(nTax)

    // Store the data.
    Handling.value = nHandling
    Tax.value = nTax
    Total.value = nTotal
    }
}
//-->
</SCRIPT>

</HEAD>
<BODY>
<!Add a heading.->
<CENTER><H1>Sam's Special Order Form</H1><CENTER>
<H3><MARQUEE WIDTH=50% LOOP=INFINITE>
    Get It While It's Hot!  Sam's is known the world over for really HOT items!
    Sams will not be held responsible for stolen items,
    but then you're not really worried about that if you're shopping here.
</MARQUEE></H3>

<!Create a form.->
<FORM NAME="DataEntry">
```

9

```
<!Place a table of order items within the form.  The table will->
<!include four columns: quantity, description, unit price, and->
<!extended price.  The user will only have to type something->
<!in the quantity column.->
<TABLE WIDTH=100% BORDER=1>
<TR>
    <TH WIDTH=30> Quantity </TH>
    <TH> Description </TH>
    <TH WIDTH=75> Unit Price </TH>
    <TH WIDTH=75> Extended Price </TH>
<TR>
    <TD><INPUT TYPE="text" NAME="Item1" VALUE="0" SIZE=3
        ONCHANGE=CalculateItem1(24.99)></TD>
    <TD>Remove It Shaving Mug</TD>
    <TD>$24.99</TD>
    <TD>$<INPUT TYPE="text" NAME="Item1Ex" VALUE="0" SIZE=7></TD>
<TR>
    <TD><INPUT TYPE="text" NAME="Item2" VALUE="0" SIZE=3
        ONCHANGE=CalculateItem2(39.99)></TD>
    <TD>Rampaging Willy Doll</TD>
    <TD>$39.99</TD>
    <TD>$<INPUT TYPE="text" NAME="Item2Ex" VALUE="0" SIZE=7></TD>
<TR>
    <TD><INPUT TYPE="text" NAME="Item3" VALUE="0" SIZE=3
        ONCHANGE=CalculateItem3(19.95)></TD>
    <TD>You Said It! Game</TD>
    <TD>$19.95</TD>
    <TD>$<INPUT TYPE="text" NAME="Item3Ex" VALUE="0" SIZE=7></TD>
<TR>
    <TD><INPUT TYPE="hidden"></TD>
    <TD ALIGN=Right><H3>Shipping and Handling (@ $5.00 / Item)</H3></TD>
    <TD><INPUT TYPE="hidden"></TD>
    <TD>$<INPUT TYPE="text" NAME="Handling" VALUE="0" SIZE=7></TD>
<TR>
    <TD><INPUT TYPE="hidden"></TD>
    <TD ALIGN=Right><H3>Tax (@ 5%)</H3></TD>
    <TD><INPUT TYPE="hidden"></TD>
    <TD>$<INPUT TYPE="text" NAME="Tax" VALUE="0" SIZE=7></TD>
<TR>
    <TD><INPUT TYPE="hidden"></TD>
    <TD ALIGN=RIGHT><STRONG><H3>Total</H3></STRONG></TD>
    <TD><INPUT TYPE="hidden"></TD>
    <TD>$<INPUT TYPE="text" NAME="Total" VALUE="0" SIZE=7></TD>
</TABLE>
</FORM>
</BODY>
</HTML>
```

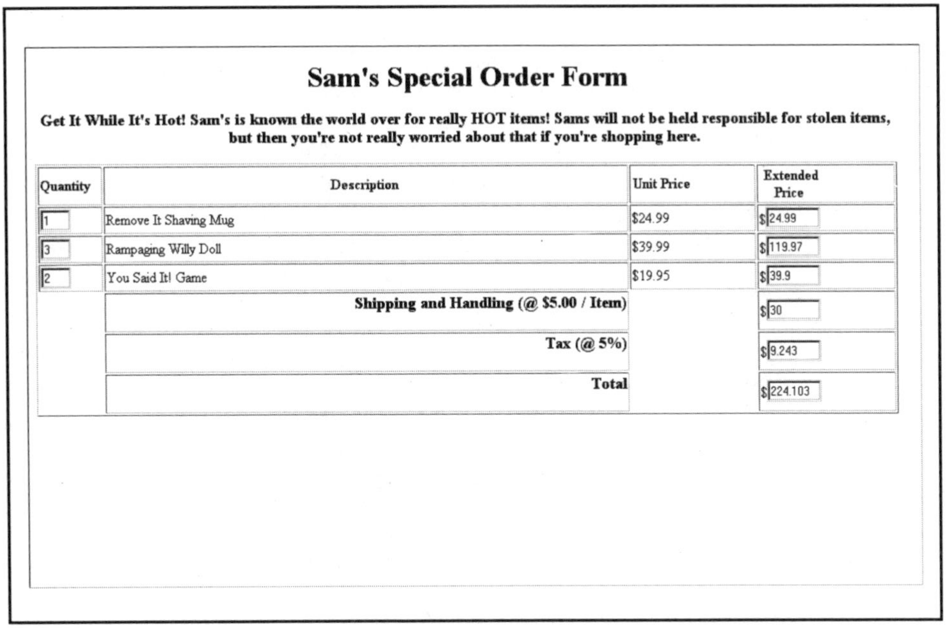

Sam's Special Order Form

Get It While It's Hot! Sam's is known the world over for really HOT items! Sams will not be held responsible for stolen items, but then you're not really worried about that if you're shopping here.

Quantity	Description	Unit Price	Extended Price
1	Remove It Shaving Mug	$24.99	$ 24.99
3	Rampaging Willy Doll	$39.99	$ 119.97
2	You Said It! Game	$19.95	$ 39.9
	Shipping and Handling (@ $5.00 / Item)		$ 30
	Tax (@ 5%)		$ 9.243
	Total		$ 224.103

The order entry form for Sam's automatically calculates the totals for all of the items ordered by the user.

Figure 9-3.

Let's begin by looking at the HTML code in this example. First, it contains a new tag, <MARQUEE>, that allows you to display scrolling text. You can also use this tag to scroll an image—which is what the vast majority of programmers do. The text capabilities you get with this tag are a little limited. Any "fancy" text that you add within the <MARQUEE> tag won't appear onscreen. The text that you start with is the text you keep throughout. This means doing any formatting you want before you actually display the marquee (it also explains why so many programmers prefer to use an image).

CAUTION: The <MARQUEE> tag won't work with Netscape Navigator browsers. What you'll see in a Netscape Navigator browser, at least if you format the tag correctly, is a centered version of the marquee text as shown in Figure 9-3. You'll also want to provide a LOOP attribute whenever you use this tag because some browsers that do support it react strangely if you don't. It's important to get user feedback when you first implement this particular tag, since it is so prone to causing problems with older browsers. A little tweak here or there could make the tag work for everyone's browser that does support it at your site.

9

The next piece of HTML code you'll see provides a typical example of how to use a table. We're using the table to create the order form. Notice the use of the WIDTH attribute in several areas. There are two ways to use it: as a percentage of the total screen or as a specific amount of screen real estate. If you use the percentage method, the amount of space used will remain proportional as the user resizes the display. Also notice that three of the four table headings use a WIDTH attribute. The Description heading gets whatever is left after the other three take what they need. You'll find that this is a very convenient way to present users with an appealing form no matter what their screen resolution or how they resize the browser window.

There are a few changes in the <INPUT> tag as well. Notice that the code uses the SIZE attribute to keep the text input to a specific size. You'll also find a new type of <INPUT> tag. The "hidden" control can get rid of those raised areas in a table. If you look at Figure 9-3 again, you'll notice that the hidden control keeps the Quantity field from retaining a raised appearance when we calculate the totals.

Now let's look at the JavaScript. Notice that we keep all of the functions within an HTML comment. The reason is simple—to prevent older browsers from having problems reading the form. You should also notice that the second part of the HTML comment looks like this: //-->. If you left off the double slash, which is a comment in JavaScript just like it is in Visual C++, then the Netscape Navigator JavaScript interpreter would try to do something with that line—as if it were a line of code. Internet Explorer ignores this comment line, which means you could simply end the line like this: -->. It's important to realize that even a small thing like a comment can make the difference between your code working with just one or a variety of browsers.

The first three functions are pretty simple. All each one does is monitor each of the three Quantity row entries for any change. When a change does occur, it calculates the total amount ordered for that item and then calls a function that recalculates the totals at the bottom of the order form. It may have been possible to combine all three calculations into one function, but this approach is somewhat faster and does reduce the complexity of the code. There isn't even any added function calling overhead.

PORTABILITY: You're going to find that the version of JavaScript for Netscape Navigator is much stricter than the one provided with Internet Explorer. You need to be aware of two extremely important differences between the browsers. Here's a line of JavaScript code from the previous example (CalculateItem1() function in Listing 9-1) that works fine in Internet Explorer: Window.DataEntry.Item1Ex.Value = nAmount * Window.DataEntry.Item1.Value. If you look at the same line in Listing 9-1, you'll see two differences. First, this version of the code isn't case sensitive. Look at the Window object—it's lowercase when you view it in the Script Wizard in ActiveX Control Pad. Netscape, on the other hand, is case sensitive. You'll absolutely have to type "window" in lowercase to make the script work. Also notice that DataEntry directly follows Window in this case. Internet Explorer doesn't require you to use fully qualified object paths; Netscape Navigator does. The fully qualified version of the object path to the DataEntry form is window.document.DataEntry. Make sure you keep these differences in mind as you write your code; otherwise, you may find yourself spending a Sunday looking for that mystery error in your script.

The CalculateTotals() function is the one that you'll want to look at closely, because there are a few tricks that you may not figure out at first when using JavaScript on forms. Notice that you can reduce the amount of typing you need to do by using the with() function. Instead of constantly typing "window.document.DataEntry," you only have to type it once if you use this approach.

9

You may have wondered at the beginning of this section how JavaScript managed to keep the actual type of a variable straight since it's a loosely typed language. In fact, it doesn't do a very good job in some places—which makes it necessary to go through a little extra work. Take a look at the first set of calculations. You'll notice that the three object values are within a parseInt() function call. This call tells JavaScript that you want to convert the string to a number. If you don't use this function, you'll end up concatenating the three strings into one large string instead of adding them as intended. The same note holds true for the next line. In this case, we need to use the parseFloat() function, though, since these are dollar values. It's not the most elegant solution, but it works.

The last thing you should notice is that the CalculateTotals() function uses a lot of intermediate variables. In this case, the intermediate variables help JavaScript keep the types of the variables straight and make the code a little easier to read. There isn't any reason you couldn't get rid of one or two of the intermediate variables if the memory they took was cause for concern.

 TIP: Make sure you use the Tools | Options | Script command to change your language type if you intend to use JavaScript instead of VBScript with the ActiveX Control Pad. The current version tends to lose this setting after each session, and reversing any changes made by Script Wizard can become time consuming.

Working with ActiveX Controls

Believe it or not, you have just about everything you need to create some really astounding Web pages using a combination of scripts, HTML, and ActiveX controls. The only thing you need to do now is put together everything you've learned so far and add just a tad more information to it.

As with the previous section, we're going to look at an example using JavaScript. The difference is that this time we'll put everything together along with objects. The example is purposely simple because we'll explore more complex avenues throughout the rest of the book. It's very important to get the basics down for now.

In this section, we'll look at one of the ways you can use ActiveX Control Pad to make things easier (though it may seem more complicated at first). We'll create a semifunctional form using all ActiveX controls (no more <INPUT> tags for now). This entire section assumes that you're using ActiveX Control Pad. However, it also contains all of the required source code so that you could potentially create it using other methods. The first thing you'll need to do is create another new HTML page and an HTML layout using ActiveX Control Pad. The New button will allow you to create either document.

Save the empty HTML layout. Use the Edit | Insert HTML Layout command to insert the layout into your HTML page. Now add a heading that explains what this document is all about. The HTML page itself is finished at this point—you won't do anything more with it in this example. Listing 9-2 shows what your HTML page code will probably look like.

NOTE: This example shows an Internet Explorer-only version of the Web page. You'd need to use a plug-in like NCompass ScriptActive to make the page work with Netscape Navigator. We'll look at this process later in the book. For right now, the Internet Explorer-only orientation will help keep the code simple so that you can see exactly how things work.

Listing 9-2:

```
<HTML>
<HEAD>
<TITLE>Using ActiveX Control with JavaScript and HTML Layout</TITLE>
</HEAD>
<BODY>

<!-Add a heading->
<CENTER><H1>Using JavaScript with ActiveX Controls on an HTML Layout</H1>

<!-Insert our layout->
<OBJECT CLASSID="CLSID:812AE312-8B8E-11CF-93C8-00AA00C08FDF"
    ID="Layout1_alx" STYLE="LEFT:0;TOP:0">
    <PARAM NAME="ALXPATH" REF VALUE="Layout1.alx">
</OBJECT>

</BODY>
</HTML>
```

9

Now that we've gotten the easy part out of the way, let's start looking at the HTML layout. Figure 9-4 shows the set of ActiveX controls used for this example. All you need to do is click on a control in the Toolbox, and then drop it onto the canvas. (ActiveX Control Pad also allows you to use a drag-and-drop operation to add controls to the canvas if you prefer that method.) Once the control is placed on the canvas, you can drag it to wherever it's needed, and then resize it to match other controls in the same area. A functional layout would differ from the one shown in Figure 9-4, but this one is designed to show you specific features for using ActiveX controls and JavaScript together. Notice that all the controls are ActiveX controls taken from the Toolbox.

It's time to make this example functional. Like VBScript, JavaScript requires that you perform some special function name formatting before you attach a function to a button or other control. There's also an easy way to come up with the name. In this case, though, we'll use Script Wizard to get it for us.

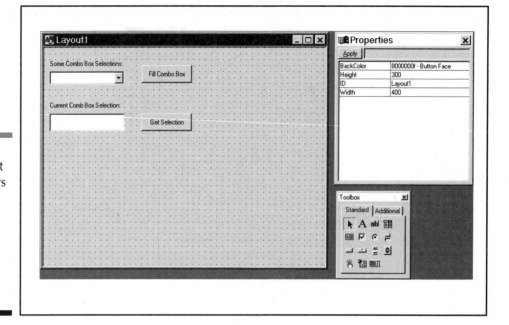

Using an
HTML Layout
control allows
for precise
placement
of ActiveX
controls
on your
Web page.

Figure 9-4.

Open Script Wizard using the Tools | Script Wizard command. Select the Click event for one of the pushbuttons. At the bottom of the Script Wizard dialog, you'll see List View and Code View radio buttons. Click on the Code View radio button and you'll see the bottom of the dialog change, as shown in Figure 9-5. Look at the gray bar in the lower third of the dialog—notice that it now shows you precisely how to format your function call for JavaScript. If you had selected VBScript in place of JavaScript as your language of choice, the dialog would show the VBScript version of the procedure call.

Now it's time to add some JavaScript to make our controls functional. Close Script Wizard (if you haven't already). Right-click on the layout and select View Source Code from the context menu. ActiveX Control Pad may ask you to save the layout first; do so if it does. What you'll see next is a Notepad or Wordpad (depending on how large your layout is) text file. Don't disturb the <OBJECT> tags already in place. Add the script code shown in Listing 9-3. (The listing also shows the <OBJECT> tags, should you wish to create this file

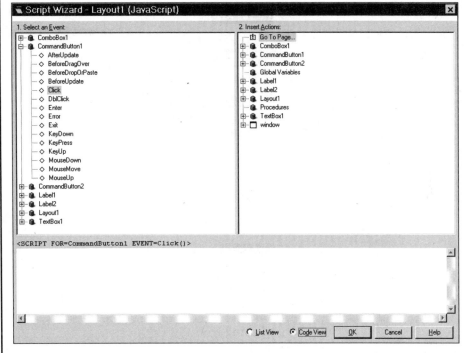

Script Wizard will help you figure out the required procedure or function names for accessing an object.

Figure 9-5.

9

by hand.) Figure 9-6 on page 320 shows how the combination of HTML, scripts, and layout page look in a browser.

Listing 9-3:

```
<!-This script fills the combo box with data.->
<SCRIPT FOR="CommandButton1" EVENT="Click()">
    for (nCount = 1; nCount < ComboBox1.ListRows; nCount++)
        {
        ComboBox1.AddItem("Item " + nCount)
        }
    ComboBox1.ListIndex = 0
</SCRIPT>

<!-This script retrieves the current combo box value.->
<SCRIPT FOR="CommandButton2" EVENT="Click()">
```

```
     TextBox1.Text = ComboBox1.Text
</SCRIPT>
<!-All of these objects are machine created, don't touch.->
<DIV ID="Layout1" STYLE="LAYOUT:FIXED;WIDTH:400pt;HEIGHT:300pt;">
    <OBJECT ID="Label1"
     CLASSID="CLSID:978C9E23-D4B0-11CE-BF2D-00AA003F40D0"
     CODEBASE="http://aux/controls"
STYLE="TOP:17pt;LEFT:8pt;WIDTH:124pt;HEIGHT:17pt;ZINDEX:0;">
        <PARAM NAME="Caption" VALUE="Some Combo Box Selections:">
        <PARAM NAME="Size" VALUE="4374;600">
        <PARAM NAME="FontCharSet" VALUE="0">
        <PARAM NAME="FontPitchAndFamily" VALUE="2">
        <PARAM NAME="FontWeight" VALUE="0">
    </OBJECT>
    <OBJECT ID="ComboBox1"
     CLASSID="CLSID:8BD21D30-EC42-11CE-9E0D-00AA006002F3"
     CODEBASE="http://aux/controls"
STYLE="TOP:33pt;LEFT:8pt;WIDTH:107pt;HEIGHT:18pt;TABINDEX:1;ZINDEX:1;">
        <PARAM NAME="VariousPropertyBits" VALUE="746604571">
        <PARAM NAME="DisplayStyle" VALUE="3">
        <PARAM NAME="Size" VALUE="3775;635">
        <PARAM NAME="MatchEntry" VALUE="1">
        <PARAM NAME="ShowDropButtonWhen" VALUE="2">
        <PARAM NAME="FontCharSet" VALUE="0">
        <PARAM NAME="FontPitchAndFamily" VALUE="2">
        <PARAM NAME="FontWeight" VALUE="0">
    </OBJECT>
    <OBJECT ID="CommandButton1"
     CLASSID="CLSID:D7053240-CE69-11CD-A777-00DD01143C57"
     CODEBASE="http://aux/controls"
STYLE="TOP:25pt;LEFT:140pt;WIDTH:72pt;HEIGHT:24pt;TABINDEX:2;ZINDEX:2;">
        <PARAM NAME="Caption" VALUE="Fill Combo Box">
        <PARAM NAME="Size" VALUE="2540;847">
        <PARAM NAME="FontCharSet" VALUE="0">
        <PARAM NAME="FontPitchAndFamily" VALUE="2">
        <PARAM NAME="ParagraphAlign" VALUE="3">
        <PARAM NAME="FontWeight" VALUE="0">
    </OBJECT>
    <OBJECT ID="Label2"
     CLASSID="CLSID:978C9E23-D4B0-11CE-BF2D-00AA003F40D0"
STYLE="TOP:74pt;LEFT:8pt;WIDTH:107pt;HEIGHT:17pt;ZINDEX:3;">
        <PARAM NAME="Caption" VALUE="Current Combo Box Selection:">
```

```
        <PARAM NAME="Size" VALUE="3775;600">
        <PARAM NAME="FontCharSet" VALUE="0">
        <PARAM NAME="FontPitchAndFamily" VALUE="2">
        <PARAM NAME="FontWeight" VALUE="0">
    </OBJECT>
    <OBJECT ID="TextBox1"
     CLASSID="CLSID:8BD21D10-EC42-11CE-9E0D-00AA006002F3"
STYLE="TOP:91pt;LEFT:8pt;WIDTH:107pt;HEIGHT:25pt;TABINDEX:4;ZINDEX:4;">
        <PARAM NAME="VariousPropertyBits" VALUE="746604571">
        <PARAM NAME="Size" VALUE="3775;882">
        <PARAM NAME="FontCharSet" VALUE="0">
        <PARAM NAME="FontPitchAndFamily" VALUE="2">
        <PARAM NAME="FontWeight" VALUE="0">
    </OBJECT>
    <OBJECT ID="CommandButton2"
     CLASSID="CLSID:D7053240-CE69-11CD-A777-00DD01143C57"
STYLE="TOP:91pt;LEFT:140pt;WIDTH:72pt;HEIGHT:24pt;TABINDEX:5;ZINDEX:5;">
        <PARAM NAME="Caption" VALUE="Get Selection">
        <PARAM NAME="Size" VALUE="2540;847">
        <PARAM NAME="FontCharSet" VALUE="0">
        <PARAM NAME="FontPitchAndFamily" VALUE="2">
        <PARAM NAME="ParagraphAlign" VALUE="3">
        <PARAM NAME="FontWeight" VALUE="0">
    </OBJECT>
</DIV>
```

9

The two scripts shown in Listing 9-3 are fairly simple. The first script shows how you would fill a combo box. All you really need to do is use the AddItem method to tell the combo box what you want to add. Once you do fill the combo box, use the ListIndex property to set the default selection. If you don't do this, the user will continue to see a blank combo box, even after you fill it. The list index starts at 0.

One of the problems with using ActiveX objects is that you can't do certain setups until run time. For example, you can't fill a combo box with values until run time (just try doing it with the Properties dialog sometime). The whole idea behind using a scripting language with ActiveX is to give you a margin of flexibility you've never seen before.

There are quite a few ways to figure out what selection the user made. If you need a numeric selection number, you can get it from the ListIndex property.

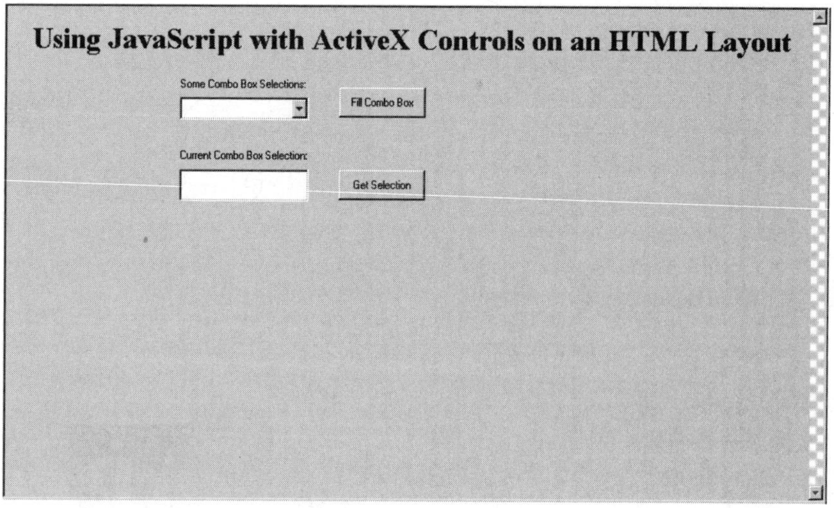

The HTML
layout isn't
visible in the
browser, but
the effects of
using it are.

Figure 9-6.

We needed a string value, so the Text property was the best place to go.
That's what the second script does. It merely copies the value of the
ComboBox1.Text property into the TextBox1.Text property.

CHAPTER 10

Creating an ActiveX Control

ActiveX controls use an OCX extension, just like the OLE controls they're designed to replace.

Some people hate the idea of learning anything new, especially when it looks hard or complicated. OCXs fall into that category for many people. The idea of writing an OLE control fits into the same category as writing device drivers under DOS. Now that Microsoft has changed the name for what amounts to a new version of the OCX to ActiveX, many people will find even more excuses for not trying out this technology.

Since you're already reading this chapter, I have to assume that you're at least mildly interested in the technology behind ActiveX controls. We're not going to deal with anything in this chapter that will dazzle your buddies. In fact, both of the programming examples I've created (while very useful) fall into the category of the mundane. We'll look at one way of creating a new type of pushbutton; an on/off switch.

The reason for choosing this example is easy to figure out: Most people find that working with something familiar eases the burden of learning something new. In addition, this particular coding example is extremely simple to implement. You'll find that learning how it works only takes a modicum of time.

NOTE: The examples in this chapter were developed using Microsoft Visual C++ Version 6.0, but you should be able to use Microsoft Visual C++ Version 5.*x* or 4.*x* without too much trouble. The code shown won't work with Borland C++ or any version of Microsoft C++ older than 4.*x* without at least some modifications. Trying to create a generic example that works with everyone's product didn't prove viable. The examples in this chapter will provide you with valuable hints and tips on developing your own OCXs no matter which programming language product you decide to use.

Complete testing of an ActiveX control means checking that it works in the application, local HTML, and remote HTML environments. You may want to test it with WSH as well.

Once the first version of the example is written, you'll learn several ways to test your new ActiveX control to make sure it's completely safe. ("Safe" in this case means being able to use the control in a production environment, not necessarily checking for security gaps, though you'll definitely want to consider doing so.) Some people may want to rush the control out the door and onto the nearest HTML page or production application program. That really isn't the best way to do things. A three-step approach usually works best for in-house testing with a step added during actual implementation. Since Windows Scripting Host (WSH) offers additional opportunities to use ActiveX controls, you may want to test them in this environment as well. (Given the lack of success for ActiveX controls on the Internet, you may find that you want to restrict their use to the company intranet, WSH add-ons, or as application components.)

This chapter will also spend some time looking at the two APIs that begin to define an ActiveX control versus its counterpart, the OCX. You'll find that the vast majority of your OCXs already work great as ActiveX controls. About the only thing that will hold you back from using them is the way the vendor licensed the control for use. The public nature of the Internet makes it more difficult to use the current set of controls you may have—most vendors allow you to include them with applications you create, not as part of a Web page. There's also a lot of concern these days about the way some controls are constructed—they're just too large to download in a reasonable amount of time. Remember that users won't be willing to download a huge file just so they can see a fancy pushbutton onscreen.

WEB LINK: Appendix A tells you about some third-party ActiveX controls you may want to consider adding to your toolbox. Besides the vendors you'll find there, you may want to take a look at the CaptiveX controls that NCompass is putting together. CaptiveX is a set of six controls that allow you to display information in a variety of ways like a billboard and a light panel. Look at **http://www.ncompasslabs.com/captivex/ index.htm** to get a full demonstration of the CaptiveX controls. Unlike many demonstration sites, you can even use this site with Netscape Navigator if you have the ScriptActive plug-in installed (it's available for download at the demonstration site).

The final section of this chapter is going to examine an offering by RealAudio. I've found that looking at what other people are doing is at least as important as learning the programming techniques we'll explore in this chapter. RealAudio provides a control that allows you to play music or other kinds of sound on the Internet. In fact, you'll find this control used all over the Internet because it meets two criteria that you'll want to know about. First, it's a small control that gets the job done with a minimum of download time. Second, it provides streaming audio, which means that users will get instant feedback. In essence, they won't notice how long it takes to download the entire sound file because the RealAudio control only needs part of the file in place before it can start playing the music (or other sound information).

10

Some Prerequisites to Understanding ActiveX Controls

Before we actually start creating ActiveX controls, there are three topics that you need to think about. The first, of course, is what is ActiveX control? There's more than a little confusion about this topic and it's important to have a definition we can work with. Remember that this is the book definition—you're going to find all kinds of other answers once you start frequenting newsgroups that cater to ActiveX programmers. The second thing we need to talk about is what you're going to get out of an ActiveX control once you create it. Part of this discussion will also look at what the user will expect. Finally, we'll need to look at what differentiates an ActiveX control from any other control that you've used. Most important are the differences between an OCX and an ActiveX control. Each of the following sections will help you explore one of the topics I've just mentioned.

What Is ActiveX?

Here's the simplest definition of ActiveX you'll ever find. ActiveX is an advanced form of OCX (maybe a simpler form of OLE is a better way to look at it). However, this simple definition doesn't even begin to scratch the surface of what you'll actually find under the hood of an ActiveX control. OLE is the user's view of ActiveX. For the programmer, ActiveX is also a set of enabling technologies for the Internet. It provides a method for exchanging information that you didn't have in the past.

NOTE: Microsoft is currently working on a new Internet-specific component technology named COM+. ActiveX was never widely adopted on the Internet, though many intranets use it and ActiveX controls will always be used as application components. There were three reasons for the failure of ActiveX on the Internet: component size, security concerns, and lack of non-Microsoft browser compatibility. With this in mind, you should probably consider ActiveX controls as solutions for your company's internal use and not as an enabling technology for the Internet.

To really appreciate ActiveX as a programmer, you have to look at OLE from the programmer's perspective, and that means looking at OCXs. From the user's perspective, all that an OCX does is exchange data between two applications (or between the operating system and an application). OCXs are a lot more than just data exchange. They include an idea called the Component Object Model (COM). COM is a specification that defines a standard binary interface between object modules. This interface defines a function-calling methodology, standard structure-based data-passing techniques, and even a few standard function calls. Using COM means that it doesn't matter which language you use to write an application module such as an OCX; the interface for that module is the same at the binary level.

NOTE: At the time of this writing, Microsoft was working on WebView, an integration technology between Internet Explorer and Windows 95's system Explorer. This new technology will make Web sites as easy to access as the drives and other resources listed in Explorer right now. You'll also see plain English names in place of the more familiar URLs that you need to know now. The first place you'll see this technology in action is in Windows 98.

So how does COM affect applications you write? The answer is fairly complex because of the number of ways in which COM gets used, not because the technology itself is so overwhelming. When a user places a graphic image object within a container controlled by your application, what do you know about that object? The only thing you really know about it is who created it in the first place. Knowing this information allows you to call on that application for a variety of services, such as displaying the graphic or allowing the user to edit it. In reality, what you're doing is sharing that application's code.

Programmers benefit from using COM as well. When you install an OCX into your programming environment, what have you really accomplished? In most cases, you have a new control that you stick on a form somewhere. You really don't need to know about the control's inner workings. The only important factors are what the control will do for your application and how you interact with it. Again, you're calling a particular module of code installed on your machine using a standard interface—that's what COM is all about.

ActiveX is an extension of this idea. You're still using a standard interface. However, instead of simply calling that code from the local machine environment or over the persistent connection of a LAN/WAN, you'll call it from the Internet. In addition, this new code can take the form of applets or mini-applications.

10

What Will ActiveX Do for You?

ActiveX will do for the Internet what OCXs have done for the desktop. However, you'll find ActiveX controls in places that you hadn't really thought about in the past. For example, NetManage, Inc. plans to create a new e-mail client called Z-Mail Pro. This package supports ActiveX technology in a way that allows users to exchange, create, and view HTML documents directly in the message-viewing window. What this means to users is that they now have the ability to create dynamic Web pages, something that you have to really work at today.

Remote connections will also benefit from the use of ActiveX. For example, Proginet Corporation is currently working on ActiveX technology that will bring mainframe data to the desktop. Its Fusion FTMS (File Transfer Management System) will work with any development language that supports OLE containers, such as Delphi, Visual C++, and PowerBuilder. Essentially, you'll place an ActiveX control on a form, define where to find the data, and then rely on the control to make the connection. No longer will remote access over the Internet require the user to jump through hoops. A special transfer server on the mainframe will complete the package by automating all transfer requests. No longer will an operator have to manually download a needed file to the company's Web site before a client can access it.

Even Microsoft Exchange will benefit from ActiveX. Wang Laboratories, Inc. and other companies are creating new add-ons that mix Exchange and ActiveX together. Wang's product is a client/server imaging add-on. It will allow users to scan, view, annotate, manipulate, or print graphic images no matter where they are located. This same product will include a hierarchical storage management ActiveX control. The two technologies will work together to make graphics easier to access and use in a large company. They'll also make it easier to find a needed graphic—which should ultimately result in a storage savings to the company.

Microsoft itself has issued a whole slew of ActiveX controls. Some of these controls are free for downloading from Microsoft's Internet site (**http://www.microsoft.com**). Examples of these new controls include Animation Player for PowerPoint and Internet Assistant for both Access and Schedule+. The Internet Assistant for Access will create a snapshot of a database table that gets uploaded as a static image. The snapshot automatically updates every time the user accesses the page. The Internet Assistant for Schedule+ will allow you to upload scheduling information to a Web page. Since the data gets updated every time a user accesses the site, you no longer have to worry about compute-at-home employees missing meetings. Finally, the PowerPoint Animation Player will allow you to play a PowerPoint presentation from within any ActiveX-compliant browser.

Finally, if you think ActiveX won't help with security, think again. A lot of new firewall and certificate strategies are making the rounds these days. One of them is Net2000. It's a set of APIs that will allow developers to tie NetWare core services (including directory, security, and licensing) into their applications. You'll be able to tap this API through ActiveX controls over an intranet. How will this help users and developers alike? It means that with the proper programming constructs, a network administrator will be able to track license usage throughout the entire network, even across Internet connections. This is going to become a much bigger issue as more people begin to compute from home rather than the office.

ActiveX Versus OCX Controls

For the most part, ActiveX and OCX controls are totally interchangeable. You'll see ads for ActiveX controls that have nothing to do with the Internet. Look a little closer, and you'll find that those controls probably appeared in an OCX listing sometime in the not-too-distant past. Of course, you'll have to watch these ads carefully. An ActiveX control isn't the same thing as an OCX—even if they do share the same heritage. Remember that an ActiveX control has to be able to work with the Internet.

One major difference between an OCX and an ActiveX control is that ActiveX controls are usually smaller (lighter).

The Internet places some special challenges on the programming environment. For one thing, you don't have the luxury of high-speed loading anymore. The size of an OCX becomes a critical issue when used within the Internet environment. Downloading a 60KB OCX may test a user's patience—trying to download a 200KB OCX will probably result in the user stopping the download altogether. ActiveX controls are small versions of OCXs.

ActiveX controls also suffer from various machine-specific requirements. When you install an OCX on your machine, the installation program can check the machine and make allowances as needed. The same can't be said about an ActiveX control. You can't assume anything about the client machine at all. It could be anything from a new Pentium to yesterday's 80386. (If your ActiveX control does have some kind of platform limitation, you'll have to either find some way to work around it or make certain that everyone who uses it knows about the limitation.)

10

You'll also need to deal with some situations that an OCX programmer would never have to think about. For one thing, what happens if the browser doesn't support ActiveX at all? The current method of dealing with this is that the browser would simply ignore any HTML tags that it doesn't know how to work with. Dealing with a browser that is non-ActiveX-compliant is easy in this case—just leave a message telling users that their browser won't work with the current page, and direct the users to an alternative.

MFC Versus ATL-Based Controls

One of the ways that Visual C++ shows its robust development environment compared to other programming languages is the inclusion of two ways to create ActiveX controls: MFC or ATL (Active Template Library). Unfortunately, this flexibility can cause some problems that other developers don't have to face. For one thing, how do you determine which type of control to create? Some developers have rendered the question moot by using the same technology for all their controls, but following this route means that you haven't really explored and used Visual C++ to its full potential.

There really isn't any way to say definitively that one method of creating a control is better in a given situation. What you really need to do is define what you expect the control to do, what you're willing to invest to get that functionality, and your level of expertise. Obviously, there are situations where one control creation method is preferred over another, as the two methods do have distinctly different advantages and disadvantages. To give you some idea of what you need to consider when looking at an ATL ActiveX control versus one created using MFC, read through the following list. What you'll find is ideas that you can use to help you make a decision on which route is best for you.

◆ *Development speed*   Using the MFC ActiveX Control Wizard is the fastest method to create a control. The Wizard takes care of most of the interface details so that what you end up with is a skeleton that's ready for some control logic. In fact, it usually takes the developers twice as long to use the ATL method for creating a control. Obviously, your results will vary depending on factors like control complexity and your programming experience.

◆ *Maintenance*   Both MFC and ATL offer features that make maintenance of your code a lot easier than writing the code from scratch. However, there are some things to consider when it comes to making maintenance-related changes to an original control like bug fixes. An ATL control normally contains less "boiler plate" code generated by a wizard. Since you're more familiar with the code that you're working with, changes that you have to make are much faster and easier. On the other hand, Microsoft maintains all of the MFC libraries that you'll use. This means that many bug fixes and other kinds of updates get made automatically for you with a simple recompile of the code. Which choice is better in this case? It's a really hard call because there isn't any way to determine exactly what kinds of maintenance changes you'll need to make to your control in the future.

There are two ways to create ActiveX controls using Visual C++: ATL and MFC.

◆ *Control size* If you want to create the smallest possible ActiveX control, then go the ATL route. ATL gives you full control over every aspect of the control and makes it feasible for you to hand-tune every control element without getting bogged down in MFC-specific code. Not only are MFC-based controls larger, but remember that clients may also have to download the MFC libraries before they can use the control, which is a significant amount of code.

◆ *Learning curve* ATL controls are much harder to create than MFC controls, simply because you have to consider more things like interfaces. In most cases it pays to create your first couple of controls using the MFC ActiveX Control Wizard so that you can learn the ropes of creating the control logic.

TIP: If you're used to the Visual C++ Version 5.0 ATL support, try the new ATL COM AppWizard in Version 6.0. The new ATL COM AppWizard helps you create controls much faster than the manual techniques of the past. However, using the MFC ActiveX Control Wizard is still far faster than using the ATL COM AppWizard to create a control.

◆ *Compatibility* By definition, MFC-based ActiveX controls require clients to have the MFC libraries installed on their machine. However, there are more than a few versions of those libraries floating around, and they aren't all compatible. What happens when users download your control and the associated libraries, then can't use an important application because the new libraries are incompatible with their application? Since the MFC libraries are stored in the SYSTEM directory, a client machine can have only one version. That's where the compatibility problems come into play.

◆ *Ease of use* The MFC ActiveX Control Wizard tends to throw everything but the kitchen sink into a control because it assumes nothing about your ability to write control code. What this means is that you end up with a wealth of interfaces you may not need or use. All of this wasted functionality bloats the size of the control and makes it harder to use.

◆ *Ease of code modification* Creating an MFC-based control is very easy the first time around. Since the Wizard adds much of the code for you, application development goes quickly—you only have to worry about the details that make your control unique. MFC is a good choice if you're creating a control that will require few modifications once you get it working. However, what happens when you decide to update that

10

control? Now you have source files that may contain a good deal of code that wasn't written by a staff programmer and that may require additional time to research and understand. If you're planning on modifying your code often, then ATL may be the better choice since it allows the programmer to maintain better contact with exactly what is happening with the programmer generated code in the control.

A Basic MFC-Based Pushbutton Programming Example

The pushbutton is the one control that every application uses and is the best place to start looking at the potential for custom controls.

I can't think of a single application on my machine that doesn't rely on a pushbutton or two. In fact, the pushbutton is one of the very few Windows controls that you could say every application has. Even an application that displays information in a simple dialog usually relies on an OK button to close the dialog once you're done with it. Suffice it to say then that the pushbutton (or command button, as some programming environments refer to it) is the one control on your machine that has to work well. It's also the control that absolutely has to provide all of the features you need and the one that programmers change the most.

With this much emphasis on the utility of one control by programmers, it didn't take me too long to figure out which control to show you how to modify in this section of the chapter. I also wanted to add a new feature, though, that you may not find very often in a pushbutton, something that everyone will need eventually. That's why I chose an on/off button as the basis for the control in this chapter—just about everyone needs to turn something on or off during the course of programming an application. It's nice having that feature built right into the control you're using. I also added a few other bells and whistles to the default pushbutton that you get with Visual C++. Even though my pushbutton may not contain all of the fancy features of commercially available controls, it'll get you started creating your own custom controls.

Defining a Project

We looked at some of the criteria for developing an ActiveX control from the user's and the programmer's perspective earlier in this chapter. Now it's time to take a more in-depth look from the programmer's perspective. Before you start looking at the first programming example, let's take a quick look at some of the criteria you need to keep in mind when defining a specific ActiveX control. The following advice should provide some insights into the special constraints you'll have to observe for ActiveX controls.

TIP: Although you can create an ActiveX control using just about any compiler that will produce OCXs, you'll find that using Microsoft's Visual C++ (Version 4.2 or higher) product will save you considerable time. You'll see in this chapter that some extra steps are needed to make an OCX work properly as an ActiveX control even in the best of circumstances. Using an older compiler means that you'll need to rely on DOS command line tools to perform the extra steps. The newer 4.2 and 5.*x* versions of the Microsoft Visual C++ compiler include these tools as part of the package and automate their use.

◆ *Keep code small* A good rule of thumb is to keep your ActiveX controls to 40KB or less. The average user won't want to download a huge control that animates some graphic on the page. If at all possible, break a large component into smaller, functional pieces.

TIP: You can also reduce the download size of a control by compressing it into a CAB file. We look at the process for doing this in Chapter 8.

◆ *Use a minimum of persistent data* Some OCXs require a huge amount of persistent data to accomplish their task. For example, you might stick a spreadsheet control on a form and not think twice about the amount of persistent data that it contains. ActiveX controls don't have this luxury since you can't assume much about the client machine. Persistent data not only increases load time and memory requirements; it also boosts the size of the control itself.

◆ *Keep bells and whistles to a minimum* Bells and whistles can really make an onscreen presentation sparkle. When you're writing an OCX for local machine use, a few extra features don't really create any problems. In fact, most programmers would be surprised if you didn't include them. Transfer time is a really big issue on the Internet. Every time you add graphics that you really don't need to a control, or some special sound effect, you're increasing load time and decreasing the value of your control. An ActiveX control can't even assume that some special effects will work correctly on the client machine (it may not include a sound board, for example).

10

◆ *Single function is key* One of the original purposes for libraries was to store a large number of function calls in a precompiled and easily accessible form. DLLs, one of the predecessors to OCXs, exist for this very reason. You'll find that many OCXs on the market, like DLLs, contain more than one object, such as a pushbutton. In fact, some of them contain a whole family of objects. This strategy works fine on the desktop but not on the Internet. Make sure you maintain one object in each ActiveX control. Doing so modularizes the controls and ensures that users don't download any more functionality than they absolutely need.

NOTE: We're going to talk about objects quite a bit in this chapter. Every object in this chapter is a Windows object (or a special form of it used by COM). Some C++ programmers might get the idea that a Windows object is precisely the same as a C++ object. Since COM uses a special form of Windows object, these same programmers might think that they won't run into any problems using any C++ object on hand to write an OCX. Nothing could be further from the truth. Although you can use a C++ object to create a Windows object, there are limitations. There isn't space in this chapter to get into a full discourse on the intricacies of objects in C++ programming—that's a topic that some authors take an entire chapter (or two) to cover as an overview—but it's important to know that there are limits to what you can and should do when writing an OCX using C++. Following the examples in this chapter is the best way to get started writing OCXs without running into problems.

◆ *Test, test, test* It isn't enough to test an ActiveX control locally or on the network. You've got to test in a variety of situations using different connections. We'll eventually look at three levels of local testing and one level of Internet-specific testing in this chapter. You may want to add more levels than this. The bottom line is that you can't test an ActiveX control too much. (It's important that you test before releasing the control, but invariably you'll also have to do some bug hunting after the fact. Keeping accurate problem logs is essential in making your ActiveX control work properly.)

Writing the Code

It's time to take a look at a simple coding example. This chapter uses Microsoft Visual C++ Version 6.0 (though you can also use Versions 4.2 and above), as mentioned earlier. Let's begin with a new C++ project. However, unlike other projects you may have created, you'll want to start with the MFC ActiveX Control Wizard to create your workspace. To do that, use the File | New command to display the New dialog. Select the Projects tab, and you'll see a dialog like this one.

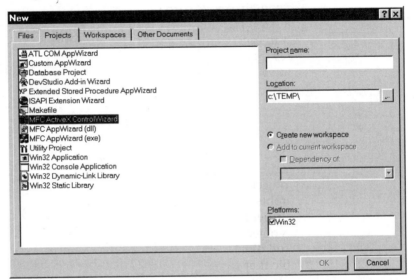

Notice the MFC ActiveX Control Wizard entry in this dialog. That's the one you'll need to start the project. The wizard provides you with an OCX framework that you can build on to create the final version of this example.

NOTE: I used the new Microsoft Developer Studio setup for this example. All the screen shots you see will reflect the Windows 95 orientation of that setup. If you choose to use the older interface, your screen shots won't match mine at all. There may be subtle differences even if you do use the Developer Studio interface due to the variety of configuration options this product provides.

10

To get the project started, you'll have to type something in the Project Name field. This example uses OCXExmpl for a project name. You'll also need to click on the MFC ActiveX Control Wizard entry in the project list, and then click on OK. Microsoft Visual C++ automatically selects the Win32 option for you. It also creates a project directory.

What you'll see next are two dialogs of MFC ActiveX Control Wizard screens. I accepted the defaults on both screens except for the subclass entry on the second one. You'll want to select the BUTTON class here if you want to create an example like this one. Otherwise, look through the list of available classes to determine what you want to use as a basis for your control. Notice that Visual C++ allows you to create your own basic class.

Once you click on the Finish button in the second wizard screen, you'll see a New Project Information dialog like the one shown here.

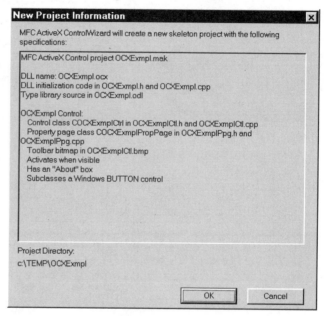

You'll want to look through the list of features presented here just to make certain the project contains everything you need. After you verify that the project setup is correct, click on OK to get the project started. Visual C++ will churn your disk for a few moments, and then you'll see the project framework.

Modifying the Default About Box

Now that you have a framework put together, it's time to start filling it out. I usually start by tackling the easy stuff first (who doesn't?). The first thing you'll want to do is modify the About box. Yes, Visual C++ creates one of those for you automatically—all you need to do is customize it. Getting access to the About box is easy. Just use the View | Resource Symbols command to display the Resource Symbols dialog shown here.

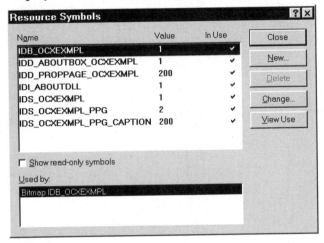

You'll want to select the IDD_ABOUTBOX_OCXEXMPL entry, and then click on the View Use button to display it. Figure 10-1 shows one way to modify the About box for this example. You'll probably want to include additional copyright and company information in your About box. Notice the variety of tools that Microsoft provides for the dialog box. One of them is the custom control button. You can stick another OCX within the About box or any other dialogs you create.

TIP: Right-click on a control, and then choose Properties from the context menu to make its Properties dialog appear. You alter the text for a static text control by changing the Caption property on the General page of the Properties dialog. Right-clicking on most objects in Visual C++ will display a context menu—most of which have a Properties option. The whole purpose of right-clicking on objects in Visual C++ is to see what you can do with a particular object. Remember that objects aren't limited to controls; they also include lines of code, the toolbar, and even the various windows.

10

The latest version of Visual C++ may require you to take an additional step for the About box that you didn't have to do in the past. You may need to create a class for the About box—previous versions of Visual C++ just assumed that you wanted to do so. Double-click on the About box and you'll

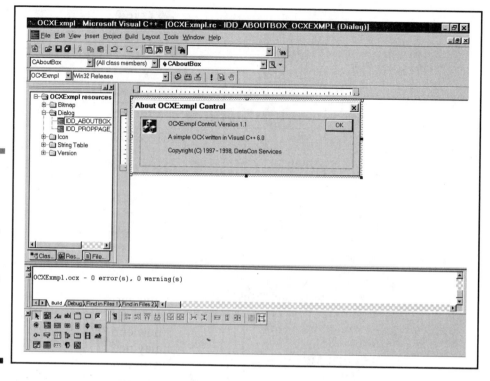

The dialog
editor looks
like the one
provided with
Visual Basic—
the difference
is that you'll
have to access
it separately
from the main
editor screen.
Figure 10-1.

see an Adding a Class dialog like the one shown here (if you don't see this
dialog, you'll know that there's already a class assigned to the About box and
you don't need to go any further).

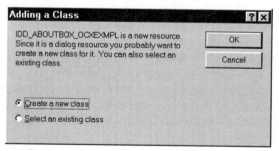

Make sure the Create a New Class option is selected, and then click OK.
Visual C++ will display a New Class dialog like the one shown here.

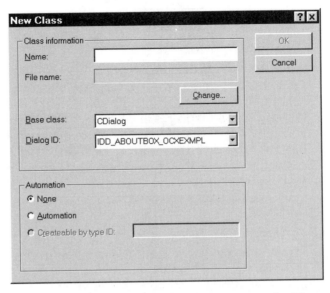

We'll use **CAboutBox** as the class name; just type it in the Name field. Everything else needed for this example is already added for you. Click OK to create the required class. You'll see a new entry in the MFC ClassWizard dialog like the one shown here (you may need to select the ClassInfo tab before your screen will match the illustration).

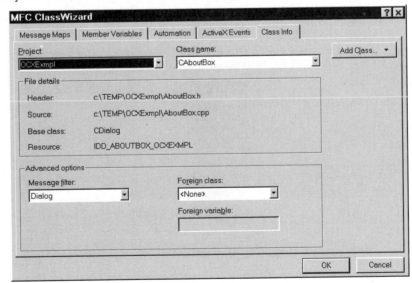

10

This dialog tells you about the new class. For example, the Header and Source entries tell you the location of the files associated with this class. You'll also see that IDD_ABOUTBOX_OCXEXMPL is the dialog resource associated with this class. Go ahead and click OK to close the MFC ClassWizard dialog.

Adding Properties and Events

Visual C++
assumes very
little about the
control you
want to create,
not even which
properties and
methods you
want to
make visible.

Customizing the About box is fun, but let's get down to the business of creating an OCX. The first thing you'll want to do is make some of the button control properties and events visible to someone using the OCX. For example, it might be nice to be able to detect when the user clicked the button. You'll definitely want to be able to change default properties like the caption displayed on the button front. There aren't very many properties visible when you first create a button. To make these various elements visible, you'll need to use the Class Wizard. Use the View | ClassWizard command to display the MFC ClassWizard dialog. Choose the Automation page, and then select OCXExmplCtrl in the Class Name field.

Stock
properties are
part of the base
class, while
custom
properties are
created for the
subclassed
control.

We'll use two different kinds of properties in this example—Microsoft provides access to a lot more. The first type is a stock property. You'll find that things like the Caption property that we all take for granted aren't visible when you first create an OCX. A *stock property* (denoted by an S in Figure 10-2) is one that the parent class supports by default. The second type is a custom property (denoted by a C in Figure 10-2). A *custom property* is one that you've added to a particular class when you subclass it. One of them is the OnOff property that we'll use to create an OnOff control. We'll look at the process for doing that later in this chapter. Figure 10-2 shows a complete list of all the properties that we'll create in this example.

Creating a new property is fairly simple. All you need to do is click on the Add Property button to display the Add Property dialog shown here.

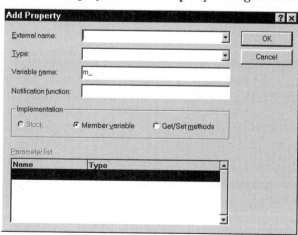

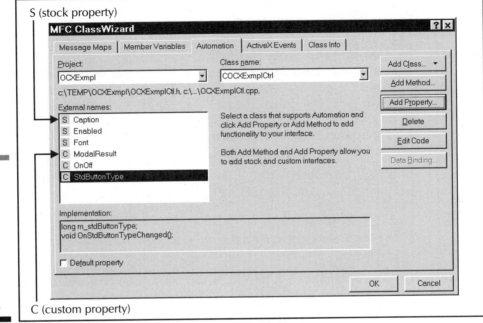

S (stock property)

C (custom property)

The MFC ClassWizard allows you to make properties and events visible to the OCX user.

Figure 10-2.

The Add Property dialog has some important features that you might not see at first. The External Name combo box contains a complete list of the default properties for the base class that you selected when creating the OCX. In this case, you'll see things like the Caption property. To create a stock property, just select one of the items from this list and click on OK. Visual C++ will take care of the details for you in this case. Go ahead and create all of the stock properties for this example program now (refer to Figure 10-2).

We'll also need three custom properties: ModalResult, OnOff, and StdButtonType. To create these properties, type the names I've just mentioned into the External Name field. You'll need to select a data type in the Type field as well. In this case the ModalResult and StdButtonType properties are the long type, while OnOff is a BOOL. (At this point you may want to close and then reopen the MFC ClassWizard dialog—there are some situations where your property selections won't get recorded otherwise.)

All of the events we'll use in this example are stock—they come as part of the button base class. All you need to do is click on the ActiveX Events page to display the dialog shown in Figure 10-3. Adding a stock event is about the same as adding a stock property. Just click on the Add Event button to display the Add Event dialog. Select a stock name from the External Name combo box, and click on OK to complete the process. Figure 10-3 shows all of the stock events you'll need for this example.

Defining the Property Page

Now it's time to add some functionality to the property page. You access it the same way that you did the About box, using the View | Resource Symbols command. In this case, you'll select the IDD_PROPPAGE_OCXEXMPL entry in the Resource Symbols dialog. The property page is used for a wide variety of purposes—most of them configuration oriented.

There are two standard sizes of property page supported by Visual C++. The small size, which is the default for an OCX, is 250×62. This is going to be too small for our purposes, so we'll need to resize it to the large property page size of 250×110. Make sure you use one size or the other when creating a control. Nothing bad will happen if you don't use a standard size, but users get warning messages saying that you didn't use a standard-sized property page.

What we'll do now is add a method for defining standard button types to the page, as shown in Figure 10-4. These are radio buttons. You'll need ten of them. (Don't worry about how to configure them just now; I'll tell you how in the paragraphs that follow.) Each radio button should have a different ID

The ActiveX Events page shows all the stock events added to our OCX programming example.

Figure 10-3.

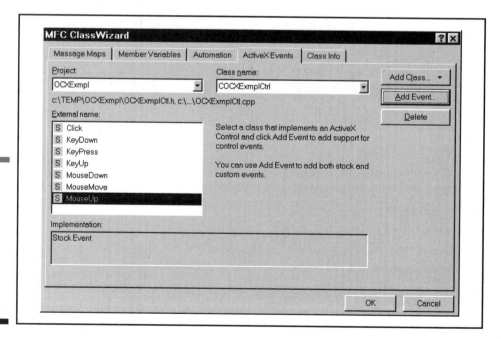

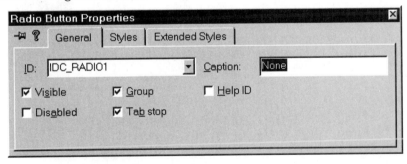

The Property Page dialog allows the user to create standard button types in addition to the on/off button.

Figure 10-4.

so that you can detect which one the user clicks (see the ID field on the General page of the Radio Button Properties dialog).

Now that you have ten standard radio buttons sitting on your property page, it's time to do something with them. Right-click on a radio button, and then choose Properties from the context menu to display the Radio Button Properties dialog shown here.

You'll need to make a few subtle changes to your radio buttons before they look like the ones in Figure 10-4. First, select the Styles page of the Radio Button Properties dialog, and select the push-like checkbox for each button. You'll also need to place the radio buttons into a group so that the current selection gets deselected when you choose a new button. To do that, check the Group and the Tab stop checkboxes on the first radio button in the group that uses the default ID of IDC_RADIO1. Check only the Tab stop checkbox for all of the other radio buttons, or you'll end up with ten groups of one button instead of one group of ten buttons. Visual C++ starts with the first button it sees that has the Group checkbox selected as the starting point for

10

the group. The group continues with each radio button in tab order until Visual C++ sees the next one with the Group checkbox selected.

TIP: Most Microsoft products prefer that you use a property page size of 250×62 or 250×110 dialog units. However, you can use any size you need. When you try to access the property page, the only thing you'll see is a message stating that you used a nonstandard size. Simply clear the message, and the property page will appear as usual.

We have to do one more thing with the radio buttons in this dialog. To create an OLE connection between the radio buttons and the OCX control, you have to assign their output to an OLE property. CTRL-double-click on the first radio button (None) in the group to display the Add Member Variable dialog shown here.

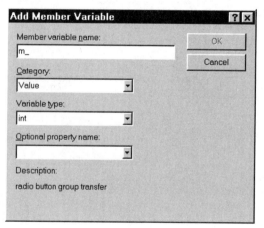

TIP: You can also access this dialog by pressing CTRL-W to display the MFC ClassWizard dialog, selecting the Member Variables page, and then clicking the Add Variable button.

The entries you make here are crucial, because Visual C++ doesn't check them for errors and there isn't any way to select them from a list. In the Member Variable Name field, type **m_stdButtonType**. That's the internal name for one of the custom properties that we created earlier. Leave the Category and

Variable Type fields alone. Type **StdButtonType** in the Optional Property Name field. This is the entry that links the property page to your OCX control. Remember that C++ is case-sensitive—capitalization is important.

TIP: The drop-down list box for the Optional Property Name field normally contains a complete list of the properties inherited from the base class of your control.

Adding Some Code

Up to this point we haven't added a single line of code to our application. That's because we've been building a framework for the code. Now it's time to start adding code to the OCX. The first thing we want to do is add some code so our control can exchange data with the client it's being used with. For example, when you see a properties dialog for a control, you normally want to see the current values of those properties. Likewise, when you change a property value, you want to be sure that the actual control state will change. Listing 10-1 shows the code you'll need to add.

Listing 10-1:

```
void COCXExmplCtrl::DoPropExchange(CPropExchange* pPX)
{

    // Default actions on the part of the Class Wizard.
    ExchangeVersion(pPX, MAKELONG(_wVerMinor, _wVerMajor));
    COleControl::DoPropExchange(pPX);

    // Make all of our properties persistent.
    PX_Bool(pPX, "OnOff", m_onOff, FALSE);
    PX_Long(pPX, "ModalResult", m_modalResult, mrNone);
    PX_Long(pPX, "StdButtonType", m_stdButtonType, 0);

}
```

10

Now let's say that you don't like the default size of the button and you want it to display a specific caption when the user inserts it onto a Web page or other layout. You can change both properties in the OnReset() function. Listing 10-2 shows the code you'll need to change. Notice that we use the COleControl class functions to make the required changes. The SetText() function allows us to change the caption of the button. Every time the user inserts this control, the caption of "Button" will appear. The SetControlSize() function allows you to set the control size of 75×25 pixels. Obviously, you

can set these properties any way you wish and can even select one of the
default buttons if you so choose.

Listing 10-2:

```
void COCXExmplCtrl::OnResetState()
{
    COleControl::OnResetState();   // Resets defaults found in DoPropExchange

    //Modify the Microsoft control to match custom size settings.
    COleControl::SetText("Button");
    COleControl::SetControlSize(75, 25);
}
```

Now that we have a method for exchanging information and we've set the
control up the way we want it to look, it's time to implement the three
custom properties that we created. That's right, every time you create a
custom property, you'll need to define some code to make that property do
something. Otherwise, it'll just sit there and do nothing at all. Listing 10-3
shows the code you'll need to add to implement the ModalResult, OnOff, and
StdButtonType properties. I'll explain the inner workings of this code in the
next section. For right now, all you need to know is that it implements the
properties we created.

Listing 10-3:

```
void COCXExmplCtrl::OnModalResultChanged()
{
    // We don't need to do anything here except set the modified flag.
    SetModifiedFlag();
}

void COCXExmplCtrl::OnOnOffChanged()
{
    //If the programmer set the OnOff property true, take appropriate action.
    if (m_onOff)
    {
        COleControl::SetText("On");         //Change the caption.
        m_SetOn = TRUE;                     //Set an internal caption flag.
        m_modalResult = mrOn;               //Set the modal result value.
    }
    else
    {
        COleControl::SetText("Button");     //Restore default caption.
        m_SetOn = FALSE;                    //Turn our caption flag off.
        m_modalResult = mrNone;             //Use the default modal result.
    }
```

```
    //Perform the default action.
    SetModifiedFlag();
}

void COCXExmplCtrl::OnStdButtonTypeChanged()
{
    // Change the modal result and button caption to match the user selection.
    switch (m_stdButtonType)
    {
    case 0:
        m_modalResult = mrNone;
        COleControl::SetText("Button");
        break;
    case 1:
        m_modalResult = mrOK;
        COleControl::SetText("OK");
        break;
    case 2:
        m_modalResult = mrCancel;
        COleControl::SetText("Cancel");
        break;
    case 3:
        m_modalResult = mrAbort;
        COleControl::SetText("Abort");
        break;
    case 4:
        m_modalResult = mrRetry;
        COleControl::SetText("Retry");
        break;
    case 5:
        m_modalResult = mrIgnore;
        COleControl::SetText("Ignore");
        break;
    case 6:
        m_modalResult = mrYes;
        COleControl::SetText("Yes");
        break;
    case 7:
        m_modalResult = mrNo;
        COleControl::SetText("No");
        break;
    case 8:
        m_modalResult = mrOn;
        COleControl::SetText("On");
        break;
```

10

```
case 9:
    m_modalResult = mrOff;
    COleControl::SetText("Off");
}

//Set the OnOff property to false since the user selected another type.
m_onOff = FALSE;

//Set the modified flag.
SetModifiedFlag();
}
```

We need to do one last bit of coding in the OCXEXMPLCtl.cpp file. What
happens when a user clicks the button? If he or she is using one of the
standard button types, the OnOff control will return a standard modal result
value. However, the OnOff control also has a special behavior. If you set the
OnOff property to True, the button should switch between on and off as the
user clicks it. We need to add some special event code to handle this
situation. Use the View | ClassWizard command to display the MFC
ClassWizard dialog. Choose the Message Maps page, and then choose the
COCXExmplCtrl entry in the Class Name field. Highlight the OnClick entry
in the Messages list. Click Add Function to add a function skeleton to the
class. Your MFC ClassWizard dialog should look like the one shown here.

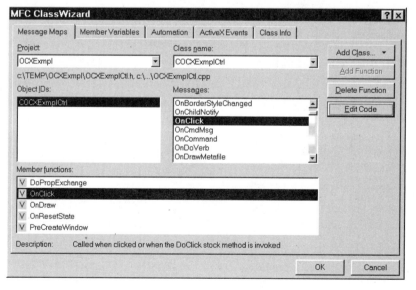

Now it's time to add some code to the OnClick() function. Click the Edit Code button, and Visual C++ will take you to the new function. Listing 10-4 shows the code you'll need to add.

Listing 10-4:

```
void COCXExmplCtrl::OnClick(USHORT iButton)
{
    // See if the OnOff flag is set.  If so, change the caption and internal
    // caption flag.  The effect you should see from this code is a toggling
    // of the caption text.
    if (m_onOff)
    {
        if (m_SetOn)
        {
            COleControl::SetText("Off");
            m_SetOn = FALSE;
            m_modalResult = mrOff;
        }
        else
        {
            COleControl::SetText("On");
            m_SetOn = TRUE;
            m_modalResult = mrOn;
        }
    }

    // Call the default OnClick processing.
    COleControl::OnClick(iButton);
}
```

10

Now that we've taken care of the function-coding part of the picture, we do need to add two support items to the OCXEXMPLCtl.h file. The first is an enumerated type. Its only purpose is to make the source code easier to read. Each entry corresponds to a standard button type. The second item is a special variable. If you'll notice in the code, I keep referring to an m_SetOn member variable, but this variable isn't part of the class right now. Listing 10-5 shows how you'll need to add the enumerated type and special variable to your header file—right between the Event maps and the Dispatch and event IDs entry.

Listing 10-5:
```
// Event maps
//{{AFX_EVENT(COCXExmplCtrl)
//}}AFX_EVENT
DECLARE_EVENT_MAP()
```

```
// Create a new enumerated type for the modal result.
    typedef enum
    {
        mrNone = -1L,
        mrOK = 1L,
        mrCancel = 2L,
        mrAbort = 3L,
        mrRetry = 4L,
        mrIgnore = 5L,
        mrYes = 6L,
        mrNo = 7L,
        mrOn = 8L,
        mrOff = 9L,
    }MODALTYPE;

// Special On/Off state variable.
    BOOL     m_SetOn;

// Dispatch and event IDs
public:
    enum {
    //{{AFX_DISP_ID(COCXExmplCtrl)
    dispidModalResult = 1L,
    dispidOnOff = 2L,
    dispidStdButtonType = 3L,
    //}}AFX_DISP_ID
    };
```

Breaking the Code into Pieces

Your initial reaction to all this code might be one of sheer terror, but it's actually pretty easy to figure out if you take it one function at a time. The fact is that you haven't written much more code than you would have for a standard application, since Visual C++ writes most of it for you as part of the ActiveX control definition process. The functions we did have to add are to address the special things that we want this control to do.

Let's start taking this code apart. The first function that you modified is DoPropExchange(). This function only performs one service in this example—it allows you to make your custom properties persistent. Essentially, the PX_ series of function calls allow you to store the value of a particular property from one session to the next. There's one function call for each variable type that you define. Each one of them accepts four variables like this:

```
PX_Bool(pPX, "OnOff", m_onOff, FALSE);
```

The first variable is a pointer to a property exchange structure. Visual C++ defines this structure for you automatically—all you need to do is use it. The second parameter contains the external name of the property, the one that the user will see in the Property Inspector. (There are a variety of names for the Property Inspector—Visual C++ uses the Properties dialog and Delphi uses the Object Inspector, for example.) The third parameter is the internal name for the property. That's the one you'll use throughout the program to define the property. Finally, we have to define a default value for the property (unless you want the user to see a blank field in the Property Inspector).

The next function you have to modify is OnResetState(). This function provides some of the aesthetic details that users will see when they add the component to a form. In this case, we'll give the component a default caption and resize it to match a custom size that works well on Web pages, since this is the place we intend to use the control most often. You'll need to change this setting to meet the needs of the programming language you use most often if you design an ActiveX control for some other purpose. The important thing to remember is that the OnResetState() function allows you to perform any setup required to use your control.

TIP: The default component size used by Microsoft is about twice the size of the one provided by Borland products such as Delphi. Internet controls vary in size, but the 75×25 (width×height) we use in the example works in most cases.

10

Two of the three modified functions in the message handlers section of the code require some kind of change. The ModalResultChanged() function doesn't require any modification, so I won't talk about it here. The property associated with the ModalResultChanged() function, ModalResult, gets changed by the other two functions. The OnOffChanged() function is the first one we'll look at. What we need to do is set an internal caption flag and the initial caption. If the programmer set the OnOff property to True, we'll set the control up as an on/off switch button by setting its caption to On. We also provide a different modal result value when the pushbutton is used as an on/off switch. Notice that the m_onOff internal property variable tracks the status of the flag. The m_SetOn internal property tracks the current condition of the OnOff control (on or off). Since the button is initially On, we set the m_SetOn flag to True.

Now it's time to look at the processing required for the property page feature of this OCX. The OnStdButtonTypeChanged function is nothing more than a simple case statement. It changes the button's Caption and ModalResult properties as needed to create various default button types. Notice that we also have to turn off the OnOff pushbutton processing if the user selects a default button type.

The OnClick() message-handling function is active during run time. There are two levels of action here. First, we need to determine whether the programmer defined this button as an on/off switch. If so, we change the internal state variable (m_SetOn) and the button caption. The function switches the button state between on and off as needed. Once we finish with the internal processing needed to make the button work, we call the default OnClick processing routine. Failure to call this default routine will cause the OCX to skip any code specific to the programming environment that you attach to button events. For example, if you were to use this control in a Visual C++ application, any code attached to the exposed events in Visual C++ would be ignored.

Before you can use this component, you'll have to build it within Visual C++. Part of the build process automatically registers the OCX for you with Windows. I really liked this feature because it saved me some time when testing the OCX later. The only downside is that preregistration contaminates your working environment. You'll have to go to another machine to test this component from an Internet point of view as an ActiveX control.

Testing the Control

Once you create a new ActiveX control of any kind (whether your compiler calls it an OCX or not), you have to perform some type of testing to make sure it works as anticipated. The best way to do this for an ActiveX control you want to use on the Internet is to follow a four-phase approach: three levels of internal testing and a fourth level of external testing. The following list illustrates the importance of each phase.

◆ *Internal testing phase 1* Use the control in a standard environment. You'll want to see if the control is going to work at all before you move it off your standard programming platform. The reason is simple: testing an ActiveX control from within a browser leaves you without a debugger. Testing the basic functionality of an ActiveX control before you move it out of the C++ (or other OCX/ActiveX) programming environment means that you'll have a debugger handy for finding the really critical problems.

◆ *Internal testing phase 2*   Test locally within a browser. Setting up a very short test on your local machine to see if the ActiveX control will even load into an HTML page could save some time later. You'll want to verify that enough properties are available to actually use the control and that it works when you view your test page.

◆ *Internal testing phase 3*   Use a network connection to test a full Web page. Once you've tested the basic functionality of the ActiveX control and verified that it works with your browser, you have to determine whether it works with a full page of HTML tags. After all, what good is a control that won't work with other controls on the same page? Interaction between controls can cause some really odd problems. You could test for interaction problems using a standard form in an application, but that really won't help much. The problem is that a browser won't look at the ActiveX control the same way that your favorite compiler will.

◆ *External testing*   Check control functionality on an uncontaminated machine. One of the biggest problems you're going to run into is contamination. Remember that most compilers automatically register an OCX or ActiveX control that you create. Someone checking into your Internet site won't have the same advantage. It's crucial to have an uncontaminated client and server handy to test your new control within the context of a Web page. In other words, this final stage of testing will look at the control the same way that anyone accessing your Internet site will see it.

Now that you have a good idea of where we're headed, let's look at some testing for the control we just created. I'm going to use Visual C++ 6.0 throughout the following sections. You could use any programming environment that supports OCXs. For example, you might want to test the OnOff control with Visual Basic or Delphi to see how it works with those languages. The important consideration is not the language you use for testing but that you test the control fully with some programming language that includes full debugging support. You want to make sure that the control you've created actually works as anticipated in the safest possible environment designed to do so. Since many Internet tools are in the testing stage, you may find that a control that seems like it should work doesn't. Being able to eliminate the control itself by testing it in a known environment is one step toward troubleshooting the problem.

10

Internal Testing Phase 1: Use the Control in a Standard Environment

Performing the first phase of internal testing doesn't have to be a long, drawn-out affair. All you really need to do is create a project using your

Remember that you need to use the Project | Add to Project | Components and Controls command to display the Components and Controls Gallery dialog, which is used to add the OCXExmpl control to the current project.

standard programming environment, and then add the ActiveX control (OCX) you've created. You'll want to make sure all of the properties work as expected. Take time to check out the property page thoroughly as well.

Start by creating a new project in your favorite programming environment (it has to support OCXs to work). For the purposes of this example, you could easily test the control by creating a dialog-based application in Visual C++. The MFC AppWizard takes care of most of the work for you. (We look at the process for creating a dialog-based application using Visual C++ in Chapter 2.) I gave my project the name OCXTest.

Once you have a new project in place, create a form (if needed) and add the ActiveX control to it. Visual C++ automatically registers ActiveX controls for you, so the control we created in the previous section should appear in the list of controls available to you. (Other programming environments may force you to register your ActiveX control separately.) Figure 10-5 shows the dialog for the test program I created to debug this example. It also shows the Properties dialog with the Control page selected.

Most programming environments also provide a way to view all of the properties associated with a control at one time. Here's the All page of the OCXExmpl Control Properties dialog; notice that the OnOff property is set to True.

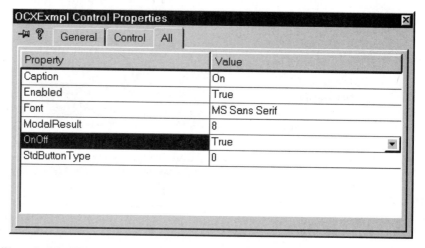

Property	Value
Caption	On
Enabled	True
Font	MS Sans Serif
ModalResult	8
OnOff	True
StdButtonType	0

You'll probably want to add some test code to the program as well. That way you can check the effects of various control events. For example, the on/off switch button in our example provides a variety of modal result return values depending on how you set the button properties. Setting the OnOff property to True creates a special switch button. The ModalResult property switches

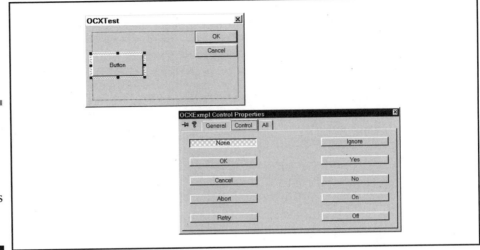

The Control page of the Properties dialog shows the special features for this pushbutton.

Figure 10-5.

between two values. However, you could just as easily select one of the standard button values from the Control page of the Properties dialog.

The first thing you'll want to do is CTRL-double-click on the control. You'll see an Add Member Variable dialog. Type **m_OnOffButton** in the Member Variable Name field. You'll also want to make sure that the Category field is set to Control and the Variable Type field is set to COCXExmpl. Now that we can access the control's properties from within the test application, right-click on the control, and then choose Events from the context menu. You'll see a New Windows Message and Event Handlers dialog like the one shown here.

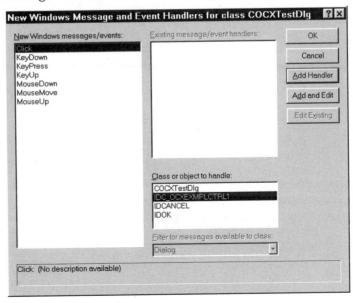

Notice that Visual C++ automatically selects the Click event and the IDC_OCXEXMPLCTRL1 object. All you need to do is click the Add and Edit button to add a new function to your program. Click OK when you see the Add Member Function dialog to accept the default function name. At this point you'll see the function skeleton for this button.

Listing 10-6 shows the C++ test code for this example. Notice the use of the GetModalResult() wrapper class function that Visual C++ automatically creates for the control. You'll find all of the declarations that Visual C++ makes for you in the OCXEXMPLE.H file. It's educational to look at this header file, since it shows how Visual C++ is interacting with your control. Looking at this file could help you find interface problems that you might not otherwise see (especially if you don't test every property of the control completely).

NOTE: You can create the OnClickOcxexmplctrl1() function in several ways. The easiest way to do it is using the MFC ClassWizard (which you can display using the View | ClassWizard command). Highlight the IDC_OCXEXMPLCTRL1 entry in the Object IDs list box, and then the Click entry in the Messages list. Clicking the Add Function button at this point will add the function to your program.

Listing 10-6:

```
void COCXTestDlg::OnClickOcxexmplctrl1()
{
    //Get the current ModalResult value.
    long liModalResult;
    liModalResult = m_OnOffButton.GetModalResult();

    //Determine which modal result was returned and display a message.
    switch (liModalResult)
    {
    case -1:
        MessageBox("None button pressed", "State of Control", MB_OK);
        break;
    case 1:
        MessageBox("OK button pressed", "State of Control", MB_OK);
        break;
    case 2:
        MessageBox("Cancel button pressed", "State of Control", MB_OK);
```

```
        break;
case 3:
        MessageBox("Abort button pressed", "State of Control", MB_OK);
        break;
case 4:
        MessageBox("Retry button pressed", "State of Control", MB_OK);
        break;
case 5:
        MessageBox("Ignore button pressed", "State of Control", MB_OK);
        break;
case 6:
        MessageBox("Yes button pressed", "State of Control", MB_OK);
        break;
case 7:
        MessageBox("No button pressed", "State of Control", MB_OK);
        break;
case 8:
        MessageBox("Button is On", "State of Control", MB_OK);
        break;
case 9:
        MessageBox("Button is Off", "State of Control", MB_OK);
        break;
    }
}
```

Now that you have a simple form with your control attached to it, try testing it. The example program will display a simple dialog box with the ActiveX control on it. Click the control and you'll see another dialog telling you the state of the button, as shown in Figure 10-6. A click on either the OK or Cancel button (provided free of charge by Visual C++) will end the program. As previously stated, this is a simple test of basic control functionality. What we've done so far is check the property page, the properties, and the results of using the control.

10

Internal Testing Phase 2: Test Locally Within a Browser
So far, we haven't done anything even remotely close to working with a Web page in this chapter, much less adding an ActiveX control to one. (We do explore the topic of working with Web pages in Chapter 8; make sure you read that chapter if you want a good overview of how to work with the Internet.) That's about ready to change. The next step in the testing process is to insert the control into an HTML document. We'll use a very simple setup again.

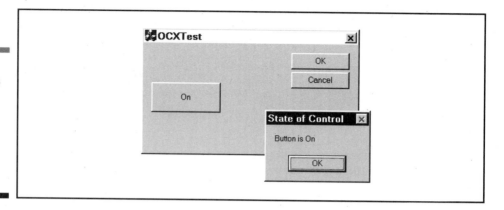

The OnOff
control works
as predicted
by returning
alternate
modal result
values.

Figure 10-6.

NOTE: We're using a very simple and easy-to-use utility in this section. If you plan on designing more than a few Web pages of average or higher complexity, then you may want to consider a tool like Visual InterDev. ActiveX Control Pad is better used as a test tool or as a means of designing simple Web pages.

Microsoft provides the ActiveX Control Pad utility as one of the ways you can quickly build HTML pages for testing your controls. Figure 10-7 shows what this utility looks like the first time you open it. You can also use it to create full-fledged Web pages (a process we look at in Chapter 8).

To create a test HTML page for your ActiveX control, use the Edit | Insert ActiveX Control command to display the Insert ActiveX Control dialog. Select your control from the list provided. Click on OK and you'll see the ActiveX Control loaded, as shown in Figure 10-8. Normally, you'd place the control within a form somewhere, but our only purpose right now is to test it alone.

Every time you load a new control, ActiveX Control Pad will automatically display the Properties dialog shown in Figure 10-8. It contains the standard list of published properties for the control. Notice that Figure 10-8 also shows the General properties page. You display it by right-clicking on the control and selecting the desired context menu entry. For our example, you'll want to select the second Properties entry.

The only property we need to change is the OnOff property in the Properties dialog. Change it to True, and then close the dialog containing the Control.

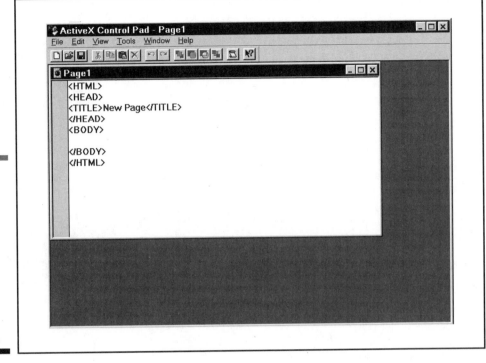

The ActiveX Control Pad utility allows you to design an HTML page for testing your ActiveX control quickly.

Figure 10-7.

ActiveX Control Pad is going to add a tag to the HTML page script. (If any of this HTML page lingo seems foreign right now, check out Chapter 8's description of the HTML tags.) Notice that the entry includes the control's CLASSID along with all of the properties needed to set it up.

10

TIP: You'll see a little button next to the <OBJECT> tag in the HTML script. Clicking this button displays the control again so that you can edit its properties. Whenever you place an ActiveX control or an HTML page layout in a script, ActiveX Control Pad will display this button, making it easy for you to edit the control or page layout as needed.

Save the sample HTML page using the Save button on the toolbar—I used TestPage.HTM for the sample page. Close ActiveX Control Pad, and then open the sample HTML page using your favorite ActiveX-compatible Web browser (which is limited to Internet Explorer or Netscape Navigator with the NCompass ScriptActive plug-in, as of this writing). If you're using Internet

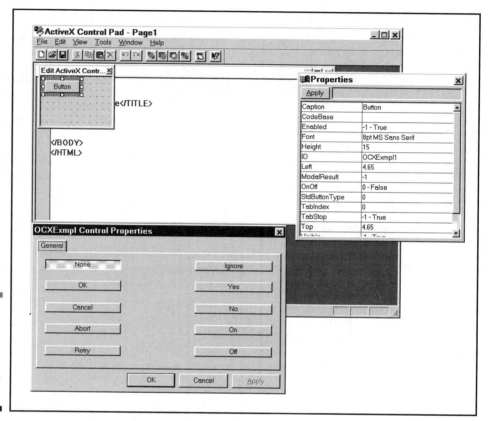

The ActiveX
Control Pad
utility displays
your control
after loading it.
Figure 10-8.

*Make sure you
save any test
Web pages using
the HTM
extension.*

Explorer, make sure you set the security level of your browser to medium. You can do this by displaying the Options dialog using the View | Options command, selecting the Security page, and then clicking the Safety Level button on the Security page.

Once you load the TestPage.HTM file, you'll see something like Figure 10-9. It doesn't look very awe-inspiring right now, but that control can do something that a standard HTML page button can't do. Click on the button, and you'll see that the caption switches between On and Off. You could monitor the modal result value of that button as well and determine what state it was in—all without writing a single line of CGI script code. (We'll look at getting information from an ActiveX control later in the chapter.)

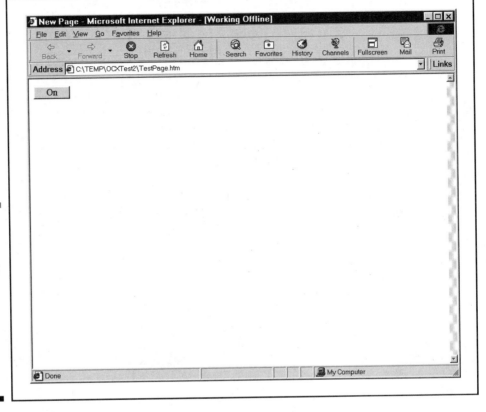

The ActiveX control on this page does something that you couldn't normally do— it changes between two states as you click it.

Figure 10-9.

NOTE: You'll probably see a Safety Violation dialog telling you that the ActiveX control in this page contains unsafe code. That's because we haven't marked it as safe. You'll learn all about security in Chapter 14, and that includes marking your controls as safe once they're fully tested. Just ignore the message for now. Versions 4.2 and above of Microsoft Visual C++ provides tools that take care of this detail for you (or at least provide a menu item so you don't have to resort to using the DOS prompt). This is one of the areas that I talked about at the beginning of the chapter in which you could write an ActiveX control using an older compiler but a newer compiler would make doing so more convenient.

10

At this point, we've tested the control's basic functionality within C++ and a local ActiveX document. Before you move to the network, you may want to try various permutations of the control. For example, the OnOff control can also work in several standard configurations. Try them out to see if they actually work.

It's interesting to see that all of the controls in the Toolbox are actually ActiveX controls and not the standard HTML equivalents.

Now it's time to use the OnOff control with other controls. Let's start a new HTML page in the ActiveX Control Pad. We're going to create a new HTML layout and then place the OnOff control within the layout. Use the File | New HTML Layout command to create a form like the one shown in Figure 10-10 (this figure also shows the On/Off control, which we'll add in the next few paragraphs). This is where you'll draw the components that will work with the OnOff control. Notice that the example layout places a few controls on the form for testing purposes. At this point you really don't need to add a lot of complexity, just enough information to make sure the control will work within a standard HTML environment.

Adding our ActiveX control is a bit different in this situation than it was the last time around. Right-click on the Toolbox and you'll see a context menu. Select the Additional Controls option, and you'll see an Additional Controls dialog like the one shown here.

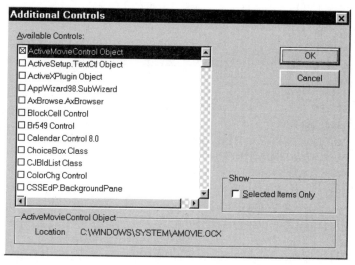

The Additional Controls dialog contains a complete list of all the ActiveX controls on your machine (it doesn't really care that these controls could be OCXs). You can also choose to display a complete list of insertable objects.

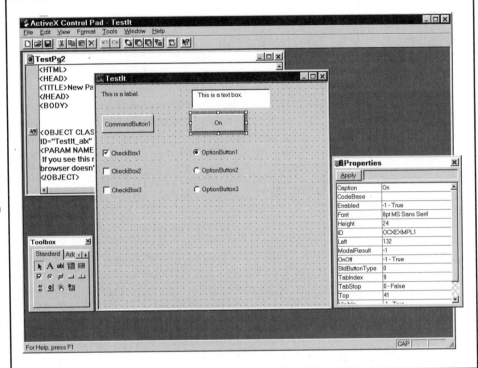

The second step in testing the ActiveX control is to see if it works with other HTML controls present.

Figure 10-10.

For example, you could place a Microsoft Word document or an Excel spreadsheet into a form. We take a look at this particular process in Chapter 11.

Select the OCXExmpl option (or whatever you named your control) from the list. Make sure you actually check the box next to the control, or ActiveX Control Pad won't install it. Click on OK to complete the process. You'll see a new control added to your Toolbox. Just grab it and place it next to the Command button as shown in Figure 10-10. As before, make sure you set the OnOff property to True if you're using the example control in this chapter.

Once you complete all your edits, save your layout and then close the page. ActiveX Control Pad will add an <OBJECT> tag to the HTML script, just like it did for the ActiveX Control page we tested earlier. Of course, the difference in this case is that we're looking at a whole page of controls, not just a single control sitting on the page by itself. You'll want to save the new test page and

10

then open it with your browser to see if the control works. After you've tested the ActiveX control in this environment, you can move on to network testing using the two pages we've just constructed.

Internal Testing Phase 3: Use a Network Connection to Test a Full Web Page

There are quite a few ways to go about testing your control on a network. The only criteria is to have two machines: a server and a client that are connected using the TCP/IP protocol. You'll also want to run an HTTP server on the server. Fortunately, both versions of Windows NT 4.0 are going to ship with a small HTTP server that you can use for testing purposes. In fact, this new version of Windows NT will include FTP and Gopher servers as well.

WEB LINK: Windows 95 users no longer have to envy their Windows NT neighbors when it comes to local testing of Web pages. You can get a copy of Personal Web Server for Windows 95, too. Owners of the OSR2 version of Windows 95 already have this feature available as part of the package—just go to the Network Properties dialog and install it. If you have an older version of Windows 95, you can download the required support from **http://www.microsoft.com/msdownload/ieplatform/ iewin95/10000.htm.** You can find out what other OSR2 features you can download for Windows 95 at **http://www.microsoft.com/windows/ pr/win95osr.htm.**

You'll want to make sure that you can communicate with the server using a standard browser and the domain name that you've assigned. Don't make the mistake of accessing the server drive through something like Explorer and then double-clicking on the test pages. Sure, this will open the browser and you'll see your test pages, but you'll defeat the whole purpose of this test phase. Opening the page through Explorer or File Manager will place the browser in file mode. It won't allow you to test the HTTP server capabilities. The reason for this phase of the test is to simulate, as closely as possible, the environment typical users will have when they access your Web site.

Once you've established a link to the server and can see the default Web page that it provides, add a link to your test page. Use this link to test both the single control and the full HTML pages that we created in the previous section. In most cases, you'll find that simply testing the link is going to be sufficient for this phase of the test. In other words, if your control works in one mode, it should work in all of the other modes that you've provided for it as well. For example, in the case of our example control, I simply tested it as an on/off switch. The standard button modes worked just fine because I had already tested them thoroughly during the first two phases of testing. That's why local testing is so important—it saves you time at this phase. (Imagine having to recreate several versions of that same Web page and test them over a server connection—that's a pretty counterproductive way to program.)

External Testing: Check Control Functionality on an Uncontaminated Machine

We've completely tested the control in our private environment. Every type of control access was looked at, and we made sure that the control worked with standard HTML controls. Now it's time for the external testing phase.

Actually, this is just an extension of the third internal phase. However, instead of accessing the Web site from the network, you'll want to access through a phone connection, just like your users will. In addition, you've been testing the control using a contaminated machine—one that has the control installed on it and all the appropriate registry entries.

The purpose of this testing phase is twofold. First, you want to make sure that the control still works when accessing from an uncontaminated machine. Otherwise, you may find that your control relies on some registry entries or other criteria that the client machines accessing your Web site won't meet. Second, you want to check the download time of your page. To this point we've been accessing the test pages using high-speed connections. People using your site won't have that privilege. The majority of them will access your site through a dial-up connection.

TIP: You'll want to install your test pages in a private section of your Web site to prevent other people from accessing them. Unlike in the network testing phase, don't place an actual link to the test pages on your main Web page. Use direct addresses to access the test pages since you've already tested connectivity in the previous testing phase.

10

To complete this portion of the testing process, move the test pages to the private section of your Web server. Dial into your Web server from an uncontaminated machine using an ActiveX-enabled browser. You'll need to use the URL for the private section of your network instead of the URL for the main page. Try accessing the single-control test page first to see if the ActiveX control works at all. You'll also want to see how long it takes to download the control outside the influences of a full-page implementation. Once you've checked out the single-control test page, move on to the second page that uses a full HTML layout. If this connection works, you've got a working ActiveX control that you can use to enhance your regular HTML pages.

Using ActiveX Controls with Netscape Navigator and Internet Explorer

Playing music and other forms of audio enhancements is probably the most common way of making a Web site more attractive. RealAudio makes this process at least a little easier while enhancing the quality of sound that you'll get. RealAudio has several different forms, not just an ActiveX control. The current version of this multimedia player also comes as a plug-in for Netscape Navigator. You can contact the makers of RealAudio at **http://www.realaudio.com/** for details on the player, SDK, and utility support. The SDK, RealAudio Encoder, RealAudio Timeline Editor, RealAudio Personal Server, and RealAudio Content Creation Guide are free for the price of a download. The RealAudio Personal Server supports two data streams—more than enough for demonstration or experimentation purposes.

Multiple levels of player support are only one of the things that makes using this particular technology worthwhile. It's also in use by quite a few Web sites. One of the more interesting sites that you can look at is **http://www.cdnow.com/** (which connects to Magazine Warehouse). This is a CD/movie store that uses multimedia to good effect. For example, if you want to purchase a CD, you can hear selected tracks over your PC's speaker before you do so. It also sells T-shirts. You can view them before you buy. About the only thing missing is the ability to view movie segments before you buy, but it's almost certain it'll add this capability eventually.

Getting started with RealAudio shouldn't be a problem. All you need to do is set up the server, encode your files, and then set up a Web page. The RealAudio Encoder utility dialog is shown in the following illustration. All you need to do is select the file you want to encode, enter any information needed in the Description area, and then click the Encode button to encode the file. (The RealAudio Encoder utility will automatically enter a destination filename for you.)

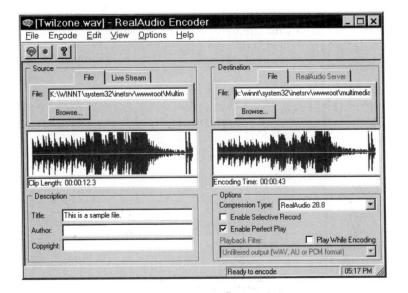

Adding the control to your Web page is pretty easy as well. All you need to do is select the RealAudio control from the list of controls in the Insert ActiveX Control dialog in ActiveX Control Pad—the same process that we've followed before. The only property you need to change other than CodeBase is shown here. Simply enter the URL where your sound file is located.

10

Listing 10-7 shows the code we'll use for this example. Notice that it contains the <EMBED> tag required by NCompass ScriptActive. This is one of the few controls that works absolutely flawlessly in both Netscape Navigator and Internet Explorer.

NOTE: You may need to change the HEIGHT and WIDTH attributes for the RealAudio1 <OBJECT> tag to work with your particular display configuration. The current values represent a default sizing that some people may find too small on high-resolution displays.

Listing 10-7:

```
<HTML>
<HEAD>
<TITLE>RealAudio Test</TITLE>
</HEAD>
<BODY>

<!-Display the heading.->
<CENTER><H2>Test of RealAudio ActiveX Control</H2></CENTER>

Click here to test the control:<BR>
<!-Display the control.->
<OBJECT ID="RealAudio1" WIDTH=49 HEIGHT=39
    CLASSID="CLSID:CFCDAA03-8BE4-11CF-B84B-0020AFBBCCFA"
    CODEBASE="http://aux/controls">
    <PARAM NAME="_ExtentX" VALUE="1296">
    <PARAM NAME="_ExtentY" VALUE="1032">
    <PARAM NAME="SRC" VALUE="http://aux/multimedia/TwilZone.RA">
    <PARAM NAME="AUTOSTART" VALUE="0">
    <PARAM NAME="NOLABELS" VALUE="0">
<EMBED NAME="RealAudio1" WIDTH=49 HEIGHT=39
    CLASSID="CLSID:CFCDAA03-8BE4-11CF-B84B-0020AFBBCCFA"
    CODEBASE="http://aux/controls"
    TYPE="application/oleobject"
    PARAM__ExtentX="1296"
    PARAM__ExtentY="1032"
    PARAM_SRC="http://aux/multimedia/TwilZone.RA"
    PARAM_AUTOSTART="0"
    PARAM_NOLABELS="0"  >
</OBJECT>
```

```
</BODY>
</HTML>
```

Now that you have the code put together, let's look at the final result. Figure 10-11 shows how the example page will look. The user can simply click the RealAudio button to open the sound file. This particular control offers more than that, however. Right-click the control, and you'll see the context menu shown in Figure 10-11. Users can customize the control to meet their specific needs.

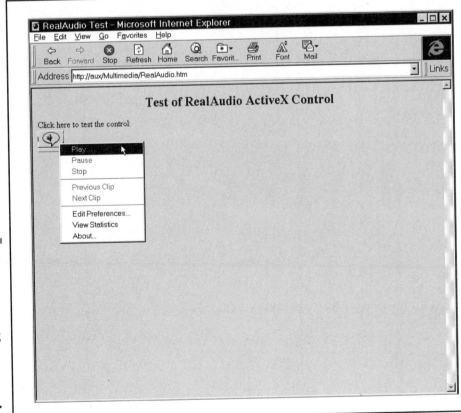

The RealAudio control provides a distinct pushbutton interface along with a context menu for user settings.

Figure 10-11.

10

So, what does the control look like in action? Here's how our sample WAV file looks from the user's perspective:

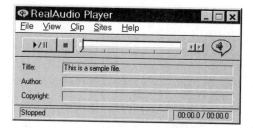

Notice that the dialog shows the description information added while in the RealAudio Encode utility. Unfortunately, the amount of information you can add is somewhat limited. It would have been nice to have one user-configurable field in addition to the default fields offered by the control.

CHAPTER 11

Creating an ActiveX Document Application

So far, we've talked about all kinds of new technology, including ActiveX and COM+, which promise to make the Internet a business tool for everyone. There are a lot of different ways in which ActiveX is being used (and COM+ will be used in the future). For example, Microsoft released a new ActiveX API called ActiveX Accessibility. This API is designed to add to the Internet what the Accessibility applet added to Windows 95. Things like Sticky Keys (a method for creating CTRL-key combinations by pressing one key at a time instead of all the keys simultaneously) will appear not only on your Windows 95 and Windows NT 4.0 desktop, but also within your ActiveX-compatible Internet browser.

ActiveX provides the means for moving exciting new technologies from the desktop to the Internet.

There are other ActiveX-based technologies in the works as well (by Microsoft and other companies)—too many to talk about here. One of the more important ActiveX technologies is ActiveMovie. In fact, the MSNBC Internet site is already using ActiveMovie to show you clips from the NBC news network. Essentially, ActiveMovie allows you to view film clips on the Internet and play AVI and other kinds of movie files.

WEB LINK: There is more information available about the technologies just described. You can find out about ActiveX Accessibility at **http://www.microsoft.com/enable/dev/msdn4.htm.** Usage instructions and technological description of the ActiveMovie control appear at **http://www.microsoft.com/msdn/sdk/inetsdk/help/complib/ activemovie/activemovie.htm.**

Some of the best ActiveX technology answers the same kinds of needs as a standard desktop application would.

The most important ActiveX technology, though, isn't a new and exciting one. It relates to that old and mundane problem: sharing documents on the Internet. This has always been a problem, because the interface is static—just consider the number of tags you'd need and the complexity of the program required to create any kind of a dynamic interface after reading Chapter 8. Sure, you can export a word processing document into HTML and come up with a realistic representation of the data, but that data won't change and it will be difficult for the user to edit it. The same holds true for spreadsheet data. Showing the data isn't too hard as long as you're willing to sacrifice up-to-the-minute information. ActiveX provides an answer in this case. It allows you to create a dynamic document—one that you can edit and see change in real time.

You'll hear
ActiveX
Document
referred to as
OLE Document
Objects by some
people and
ActiveDocument
by others.

So, where did this technology mysteriously appear from? It's not new at all: Microsoft has simply modified the technology found in Microsoft Office. The original name for ActiveX Document is OLE Document Objects. (Most people, including Microsoft, have now shortened ActiveX Document to simply ActiveDocument—the term we'll use throughout the book since it's clearer and more explicit.) It's part of the Microsoft Office Binder technology and was never meant to become a public specification. Originally, you had to sign up for the Office-compatible program before you could even get a specification for OLE Document Objects. It was only after the appearance of Windows 95 that this specification became something that anyone could get. However, it only makes sense that Microsoft would make this specification public, since it's the next logical step in the evolution of OLE.

ActiveDocument is what this chapter's all about. We're going to examine what will be the most important use of ActiveX besides database applications. You'll learn just how easy it is to create ActiveDocuments for browser use. We'll also examine what you need to do to create custom document setups of your own.

We'll examine three main ActiveDocument topics in this chapter. First, we'll look at using the Web Publishing Wizard. If you don't know how ActiveDocument works from the user perspective, you'll want to pay close attention to this section. After all, how can you be expected to write an application for something you don't understand? Next, we'll look at some of the theory behind ActiveDocument—most notably, the interfaces you have to implement. Finally, we'll create a simple program that implements the interfaces required for ActiveDocument.

NOTE: All of the examples in this chapter use Visual C++ 6.0, though you can easily use versions 4.2 and above as well with a few small procedural changes. (The code itself should work just fine.) You must have one of these versions of Visual C++ (the 6.0 version is preferred) to follow the examples in this chapter from start to finish. There are ways to at least use the examples with Visual C++ 4.1, but you may need to work with them a little first. For example, you'll need to add references to the various new classes supported as a default by Visual C++ versions 4.2 and above. In addition, creating the examples won't be as automatic as when using the newer products. Theoretically, it's possible to create these examples with Visual C++ 4.0 as well, but the amount of work required will certainly make getting an updated version of the compiler seem like a good idea.

11

What Are ActiveDocuments (OLE Document Objects)?

Up to this point, we haven't looked very much at the kinds of documents users would be familiar with in regard to the Internet. For example, while users are going to be very familiar with the Word document they just modified on their local hard drive, the really neat ActiveX control they used on the Internet is going to be totally unfamiliar. We've also looked at the scripting language used to display specific page elements in a way that only a programmer would love (a user probably isn't all that interested in the latest techniques for creating JavaScript). Of course, this begs a question that nearly everyone will ask: What's in the Internet for the user besides a bit of information, a few forms, and your dazzling ActiveX controls? ActiveDocuments provide part of the answer. They're a means for just about anyone to create content and display it on a Web page.

However, ActiveDocuments are more than merely a way to share information—you can actually use them to get real work done. Think about this scenario: Your company has its own intranet that employees can contact as needed from anywhere in the world. They use it to get their e-mail and perform a variety of other tasks. Now your boss tells you that the marketing department has to create a report and that most of the sales representatives are on the road. How do you get the job done?

NOTE: Netscape Navigator and earlier versions of Internet Explorer let you view nonstandard documents through the use of helpers. The browser would start a full copy of the application and then pass it the contents of the file on the Web site. The problem with this approach is that you use more memory to start another application and you don't have a live connection to the Internet server. Changes made to the file wouldn't be reflected in the server copy. Even though Microsoft still uses the term "helpers" with regard to Internet Explorer 3.0 and above, the view from the user's standpoint is completely different.

ActiveDocuments are the answer in this case. Simply place a link to the document in an HTML document using the tags we discuss in Chapter 8. When users click on the document reference, they'll see an editable copy of the document in their browser with the appropriate changes to their menu and toolbar. Figure 11-1 shows a Word for Windows document displayed in

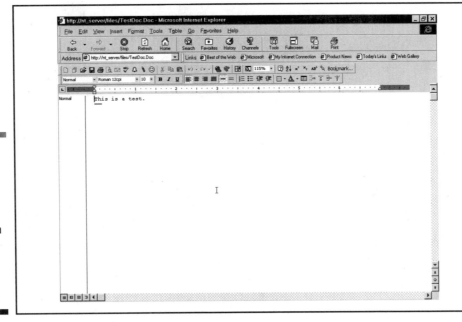

Internet Explorer 4.0 shows the effects of in-place editing, which is an OLE 2 feature of COM.

Figure 11-1.

ActiveDocument uses an OLE 2 feature known as in-place editing, which allows you to edit the document in the client rather than display a separate server.

an Internet Explorer browser window. Notice that all of the browser features are still intact; the only thing that's changed is the way the document gets displayed. This particular technique isn't new—it's called *in-place editing*. Most OLE 2 servers can now provide this capability to an OLE 2 client. Try it out in Word for Windows or CorelDRAW! sometime. The menu and toolbar will change to match that of the client anytime you click on an OLE object. The big difference is that this is happening in a browser through an Internet connection.

NOTE: If you test this sample on a LAN-based Internet server, you may get a dialog asking whether you want to open or save the file. In most cases, you'll definitely get it when testing the connection over a live Internet connection (depending on how you set up security for your browser). Simply open the file to see it, as shown in Figure 11-1.

11

You'll notice another difference as well. If you were to make a change to this document, and then click the Back button on the Internet Explorer browser toolbar, you'd see the following dialog asking if you want to change the file.

If you click on Yes, you'll see a typical File Save dialog. The unfortunate part of this setup is that saving the file using this technique will place it on your local hard drive—something that won't work in our scenario but possibly could in other circumstances. There are other ways of saving the file. You could use the File I Save As command. You could also use the File I Send To I Web Publishing Wizard command to actually send it back to the Web server—that would be our choice in this situation. (Some combinations of Internet Explorer and Windows won't provide a File I Send To I Web Publishing Wizard command, which means that you'll need to save the file locally and use the Web Publishing Wizard to send it to the Web server as a separate step.) We'll look at the steps needed for using the Web Publishing Wizard in the section, "Using the Web Publishing Wizard" later in this chapter.

T IP: There are some situations where none of the techniques in this section will help very much. For example, you may want to post the document on the Web server, but you may want each post to arrive individually. In that case, you could tell the user to use the File I Send To I Mail Recipient command. Obviously, this would mean coordinating all of the documents you receive, but this method will work when others won't.

T IP: The current HTTP 1.0 specification doesn't allow the user to publish a document to the WWW server. The newer 1.1 specification remedies this oversight. If you want to allow users to publish documents back to the server from a Web page, then providing a server that uses the 1.1 specification is the way to go. Not only will you save time and effort by not having to write mundane scripts or jump through other hoops, you'll also reduce support calls by making things easier for the user as well. (All current versions of both Netscape and Microsoft products support this 1.1 specification—check your documentation if you own an older version of either vendor's product.)

ActiveDocument also presents some changes in the way a programmer has to think about OLE. There are three levels of object participation within a client. An object can simply appear in the viewing area, or it can take over the window, or it can take over the entire application frame. Let's look at how these three levels differ.

Originally, you could create an object and place it in a container. When OLE 1 came out, the container would simply display an icon showing the presence of the object and nothing more. To edit an object, you double-clicked on its icon within the container. Windows would bring up a full-fledged copy of the document in a separate window. This is what's meant when someone says an object simply appears in the viewing area.

OLE 1 only displays an icon when you create a link to an external document; OLE 2 displays the actual document contents and allows you to perform in-place editing.

OLE 2 changed the way clients and servers interact. Now you could actually see the contents of the object. For example, if you placed a spreadsheet object within a word processing document, you could see its contents without double-clicking on the object. This is the window level of participation. The client and server share a window; the client displays its data, and then relies on the server to display any information within an object. OLE 2 also provides in-place activation. In most cases, double-clicking on the object starts an out-of-process server that actually takes over the entire client frame. The server takes over the menus and toolbars normally reserved for client use. From a user perspective, the application was the same; the tools just changed to meet the user's needs for editing an object.

ActiveDocument moves this technology from desktop to the Internet through the use of a browser. Now your browser tools will automatically change to meet the needs of the user, and they no longer need to open a separate program to edit a document. An out-of-process server will take care of changing the browser menus and toolbars to match the ones normally used by the application. In fact, future versions of Windows will go still farther.

Out-of-process servers implement the menu and toolbar changes that you see when you click on an object within a container application.

Windows 95 and Windows NT 4.0 both use the Explorer interface. If you right-click on just about any document that's associated with a registered application, you'll see a menu with a variety of choices. The most common choices are to open or print the document. In some cases, you'll also see an option to use the Quick View utility to see what the document contains.

The interface will probably change in the near future. Double-clicking on a document will perform an in-place activation. The server will actually take over the Explorer menus and toolbars. No longer will the user leave Explorer to open another application window. In addition, Internet sites will appear within Explorer as hard drives, combining the functionality of a browser with what we have today.

Are all of these changes welcomed by the programmer community? Not by a long shot. A few people are already claiming that this technology is only tightening Microsoft's grip on the computing world. Of course, that would only happen if you couldn't install another server in the place of Internet Explorer—which is something that definitely won't happen. ActiveDocument is going to be an extremely important technology as computing matures. That's why this chapter is so important—its purpose is to get you up to speed on this emerging technology so that you can use it to meet your current computing needs.

Creating the Connection

Now that we've seen the result of using ActiveDocument and discussed why this technology is important, let's take a look at the HTML code required to implement it. Listing 11-1 shows the code used to create this example; it's short and to the point. I didn't add any bells or whistles, so you can see the absolute minimum required to create an ActiveDocument link. As you can see, the code uses a simple link and nothing more. All of the "magic" behind this application is located in Internet Explorer. We've used this kind of link to display other pages on a Web site in Chapter 8.

Listing 11-1:

```
<HTML>
<HEAD>
<TITLE>ActiveX Document</TITLE>
</HEAD>
<BODY>
<Center>
<H2>ActiveX Document Test Page</H2>
<EM>Requires Microsoft Word or WordPad</EM><P>
</Center>
<A HREF="http://nt_server/files/TestDoc.Doc">Test Document</A>
</BODY>
</HTML>
```

OK, so you've got a document displayed in your browser that you can edit. That really isn't such a big deal, is it? Sure it is. Since the document remains in the browser, you save memory. There is only one application running, and although you do have to pay the cost of some additional processing overhead and memory to view and process the document, it's a lot less than running two applications. For example, the in-place activation features are the result of using an out-of-process server. An *out-of-process server* is essentially a fancy form of DLL that provides the right kinds of interfaces to communicate with

ActiveDocument uses an out-of-process server, which is normally a DLL, to implement in-place editing.

the client application. The point is that the DLL will take less memory than a full-fledged application if for no other reason than it doesn't have to worry about displaying anything (that's the job of the client). We'll take a look at some of the requirements for this DLL in the section, "An Overview of ActiveDocument Architecture" later in this chapter.

There are two other ways to create an ActiveDocument connection that we won't spend much time looking at here. The Microsoft Web Browser Control allows you to browse the Internet looking for any kind of document—including those that you don't normally associate with the Internet, like Word for Windows documents. There are several advanced <OBJECT> tag attributes that will help you in this regard as well. You'll want to take the time to look at the <OBJECT> tag information in Chapter 8 and then go to the Web site listed there to download the associated specification. The advanced attributes for the <OBJECT> tag are currently in a state of flux, which is why we won't look at them here.

Using the Web Publishing Wizard

You don't have to settle for the old methods of keeping documents up to date. It takes only a little bit of effort to use the Web Publishing Wizard to keep a document current on the Web server. These changes to the document won't appear solely on your local machine as they would with older browser technology. They'll actually appear on the Internet server. By providing a written procedure for using the Web Publishing Wizard (and possibly setting up the connection information in advance), you've allowed an employee to make a change to what's essentially an HTML page from a remote location.

WEB LINK: You'll need a copy of the Web Publishing Wizard to work with this section of the chapter. You should see the Web Publishing Wizard on the Explorer Send To menu (right-click on a file and then look at the context menu entries). You'll also see the Web Publishing Wizard entry in your Word File | Send To menu when you open a document in a browser (but not when you open Word normally). You can download the Web Publishing Wizard at **http://www.microsoft.com/windows/software/webpost/default. htm.** Windows 98 users will find that the Web Publishing Wizard appears in the Internet folder on the Windows Setup tab of the Add/Remove Programs Properties dialog. The Web Publishing Wizard gets installed as part of various Internet programming tools offered by Microsoft, so you'll want to see if the Web Publishing Wizard is available before you install it.

So how do you start the process? The following procedure will get you going the first time around. You can make this an easy four-step process after this first attempt—we'll look at that part of the procedure once we go through this first phase. We'll start with a document like the one shown in Figure 11-1 and assume that you've already edited it. Now you want to save the change to your Internet site.

1. Use the File | Save As command to display a File Save dialog. You'll need to save the file locally before you can send it to the Web server. Perhaps Microsoft will change this part of the procedure later, but for now you'll have to take the time to make a local copy. Give the file the same name as the Web site page. In the case of our sample Internet site, the name of the file is TESTDOC.DOC (as shown on the Internet Explorer title bar in Figure 11-1).

2. Use the File | Send To | Web Publishing Wizard command within Word or Windows Explorer to display the Web Publishing Wizard dialog (make sure you highlight the file or folder first if you send it using Windows Explorer).

3. Click Next. You'll see the next page, as follows, if you're using an older version of Web Publishing Wizard or if you started Web Publishing Wizard from the Start menu.

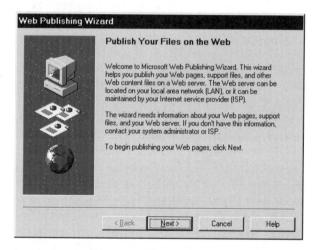

In some cases, Web Publishing Wizard automatically places a filename in the File or Folder Name field. You won't want to use this filename right now. (If you're using a newer version of the product and you did select a file before starting the Web Publishing Wizard, you'll see a dialog that asks which Web server connection to use; skip to step 5 in this case.)

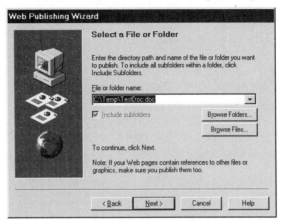

4. Click the Browse Files button to display a Browse dialog (it looks like a standard File Open dialog). Locate the local copy of the document you just saved, and then click on Open. Now you'll see the name of the Web document in the Field or Folder Name field. Click Next.

5. If you've defined a Web server connection in the past, you'll see a single drop-down list box that contains names of the connections. You can select one of those connections or define a new one by clicking the New button. We'll assume that you need a new connection for the purposes of this example. (If you don't need a new connection, select an existing one and skip to step 14.) Whether you click the New button or you've never defined a server connection in the past, you'll see the next page, as shown here.

11

(This page is from the latest version of Web Publishing Wizard, which includes one field and one command button; older versions have two fields.) This page is where you begin to define the connection between the client machine and the Internet server. Fortunately, you have to do it only once.

NOTE: Older versions of Web Publishing Wizard provided two fields in this dialog. The first contained the connection name, the second the type of connection to create. You can access this second field on newer versions of Web Publishing Wizard by clicking the Advanced button shown in the dialog.

6. Type the name you want to use for your Internet connection. In most cases, leaving My Web Site is just fine if you need only one entry. Select an Internet Service Provider from the second list box. (Users of the latest version of Web Publishing Wizard will need to click the Advanced button.) If you're creating a connection for a LAN intranet site, then select Other Internet Provider when using an older version of Web Publishing Wizard or Automatically Select Service Provider when using a new version of Web Publishing Wizard.

7. Click Next. You'll see the next page, as shown here.

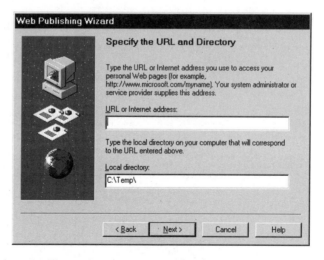

Notice that you'll need to define a connection to the Internet server. Simply type in the URL for your site. Users of the newer version of Web

Publishing Wizard will also need to provide a local directory that corresponds to the remote Web site. This is where Web Publishing Wizard will look for files to publish to the Web server. Use the default directory in most cases. If you're using an older version of Web Publishing Wizard, skip to step 9.

8. Click Next. Web Publishing Wizard will ask you for the URL that you want to use for publishing the information. Unless you're using an unusual setup, the default URL provided by Web Publishing Wizard will work fine.

9. Click Next. You'll see the next page, as shown here.

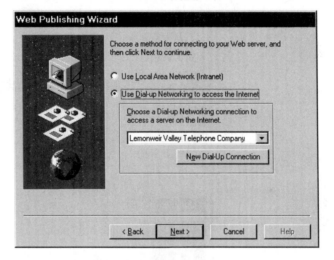

This page allows you to select a connection type: LAN or dial-up. Don't be fooled by the description provided by the dialog. You can create a dial-up connection for an intranet just as easily as you can for an Internet.

11

10. Choose between a LAN connection (no modem connection) or a dial-up connection. If you pick a dial-up connection, you'll also need to select one of the dial-up connections in the list box. Clicking the New Dial-Up Connection button allows you to create a new connection definition.

11. Click Next. The Web Publishing Wizard displays the next page, which simply states that it needs to verify the information you provided. Click Next to begin the verification process. If you're trying to create a LAN

connection, you'll almost certainly get the error message shown here when using an older version of Web Publishing Wizard.

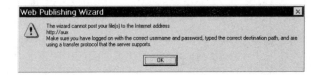

Don't worry about it—the next few steps will show you how to fix the problem. If the Web Publishing Wizard successfully finds your site, you can proceed to step 15.

12. Click OK to clear the error message dialog. You'll see the first page of an extended connection configuration, as shown here.

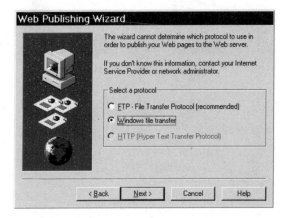

This is where you'll select a file transfer method. If you're working with an Internet site through a dial-up connection, you can choose between an FTP or HTTP file transfer. The HTTP method is only available to Web sites using HTTP version 1.1 or above. If you're working with a LAN, the FTP and Windows File Transfer options are available. At this point, the various connections require a bit more definition. The procedure will continue by showing you the Windows File Transfer option, since it's the one you'll need most often.

T IP: When configuring a LAN connection, use the Windows File Transfer method whenever possible, since it's faster. The FTP connection requires an added file transfer layer that really isn't needed in the LAN environment. However, on a WAN, the FTP method could provide an added layer of security.

13. Click Next. You'll see the next page, as shown in Figure 11-2. This is where the connection problem will become obvious. Web Publishing Wizard almost never gets the UNC (universal naming convention) destination for your file right. The reason is pretty simple: the name is obscured by the server in most cases. You'll need to provide a fully qualified UNC to your storage directory, like the one shown in Figure 11-2. Make absolutely certain that you provide a UNC name, not a standard DOS drive and directory location. The reason for using a UNC is that it allows you to use the same entry technique no matter what file system the server is using.

14. Click Next. The Web Publishing Wizard displays the next page, which simply states that it needs to verify the information you provided. Click Next to begin the verification process. This time you should see a success message.

15. Click Finish. This will allow you to complete the file transfer process. You'll see a file transfer dialog while Web Publishing Wizard copies the file for you. Once it's finished, you'll see the success dialog shown here. You've just modified this document—anyone visiting the Web site will see the changes automatically.

This page shows the source of almost every problem you'll have configuring Web Publishing Wizard.

Figure 11-2.

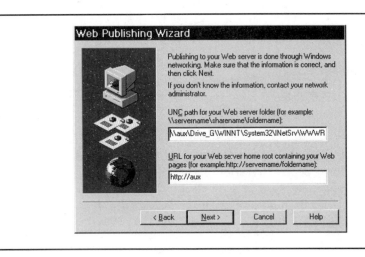

11

Once you finish these setup steps the first time, the user can complete the process in four easy steps. All you need to do is save the document to a local drive, use the File | Send To | Web Publishing Wizard command to start the Wizard, select the file, select a connection, and then click Finish to complete the process, which are steps 1 through 4 and 15 if you want to look at it from a procedural view.

TIP: A network administrator could perform this task once on each machine to reduce support calls from users. Unfortunately (at least as of this writing), there doesn't appear to be any way of doing this automatically like making a registry change or copying a file to the target machine.

An Overview of ActiveDocument Architecture

It's important to understand how the controls that you use work—at least to a certain extent—so that you can easily troubleshoot them when the time comes. There isn't room in this book to go over the theory behind OLE in detail; whole books are devoted to that task and have a hard time doing it even in 1,000 pages. However, an ActiveDocument control requires some special features, and those are the ones we'll look at in this section.

OLE controls work because they use standard interfaces that a client can learn about and use.

The first thing you need to understand is that an OLE control works because it uses a common interface. Every OLE control that you'll ever use must support specific classes (actually interface elements) to allow applications to access it. For example, if a client needs to ask the server for in-place activation support, it makes a call to one of the methods associated with IOleInPlaceActivateObject. Every server that supports in-place activation has to provide a class of this name and expose it for the client to use. The equivalent client class in this case is IOleDocumentSite. There are literally hundreds of classes (and associated methods) that you could support to provide various kinds of OLE functionality (it's inconceivable that you would need to support them all, though, since some forms of functionality simply aren't needed by specific controls). Figure 11-3 shows the classes (interface elements) for Excel Worksheet using

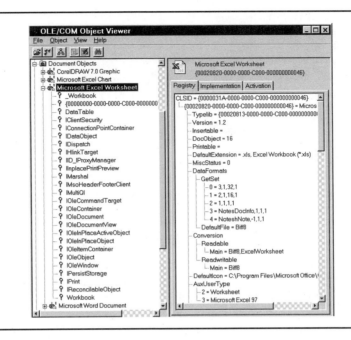

OLE/COM Object Viewer provides a convenient method for seeing what kind of interface elements you need to support when creating a control.

Figure 11-3.

OLE/COM Object Viewer (the utility we discuss in Chapter 9). Notice that each one of them begins with an *I* instead of the more familiar *C*. This represents the exposed interface classes—the ones that a client would access to gain some type of functionality from the server.

NOTE: Older versions of the OLE/COM Object Viewer are named OLE/COM Object Viewer. Both utilities will provide you with about the same information.

11

NOTE: Figure 11-3 shows the latest ActiveDocument functions for Microsoft Excel. You may see four IMso functions. This represents the prespecification names for the ActiveDocument functions. The ActiveX specification now states that these are standard IOle classes. Fortunately, it appears that Internet Explorer 3.0 will support document objects using either interface. However, this support may not last long, and you should use the IOle versions of the calls we'll talk about in this chapter.

Obviously, you could drive yourself crazy trying to remember if you implemented all of those calls in your control. Fortunately, an IDE like Visual C++ that provides direct support for building ActiveX controls (or OCXs) normally takes care of creating the myriad of classes for you. (There are more than a few compiler vendors creating ActiveX add-ons for their products as you read this. Products like Borland's Delphi already include an Internet control pack add-on to help you build Internet-aware applications.) It implements a default behavior for each of the required classes as well. The only time that you really need to change a behavior is if you want to add some special kind of functionality not supported by the compiler. We see in Chapter 10 that building a simple control doesn't have to involve a lot of work if you build an appropriate application framework. That's why the example spends so much time getting everything set up before adding even a single line of code.

There's actually an easy way of looking at the OLE interface functions required to create ActiveDocuments. In fact, we can summarize the functionality of an ActiveDocument using what you've learned so far in the book. If you want your application to support this specification, it must do the following:

◆ *Implement IPersistStorage*   Your application must support this class and associated methods so that it can use OLE compound files as a storage medium.

◆ *Support OLE Document Embedding Features*   This feature is implemented in many different ways. The current trend is toward providing the user with two embedding methods through menu functions: Insert Object and Paste Special. The functions used to do this are IPersistFile, IOleObject, and IDataObject.

◆ *Provide In-Place Activation Support*   There are two classes that you need to implement in order to support in-place activation: IOleInPlaceObject and IOleInPlaceActivateObject. To implement these classes, you'll have to gather information about the container using methods provided by the IOleInPlaceSite and IOleInPlaceFrame classes.

◆ *Add the ActiveDocument Extensions*   Most OLE 2 servers perform the first three steps right now. To make them work on the Internet, you have to add four functions, IOleDocument, IOleDocumentView, IOleCommandTarget, and IPrint, which we'll discuss shortly.

Let's talk about the final item on this list in greater detail. ActiveDocuments are fairly new in some ways. Since Microsoft kept the specification for them a secret for so long, few compilers out there provide direct support for an ActiveDocument server. What this means to you as a programmer is that you'll have to either build the added interfaces yourself (not really too difficult) or upgrade your compiler. What we'll look at in the next four sections are the four added interface calls that you'll have to support in order to create a fully functional ActiveX Document server. (Fortunately, they aren't all required—Figure 11-3 shows that Excel only implements three of them.) The good news is that the ActiveX SDK provides the header and other support files needed to create these interface elements. We'll take a look at those in this section as well.

TIP: Microsoft Visual C++ versions 4.2 and above include direct support for creating most ActiveX object types, including ActiveDocument. This means that these versions will literally build all of the elements we'll talk about in this section for you—reducing the time it will take for you to create your new control or application.

IOleDocument
tells the client
that your
application can
act as an
ActiveDocument
server and
provides
communication
services.

IOleDocument

Whenever an Internet client sees a server that implements the IOleDocument class, it knows that the server can act as an ActiveDocument server. This is the first thing that Internet Explorer and other Internet client applications will look for when they see a document that's associated with your application. Don't confuse standard in-place activation with the kind used by an ActiveDocument server. You can build an application that supports in-place activation alone and it will work fine on a local machine, but it won't support in-place activation over the Internet.

11

NOTE: In many cases, it doesn't matter if you implement this interface—you can still support OLE 2 without it. A server that's missing this interface will simply be opened in a separate window, even if it normally supports in-place activation with local clients like Word for Windows.

A server view is a single instance of the server itself—it allows communication between the client and server.

So what does this class do besides tell Internet Explorer that your application supports ActiveDocuments? The methods it supports are called every time the client needs to create new server views (CreateView method), enumerate those views (EnumViews method), or retrieve the MiscStatus bits associated with the ActiveDocument (GetDocMiscStatus method). In essence, this class helps you manage the server as a whole. It provides the low-level functionality required for the client and server to communicate.

A server view isn't the same thing as the view that the user sees when clicking on a link to one of your documents—that's managed by the IOleDocumentView interface, which we'll talk about next. What a server view provides is a single instance of the server itself. A client application uses this view for communication purposes. For example, if the client needs to find out what features the server supports, it would use a server view to do so. We'll see how this works when we get into the actual application code.

There are four standard miscellaneous status bits. The following list describes each of them in detail.

◆ *DOCMISC_CANCREATEMULTIPLEVIEWS*   Tells the client whether the server can create multiple views. In other words, this bit defines whether you can run multiple copies of the application at one time. In most cases, a modern server can do this. About the only exceptions are for CAD or drawing programs where the memory requirements might be prohibitive. Another class of application that may not support this is a communications program, since most people only have one modem.

◆ *DOCMISC_SUPPORTCOMPLEXRECTANGLES*   Tells whether the server can support complex view area commands. An example is whether or not the server will allow the client to determine the position of things like scroll bars and sizing boxes.

◆ *DOCMISC_CANOPENEDIT*   Used to tell the client whether the server can open a document for editing. Setting this bit prevents the user from editing a document online (something you may want to consider for security reasons or if you want to create a server for viewing purposes only).

◆ *DOCMISC_NOFILESUPPORT*   Tells whether the server supports any kind of file manipulation. Setting this bit usually forces the client to display an error message since the user won't even be able to read the selected file.

IOleDocument
View provides a
single instance
of the document
that the user
wants to see.

IOleDocumentView

Like the IOleDocument class, you must implement IOleDocumentView to make ActiveDocument work. This particular interface element is reliant on the IOleDocument class. You need to have a server running before you can open a document. In addition, the client relies on information it gets from the GetDocMiscStatus method of IOleDocument to know how to interact with this class. Each copy of the IOleDocumentView class controls a single instance of an ActiveDocument view. In most cases, this means that the single instance of the IOleDocumentView class controls a single document. However, you could just as easily create one instance of the class for each view of the single document you have opened.

The IOleDocumentView class supports a variety of methods. Table 11-1 lists the most common methods that you'll find. As you can see, these methods allow you to resize the screen, create another copy of the view that you're looking at, reset the view's bounding area, or determine which document is currently displaying within the view.

Method	Action
SetInPlaceSite	Associates a view site object with this view. The client supplies the view site object. In essence, this is the method that will associate a document with the current view.
GetInPlaceSite	Returns a pointer to the view site object associated with the view.
GetDocument	Returns a pointer to the document associated with the view.
SetRect	Defines the bounding area for the view. In other words, this method sets the size of the window that the user will see.
GetRect	Returns the coordinates for the view's bounding area.
SetRectComplex	Defines a complex bounding area for the view. This method determines not only the size of the window the user will see, but things like the placement of scroll bars and other view elements. A view doesn't have to support this feature. You do need to set a miscellaneous status bit if your application doesn't provide the support. (See the IOleDocument class description for more details.)
Show	Lets the client either show or hide the view.

Methods
Associated
with the
IOleDocument
View Class
Table 11-1.

11

Method	Action
UIActivate	Determines whether the user interface is active or not. Normally the user interface is only active when the view has the focus. It is usually deactivated at all other times, to prevent conflicts with the view that does have focus.
Open	Requests that the server open the view in a separate window. You can turn off this feature using a miscellaneous status bit. (See the IOleDocument class description for more details.)
CloseView	Shuts down the view.
SaveViewState	Writes the current view status information to an IStream.
ApplyViewState	Requests that a view return its state to the settings defined in a previously saved IStream.
Clone	Creates a copy of the current view. The cloned view will have the same context but will use a different view port (instance of the IOleDocumentView class).

Methods Associated with the IOleDocument View Class (*continued*)

Table 11-1.

IOleCommandTarget

IOleCommand
Target allows
the server and
client to
communicate
without using
things like
fixed-menu IDs.

This is one of the classes you don't have to implement to make ActiveDocument work. However, it's a lot more than a simple convenience item. IOleCommandTarget allows the client and server to talk with each other without resorting to tricks like assigning fixed-menu IDs. Of course, there are limitations to this communication. For one thing, the communication is still limited to a fixed number of commands (which we'll talk about a little further down). There is a two-step procedure required to make this part of the interface work.

The first part of the client-to-server communication is to find out what commands the server supports. The client does this using the Query method. Table 11-2 provides a complete list of the commands that the server can support along with their associated identifiers. The first thing you should notice is that most of the commands are standard menu entries.

The second phase of the client/server communication uses the Exec method. The client passes the server one or more OLECMD structures. Each structure contains a single command, any required input arguments, and a place to put informational flags on return from the call. You won't need to provide any

Command	Identifier
Edit Clear	OLECMDID_CLEARSELECTION
Edit Copy	OLECMDID_COPY
Edit Cut	OLECMDID_CUT
Edit Paste	OLECMDID_PASTE
Edit Paste Special	OLECMDID_PASTESPECIAL
Edit Redo	OLECMDID_REDO
Edit Select All	OLECMDID_SELECTALL
Edit Undo	OLECMDID_UNDO
File New	OLECMDID_NEW
File Open	OLECMDID_OPEN
File Page Setup	OLECMDID_PAGESETUP
File Print	OLECMDID_PRINT
File Print Preview	OLECMDID_PRINTPREVIEW
File Properties	OLECMDID_PROPERTIES
File Save	OLECMDID_SAVE
File Save As	OLECMDID_SAVEAS
File Save Copy As	OLECMDID_SAVECOPYAS
Not a standard command. This identifier asks the server if it can perform the following three tasks: return a zoom value, display a zoom dialog, and set a zoom value. This identifier is normally associated with View menu commands (or their equivalent) if the server supports them.	OLECMDID_ZOOM
Not a standard command. This identifier retrieves the zoom range supported by the server. It's normally associated with the View Zoom command if the server supports it (or an equivalent).	OLECMDID_GETZOOMRANGE
Tools Spelling	OLECMDID_SPELL

11

Common Commands Supported by IOleCommand Target

Table 11-2.

IPrint performs the task that its name implies—it allows an object to support programmatic printing.

input arguments, so that part of the structure will contain a NULL. The standard options appear in Table 11-3. Table 11-4 describes the flags that you'll see on return from an Exec call.

IPrint

IPrint is another optional class that you can implement. This class allows an object to support programmatic printing. There are three methods supported by IPrint: print (Print), retrieve print-related information (GetPageInfo), and set the initial page number for a print job (SetInitialPageNum). Of the three methods, only the Print method accepts any flags as input. Table 11-5 provides a list of these flags and tells how to use them.

Flag	Action
OLECMDEXECOPT_PROMPTUSER	Prompts the user for some kind of input prior to executing the command. For example, you'd want to use this option with a File Open command.
OLECMDEXECOPT_DONTPROMPTUSER	Don't ask the user for any kind of input. For example, you might want to use this option when the user asks you to print a document.
OLECMDEXECOPT_DODEFAULT	You're not sure whether to prompt the user or not. In this case you want the application to perform the default action. In most cases this means it will prompt the user for input.
OLECMDEXECOPT_SHOWHELP	Don't execute the command at all; display its help screen instead. You might want to use this command if your ActiveDocument provides an alternative help button.

Standard Exec Method Input Arguments

Table 11-3.

Flag	Action
OLECMDF_SUPPORTED	The view object supports the requested command.
OLECMDF_ENABLED	The command is available and the view object has enabled it.
OLECMDF_LATCHED	This command uses an on-off toggle and it is currently set to On.
OLECMDF_NINCHED	The view object can't determine the state of a command that uses a toggle state. In most cases this means that the command uses a tri-state configuration and that it's in the indeterminate state. For example, a three-state checkbox will return this value if the user has selected some suboptions for an install program but not others. (The checkbox appears grayed onscreen.)

Standard Exec
Method Return
Values
Table 11-4.

Flag	Action
PRINTFLAG_MAYBOTHERUSER	Tells the server that user interaction is allowed by the client. If this flag isn't set, then any print requests have to run by themselves. In most cases the client will allow user interaction—the only exception will probably involve batch printing jobs or situations where the print operation proceeds in the background.
PRINTFLAG_PROMPTUSER	Prompts the user for input regarding the print job using the standard print dialog (like the one supported by Windows). For example, the user can select the number of copies when this option is specified. You must also specify the PRINTFLAG_ MAYBOTHERUSER flag to use this option.

Flags
Supported by
the Print
Method of
IPrint
Table 11-5.

11

Flag	Action
PRINTFLAG_USERMAYCHANGE PRINTER	Allows the user to change the printer. There are some situations where you won't want to enable this option—like network setups where the user can't easily access the printer. You must also specify the PRINTFLAG_PROMPTUSER flag to use this option.
PRINTFLAG_RECOMPOSETODEVICE	Tells the print job to recompose itself for the target printer. For example, if the target printer supports a higher resolution than is currently specified as part of the print job, then the print job should make use of that higher resolution.
PRINTFLAG_DONTACTUALLYPRINT	Tests the print job but does not actually create any output. This option allows you to test a user interface feature like prompting without wasting paper in the process.
PRINTFLAG_PRINTTOFILE	Sends the printed output to a file instead of to a printer.

Flags
Supported by
the Print
Method of
IPrint
(*continued*)
Table 11-6.

Creating an ActiveDocument

In the previous section, we looked at what you can do with an ActiveDocument application such as Word for Windows or Excel. That's fine if you're a power user who needs to get a little added performance or a webmaster who wants to optimize a Web site, but you're a programmer who needs to create an application with these capabilities.

Trying to manually add all four of the required interfaces that we looked at in the previous section might prove troublesome even to the most accomplished programmer. In addition, there really isn't any need to go through the trouble now that Microsoft has released its new version of C++ (versions 4.2 and above work, but you'll find that 5.0 works with fewer glitches than 4.2, and version 6.0 is completely seamless). What we'll look at in this section is the quick method for creating an ActiveDocument-enabled application. We'll skip some of the details that you'd find in just about any application and concentrate on the ActiveX-specific portions of the project instead.

The first thing you need to do is create a new project workspace. We saw how to do that in Chapter 2. You'll want to select the MFC AppWizard and give your application a name—the sample application uses ActivDoc. Click on OK to start the process, and you'll see the first page of the MFC AppWizard. To make life a little simpler, check the Single Document option on the first page of the wizard. Click Next twice to get past the first and second pages of the wizard. What you'll see next is the third page.

The third page is where you'll do most of the ActiveDocument configuration for the application. You can provide five different levels of OLE support with your application. The last three levels also allow you to add ActiveDocument support. The Mini-Server option won't allow you to run the application alone—you'd have to run it from Word for Windows, Internet Explorer 3.0, or some other container. This level of support is fine if you want to create a file browser. The next option is Full-Server, which allows the application to execute by itself. You can use this kind of application to support objects but not to display them. Paint programs are usually good examples of an application that acts as a server but not necessarily as a container. The final level, Both Container and Server, is the one that we'll select for this application. It allows you to provide full OLE 2 capabilities in your application, including embedding objects. You'll also want to check the ActiveDocument Server option. Make sure you also check the Automation and ActiveX Controls options. Here's what your dialog should look like at this point.

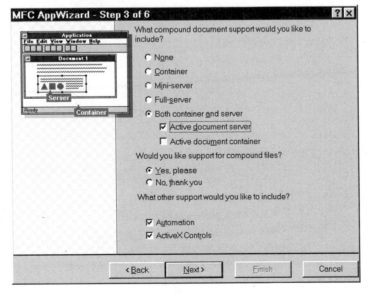

11

NOTE: The Active Document Container option is new to Visual C++ 6.0. It allows you to build applications that can contain other ActiveDocuments. For example, you could use this capability to display an Internet Explorer document within your application without actually providing HTML capabilities.

Click Next to see the fourth page of the MFC AppWizard. Most of the settings on this page are just fine. You may want to set the Recent File List setting higher since most people really like this feature (it sure beats hunting around on the hard drive). A setting of 9 or 10 works fine in most cases; the example program uses a setting of 10.

This page also contains an Advanced button—which most programmers might whiz right by if they didn't look hard enough. Unfortunately, this button really shouldn't be labeled Advanced (or perhaps Microsoft should consider reworking the Application Wizard a bit to make one of the required settings more obvious). Click on the Advanced button and you'll see an Advanced Options dialog similar to the one in Figure 11-4.

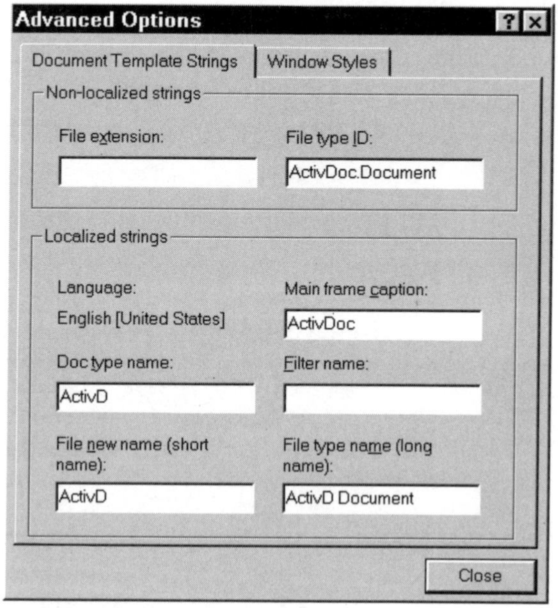

The Advanced Options dialog contains at least one entry that you really need to change before creating an application.

Figure 11-4.

Advanced Options

Document Template Strings | Window Styles

Non-localized strings

File extension: | File type ID:
| ActivDoc.Document

Localized strings

Language: | Main frame caption:
English [United States] | ActivDoc

Doc type name: | Filter name:
ActivD |

File new name (short name): | File type name (long name):
ActivD | ActivD Document

Close

The Document Template Strings page of the Advanced Options dialog allows you to set the file extension for your application. It also performs some important behind-the-scenes work for you automatically. The example program uses a file extension of AXD. All you need to do is type the extension in the first field (which starts out blank). You may want to change some additional strings, for example, the Main Frame Caption field. The example uses ActiveX Document Editor. You may want to make the entry in the Filter Name field a little more descriptive as well. It starts out as ActivD Files (*.axd), but changing it to ActiveX Document Files (*.axd) is a lot more readable. Some people really don't care too much about the long File Type Name field (which defaults to ActivD Document), but changing it to ActiveX Document will certainly help later as you search through the registry. In addition, this is the string used to display your new document within the Windows context menu (more on this in a few paragraphs). Once you make all of these changes, your Advanced Options dialog should look like the one here.

At this point, we've made all the selections required to create a simple ActiveDocument server, but we'll want to make one additional change. Click on Close to close the Advanced Options dialog. Click Next twice to get to the MFC AppWizard - Step 6 of 6 dialog. Choose the CActivDocView entry in the classes list, and then select CRichEditView in the Base Class field. Your dialog should look like the one shown here.

11

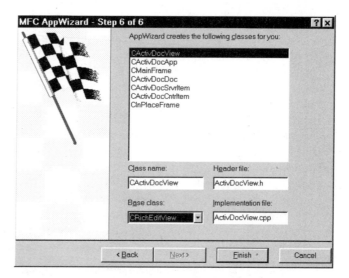

The whole purpose of this last step is to allow you to use the sample application as a simple editor, should you wish to do so. You could have implemented the standard CView class if you had wanted to—it wouldn't affect the ability of the program to act as an ActiveDocument server. Now click on Finish to complete the project shell. You'll see a New Project Information dialog like the one shown here.

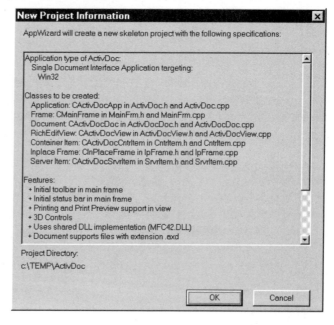

Take a few seconds to look through the list of features to ensure that the ActiveX support is complete. (After working with a few projects, you'll find that you can detect any problems very quickly by looking at this dialog.) Click on OK to generate the project shell.

Testing the Default Application

Right now our sample application can't do much, but there are a few things it can do right out of the Wizard. Compile and run the application once the MFC AppWizard finishes creating it. Running the application is important because the application makes some registry entries the first time you do so. The first change you'll notice is that the Windows context menu now contains an entry for your application file type, as shown here.

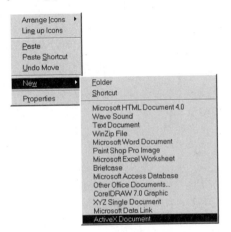

Notice that this is the same name that we typed in the File Type Name field of the Advanced Options dialog from the preceding section.

You'll see another change as well. Figure 11-5 shows the ActiveX Document application type within the OLE/COM Object Viewer utility (we worked with this utility in a previous section). As you can see, it's listed with the other Document Objects, such as Word for Windows. You should immediately notice that none of the four interfaces we talked about earlier in the chapter are listed here, as they would be for Word for Windows or other Binder programs. We'll see later in this section that checking your interfaces before saying that a program is ready for testing can save you a lot of time and effort later.

The ActivDoc program can also create a basic container file. All you need to do is use the Insert I Object command to add an existing object to the current

11

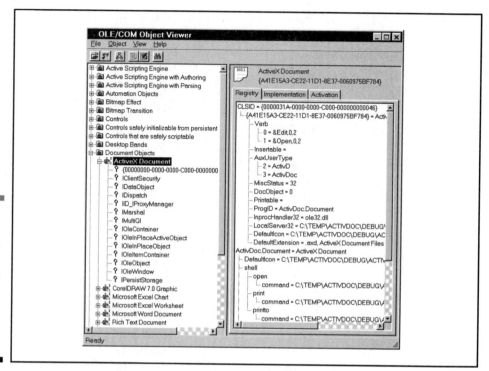

The ActivDoc application appears within the OLE/COM Object Viewer utility as a Document Object.

Figure 11-5.

document. You can save the file to disk. Try creating one now so that you can test the application frame with Internet Explorer. Make sure you insert an object and then save the file, or you won't see anything when opening the document. This example uses the ColorBlk.BMP file as the object—the file itself is saved as TESTDOC.AXD. Once you create the test document, you'll need to create an HTML page to test it. Listing 11-2 shows the code we'll use in this case.

Listing 11-2:

```
<HTML>
<HEAD>
<TITLE>New Page</TITLE>
</HEAD>
<BODY>

<!-Display a heading.->
<CENTER><H2>ActiveX Document Test</H2></CENTER>

<!-Create a link to the test document.->
Click <A HREF="TestDoc.AXD">Here</A> to test the AXD file.

</BODY>
</HTML>
```

Now that we have a test bed, let's see how the application works. Open the test Web page in Internet Explorer, and then click on the test link. What you should see is a copy of our test application within Internet Explorer, as shown in Figure 11-6, just as you saw when working with Word for Windows. Notice that the sample application has taken over the menus and toolbar of the browser, just as a Word for Windows document would. In addition, you can insert new objects and perform other tasks using the menu, just as if the application were working on a local document. You can also use the Web Publishing Wizard to save changes (see the section, Using the Web Publishing Wizard" earlier in this chapter for details on this utility).

NOTE: If everything works properly, you'll see a dialog asking if you want to either save or open the file (assuming, of course, that you haven't turned the dialog off during a previous session). Make sure you tell the browser to open the file so that you can actually view it.

Converting an Existing Application

Don't worry if you have a perfectly good application lying around that just doesn't happen to support ActiveDocument. You can convert it to provide this level of support with a minimum of effort—well, at least a lot less effort than writing the program from scratch. In this section we're going to look at a five-step process that you can use to convert just about any existing OLE server to a rudimentary ActiveDocument server. However, it's important to remember that you'll only provide rudimentary support. Some applications will work just fine with this; others won't. Spend some time reading once more the overview of ActiveDocument architecture in this chapter to get the theory down before you start adding support items. Once you do get the additional support items worked out, make sure you test them using an actual Internet setup rather than a local drive. This ensures that you test the complete interface and that the application won't try to do an end around by

11

Our sample document appears within the browser window, just as any Active-Document would.
Figure 11-6.

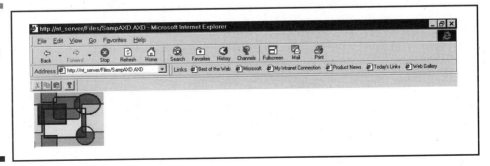

using standard OLE interfaces rather than the ActiveDocument interfaces that you really want to test.

Step 1: Implement the Classes

The first and most obvious step is to implement the classes required to create an ActiveDocument server. If you look at the example we just created in the previous section and any pre-C++ 4.2 application, you'll notice some very basic differences in the way the classes are declared. That's because Microsoft has subclassed the original MFC classes and added some functionality to them. Table 11-6 shows which classes have changed and how. The first column shows the class declarations used in a pre-C++ 4.2 application. The second column shows the new declarations. The third column tells you which file is affected. The fourth column shows an alternate class declaration that you may find implemented in older MFC class files—they're based on the Microsoft Office Binder declarations.

Once you replace these declarations in your header files, you'll also need to replace them in the associated CPP files. Using the search-and-replace capability of Microsoft Developer will make this easier. You won't have to worry too much about missing any of the places where the new class names are used—the compiler will point out any discrepancies automatically once you make the header file changes. Therefore, it's important to make the header file changes first and double-check them before you move on. (Notice that if you're trying to implement an ActiveDocument server using the ActiveX SDK and an older set of MFC files, you'll need to change three header

Active Document Class Declarations
Table 11-7.

Original Class Declaration	New C++ 4.2 and Above Declaration	ActivDoc Example Program File	Alternate MFC Class Declaration
class CInPlaceFrame : public COleIPFrameWnd	class CInPlaceFrame : public COleDocIPFrameWnd	IPFrame.H	class CInPlaceFrame : public CDocObjectIPFrameWnd
class CActivDocDoc : public COleServerDoc	class CActivDocDoc : public COleServerDoc	ActivDocDoc.H	class CActivDocDoc : public DocObjectServerDoc
class CActivDocSrvr : public COleServerItem	class CActivDocSrvr : public CDocObjectServer	SrvrItem.H	class CActivDocSrvr : public CDocObjectServerItem

files, whereas moving to Visual C++ 4.2 or above requires a change of only two header files.)

Step 2: Add a Simple Declaration
The second step is to add a simple declaration to the STDAFX.H file for your application:

```
#include <afxdocob.h>
```

This header file contains all of the declarations needed by your application to get document object support. In fact, a quick look at this file can be quite educational, as it shows exactly how the four ActiveDocument interface elements get implemented.

Step 3: Change a Registry Entry
The third step is to change the way you make one of the registry entries. The application you're creating is no longer just an in-place server, so you'll need to change the registry entry in your CWinApp.CPP file (in the case of the example program, it's the ActivDoc.CPP file) from OAT_INPLACE_SERVER to OAT_DOC_OBJECT_SERVER. The actual line of code looks like this:

```
m_server.UpdateRegistry(OAT_DOC_OBJECT_SERVER);
```

Step 4: Change the Parse Maps
The fourth step is to change some of the parse maps, since you'll need to tell your application where to send the print commands and other OLE-related information. You'll need to change two files. The first is the application document header file—ActivDocDoc.H in the case of our sample program. You'll need to add the following highlighted line:

11

```
// Generated message map functions
protected:
    //{{AFX_MSG(CActivDocDoc)
        // NOTE - the ClassWizard will add and remove member functions here.
        //    DO NOT EDIT what you see in these blocks of generated code !
    //}}AFX_MSG
    DECLARE_MESSAGE_MAP()
DECLARE_OLECMD_MAP()
};
```

If the message map includes a DECLARE_MESSAGE_MAP() message map function, make sure the DECLARE_OLECMD_MAP() line appears after it. The second file is the application-document CPP file. At the very beginning of the file, you'll find at least one mapping area for messages. You'll need to add another mapping area, as shown here:

```
BEGIN_OLECMD_MAP(CActivDocDoc, COleServerDoc)
    ON_OLECMD_PAGESETUP()
    ON_OLECMD_PRINT()
END_OLECMD_MAP()
```

As you can see, these additions allow the application to print by routing the print functions through their handler functions using the ID_FILE_PAGE_SETUP and ID_FILE_PRINT standard identifiers. All you need to do to complete the picture is add command maps for the actual handler functions, like this:

```
ON_COMMAND (ID_FILE_PRINT, OnFilePrint)
```

Step 5: Add a New Function

The fifth (and last) step is to add a new function to your application document header and CPP files.

Once you've completed these modifications, you'll need to compile and test the updated application. In most cases, you'll want to test it locally first to make sure you haven't broken anything with the changes. After you're satisfied that the changes haven't affected local performance, try to open a document from the browser. You should see the document open within the browser instead of within a separate window (just as the example program does in Figure 11-6). Make sure the application provides the same level of functionality (sans File | Save command) as it would when used locally.

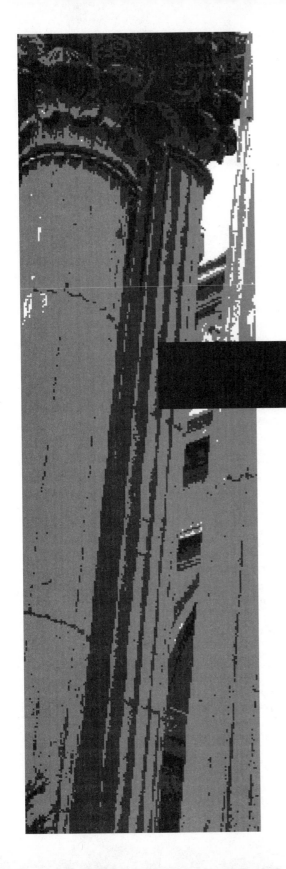

CHAPTER 12

Using URLs
and Monikers

People in the northeastern part of the United States are famous for saying "You can't get there from here; you have to go somewhere else first." Some people feel the same way about the Internet. It always seems as if you have to cross a minimum of four or five Web pages before you find the one site you were looking for to begin with.

It's this very principle that has caused some webmasters to place a number of links on their Web sites. Each link points to information related to the current topic—information that augments the Web site in some way. There isn't a single user who will complain about the presence of these added links. In fact, you'll find that they would complain if the links were missing.

> A uniform resource locator (URL) specifies where to find something on the Internet.

There's a problem with the current system of links, though. Just like everything else on the Internet, they're static. You get the same set of links on a particular site no matter how you entered it or what set of conditions you're operating under. Wouldn't it be nice if the Web site had at least a little intelligence to help you find what you needed? In addition, wouldn't it be nice if you could enter some criteria to make the process of moving from one site to the other a bit easier? For example, you could type in some kind of criteria to locate a specific kind of site based on current needs. ActiveX provides a way to take care of this dynamic need through the use of the URL (a string that defines where to find something) and the moniker (the actual resource object provided by the system).

> A moniker, in the context of the Internet, is the resource used to store a location object.

Overview of URL Monikers

Let's begin this section by looking at what those two terms, URLs and monikers, mean. A *URL* (uniform resource locator) is the method we've all become accustomed to using for getting from one site to another. It's the **http://www.mycompany.com** that you type when using a browser. URLs have three essential parts: the *protocol* (http in this case), the *host* (www), and the *domain* (mycompany.com). The rest of any URL you type is a location (like a directory) on the resource that you've identified. What makes this scheme so useful is that you can extend it almost infinitely. For example, if you want to use another protocol, just specify it at the beginning of the URL. The Internet has quite a few such protocols, including HTTP, FTP, Gopher, and News.

> URLs consist of three main parts: protocol, host name, and domain.

NOTE: The discussion of URLs in this section is meant to include all URLs, not just the general case discussed. For example, some URLs use home or another name for the host, like **http://home.netscape.com**. In addition, some domains are becoming increasingly complex so they can provide more precise information, like **http://www.wisconsin.edu.k6.us**, which is a URL for primary schools in the state of Wisconsin in the United States. Some browsers don't require the user to type a protocol; they simply check all appropriate protocols for the resource. In sum, don't assume anything about the URLs in this section other than the general case example they provide.

Monikers originated with the OLE 2 specification. Essentially, a *moniker* is a system-generated object. You can use this object to find another object or to retrieve data from it. Some types of custom monikers may support other operations as well, but these are the two basic operations that are provided by any moniker. The OLE 2 specification introduced synchronous monikers, which means that the application would wait until the system had retrieved whatever data it was looking for from the specified object.

WEB LINK: You may want to invest in a little specialized training if you plan to use URL monikers in a commercial application. Developer Solutions has a course you can read about at **http://www.devsolutions .com/** that deals specifically with the topic of monikers. The three-day course also covers a variety of other OLE-related topics like DCOM and marshalling. If you're really interested in finding out about the full details of the OLE standard that Microsoft has submitted to ANSI for approval, look at **http://info.gte.com/ftp/doc/activities/x3h7/by_model/ OLE2.html**.

If you combine the idea of a URL with that of a moniker, you get the *URL moniker* provided by the ActiveX API, which is included as part of Visual C++ versions 4.2 through 6.0. So what's the difference between the URL moniker used by ActiveX and the synchronous monikers that the OLE 2 specification talks about? For one thing, URL monikers provide both synchronous and asynchronous binding. This is important for looking on the Internet because

12

you don't know how long it will take to find something. If you use synchronous binding for an Internet search, the application could get blocked and cause all kinds of problems on the client machine (not the least of which is that the user will sit there and wait while looking at an unchanging application). A URL moniker also provides a framework for building and using URLs—something the OLE 2 specification didn't have to take into account. If you want to access remote data using a standard OLE 2 application, it has to support UNC (universal naming convention) drive locations across a network. This implies mapped drives of some sort, which you obviously can't get with an Internet location.

You'll need three pieces to create a URL moniker: client, system, and transport. The *client* part of the equation is built into your application. We'll look at the client end of the picture later in the section on working with URL monikers. The *system* component is part of the operating system (you don't have to worry about this part because Microsoft takes care of it). A *transport* simply specifies how you plan to get the information from the server to the client. The transport part of the equation is variable—it depends on what transport you want to implement. When it comes to the Internet, you'll probably use TCP.

Just like every other special OLE capability discussed in this book so far, implementing URL monikers requires you to create or use some special interfaces. There are two each in the client, system, and transport components of the URL moniker. The following list describes each interface.

◆ *IEnumFormatETC (client)*   This optional interface allows you to provide protocol-specific information that affects the bind operation. For example, if you want to supply MIME capabilities, you'd need to provide this interface to enumerate the formats your application supports.

◆ *IBindStatusCallback (client)*   The transport uses this interface to notify the client about specific events such as the progress of a download. More importantly, once the binding from the client through the system to the transport is complete, the transport uses the IBindSystemCallback:: OnStartBinding method to pass back an IBinding interface.

◆ *IBindCtx (system)*   You'll begin the process of finding an Internet resource by passing a pointer to your IBindStatusCallback interface (and optionally, the IEnumFormatETC interface) using the CreateAsyncBindCtx ActiveX API call. This returns a pointer to the IBindCtx interface, which performs the actual binding between client and transport.

Remember that Windows provides the two system-level interfaces that you'll need to implement URL monikers.

◆ *IMoniker (system)*   You use this interface element for a lot of purposes. The main functions it performs include retrieving moniker names in human-readable form using the GetDisplayName method and transport instantiation using the BindToStorage or BindToObject method.

◆ *IParseDisplayName (transport)*   The current version of the MkParseDisplayNameEx() function supported by ActiveX will allow you to create monikers from either files or URLs. You may find that you need to create monikers from other kinds of objects. This interface allows your application to work with the transport to create new moniker types. You'll also need to register these new moniker types with the registry.

◆ *IBinding (transport)*   The system creates a transport defined by the type of protocol that the application wants to access. IBinding is the resulting protocol-specific transport interface. It parses the protocol string, drives any download of data, and provides status information to your application through its IBindStatusCallback interface. The application can use the IBinding interface to start, stop, pause, or resume the binding operation.

IN DEPTH

The Relationship Between Port Numbers and URLs

I'm not going to spend a lot of time bending your ear about a topic best left to engineers, but at the same time it's kind of handy to know a little about how that "http" in a URL works when it comes to the hardware/software connection. The Internet uses the concept of a port number. In other words, when you make a connection to IP address 200.100.100.1, you can choose a particular port on that location.

Actually, this concept is a leftover from the days when people used mainframes on the Internet to the exclusion of everything else. You could plug a terminal into a specific port on the back of the mainframe to access specific services. Fortunately, you can downsize this concept to the PC. Like the serial and parallel port on your computer, the ports on the Internet have a specific purpose.

12

The software part of the picture is pretty easy to understand as well. Anyone who has done assembly-level programming on the computer knows that you need to access a specific port number to grab information from the keyboard. Even if you haven't done any assembly-language programming, you've probably spent time configuring a card, like a sound board, to use a specific port. Any software you want to use with the sound board, like a game, needs to know the port number of the sound board before you'll hear any sounds. Likewise, if you want to grab a specific piece of information from the Internet, you'll need a port number.

Specifying a particular protocol in a URL is equivalent to asking for a particular port number. Older communication programs required you to enter the port number; thankfully, URLs have solved that problem. For example, when you type "http" as part of a URL, you're requesting access to port number 80 on the host computer. (Other examples include TelNet, which uses port 23, and some types of interactive games, which use port 4201—in short, every protocol has a specific port number.) Remembering http is a lot easier than remembering you need to use port 80. Since everyone on the Internet uses the same port numbers for specific common services, using http in a URL actually works.

OK, so now it's time to figure out why this information is important for you to know. A network administrator isn't stuck using the default port numbers for services. You could add a special port number for specific company services on the Internet—provided your server software allows such a configuration. While using special port numbers isn't a replacement for firewalls and other security aids, it is one way to set a spot on your Internet server aside from the prying eyes of the world. Knowing the port numbers is also handy when performing certain configuration tasks like setting filters for your firewall. Finally, and this is a big deal for programmers, knowing how an Internet connection works can help you troubleshoot applications when everything seems like it should be working, but isn't.

Creating a URL Moniker

As with every other kind of OLE communication, creating an URL moniker follows a pretty standard routine. There are several levels of communication, and you can choose whether or not to implement some interfaces fully or at all (IEnumFormatETC). The following steps outline a typical communication session using the minimum number of interface elements. In other words, this procedure tells you what you'll always see—anything else either increases flexibility or provides additional information exchange.

1. Create a binding context. You can do this using the CreateAsyncBindCtx() function call provided with the ActiveX API. This call requires that you provide a pointer to your application's IBindStatusCallback function. Without this interface, there isn't any way for the system and transport to communicate with your application. You can also pass a pointer to the optional IEnumFormatETC interface if your application implements special features such as MIME. The format enumerator allows the server and transport to determine what data formats your application can handle (they always assume you can handle text data).

2. The system will pass back a pointer to its IBindCtx interface. This interface also registers your IBindStatusCallback with the bind context.

3. Once your application has an IBindCtx to work with, it can use either the CreateURLMoniker() or the MkParseDisplayNameEx() function call to create a URL moniker. The choice of which function to use is simple. If you have a moniker, use the CreateURLMoniker() function. Otherwise, use the MkParseDisplayNameEx() function that parses the text string, creates a moniker from it, and then passes this information to the CreateURLMoniker() function.

NOTE: Users of older versions of Visual C++ will need the updated version of the Win32 API provided with the MSDN subscription to implement the MkParseDisplayNameEx() function—this support comes with Visual C++ 5.0 and 6.0 as part of the package.

4. The next step is to create a transport capable of working with the URL moniker by using the system's IMoniker interface. There are two methods for doing this: BindToObject() and BindToStorage(). The BindToObject() call allows you to instantiate an object that points to the moniker. This object allows you to interact with the moniker. Normally, you'd use it with a Web site or other live connection. The BindToStorage() call retrieves the data pointed to by the moniker and stores it. This process is referred to as *binding* the moniker. Essentially, you grab the information and stick it on disk. You'd use this call with

12

something like an FTP site. In either case, you have to pass the pointer to the IBindCtx that you received in step 2 as part of the call.

5. The system's IMoniker interface will launch a transport-specific server for whatever protocol you requested. It determines which protocol to use based on the moniker you passed. As soon as the transport-specific server becomes active, it sends the application a pointer to its IBinding interface using the application's IBindStatusCallback::OnStartBinding() method.

6. Now that you've established communication between all three elements—application, system, and transport—and provided the application with two interfaces for working with the other elements (IBindCtx and IBinding), your application can begin the process of downloading a file, Web page, or other resource. There's one other piece to the communication puzzle, though. Whenever the application requests data, the transport will tell it the progress of the download using the IBindStatusCallback::OnDataAvailable() method. The application uses the status information passed through this method to determine whether or not the download is complete. (You can also use this status information to update a progress bar or other status indicator for the user.)

Hyperlinking Basics

The user-specific part of a URL moniker interface could be as simple as the hyperlink on a Web page.

URL monikers are the low-level part of an OLE implementation for getting from one place to the other on the Internet. There's a higher-level interface as well: the one seen by the user. Whenever you see a bit of underlined text in your browser, you're probably looking at a hyperlink to another site. We've already covered the HTML part of this process in several chapters of the book (see Chapter 8 for an overview of HTML).

Microsoft provides an ActiveX hyperlink interface you can use to emulate a specific browser's actions within an ActiveX control. Like other forms of OLE, this means that you can extend browser technology to an application or simply use it within an HTML page to provide an added level of functionality for an ActiveX control. Wherever you use ActiveX hyperlinks, you can perform a few basic services that include the items in the following list.

◆ *Application to application* You can create a hyperlink between two applications in the absence of a browser. This is an especially handy feature if you implement some type of intranet site on your LAN.

◆ *Application to ActiveX/HTML document* We saw how ActiveDocuments work in Chapter 11. The document is actually displayed in the browser window. You make the connection from the Internet to the document using a standard HTML <A HREF> tag. What if you could place a control in an application that automatically connects you to a document on the Internet? In other words, this link would act just like an HTML <A HREF> tag in reverse. ActiveX hyperlink controls can help you accomplish this task. For example, you can use this capability to provide links from a company policy document to sources of additional information on the Internet.

◆ *ActiveDocument to ActiveDocument* You're in a browser looking at a document. Wouldn't it be nice to be able to move from one place to another in that document using anchors, just like you can on an HTML page? ActiveX hyperlinks allow you to do just that. You can also use this capability to move from one document to the next, just as you would move from one HTML page to the next on the Internet.

A navigation stack is a list of URLs visited during the current session and is maintained by the browser.

◆ *Browser ActiveDocument to Microsoft Office Binder ActiveDocument* A company could potentially use this capability on a local intranet. It would allow users to move from a document displayed in a browser to one located on the local machine through the Microsoft Office Binder. For example, you could use this capability to provide links to a local glossary. Whenever users didn't know the meaning of a word, they could follow a link located on the Internet to the local copy of the glossary for clarification.

Before you can perform any of these neat tricks, you need to create a URL moniker. We looked at this process in the previous two sections. You'll also need to work with the hyperlink interface provided with the ActiveX API. Fortunately, you don't have to resort to using a low-level interface like that provided for URL monikers. If all you want to do is get from point A to point B, you can use a set of four functions that Microsoft thoughtfully provided.

12

Function	Description
HLinkSimpleNavigateToString()	This function allows you to go to a new location based on a string—one that's formatted just like the strings you would type in at the browser. You'll normally use this function to go to a new HTML document or another location within the same HTML document, but you could use it with objects as well.
HLinkSimpleNavigateToMoniker()	This function moves you from one place to another using a moniker as a source of information. Normally, you'd use it with objects.
HLinkGoBack()	This function emulates the Go Back button on a browser's toolbar. It moves you to the previous position in the navigation stack.
HLinkGoForward()	This function emulates the Go Forward button on a browser's toolbar. It moves you to the next position in the navigation stack.

TIP: The simple hyperlink functions are located in the URLHLINK.H header file. (For users of Visual C++ versions older than 5.0, this file is provided with the ActiveX SDK.) You'll find the actual functions in the URLMON.DLL file.

Using these functions is fairly simple. Let's begin with the easier functions: HLinkGoBack() and HLinkGoForward(). Both of these functions require a single argument, a pointer to the IUnknown interface for the current document. To retrieve it, simply use the ExternalQueryInterface() function with IID_IUnknown as the first argument and a pointer variable as the second argument.

The HLinkSimpleNavigateToString() and HLinkSimpleNavigateToMoniker() functions are a bit more complicated. The following command lines show what arguments the functions will accept.

```
HLinkSimpleNavigateToString(szTarget, szLocation, szTargetFrame,
    pIUnknown, pIBindCtx, pIBindStatusCallback,
    grfHLNF, dwReserved)
HLinkSimpleNavigateToMoniker(pmkTarget, szLocation, szTargetFrame,
    pIUnknown, pIBindCtx, pIBindStatusCallback,
    grfHLNF, dwReserved)
```

Except for the first argument, both functions allow you to use the same list of arguments. The first argument for HLinkSimpleNavigateToString() is a string containing the URL (or other identifying information) of the site you want to visit. The first argument for HLinkSimpleNavigateToMoniker() is a pointer to a moniker.

Let's look at the common arguments. szLocation contains the name of a location on the same page. We looked at how this works in Chapter 8. The szTargetFrame argument contains the name of a frame within the document. This is HTML specific and works only with pages that use frames. Neither of these arguments is required; you need to provide them only if you want to furnish extended navigation information. Use a value of NULL for both arguments when you don't want to include them.

There are three interface-specific arguments: pIUnknown, pIBindCtx, and IBindStatusCallback. Of these three, only the pIUnknown argument is required. You can retrieve it using the ExternalQueryInterface() function. You'd need to specify a pIBindCtx value only if you wanted to provide additional processing information. For example, if your application provides MIME capability, you could use this parameter to pass the location of the IEnumFormatETC interface (it's passed as part of the IBindCtx parameter—don't pass a pointer to the IEnumFormatETC interface itself). You'll want to pass a pointer to the IBindStatusCallback interface for your application if you want status information during the transfer.

12

The grfHLNF argument is the only one remaining. It allows you to specify certain behaviors on the part of the browser. For example, if you provide HLNF_OPEN_INNEWWINDOW for this argument, the browser will display the specified site in a new window. You can see a complete list of HLNF values in the HLINK.H header file. (For users of Visual C++ versions older than 5.0, this file is provided with the ActiveX SDK.)

Understanding the Hyperlink Interface

In some situations, the simple hyperlink function calls discussed in the previous section won't do the job. For example, you may want to implement a full-fledged browser as part of your application. Another situation in which the simple calls won't work is if you want to provide some type of extended functionality not supported by the calls, for example, working with a history list. The calls in the previous section are best used in situations where navigation is the only concern.

As with any ActiveX control, you'll need to provide a few additional interfaces to implement hyperlinking within an application. In fact, there are five new interfaces, as follows:

◆ *IHLink (mandatory)*   This is the center point of the ActiveX hyperlinking interface. It's the interface that provides everything another application would need to hyperlink. This includes the target moniker (actual object identification), URL-style string, and a friendly name. You'll find that it also provides other kinds of information, but they're not normally needed to create a simple hyperlink. All simple hyperlinking is done through the Navigate method, which is what the simple functions described in the previous section use.

◆ *IHLinkTarget (optional)*   You'll use this to find your way around the document or to download additional information. For example, this interface would allow you to point to a specific cell within a spreadsheet. IHLinkTarget also provides the means for passing a pointer to the document's IBrowseContext interface to the calling application. An application can still hyperlink to a document that doesn't provide this interface, but that's about it.

◆ *IHLinkFrame (optional)*   Remember that in OLE, a frame is an application's container for an OLE container. It contains the menu and the outside box. This interface allows the frame to maintain contact with the OLE container (usually a document of some sort).

◆ *IHLinkSite (optional)*   This is the interface that manages the hyperlink site. It performs two essential services and many miscellaneous ones. The first major task is gaining access to a document's HLink object. Gaining access to this object provides a wealth of information, such as the current site name. The second major purpose for this interface is to provide feedback to the client application. For example, the OnNavigationComplete method will tell the client that a download or other task is complete.

◆ *IBrowseContext (optional)*   An application gains access to the browse context object through this interface. All the browse context object does is keep track of the navigation stack—the sites visited during the current session. The HLinkGoForward() and HLinkGoBack() functions described in the previous section rely on this interface to do their work.

There are actually two levels of implementation within this group of interfaces. We'll assume that the first level is an application—a browser in this case. The second level is an OLE container—a document in this case. The browser implements the IHLinkFrame and IBrowseContext interfaces. There is only one occurrence of both of these interfaces—the browser either implements them or it doesn't. The document implements the IHLinkTarget, IHLink, and IHLinkSite interfaces.

The document is a little more difficult to define in terms of interfaces. The container portion of the document implements the IHLinkTarget interface, so you'll only see one of them even when working with a document containing more than one object. Likewise, there is only one IHLinkSite interface per document no matter how many objects it contains. You can, however, have more than one hyperlink within a document.

Let's take a quick look at hyperlinks. Each hyperlink requires a separate IHLink interface, and there are four functions you can use to create one: HLinkCreateFromMoniker(), HLinkCreateFromString(), HLinkCreateFromData(), and HLinkQueryCreateFromData(). HLink objects can use persisted data, meaning that the control must implement an IPersistStream interface. Since you can create an HLink from data, you can also cut, copy, and paste it using the clipboard. In addition, since an HLink uses monikers, you can point to any kind of OLE document, including things you don't normally see displayed in a browser, such as a Word for Windows file.

Working with URL Monikers   12

With the special focus that some companies are placing on the Internet today, it won't be long before the information on the Internet becomes as easy to access as the data on a local hard drive. In fact, Microsoft has partially blurred this distinction as part of the Internet Explorer 4.0 release included with your copy of Visual C++ 6.0. You'll find that your hard drive and favorite places on the Internet share a common Explorer view.

WEB LINK: Getting the information you need often means making a visit to your local newsgroup for help from other programmers. Needless to say, you'll find that some newsgroups spend more time talking about URL monikers than others—after all, it's a somewhat esoteric subject. For example, the **microsoft.public.win32.programmer.ole** newsgroup had a fairly long thread on binding a moniker to a specific control. There's even a newsgroup devoted to the topic of URL monikers: **microsoft.public. activex.programming.urlmonikers**. If you want to make sure you'll get Visual C++-specific help from the people on the newsgroup, look at **microsoft.public.vc.mfcole**.

Of course, this blurring of data sites will open up some new opportunities for the user and programmer alike. For example, as a user you'll find it less cumbersome to get the data you need into the application you need in order to edit it. As a programmer, you'll find that there are now additional ways to tweak a program and make it special.

NOTE: You must install the ActiveX SDK if you're not using Visual C++ 5.0 or above to create the example in this section. The SDK provides the URLMON.H, HLINK.LIB, and URLMON.LIB files required to make the code work.

One of the most common ways that you'll probably find to make your application special is to add hyperlink capability to it. The easiest way to do this is to stick a button on the application's toolbar that takes the user to the company's intranet. You could extend this idea with another button that would allow the user to select a specific site or choose from a list of company-authorized Internet sites. That's what we'll look at in this section. The sample program will show you how to add two buttons to a typical application that will give the user a fast and easy way to make a link to the Internet.

The first step, of course, is to create a new application. As with the ActiveDocument example in Chapter 11, you could create this code using older versions of Microsoft's Visual C++ compiler. The text in this section assumes that you're using the 5.0 or above version of that product, though you'll be able to create it using the 4.2 version with relative ease. Since we looked at the process of creating an application with MFC Application

Wizard in Chapter 2, we'll use an abbreviated procedure here. There are a few options you'll need to select during the creation process in order for the example to work. First, the name of the example is ViewURL (though you could choose any name you want). Second, you'll want to select Single Document on the first page of the Wizard. Third, you'll want to select Windows Sockets support on the fourth page of the Wizard. Finally, set the Base Class field on page 6 of the MFC AppWizard to CEditView. This will allow you to edit text within the main window of the sample application.

TIP: There are some situations, like this one, where you don't need the full capabilities of the CRichEditView class. Not only is the CRichEditView class fairly large when compared to CEditView, but using the CRichEditView class also requires you to add OLE container support to the application—further increasing application size. The CEditView class will still allow you to display unformatted text and keep the size of the application small—an important consideration for utility-class applications.

Adding Library Support

Once the Wizard finishes creating the application, you'll need to start making a few changes. The first thing you'll want to do is add hyperlink support to the application. To do this, add the following #include in the STDAFX.H file.

```
//Added for URL support.
#include "URLMon.h"
```

This header file contains all of the #defines that you'll need in order to use the various URL moniker-related commands. We discussed a few of these commands earlier in the chapter—you'll get to see them in action here.

NOTE: The next thing users of older versions of Visual C++ will need to do is add some static library support (Visual C++ 5.0 or above users won't need to take this step). The two libraries, HLINK.LIB and URLMON.LIB, are in the LIB folder of the ActiveX SDK. Use the Insert I Files Into Project command of Visual C++ to add the required library support to your application. Double-check that the support was actually added by looking at the list of included files in FileView (just click the FileView tab on the left side of your display work area).

12

TIP: Microsoft intends to fold the static library support found in HLINK.LIB and URLMON.LIB into URLMON.DLL at some future date. Make sure you check for this dynamic library support before writing a URL moniker–enabled application.

Creating the Required Resources

Now that you've added the required library support, let's add the buttons to the toolbar. Click on the ResourceView, open the Toolbar folder, and then double-click on the IDR_MAINFRAME entry. You'll see the standard toolbar, shown in Figure 12-1. Adding a new button is easy—just click on the blank button at the end of the toolbar and start drawing on the blank button displayed in the drawing area.

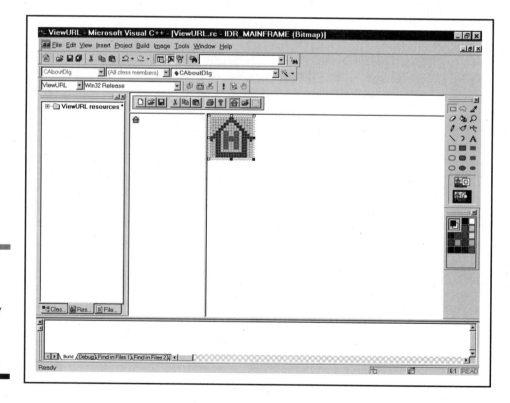

The standard toolbar with the Home Page and Any Web Page buttons

Figure 12-1.

Moving the button a little to the right will separate it from the other button groups already displayed on the toolbar. Figure 12-1 shows the two buttons added for this example program.

NOTE: Adding the buttons will provide the user with a visual display. You also need to add some button identification information for the application. Simply double-click on the toolbar representation of the button you wish to configure (don't click on the button icon you just created). What you'll see is a dialog like the one shown here. Use the settings shown in the following table for the two buttons.

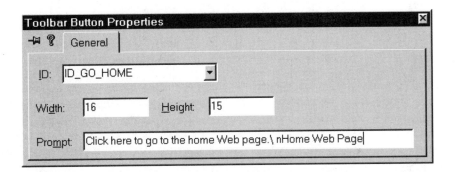

Button	Description	Height	Width
ID_GO_HOME	Click here to go to the home Web page.\nHome Web Page	15	16
ID_GO_SITE	Click here to go to any Web page.\nAny Web Page	15	16

TIP: Notice that the Caption has a long description, a \n, and then a short description. The long description will appear on the application's status bar. The short description appears as bubble help when you rest your mouse over the control. Make sure you include the \n to separate the two entry types. You can use this particular entry method just about anywhere you normally see bubble help in a Visual C++ application.

12

Clicking the first button will take the user to the company's home page—so you don't really need anything more in the way of resources to make this button work. All you need to add is a little code to perform the actual work. The second button, however, will allow users to type in their own site and, if they so desire, a location within that site. This button will also support frames for those sites that use them. This means adding a special dialog box. Open the Dialog folder in the ResourceView. Right-click on the Dialog folder, and you'll see a context menu. Select the Insert Dialog entry, and you'll see a new dialog named IDD_DIALOG1 added to the list in the folder (the only other dialog currently provided with the application is the About Box dialog).

Let's rename the dialog. Right-click on the IDD_DIALOG1 entry and select Properties from the context menu. Type **IDD_SITE_SELECT** in the ID field, and then click on the properties dialog. You'll see the new name appear in the list of dialogs within the Dialog folder.

Adding the required controls to the dialog is fairly easy. The first thing you'll want to do is resize the dialog to 25×120 pixels (the current dialog size appears on the right-hand side of the status bar). This will buy you a little room for those long URLs the user may want to type. Once you resize the dialog, add three labels and three edit controls, as shown in Figure 12-2.

Double-click on each of the edit controls to display their property dialogs. We'll want to give them IDs that are easy to remember. The first control ID is IDC_URL, the second is IDC_ANCHOR_NAME, and the third is IDC_FRAME_NAME. You'll see how these names come into play later.

Defining New Classes and Writing Code

All of the resources we'll need are defined. It's time to create some code to go with the two buttons we've added to the toolbar. Make certain you have the IDD_SITE_SELECT dialog selected. Use the View | Class Wizard command to display the ClassWizard dialog. In this case, you'll see a dialog like the one shown here telling you that the IDD_SITE_SELECT dialog is new and you need to create a class for it.

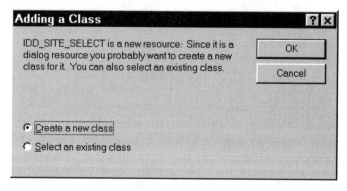

Figure 12-2.

Our sample program will display this dialog when the user chooses to visit something other than the home Web site.

Figure 12-2.

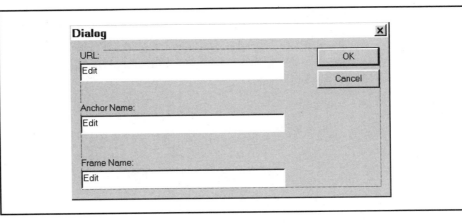

Click on OK, and you'll see the New Class dialog. All you need to provide is a class name. The example program uses CSiteSelect—which makes the class name and its associated resource very easy to identify. Use the default CDialog base class in this case. Click OK to complete the action.

Select the Message Maps tab of the ClassWizard. Select the CMainFrame class name from the Class Name field. Scroll down the list of Object IDs on the left side of the dialog until you find ID_GO_HOME. Click on this entry and then on the COMMAND entry in the Messages field on the right side of the dialog. Click Add Function to add the required function to your application. You'll see an Add Member Function dialog box. Click OK to accept the default function name. Follow this same procedure for the ID_GO_SITE object identifier. Your MFC ClassWizard dialog should look like this when you get through:

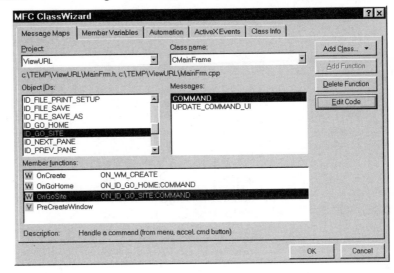

12

Select the OnGoHome entry and click Edit Code. The MFC ClassWizard will take you right to the shell for the new function. Listing 12-1 shows the code for this button. Make sure to set the first parameter in the HLinkSimpleNavigateToString() function call to match your Web server's default page address.

Listing 12-1:
```
void CMainFrame::OnGoHome()
{
    // Go right to the company's home page.
    HLinkSimpleNavigateToString(L"http://aux/default.htm",
        NULL, NULL, NULL, 0, NULL, NULL, 0);

}
```

You'll see the OnGoSite() function right below the OnGoHome() function. Add the code shown in Listing 12-2 to it. Make certain that you include SiteSelect.H at the beginning of the MainFrm.CPP file (you could also include it in the STDAFX.H file if desired).

Listing 12-2:
```
void CMainFrame::OnGoSite()
{
    // Create a copy of the dialog.
    CSiteSelect   NewSiteSelect;

    // Display it.
    NewSiteSelect.DoModal();

}
```

So far we have enough code to send the user to the home page (Listing 12-1) or display a dialog (Listing 12-2). You'll also need to add some code to the CSiteSelect dialog. When users click on OK, you'll want to take them to the site they selected. The first thing we'll need to do is add some memory variables to record what the user types. Look at the IDD_SITE_SELECT dialog box again. CTRL-double-click the first edit box. You'll see an Add Member Variable dialog like the one shown in the following illustration.

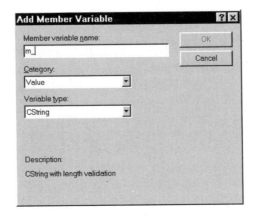

It'll allow you to assign a variable to the IDC_URL edit box. For the purposes of this example, name it URL (the name will actually appear as m_URL in the dialog box). Select Control in the Category field—this will change the Variable Type field to CEdit, which is the variable type we need for this example. Click OK to complete the process. Do the same thing for the other two edit boxes. Name the second variable Anchor and the third variable Frame.

Now that we have variables to work with, it's time to add another function. Open the MFC ClassWizard using the View | Class Wizard command. The dialog should still show the Message Maps tag; if not, select it. Select the CSiteSelect entry in the Class Name field. You'll see the list of Object IDs on the left side of the dialog change to match those provided by the CSiteSelect dialog. Highlight the IDOK object identifier and then the BN_CLICKED entry in the Messages field. Click Add Function and then OK on the Add Member Function dialog. Your MFC ClassWizard dialog should look like the one shown here.

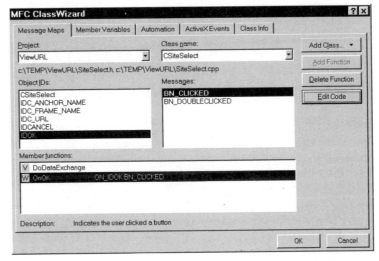

12

Now display our function skeleton by clicking Edit Code. This function has to accept the information users type in the dialog and then send them to the specified location on the Internet. Listing 12-3 shows the code to accomplish this task.

Listing 12-3:

```
void CSiteSelect::OnOK()
{
    LPCWSTR    pszURL = NULL;        //Local copy of URL string.
    LPCWSTR    pszAnchor = NULL;     //Local copy of Anchor string.
    LPCWSTR    pszFrame = NULL;      //Local copy of Frame string.
    LPTSTR     pszBuffer = "";       //Conversion buffer.

    // Get the URL string and convert it.
    if (m_URL.LineLength(0) > 0)
    {
        m_URL.GetLine(0, pszBuffer, m_URL.LineLength(0));
        pszURL = LPCWSTR(pszBuffer);
    }
    else
    {
        MessageBox("You must enter a URL", "Error", MB_OK);
        return;
    }

    // Get the Anchor string and convert it.
    if (m_Anchor.LineLength(0) > 0)
    {
        m_Anchor.GetLine(0, pszBuffer, m_Anchor.LineLength(0));
        pszAnchor = LPCWSTR(pszBuffer);
    }

    // Get the Frame string and convert it.
    if (m_Frame.LineLength(0) > 0)
    {
        m_Frame.GetLine(0, pszBuffer, m_Frame.LineLength(0));
        pszFrame = LPCWSTR(pszBuffer);
    }

    // Go right to the selected page.
    HLinkSimpleNavigateToString(pszURL,
        pszAnchor, pszFrame, NULL, 0, NULL, NULL, 0);


    CDialog::OnOK();
}
```

There are a few little tricks in this code, but nothing that most C programmers wouldn't already do. First, you need to set all three of the variables used to hold location information to NULL. That way they'll be ready to go if there isn't any information for them to hold. In this case the code also forces users to provide a URL. There's only one situation in which they wouldn't need to do this. If you wanted to let users jump to an anchor on the same page that they're currently on, you could leave the URL parameter NULL and simply have them specify the anchor name instead. The method used to store the information on the dialog requires the use of a buffer variable. However, the conversion from LPTSTR (long pointer to either a Windows or Unicode null-terminated string) to LPCWSTR (long pointer to a null-terminated Unicode string constant) is fairly straightforward. The meat of this particular routine is the call to HLinkSimpleNavigateToString, which converts the location information into an actual URL.

Let's take a look at how this application looks. Compile and run your application as usual. If you click on the Home Web Page button, you'll see a copy of Internet Explorer (or other default browser) start, then take you to whatever Internet site you set as a home page. Figure 12-3 shows the results of pressing this button for the example program. (The home page shown in the figure reflects the author's Internet server setup—your screen should reflect your setup.) Make sure you set the address in the HLinkSimpleNavigateToString() call in Listing 12-1 to your home Web site, or you may get some unusual results.

Clicking the Any Web Page button will display a dialog like the one shown here.

It allows you to enter a URL, along with an optional anchor name or frame name. Your target Web page must support the anchor or frame name you

12

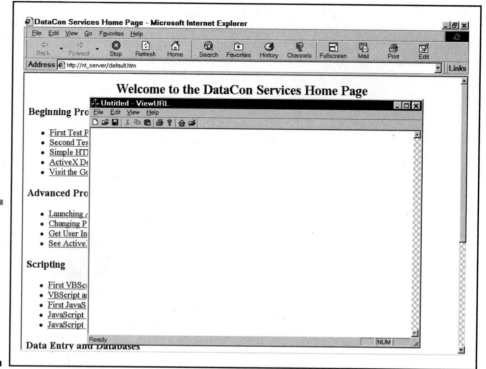

You can add
buttons like
this to any
application
and allow
users to access
the Internet
with ease.

Figure 12-3.

specify, or the function call will fail. The application also requires a live
Internet connection if you enter any URL values outside the addresses
supported by your local test machine.

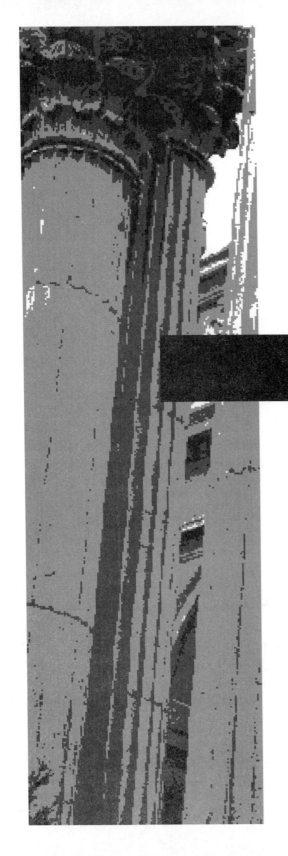

CHAPTER 13

Working with Internet Information Server (IIS)

There are a lot of different ways in which to work with IIS. Most of them are along the traditional static HTML route, which requires the use of scripts of various types. For example, you can use a CGI (Common Gateway Interface) script to query a database through a C/C++ program. The script would then format an HTML page containing the results of the query and upload it to the client. We aren't going to cover any of these more traditional routes in this chapter since there are entire books available on the topic. However, it's important to mention that the traditional methods exist because they do work and you may find you need one when the newer methods we'll talk about in this chapter just don't fit the bill. For example, you may already have an existing infrastructure and trying to reprogram everything using new technology may not be cost effective.

WEB LINK: There's a fast way to learn the bare essentials of some types of IIS access techniques including ODBC. Dynamic Systems International provides a series of lessons you can download about IIS from **http://www.dsi.org/dsi/iis.htm**. These lessons include an overview of just about everything you'll need to make some of the older technology access methods work. You may also want to visit the Microsoft IIS FAQ site (sponsored by Stephen Genusa) at **http://www.genusa.com/iis/**, which includes topics like CGI. In addition, the KLV site at **http://www.Adiscon. com/IIS** contains links for various Visual C++ programming considerations when using older technology. The same site includes links to places where you can find out the latest information on Internet specification efforts and security concerns like user authentication.

On the other hand, using new technology like Active Server Pages (ASP) can give you better flexibility and could greatly enhance your ability to provide content on the Internet. That's what we'll talk about in this chapter—the new technology you can use to provide great content on your Web site. We'll also look at a specific way to provide that increased flexibility to the users of your Web site. What we'll look at in this chapter is the Internet Server Application Programming Interface (ISAPI). More important, we'll look at some of the enabling technologies that go with ISAPI, like ISAs (ISAPI server applications). When you complete this chapter you'll have a good overview of how this technology will work in a real-world situation. You'll also have a good idea of when you'll need to use those older technologies instead. I'll be sure to tell you about any problem areas you'll need to watch as you implement these new technologies on your own server. Knowing these pitfalls may help you decide whether to go the new-technology route or stick with what you've used in the past.

ISAPI is a set of special MFC extensions that allow you to work with IIS.

So what is ISAPI? For the purposes of this book, ISAPI is a set of MFC extensions that allow you to work directly with IIS. We'll work with a new kind of project to implement ISAPI in this chapter, the ISAPI Extension Wizard. There are also five new classes that we'll look at: CHttpServer, CHttpServerContext, CHttpFilter, CHttpFilterContext, and CHtmlStream. You'll use these classes to create ISAs—which are called by a whole variety of other names, like ISAPI server extension DLLs in the Microsoft documentation. We'll use ISA throughout the text just to keep things simple.

By necessity, ISAs rely on ISAPI. You'll use ISAPI classes to create ISA extensions and filters for IIS. However, you're not limited to ISAPI classes; there are also WinInet classes for controlling Internet communication and all of the standard MFC classes to provide things like an interface. A filter allows you to keep something out or in by monitoring events on your server. For example, you could create an ISA filter that keeps people out of your Web site unless they enter the right password. Another type of filter could prevent files larger than a certain size from getting uploaded to the FTP server on your Web site. Extensions are more like applications or background processes. For example, you could create an extension that allows the user to interact with a database without resorting to using scripts. The same extension could create Web pages dynamically based on the user input and the contents of the database on your server.

An ISA can either filter information/ access or extend the services offered by IIS.

Before you begin reading the information in this chapter, you may want to look at the client-side information in Chapters 8 through 12. Chapter 8 will help you understand the basics of HTML, Chapter 9 will help you understand JavaScript, Chapter 10 will enlighten you on the basics of ActiveX control programming, Chapter 11 will help you understand ActiveX Document programming, and Chapter 12 contains a very important discussion about URL monikers. All of these chapters help you understand what the client expects of the server—an important piece of information if you plan to modify the server in some way. Chapter 12 is especially important because it helps you understand the connection between the client and the server—the underlying mechanism that helps one talk to the other.

NOTE: The code in this chapter was developed using Visual C++ Version 6.0 exclusively and hasn't been tested extensively on older platforms (the code should work fine with Visual C++ 5.0). While the code may work without modification with Visual C++ 4.2, you'll probably need to make allowances in the procedures I've provided. The code itself will require change to work with versions of Visual C++ older than Version 4.2.

13

The following sections will take you through five important areas of ISAPI programming. First, I'll give you an overview of ISAPI itself. This is a theory section you could skip if you already have a good idea of how ISAPI works and want to get right into creating your own programs. I've purposely separated discussion of the creation of filters and extensions from their implementation in this book to make it more generic. Besides, creating an ISA is a different step from implementing it. The second section of the chapter tells you how to create an ISAPI extension, while the third tells you how to implement it on the server. Likewise, the fourth section of the chapter tells you how to create an ISAPI filter, while the fifth tells you how to implement it.

The last two sections of the chapter will show you how to create additional kinds of ISAPI extensions and filters. The sixth section provides another ISAPI extension programming example, while the seventh section provides a second ISAPI filter programming example. These additional examples should give you a better idea of what you can do with ISAPI to enhance server performance, provide the user with better output, or make your network more secure.

WEB LINK: There are a lot of newsgroups you can visit to get help with your IIS, ASP, or ISA problem. In fact, there are too many to list them all in this chapter, so you'll want to spend a little additional time looking around. For the best Microsoft-specific support for IIS, take a look at **microsoft.public.inetserver.iis**. There are other newsgroups in the **microsoft.public.inetserver** area that you'll want to take a look at too, but this one usually has the most messages. You'll find Microsoft-specific ASP help at **microsoft.public.inetserver.iis.activeserverpages**. One of the more interesting non-Microsoft IIS sites is **comp.lang.java**. I was amazed to find message threads about everything from ASP to ActiveX on this site. Another good non-Microsoft site for IIS-specific help is **comp.infosystems. www.servers.ms-windows**. I found a great ISAPI thread on this newsgroup at the time of this writing. Needless to say, there are other **comp.infosystems.www** newsgroups you'll want to check out as well. If you're using FrontPage as one of your Web page maintenance tools, you'll want to take a look at **microsoft.public.frontpage.client** for ISAPI-specific help. It's hard to find out what the bugs are in some software, but you won't find it very difficult to do with IIS if you look at **comp.os. ms-windows.nt.software.compatibility**. Finally, if you're searching for that hidden ASP newsgroup, take a look at **microsoft.public.activex. programming.scripting.vbscript**.

An Overview of ISAPI (Internet Server API)

Before you can understand ISAPI, you have to understand where it fits into the Microsoft scheme of things. There are actually five levels of Internet support provided with Visual C++, three of which can reside on the server. The other two levels of support are client specific—you'll never see them on the server. The following list defines each level of support and tells where you'll find it.

- *ISAPI (server)*   This is the level of support we're talking about in this chapter. You need it to provide an extension or filter for the server itself. In other words, the client won't directly interact with this level of support; it'll merely see the results of the interaction.

- *WinInet (server or client)*   We don't cover this level of support in the book directly, but we do cover it indirectly. This set of classes allows you to use a specific method of data transfer between the client and the server. There are three levels of protocol support: HTTP, FTP, and Gopher. Essentially, you'd use these classes to create a session (CInternetSession), which is one connection to the server, and then specify a connection type (CFtpConnection, CHttpConnection, or CGopherConnection). After establishing a connection, the user can do things like look for a file (CFtpFileFind or CGopherFileFind). Normally, you don't have to interact with these classes directly because Visual C++ takes care of everything for you, as we saw in Chapter 12 when creating an URL moniker application.

- *Asynchronous URL monikers (server or client)*   We looked at this particular area of Visual C++ Internet support in Chapter 12. The important aspect for you to remember is that an asynchronous URL moniker allows you to perform tasks on the Internet without waiting. You simply tell the target application what you want, and then go on doing whatever else you wanted to do. The whole idea is that the Internet doesn't provide an instantaneous response in most situations and even if it does, a long download could render the user's machine useless for hours at a time without the use of asynchronous URL monikers.

- *ActiveX documents (client)*   Displaying a document in your browser and allowing the user to edit it is what this level of support is all about. We visited it in Chapter 11.

- *ActiveX controls (client)*   Creating the basic elements of a Web page used to involve lots of scripting, and even then you got a static image. Using ActiveX controls on a Web site means that old technology and static displays no longer hold you back—your Web page can change to meet a specific situation. We took a look at this technology in Chapter 10.

13

WEB LINK: There are a lot of places you can visit on the Internet to find out more about IIS, ISAPI, and other Internet server-related technologies like Active Server Pages (ASP). The main Web site to visit for IIS information is **http://www.microsoft.com/ntserver/Basics/WebServices/ default.asp**. This Microsoft-supported Web site contains links to just about everything you'll need to use IIS itself and even a few of the more common links for enabling technologies like ISAPI. If you value non-Microsoft assistance, take a look at the ASP Developer's Site at **http://www.genusa. com/asp/**. This Web site contains a lot of valuable information about using Active Server Pages on your Internet server. This same site has non-Microsoft links to both IIS and ISAPI sites.

Using ISAPI in the Real World

There a few things you need to know about ISAPI when it comes to a real-world production environment. For example, your ISA will be a DLL that loads on the server, just like any other DLL. This DLL will share the same address space as the HTTP server does, and you can unload it later if you need the memory it's consuming for something else. So what does that buy you? The following list tells you about the advantages of using ISAs to other techniques like CGI.

◆ *Lower memory costs* Since your ISA loads as a DLL on the server and uses the same memory space as the HTTP server, you won't have to waste the memory normally associated with CGI overhead. All you'll really need to load is the logic required to perform the task you're asking the ISA to do.

◆ *Speed* Loading a DLL or C application the first time will take essentially the same amount of time, though the DLL will be slightly faster due to its smaller size. However, once you've loaded the DLL the first time, it'll stay in memory until you unload it, which means that you don't have to pay that loading cost more than one time if you don't want to. A CGI script will load the C application every time you call it. That's not the best news, though. Since the ISA DLL shares the same memory space as your HTTP server, you won't have to pay a time penalty for interprocess calls or any of the overhead normally associated with using a C application in a separate address space.

◆ *Code sharing* All the server needs to do is load your DLL one time. Any application that requests the services of that DLL has access to it. Obviously, code sharing is one of the factors that leads to the lower memory costs and speed improvements over CGI mentioned in the first two points. However, code sharing results in some not-so-obvious benefits as well. For example, code sharing reduces administration time for your server, since the administrator only needs to replace one copy of any given DLL to affect every application that uses it. The C applications typically used by CGI have a lot of redundant code in them. Change a single routine and you'll need to change every C application that uses the routine on your server, which means greatly increased administrator time and the need for additional application tracking by the programmer.

◆ *Reliability*   C applications used by CGI scripts load and execute on the server without having much access to the server itself. As a result, it's harder to create a C application that can monitor server events and recover from errors. What usually happens is that the server will terminate an errant CGI script and the client will end up with nothing. ISAs have full access to the server, which means that they can recover from errors more easily. As a result, the client very seldom (if ever) ends up having to make a request the second time.

◆ *Filtering capability*   You can't provide an event-driven equivalent to an ISA using CGI and a C application. The reason's simple: a C application gets called, does its work, and then unloads. There isn't any way that it can monitor server events over the long term.

◆ *Multiple tasks in one DLL*   Every task that you want CGI to perform requires a separate executable for each task you perform. As a result, you incur the overhead of calling each routine. ISAs, on the other hand, can contain multiple commands, each of which is a member of the CHttpServer class.

Getting these six capabilities doesn't mean that you have to pay a big price in either learning curve or excess coding. ISAs are just as easy to use as the CGI equivalent. Here's what the two lines of code would look like in an application:

```
<!-This is a call to a CGI routine with one parameter.->
http://aux/controls/sample.exe?Param
```

```
<!-This is a call to an ISA routine with one parameter.->
http://aux/controls/sample.dll?Param
```

13

As you can see, working with ISAPI doesn't have to be difficult. We called our ISA control using about the same code as we would a CGI routine. In fact, the only difference from a coding perspective is that our ISA control uses a DLL extension, while the CGI routine uses an EXE extension. Theoretically, you could switch your server to ISAs, make a few search-and-replace changes to your Web pages, and no one would notice the difference from an interface perspective. Of course, everyone would notice the higher efficiency of your Web site due to the advantages of using ISAPI.

The last advantage that I mentioned for using ISAs was the fact that you can perform more than one task with a single ISA. We'll see later how you implement this behavior. For right now all you really need to know is that the calling syntax still doesn't differ much from standard CGI calls you may have used in the past. Here's an ISA routine call that specifies that you want to use the DisplayStr function:

```
<!-Call the DisplayStr function in an ISA routine with one parameter.->
http://aux/controls/sample.dll?DisplayStr?Param
```

You can call something other than the default function in an ISA by adding a second question mark to the calling syntax.

As you can see, we called something other than the default task using a second question mark (?) in the calling string. The first parameter now tells which function you want to call within SAMPLE.DLL, and the second parameter contains a list of parameters. This method of calling functions is known as a parse map, which you'll learn how to create in the section later on creating an ISAPI extension.

ISAs do share some qualities that you'll find in CGI. For one thing, your application executes on the server, not the client. This makes updating your application easy—all you need to do is replace one DLL file on the server. (You do need to stop the service to update the DLL, but this is a small price to pay for the convenience of one machine update.) Obviously, this is a lot easier than trying to replace an application on every client machine that accesses your Web site. It's also one of the reasons that companies are taking a serious look at intranets to host things like a help desk and custom database applications—updating one server is a lot easier than updating a lot of clients.

ISAs run on the server, meaning you update only one server instead of many clients every time you update a custom application.

T IP: IIS Version 4 adds some new capabilities that make working with ISAs easier. For one thing, you can tell the server to unload the ISA after each call. This means that you can try the ISA to see if it works and replace it with a new copy if necessary, all without stopping the service. The disadvantage of this new capability is that you'll see a slight performance hit because the server will need to reload the ISA every time it gets called by a client.

Choosing Between a Filter and an Extension

You don't have to spend a lot of time deciding whether to create an ISA filter or an ISA extension (or even both). The differences between the two types of ISA are pretty easy to figure out. Once you do so, choosing the one you need becomes fairly simple.

A filter will always react to events on the server itself. A user attempting to log into your Web site will generate an event that an ISA filter can monitor. You'll normally use it to modify the data flow between the client and server. For example, if your application saw an SF_NOTIFY_AUTHENTICATION event take place, it could display a dialog for the user to enter a name and password. If these were correct, the user would gain access to the Web site.

Extensions are used in the same situations as their CGI counterparts. For example, if you wanted to create an order entry system, you would likely use an extension. The extension would receive data from a form that the user filled out, process the information, add it to the database, and finally send some type of receipt back to the user. This is the same process that you would follow when using a CGI script; the only difference is that now you're using a DLL instead. Unlike a filter, an extension doesn't monitor events on the server—it acts in every way like an application would.

There are some types of ISA applications like a visitor counter where you can choose to create a filter or an extension.

There are some situations where the choice of filter or extension doesn't really matter very much. For example, consider a simple Web counter. Every time someone accesses your Web site, you update the counter to show what number visitor that person is. You could call an ISA extension from the Web page to update this counter if so desired, or have a filter monitor the SF_NOTIFY_LOG event on the server and send the information automatically. The choice is a matter of personal taste.

Some ISA applications like specialized browser support require you to create complex DLLs that include both filters and extensions.

You'll run into situations where you need to use both an extension and a filter. For example, you might want to display one Web page for an authorized Netscape user, another for an unauthorized Netscape user, and two others for authorized and unauthorized Internet Explorer users. This situation requires some scripting within the HTML form to detect the browser type, a little bit of work on the part of a filter to detect whether the user is authorized or not, and a little work on the part of an extension to generate the proper page. Using this combination of client scripting and ISA extensions to your server represents one way to fully extend your Web site and make it convenient for everyone to use.

13

Working with the Five ISAPI Classes

Previously, I mentioned that you would be working with five new MFC classes in this chapter. That doesn't mean you won't continue to work with the classes you're already familiar with, but these classes do provide special capabilities you'll need to design an ISA filter or extension. The following list is meant as an overview of the classes that you'll work with in the sections that follow. Obviously, you'll get a much better view of these classes when we begin to work with the example code.

- ◆ *CHttpServer* This is the main class that you'll need to use to create either a filter or an extension. The CHttpServer class defines an object that works as a server extension DLL or an ISA. The main purpose of the CHttpServer object is to handle the messages generated by the server and the client. As a result, you'll only find one CHttpServer object in any ISA DLL.

- ◆ *CHttpServerContext* The CHttpServer class actually creates this object. It's a single instance of a single request from the client. In other words, you'll see one CHttpServerContext object for every active client request. The object gets destroyed when the client request has been fulfilled.

- ◆ *CHttpFilter* ISA filters require the use of a special CHttpFilter object to monitor server events. This object will look for all of the SF messages that the server generates as the client interacts with it. For example, the client will generate an SF_NOTIFY_LOG message every time a user tries to access the Web site.

- ◆ *CHttpFilterContext* The CHttpFilter object will create one CHttpFilterContext object for each active server event. The CHttpFilterContext class represents a single event generated by a single client during a specific session.

- ◆ *CHtmlStream* You'll use this class to manage data from between the client and the server. The CHttpServer class will create an object of this type whenever it needs to transmit information between the client and the server. In most cases there is only one of these objects per DLL. However, the CHttpServer object can create as many CHtmlStream objects as it needs to transfer data safely. A typical CHtmlStream object contains data and all the tags required to create the content for an HTML page. For example, if you performed a search of a database, the resulting CHtmlStream object would contain not only the data but also the HTML tags required to actually create the Web page used to display the data. (See Chapter 8 for more information about HTML tags.)

Creating an ISAPI Extension

OK, it's time to look at our first ISA. In this case, we'll create a very simple ISAPI extension using the ISAPI Extension Wizard. The whole purpose of this particular example is to get you used to the idea of working with ISAPI and show you some of the techniques you'll need to make ISAPI work. The example program will accept a string from the client, change it a little, and then display a new page showing the string that the client sent. The following procedure will take you through all the steps required to create the sample ISA. You can use the same procedure to start any ISA extension that you need to create. I'm assuming that you already have Visual C++ running and that you're using the 6.0 version of the product.

WEB LINK: One of the best places to look for ideas for your own ISAPI extension or filter is freeware produced by other programmers. The **alt.comp.freeware** newsgroup lists quite a few of these offerings. For example, at the time of this writing, AAIT Incorporated introduced a new freeware product named CGI Expert. It supports the CGI, win-CGI, ISAPI, and NSAPI interfaces simultaneously. Obviously, you'll want to use freeware products, like any other product, with care. However, they do provide excellent ideas on how to create your own custom extensions when needed (or a solution so you don't have to do any programming at all).

1. Use the File | New command to display the New dialog shown here. Notice that I've already selected the ISAPI Extension Wizard.

13

2. Type the name of the ISA you want to create in the Project name field. I used DispStr for the example ISA, but you could use any name that you want.

3. Click OK. You'll see the ISAPI Extension Wizard - Step 1 of 1 dialog shown here.

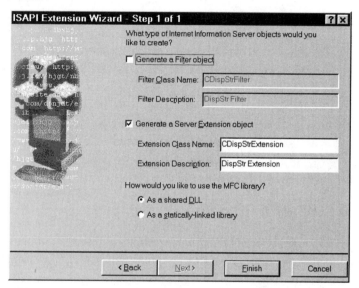

This is where you'll select the various characteristics for your ISA. Notice that there are three main areas to the dialog. You can choose to create a filter by checking the first checkbox and an extension by checking the second checkbox. The third area defines how you'll link MFC into your application.

4. Check the extension option, and uncheck the filter option. You'll want to provide a short, concise statement of what your ISA does in the Extension Description field. The description appears as a string that you can use within the DLL as needed. This description won't show up in the Properties dialog when someone opens it for your ISA, so you'll want to add some additional text to the version information for your DLL as well.

5. Type **Display a string from the client** in the Extension Description field.

6. Click Finish. You'll see a New Project Information dialog like the one shown here.

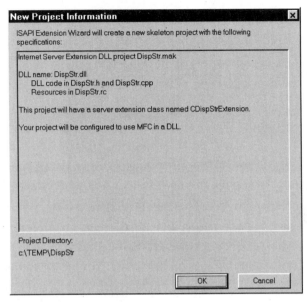

7. Click OK. The ISAPI Extension Wizard will create the required program shell for you.

At this point we need to do three things to the skeleton that the ISAPI Extension Wizard has created for us to make the extension functional. The first task is to create a parse map for the new function we want to add. You'll find the parse map near the beginning of the DispStr.CPP file. Listing 13-1 shows the code you'll need to add to the parse map so that we'll be able to access the new function from the HTML page.

Listing 13-1:

```
////////////////////////////////////////////////////////////////////////
// command-parsing map

BEGIN_PARSE_MAP(CDispStrExtension, CHttpServer)
    // Our special DisplayStr parse command.
    ON_PARSE_COMMAND(DisplayStr, CDispStrExtension, ITS_PSTR)
    ON_PARSE_COMMAND_PARAMS("string='No String Supplied'")

    // Default parse command
    ON_PARSE_COMMAND(Default, CDispStrExtension, ITS_EMPTY)
    DEFAULT_PARSE_COMMAND(Default, CDispStrExtension)
END_PARSE_MAP(CDispStrExtension)
```

13

Even though you only had to add two lines of code to make this example work, we're actually concerned with three lines of code. The ON_PARSE_COMMAND() macro allows you to define a new function. Notice that we supply a function name, the class in which the function is supplied, and the type of parameters the function will use. The ON_PARSE_COMMAND() macro requires a parameter entry, even if you don't need any parameters to make the function work. Notice that the Default function uses a value of ITS_EMPTY since it doesn't need any parameters, but that our new function, DisplayStr, has a parameter of ITS_PSTR because it requires a string pointer.

That brings us to the ON_PARSE_COMMAND_PARAMS() macro on the next line. You have to tell Visual C++ how to deal with the parameters for your function. For example, if we had wanted to force the user to supply a string value for our function, we would simply have "string" in the ON_PARSE_COMMAND_PARAMS() macro. Since we don't absolutely have to have the user supply a string to use our function, I've supplied a default value of "No String Supplied." Be aware that the query will fail if you require a parameter and the user doesn't supply it. Finally, you need to tell Visual C++ which function to use as a default using the DEFAULT_PARSE_COMMAND() macro. Since the Default function is just fine in this case, I didn't change the default setting.

The second thing you'll need to do to the code is add the function entry to the DispStr.H file. Unless you modify the class specification to include your new function, Visual C++ won't know anything about it and the DLL won't compile. Fortunately, all we need is the single line entry shown in bold in Listing 13-2. I've included the surrounding code so that you know where to place the new entry.

Listing 13-2:

```
{
public:
    CDispStrExtension();
    ~CDispStrExtension();

// Overrides
    // ClassWizard generated virtual function overrides
        // NOTE - the ClassWizard will add and remove member functions here.
        //    DO NOT EDIT what you see in these blocks of generated code !
    //{{AFX_VIRTUAL(CDispStrExtension)
    public:
    virtual BOOL GetExtensionVersion(HSE_VERSION_INFO* pVer);
    //}}AFX_VIRTUAL
```

```
    // TODO: Add handlers for your commands here.
    // For example:

    void Default(CHttpServerContext* pCtxt);
    void DisplayStr(CHttpServerContext* pCtxt, LPTSTR pszString);

    DECLARE_PARSE_MAP()

    //{{AFX_MSG(CDispStrExtension)
    //}}AFX_MSG
};
```

As you can see, adding the function call declaration is a pretty simple matter. At this point, though, you may be wondering where the CHttpServerContext* pCtxt part of the declaration came in. We certainly didn't declare it previously in any of the parse map macros. It turns out that the pCtxt parameter gets passed to your function by default. Remember from our previous discussion that the CHttpServer class automatically creates a CHttpServerContext object for every user request. This is where the parameter comes from. What you're getting is a pointer to the CHttpServerContext object associated with the user's call to your function. It's also the way that you keep multiple calls to your function separate—each call has a completely different object associated with it.

There is one last thing that we need to do to make this DLL function: add the function code to the DispStr.CPP file. I added the function code right after the existing Default() function code. Listing 13-3 shows the very short function that I created for this example. There isn't anything fancy here; the whole purpose is to show you how to put things together.

Listing 13-3:

```
void CDispStrExtension::DisplayStr(CHttpServerContext* pCtxt, LPTSTR pszString)
{
    // Start sending information to the new Web page including a default title.
    StartContent(pCtxt);
    WriteTitle(pCtxt);

    // Display the body of the new page.
    *pCtxt << _T("<H3><CENTER>ISAPI Server Extension Example</CENTER></H3><P><P>");
    *pCtxt << _T("This was the string you entered:<P><EM>");
    *pCtxt << _T(pszString);
    *pCtxt << _T("</EM>");
```

13

```
    // End the display area.
    EndContent(pCtxt);
}
```

The function itself is pretty easy to figure out. The first thing we do is tell Visual C++ to start a Web page. That's like adding the <HTML> and <HEAD> tags to a document. The second thing we do is output a title—just as if we were typing the <TITLE> tag into a document. The only way to override the default title is to override the WriteTitle() function—something that you can do if you'd like. Now that we've got a heading, it's time to create some body content. We have to use the stream operator to send the information. Notice that I freely use all of the tags that we covered in Chapter 8 in this example. Anything you can do with a standard HTML document, you can do with your ISAPI extension. We'll see in just a few moments how all these tags work together to produce a Web page. You'll also want to notice that we send the string we got from the Web page back to the new Web page—you don't even have to convert the values to text to make them work. The final function call we use, EndContent(), tells Visual C++ that we're done sending information. It's like adding the </HTML> to the end of the document.

At this point you can compile the ISAPI extension we've created. Once you successfully compile it, move the DLL to your Web server. There are several logical places to put the DLL, but the two most common would be a Scripts directory or a special Controls directory. I normally keep all my controls in one place in a Controls directory to make them easy to locate, but the actual location you use isn't all that important. The only criteria are that the user be able to access the directory containing the DLL through your Web site and that you've marked the directory as executable using the Internet Service Manager provided with your Web server.

Using an ISAPI Extension within a Web Page

Now that you have a new ISAPI extension loaded on your Web server, it's time to test it out. Remember that our ISA has two functions: the default function provided by the ISAPI Extension Wizard (Default) and the one that we added (DisplayStr). In addition, our DisplayStr() function will react one of two ways depending on whether the user provides some data for the function to work with. Listing 13-4 shows the HTML code you'll need to create a test Web page for our ISA. I used a name of Extend.HTM for the resulting file.

Listing 13-4:

```
<HTML>
<HEAD>
<TITLE>ISAPI Extension Example</TITLE>
```

```
</HEAD>
<!-Create a form to display our pushbuttons.->
<FORM NAME="MyForm">
<!-Display a heading.->
<H3><CENTER>Display a String ISAPI Extension</CENTER></H3>

<!-Display an edit box.->
Type a string value:
<INPUT TYPE=TEXTBOX NAME="StringValue" SIZE=40><P>

<!-Display a couple of buttons.->
<CENTER>

<!-Perform the default action.->
<INPUT LANGUAGE="JavaScript"
    TYPE=BUTTON
    VALUE="Default"
    ONCLICK="window.location.href = 'controls/DispStr.dll?'">

<!-Perform a special action with a string.->
<INPUT LANGUAGE="JavaScript"
    TYPE=BUTTON
    VALUE="Display String"
    ONCLICK="window.location.href = 'controls/DispStr.dll?DisplayStr?'
        + MyForm.StringValue.value">

</CENTER>
</FORM>
</HTML>
```

PORTABILITY: While Internet Explorer is perfectly happy displaying <INPUT> tags that appear in the body of an HTLM document (between the <BODY> and </BODY> tags), Netscape Navigator won't even recognize them. To make a form usable with all browsers, you must place the <INPUT> tags within a form (between a <FORM> and </FORM> tag pair).

The sample code isn't that complex. It consists of a heading, a text box, and two pushbuttons. The text box will contain the string value that the user wants to display. Notice that we don't include a submit action for our form but use standard pushbuttons and JavaScript to initiate an action. This

13

arrangement seems to work better than a submit when using an ISA that contains more than one function, as ours does.

There are a couple of things you should note about the JavaScript provided for the ONCLICK event of each pushbutton. Notice that with the Default pushbutton we only call the DispStr.DLL itself—we don't specify a particular function. On the other hand, the Display String pushbutton includes both a function name and a string parameter as part of the DispStr.DLL call. We'll see how this works shortly.

TIP: HTML doesn't send any text after a space in a text box to the server. For example, if you type Hello World in the text box, the server will only receive "Hello." You must place plus signs (+) between words to send them to the server. For example, if you send Hello+World to the server, it'll see "Hello World" (the Web server log will still show the + sign, which indicates the + sign is replaced with a space after it arrives at the server). This means adding some text manipulation code not shown in the example program to replace the spaces in the text box with plus signs before sending the string to the server.

Open the test Web page and you'll see something like the page shown in Figure 13-1. As previously mentioned, this is a test page, so I didn't add too much formatting code, in order to keep things simple.

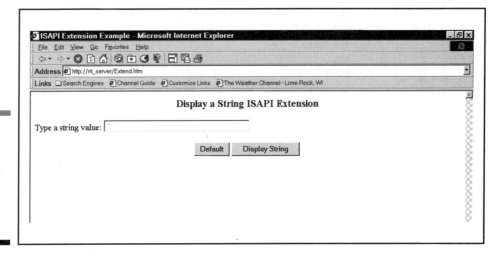

This simple test page allows us to check the full capability of DispStr.DLL.

Figure 13-1.

NOTE: Make absolutely certain that the directory you use to store DispStr.DLL on the server is marked for execute privileges from within the Internet Service Manager for your Web server. Otherwise, you'll see any number of errors from the browser as it attempts to execute the file—most of which won't tell you that it can't execute the file (the most common error is that the service isn't supported). Marking the directory for execute privileges within the operating system isn't sufficient to allow a visitor to your Web site to use the ISA you've created. In most cases you can avoid any problems by ensuring the ISA DLL appears in the script directory for your Web server (assuming it has one).

Let's test the DispStr.DLL. Begin by clicking the Default button. What you should see is a default string like the one shown here that the ISAPI Extension Wizard provides. (In essence it tells you that you need to add some code to the default function.)

This default message was produced by the Internet Server DLL Wizard. Edit your CDispStrExtension::Default() implementation to change it.

Click the Back button (or the equivalent on your browser) to get back to the Extend.HTM page. Now click the Display String button and you'll see something like this.

ISAPI Server Extension Example

This was the string you entered:

No String Supplied

In this case we called DispStr.DLL with the DisplayStr function, but since there wasn't any value in the text box, the function had to display the default string we defined as part of the ON_PARSE_COMMAND_PARAMS() macro. Now you can see the importance of providing a default value in most cases. Users don't have to worry about your ISA causing problems if they forget to provide a needed value. What they'll get instead is a return value that could help them troubleshoot their Web page. In this case, the user will know precisely what went wrong and can fix it in a matter of minutes instead of the hours that debugging normally takes.

Click the Back button again to get back to the Extend.HTM display. This time, type **Hello+World** into the Type a String Value field. Click the Display String button and you'll see something like what is shown here. In this case, we asked to use the DispStr.DLL DisplayStr function and provided it with "Hello+World" as a string value.

It's important to note that you must supply the plus sign between words when sending a string value to the server; otherwise, just the first word will get displayed. (You may want to experiment a little to see this for yourself—make sure you check the Web server logs as you try various combinations.) If you look at the Location field on the browser, you'll notice that we have supplied a + sign between words, yet the content of the page shows a space between the words. This is because the Web server replaces the plus signs with spaces for you—that's why we didn't have to add any additional code to the ISA.

Creating an ISAPI Filter

The previous two sections showed how you could use an ISAPI extension to your advantage when constructing a Web site. What we'll do in this section is look at the process for building your own ISAPI filter. The process for starting

Remember that an ISAPI filter reacts automatically when a specific event happens, unlike an extension, which gets called much like an application would.

the ISAPI filter is just about the same as the one for creating an extension. The following steps will help you create a program shell.

1. Use the File | New command to display the New dialog. Select the ISAPI Extension Wizard. (Even though we're creating a filter, you'll still need to use the ISAPI Extension Wizard to do it.)

2. Type the name of the ISA filter you want to create. I used NoLog for the example ISA, but you could use any name that you want.

3. Click OK. You'll see the ISAPI Extension Wizard - Step 1 of 2 dialog. This is where you'll select the various characteristics for your ISA. There are three main areas to the dialog. You can choose to create a filter by checking the first checkbox and an extension by checking the second checkbox. The third area defines how you'll link MFC into your application.

4. Check the filter option, and uncheck the extension option. (Notice that adding the filter also adds another step to the process.) You'll want to provide a short, concise statement of what your ISA does in the Filter Description field. The description appears as a string that you can use within the DLL as needed. This description won't show up in the Properties dialog when someone opens it for your ISA, so you'll want to add some additional text to the version information for your DLL as well.

13

5. Type **Classify some log entries for security reasons** in the Filter Description field.

6. Click Next. You'll see the ISAPI Extension Wizard - Step 2 of 2 dialog shown here.

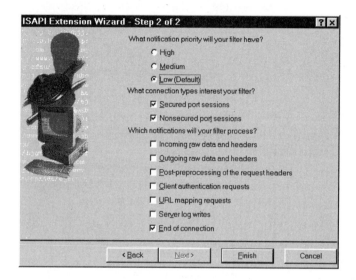

This is the page you'll use to select the events and type of monitoring your filter will provide. There are three areas to consider. See the In Depth box entitled "Choosing Filter Options" to get more details about these options.

7. Check the Server Log Writes checkbox, and uncheck the End of Connection checkbox. We want to activate our filter when the user requests specific kinds of access to the server since we're creating a simple filter to keep some log entries classified.

8. Click Finish. You'll see a New Project Information dialog like the one shown here. Make sure you double-check all the settings for your filter because the New Project Information page provides a detailed breakdown of the events that it'll get to see.

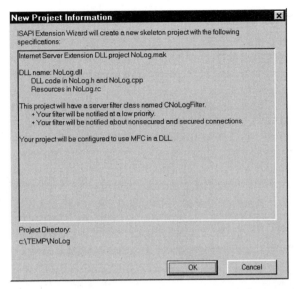

9. Click OK. The ISAPI Extension Wizard will create the required program shell for you.

The coding portion of this example is short and to the point. Filters can quickly get out of hand in the complexity department, and debugging them is fairly difficult. In most cases you'll want to make your filter programs as short as possible. Modularization is a big help as well when it comes time to troubleshoot a faulty filter. Listing 13-5 shows the code you'll need to add to the OnLog() function to make it work.

Listing 13-5:

```
DWORD CNoLogFilter::OnLog(CHttpFilterContext *pCtxt, PHTTP_FILTER_LOG pLog)
{
    // Check for a specific notification.
    if (strstr(pLog->pszTarget, "NoLog.htm") != NULL)
    {
        // Change the target information to Classified.
        pLog->pszTarget = "Classified Target";
        pLog->pszParameters = "Classified Parms";
```

13

```
   }

      // Pass control to the next filter.
      return SF_STATUS_REQ_NEXT_NOTIFICATION;
}
```

As you can see, we'll simply monitor the log entries for a particular target, which could be any number of things but is normally another Web page. Once we find the log entry we're looking for, we'll change two members, pszTarget and pszParameters, to their classified setting. Obviously, this whole idea is very simplified, but it does have practical uses. You might want to hide specific log entries from prying eyes, and this is one way to do it. Remembering that hackers often use log files they find on a server to dig deeper into a company's resources is justification enough, but you'll find other reasons as well for keeping some log entries classified. In some cases, you may even want to eliminate certain log entries totally simply because you don't want to monitor them. Suffice it to say that you'll want to exercise care when using this kind of filter, but it's a good place to start.

At this point you can compile the new ISAPI filter. However, even after you move it to the Controls or Scripts directory on your server, you'll still have to perform one other task. Unlike an extension, an ISA filter gets loaded when you start the service. This means stopping the target service, making a registry entry, and then starting up the service again if you're using an older version of IIS. The filter will get loaded as part of the starting process.

The WWW service stores its filter entries in the following registry value: HKEY_LOCAL_MACHINE\SYSTEM\CurrentControlSet\Services\W3SVC\Parameters\Filter DLLs. You'll probably find one or more values in this location already. All you need to do is add a comma and then type the location of your new ISA filter. Make absolutely certain you perform this step before going on to the next section, or the filter won't load. In fact, this is the setting you'll want to check first if you have trouble getting the filter to work.

Users of IIS Version 4.0 and above will really appreciate the fact that they no longer have to edit the registry manually to load an ISAPI filter. All you need to do is open the Microsoft Management Console, right-click on the Web site that you want to add the filter to, and choose Properties from the context menu. Select the ISAPI Filters tab and you'll see a dialog like the one shown here.

Click the Add button and you'll see a Filter Properties dialog. Type the human readable name in the Filter Name field. Use the Browse button to find the NoLog.DLL file (or whatever ISAPI filter you want to add to the Web site). Once you select the file, its name will appear in the Executable field. Click OK once to close the Filter Properties dialog, and click OK again to close the Default Web Site Properties dialog. IIS will automatically load the filter for you.

IN DEPTH

Choosing Filter Options

The second page (Step 2 of 2) of the ISAPI Extension Wizard dialog is very important as far as filter designers are concerned, because it contains the options you'll need to set the filter's monitoring options. There are three sections of options on this page. The first section determines the filter's priority. Low, the default, works just fine in most cases. You'll want to use this level for any kind of filter that performs a general background task. A security filter may require that you set the filter's priority to medium. After all, you don't want the filter to react after the event—a reaction during the event would be much better. Finally, the high priority setting should be reserved for emergency-level filters. For example, you might want to send a message out to everyone that the server is going down due to a power failure.

The second section of the ISAPI Extension Wizard - Step 2 of 2 dialog contains two entries. Check the first entry if you want to monitor events when a user has a secure connection. For example, if you plan to provide extra services to a registered user that an anonymous user doesn't get, you may want to check this option. The second option, Nonsecured Port Sessions, allows you to monitor events when a user doesn't have a secure connection to the server. That's the way most users will access your site if you have a general Web site on the Internet.

The third section contains a list of notifications (events) that your filter will track. Every time the specified event happens, your filter will get called. However, there are two things that will affect it when it gets called. If you set the priority of your filter to low, then any high- or medium-priority-level filters will get to react to the event first. In addition, your filter has to be set to monitor the event with the user's current security level. In other words, your filter won't get called at all if you set it to monitor nonsecured activity and the user is in secured mode.

Using an ISAPI Filter to Keep Your Web Site Classified

By now you should have your ISA filter completed and compiled. You should have placed it in a location where you normally keep filters—which could be a Controls, Scripts, or even the System32 directory. Remember to make the required registry entry while the server is stopped, and then restart the server when you're finished. Now we're ready to test the filter out.

The first thing we'll need are three Web pages. The first is a central Web page we'll use to switch between two others—one logged normally and the other logged as classified. Call the first Web page Filter.HTM. Listing 13-6 shows the source code for this part of the test setup.

Listing 13-6:

```
<HTML>
<HEAD>
<TITLE>ISAPI Filter Test</TITLE>
</HEAD>
<BODY>

<!-Display a heading.->
<H3><CENTER>ISAPI (NoLog) Filter Tester</CENTER></H3>
```

```
<!-Display the links and some explanatory text.->
Choosing the first link will create a classified log entry,
while the second one creates a standard log entry.<P>

Log this Link as <A HREF="NoLog.htm">Classified</A><P>
Log this Link <A HREF="LogIt.htm">Normally</A>

</BODY>
</HTML>
```

There shouldn't be anything too mysterious about this code. We've used it all before. All this page contains is a heading, some explanatory text, and a couple of links. We'll use it to switch between the two test pages without going through a lot of extra work.

The names for the two test pages are important; you must name the first test page NoLog.HTM or the filter won't work. (Since it's looking for a target by this name, you have to provide one for testing purposes.) Listing 13-7 contains the source code for this page. The second text page is named LogIt.HTM. Listing 13-8 contains the source code you'll need to create it. Both test pages contain a header and some text, but that's about it.

Listing 13-7:

```
<HTML>
<HEAD>
<TITLE>ISAPI Filter Test</TITLE>
</HEAD>
<BODY>
<H3><CENTER>This Page is <EM>Not</EM> Logged</CENTER></H3>
Which means that you won't see any of the normal entries in the log.<P>
What you will see are a bunch of classified entries instead.
</BODY>
</HTML>
```

Listing 13-8:

```
<HTML>
<HEAD>
<TITLE>ISAPI Filter Test</TITLE>
</HEAD>
<BODY>
<H3><CENTER>This Page is Logged</CENTER></H3>
Which means that you'll see all the normal entries in the log.
</BODY>
</HTML>
```

We're all ready to check out the ISA filter. All you need to do is open the Filter.HTM Web page using your Web browser. Make absolutely certain you

13

access the Web server through an intranet connection. Double-clicking on the Filter.HTM file in Explorer and opening it as a file won't force the Web server to make the appropriate log entries. Once you've gone between the two test pages several times, open the log file. If you have your Web server set up like I do, there's one log file for each day in the System32\LogFiles directory on your Web server. Here's what the log entries looked like when I tried the NoLog ISA filter out.

```
in980430 - Notepad                                                              _ □ ×
File  Edit  Search  Help
SUC1, NT_SERVER, 200.100.100.1, 752, 288, 5212, 200, 0, GET, /, -,
SUC1, NT_SERVER, 200.100.100.1, 28811, 326, 668, 200, 0, GET, /Filter.htm, -,
SUC1, NT_SERVER, 200.100.100.1, 9784, 335, 499, 200, 0, GET, Classified Target, Classified Parms,
SUC1, NT_SERVER, 200.100.100.1, 2223, 314, 121, 304, 0, GET, /Filter.htm, -,
SUC1, NT_SERVER, 200.100.100.1, 8182, 335, 419, 200, 0, GET, /LogIt.htm, -,
SUC1, NT_SERVER, 200.100.100.1, 60136, 314, 121, 304, 0, GET, /Filter.htm, -,
```

Notice that all of the log entries show the appropriate Web page except the ones for NoLog.HTM. The only NoLog.HTM entry shown here is on the third line from the top. These entries are marked as classified because the NoLog filter changed them. On the other hand, the LogIt and Filter entries appear just as they should. Obviously, all this was done automatically—the filter responded to the log event in the background.

Using an ISAPI Extension to Relay Server Information

Just about everyone knows the local time and date—all you need to do is look at a clock. However, if you're a network administrator or webmaster, it's often not enough to know what time it is locally if you're managing remote resources. It's actually more important to know the time and date of the location that you're administering.

This example is going to show you how to grab the time and date from the server and display it in a browser window. You could use this particular ISAPI extension in a variety of ways, but we'll look at it when used on a simple Web page. The most important concept you should walk away with is that using an ISAPI extension allows you to access every piece of information that you could with a regular program while sitting at the console. In other words, anything you could do while sitting at the computer is also available when managing it remotely. The only real limitations are those that standard Windows NT security would place on your account.

T IP: Flexibility is a two-edged sword. There are some limitations you should place on ISAPI extensions that you wouldn't place on an ordinary program. For example, you may want to think twice about allowing remote backups unless you have all of the capability in place for actually managing the entire process. An administrator sitting at the Windows NT console could see that the tape you're trying to use isn't the one you should be using for backup by physically verifying the tape number or other identifying information. The question you have to ask yourself is whether a remote administrator has the same capability. In many cases the answer is no.

Creating the Get Time/Date ISAPI Extension

Let's begin by getting the basic program put together. Since we've already put a basic ISAPI extension together in this chapter, I won't spend a lot of time on procedural details in this section. The following procedure will get you set up.

1. Create a new ISAPI extension project. I used GetTD as the name for my extension, though you could use any name you like.

2. We don't need to do anything special on the ISAPI Extension Wizard, Step 1 of 1 dialog, so click Finish when you get to this point.

3. Clear the New Project Information dialog by clicking OK. Make sure you verify all the program parameters first.

Creating the code comes next. As with any ISAPI extension, you'll need to add three major pieces of code to this example. The following list shows what you'll need to add.

◆ *Parse map* The parse map defines how the functions in your DLL get called. It also defines the variables you need and the way they get mapped to your functions.

◆ *Functions* Obviously your DLL is useless without some code that provides output to the browser.

◆ *Function definition* You'll need to add a function declaration to your ISAPI extension header file.

As you can see, we have to make two changes to the GetTD.CPP file and one to the GetTD.H file. Listing 13-9 shows the pertinent code from the GetTD.CPP file. Make sure you look for both the parse map and the GetTD() function. You'll also want to note the change I made to the Default()

13

function, which makes it a bit more useful when you have more than one function in a single ISAPI Extension file. Listing 13-10 shows the entire GetTD.H file.

Listing 13-9:

```
///////////////////////////////////////////////////////////////////
// command-parsing map

BEGIN_PARSE_MAP(CGetTDExtension, CHttpServer)
    // Get the system time and date.
    ON_PARSE_COMMAND(GetTD, CGetTDExtension, ITS_EMPTY)

    // Default parse map.
    ON_PARSE_COMMAND(Default, CGetTDExtension, ITS_EMPTY)
    DEFAULT_PARSE_COMMAND(Default, CGetTDExtension)
END_PARSE_MAP(CGetTDExtension)


///////////////////////////////////////////////////////////////////
// The one and only CGetTDExtension object

CGetTDExtension theExtension;


///////////////////////////////////////////////////////////////////
// CGetTDExtension implementation

CGetTDExtension::CGetTDExtension()
{
}

CGetTDExtension::~CGetTDExtension()
{
}

BOOL CGetTDExtension::GetExtensionVersion(HSE_VERSION_INFO* pVer)
{
    // Call default implementation for initialization
    CHttpServer::GetExtensionVersion(pVer);

    // Load description string
    TCHAR sz[HSE_MAX_EXT_DLL_NAME_LEN+1];
    ISAPIVERIFY(::LoadString(AfxGetResourceHandle(),
```

```
            IDS_SERVER, sz, HSE_MAX_EXT_DLL_NAME_LEN));
    _tcscpy(pVer->lpszExtensionDesc, sz);
    return TRUE;
}

//////////////////////////////////////////////////////////////////////
// CGetTDExtension command handlers

void CGetTDExtension::Default(CHttpServerContext* pCtxt)
{
    StartContent(pCtxt);
    WriteTitle(pCtxt);

    // Display an informational message on how to use this extension.
    *pCtxt << _T("<H2><CENTER>How to Use This ISAPI Extension</CENTER></H2>");
    *pCtxt << _T("Use the <STRONG><EM>GetTD</EM></STRONG> function to");
    *pCtxt << _T("retrieve the current Web server date and time.<P>");

    EndContent(pCtxt);
}

void CGetTDExtension::GetTD(CHttpServerContext* pCtxt)
{
    // Create a couple of local variables.
    CString    cDate;        // String representation of date.
    CString    cTime;        // String representation of time.
    CTime      oCurDate;     // Current date and time.

    // Get the current date and store it in a string.
    oCurDate = CTime::GetCurrentTime();
    cDate = oCurDate.Format("%A, %d %B %Y");
    cTime = oCurDate.Format("%I:%M %p");

    // Start an HTML page.
    StartContent(pCtxt);
    WriteTitle(pCtxt);

    // Display the time and date.
    *pCtxt << _T("The system date is: ");
    *pCtxt << _T(cDate);
    *pCtxt << _T("<P>");
    *pCtxt << _T("The system time is: ");
    *pCtxt << _T(cTime);
```

13

```
    *pCtxt << _T("<P>");

    // End the HTML page.
    EndContent(pCtxt);
}
```

Listing 13-10:

```
if !defined(AFX_GETTD_H__E8B71025_2785_11D1_8E36_444553540000__INCLUDED_)
define AFX_GETTD_H__E8B71025_2785_11D1_8E36_444553540000__INCLUDED_

// GETTD.H - Header file for your Internet Server
//     An ISAPI Extension that retrieves the time and date.

#include "resource.h"

class CGetTDExtension : public CHttpServer
{
public:
    CGetTDExtension();
    ~CGetTDExtension();

// Overrides
    // ClassWizard generated virtual function overrides
        // NOTE - the ClassWizard will add and remove member functions here.
        //     DO NOT EDIT what you see in these blocks of generated code !
    //{{AFX_VIRTUAL(CGetTDExtension)
    public:
    virtual BOOL GetExtensionVersion(HSE_VERSION_INFO* pVer);
    //}}AFX_VIRTUAL

    // Default handler.
    void Default(CHttpServerContext* pCtxt);

    // Special time and date handlers.
    void GetTD(CHttpServerContext* pCtxt);

    DECLARE_PARSE_MAP()

    //{{AFX_MSG(CGetTDExtension)
    //}}AFX_MSG
};
```

```
//{{AFX_INSERT_LOCATION}}
// Microsoft Developer Studio will insert additional declarations immediately
before the previous line.

#endif // !defined(AFX_GETTD_H__E8B71025_2785_11D1_8E36_444553540000__INCLUDED)
```

Let's talk about the code in Listing 13-9 first. The parse map shouldn't be too much of a surprise. We don't need to pass any data from the client to the server, so we use the ITS_EMPTY constant for the GetTD function.

Notice how I've modified the Default() function. Normally you'd use the Default() function for your code if there was only one function in the DLL. However, I've found it quite handy to use the Default() function as a method of documenting my ISAPI Extension interface when there is more than one function. That way a coworker can quickly construct a Web page, view the documentation the ISAPI extension provides, and then get down to the business of creating a real page.

The GetTD() function is pretty basic. All it does is grab the system time and then format it into two strings: one for time and another for date. Notice how I use the Format() function to obtain both strings. Once I have my two string variables, I create a basic Web page containing the values.

Listing 13-10 isn't much different than our previous example either. All I did was declare the GetTD function. The only data in this case is pCtxt since I don't have to pass the function any data.

Creating a Test Web Page for GetTD

Now let's look at some HTML code to access this ISAPI extension. Listing 13-11 contains a very simple test page.

Listing 13-11:

```
<HTML>
<HEAD>
<TITLE>Get Time/Date ISAPI Extension Example</TITLE>
</HEAD>
<BODY>

<!- Display a heading. ->
<CENTER><H2>Getting Time and Date from Your Server</CENTER></H2>
```

13

```
<!- Display a link for the Default() function. ->
Click <A HREF="Controls/GetTD.DLL?Default">here</A> to see the
Default() function message.<P>

<!- Display a link for the Get Time/Date page. ->
Click <A HREF="Controls/GetTD.DLL?GetTD">here</A> to see the Time() and Date()
function messages. <P>

</BODY>
</HTML>
```

You should notice a major change in Listing 13-11 from the previous example (Listing 13-4). I'm using an anchor this time to get to the ISAPI extension. When users click on the link, they'll get a page generated by the ISAPI extension rather than linking to a static page on the Web server as usual. There are some significant advantages to this approach:

◆ You can create browser-specific pages by detecting the browser type and passing it as a parameter to the ISAPI extension. Most browsers do provide unique identification information.

◆ An ISAPI extension allows you to customize the content of the Web page to reflect a particular user's needs.

◆ Using an ISAPI extension allows you to create links based on some criteria like the day of the week. For example, you could have a Monday Welcome page and a Friday Meeting page connection to the same home page link.

Obviously, you could get similar results using other technologies like ASP or older scripts. The fact remains that you could use the anchor technique in a variety of ways that you normally wouldn't use on a Web site.

 NOTE: Remember to test this ISAPI extension on an intranet. You can't open the extension locally, so the link will fail if you simply open the test Web page as a file in your browser.

Let's look at the output of this ISAPI extension. Figure 13-2 shows the page when you first look at it. As you can see, it contains a simple heading and two links—one for each function in the ISAPI extension.

Our initial test page gives you two options: one to look at the Default() function output and the other to view the GetTD() function output.

Figure 13-2.

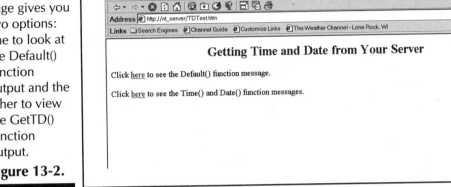

If you click on the first link, you'll see something like this.

How to Use This ISAPI Extension

Use the *GetTD* function to retrieve the current Web server date and time.

Even though this page doesn't give explicit usage instructions for the ISAPI extension, you do get an idea of what it can do. Obviously, you would provide more details in a production extension. You'll also want to include a list of parameters, if any, as part of your Default() function page. There are some situations where you may even want to include contact information for the ISAPI extension's creator.

Click the Back button on your browser to get back to the original Web page shown in Figure 13-2. Now we'll try the second link. Before you try the link though, change the time and date on your test server. You'll want to do this to be certain that the ISAPI extension is working as anticipated. Here is a typical example of the time and date output from the GetTD() function. As you can see, the Web page contains the changed system time, not local time, for your server.

13

The system date is: Saturday, 02 May 1998

The system time is: 03:13 PM

Using an ISAPI Filter to Request a User Name and Password

There are a lot of different ways to use a security filter with IIS. Before you can do anything, though, you have to have some understanding of how to put a very simple filter together. This section will help you understand how to create a filter that will pass values onto the server and rely on it to validate the user.

The first thing that a filter would need to do is get some input from the user, which usually consists of a user name and a password. Once a filter has determined that the user has provided some input, it can simply pass control to the server for verification. Of course, this isn't always what you want. You may want to perform some additional processing within the filter that the server doesn't normally do. The filter may also have to provide some additional functionality in the form of decryption or perhaps even specialized error message handling. The following list gives you some ideas on the additional features that a security filter can provide.

◆ *Decryption* You can always choose to encrypt the password and user name at the client end. This means decrypting it at the server end as well. An ISAPI filter is perfect for this purpose.

◆ *Authentication* Windows NT doesn't force you to use the built-in authentication. You can always choose to authenticate users yourself and give them an appropriate level of security. For that matter, you could perform an authentication, then assign the user to a group and let Windows NT take care of the details. There are a number of different authentication scenarios.

◆ *Custom error handling* You may not like the way that Windows NT handles errors. An ISAPI filter can provide at least limited error handling. Of course, the precise level of error handling you provide is determined by the client as well as the server, which means you'll want to have control over which browser the user uses for access.

◆ *Specialized access handling* There are situations where you may not want everyone to have 24-hour access to your Web site. Neither IIS nor Windows NT currently provides any method for shutting down your Web server to the average user while keeping it open for everyone else. An ISAPI filter can provide access based on the current time or any other criteria for that matter. You may even restrict access to certain sites based on server load.

Now that you have some idea of what a filter can do for you, let's create an example. The first thing you'll need to do is create a shell using the same process as in the previous ISAPI filter section of the chapter. The only difference when creating the project in this case is that I have given my program the name of AuthUser, though you could use any name you like. In addition, you'll need to check the Client Authentication Requests option and uncheck the End of Connection option on the ISAPI Extension Wizard - Step 2 of 2 dialog. Listing 13-12 shows the code you'll need to add to the OnAuthenticate() function. I'll describe how the code works after the listing.

NOTE: You must set up your test Web server to allow challenge/ response security for this example to work. It won't work if you use the Windows NT Authentication method in most cases. In addition, you must set the target directory to disallow anonymous access in some cases.

Listing 13-12:

```cpp
// AUTHUSER.CPP - Implementation file for your Internet Server
//     AuthUser Filter

#include "stdafx.h"
#include "AuthUser.h"

/////////////////////////////////////////////////////////////////////
// The one and only CWinApp object
// NOTE: You may remove this object if you alter your project to no
// longer use MFC in a DLL.

CWinApp theApp;


/////////////////////////////////////////////////////////////////////
```

```
// The one and only CAuthUserFilter object

CAuthUserFilter theFilter;


/////////////////////////////////////////////////////////////////////////
// CAuthUserFilter implementation

CAuthUserFilter::CAuthUserFilter()
{
}


CAuthUserFilter::~CAuthUserFilter()
{
}


BOOL CAuthUserFilter::GetFilterVersion(PHTTP_FILTER_VERSION pVer)
{
    // Call default implementation for initialization
    CHttpFilter::GetFilterVersion(pVer);

    // Clear the flags set by base class
    pVer->dwFlags &= ~SF_NOTIFY_ORDER_MASK;

    // Set the flags we are interested in
    pVer->dwFlags |= SF_NOTIFY_ORDER_LOW | SF_NOTIFY_SECURE_PORT | SF_NO-
      TIFY_NONSECURE_PORT
              | SF_NOTIFY_AUTHENTICATION;

    // Load description string
    TCHAR sz[SF_MAX_FILTER_DESC_LEN+1];
    ISAPIVERIFY(::LoadString(AfxGetResourceHandle(),
            IDS_FILTER, sz, SF_MAX_FILTER_DESC_LEN));
    _tcscpy(pVer->lpszFilterDesc, sz);
    return TRUE;
}


DWORD CAuthUserFilter::OnAuthentication(CHttpFilterContext* pCtxt,
    PHTTP_FILTER_AUTHENT pAuthent)
{
    CString    oBuffer;         // Buffer for client output.
    DWORD      dwSize;           // Size of the buffer.
    LPVOID     pvInOut;         // Client input or output.
```

```
// See if we're getting an anonymous request.
if (strlen(pAuthent->pszUser) == 0)
{

    // Get the user's name.
    dwSize = 100;
    pvInOut = " ";
    pCtxt->GetServerVariable("REMOTE_USER", pvInOut, &dwSize);
    dwSize = strlen(LPTSTR(pvInOut));

    if (strncmp(LPTSTR(pvInOut), " ", 1) == 0)
    {

        // Set an error condition.
        pCtxt->ServerSupportFunction(SF_REQ_SEND_RESPONSE_HEADER,
            "401 Access Denied",
            NULL,
            NULL);
    }
    else
    {

        // Indicate the user has supplied a password.
        pCtxt->ServerSupportFunction(SF_REQ_SEND_RESPONSE_HEADER,
            NULL,
            NULL,
            NULL);

        // Store the user's name.
        strncpy(pAuthent->pszUser, LPTSTR(pvInOut), dwSize);

        // Get and store the user's password.
        dwSize = 100;
        pvInOut = " ";
        pCtxt->GetServerVariable("AUTH_PASS", pvInOut, &dwSize);
        dwSize = strlen(LPTSTR(pvInOut));
        strncpy(pAuthent->pszPassword, LPTSTR(pvInOut), dwSize);
    }
}

// return the appropriate status code
return SF_STATUS_REQ_NEXT_NOTIFICATION;
}
```

13

```
// Do not edit the following lines, which are needed by ClassWizard.
#if 0
BEGIN_MESSAGE_MAP(CAuthUserFilter, CHttpFilter)
    //{{AFX_MSG_MAP(CAuthUserFilter)
    //}}AFX_MSG_MAP
END_MESSAGE_MAP()
#endif    // 0


/////////////////////////////////////////////////////////////////////////
// If your extension will not use MFC, you'll need this code to make
// sure the extension objects can find the resource handle for the
// module.  If you convert your extension to not be dependent on MFC,
// remove the comments around the following AfxGetResourceHandle()
// and DllMain() functions, as well as the g_hInstance global.

/****

static HINSTANCE g_hInstance;

HINSTANCE AFXISAPI AfxGetResourceHandle()
{
    return g_hInstance;
}


BOOL WINAPI DllMain(HINSTANCE hInst, ULONG ulReason,
                    LPVOID lpReserved)
{
    if (ulReason == DLL_PROCESS_ATTACH)
    {
        g_hInstance = hInst;
    }

    return TRUE;
}


****/
```

As you can see, this code is a lot more complex than the code in the previous ISAPI filter example. One of the things we need to do is pass information from the filter directly to the server, which in turn passes it onto the client. It takes three passes to complete the trip through this filter, as listed here.

1. Determine if the user is trying to access the server anonymously by using the GetServerVariable() function to retrieve the user name. (A blank return value for the user name indicates that the user is trying to access the server anonymously.) If so, tell the server to send a 401 error message to the client using the ServerSupportFunction() function. This displays the browser's password dialog where the user can enter a password and name.

2. Once the user enters a password and name, retrieve it from the input stream using the GetServerVariable() function. Pass the name and password along to Windows NT security for verification.

3. Tell the server that the filter has successfully completed its mission using the SF_STATUS_REQ_NEXT_NOTIFICATION return value.

Since you have three loops to work with, there are always a few surprises when working with a security filter. For example, any decryption will happen during the second pass through the filter between the time you retrieve the user name and password using the GetServerVariable() function and the time you copy this information to the pAuthent structure using the strncpy() function. Some things happen during the third loop. For example, you may decide that you need to interact with the user directly. This usually happens during the third pass through the filter.

Notice that I provided a return value of SF_STATUS_REQ_NEXT_NOTIFICATION. That's the server's signal that you want it to handle the details of validating the user and displaying a Web page. If you want to perform all of the validation yourself, you'll also need to display the requested information. There isn't any middle ground when it comes to this step.

TIP: IIS normally gives you three chances to enter the password correctly before it displays an error message. You could circumvent this behavior in two ways. First, you could perform your own authentication between the second and third passes of the security filter. This way you could give the user additional chances to provide the correct password and pass the correct user name and password to the server the first time around. The second method is to use the SF_STATUS_REQ_ERROR return value to stop any attempt to access the Web server after the first failed attempt. This will display a server error message and could possibly convince less knowledgeable users that the server is down, reducing further attempts at access.

13

Once you compile this filter, you'll need to install it using the same technique we used for the first ISAPI filter example in the chapter. When you run this example, you'll see a password dialog like the one shown here.

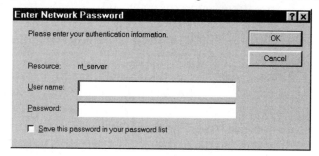

If you enter a nonexistent user name or password, you'll see a server-generated error message like the one shown here.

HTTP Error 401

401.1 Unauthorized: Logon Failed

This error indicates that the credentials passed to the server do not match the credentials required to log on to the server.

Please contact the Web server's administrator to verify that you have permission to access the requested resource.

Entering a valid name and password will give you access to the Web site.

PART IV

The Developer's View of
Visual C++

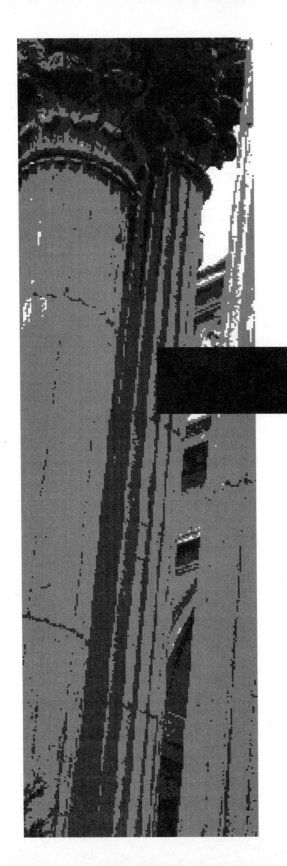

CHAPTER 14

Designing with Security in Mind

Just about everyone knows what kinds of problems face the network administrator trying to enforce security on a network today. We all know that short/common passwords, users who don't understand security procedures, and outright neglect on the part of the administrator can all work toward making your LAN a security risk. Fortunately, operating systems like Windows NT make it much easier to enforce security on the local machine and the LAN, regardless of user habits. Knowing how to access these security features and build them into your applications is essential to ensuring the safety of both your data and applications.

Security is also one of the major issues facing anyone building an Internet or intranet site today. It's hard to know who's harder pressed: the company building a public access Internet or the one trying to hide its presence with an intranet. No matter which environment you work in, a host of companies are preparing tools of various kinds and capabilities to address the needs of those who want to protect their data from harm. Unfortunately, all the nifty tools in the world won't prevent you from shooting yourself in the foot when building your own controls and application programs. (These tools also don't work very well when you use them in the wrong way.) Again, knowing the security features that Windows NT provides can help you improve the security of remote access technologies like ActiveX.

What you shouldn't be looking for in this chapter are concrete answers that are going to work in your specific situation. It would be silly to try to cover in one chapter all of the various technologies available today, or even every security issue you'll ever run into. What we'll concentrate on instead is the programmer's perspective on security matters. We'll talk about the technologies that are available to you as a programmer, but we won't get into specific solutions to a specific problem. The solution you finally decide to use will have to be based on your company's needs and the tools you have at your disposal.

In fact, the focus will be even tighter than on Internet security as a whole—we'll spend most of our time looking at Windows NT security in particular. We'll also look at what you'll need to know about security when using remote access technologies like ActiveX controls, Distributed Component Object Model (DCOM), and Component Object Model Plus (COM+). This chapter will answer the question of what a programmer can do to protect not only data but also application code from harm. From a programmer's perspective, an ActiveX control isn't only a source of new browser capabilities, it's also a potential source of viruses. Even the most careful attempts at protecting a control could prove inadequate unless the browser, programmer, and Internet site all work together to make security a reality. Likewise, while DCOM may allow you to better use LAN resources, it also means exposing your server to potential damage from an inept user. And since COM+ is still looming in the future, you'll want to be especially careful when using this new technology.

The first thing we'll do is spend some time looking at the various APIs and other tools that Microsoft has provided to make writing all kinds of applications, both local and remote, at least a little safer. Especially important is a look at the native security provided by products such as Windows NT. Since you have full access to the operating system, why not use the security features that it provides to your advantage? The benefits of operating system security in a normal application environment are obvious to everyone—except perhaps when you're looking at the Internet. Remember that you can use ActiveX controls to do things like manipulate the registry or at least query it for information like a user's name and company. If you can use an ActiveX control to grab the user's name and company from the registry, you can also use an ActiveX control to help implement security through the operating system services that Microsoft provides. It doesn't take long to figure out that some added security measures on your part will keep the burden of security on an Internet site pretty much out of view.

The next thing we'll look at in this chapter are the kinds of problems that a programmer needs to think about in regard to security. Just who is involved with an Internet site and how? It's also important to know about the weak links in your organization and what harm they could cause by downloading controls from the Internet without too much thought. Unless you know who you're protecting and from what, the effort is a lost cause from the start.

Once we get past some of the more mundane concerns of Internet security, we'll start looking at what you can do to implement it. Here's the problem. When Sun started creating Java applets, it took what's termed the "sandbox" approach to security. A Java applet can only play in its own sandbox—it can't access the operating system or even the hardware hosting the applet outside the strict areas that Sun thought the applet should access (which is pretty close to no access at all). The run-time engine you need in order to use a Java applet ensures that access is strictly controlled. The advantage of this approach is immediately clear: lack of access also means lack of security concerns. Unfortunately, it also severely limits what you can do with a Java applet, especially when it comes to data exchange of various sorts.

Java takes the "sandbox" approach to security.

14

W EB LINK: Even Java isn't bulletproof. Hackers have already found holes in its implementation that make Java a less-than-perfect solution. For example, on March 22, 1996, Drew Dean (ddean@ICS.Princeton.EDU) and Ed Felton (felten@ICS.Princeton.EDU), of the Princeton Department of Computer Science, found a bug in Java that allowed them to create an applet that deletes a file on the user's local disk. They did this by downloading a file to the user's machine through the Netscape caching mechanism and then fooling Java into running the applet. Fortunately, this bug was fixed in the 2.01 release of Netscape. You can find out about other potential security problems with Java at **http://www.cs.princeton.edu/sip/pub/secure96.html**.

Microsoft took another tack with ActiveX controls, called the "shrink-wrap" approach. With an ActiveX control, you have full access to the system, just as you would with any shrink-wrapped piece of software. What this means is that you can write some extremely flexible controls that make full use of what the system has to offer. There are no limitations from a data access standpoint either. However, from a security perspective, ActiveX could turn into a nightmare. What would prevent a control that you downloaded from completely trashing your system as you watched in horror? There's another aspect to this approach: vendor identification. When you buy a piece of

ActiveX controls take the "shrink-wrap" approach to security.

software at the store, you know who produced it. If the software contains a virus or even a nasty bug, you know whom to contact. We'll look at a certification method that Microsoft is proposing for ActiveX controls that does the same thing as the packaging for a piece of software you buy in the store—it identifies with certainty the vendor who created the software you're using.

W EB LINK: All the vendors involved in both VBScript and JavaScript are constantly working to improve the security of these two scripting languages. Unfortunately, it's a little difficult to find out what's going on with VBScript. You can read about the currently known security problems with JavaScript at **http://www.osf.org/~loverso/javascript/**.

Lest you think that scripts are easily monitored, we'll look at some of the security concerns about running them. The short version is that neither VBScript nor JavaScript are even close to safe (though more work has been done finding the security holes in JavaScript). The following list presents three of the most common problems.

◆ *Tricking the user into uploading a file*   Even though JavaScript has to ask the user's permission to upload a file, a hacker could hide this request in a variety of ways. All a hacker really needs is a button with an interesting caption. Uploaded password files like those used for Windows 95/98 are easily cracked—making the hacker's job of breaking into your system easy.

◆ *Obtaining file directories*   A JavaScript doesn't have to ask anyone's permission to upload a directory of your machine. In fact, it can upload the directories of any network machines you have access to as well. A hacker who knows the organization of your hard drive has gone a long way toward being able to break into your system.

◆ *Tracking sites visited*   Hackers can learn a lot about you by keeping track of the Web sites you visit. A JavaScript makes this easy to do. It can track every URL you visit and send the addresses to the hacker's machine. As with the file upload problem, the user has to give permission to do this, but the hacker can disguise this permission as just about anything.

The chapter will also spend some time on security standards. Some programmers view standards of this type as a nuisance because they don't directly relate to programming. We won't waste a lot of time covering the content of those standards, but it's important to know that they exist and where you can find them. Most of you will agree that there isn't a good reason to reinvent the wheel when it comes to security. If someone else has already figured out a way to prevent harmful access in a standardized way that everyone can use, why not make use of that information? That's what the standards section is all about: letting you know what's available and how you can use the information that the standards contain.

Understanding the Windows Security API

Windows NT provides a level of security that almost verges on paranoia for an operating system. It allows you to set security in a variety of ways, including both the familiar user and file levels. You can also create groups and assign security by using groups instead of individuals. In addition, you can monitor every aspect of the security system using various alarms and log files. Windows NT excels in the way that it actually monitors system activity. Not one event goes without some kind of scrutiny. In fact, the simple act of passing information from one process to another undergoes some level of scrutiny by Windows NT.

As for applications, the level of security that Windows NT provides is a two-edged sword. On the one hand, there aren't too many things that an

14

application can do to break security. In most cases Windows NT will simply terminate an errant application before any kind of security breach can occur. On the other hand, such stringent security actually breaks some older applications that work fine when using less stringent forms of Windows like Windows 95/98. In essence, the security that Windows NT provides can actually affect the compatibility your machine can provide.

TIP: If your only intent is to design an application that performs a useful, non-security-related service, you may want to design with Windows 95/98 in mind. On the other hand, Windows NT provides so many security-related services that you can create an application with an almost impenetrable interface. However, the price you'll pay is forfeiting the ability to run the application on a wide range of machines. Windows NT and Windows 95/98 put two almost completely different faces on the issue of security—Windows NT furnishing almost too much security and Windows 95/98 almost none.

A famous hacker once said it's not a matter of if, but when, someone will break into your Web site— tracking security events will allow you to detect security failures before they become a problem.

The overabundance of security provided by Windows NT is a big plus for Internet users and sites. It's the level of native security that makes Windows NT an excellent platform for a Web site. In addition, you can improve on most of the standard features provided by a Web site if you go to the added trouble of writing code to use the features that Windows NT provides. For example, we see in Chapter 13 that you can write ISAPI filters to monitor events in the background. Combining an ISAPI filter with the security features of Windows NT could provide everything you need to at least track significant security events. In other words, if you can't prevent a hacker from breaking your security, you can at least track what he or she is doing to keep damage to a minimum. In addition, knowing where someone did break in is one way to improve security in the future.

Security features need not be limited to ISAPI filters or desktop applications; you can also incorporate Windows NT security into an ActiveX control or an ISAPI extension. For example, you could write an ActiveX control that tests whether a person logging into the system is actually allowed access to the server. Likewise, an ISAPI extension could display a login screen for the user and then check for access level in a system database. You could even write an ISAPI extension that would send different kinds of HTML pages back to the client based on the level of access the user is allowed by the system.

ActiveX controls
always act from
the client side of
the Internet,
while an ISAPI
extension works
from the server
side.

Theoretically you could also add Windows NT security into DLLs designed to be accessed from a client machine (even a Windows 95/98 client) using DCOM. Since the DLL will execute on the Windows NT server rather than being downloaded to the client (as is normally done), the client could be protected using standard Windows NT security features. Realistically, adding this kind of security to an application would prove expensive when it comes to network bandwidth and server processor cycles. You'd want to implement security through DCOM in the minority, rather than the majority, of cases.

So why would you want to go to all the effort of building additional Windows NT-specific security into your application? For one thing, there are holes in the current API specifications for Internet security. For example, we've talked about Internet Component Download service—we look at the process itself in Chapter 8 as part of the discussion on downloading from the Internet. There are methods that an unscrupulous person could use to bypass all of the security features we discuss in that chapter as a result of holes in the current defenses provided by the various browsers on the market. (We'll concentrate on Internet Explorer, but you can be sure Netscape and other browsers have the same, slightly different, or even worse problems.) These security holes aren't in the API itself, but in some of the creative solutions people used in the past to make the Internet work. In essence, problem-solving in the past created security back doors in the present. The following list tells you about three of the holes in the Internet Component Download service (though it's almost certain that more holes exist).

◆ *HTML <A HREF> tag*   There are ways to download and run an EXE file using the <A HREF> tag. The current method used by Internet Explorer 3.*x*/4.*x* to keep this problem in check is to have the HTML parser use the URL moniker directly to download the code and then to call WinVerifyTrust to check code validity (this is the same technique described in Chapter 8). Is this method 100 percent safe? No, because you're using something other than the standard procedure to verify the contents of a file. In this case you're relying on the HTML parser.

◆ *Scripts*   Right now scripts are totally free of any kind of security check. There is no way to verify who created the script or what it might do to your machine. More important, there isn't any way to verify what information the script might retrieve from your machine. (At the beginning of this chapter, we looked at two kinds of information a JavaScript could retrieve from your machine: the directories on the user's hard drive and the sites the user visits.) Microsoft is working right now to create some kind of script certificate. Once script certificates become a reality, the browser can call WinVerifyTrust to check a script before running it.

◆ *Full applications or other complex download situations*   Internet Explorer does a good job of checking specific kinds of downloads right now. For example, downloading an OCX initiates a WinVerifyTrust sequence. What happens if the download parameters fall outside the limited scope of things checked by Internet Explorer? For example, a user might want to download and install Doom or some other game program. The installation sequence might include unpredictable actions such as making registry entries and rebooting the machine. Internet Explorer can't handle that situation at the moment. Microsoft plans to make future versions of component download more robust so that it can handle such events.

WEB LINK: Part of your protection strategy is going to include testing multiple browsers to see how they react—especially if you're creating a public access Web site. As a programmer working with multiple products, you still have to keep track of all the Web sites you visit on a regular basis for ideas. A product called NavEx allows you to create copies of your Internet Explorer Favorite Places folder as Netscape bookmarks and vice versa. You can download it at **http://mach5.ocs.drexel.edu/navex/**.

NOTE: We'll also look at holes in other types of Internet technology in this chapter. For example, Table 14-1 is full of new specifications designed to plug the holes in the technology we use today. SHTTP, S/WAN, and other technologies like them wouldn't be needed if security didn't present a problem. There's even a new version of MIME called S/MIME to make sure that no one reads your mail.

One of the first steps in understanding how Windows NT can help you enhance the security of your Internet site is to look at the basic security features offered by the operating system itself. Every security feature like drive mapping that Windows NT has to offer can be accessed using an application. What many programmers seem to forget is that you can also access those features using an ActiveX control. For example, you could create a button similar to the one we create in Chapter 10 whose whole purpose is to display a Map Network Drive dialog where the user can choose a drive to map on the network.

Of course, some Windows NT security features, such as mapping a drive, don't make much sense in the realm of Internet security—creating a drive-mapping pushbutton would only make sense if you intended to use it in an application. However, adding other Windows NT security features to an ActiveX control does make sense. For example, you could use the password protection features of Windows NT to display a logon dialog every time someone requests secure access to your site.

Creating an ActiveX control to display a logon dialog actually accomplishes two things in an Internet application. First, the password security provided by Windows NT is a lot better than that provided by Windows 95/98. A hacker will have a pretty tough time getting past the logon dialog without the right password. Second, you can tell the server to log every secure access—remember that Windows NT gives you the capability of monitoring everything. If someone does manage to break into your system, you'll at least know which account was used. Having an account name will allow you to assess the level of damage the hacker could inflict based on the security level of the person whose account was broken into.

The bottom line, then, is that the Windows NT Security API can help you create a more secure Internet environment. You can use ActiveX controls to access these security features from the client site, ISAPI extensions to access them from the server side, and ISAPI filters to perform behind-the-scenes monitoring of security events.

Making Windows NT Security Work for You

One of the main reasons to use Windows NT as your Internet server is to gain access to the Windows NT Security API.

The previous section explored some of the reasons you would want to use Windows NT as a Web server—the most important being to gain access to the Windows NT Security API. Understanding why the Windows NT Security API exists is only part of the picture. Now it's time to look at how you can actually implement those security features in the real world. In other words, it's time to take a look at the nuts and bolts of working with security in Windows NT. There are actually five different types or levels of security we'll explore in this chapter. The following list defines each type.

14

◆   *Built-in security*   Windows NT comes with a certain level of security as part of the operating system. Every object has some type of security associated with it under Windows NT, and we'll look at how that security is implemented. Using object-level security means that there is little chance that anyone could access any part of the operating system or its data without the proper authorization. Of course, little chance doesn't mean there is no chance at all—it always pays to assume your security is less than perfect.

◆ *Private Communication Technology (PCT)*   This is a special level of Internet security that Microsoft and the IETF are working on together. The short version is that PCT will enable a client and server to engage in private communication with little chance of being overheard. This level of security depends on digital signatures and encryption methodologies to do its work.

◆ *Windows NT authentication over HTTP*   Many people are under the mistaken assumption that security has to be convoluted or overly complex to work. In some cases it's the simple solution that provides the best answer. Authentication can take two forms under Windows NT when looked at from the Internet perspective. First, you could simply ask for the user's name and password, and then check that information against an access list on the server. There are two ways of doing this: the basic method that's used during a standard login and Windows NT Challenge/Response. The latter method relies on the client to supply the required user name and password based on the current session settings. In other words, the client supplies the information that the user used to log into the machine in the first place. The other method is equally simple. It relies on an existing technology called Secure Sockets Layer (SSL). SSL relies on encryption and digital certificates to do its work. If you're really paranoid about security, you can even combine these two security methods—they're not mutually exclusive.

◆ *Digital signatures*   A digital signature works as its name implies. The sender of a document or executable file signs it. You know that the work is genuine by examining the signature. You'll use a series of private and public keys to implement this level of security.

◆ *Cryptography API*   Some types of security rely on layers of protection to work. In other words, if a hacker were to break through one layer of protection, another layer would exist to prevent further access. That's just what the Cryptography API (also called CryptoAPI) is all about: it's a layer of protection added to all the layers that currently exist. It serves to keep someone from further penetrating your security.

The next few sections of the chapter explore several new technologies that you'll find embedded in either Windows NT, one of the Internet servers that it supports such as Microsoft Internet Information Server or Peer Web Services (provided free with Windows NT 4.0 and the OSR2 version of Windows 95/98), or one of the new browsers. It's interesting to see that Microsoft Internet Explorer 3.*x*/4.*x* provides built-in SSL support, as does the new version of Netscape Communicator. You'll also find PCT support in at least Internet Explorer. We'll also take a look at the Authenticode (digital signature) technology used by several vendors now to allow programmers to digitally sign their work. Any tampering with the code after that will show up when the user tries to download the program. The result is that it's less likely that you or one of your users will download a virus-infected program.

WEB LINK: You can download a version of Personal Web Server (PWS) for Windows 95 from **http://www.microsoft.com/iis/guide/pws.asp?A=2&B=5** (Windows 98 comes with PWS as part of the package). This is the version of PWS that shipped with the OSR2 version of Windows 95 and the Microsoft Windows NT Option Pack (there is a Windows 95/98 version of the option pack as well). While PWS won't fulfill the needs of a production Web site, it works fine for a developer who wants to test an Internet application. Remember that since Windows 95/98 doesn't provide the same security features that Windows NT does, you won't be able to test any security features of your application using the Windows 95/98 version of PWS. (Fortunately, the version of PWS that ships with Windows NT 4.0 Workstation will allow you to fully test security features.)

Encryption is another potential way of keeping your data safe, so we'll visit the CryptoAPI that Microsoft has developed. This particular bit of technology is included in at least a rough form in Internet Explorer. However, even though you can do some work with it now, the CryptoAPI is really a work in progress. In addition, the development kit required to expand on the CryptoAPI is only available in the United States and Canada—making this feature of limited appeal for the moment.

Built-in Security Features

Windows NT is about the most overengineered operating system on the market today when it comes to security. If you have any doubt as to the importance of security with Microsoft, just look at some of the qualifications that Windows NT presents. You can use that capability to your advantage. For example, you could make use of those advanced capabilities within an

14

OCX or grant access to specific features over the Internet. You'll have to use a lot of restraint in doing this because you don't want to damage your security net. In addition, it's impractical to use some features from the Internet because they just aren't important.

Fortunately, ActiveX controls aren't necessarily restricted to the Internet either. There's no rule saying that you can't create a control designed specifically for use within applications. An ActiveX control in a database or other application normally used by a network administrator (or other qualified person) could make that task a lot easier and more secure. In fact, an ActiveX control can take on multiple personalities if you want it to. You could even add the capability to detect the control's current location or perhaps add a special location field as part of a property page setup. Someone could choose a subset of features for Internet use, another set of features for LAN use, and still another set of features for local use.

One of the better uses for ActiveX controls in the LAN environment is to provide a subset of network security management capabilities to less-qualified managers.

About now, many of you are asking what kind of administrator would need to access security but wouldn't use the tools furnished by the NOS to do so. Windows NT actually provides a lot of very easy-to-use tools, so adding a lot of functionality isn't worthwhile in the minds of some programmers. There are actually a few good answers to this, but there's one situation that almost always comes to mind when most people think about security under Windows NT. What if the person administering the application isn't a network administrator—someone with the training to work with the NOS itself? Say that person is a workgroup manager or other individual who doesn't need to see the whole network picture, but just requires enough information to maintain the application he or she is responsible for managing. You'll find yourself in that situation a lot more often than you might think. Large companies with a lot of small workgroups frequently fall into this category. The network administrator doesn't have the knowledge needed to administer the application correctly, but doesn't want the workgroup manager crawling around the network either.

Whether you're creating a control for Internet, local, WAN, or LAN use, you'll find that a good understanding of the underlying network security architecture is essential. Windows 95/98 doesn't provide the same level of security that Windows NT does, so you'll find yourself doing without added security under Windows 95/98 at times. However, when Windows 95/98 does provide a security feature, it uses the same setup as Windows NT, so one security module will work with both of them. (In other cases you'll definitely want to use a separate module for Windows NT to make better use of its enhanced security capabilities—see the following note for details.)

NOTE: Windows NT does support a lot more Windows security API calls than Windows 95/98 does, because its security is much more robust. In fact, you'll find that your ability to manage security when using Windows 95/98 is severely hampered by its lack of support for Windows NT security features. For example, you can't use the GetUserObjectSecurity call under Windows 95/98. Most of the access token calls that we'll look at in the next section won't work either. The best way to figure out whether a call is supported or not is to test it. If you get ERROR_CALL_NOT_IMPLEMENTED (value 120) returned from the call, you know that you can only use it under Windows NT.

Windows NT and Windows 95/98 both use the term "object" rather loosely. It's true that a lot of objects are lurking beneath the surface, but you may find that they don't fit precisely within the C++ usage of the term. In general, in the next few sections, we'll look at an object as the encapsulation of code and data required to perform a specific security task. In other words, each security object is a self-contained unit designed to fulfill a specific role. (In many places in both Windows 95/98 and Windows NT, Microsoft chose to use the full C++ version of an object mainly because it implemented the required functionality as part of MFC. However, when reading either the Microsoft documentation or this chapter, you shouldn't depend on the definition of an object to mean a strict C++ object—think of objects more in the COM sense of the word.)

Knowing that everything is an object makes security a bit easier to understand—at least it's a starting point. However, objects themselves are just a starting point. Users are the other part of the security equation. An object is accessed by a user, so security in Windows is a matter of comparing the object's protection to the user's rights. If the user has sufficient rights (rights that meet or exceed those of the object), then he or she can use the object. The Windows documentation refers to an object's level of protection as a *security descriptor*. This is the structure that tells the security system what rights a user needs to access the object. Likewise, the user has an *access token*, which is another structure that tells the security system what rights a user has in a given situation. "Token" is a good word here because the user will give Windows NT the token in exchange for access to the object. (Think of the object as a bus, with Windows NT as the driver and the user presenting the required token to board.) Figure 14-1 shows both of these structures.

This is the shortest look you can take at security under either Windows 95/98 or Windows NT. Simply knowing that there are security objects and user

14

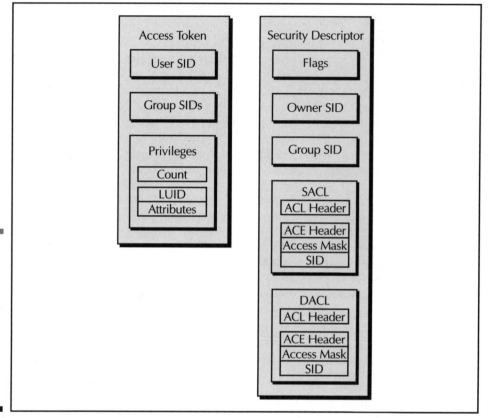

Access tokens
define the
user's rights,
while security
descriptors
define the
protection
level for a
process.

Figure 14-1.

tokens will go a long way toward helping you make sense out of the
Windows security API calls. In the following sections we'll take a more
detailed look at precisely what a token is and how it works. We'll also look at
the security descriptor. You don't absolutely have to know this information
to implement security using ActiveX if your only interest is the Internet, but
knowing it can help you design ActiveX controls of a more general nature
and wider appeal.

Understanding Access Tokens

You'll find that there are two ways of looking at a user's rights under
Windows; both are related to objects in one form or another. The user's
access token has a security identifier (SID) to identify the user throughout the
network—it's like having an account number. The user token that the SID

Windows NT supports two types of SIDs: user and group.

identifies tells what groups the user belongs to and what privileges the user has. Each group also has a SID, so the user's SID contains references to the various group SIDs that the user belongs to, not to a complete set of group access rights. You would normally use the User Manager utility under Windows NT to change the contents of this access token.

So what's the privileges section of the access token all about? It begins with a count of the number of privileges that the user has—not the groups that the user belongs to, but the number of special privilege entries in the access token. This section also contains an array of privilege entries. Each privilege entry contains a locally unique identifier (LUID)—essentially a pointer to an object—and an attribute mask. The attribute mask tells what rights the user has to the object. Group SID entries are essentially the same. They contain a privilege count and an array of privilege entries.

TIP: Now would probably be a good time to look at the Windows API help file provided with your copy of Visual C++ to see what kind of SID- and token-related API calls you can find. Examples of SID-related calls include CopySID and AllocateAndInitializeSID. You'll also find that the OpenProcessToken and GetTokenInformation calls are essential to making security work correctly with any language you use.

IN DEPTH

Observing the Flow of Access Rights

One of the things that you need to know as part of working with some kinds of objects is that object rights flow down to the lowest possible node unless overridden by another SID. For example, if you give a user read and write rights to the \Temp directory on a hard drive, those rights would also be applied to the \Temp\Stuff directory unless you assigned the user specific rights to that directory. The same holds true for containers. Assigning a user rights to a container object like a Word document gives the user the right to look at everything within that container, even other files in most cases. As you can see, it's important to track a user's exact rights to various objects on your server through the use of security surveys, since you could have inadvertently given the user more rights than he or she needs to perform a certain task.

14

Using Access Tokens

Let's talk briefly about the Token calls that the Windows API provides, since they are the first stepping-stone that you'll need to know about when it comes to security. To do anything with a user's account—even if you want to find out who has access to a particular workstation—you need to know about tokens. As previously stated, tokens are the central part of the user side of the security equation. You'll almost always begin a user account access with a call to the OpenProcessToken call. Notice the name of this call—it deals with any kind of a process, user or otherwise. The whole purpose of this call is to get a token handle with specific rights attached to it. For example, if you want to query the user account, you need the TOKEN_QUERY privilege. (Your access token must contain the rights that you request from the system, which is why an administrator can access a token but other users can't.) Any changes to the user's account require the TOKEN_ADJUST_PRIVILEGES privilege. There are quite a few of these access rights, so we won't go through them all here.

Once you have an access token handle, you need to decide what to do with it. If you decide you want to change a user's privilege to do something, you need the LUID for the privilege you want to change. All of these appear in the WINNT.H file with an SE_ attached to them. For example, the SE_SYSTEM_PROFILE_NAME privilege allows the user to gather profiling information for the entire system. Some SE values aren't related to users (for example, the SE_LOCK_MEMORY_NAME privilege that allows a process to lock system memory). You get the LUID for a privilege using the LookupPrivilegeValue call. Now you can combine the information you've gotten so far to change the privilege. In general, you'll use the AdjustTokenPrivileges call to make the required change.

Querying the user's account (or other access token information) is fairly straightforward. You use the GetTokenInformation call to retrieve any information you might need. This call requires a token class parameter, which tells Windows what kind of information you need. For example, you would use the TokenUser class if you wanted to know about a specific user. You'll also need to supply an appropriate structure that Windows can use for storing the information you request—which differs based on the token class you request.

Understanding Security Descriptors

Now let's look at the security descriptor. Figure 14-1 shows that each security descriptor contains five main sections. The first section is a list of flags. These

Look in the WINNT.H file for a list of Windows NT-defined privileges that you can change.

flags tell you the descriptor revision number, format, and ACL (access control list) status.

The next two sections contain SIDs. The owner SID tells who owns the object. This doesn't have to be an individual user; Windows allows you to use a group SID here as well. The one limiting factor is that the group SID must appear in the access token of the person changing the entry. The group SID allows a group of people to own the object. Of the two SIDs, only the owner SID is important under Windows. The group SID is used as part of the Macintosh and POSIX security environment.

The final two sections contain ACLs. The security access control list (SACL) controls Windows' auditing feature. Every time a user or group accesses an object and the auditing feature for that object is turned on, Windows makes an entry in the audit log. The discretionary access control list (DACL) controls who can actually use the object. You can assign both groups and individual users to a specific object.

NOTE: There are actually two types of security descriptors: absolute and self-relative. The absolute security descriptor contains an actual copy of each ACL within its structure. This is the type of security descriptor to use for an object that requires special handling. The self-relative security descriptor only contains a pointer to the SACL and DACL. This type of descriptor saves memory and reduces the time required to change the rights for a group of objects. You would use it when all the objects in a particular group require the same level of security. For example, you could use this method to secure all the threads within a single application. Windows requires that you convert a self-relative security descriptor to absolute format before you can save it or transfer it to another process. Every descriptor you retrieve using an API call is of the self-relative type—you must convert it before you can save it. You can convert a security descriptor from one type to another using the MakeAbsoluteSD and MakeSelfRelativeSD API calls.

An ACL consists of two types of entries. The first entry is a header that lists the number of access control entries (ACEs) that the ACL contains. Windows uses this number as a method for determining when it has reached the end of the ACE list. (There isn't any kind of end-of-structure record or any way of determining a precise size for each ACE in the structure.) The second entry is an array of ACEs.

CAUTION: Never directly manipulate the contents of an ACL or SID, since Microsoft may change its structure in future versions of Windows. The Windows API provides a wealth of functions to change the contents of these structures. Always use an API call to perform any task with either structure type to reduce the impact of changes in structure on your application.

So what is an ACE? An *ACE* defines the object rights for a single user or group. Every ACE has a header that defines the type, size, and flags for the ACE. Next comes an access mask that defines the rights that a user or group has to the object. Finally, there's an entry for the user's or group's SID.

There are four different types of ACE headers (three of which are used in the current version of Windows). The *access-allowed* type appears in the DACL and grants rights to a user. You can use it to add to the rights that a user already has to an object on an instance-by-instance basis. For example, say you wanted to keep the user from changing the system time so that you could keep all the machines on the network synchronized. However, there might be one situation—such as daylight savings time—when the user would need this right. You could use an access-allowed ACE to give the user the right to change the time in this one instance. An *access-denied* ACE revokes rights that the user has to an object. You can use it to deny access to an object during special system events. For example, you could deny access rights to a remote terminal while you perform some type of update on it. The *system audit* ACE type works with the SACL. It defines which events to audit for a particular user or group. The *currently unused* ACE type is a system alarm ACE. It allows either the SACL or DACL to set an alarm when specific events happen.

The three types of ACEs currently in use under Windows NT include: access-allowed, access-denied, and system audit.

TIP: Now would be a good time to look through the Windows API help file to see what types of access rights Windows provides. You should also look at the various structures used to obtain the information. Especially important are the ACL and ACE structures. Look for the ACE flags that determine how objects in a container react. For example, check out the CONTAINER_INHERIT_ACE constant that allows subdirectories to inherit the protection of the parent directory.

Using Security Descriptors

Understanding what a security descriptor is and how the various structures it contains interact is only one part of the picture. You also need to know how to begin the process of actually accessing and using security descriptors to write a program. The first thing you need to understand is that unlike tokens, security descriptors aren't generalized. You can't use a standard set of calls to access them. In fact, there are five classes of security descriptors, each of which uses a different set of descriptor calls to access the object initially. (You must have the SE_SECURITY_NAME privilege to use any of these functions.)

◆ *Files, directories, pipes, and mail slots*   Use the GetFileSecurity and SetFileSecurity calls to access this object type.

NOTE: Only the NTFS file system under Windows NT provides security. The VFAT file system provides it to a lesser degree under Windows 95/98. You cannot assign or obtain security descriptors for either the HPFS or FAT file systems under either operating system. The FAT file system doesn't provide any extended attribute space, one requirement for adding security. The HPFS file system provides extended attributes, but they don't include any security features. Of all the file systems described, NTFS is the most secure. However, never assume that any file system is completely secure. There are utility programs on the Internet that will read the contents of an NTFS file partition even if the user hasn't logged in properly to Windows NT.

◆ *Processes, threads, access tokens, and synchronization objects*   You need the GetKernelObjectSecurity and SetKernelObjectSecurity calls to access these objects. All of these objects, even the access tokens, are actually kernel objects. As such, they also have their own security descriptor for protection purposes.

◆ *Window stations, desktops, windows, and menus*   GetUserObjectSecurity and SetUserObjectSecurity calls allow you to access these objects. A *window station* is a combination of keyboard, mouse, and screen—the hardware you use to access the system. *Desktops* contain *windows* and *menus*—the display elements you can see onscreen. These four objects inherit rights from each other in the order shown. In other words, a desktop will inherit the rights of the window station.

14

◆ *System registry keys*   This object type requires use of the RegGetKeySecurity and RegSetKeySecurity calls. Notice that these two calls start with Reg, just like all the other registry-specific calls that Windows supports.

◆ *Executable service objects*   The QueryServiceObjectSecurity and SetServiceObjectSecurity calls work with this object. For some strange reason, neither call appears with the other security calls in the Windows API help file. You'll need to know that these calls exist before you can find them. An executable service is a background task that Windows provides—such as the UPS monitoring function. You'll find the services that your system supports by double-clicking the Services applet in the Control Panel.

Once you do gain access to the object, you'll find that you can perform a variety of tasks using a generic set of API calls. For example, the GetSecurityDescriptorDACL retrieves a copy of the DACL from any descriptor type. In other words, the descriptors for all of these objects follow roughly the same format—even though the lengths of most of the components will differ. One reason for the differences in size is that each object will contain a different number of ACEs. The SIDs are different sizes as well.

The next step in the process of either querying or modifying the contents of a security descriptor is to disassemble the components. For example, you could view the individual ACEs within a DACL or a SACL by using the GetACE API call. You could also use the owner and group SIDs for a variety of SID-related calls (we discussed these calls in the access tokens sections of the chapter). Suffice it to say that you could use a generic set of functions to manipulate the security descriptor once you obtain a specific procedure. In essence, any security descriptor access will always consist of the same three steps:

1. Get the descriptor.
2. Remove a specific component.
3. Modify the contents of that component.

To change the security descriptor, you reverse the process. In other words, you use a call like AddACE to add a new ACE to an ACL, then use SetSecurityDescriptorSACL to change a SACL within a descriptor, and finally, save the descriptor itself using a call like SetFileSecurity (assuming that you want to modify a file object).

ACEing Security in Windows

Once you start thinking about the way Windows evaluates the ACEs in the DACL, you'll probably discover a few potential problem areas—problems that the Windows utilities take care of automatically, but which you'll need to program around in your application to derive the same result. (The SACL has the same potential problem, but it only affects auditing, so the effect is less severe from the standpoint of system security.)

The order in which ACEs appear in an ACL is important, since Windows evaluates them in order and stops when it finds the first ACE either granting or denying access to an object.

Windows evaluates the ACEs in an ACL in the order in which they appear. At first this might not seem like a very big deal. However, it could become a problem in some situations. For example, what if you want to revoke all of a user's rights in one area, but his or her list of ACEs includes membership in a group that allows access to that area? If you place the access-allowed ACE first in the list, the user would get access to the area—Windows stops searching the list as soon as it finds the first ACE that grants all the user's requested rights (or an ACE that denies one of the requested rights). Granted rights are cumulative. If one ACE grants the right to read a file and another the right to write to it, and the user is asking for both read and write rights, Windows will view the two ACEs as granting the requested rights. The bottom line is that you should place all your access-denied ACEs in the list first, to prevent any potential breach in security.

You also need to exercise care in the ordering of group SIDs. Rights that a user acquires from different groups that he or she belongs to are cumulative. This means a user who is part of two groups, one that has access to a file and another that doesn't, will have access to the file if the group granting the right appears first on the list.

Obviously, you could spend all your time trying to figure out the best arrangement of groups. As the number of groups and individual rights that a user possesses increases, the potential for an unintended security breach does as well. That's why it's important to create groups carefully and limit a user's individual rights.

Other Security Concerns

There are two other concerns when you look at security under Windows 95/98 or Windows NT: data protection and server protection. The first deals with a client's ability to access data he or she isn't supposed to when accessing data through a server. (I'm not talking about a file server here, but some type of DDE or other application server.) Think about it this way: What if a client didn't have rights to a specific type of data, but accessed the data through a DDE call to a server that did have the required rights? How could the server protect itself from being an unwilling accomplice to a security breach?

Windows provides several API calls that allow a server to impersonate a client. In essence, the calls allow a server to assume the security restrictions of the client in order to determine whether the client has sufficient rights to access a piece of data or a process. For example, a Word for Windows user might require access to an Excel data file. The user could gain access to that file using DDE. In this case, the server would need to verify that the Word for Windows user has sufficient rights to access the file before it sends the requested data. A server might even find that the client has superior rights when he or she uses this technique. The bottom line is that the server's only concern is for the protection of the data, resources, and environment that it manages.

This set of API calls supports three different types of communication: DDE, named pipes, and RPCs. You need to use a different API call for each communication type. For example, to impersonate a DDE client, you would use the DDEImpersonateClient call. There are some limitations to the level of impersonation support that Windows currently provides. For example, it doesn't currently support TCP/IP connections, so you'd have to resort to using other methods to verify that a user has the proper level of access rights in this case.

The other security concern is protecting the server itself. What prevents a user who calls Excel from Word for Windows from doing something with Excel that damages the server itself? Ensuring that security concerns are taken care of isn't difficult to do with files and other types of named structures, since the file server automatically attaches a security descriptor to these objects. (A DDE server like Excel wouldn't need to do anything in this case because the file is under the control of the file server.) However, many of the DDE or application server's private objects aren't named and require special protection. Windows also provides API calls to help a server protect itself. For example, the CreatePrivateObjectSecurity call allows the server to attach a security descriptor to any of its private objects—say, a thread or other process. The security descriptor would prevent anyone other than the server from accessing the private object.

Private Communication Technology (PCT)

Microsoft and the IETF are working together to create a new low-level protocol named PCT. Like SSL, PCT is designed to prevent hackers from eavesdropping on communications between a client and server through the use of encryption, authentication, and digital signatures. As with SSL, client authentication is optional.

WEB LINK: If you want to find out about the current status of PCT, look at **http://www.lne.com/ericm/pct.html**. This document contains the current draft of the second version of PCT. In addition, you'll want to reference the W3C Web site at: **http://www.w3.org/Security/** for details on current Internet security technologies including PCT and SSL.

PCT assumes that you have a reliable transport protocol in place such as TCP. Some people look at TCP/IP as a single protocol, but it isn't. TCP is the transport part of the protocol, while IP is the data transfer portion of the protocol. IP doesn't provide any form of data encryption. So, when you use TCP/IP, your data is open to anyone who wants to see it. Using a protocol such as TCP/PCT or TCP/SSL makes your communications secure. The first version of PCT corrects several problems with SSL, as described in the following list.

◆ *Simplified message and record structures*   Reconnected sessions require a single message in each direction if you don't enable client authentication. Even with client authentication, a reconnection requires only two messages in each direction.

◆ *Extended cryptographic negotiation*   PCT supports a wider variety of algorithms than SSL. This means it can support a broader range of protocol characteristics and that those characteristics get negotiated individually. For example, the common characteristics include cipher type, server certificate type, a hash function type, and a key exchange type.

◆ *Improved message authentication keys*   The message authentication keys are separate from the encryption keys under PCT. This means that messages can use a very long key, ensuring secure transmission even if the encryption key is short or nonexistent. The main reason for this feature is to circumvent the 40-bit key limitation imposed by the U.S. government for secure transmissions.

◆ *Patched security hole*   PCT uses a client authentication based on the cipher negotiated during a session. This prevents someone from capturing the client authentication key, disconnecting the original client, and then reconnecting to the server using the stolen key. The client must know both the cipher and the key to gain access to the server.

14

◆ *Addition of Verify Prelude field*   During the original handshaking process, communication between the client and server is carried out in the clear. The addition of this field makes it possible for the client and server to detect any tampering with these "in the clear" communications.

NOTE: Even though SSL version 3 also provides a Verify Prelude field type capability, a hacker can get around it by changing the protocol version number to 2, which didn't include this feature. Since SSL version 3 is fully version 2 compliant, neither client nor server will notice the change.

Microsoft is currently working on the second version of PCT. It's fully compatible with the first version, but offers several important features that the first version didn't. The following list provides an overview of these features.

◆ *New datagram record type*   Individual records are sent independently as "datagrams." In essence, this means that the protocol doesn't guarantee an order of delivery or that the record will even get to its destination. It's up to the client to put the records it receives in order and then verify that they're all present. The main advantage of this approach is speed.

◆ *Recognizable record types*   The record header contains information that tells the receiver what kind of record to expect.

◆ *Continuation records*   PCT version 1 allows data to span more than one record even though the record header didn't indicate any form of continuation. Version 2 adds a continuation field to the record header, which allows protocol messages to span more than one record as well.

◆ *Intermediate processing of data records*   Data records are encapsulated now, which allows the sender to perform some form of intermediate processing, such as compression.

◆ *Independent decryption of datagram records*   Since datagram records could be sent across an unreliable transport, this particular feature is essential to secure communication. Each record is encrypted individually, making it possible for the receiver to decrypt them one at a time even if they're received out of order.

◆ *New key management record type*   This record type allows the sender to temporarily change either the encryption or message authentication keys during a session. In essence, this allows PCT to transmit pre-encrypted data.

- *New closing connection key management message*   This is a special message that tells the other party to close a connection. Since this is an encrypted message, it's harder for a hacker to send a simulated message and close the connection prematurely.

- *Enhanced message authentication*   Message authentication now includes record headers.

- *Improved handshaking*   Both the client and server authentication phase include a wider variety of options, including key exchange, signature public key, and certificate.

- *New private authentication feature*   This feature allows a client and server to authenticate each other using a previously shared identity-associated private key rather than a certified public key.

Now that we have a few of the basics down, let's look at how PCT works. PCT uses variable-length records as a means of communication. Every record contains a header that defines the kind of message it contains. There are two kinds of messages: application and protocol. *Application* messages always contain data and can use either the standard PCT or datagram formats. A *protocol* message can key management, error, or handshake information. PCT uses two additional layers. Records are always transmitted using a connection. Normally, there is one connection between a client and server, but there isn't any reason why there can't be more. Every connection is part of a session. Again, normally you'll only see one session between a client and server, but you could have more. (Multiple sessions would require more than one physical connection between the client and server.)

A PCT protocol connection begins with a handshake phase. This is where the handshake management message type comes into play. The client and server exchange several pieces of information, beginning with the negotiation of a session key for the connection. In other words, the client and server decide on a secret password to use for talking to each other. The client and server authenticate each other during this time as well. It doesn't pay for them to talk if the client or server doesn't know who the other party is and that it can be trusted. Once the client and server determine that they can trust each other, they decide on a master key that is used for encrypting all other messages.

Windows NT Authentication over HTTP

14

Windows NT authentication is less a programmer issue and more a network setup issue. However, it does pay for you as the programmer to know about authentication issues, especially if you plan to work with intranets or

Internets. There are two basic types of authentication supported by Windows NT right now, though there's nothing stopping someone from coming up with another method.

TIP: If you want to use Windows NT Challenge/Response, you must use Internet Explorer 2.0 or above as a browser. Other browsers don't currently support the Windows NT Challenge/Response method of implementing security.

The two forms of authentication supported by Windows NT are basic and challenge/ response, with challenge/ response being the most secure.

The first method of authentication is Windows NT Challenge/Response. This method relies on communication between the server and the client without any form of user input. The server asks the client to provide the user name and password the user supplied during initial login to the system. The client provides a specially encrypted user name and password. It must also supply a domain name since the client must be part of the server's domain or exist in one of the trusted domains that the server recognizes. Since Windows NT Challenge/Response automatically uses encryption to pass information between the client and server, it's much more secure than the basic authentication provided by the server.

WEB LINK: Sometimes it's handy to have a ready source of detailed information about how Windows NT works with regard to Internet security. One source of information is Rick's Windows NT Info Center at **http:// rick.wzl.rwth-aachen.de/cgi-bin/isindex3.cmd**. This Web site covers a lot of ground you won't find in the Microsoft manuals. For example, you'll learn how to use various third-party products with Windows NT—something that's nice to know when the Microsoft solution doesn't work as anticipated.

So how does the client know that it's supposed to send the user name and password to the server? The server requests the information as part of a header. The server actually sends an error message (401 Access Denied) that tells the client it's supposed to request secure access. It's important to realize that what you see in the browser doesn't include everything that the browser actually receives from the server. What you see in the browser is the information that the server wants you to see after the browser strips off any header information. For example, the server normally has to tell the browser what type of information it's receiving so that the browser can activate a helper application if necessary. Keeping this header in mind is very important when you're trying to understand the dynamics of data transfer between the client and the server.

CAUTION: If you choose to implement basic security on your Internet site, you must use SSL to ensure secure transmission of user name and password information. Using basic security without SSL transmits the user name and password in plain text, making it very easy for someone to intercept the user name and password and use them to gain access to your secured Internet site.

The second method relies on a digital signature technology known as SSL. Essentially, Windows NT will request a digital certificate from the client machine. The client can likewise request a digital certificate from Windows NT. These digital certificates are obtained from a third-party vendor like VeriSign that can vouch for the identity of both parties. We'll look at the precise procedure for using digital signatures in the next section of this chapter. All you need to know for right now is that the digital signature is a secure method of identifying another party who is trying to access your machine.

Essentially what happens when using SSL is that the Windows NT server requests the identity of the client. What Windows NT gets is a certificate issued by a third party like VeriSign along with a public key. There is a six-step process for SSL authentication as follows:

1. The client sends Windows NT an unencrypted random message along with its VeriSign-issued certificate (which contains the client's public key). The VeriSign-issued certificate was encrypted using VeriSign's private key. Since everyone has VeriSign's public key, Windows NT can decrypt the certificate and check it for accuracy. Also, since the certificate was encrypted using VeriSign's private key, no one can forge a public key of their own—they have to get it from VeriSign.

2. Once Windows NT confirms it has received a valid certificate and public key from the client, it tells the client to send an encrypted version of its original message.

3. The client computes a digest of its original random message and then encrypts it using its private key.

4. Windows NT uses the client's public key to decrypt the digest.

5. Windows NT compares the decrypted digest to a digest it generates from the random message originally sent in unencrypted form by the client.

6. If the two digests match, the client is authenticated.

14

At this point you might ask how a programmer would get involved with what appears to be an administrator issue. Even though Windows NT comes with these two built-in methods for controlling access to the server, there isn't anything stopping you from creating an ISAPI filter to either augment or even replace the standard security. We look at a very basic filter in Chapter 13, but there are definitely other ways in which to use them. All you really need to do is monitor the security-related events generated by the server. The most important of these events are the client authentication requests. Monitoring client authentication requests allows you to add any requests needed to make sure the party on the other end is actually someone you want wandering around on your Web site.

An ISAPI filter will allow you to modify the method that a Web server uses to authenticate users.

Using Digital Signatures

Figuring out the precise technology behind digital signatures right now is a little like nailing JELL-O to the wall—you might be able to do it, but who would want to try? The first thing you need to understand is that the digital signature is also referred to as a *certificate*. Think of it as you would a driver's license, since it has the same function. A digital signature identifies some Internet object, who created it and when, and could potentially provide a wealth of other information. If the object happens to be a client or server, a digital signature shows the current owner of that object. The digital signature certificate, like a driver's license, also expires—forcing vendors to keep proving they are who they say they are. The expiration date also gives hackers a lot less time to figure out how to steal the certificate. (Since each certificate is a separate item, learning to steal one won't necessarily buy the hacker anything.) Using a digital signature helps to keep everyone honest because it forces everyone to go through a central verification point. A digital signature avoids the one big problem with the honor system used by the Internet to date: it doesn't rely on one person to maintain the security of your machine. Now you have direct input into who gets access and when. (This implies some level of user training to ensure that people actually know how to use this feature.)

The code-signing process (described later in the section on downloading Internet components) will eventually incorporate a digital certificate, even though it doesn't do so now.

Implementing a digital signature—especially from the client end—is pretty straightforward. In most cases you'll find that vendors provide a standard certificate recognized by any browser or server designed to do so, but that there are some differences in the way the certificates actually accomplish the task. For example, the Web page shown in Figure 14-2 shows one of the potential problem areas. If you're getting a client certificate, how do you determine what level to get? (Most people will go for the Class 1 Digital ID certificate since it's the lowest cost option.)

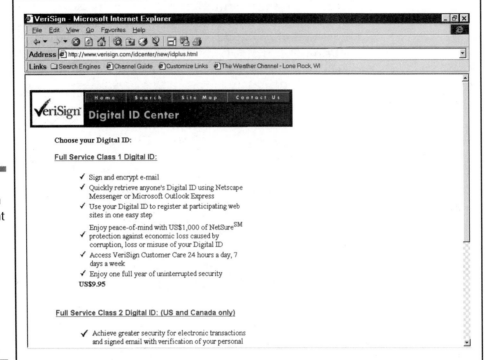

Client-side authentication is an important part of future Internet security, but figuring out what to get can be confusing.

Figure 14-2.

From an implementation standpoint, it doesn't matter whether you get a Class 1 or 2 certificate in this case—even the vendor doesn't really matter, though you'll probably want to stick with VeriSign (the place you end up when you follow the prompts) for compatibility purposes. The methods for using digital signatures are pretty much the same from vendor to vendor since the interface is defined by the Web server or browser vendor. What you'll do is submit an application, and once the vendor verifies who you are, you'll get a PIN or other means of identification in your e-mail. Installing the certificate is a matter of following the instructions provided with your browser or Web server. In the case of VeriSign, you go to its Web site and plug in your PIN, and the browser will take care of the download and installation details. The following list provides a very basic description of the classes of certificates you can get from VeriSign.

◆ *Class 1* Provides the user with a unique name and address within a repository. VeriSign (or whatever certificate vendor you choose) will be able to verify that the person and the address go together. The mail-back

14

process is the only verification that VeriSign uses in this case. You have to own an e-mail address to receive the certificate, making it hard for a hacker to obtain a fake certificate. This class of certificate costs $9.95 per year to maintain. (You can get a free trial version of the Class 1 certificate.)

◆ *Class 2*   To obtain a Class 2 certificate, you must provide third-party evidence of your identity. (This limits access to a Class 2 certificate to people in the United States and Canada at the moment.) The big difference between a Class 2 and a Class 1 certificate is that VeriSign actually checks information you provide against a consumer database maintained by EquiFax. You'll also go through a hardware signing process, which requires multiple keys instead of one. This class of certificate costs $19.95 per year to maintain.

Browser compatibility isn't the only reason that you can get a certificate and expect it to work with a variety of software. There's also a plethora of digital signature-oriented specifications in the works (see Table 14-1), and you'll find that most digital signature certificate vendors are adhering to those standards now.

OK, so now you have a digital certificate assigned to your ActiveX control, a Web server, or your browser (or all of the above). How do you identify someone who has a certificate versus someone who doesn't? You'll always see some kind of warning dialog when accessing a nonsecure site. Likewise, accessing a site with a digital certificate always looks the same. You'll see a digital certificate dialog like the one shown here.

Notice that the dialog gives you a few options for optimizing your system. First, you'll want to check the certificate to make sure it's valid. For example, check to see that the vendor listed is the one that you expected. Also check the date to make sure that the certificate hasn't expired. Second, you'll have the ability to bypass the verification stage for this vendor if you want to. The first checkbox below the certificate always allows you to add a particular company to the list checked by WinVerifyTrust (we cover the download process in Chapter 8). If you check this box, you won't get asked each time you request a download from that particular vendor. This is a good risk with some vendors, but may not be such a smart thing to do with others. What you have to determine is how far you trust the vendor. The second checkbox always allows you to accept all access from any vendor certified by a specific certificate authority, such as VeriSign (the vendor shown in this case). Unless you're very comfortable with the certification process, you'll probably want to leave this box unchecked.

You're probably wondering what all this has to do with ActiveX controls. Like users and webmasters alike, you'll find yourself requesting certificates somewhere along the way if you decide to make your site public. People won't want to download the controls you create unless they're digitally signed and they see the certificate associated with your company. The process for getting a certificate shouldn't be too much different than the one we just looked at for browser users. Right now you don't actually need a certificate to sign your controls, but you will in the near future. We'll cover the process for actually signing your ActiveX control in the section on downloading Internet components later in this chapter.

Understanding the Cryptography API

Preventing someone from reading your data has been the topic of just about every area of this chapter so far. We've studied protocols and a variety of security techniques that are going to help you make the work of a hacker nearly impossible. However, there isn't a lock that can't be picked given enough time. In fact, that's the whole purpose behind using a 128-bit key instead of a 40-bit key. Picking the 128-bit lock is too time intensive (at least at the moment) to make the data contained in a record attractive to a hacker. It's not that the hacker can't pick the lock; it simply isn't efficient to do so.

Layers of Protection

Adding layers of protection is another way to guard against hackers. Encrypting the data at several different levels adds "doors" that the hacker must pass through to get to the data. Put enough doors between your data and the hacker, and the hacker will find something easier to break.

14

Microsoft's CryptoAPI (or Cryptography Application Programming Interface) falls into the layer category of protection. It's a means of adding yet another layer of protection to your sensitive data. Are the encryption techniques you'll find supplied here unbreakable? No, but they do extend the time required for someone to unlock your data and read it. Using the routines in the CryptoAPI will help you better protect the data transferred between a client and server on the Web.

WEB LINK: As with just about everything else dealing with the Internet, the CryptoAPI is brand new and evolving. At the time of this writing, the CryptoAPI is only mentioned as part of the ActiveX SDK—you'll need to download a copy of the specification from the Internet. Even though this section provides the best overview possible at the time of writing, you'll want to visit the CryptoAPI site at **http://www.microsoft.com/ security/tech/misf6.htm** for the latest information.

The CryptoAPI has another purpose, though. It's a general-purpose tool designed to allow encryption of data in any environment, not just the Web. For example, you could build an application that stores data using the same encrypted format whether the information was stored locally, transferred through a modem, uploaded to a Web site, or sent through the mail on a disk. That's a big advantage to your company. Using encryption all the time for sensitive data means that a hacker breaking into your system will find that the job has suddenly gotten a lot harder, yet a common encryption technique means that your users won't be inconvenienced by the added security. You can bet that a user is more likely to use encryption when it's convenient (and for the most part automatic). Making things difficult, hard to understand, or simply too time consuming is the best way to convince the user that it's too much trouble to protect the data on your system.

NOTE: Windows NT 4.0 comes with CryptoAPI 1.0 support built in. When you install Service Pack 3, the level of support gets upgraded to CryptoAPI 2.0. One of the major differences between the two versions is that CryptoAPI 2.0 provides core cryptographic support, which allows a developer to incorporate cryptography within an application. CryptoAPI 2.0 supports X.509 certificates, ASN.1 encoding, and both PKCS #7 and #10 encapsulation. You'll find the Visual C++ support required to implement CryptoAPI 2.0 support in the WINCRYPT.H and CRYPT32.DLL files.

Microsoft has also moved to a modular approach to its operating design in the past few years, so it's no surprise that the CryptoAPI is modular as well. The CryptoAPI could be compared to the GDI (Graphics Device Interface) API under Windows. Any vendor can add a new device driver that tells the GDI how to work with a particular display adapter. The same holds true for the CryptoAPI. It uses the idea of a Cryptographic Service Provider (CSP) just as you would a display adapter device driver. Windows will come with one CSP—the one provided by Microsoft. However, if Microsoft's encryption feature set doesn't meet your needs, you could either design a new CSP yourself or buy one from a third party. The installation procedure would work much like the one you currently use to add a device driver. In fact, this device driver approach makes it easy for you to mix encryption hardware and software on your machine—a real plus in a world where you normally install hardware and software as separate entities.

W **EB LINK:** Microsoft has developed a DDK (device driver development kit) for the CryptoAPI called the Cryptographic Service Provider Developer's Kit (CSPDK). You can get more information about it at **http:// www.microsoft.com/devnews/novdec96/crypto5_6.htm**.

Encrypting a File

One of the easiest ways to show you the functionality provided by the CryptoAPI is to give an example. Encrypting a file is fairly simple. Microsoft follows a straightforward procedure using an eight-step process (six of the steps involve cryptographic-specific calls). You begin by opening a source and destination file, just as you would in any program. (The example code in this section is written in C, but you could easily port the required header files to other languages.) Once you have valid file handles, you need to get the handle for a CSP, like this:

```
// Get handle to the default provider.
if(!CryptAcquireContext(&hProv, NULL, NULL, PROV_RSA_FULL, 0))
{
   MessageBox("Error during CryptAcquireContext", NULL, MB_OK | MB_ICONEXCLAMATION);
   PostQuitMessage(1);
}
```

14

NOTE: You'll find a complete list of cryptography-related functions, structures, and defines in the WINCRYPT.H file.

CryptAquireContext( ) can accept up to five parameters, but only two of them are essential in this case. The first parameter stores a handle for the CSP. The second parameter specifies the type of CSP that you're looking for. Every CSP has both a name and a type. For example, the name of the CSP currently shipped with Windows is Microsoft Base Cryptographic Provider v1.0, and its type is PROV_RSA_FULL. The name of each provider is unique; the provider type isn't. The second parameter contains the key container name. If you specify a value here, Windows will look for a specific key container. A vendor can store the key container in hardware, within the registry, or on the hard drive, so you normally won't know the name of the key container. Using NULL (as shown) tells Windows to return the default key container. The third parameter contains the name of a CSP. You can retrieve the values of any installed CSPs using the CryptGetProvParam( ) function. Supplying a NULL value returns the default CSP. The final parameter contains one or more flags. Normally, you'll set this value to 0 unless the CSP provides specific flag values for you to use. (Microsoft does provide some default flag values, but they're for administrative purposes only.)

The next step is either to encrypt the file using a random key or to generate a key using a password. The random key method is the one you'll probably use most often within an ActiveX control, so that's the one described here. The password method is similar and actually requires fewer steps than the random key method.

```
// Create a random session key.
if(!CryptGenKey(hProv, ENCRYPT_ALGORITHM, CRYPT_EXPORTABLE, &hKey))
{
    MessageBox("Error during CryptGenKey", NULL, MB_OK | MB_ICONEXCLAMATION);
    PostQuitMessage(1);
}
```

The CryptGenKey( ) function provides you with a unique key. Notice that the very first parameter is the CSP handle that we obtained in the previous step. The second parameter contains the name of an encryption algorithm. Microsoft supports two: CALG_RC2 (block cipher) and CALG_RC4 (stream cipher). You'll probably find that the algorithm names vary by vendors, so it's

important to know which vendor the user intends to use as a CSP.
The third parameter contains flags. There are three default flag values.
CRYPT_EXPORTABLE tells Windows that it can export the random key value into a blob (we'll look at blobs in a few moments). CRYPT_CREATE_SALT tells Windows to use something other than 0 for the random key seed value. Finally, CRYPT_USER_PROTECTED tells Windows to notify the user when certain actions take place while using this key. Each CSP will probably define a unique set of actions. The last parameter is a container for the returned random key.

Sometime during the process of getting a certificate, the user received a public key. This is the key that the CSP keeps stored in a central place—it identifies the user. To make data transfers absolutely safe, then, it's important to get a copy of the user's public key to use in the encryption process. That's what we do in the next step.

```
// Get handle to key exchange public key.
if(!CryptGetUserKey(hProv, AT_KEYEXCHANGE, &hXchgKey))
{
    MessageBox("Error during CryptGetUserKey", NULL, MB_OK | MB_ICONEXCLAMATION);
    PostQuitMessage(1);
}
```

The very first parameter we supply to CryptGetUserKey( ) is the handle to the CSP. The next parameter tells what kind of key to retrieve from that provider. Every CSP will support two keys: AT_KEYEXCHANGE (exchange the public key provided for a personal certificate used in an application like a browser) or AT_SIGNATURE (get a signature key like the one we'll generate later for an ActiveX control). The third parameter provides a place to store the key returned by the function.

Now comes the fun part. We take the random key and the user's public key and mix them together. Mixing them together means that even if the user's key has been compromised in some way, the data will still get encrypted in a way that forces the hacker to start from scratch every time. It's the random element that makes this encryption technology at least a little more secure than other methods.

```
// Determine size of the key blob and allocate memory.
if(!CryptExportKey(hKey, hXchgKey, SIMPLEBLOB, 0, NULL, &dwKeyBlobLen))
{
    MessageBox("Error computing blob size.", NULL, MB_OK | MB_ICONEXCLAMATION);
```

14

```
    PostQuitMessage(1);
}
if((pbKeyBlob = malloc(dwKeyBlobLen)) == NULL)
{
    MessageBox("Error allocating memory for blob.", NULL, MB_OK | MB_ICONEXCLAMATION);
    PostQuitMessage(1);
}

// Export session key into a simple key blob.
if(!CryptExportKey(hKey, hXchgKey, SIMPLEBLOB, 0, pbKeyBlob, &dwKeyBlobLen))
{
    MessageBox("Error during CryptExportKey", NULL, MB_OK | MB_ICONEXCLAMATION);
    PostQuitMessage(1);
}
```

Notice that the process of exporting the *blob key* (the combination of the user's public key and the random key) is actually a three-step process. We call the CryptExportKey( ) function twice. The first two values are the keys we created: random and user. The third parameter tells Windows what kind of blob to create. Most CSPs support two values: SIMPLEBLOB or PUBLICKEYBLOB. The fourth parameter is for flags. Always set this value to 0 unless a CSP uses it for some purpose. The fifth parameter points to a buffer used to store the blob. If you call CryptExportKey( ) with this parameter set to NULL, it simply returns the size of the buffer you need in the sixth parameter. That's what we've done in the first call to the function. The sixth parameter normally contains the size of the buffer when you actually call CryptExportKey( ) to create the blob. (The source code displayed here also contains a memory allocation function call.)

Now that we have a blob to work with, it's time to do a little maintenance. One of the things you'll want to do without waiting around too much is destroy the user's public key. Just think about a hacker looking around in memory for some way of breaking down your code. Leaving the key in memory is one of the fastest ways to do this. Killing the key, then, isn't only a good idea from the standpoint of memory and good coding practice; it's a necessary part of maintaining a secure environment. The following source code calls the CryptDestroyKey( ) function to get rid of the public key.

```
// Release key exchange key handle.
CryptDestroyKey(hXchgKey);
hXchgKey = 0;
```

At this point you would send the blob data to the destination file on disk. The blob actually forms a header that the receiving computer will use later to decrypt the file. However, a header isn't much good without some data, so that's what we'll take care of next. The first thing you'll want to do is define a block size for the data. If you're using a *block cipher,* the CSP will provide a block size for you to use. A block cipher normally requires you to add one additional blank block at the end of the file as well. When using a *stream cipher,* you can define any convenient block encryption size (though Microsoft recommends a block size of 1,000 bytes). Now you'll read the data into a buffer one block at a time, use the following code to encrypt it, and then write the block to the destination file.

```
// Encrypt data.
if(!CryptEncrypt(hKey, 0, eof, 0, pbBuffer, &dwCount, dwBufferLen))
{
    MessageBox("Error during CryptEncrypt", NULL, MB_OK | MB_ICONEXCLAMATION);
    PostQuitMessage(1);
}
```

You can process the data in a loop until you run out of blocks. Make sure you pad the end of any incomplete blocks. The CryptoAPI depends on an even block size as part of the decryption process.

The Internet: Wild and Untamed

Some people view the Internet as today's Wild West of computers. There are few standards in place and even fewer security measures. Growth is exponential as more people move onto the Internet to sell their wares. Unfortunately, the Wild West nature of the Internet has kept some of the more conservative businesses like banks and larger retail stores from participating very much. The problem for these well-established firms is simple: they don't want to risk the bad press that a security breach would generate. So, while many new companies like CD-Now are embracing the Internet with gusto, older companies that really need an Internet presence are taking a wait-and-see stance.

Even the growth of Internet technology reflects the kind of environment that we often associate with the Wild West. It's the combination of home-grown, new, and old technology, however, that threatens the Internet the most. For example, the current version of IP (Internet protocol) doesn't provide any method for encrypting data (at least not at the protocol level). The problem with this is that people need to send data over the Internet in such a way

14

that no one else can easily read it, and you just don't have the tools to ensure that security 100 percent right now. Future versions of IP are supposed to fix this, but they aren't available today. The theme of future fixes prevails on the Internet—just as it did in the Old West, when people looked toward the promise of a brighter tomorrow. A lot of upgrades have been promised, but few are in place today. Surfing the Internet is fun for some people in part because it's so wild and untamed.

WEB LINK: You can find out what kinds of security risks you're facing, especially when running a Web server, by reading the World Wide Web Security FAQ at **http://www.genome.wi.mit.edu/WWW/faqs/ www-security-faq.html**. This white paper is a work in progress and includes specifics about the security risks of using certain browsers and servers. It includes Windows NT, Unix, and Macintosh servers at the moment, with a definite bias toward the Unix end of the spectrum. The paper also addresses many general questions, such as trying to find a balance between user privacy and your need to know who's accessing your site. You'll even find a What's New section to tell you how the document is growing as the Internet matures.

Just as the Wild West eventually became a much tamer environment, we'll eventually see similar progress in the Internet as well. Technologies such as ActiveX will help shape that future and make the Internet a place where people can transact business without fear of loss. These technologies will also make the Internet a friendlier place; just as cars and highways have made the West a lot easier to travel, these new technologies will help speed people on their way from one point to another.

One thing that will never change in the West—or on the Internet for that matter—is the need for security. Working in a secure environment is one of the ways in which society fosters innovation and all of the good things we associate with modern times. After all, if you're not spending all your time fighting the enemy (whoever that might be), you actually have time to work on artistic goals. The following sections discuss some of the concerns behind Internet security. It's important to define the security problem before you try to tackle it within an application. If you've already defined your security problems and want to get on with the task of implementing security, take a look at the section on Internet security standards. Otherwise, let's take some time to consider a few of the problems you'll face as you try to make the Internet a viable tool for your company.

The Business Perspective of the Internet

As previously mentioned, part of the thrill of the Internet for many users is the fact that it's untamed—you can literally find anything on the Internet because no one's regulating it. (Recent efforts by the U.S. government to regulate online services weren't very successful.) If you're a programmer, the untamed environment of the Internet may have a certain appeal, but you won't be building applications for yourself. You must consider the needs of the businesspeople that you'll work with. Businesspeople tend not to be part of the crowd searching for cheap thrills. The idea of an untamed environment is more of a nightmare than a fantasy for your typical business user, who wants everything defined, well ordered, and most of all, secure.

The extreme growth rate of the Internet isn't doing anything to instill confidence in business users either. New and untested technology is simply an accident waiting to happen in some business users' minds. Consider the potential gains and losses of ActiveX controls. Sure, they'll allow business users to get things done more quickly, but there's still that security element to consider. Anyone with a modicum of programming skills could create a potentially devastating control that would destroy everything that a company holds dear.

Recent trade paper surveys show that big companies are taking things slow when it comes to the Internet. One of the biggest factors they cite for this slow approach is the lack of security. Businesses want to be sure that the technology is stable and that their data will be safe before making any kind of commitment. One way to build the perceived trust level of the Internet is to write good applications in-house. Stated another way, building ActiveX controls that really work is even more critical than for many other application classes.

NOTE: Business users will need to deal with a host of issues that don't affect the programmer in a general sense, such as whether to allow employees to access the Internet and what level of access to allow. Certainly the debate over these issues will remain heated for quite some time, but we won't cover them in this chapter. Only the programmer-specific issues appear here.

So how do you tackle this problem of security? Talking with management at the company you're working for is one way to pursue things. If you can find out what concerns management has in regard to the applications you write, you can likely address those needs specifically as part of the application. For example, we'll look at the methods you can use to access the built-in security provided with a Windows NT server later in this chapter. The downside to this approach is that addressing security concerns with a lot of added code will definitely slow the application down and could make it harder for users as well. Make sure you also tell management the trade-offs they're making during the design phase of the application (and ultimately the Web site).

Communication between the various levels of a corporation is one requirement to creating a secure Internet or intranet environment.

Defining the Object of Protection: Data

So what are you trying to protect? You'll get a surprising number of answers, but they all point to one thing. When all is said and done, keeping data safe is the most important reason for security on the network. Hardware and application concerns take a back seat to data concerns. Lose a hard drive and you can replace it; kill a software configuration and you can reinstall it; lose last week's report on the company's finances and you're the only person who can reproduce it. Data is the most precious part of the computing environment simply because you will have to fight hard to replace it once it's lost.

Data protection is the main security concern on the Internet.

Securing data has always been a major concern for anyone responsible for its use (and potential misuse). Some network administrators spend more time looking after security concerns than just about anything else. In most cases, the security concerns deal with who has access to what data and why. Look in any trade press, and you'll find article after article on data security—it doesn't matter whether you're looking at a magazine or weekly paper, the effect is the same. The data we produce with computers fills every second of every day; there isn't any doubting its value to you and your company. When you build an ActiveX control and attach it to an HTML page, your major security concern is the data that you'll provide access to.

Data security revolves around access. Whether it's access to a local machine or access to your network, the goal of preventing unauthorized access is the same. Trying to create a secure environment on a local machine is fairly easy. Besides all of the software mechanisms available, many computers also come with BIOS-level password protection. If this isn't enough, you can always resort to physical security to make sure that no one can access your system. Keeping things secure on a LAN gets a little harder, but you can still do it without too much effort. Network operating system products such as Novell's NetWare and Windows NT are rife with various kinds of security measures designed to make local data access difficult at best (unless someone physically cuts through the cabling and starts to ferret things out with a network sniffer). Implementing security on a WAN can be a nightmare, especially if you have a lot of dial-in connections. No longer are all your connections in one place—software and hardware entry points abound, making it a lot easier for someone to break in without your knowing it (at least for a while). Some people have gone so far as to say that implementing security on the Internet might be impossible. Not only do you have the significant problems posed by a WAN environment, but you also have the public access provided by the Internet itself. Anyone reading recent trade presses knows how hard vendors are trying to plug security holes in their products, only to find that someone has found yet another way through the system.

Creating Some Form of Protection

Even if you try to ignore Internet-specific security problems for the moment, there are other issues to consider when it comes to data protection. For example, what kind of protection do you want to provide? Let's take a non-Internet view for a second. In this environment, you can view protection from a hardware or software perspective as a physical means for preventing access to your computer or network by unauthorized persons. Providing a secure workstation as a separate entity from everything else is one way that some companies deal with data requiring special care. This physical separation from the network means that anyone requesting access to the data on the workstation actually has to use that workstation. You can prevent access using locks if necessary in this case. Other companies deal with this issue through the use of data encryption or by performing security audits—both of which are software-specific security schemes.

Unfortunately, you can't set a computer in the corner of a room and lock it up to protect data you have on the Internet. This means that the hardware alternatives that a company used in the past are probably out of the picture as far as the Internet goes—at least when looking at the workstation view of things. The loss of hardware-level protection places an additional burden on the programmer. As a programmer, you'll be responsible for adding some measure of security to the applications (including products like ActiveX controls and ISAPI filters/extensions) you create. Fortunately, you can look at the way things are done now for dealing with the new security issues posed by the Internet. For example, document encryption is still a valuable data protection technique. An encrypted document is just as secure on an Internet site as it is on the WAN—the only difference is the number of people that your company allows to access that document.

14

Now that we've looked at workstations (which you'll find difficult at best to protect) and data (which you could protect using encryption), let's look at the server. From an Internet perspective, some companies are implementing their site using a server that's physically separate from the rest of their network (which definitely reduces the number of ways in which you can use that server for company-specific needs). Using a separate server is the hardware approach to keeping your network secure. No one can see the data on your network if there isn't any connection from your Web server to the rest of the network. The software solution comes in the form of firewalls—essentially another form of the same login procedure we've used for years on LANs.

There are practical limitations to what you can take from the setup you currently use and the one you'll need to implement. One of the main concerns as far as Internet access goes is flexibility. Sure, you can lock down your site to the point that no one can access it, but what reason would you have to do so? Resorting to inflexible and harsh tactics to enforce security probably won't buy you much because it runs counter to the free access that the Internet is supposed to espouse. Learning new ways to make security strong without impinging on the level of access enjoyed by people using your Web site is the challenge you'll face. From a programmer's perspective, this means that you'll have to learn about the capabilities of the hardware and software installed on the network before you'll even begin to make a dent in the security concerns that the Internet introduces.

Implementing a Solution

It doesn't take long to figure out that creating a secure environment is a big issue. It takes time and effort to formulate even a basic security plan. Implementing the plan takes even longer, especially if you're trying to reduce the impact on the working environment by taking a phased approach. Even if you write a great security plan and do your best to cover every contingency, you can never be quite sure that you've covered all the bases. When someone finally breaks through your security and damages some data, it could mean the end of your job. Situations like this are enough to make any network administrator paranoid.

Once you consider all of these potential problems, it's not too hard to figure out why network administrators are constantly clamping down on user freedom when it comes to even the most innocuous things. For example, some network administrators are firmly against any form of Internet access for their company, while others take a Big Brother approach to monitoring user activity once Internet access is approved.

Network administration and data protection aren't the only security issues you'll face when setting up a Web site of any kind. It's also important to consider the user end of the question. How would you like it if someone told you that a connection was secure and you found out it wasn't? A lot of credit card users really don't want to take that risk. A non-secure connection from their computer to a Web site could mean thousands of dollars in credit card charges before they get the chance to even stop payment.

When it comes time to implement a security solution, make sure you have all of the facts. The applications you create can go a long way toward ensuring that the data exchanged by a client and server is secure. Taking time to consider the full impact of all the needs of everyone using the Internet is essential if you want to make your Internet site as bulletproof as possible. Then, when the unthinkable happens and someone does break through, a security plan can help you react quickly to plug any holes in your security net.

Ensuring the Safe Download of Internet Code

It seems like every time you look in the trade press another vendor is promising to upload its application to the Internet as a series of ActiveX controls. For example, Lotus plans to migrate a series of Notes-specific viewers to the Internet in the form of ActiveX controls. Quarterdeck also plans to convert its entire line of utility programs into ActiveX controls and upload them to the Internet. Soon, you'll be able to at least view just about any kind of data you want to directly from a browser. In some cases you'll be able to edit it directly as well. (We'll probably have to wait awhile for those full-fledged editors.)

Trying to keep all of that code virus-free could cause vendors major problems if they don't have a plan in mind for ensuring it doesn't get damaged. We've already discussed some of the mechanics behind the Windows Verify Trust API (used in conjunction with the Windows Trust Provider Service) in Chapter 8. In this section we'll look at the API itself. You'll get an overview of how this technology works and ideas of places to go for detailed information.

We'll also look at the Windows Software Publishing Trust Provider in this section. It's actually an add-on to the Windows Verify Trust API that verifies the trustworthiness of downloaded software components. It does this through several different methods that include checking local rules (like the security-related checkboxes in your browser) and cryptographic information in the file itself (like digital signatures).

Finally, we'll take a look at the process for signing your ActiveX controls. Signing your control allows you to place it on the Web without forcing users to see those "not trusted" messages each time they download a page containing it. This section also takes a quick look at a procedure you can use to clean up your machine for testing—at least in a small way. You'll learn how to uninstall an ActiveX control so that you can test ActiveX control signing and other downloading features of your Web site without having to run to a clean machine every time.

Using the Windows Verify Trust API

This particular API is stable in some ways right now—Microsoft has already implemented parts of it in Internet Explorer 3.*x*/4.*x* and within Windows itself. Other sections are in a state of flux as you read this because the various software vendors are trying to hash out the best methods for checking downloaded software (along with other trust verification items).

So what precisely is the Windows Trust Verification API? It's a general method for determining whether you can trust any Windows object. It doesn't matter whether that object is a client requesting services, a server requesting information, a downloaded document, or even an ActiveX control. The final form of this API will allow you to check the trustworthiness of any object.

Like most of the APIs supported by Windows, the Windows Trust Verification API is extensible—you can add new features to allow it to perform extended checks. One of the extensions that comes as part of Internet Explorer 3.*x*/4.*x* is the Windows Software Publishing Trust Provider. We'll take a look at it in the next section. For right now, all you really need to know is that the Windows Trust Verification API is a general-purpose API and will probably require various extensions as more people use it.

The Windows Trust Verification API uses a variety of methods to check the trustworthiness of a file. Some of those methods are up for debate right now, but the two most common methods are checking system rules and verifying any certificates or digital signatures accompanying the object. You'll also find that the Windows Trust Verification API relies on external certificates. For example, many popular Internet encryption standards currently use the idea of a public and private key. The public key gets passed around in the header of a file (to see one example of how this works, look at the section on encrypting a file earlier in this chapter). The private key resides on the user's machine. To decrypt a file, you need both the public and the private key. Since only the user has that key, no one else can view the file. Obviously, there is more involved than just two keys. Some of the simpler schemes also add a random key, which when combined with the public key, makes it nearly impossible for a hacker to break into more than one file without individually decrypting each one.

System rules could reside in a number of places. For example, browsers store their "trust" information as part of a configuration file or within the registry. The system administrator also sets policy. Those settings could appear in an individual user's registry file or within the general registry files used by everyone. The exact placement of a policy depends on which version of Windows you're using, whether you have multiple users enabled (under Windows 95/98), and the type of policy that the system administrator wants to implement (system or individual). You also have the trust provider (CPS) rules to work with. (The exact term used by the specification is "trust provider" since the source of rules could be any trusted authority, not just a CPS.) For example, telling your browser that anyone certified by a certain trust provider is trustworthy places the burden for verification on the trust provider. A trust provider will always define a specific object type and level of trust provided along with a specific list of owner names as part of the trust verification rules. User actions can also affect the rules that the Windows Trust Verification API will use. For example, when a user tells the system that a certain vendor is trustworthy, that information gets placed in the registry. Every time the Windows Trust Verification Service sees that vendor's name on a certification from that point on, it passes the object without checking further.

Now that you have an overview of what this API will do for you, let's take a quick look at the API itself. The call that you'll be most interested in is this:

```
WinVerifyTrust(HWND hwnd, DWORD dwTrustProvider, DWORD dwActionID,LPVOID ActionData);
```

As you can see, the call requires four parameters. Most of you should know the first parameter by heart—it's a handle for the current window. The purpose of this parameter is to let WinVerifyTrust( ) know that there's a user available to make decisions. For example, the call may want to ask whether to download a file even though it hasn't been signed. If you want to check the trustworthiness of an object without bothering the user, simply substitute INVALID_HANDLE_VALUE for the window handle. You can also use a value of 0 if you want the user's desktop to take care of any interaction instead of the current application. The second parameter defines who to ask regarding the matters of trust. Windows recognizes two values as a default (though a vendor could certainly define any special values needed to make the actual trust provider clear): WIN_TRUST_PROVIDER_UNKNOWN (find a trust provider based on the action you want performed) or WIN_TRUST_

14

SOFTWARE_PUBLISHER (an actual software publisher). If you choose the WIN_TRUST_PROVIDER option, Windows will try to find a registry entry containing the action you want performed. If it can't find such an entry, the WinVerifyTrust( ) function will return TRUST_E_PROVIDER_ UNKNOWN. The third parameter specifies an action. For the most part it tells the trust provider what you want to do. Since each trust provider is different, you'll have to check trust provider documentation for a list of valid actions. The precise contents of the final parameter are also dependent on the trust provider you use. In most cases you'll at least need to tell the trust provider what data you want checked. Some trust providers may also request information about the level of trust required or context for the trust decision.

Once you make a call, WinVerifyTrust will usually return some kind of value specific to the trust provider. In some cases it could also return one of four standard values. You'll notice that all four of them are error values—the Windows Trust Verification API doesn't define any default success messages. The following list shows the four values and provides an explanation for each one.

◆ *TRUST_E_SUBJECT_NOT_TRUSTED*   Normally the trust provider will give you a more specific error message than this one. This return value simply states that the object wasn't trusted for the action you specified. It doesn't necessarily mean that the object isn't trusted at all, just that it wasn't trusted for the current action. Unfortunately, you'll need to call WinVerifyTrust( ) once for each action unless the trust provider supplies some type of generic action or you only need to perform a single action with this particular object.

◆ *TRUST_E_PROVIDER_UNKNOWN*   As previously stated, Windows returns this error message when it can't find a specific trust provider based on the action you requested.

◆ *TRUST_E_ACTION_UNKNOWN*   Windows returns this error value if the action you requested isn't supported by the trust provider. At the time of this writing, WinVerifyTrust uses registry entries instead of actually talking with the trust provider to verify valid actions. This means that even if a trust provider does support a specific action, you might not be able to use it if the registry has been damaged somehow.

◆ *TRUST_E_SUBJECT_FORM_UNKNOWN*   There are a variety of reasons for getting this error message. For the most part you'll get it if the data parameter isn't formatted right or contains incomplete information. A trust provider may not be able to find the object you want verified and return this message as well. If you're lucky, the trust provider will supply a more precise set of data-related error messages, but you may still see this value if the trust provider can't determine what the source of the problem is.

Understanding the Windows Software Publishing Trust Provider

The Windows Software Publishing Trust Provider is an add-on to the Windows Trust Verification API discussed in the previous section. The main purpose for this add-on is to allow an application to check whether a software component contains digital signatures or certificates. Either of these items will identify the document as being authentic software released by a publisher trusted on the local user's system. As with the Windows Trust Verification API, this API uses a variety of techniques and sources of information to determine whether a particular document is trustworthy or not.

You'll also find that the Windows Software Publishing Trust Provider uses the WinVerifyTrust( ) function that we talked about in the previous section. There are, however, a few differences. For one thing, you should always use the WIN_TRUST_SOFTWARE_PUBLISHER trust provider unless the trust provider supplies a different value. If you do use the WIN_TRUST_PROVIDER_ UNKNOWN trust provider, Windows will simply select the default trust provider. Windows also defines two actions you can perform (the trust provider you choose may offer others): WIN_SPUB_ACTION_TRUSTED_ PUBLISHER (checks to see that the publisher of the document is in the trusted list) and WIN_SPUB_ACTION_PUBLISHED_SOFTWARE (checks the document itself for the proper verification certificate). The WIN_SPUB_ ACTION_ TRUSTED_PUBLISHER action isn't supported by the current version of the Windows Software Publishing Trust Provider. If you select the WIN_SPUB_ ACTION_ PUBLISHED_SOFTWARE action, then WinVerifyTrust( ) will also expect the WIN_TRUST_ACTDATA_SUBJECT_ONLY data structure shown here:

```
typedef LPVOID WIN_TRUST_SUBJECT

typedef struct _WIN_TRUST_ACTDATA_SUBJECT_ONLY
{
    DWORD                 dwSubjectType;
    WIN_TRUST_SUBJECT     Subject;
} WIN_TRUST_ACTDATA_SUBJECT_ONLY , *LPWIN_TRUST_ACTDATA_SUBJECT_ONLY
```

14

Notice that the structure contains two variables. dwSubjectType defines the type of object you want to verify. You can choose either WIN_TRUST_ SUBJTYPE_RAW_FILE for most data file types or WIN_TRUST_SUBJTYPE_ PE_IMAGE executable files (including DLLs and OCXs). The Subject structure points to the object that you want to verify. It has the following format.

```
typedef struct _WIN_TRUST_SUBJECT_FILE
{
    HANDLE              hFile;
    LPSTR               lpPath;
} WIN_TRUST_SUBJECT_FILE, *LPWIN_TRUST_SUBJECT_FILE;
```

As you can see, the two variables in this structure point to the file and the path where it can be found. In most cases you'll find the file in one of the cache folders for the particular browser (or other application) you're using. For example, Internet Explorer 3.0 stores its cache in the Temporary Internet Files (data files) or OCCACHE (executable files) folders under the main Windows directory. Just to be different, you'll find most ActiveX controls for Netscape Navigator stored in the ActiveX Control Cache folder (also located under the main Windows directory).

Now that you have all of the information together and have made the call to WinVerifyTrust( ), how does Windows actually verify the document? The first thing it looks for is a PKCS #7 signed data structure. This is the data structure that we'll create in the upcoming section on signing your control. The next thing it does is look for a series of X.509 certificates. In the current implementation of Windows Software Publishing Trust Provider, you must provide a root private key along with the software publisher's public key. (We'll also look at what that means in an upcoming section.) In the future, Windows Software Publishing Trust Provider will also look for appropriate X509.3 extensions defining key-usage restrictions and other attributes of the certified parties. If the PKCS #7 data structure and X.509 certificates are correct, WinVerifyTrust will return a success message to your application.

Internet Component Download Mechanics

You could also entitle this section "Signing Your Code." There are actually four parts to this process, and you may have to repeat them several times to get the right results. The first action you need to take is to create a document using your ActiveX control on a local Web server. You need to access the server as an Internet site, or any testing you do won't mean a thing. We look at this process in Chapter 10, so we won't look at it here. The second action is to unregister your ActiveX control. Most programming languages automatically register the control for you when you create it. Even if they didn't, you'd have to register it as part of the testing process we discussed in Chapter 10. Unregistering the control removes all of the registry entries that WinVerifyTrust( ) would use to look for a local copy of the control. Since it won't find any, you'll see the same trust screens that the user will. The third action is to sign your ActiveX control. The fourth and final action is to visit your test Web site and take a look at the page. This action will download the control and allow you to test the signing process. You may need to perform these last three actions several times before you get the signing process right.

Unregistering Your Control

In your SYSTEM (or SYSTEM32) folder you'll find a little program called RegSvr32. It's the program responsible for adding entries for your ActiveX control to the registry. The same program can unregister your control using a little-known command line switch, -U. So if you wanted to unregister the basic control we create in Chapter 10, you'd type REGSVR32 OCXEXMPL.OCX -U at the command line. If you're successful, you'll see a dialog like this one.

Signing Your Control

Signing your control is a four-step process. The first step is to create an X.509 certificate (we talk about this certificate from a security standpoint in the previous section on the Windows Software Publishing Trust Provider). You'll use the MAKECERT utility as follows to create a basic certificate. The documentation for this utility (and all of the others needed in this section) is in SIGNCODE.TXT, which appears in the BIN folder of your ActiveX SDK installation.

NOTE: Visual C++ 5.0 provides the utility programs you'll need to sign your controls as part of the package. However, it doesn't load these utilities during the installation process. You'll find all of the files discussed in this section in the Cab&Sign directory on the Visual C++ CD. Make sure you actually copy these files to your hard drive—they won't work properly from the CD. The following procedure assumes you're using the ActiveX SDK to get the latest tools available, but the tools provided with Visual C++ 5.0 are current as of this writing.

```
MAKECERT -u:AKey -k:AKey.PVK -n:CN=MyCompany -d:A-Company TESTCERT.CER
```

All this command line does is create a random public/private key pair and associate the key pair with a friendly name. We also created a private key file (PVK) that holds a copy of the private key. Once you create a certificate, you have to combine it with a root X.509 certificate from a CSP such as VeriSign (this is step 2). Since there aren't any CSPs that deal with this kind of certificate right now, Microsoft provides a test certificate for you to use called ROOT.CER. It's in the BIN directory along with everything else.

We'll use the CERT2SPC (certificate to Software Publishing Certificate) utility to place both certificates into a PKCS #7 signature block object (we discuss this object from a security standpoint in the earlier section). Essentially, this object acts as a holder for any certificates you want to include within a signed object. Normally, there are only the two certificates that we've described so far. You use the CERT2SPC as follows:

```
CERT2SPC ROOT.CER TESTCERT.CER TESTCERT.SPC
```

The three parameters in this case are the root certificate supplied by Microsoft, the certificate we created in the first step, and the name of a new file used to store the PKCS #7 signature block object. Now that you have a completed certificate, you have to place it within the ActiveX control (step 3). You do that using the following command line.

```
SIGNCODE -prog OCXEXMPL.OCX -spc TESTCERT.SPC -pvk MYKEY.PVK
```

This command line actually performs quite a few tasks, even though you don't end up with any more files than you had before. The first thing it does is to create a cryptographic digest of the image file (OCXEXMPL.OCX in this case), and then sign it with the private key found in MYKEY.PVK. This cryptographic digest allows the client to compare the current state of the image file with the state it receives the file in. The client will use this comparison to detect any form of tampering along the way. Next, SIGNCODE removes any X.509 certificates it finds from the SPC file. It creates a new PKCS #7 digital signature object using the serial number of the X.509 certificate and the signed cryptographic digest. Finally, it embeds the new PKCS #7 digital signature object along with the X.509 certificates into the image file.

You'll want to check the work of the SIGNCODE utility, considering the amount of work it's done. That's the fourth step of the process. The first thing to check is whether the digital signature was implanted successfully. Use the PESIGMGR utility to do this. All you need to supply is the name of the file you want to check. If you get a success message, check to make sure the executable code is properly represented by the digital signature object by using the CHKTRUST utility. This utility does the same thing that a user's browser will do. It examines the digital signature object and then the X.509 certificates. If they both check out, CHKTRUST will also perform a check on the image file's code to see if it compares with the signed cryptographic digest. CHKTRUST performs one final act not usually performed by your browser. It checks the linkage between the various certificates and makes sure that the dependency chain eventually ends up at the root.

Performing a Live Test

The last step in checking your signed control is to actually use it. You have to do this over an Internet connection; nothing else will do. Simply move the control over to your Internet server, make certain that it's no longer registered at your local machine, and then try to view the test page using your browser. If everything works right, you should see a certificate displayed instead of the usual warning message when your browser goes to download the control.

There are a few ways that your test can fail even if the control was signed properly. The first error to look for is an improperly formatted <OBJECT> tag. We discuss this tag in Chapter 8. However, one reminder here is in order. Make sure your CODEBASE attribute points to the location of the control. In addition, use an URL instead of a directory location on your machine. For example, if your control is located in the CONTROLS subdirectory of the Web site root, use an URL like **http://www.*mycompany*.com/CONTROLS/OCXEXMPL.OCX** with the CODEBASE attribute.

You may want to double-check your control after signing locally as well. Even though it's unlikely that the control will get damaged during the signing process, it could happen. Make sure that the control works on your

14

local test page if it doesn't work properly the first time you test it at the remote location.

Security Standards

The previous section concentrated on telling you all of the problems you'll face when writing code for the Internet. All of those problems are real, but you don't have to face them alone. Standards groups are working even as you read this to come up with methods for protecting data. All you need to do is learn the methods that these groups come up with for managing security on your Web site. The advantages to going this route are twofold. First, you won't have to reinvent the wheel and create everything from scratch. Second, your security methods will mesh with those used by other sites, reducing the user learning curve and making it possible for you to use tools developed for other programmers.

WEB LINK: If you want to find out the latest information on where the Internet is going with security standards, take a look at **http://www.w3.org/pub/WWW/Security/**. This page of general information won't provide everything you need, but it will give you places to look and links to other sites that do provide additional material. Another good place to look for information is the WWW Security References page of Rutgers University Network Services at **http://www-ns.rutgers.edu/www-security/reference.html**. For the most part this site tells you who to contact and provides abstracts of various security meetings rather than actual specifications. Developers will want to get the commercial view of security at **http://www.rsa.com/**. The RSA site covers a pretty broad range of topics, including the current status of efforts by MasterCard and VISA to create secure credit card transactions. You can also find out the current status of IETF efforts by viewing the document at **ftp://ftp.isi.edu/internet-drafts/1id-abstracts.txt**.

Let's take a quick look at the various types of standards that either have become fact or should be emerging soon. Table 14-1 shows the standards or standards drafts that were available at the time of this writing. You may find even more available by the time you read this. It's a surprising fact that vendor standards are probably the fastest growing area of the Internet right now besides browser technology (which seems to be growing so fast that even the beta testers have a hard time keeping up). You'll also notice that the majority of standards listed here aren't from Microsoft or some other company—they

Standard	Description
Distributed Authentication Security Service (DASS) IETF RFC1507	DASS is an IETF work in progress. It defines an experimental method for providing authentication services on the Internet. The goal of authentication in this case is to verify who sent a message or request. Current password schemes have a number of problems that DASS tries to solve. For example, there is no way to verify that the sender of a password isn't impersonating someone else. DASS provides authentication services in a distributed environment. Distributed environments present special challenges because users don't log onto just one machine—they could conceivably log onto every machine on the network.
DSI (Digital Signatures Initiative)	This is a standard originated by W3C to overcome some limitations of channel-level security. For example, channel-level security can't deal with documents and application semantics. A channel also doesn't use the Internet's bandwidth very efficiently because all the processing takes place on the Internet rather than at the client or server. DSI defines a mathematical method for transferring signatures—essentially a unique representation of a specific individual or company. DSI also provides a new method for labeling security properties (PICS2) and a new format for assertions (PEP). This standard is also built on the PKCS7 and X509.v3 standards.
Extended Internet Tag SHTTP (EIT SHTTP)	This extension to SHTTP (described later) would add security-related tags to the current HTTP list. There is no standards organization support for this technology now but there could be in the future. (The Web Transaction Security, or WTS, group of the IETF was recently formed for looking at potential specifications like this one. You can contact them at **http://www-ns.rutgers.edu/ www-security/wts-wg.html**.)

Current Security Standards for the Internet

Table 14-1.

14

Standard	Description
Generic Security Service Application Program Interface (GSS-API) IETF RFC1508	This is an approved IETF specification that defines methods for supporting security service calls in a generic manner. Using a generic interface allows greater source code portability on a wider range of platforms. IETF doesn't see this specification as the end of the process, but rather the starting point for other, more specific, standards in the future. However, knowing that this standard exists can help you find the thread of commonality between various security implementation methods.
Generic Security Service Application Program Interface (GSS-API) C-bindings IETF RFC1508	This is an approved IETF specification that defines methods for supporting service calls using C. It's one of the first specific implementation standards based on RFC1508.
Internet Protocol Security Protocol (IPSec)	IETF recently created the IP Security Protocol working group to look at the problems of IP security, such as the inability to encrypt data at the protocol level. It's currently working on a wide range of specifications that will ultimately result in more secure IP transactions. You can find out more about this group at **http://www.ietf. cnri.reston.va.us/html.charters/ ipsec-charter.html**.
JEPI (Joint Electronic Payment Initiative)	A standard originated by W3C, JEPI provides a method for creating electronic commerce. Transactions will use some form of electronic cash or credit cards. Data transfers from the client to the server will use encryption, digital signatures, and authentication (key exchange) to ensure a secure exchange. This is an emerging standard—some items, such as transport-level security (also called privacy), are currently making their way through the IETF.

Current Security Standards for the Internet (*continued*)

Table 14-1.

Standard	Description
The Kerberos Network Authentication Service (V5) IETF RFC1510	This is an approved IETF specification that defines a third-party authentication protocol. The Kerberos model is based in part on Needham and Schroeder's trusted third-party authentication protocol and on modifications suggested by Denning and Sacco. As with many Internet authentication protocols, Kerberos works as a trusted third-party authentication service. It uses conventional cryptography that relies on a combination of shared public key and private key. Kerberos emphasizes client authentication with optional server authentication.
Privacy Enhanced Mail Part I (PEM1) Message Encryption and Authentication Procedures IETF RFC1421	This is an approved IETF specification for ensuring that your private mail remains private. Essentially, it outlines a procedure for encrypting mail in such a way that the user's mail is protected but the process of decrypting it is invisible. This includes the use of keys and other forms of certificate management. Some of the specification is based on the CCITT X.400 specification—especially in the areas of Mail Handling Service (MHS) and Mail Transfer System (MTS).
Privacy Enhanced Mail Part II (PEM2) Certificate-Based Key Management IETF RFC1422	This is an approved IETF specification for managing security keys. It provides both an infrastructure and management architecture based on a public key certification technique. IETF RFC1422 is an enhancement of the CCITT X.509 specification. It goes beyond the CCITT specification by providing procedures and conventions for a key management infrastructure for use with PEM.
Privacy Enhanced Mail Part III (PEM3) Algorithms, Modes, and Identifiers IETF RFC1423	This is an approved IETF specification that defines cryptographic algorithms, usage modes, and identifiers specifically for PEM use. The specification covers four main areas of encryption-related information: message encryption algorithms, message integrity check algorithms, symmetric key management algorithms, and asymmetric key management algorithms (including both symmetric encryption and asymmetric signature algorithms).

Current Security Standards for the Internet (*continued*)

Table 14-1.

14

Standard	Description
Privacy Enhanced Mail Part IV (PEM4) Key Certification and Related Services IETF RFC1424	This is an approved IETF specification that defines the method for certifying keys. It also provides a listing of cryptographic-related services that an Internet site would need to provide to the end user.
Secure/Multipurpose Internet Mail Extensions (S/MIME)	This is a specification being promoted by a consortium of vendors, including Microsoft, Banyan, VeriSign, ConnectSoft, QUALCOMM, Frontier Technologies, Network Computing Devices, FTP Software, Wollongong, SecureWare, and Lotus. It was originally developed by RSA Data Security, Inc., as a method for different developers to create message transfer agents (MTAs) that used compatible encryption technology. Essentially, this means that if someone sends you a message using a Lotus product, you can read it with your Banyan product. S/MIME is based on the popular Internet MIME standard (RFC1521).
Secure/Wide Area Network (S/WAN)	S/WAN is only a glimmer in some people's eyes at the moment. It's an initiative supported by RSA Data Security, Inc. The IETF has a committee working on it as well. RSA intends to incorporate the IETF's IPSec standard into S/WAN. The main goal of S/WAN is to allow companies to mix-and-match the best firewall and TCP/IP stack products to build Internet-based virtual private networks (VPNs). Current solutions usually lock the user into a single source for both products.
SHTTP (Secure Hypertext Transfer Protocol)	This is the current encrypted data transfer technology used by Open Marketplace Server, which is similar in functionality to SSL. The big difference is that this method only works with HTTP. There is no standards organization support for this technology now, but there could be in the future. (The Web Transaction Security, or WTS, group of the IETF was recently formed for looking at potential specifications like this one.)

Current Security Standards for the Internet (*continued*)

Table 14-1.

Standard	Description
SSL (Secure Sockets Layer)	This is a W3C standard originally proposed by Netscape for transferring encrypted information from the client to the server at the protocol layer. Sockets allow low-level encryption of transactions in higher-level protocols such as HTTP, NNTP, and FTP. The standard also specifies methods for server and client authentication (though client site authentication is optional). You can find details about SSL at **http://www.netscape. com/ info/security-doc.html**.
Universal resource identifiers (URI) in WWW IETF RFC1630	URI is an IETF work in progress. Currently, resource names and addresses are provided in clear text. An URL (uniform resource locator) is actually a form of URI containing an address that maps to a specific location on the Internet. URI would provide a means of encoding the names and addresses of Internet objects. In essence, to visit a private site, you would need to know the encoded name instead of the clear text name.

Current Security Standards for the Internet (*continued*)

Table 14-1.

come from one of two groups: the IETF (Internet Engineering Task Force) or a group known as W3C (World Wide Web Consortium). IETF has been around for a long time. It's one of the very first groups to work with the Internet. Be prepared to read a lot about the W3C group as you delve into Internet security issues (and to a lesser extent other standards areas such as HTML tags). It's the one responsible for newer standards of every kind when it comes to the Internet. For example, Microsoft is currently trying to get W3C to accept the <OBJECT> tag and other ActiveX-related HTML extensions.

NOTE: The MTS acronym is used for several purposes. The only two purposes we'll use it for in this book are: Microsoft Transaction Server and Mail Transfer System. MTS generally denotes Microsoft Transaction Server, except in Chapter 14 where it denotes Mail Transfer System.

WEB LINK: Table 14-1 tells you about a lot of the security-related standards being created by the IETF. Most of the IETF RFC documents can be found at **http://ds.internic.net/rfc/**. You can also find a list of current IETF working groups at **http://www.ietf.cnri.reston.va.us/html. charters/**. These working groups help create the standards used on the Internet.

The security standards in Table 14-1 represent the Internet end of the security picture. It's important to keep this fact in mind. All that these standards really cover is the connection between the client and server. You can still add other security measures at the client, the server, or both. Most of these standards don't cover Internet add-on products such as firewalls either. Your company can add these additional security features and at least make it more difficult for someone to break into its system.

WEB LINK: Just in case you don't have enough security information yet, you can always spend time looking at the IETF informational sites. Two of the current sites are **gopher://ds1.internic.net/00/fyi/fyi8.txt** (Site Security Handbook) and **gopher://ds1.internic.net/00/fyi/fyi25.txt** (A Status Report on Networked Information Retrieval).

Who Is W3C?

Before we go much further, let's take a quick look at the W3C organization. It first appeared on the scene in December 1994 when it endorsed SSL (Secure Sockets Layer). In February 1995 W3C also endorsed application-level security for the Internet. Its current project is the Digital Signature Initiative; W3C presented it in May 1996 in Paris. As you can see, W3C started as a standards organization devoted to security needs. Some of its other functions have evolved from that starting point.

T **IP:** There's a lot of concern over the safety of using SSL right now because some computer hackers could conceivably break the encryption in specific cases. The U.S. government restricts exported encryption technology to a 40-bit key. A computer could break such a key by trying all 2^{40} key combinations. Encryption programs made for U.S. use can use only a 128-bit key, which means that someone would have to have the patience to wait until the computer tries all 2^{128} key combinations (not in your lifetime). So how do you determine the safety level of a transaction? Netscape makes it easy. Just look at the key in the lower-left corner of the screen. A broken key means no encryption, a single-toothed key means 40-bit encryption, and a double-toothed key means 128-bit encryption. Both Netscape and Internet Explorer also offer a Document Properties dialog as part of the File menu. Simply check this dialog to see what kind of protection a particular site offers.

So why do we need yet another standards organization? The main idea is to get the major industry players to work together toward the goal of creating a secure Internet environment. In addition, some standards groups—the IETF for one—are staffed by volunteers and move too slowly to make the changes currently required by the industry. W3C is an effort to add some semblance of order by allowing change to happen faster, yet in an organized way. Finally, the W3C is there to provide the actual specifications (a place where you can find out what a specification is all about), demonstrations of applications that comply with the standards, and prototype code as needed so others can create applications that comply with the standards.

Another project that W3C is working on is the Joint Electronic Payment Initiative (JEPI), one of the standards that will affect future commerce on the Internet. It's amazing to think that people from England, France, Germany, and America could visit the same Web site and buy the exact same items for the same price. Before this can be done, there are some problems that need to be worked out. For example, do you ask "customers" to provide a method of payment before they enter your electronic store, or do you wait until they've "filled their shopping cart" before asking them for some method of payment? What kind of payment do you need to accept? You have to think beyond paper currency, since there isn't any way to exchange it electronically. Credit cards offer one solution, but W3C is also exploring other avenues such as

14

electronic checks, debit cards, and electronic cash. This is one of the smaller issues. A major issue is coming up with some kind of noncurrency-related method for pricing. How do you tell people in Germany that the price of a coat is $80? Would they really understand what a dollar is if they haven't been exposed to it? As for Americans, they could visit an English store and find that they needed to deal with the pound.

So what does JEPI have to do with security? Think about transactions as a whole. Your company may not have to deal with a customer wanting to buy a coat, but you may have to deal with other transaction-related issues. A large company may want to provide a faster, more efficient means to move money from one area of the world to another. Electronic commerce over the Internet could eventually provide an answer. OK, so that's not in your immediate future. What about travel? Just about every company has to deal with traveling employees. What do you do when they run out of cash? Right now you issue a credit card and hope for the best. Wouldn't it be nice, though, if you could get a daily report on expenditures over the Internet? Right now, it's not really a good idea to do so because there are too many security holes. These commerce standards will help companies create new methods of transferring sensitive information from one place to another.

Standard Methods of Handling Money

You may run into a situation in which you have to find a way to accept money at your Web site. The most obvious situation is if your company sells a product of any kind—whether it's something you would buy at the mall or not is probably immaterial. You could sell widgets just as easily over the Internet as you could any other way. In fact, you might even be able to sell them better. Other situations could include services. For example, you might provide a method for customers to pay their bills electronically rather than send you a check in the mail. There are rumors that at least one telephone company is looking into this possibility. A small business might find Internet transactions more trouble than they're worth, but certainly medium-sized and large companies will embrace this method at some point. Banks and credit card companies will eventually get into the picture as well. In fact, you can already get a Web Conductor VISA card by filling out a form online (check out **http://www.conductor.com/** for more details). This particular card allows you to view statements and request services online. In the near future it will also allow you to make payments online, reducing the amount of time spent filling out checks by hand.

There are currently three different common schemes for implementing a cash-handling capability on your Web server: First Virtual Accounts, DigiCash, and Cybercash. Each one has different strengths and weaknesses that we'll talk about in the next few paragraphs. The important thing to realize now is that none of these schemes is perfect, and you'll probably have to compromise in some areas to make a solution work for right now. If that statement makes you feel uneasy, it should. A lot of major financial companies are currently working toward some method of making financial transactions totally secure, but it wouldn't be safe to say they're available today.

From an implementation point of view, the First Virtual Accounts scheme is the easiest to use. Users sign up for a First Virtual Account over the phone and receive a special account number that has nothing to do with the credit card supplied. Vendors who support this scheme accept the account number using a secure certificate. Every transaction uses this special number instead of a real credit card number—reducing the risk of someone stealing your credit card and using it without your knowledge. The vendor turns any transactions over to First Virtual Accounts, which verifies the transaction with the user. When the user approves the transaction, the vendor receives payment and ships whatever product the user requested. You can find out more about First Virtual Accounts at **http://www.fv.com/**.

DigiCash has the advantage of using real money for transactions instead of credit. This means vendors don't have to pay credit card surcharges. In addition, DigiCash has the advantage of working just like an ATM debit card: vendors get real money today instead of waiting for the credit card company to honor a transaction. This particular scheme requires the user to make a deposit at a special bank. The bank sets up an account, just like a checking account, except that it works online. When the user makes a purchase, he or she uses "E-cash" instead of credit. The vendor simply turns in the E-cash and gets real money in return. Obviously, users must replenish their accounts from time to time, just as they would any other bank account. You can contact DigiCash at **http://www.digicash.nl/**.

Cybercash is a combination of the previous two transaction schemes. It provides both debit and credit capabilities—sort of like a bank account with overdraft protection. Unlike the other two schemes, Cybercash uses real account information. This represents a risk to users since their account information could end up anywhere in unencrypted form if the vendor is of the less scrupulous sort. When users make a purchase, Cybercash pops up a window that requests account information. In credit mode, users supply the name and number of their credit card. In debit mode, they provide the name of a local bank and their account number at that bank. You can find out more about Cybercash at **http://www.cybercash.com**.

 WEB LINK: The banks and credit card companies aren't the only ones talking about online transactions. Open Market, Inc., the Web server company, is also working on an online transaction scheme based on SHTTP. It will act as the bank and credit card company if you sign up for this scheme. You can find out more about this endeavor at **http://www.openmarket.com**.

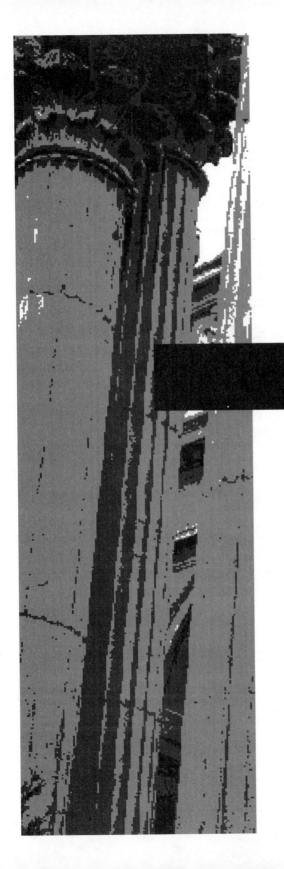

CHAPTER 15

Building a
Help File

535

Generalizations are usually dangerous to make, especially in a book. However, one truism about programmers as a whole is that they hate to write documentation—and that's fairly straightforward when compared to writing help files. Think about the last time you ran across a help file that was so difficult to use that you decided to stick with the paper documentation instead (not that it was much better). In most cases, you'll find that the help file was written by a programmer who made the task a job rather than an opportunity to help other people use a program that may have taken months to write.

HTML-based help provides easy to update, flexible documentation that some vendors are using to replace the paper equivalent.

The latest craze in help files, HTML-based help, only makes things worse. The Windows help file may not have been perfect, but at least the Windows Help engine provides a comprehensive search engine so that the user can look things up when the programmer doesn't provide every link needed. Unfortunately, a Windows help file gets out of date rather quickly when used in some situations like operating system documentation. HTML-based help has the advantage of being easy to update and modify as needed when new application features get added. Flexible help files are becoming more important as vendors move from a paper-based document to online documentation.

A help file is a guide to using your application: it should help readers understand how to use your application so they can appreciate the work you put into it.

If you think about it for a few seconds, the help file that comes with your application is just as important as the application itself. Are the users really going to care about that nifty new sort routine you added to the program if they can't figure out how to use the program in the first place? What about all those new features you added? Will the users really care if they can't even find them? Suffice it to say that help files should be as well constructed and easy to use as your application.

You're going to spend some time writing help files—there just isn't any way around it. The bigger your application, the larger and more complex the help files you'll need. In fact, a good rule of thumb is to set aside one help file development hour for every four hours you spend programming. You might be able to get by with less than that, but probably not much less. The nice part about creating a good help file is that you can normally use it as the basis for the application's manual. Some people I know use a single file for both purposes.

WEB LINK: Do you need some help getting your help file together? While this chapter will answer the major questions, you might need some assistance from other programmers. Help files get discussed in all the usual places that we've talked about so far. For example, you'll definitely want to look at the **comp.os.ms-windows.programmer.win32** and **microsoft.public.win32.programmer.tools** newsgroups. However, help files are also discussed in some less common places like the **microsoft.public.access.chat** newsgroup—a good place to talk about the special needs of database application help files. You might want to check out the **comp.lang.java.programmer** or **microsoft.public.internet.news** newsgroups if you intend to create a help file for Internet use. (You can use either HTML-based help or Windows help on the Internet, but HTML-based help is the better choice by far.) You'll even find help files discussed in general programming newsgroups like **comp.programming**.

One of the most important parts of designing a help file is to fully outline it first, just as you would do with any programming project.

The following sections are going to help you get over many of the hurdles you'll face when creating a help file of your own. For one thing, there is more than one kind of help in common use today, so the first thing you'll need to decide is what type of help will best meet your needs. The first section of this chapter talks about two kinds of help and provides you with some ideas of when to use one over the other. Obviously, there isn't any way that I can create a set of hard-and-fast rules for you to follow, but you'll at least have some idea of where each kind of help works best.

Just like any programming project, the first thing we'll cover once you decide on a specific kind of help to create is organization. You'll find that help files, like applications, are a lot easier to create when you organize your thoughts first. In fact, you'll simply replace the pseudocode that you'd normally use to represent program flow with a specially designed outline meant to show help file flow.

Once we get past the organization stage, we'll start talking about implementation. There are two Windows help implementation sections in the chapter. The first shows you how to use the Help Compiler with an RTF file. This method works well if you plan to add a lot of unique features to your help file and want the added flexibility it provides. The second method relies on using the Microsoft Help Workshop. This method has the advantages of taking less time and requiring a lot less time on your part to learn.

Building a great Windows help file isn't much use unless you actually integrate it into your application. That's what the next section of the chapter is going to talk about. We'll look at several different ways to incorporate Windows help into the single-document application we created in Chapter 2. You'll find that you might be making a mountain out of a molehill when it comes to adding context-sensitive Windows help to an application.

WEB LINK: More than a few people are abandoning the Windows Help file format in favor of a more Internet-friendly HTML approach. Even Microsoft is using this approach in some of its current products. A major problem with using HTML is that you lose some of the search capabilities and formatting features that the Windows Help file format provides. The positive side of using HTML is that you can keep it up to date a lot more easily than a help file. For a good discussion of some of the issues involved in moving to and from the Windows Help format, look at the HyperNews Forums Web Mastery Resource Lists at **http://union.ncsa.uiuc.edu/HyperNews/ get/www/html/guides.html**. This site contains a lot of helpful information about HTML converters that you can use to convert your current Windows Help files to HTML format. You'll also want to take a look at the WWWWAIS.C site at **http://www.eit.com/software/wwwwais/ wwwwais.html**. WAIS is a special search program that allows you to add search capabilities to your Web site.

HTML-based help requires an implementation phase as well. However, creating HTML-based help is more akin to building a Web page than you might think. Make sure you read Chapter 8 so that you have a basic understanding of how HTML tags work before you start on this chapter. Once you have a basic idea of how HTML tags work, this next section of the chapter will discuss special considerations for creating HTML-based help files.

The final section of this chapter will show you how to add HTML-based help to the application we created in Chapter 2. You'll find that adding HTML-based help to an application doesn't have to be hard, but it is different than adding Windows help to an application. In addition, you'll find that there are some limitations to making that help truly context-sensitive, but that you can get around most of them with a little planning. Finally, this section of the chapter will show you why so many vendors like the idea of using HTML-based help for its ease of update.

Deciding What Type of Help to Create

Microsoft would have you believe that HTML-based help is the best documentation aid to come on the market in recent history and that it's the only form of help you should consider when creating a new application. Nothing could be further from the truth. The form of help you choose to include with your application should be based on a number of factors, not just the latest fashion statement to come out of Redmond.

NOTE: Look for HTML-based help to become the de facto standard for commercial software, though, because it is relatively easy to create, which reduces the cost of creating the documentation. However, reduced documentation costs don't necessarily result in better documentation.

In fact, many Microsoft users are complaining that HTML-based help is the wrong choice for some Microsoft products. However, there are other situations where HTML-based help is the very best form of documentation you can provide to the user. So, how do you decide what form of help to use? Well, one of the things you can do is make a list of the relative merits of one technology versus another. The following list tells you some of the reasons that you would want to use HTML-based help over Windows help.

◆ *Upgradeability* When you write a Windows help file and include it with your application, you're creating a static help file that can't easily be upgraded because it resides on the user's machine. HTML-based help can reside on a Web site (either intranet or Internet), making it possible to provide the user with upgraded help by changing the contents of one file.

◆ *Reduced learning curve* As businesses move to the Internet or create intranets it becomes more likely that someone on staff will know how to create Web pages using standard tags. Windows help files, on the other hand, require the programmer to learn an entirely new set of tags.

◆ *Fewer language/special needs concerns* There are a lot of ways to make HTML-based help more language- and special need-friendly without incurring the usual programming penalty imposed by Windows help. You can ask users which language they want to use, store the required information in a cookie, then use the information to redirect users to a help page in the desired language. Language support becomes automatic without the need to build special language redirection features into each application you write. The same technology makes it easier to incorporate features like large font support for users who need it.

◆ *Enhanced customization opportunities* The open structure of HTML files makes it easier to customize HTML help files. Unlike Windows help files, where all of the graphics are frozen in the compiled file, you can substitute graphics in an HTML-based help file. This means that you could customize a help file with a client company's logo or adjust displays to reflect cultural bias without having to recreate the help file.

Using HTML-based help won't solve all of your problems. In fact, it'll actually introduce a few new ones that you may not have had to deal with before. The following list will help you understand some of the things that you'll give up when using HTML-based help.

◆ *Security* With a Windows help file you can theoretically hide information about application features available only to the administrator. Since HTML-based help is in plain text, anyone can learn that administrator features exist, making it more likely someone will try to find a way to access them.

◆ *Size* You can compress a Windows help file to consume a fraction of the disk space that the text and graphics would take. Since HTML-based help can't be compressed, hard disk usage can become an issue.

◆ *Remote access* Windows help is always available since it's located on the local hard drive. One of the features that makes HTML-based help so attractive can also turn into a nuisance. What if the user doesn't have access to the company LAN or the Internet? Suddenly that out-of-date local copy of a help file can look very attractive to a user who needs assistance.

◆ *No annotation/reduced bookmark support* Giving users the ability to add notes to their help file is extremely important, yet this is one feature you won't get with HTML-based help. Theoretically you could add an application feature that would allow the user to modify the original HTML files, but this would be a lot more work than just using Windows help in the first place. Likewise, even if you incorporate a "Favorites" feature into your HTML-based help file (akin to the Favorites feature in Internet Explorer), the user could only save the location of the page itself. Windows help allows you to mark a specific location on a page, making the bookmark a lot more useful.

◆ *Reduced search capability*   We've already discussed this to some extent. Windows help allows you to look for specific words in the help file with relative ease. The use of keywords will allow you to create custom search criteria for the user as well. HTML-based help makes it hard, if not impossible, to provide search capabilities anywhere near those found in Windows help. You definitely won't get the ability to search for single words or keywords.

At this point you should have some idea about the trade-offs of using HTML-based help versus the Windows help alternative. The two forms of help are definitely different and work better in some situations than others. You probably have additional concerns that I haven't even covered here that may make one form of help preferable over the other.

Organizing Your Help File

There are quite a few ways to design a help file. Organization is one of the first things you'll need to tackle. The way that you organize a help file can make it either easier or more difficult to use. For example, a help file that's task oriented will help users get specific tasks done more quickly—assuming of course, that you know precisely what tasks they intend to perform with your application. On the other hand, a menu-oriented help file can make searching for specific items faster.

The type of help file you intend to create will also affect its organization. For example, since a Windows help file provides superior search capabilities, you'll find that you can use a task-oriented organization more often, since users will be able to find the command information they need. In addition, it would be difficult to create a help file with a tutorial organization using an HTML-based help file. On the other hand, you'll find that it's relatively easy to use a menu flow organization with HTML-based help files because adding new menu options is almost trivial when compared to Windows help files.

Creating an Outline

It's always important to begin the help file-writing process by composing an outline of what you want the help file to contain. The outline should reflect the specific user orientation that you plan to pursue when writing the help file. This will help you organize it from the very beginning and focus your thoughts on each segment of the help file as you write it. The following list provides some of the organizational techniques that I've used in the past.

♦ *Menu flow*   The menu flow technique starts with the application menu system and works down from there. Simply list all of the menu items in hierarchical format. Once you have all the menu items listed, start listing any dialogs. Each dialog gets listed in order along with the various controls that it contains. Finally, list the Main window and any components it contains. Using this organizational method has the advantage of fast access to specific program features. The disadvantage is that you're telling the reader not how to accomplish a specific task, just what a specific item is used for. For this reason, you'll want to limit this approach to situations where users are apt to have at least a moderate level of expertise—you want to give them quick access to what the program can do for them without burdening them with information they already know. This type of help file works very well with utility programs because most readers will have a good idea of what to do when they buy the application. You'll also find that it works well with configuration modules where the questions you're asking are pretty straightforward, but the user may need a little additional help answering them.

♦ *Task*   Most users that I've talked to really don't care about the latest "gee whiz" feature in a program. All they know is that they have to get a particular job done in a limited amount of time. This is especially true of people who crunch numbers all day or perform some of the more mundane office chores in a company. They don't have time to figure out how to do something—you have to tell them. That's where this kind of help file is most useful. You work out a list of the kinds of tasks that the user will perform, and then explain each one in detail. It's a good idea to start out with an explanation of the task itself—what will the user accomplish?—and then provide a procedure to get the job done. You should expect this kind of user to have a minimum of computer talents and little desire to learn new ones. You'll find that this particular technique works well with data entry or other programs that have a fixed number of tasks to perform. Once you start getting into the freewheeling world of the word processor or other general-purpose application, you need to take a different approach.

♦ *Generalized menu/task*   There are times when you'll write an application that could perform a variety of tasks. For example, a word processor isn't used for just one purpose but several. If you wrote hard and fast rules for accomplishing tasks in this case, you'd be doing the user and yourself a disservice. What I usually do is provide a very generalized assortment of task explanations that demonstrate how to use product features but not how to accomplish specific tasks. It's also a good idea to provide an overview of the menu system rather than a detailed look. That way the user gets a general feel for what the application can do without absorbing too many preconceived ideas from the developer. Follow this up with ample use of *cloud help*—those are the little balloons that appear near a control when you place the mouse cursor on top of it for a few seconds.

◆ *Reference* Compilers and applications that provide their own macro language often include a reference-type help file. In this case, you're looking at the program not from a physical perspective but from a control perspective. It doesn't really pay to do much more than list the macro commands for a word processor in alphabetical order because there isn't any way to know how the user will use them. What you'll normally want to do is describe the command, tell what each parameter will do, and then provide some kind of example of how to use the command. Obviously, you can also add other information like hints and version-specific differences. One type of tip that users find helpful is the kind that says "If you want to do X, then use this command; otherwise, use command Y—it's more efficient."

◆ *Tutorial* This is a special-purpose help file. You'll want to use them only with applications designed for novices. In essence, you'll use a help file to teach someone how to use your application. Most programmers find that this kind of help file is effective in places where the user may not have had much previous experience using the application. A minimal amount of experience with the computer and operating system is essential to making this type of help file work. Data entry applications are one of the situations where I find this type of help file useful. I normally provide a short, task-oriented text section, followed by some type of question-and-answer section. An interactive help session where the user works with a mock-up of the real application is also helpful. You can use help file macros to make this kind of situation work. The help file actually monitors user input for correct responses. This type of help file is unfortunately difficult to put together and provides little benefit to the user over the long haul. You'd probably be better off trying to convince a company to hire a trainer or two instead of taking the time to put one of these together.

◆ *Functional area* Some applications lend themselves to this kind of help file organization because of the way that they're used. CAD and other

15

drawings fall into this area because you can group the things that they do into functional areas. A CAD program provides some commands for drawing, others that control the color palette, and still others that allow you to manipulate the drawing size and shape. Grouping like items in this case is going to help users find what they need quickly. The reason is simple: When users are creating the drawing, they'll look for drawing commands. Later, as they embellish their work of art, they'll want to know about color- and texture-related commands.

WEB LINK: If you still think that creating a help file for your application is going to be too much work, you might consider using a third-party service to do the work for you. For example, the SheepNet site at **http://www.sheepnet.demon.co.uk/helpfile.htm** offers to create quality help files. Of course, if you go this route, you'll still spend some time working with the third party to get the help file right. Somewhere along the way you'll still have to help someone understand the intricacies of working with your application to get a fully functional help file in return.

Creating a Script

Once you create an outline, you have to fill it in with some meaningful text. There are a few rules that you should follow here as well. The first is to try to keep a help section down to one screen. (The one screen rule is especially important if you want to use HTML-based help since the user won't have access to bookmarks or annotation to make finding information easier after finding it the first time.) Users won't want to page up and down in the help file as they look for that critical piece of information. In a lot of cases, you can break a large piece of the help file into subtopics, making the file easier to read. In today's computing environment you'll probably want to keep a single screen down to what you can see at 800×600 resolution (though 1024×768 resolution displays are becoming much more common). Even though many of us have larger displays, I know of more than a few people who still use these smaller ones.

You'll normally want to keep your help page size down to what you can fit on one screen at 800×600 resolution.

TIP: The vast majority of new laptop computers use a 1024×768 display, while many older laptops provide an 800×600 or even a 640×480 display. Keep this limitation in mind as you design and organize your help file.

There are some obvious exceptions to the one screen rule. For example, you don't want to divide a procedure into subtopics. It's really annoying to get a help file that works this way. It'll have instructions like "create a mail merge file—see help topic 3A for instructions on how to do this." The fact that this type of procedure exists is manifested in all the satire built around this particular kind of problem in such everyday pieces of equipment as the stereo. I know you've all heard the expression "This reads like stereo instructions."

You'll also want to exceed a single-screen help topic if there isn't any way to conveniently break it into parts. For example, procedures that require graphics for explanation purposes often require more than one screen. In most cases, complex procedures also call for more than one screen. Don't use the complexity of a procedure to avoid using subtopics, though; look for places to simplify a procedure whenever possible. What you'll want to do is reach a balance between the use of full procedures and breaking the procedure into subtopics. Make sure that the screen reads well without the subtopics. What you'll normally want to do is place amplifying information in the subtopic area. That way an advanced user can look at a single help screen and get the information he or she needs.

The entire process that I've just described could be best termed "building a script." You're creating what amounts to a book, but not in book form. One topic doesn't necessarily flow into the next as it would in a book. (It's really irritating to see a help file that is written as a book—you'll get screens that introduce a topic but don't really lead anywhere.) Each topic is designed to stand on its own merit. Of course, adding continuity between topics in a help file will always make it easier to use.

Creating a script is about half the process of building a help file. Another third of the process is to convert that script into something that the Windows Help engine or HTML browser can use to display information to the users of your application. You'll need to break the outline into screens and add hypertext links as required. Some help compilers also require the equivalent of a make file. The *make file* tells the compiler which script files to include in the help file and can add optional features like buttons.

The following sections are going to take you through the process of creating a help file from your script. Once you accomplish that task, we'll look at what you need to do to add context-sensitive help to your Visual C++ application. That's the last part of the help file creation process. You want to make sure everything else is in place before you actually start adding the help file to your application.

IN DEPTH

The Importance of a Glossary

Those of us who spend each and every hour of the work week immersed in programming or other computer-related activities learn even the most arcane terms rather quickly. A new term is something to spice up the day, not a hindrance to communication. In fact, I'm often surprised at just how many terms I learn without even realizing it.

On the other hand, most users look at the computer as a mere acquaintance—something they use to do their job, and nothing more. (A good friend of mine even says that she's "computer hostile"—how's that for a descriptive term?) For the typical user, a new term is an insurmountable obstacle to getting the work done. Help files filled with undefined jargon are worse than no help file at all. The user can read the file but doesn't really understand what it means.

Let's face it, there's no way to completely avoid jargon when writing a help file. We're working in an industry that seems to invent yet another new term (and sometimes even more) every day. You should do your best to avoid jargon when writing a help file, but it's impossible to avoid the use of standard computer terms.

What you'll normally want to do is script your help files before committing them to final form. In other words, you should create an outline, and then fill in the blanks. What I'm really talking about is a simple form of book. At this point you need to have one or two people who haven't seen the file before read it and write down any terms they don't understand. Picking nontechnical types is the best way to go because you'll get better input from someone who isn't immersed in the technology. When they're finished, take the list of "unknown" words from each reader and define them. Now you have a glossary that's hand-tuned to the user's needs, or at least closer to those needs than something you would have put together by yourself.

The last step in the process is to add hot links from every occurrence of an unknown work in the text to its entry in the glossary. A user who doesn't know what a term means only needs to click on the hot link. Windows Help or the HTML browser will take the user to your glossary entry.

Using the Microsoft Help Compiler

I'm not going to go through the entire Microsoft Help Compiler reference in this chapter; in most cases you'll find that you use a subset of the available commands to create a help file. In addition, you'll find that the help file provided with the compiler is pretty well designed as a programmer's reference. What we'll look at is a simple example of how you could put together a help file using a standard word processor and the help compiler. This section represents the method that most of us had to bear with until better tools arrived on the market. It also represents the most flexible way to create a help file, since you have the most control over the contents of the help scripts you create.

 NOTE: This section of the book talks exclusively about Windows help files. If you want to learn more about HTML-based help file construction techniques, look at the section on creating an HTML-based help package later in this chapter.

Visual C++ requires you to perform an extra step before you actually start to create your help script or make file. Fortunately, that extra step will save you some time later on, especially if you remember to do it before you start working on the RTF or make files. You need to use the MakeHM (make help map) utility located in your Visual C++ BIN directory to create a help map before you do anything else. (Visual Studio users: you'll find the MakeHM utility in the Program Files\Microsoft Visual Studio\Common\Tools directory if you've used the default directory locations during setup.) All you need to do is type the following at the command prompt to create the help map you'll need later on to link the help file to the application.

```
MAKEHM ID_,HID_,0x10000 RESOURCE.H MY.HM
```

What you'll get is a listing of the help IDs in your application like the one shown in Listing 15-1. These help identifiers will allow you to make the link between Visual C++ and your help file, as we'll see later. For right now all you need to know is that you'll include that list of help IDs in your help file. You'll also use the help ID names in your help script.

Listing 15-1:

```
HID_CANCEL_EDIT_CNTR          0x18000
HID_CANCEL_EDIT_SRVR          0x18001
HID_UNDERLINE                 0x18006
HID_STRIKETHROUGH             0x18007
HID_BOLD                      0x18008
HID_ITALIC                    0x18009
HID_FONT_DIALOG               0x1800A
HID_VIEW_FORMATTOOLBAR        0x1800B
HID_FORMAT_FONT2              0x18010
HID_HELP_CONTENTS             0x18012
HID_HELP_WHATSTHIS            0x18013
```

NOTE: It doesn't matter which word processor you use—you could even use a programmer's editor if you'd like. The only requirement to use the Microsoft Help Compiler is that the script file be in RTF format. Fortunately, RTF is really an ASCII file containing special formatting commands. You'll want to be careful about using a text editor created strictly with the CRichEdit MFC class, since older versions of this class don't implement some of the RTF commands you'll really need to create a help file. The CRichEdit class provided with Visual C++ 5.0 and above still isn't as complete as a dedicated word processor, but it should work fine for creating help files.

The Microsoft Help Compiler requires a minimum of two files: the help script and a make file. I normally use Microsoft Word to create the help script, since it provides full RTF support and it's my word processor of choice when writing. The first thing you'll want to do is separate the various help file sections. You do this by adding a hard page break before each new section. The page break is symbolized as the \page statement in an RTF file. (I'll be including some of the more important RTF statements in my discussion so that you can troubleshoot any problems in your RTF file if necessary.)

WEB LINK: If the Microsoft utilities don't fulfill all your help file writing needs, then look at the Windows 95 WinHelp Tools and Utilities site at **http://win95.daci.net/webwhelp.htm**. There are a variety of products at this site designed to meet just about every need. For example, the Help Maker Plus utility is designed as a complete replacement for the Microsoft Help Compiler. Another good site to visit is the WinHelp WWW Index at **http://www.hyperact.com/winhelp/FTP_and_file_Archives/index.html**. While this site doesn't contain any helpful information, it does have a wealth of links that take you to Windows Help-specific sites. For example, you'll find a link to the RTF file specification and another for the SHED file format. You'll also find links for places that provide alternative help file compilers and design utilities.

Adding one or more footnotes to each heading comes next. Footnotes are used for a variety of hyperlink functions. For example, the search words for your index will come from this source. You'll also use footnotes to define links between words in the glossary and the help file. Table 15-1 shows a partial list of footnotes. You'll find that these are the footnotes you use most often. You should also check the documentation for the Microsoft Help Compiler for additional ideas—there are times when those alternatives to the standard footnote come in handy.

So what do you type in the footnote? You have to add one of several things depending on the footnote types. For example, when using the # footnote, you add the name of a hyperlink. Make sure you read the text that follows each footnote in the table to learn about any requirements for using them. It's extremely important to create unique names for each of your footnotes. Descriptive names are also essential since you'll have to remember what those names mean later. One thing that you need to remember is that hyperlink

Footnote Type	Purpose
*	You'll eventually end up with a lot of RTF files on your machine and you may not want to include all of the topics they contain in every help file. For example, I have one help file that I include with a communication program that talks about online courtesy. It's very generic and most users find it helpful when trying to figure out the various acronyms they see online. It appears in an RTF file of general topics. While I wouldn't want to include that topic in a utility program, the general file does have topics I do want to include. This footnote defines a build tag. It works in concert with the help project (HPJ) file that I'll describe later. The help compiler looks at the list of help topics you want to include and then looks at the build tags in the RTF file to find them. You must include this footnote as the very first footnote for a topic. Build tags are case insensitive, but I still type mine in uppercase so that any future changes to the way that Microsoft handles help files won't break mine. A typical build tag in an RTF file looks like this: *{/footnote BUILD_TAG}.
#	This is a topic identifier footnote. Think of this as a label used by a GOTO statement. Whenever you "call" this topic identifier using a technique I'll describe in just a bit, Windows help changes the focus to this particular footnote. This is the first half of a hyperlink within the help file. You can use hyperlinks for a variety of tasks including menus and to create links to a glossary. Like build tags, topic identifiers are case insensitive, but again, I still type mine in uppercase so that any future changes to the way that Microsoft handles help files won't break mine. One example of this kind of footnote in an RTF file is: #{\footnote SOME_LINK}.
$	Use this footnote type to create a topic title. The topic title appears in the gray area above the help text in the help window. You'll also see the topic title in the Topics Found and the History dialogs. This footnote accepts any kind of text. For example, you could use ${\footnote This is a title.} as a topic title.

Standard
Footnote Styles
for the
Microsoft Help
Compiler

Table 15-1.

Footnote Type	Purpose
+	There may be times when you want to create a sequence of help topics to allow the user to move from one area of the help file to another with relative ease. For example, a lengthy procedure may be inconvenient to use if you make it fit in one window. One alternative to this is to break the procedure into window-sized elements and then allow the user to browse from one window to the next. Adding the browse-sequence identifier footnote to an RTF file does just that. It activates the two Browse buttons >> and << in the help window. Windows will allow you to use any identifier for a browse sequence—it sorts the identifiers in alphabetical order to determine which sequence to display next—but I usually use a page-numbering sequence. For example, +{/footnote Page:1} would be the first page in a sequence. The only limitation to using sequences is that you can only have one per topic. You have to enable the Browse buttons by adding a BrowseButtons macro to the HPJ file. Windows help looks for this macro as part of the help file initialization process. I'll show you how to add it in the section on creating the make file later in this chapter. The browse sequence identifier is one of the handier help file footnotes because you can use it to break up long sections of text without causing any confusion for the user. I also find it essential when I need to display a multipage graphic like a hierarchical chart. For example, one of the help files I created contained a complete hierarchical chart of all the Novell forums. Since the chart required more than one page, I used a browse sequence to make it easy for the user to move from one area to the next. You could also use this feature in a reference-type help file to move from one command to the next. The applications for this particular footnote are almost unlimited.

Standard Footnote Styles for the Microsoft Help Compiler (*continued*)

Table 15-1.

15

Footnote Type	Purpose
K	The search capability of your help file depends on the keyword footnote. You define one or more descriptive words for each topic and subtopic in your help file. I always err on the side of too many rather than too few keywords. The keywords you define appear in the Index page of the Search dialog if you're using the Windows 95/98 interface. A keyword can contain any sequence of characters including spaces. Windows also preserves the case of your keywords—making it easier for you to come up with descriptive terms that the user can identify easily. One topic can also have more than one keyword; just separate them with semicolons.

There's a flaw in the DOS version of the help compiler, HC31, that you need to compensate for when using this footnote. You'll need to add an extra space between the footnote and the next character in the RTF file, or it won't appear in the help file. In addition, if your keyword begins with a K, you'll need to precede it with an extra space or a semicolon.

One example of a keyword footnote might be: K{/footnote Control;Exit Pushbutton;Leaving the Program}. In this case the user could find the same help topic using three different routes: Control, Exit Pushbutton, and Leaving the Program. You'll find it easier to build a comprehensive yet consistent help file if you maintain a sorted list of keywords as you build the RTF files. Make sure that you use the same keyword in every place a topic appears. For example, if you say "Control" in one place, don't use the plural form or a different term in another place. A user can adapt to a help file that's consistent—it's when the help file uses terms inconsistently that you start running into problems. |

Standard Footnote Styles for the Microsoft Help Compiler (*continued*)

Table 15-1.

Footnote Type	Purpose
@	What would a program be without comments? You couldn't figure out what you did during the previous build the next time you needed to add a new feature. As you can tell by looking at the examples in this book, I like to add a lot of comments. I've found that comments are an essential part of any programming effort. Help files can get quite complex. You could easily forget why you added a macro or did something in a particular way between editing sessions. The author-defined comment footnote solves this problem. It's like adding comments to your help file. The only difference is that you won't see the comment in most cases until you open the footnote for viewing (assuming, of course, that you're using a standard word processor to create the file). A typical author-defined comment footnote looks like this: @{/footnote This is a comment.}. Needless to say, since the help compiler ignores this footnote you can include any kind of text within it.

Standard Footnote Styles for the Microsoft Help Compiler (*continued*)

Table 15-1.

names, like variables, don't contain spaces. Footnotes are symbolized by the <footnote type>{\footnote <text>} RTF file statement.

What you should do at this point is compile a list of the topic identifier (#) footnotes you've created. Armed with this list, you can go through the rest of the help file and create the appropriate hyperlinks. Just how do you go about doing this? When you look at a standard help file and see the green text that signifies a hyperlink, what you're looking at is a double underline (/uldb in an RTF file) or a strike-through (/strike in an RTF file). So the first part of creating a hyperlink is to double-underline or strike through the text that you want the user to see as green text. Right after the double underline, add the topic identifier of the hyperlink in hidden text (use the /v statement in an RTF file). This is the same identifier that you typed in the # footnote.

At this point you'll probably need to decide a variety of things. For example, do you want to add graphics to your help file? A few graphics in the right places can go a long way toward making your help file truly user-friendly. Some people like to add sound or other multimedia. Unless you're proficient at using these mediums, I'd probably avoid them for the first few projects. You'll also need to decide what types of things to include in your make file. The following sections provide you with the details of completing your help file. I'll spend some time talking about the various options you have and what I normally do with specific types of help files.

Adding Special Effects to a Help File

There are a variety of enhancements you can add to a help file. One that I usually add is graphics. For example, you can grab a screen shot of your application and then define hotspots on it with the Hotspot Editor utility (SHED.EXE). You can use BMP, DIB, WMF, and SHG graphics formats with the Hotspot Editor. Files containing hotspots always use the SHG extension.

T IP: One of my favorite graphics additions to tutorial-style help files are Answer buttons. These look like standard Windows pushbuttons that I create as a graphics image. Users read the question, answer it, and then click the Answer pushbutton to see if they made the correct response. You can also use this technique to simulate a variety of other application controls—the Windows Help utility doesn't provide very much help in this regard. It does, however, provide the {BUTTON [LABEL], Macro1[: Macro2: ... : MacroN]} macro that allows you to create a standard pushbutton. Label contains the caption you want to see on the pushbutton. The macro parameters allow you to attach one or more macros to the pushbutton.

Let's take a look at the Hotspot Editor. Figure 15-1 shows a typical view. I've opened a screen shot of the example program we'll use later to test the help file. In this case we're looking at a picture of the main form. I plan to add hotspots for each control to make it easy for the user to find out about the application. Remember that you can't use the Hotspot Editor to create a new drawing—you'll need some type of graphics application to do that. The whole purpose of using the Hotspot Editor is to add places where the user can point and expect something to happen. Every time you see the cursor change from a pointer to a pointing hand in a help file, you're seeing the effect of using the Hotspot Editor.

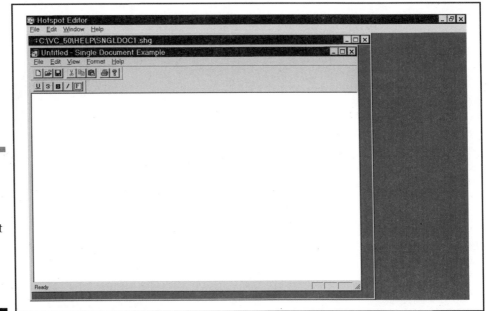

The Hotspot
Editor won't
allow you to
create a new
drawing, but it
does add
hotspots to
existing ones.

Figure 15-1.

The Attributes
dialog contains
the entries
needed to define
the type of
hotspot you
want to create
for the
graphic image.

Creating a new hotspot is as easy as dragging the mouse. All you need to do is create a box like the one shown in Figure 15-2. The area within the box is the hotspot.

Once you create a hotspot, you need to define it. Just double-click on the hotspot and you'll see the Attributes dialog shown here.

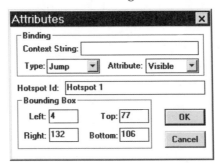

There are only three mandatory entries in this dialog: Context String, Type, and Attribute. A context string works just the same as the double underlined (or strike-through) text in the previous section. It acts as the second half of a hyperlink. When the user clicks on the hotspot, Windows Help will transport

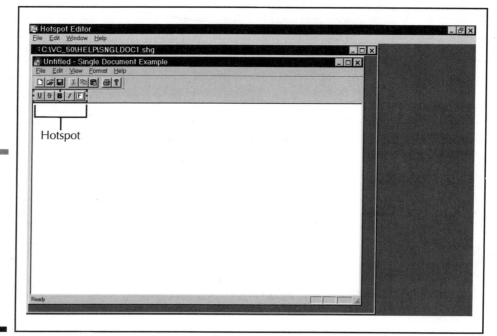

Creating a hotspot is as easy as dragging the mouse—a square shows where the hotspot will appear.
Figure 15-2.

him or her to the place in the help file that you've defined. You can choose to make the box surrounding the hotspot visible or invisible. I normally make them invisible and can't say that I've seen anyone else do otherwise. There are three different types of hotspots. The following list tells you where they're used.

T IP: You can define a standard set of hotspot attributes using the Edit | Preferences command. What you'll see is a dialog that allows you to define a default Context String, Type, and Attribute. You can also use this dialog to define a default Hotspot ID.

◆ *Jump* Windows Help will replace the contents of the current window with whatever help topic is pointed at by the context string. A jump moves the user from one area of the help file to another. I find that this type of hotspot works well for icons that tell users what other kinds of information they can find on a given topic. You could use it to create a See Also icon. I also use this type of jump when creating links between a multipage hierarchical chart. Hotspots allow the user to jump directly from one place to another without using the Browse buttons. This is also the kind of jump that I use with control pictures used to simulate the real thing that you'll find in an application.

◆ *Pop-up*   You'll find that this kind of a jump is used most often with control descriptions or other pictorial-type hotspots. The help topic associated with the hotspot is displayed in a pop-up window. Since the user doesn't leave the picture, he or she can easily select other controls to look at. I also use this in tutorial-type help files in the question-and-answer section. The Answer button displays a pop-up window containing the answer to a question.

◆ *Macro*   There are times when you won't want a picture to display a help topic. The macro type of hotspot allows you to play back a predefined macro. I'll show you examples of macros later in the section on creating the make file. You'll find that macros are a powerful (and underused) feature of Windows Help. You can even use macros to call programs or reprogram the way that Windows Help works.

T IP: The Microsoft Help Compiler provides a lot of predefined macros. For example, you can use the SetPopupColor macro to change the color of a pop-up window. Attaching these macros to a button or menu will give users a specific level of control over the help window and enhance their ability to use it. One way to combine a macro with a bitmap is to create a bitmap of colored squares. When the user clicks on a colored square, the color of the help windows changes to match it.

There are several other entries on the Attribute dialog that you need to know about but will not necessarily have to change. One is the Hotspot ID field. It tells the Hotspot Editor how to identify this particular hotspot. I'll show you momentarily how this comes into play for you as a programmer. The other four entries define the bounding box for the hotspot. You can use these entries to fine-tune a box's position or size. I find that using the sizing controls is a lot faster and easier for the most part. The user probably won't notice if the hotspot is a pixel or two off, as long as the hotspot is available for use.

You may find that you need to redefine a hotspot somewhere along the way. Hotspots are easy to find if you make them visible, but I've already noted that most people don't. So how do you find a hidden hotspot on a complex drawing? The Edit | Select command provides the answer. It displays the Select dialog shown here.

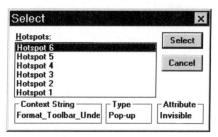

Notice that this dialog lists the various hotspots in the current drawing by hotspot identifier, not by context string. Selecting a particular hotspot will display its context string, though, so that you can be sure you have the right one without actually going to that location on the drawing. Along with the context string, the Select dialog displays the jump type and attribute information. I wish Microsoft had added bounding box information to this dialog as well, but there's sufficient information to allow you to find what you need in most cases.

Make sure you use the File | Save As command to save your edited graphics file, or you may find when you need it later that you have overwritten the original graphic.

After you get all the hotspots defined, you may be tempted to save your graphic using the current name with the File | Save command. I always save it with an SHG extension using File | Save As. For some reason the Hotspot Editor doesn't insist that you do this. However, if you don't, you'll find that you've overwritten your drawing with information that some drawing programs can't read. Since you can't modify your drawing within the Hotspot Editor, you're stuck with an image that you can't change. I always retain the original drawing in its pristine state so that I can modify it later.

Now that you have a drawing (or other multimedia element), how do you add it to your help file? Microsoft has defined a set of commands that allow you to add graphics or other elements to your help file. The same commands allow a certain level of control over the placement of these graphics, but I find that the positioning mechanism is crude at best. Table 15-2 shows a complete list of the commands you'll need to add multimedia elements to your help file.

TIP: You can add a *T* (for transparent) to the three graphics commands listed in Table 15-2. This changes the background color of the image to match that of the help window. For example, the {BMRT FIGURE.BMP} command would display a bitmap named "figure" on the right side of the screen and change its color to match that of the help window. Windows Help only allows you to use this feature with 16-color graphics.

Command	Description
{BMR <Filename>}	Display a graphic on the right side of the display window. You must provide a full filename and extension. Windows Help recognizes bitmaps (BMP, DIB, and WMF files), multiple-hotspot bitmaps (SHG files), and multiple-resolution bitmaps (MRB files). Unfortunately, you can't use PCX files within a help file.
{BMC <Filename>}	Display a graphic in the center of the display window.
{BML <Filename>}	Display a graphic on the left side of the display window.
{MCI_LEFT [<Options>,] <Filename>}	Displays a media control interface (MCI) file on the left side of the display. There's a mistake in the Microsoft Help Workshop help file that says you can only use this option with AVI files like those provided on the Windows 95/98 CD. The current version of Windows help supports all MCI formats including WAV, MID, and AVI files. Sticking with these three formats is probably a good idea, though, unless you know that the target machine supports other formats. You can also specify one or more options with this command, including EXTERNAL, NOPLAYER, NOMENU, REPEAT, and PLAY. The EXTERNAL option keeps the file outside the help file, reducing the amount of memory that the help file consumes when the user loads it. The down side of this option is that you must include the multimedia file as a separate item. Normally Windows help displays a multimedia player when it displays the file—you can use the NOPLAYER option to prevent this. This option would come in handy if you wanted to automatically play or repeat a multimedia file. The NOMENU option allows you to display a play bar without the menu button, effectively keeping the display elements of the play bar but removing the user's ability to control playback. The REPEAT option tells Windows help to automatically repeat playing the file when it finishes playing the first time. The PLAY option automatically plays the file—a handy feature for splash screens.
{MCI_RIGHT [<Options>,] <Filename>}	Displays an MCI file on the right side of the display.

Multimedia
Element Help
Commands
Table 15-2.

15

TIP: You can specify more than one bitmap within a single command to compensate for differing display capabilities of the machines that use your help file. Windows Help chooses the bitmap that most closely matches the color capabilities of the machine and displays it. For example, the command {BMR CAT016.BMP;CAT256.BMP;CAT024.BMP} might allow three different computers to display bitmaps in 16-, 256-, and 24-bit colors. You can further enhance the flexibility of your help file by using MRB files to compensate for differences in resolution. The up side of this approach is that you gain a lot of flexibility in your ability to display detailed information to those users who have a machine capable of displaying it. The down side is that this approach greatly increases the size of the help file and its corresponding memory requirements.

NOTE: If you don't see everything you want in regard to multimedia capability, Microsoft also provides a special help statement you can use to further enhance a help file. The {EWx <DLLName>, <WindowName>, <Data>} statement allows you to access routines in an external DLL. The *x* in EWx specifies left (l), right (r), or center (c) placement of the output from the DLL. WindowName contains the name of the current help file window—it's the $ footnote we covered earlier. The Data parameter allows you to send data to the DLL for processing.

Use graphics and sounds sparingly in a help file to keep them from losing impact.

It doesn't take long to figure out that you aren't very limited when it comes to including bells and whistles in your help file. Just about anything you can include in an application will also go into a help file. There are some obvious things you'll need to consider, though, before you go overboard in making your help file look like someone's idea of a nightmare. A little multimedia goes a long way. Use graphics and sounds only where they really fit—where they enhance the appearance of your help file.

You'll also need to consider memory consumption when writing your help file. Windows Help loads an entire help file when the user tries to access it. One of the ways to reduce the memory load on the machine is to use a lot of external files—you can break the help file into pieces and store any multimedia externally. In the end, though, a modicum of restraint when using graphics and sounds in your help file is what you'll need to make it efficient as well as fun to use.

Creating the Make File and Compiling Your Help File

Creating a set of RTF files is probably the most time-consuming part of writing a help file unless you plan to include a lot of features in it. Unlike the make (project) files you use when writing an application, the make file used with a help compiler usually contains more than just a list of files to compile.

I'm going to show you the manual method of creating a make file in this section. The Microsoft Help Workshop utility provides a more automated method, which I'll show you later. The reason for looking at the manual method first is that you'll need it when using the older DOS utility, HC31, to create help files. It's also handy to know what a make file contains so that you can hand-tune some features like macros if necessary.

Let's begin by looking at a typical make file. Listing 15-2 contains a make file for the help file in this book. If I were using the DOS utility to write this help file, I'd have to add by hand everything it contains. The only difference is the comment at the top of the make file that says that the help compiler is maintaining the file automatically. We'll use the Microsoft Help Workshop to create an example for this book a bit later. I've included a variety of things here that you may or may not include in a typical help file. We'll take a look at these items so that you can decide whether you want to use them or not.

NOTE: Some lines of code in Listing 15-2 may be broken due to their length. When creating a make file for the help compiler, you must keep the entries on one line.

Listing 15-2:

```
; This file is maintained by HCW. Do not modify this file directly.

[OPTIONS]
HCW=0
COMPRESS=12 Hall Zeck
ERRORLOG=HELP.LOG
LCID=0x409 0x0 0x0 ;English (United States)
REPORT=Yes
CONTENTS=CONTENTS
TITLE=Single Document Application Help File Example
COPYRIGHT=1998 Some Company
```

15

```
HLP=.\Sngl_Doc.hlp

[FILES]
.\Sample.rtf
.\Glossary.rtf

[MAP]
#include ..\Resource\my.hm
CONTENTS=1            ; Main help file menu.
FORMAT_TOOLBAR=2         ; Format Toolbar explanation shortcut.
GLOSSARY=3            ; Glossary window shortcut.
HID_FORMAT_FONT=0x1E160          ; Added for ID_FORMAT_FONT in AFXRes.h file.

[WINDOWS]
Main="A Sample Help File",(0,0,800,600),52484,(r14876671),(r12632256),f7; This is the Main window.
Glossary="A Sample Help File - Glossary",(50,50,850,650),52484,(r14876671),(r12632256),f7;
The direct Glossary help window.

[CONFIG]
CB("glossary", "&Glossary", "JI('SNGL_DOC.HLP>glossary', 'GLOSSARY')")            ; Add
a Glossary button to the display.
CB("controls", "C&ontrols", "JI('SNGL_DOC.HLP>main', 'FORMAT_TOOLBAR')")         ; Add a
jump to the controls bitmap button.
RegisterRoutine("USER", "EnableMenuItem", "uuu")        ; Enable (or disable) a menu item.
RegisterRoutine("USER", "GetSubMenu", "u=uu")          ; Get the name of a submenu.
RegisterRoutine("USER", "GetMenu", "u=u")        ; Get a menu name.
RegisterRoutine("USER", "GetActiveWindow", "u=")        ; Get the active window name.
RegisterRoutine("USER", "DrawMenuBar", "u")          ; Instruct Windows Help to draw a
menu bar.
EnableMenuItem(GetSubMenu(GetMenu(GetActiveWindow()), 1), 0, 1027)         ; Disable the
Copy option of the Edit Menu.
DrawMenuBar(GetActiveWindow())            ; Redraw the menu when we're through.
```

As you can see, the make file can look a bit overwhelming the first time you view one. It helps to take the file one section at a time. For example, if you look at the FILES section, you'll see it contains a list of the script (or "topic" in Microsoft parlance) files used to create the help file. Let's take a closer look at the first section.

The OPTIONS section of the make file tells you how the help compiler will compile the file. Most of the entries here are self-explanatory. For example, the COPYRIGHT statement appears in the About box of Windows Help when the user loads the help file. The COMPRESS statement defines whether the help compiler compresses the file and what technique it'll use to do so. The HCW statement is Microsoft Help Workshop-specific; you wouldn't include it when using the DOS help compiler. The one entry you have to pay special attention to is HLP. Notice that the name of the help file is going to be the same as the name of our Visual C++ application. While this isn't an absolute requirement, you'll find that adding help to an existing application is a lot easier if you take this simple step. MFC will actually help you implement help in your application if you give your application and help file the same name—of course, they'll have different extensions.

You'll use the MAP section of the help project file to define the help context property settings that Visual C++ will ask you for (we'll take a look at this in just a bit). Each word here has to appear as a topic identifier (# footnote) in one of the script files. Associating a number with each jump that you want to export makes the topic accessible from a control. All the user needs to do is select the control and press F1 to get help on that particular control. Notice that we haven't listed all of the controls for our application—instead we included the HM file we created earlier in the chapter. Using an HM file won't only save you time typing; we'll see in the next section that it can actually help you find gaps in your help file.

There's more than one way to display the data in your help file. I usually display main topics in their own window. You'll notice that there are two windows listed in the WINDOWS section. One is the Main window, which I always display. The other is a special window for the glossary. If users click the Glossary button on the speed bar, they'll see this window. It allows them to look up a word without losing their current position in the help file. Obviously, I don't display this window every time the user accesses the glossary. If the user hyperlinks to the glossary by clicking on a highlighted word in the help file, the glossary gets displayed in the Main window—not a separate window. In this case the user can simply click the Back button on the speed bar to return to his or her former position.

The CONFIG section is the one that will take the most amount of explanation in this case. You'll find that this is the section where you'll probably spend the most time when creating your make file because it offers the greatest amount of flexibility. There are three different events taking place in my make file: button creation, function registration, and a set of Windows API calls. Obviously, you could add any number of events to your file, but let's take a look at this fairly simple example.

I begin by creating two new buttons. The first is the Glossary button I told you about before. Notice that I have to use two different macro calls to get the job done. One call creates the button. I tell the help compiler that I want to call this button "glossary." I want to use the word "Glossary" for my button label and I want the *G* underlined. This button is going to provide a jump to the identifier returned by the JI macro call. The JI macro call requires three parameters even though it looks like only two. The " SNGL_DOC.HLP> glossary " parameter actually provides two pieces of information: I'm telling the JI macro what help file to look into and then I'm telling it what window to use to display the help topic that I'm going to jump to. The other parameter provides the name of a topic identifier—remember that's a # footnote.

The next task I need to perform is to register some DLL functions with Windows Help. You can use just about any DLL function that you want as long as you register it first. Registering a DLL function is always a three-step process. First, you need to tell Windows Help what DLL to look in. Windows Help always assumes that the DLL is in the SYSTEM directory, so you'll need to either place the DLL there if it isn't already there or provide path information. I usually move the DLL, since there isn't any way to know in advance where the user will place the DLL if you don't. Second, you need to provide the name of the function you want to use within the DLL. Make sure you use the same capitalization that the DLL uses—I've had strange results when I didn't do this in the past. Third, you need to tell Windows Help what kind of parameters that function will look for. That's what the "u=uu" is all about when I register the GetSubMenu function. In this case I'm telling Windows Help that the GetSubMenu function requires two unsigned numbers as input and returns an unsigned number as output. There are four types of values that you can specify: unsigned number (u), signed number (i), string (s), or unknown (v). The equal sign (=) always delimits the input values from the output value.

Now that I have some Windows API calls registered, I can make some changes to the help display. (You could do anything that the routines that you register will allow.) In this case I disable the Edit | Copy command. You can still see it, but it's grayed out. I find there are a lot of things you can do to spruce up your help files using this technique. Notice that I use the DrawMenuBar function to redraw the menu bar when I'm done. If you don't do this, there's a good chance that any menu changes you make won't show up.

About the only thing you have left to do now is compile the help file. If you're using the DOS version of the help compiler (HC31.EXE), you'll want to make sure you specify a log file as part of the CONFIG section options. That's what the ERRORLOG=HELP.LOG statement is for in my make file. It allows me to view the errors in my help file using a text file. Unfortunate as it may seem, the DOS version of the help compiler is command line driven and doesn't provide anything in the way of an interface. If you don't specify a log file, you'd better be prepared to read fast. All you need to do to use the help compiler is type **HC31 <MAKEFILE>.HPJ**. Make sure you append the .HPJ to the end of the make filename, or the help compiler won't be able to find it. The help compiler will display a series of dots as it creates the help file. When you see the DOS prompt return, you know the help file is done.

Using the Microsoft Help Workshop

Early Windows programmers had a lot to learn to complete even the smallest projects. The tools that we had were difficult to use, and even a small program required a lot of coding. DOS was present in force during those early days, but as compilers increased in functionality, DOS all but disappeared. However, it was still present until very recently when it came to creating help files. I really hated using a DOS utility to create my help files, but it was about all I had to use until the latest Windows 95/98 compilers came around. Even the third-party products I used to create the help file required some level of interaction with the dreaded HC31 command line utility. The fact that they hid the actions of the help compiler really didn't change much.

NOTE: This section of the book talks exclusively about Windows help files. If you want to learn more about HTML-based help file construction techniques, look at the section on creating an HTML-based help package later in this chapter.

Microsoft has changed all that with the introduction of the Microsoft Help Workshop utility. No longer will you need to rely on a DOS application to build your Windows help file. The Microsoft Help Workshop allows you to create help project files (another name for a help make file that we visited in the previous section) and compile them from within Windows. Figure 15-3 shows a typical view of the Microsoft Help Workshop.

NOTE: Even if you use the Microsoft Help Workshop, you'll still need an editor that produces RTF files. I'm not quite sure why Microsoft left this feature out of an otherwise phenomenal improvement in help compiler technology, but it did. I still use Microsoft Word to create my RTF files, then I reference them from within the make file I create using the Help Workshop.

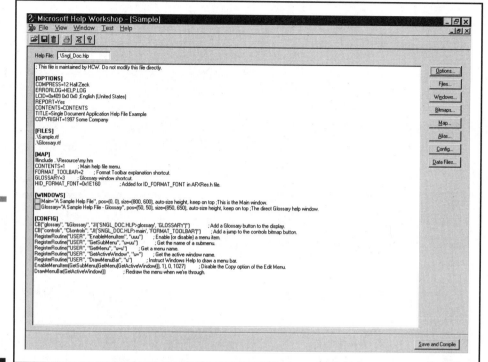

The Microsoft
Help
Workshop
provides a
convenient
GUI for
creating help
files.

Figure 15-3.

Let's look at how this tool can help reduce the complexity of creating that make file we looked at in Listing 15-2. (I'll assume that you've already created some RTF files containing a help script.) The first step is to create a new project. Simply use the File | New command to display the New dialog shown here.

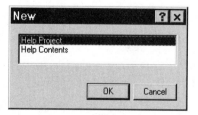

Select Help Project and click on OK to complete the action. As you can see in Figure 15-3, I've already created a new help project. It starts out as a blank page that you fill in with the characteristics of your help file.

WARNING: The files you'll create using the Microsoft Help Workshop aren't compatible with those created using the older DOS utilities I described in the previous sections. You have to decide on a single application strategy. I think that the new Help Workshop makes life a lot easier for the developer, but only if you work with 32-bit operating environments. If you still need Windows 3.*x* compatibility, you have to use the DOS utility versions of the help compiler.

Defining a Project's Options

Once I have a new project to work with, I usually start defining some of the project options. For example, you should at least have some idea of what you want to call your help file and what type of copyright information to add. I always use the contents topic as my main topic, so adding that entry at the beginning is a good idea as well. All you need to do is click on the Options button and you'll see the Options dialog shown here.

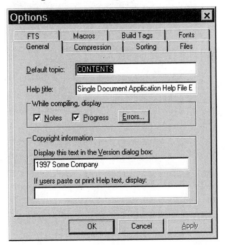

Notice that I've already defined some general options in this case. All of these options should look familiar since I described them as part of the make file discussion in the previous section. (You'll find that the options on the Compression page look pretty familiar, too—they define the type of compression you'll use to reduce the size of your help file.) Some programmers may feel at this point that they won't get much benefit out of using this tool, especially if they have a lot of predefined files sitting around on disk. It's important to remember that this dialog provides a simple form for you to fill out; no longer do you need to remember what statements to use to accomplish a specific task.

The Sorting page of the Options dialog contains two areas. The first area determines the language of the help file. Language makes a difference in the way things are sorted, since everyone's alphabet is slightly different. The second area contains two options in this page. One option allows you to ignore nonspacing characters. For example, the circumflex (^) that appears in ê would affect the sort order if you didn't select this option. The other option tells the help compiler to ignore any symbols in the help file when sorting. This comes in handy if you want to create a nonspecialized index for a data entry program or other general application. On the other hand, it would actually get in the way when creating an index for a reference help file. Consider the fact that many C functions begin with an underscore. Ignoring those underscores would make the function more difficult to find.

The next thing we'll need to look at is the Files page of the Options dialog as shown here.

Options			
FTS	Macros	Build Tags	Fonts
General	Compression	Sorting	Files

Help File: `.\Sngl_Doc.hlp`

Log File: `HELP.LOG`

Rich Text Format (RTF) files:
`.\Sample.rtf`   [Change...]

Contents file:
[Browse...]

TMP folder:
[Browse...]

Substitute path prefix:
[Edit...]

[OK] [Cancel] [Apply]

Notice that there are a lot of entries here that I've talked about before. You can change the name of the help file by changing the contents of the Help File field. Normally, the help compiler uses the name of the project file as a basis for naming the help file. The Log File field contains the name of a log file. Fortunately (as we'll see later), this particular option isn't really required with the new help compiler. I still use a log file to keep track of the status of various help file projects, but it's an option now.

One of the most important fields on this page is the Rich Text Format (RTF) files list box. You'll find a list of the files for the current help project here. Clicking the Change button next to the field displays the Topic Files dialog shown here.

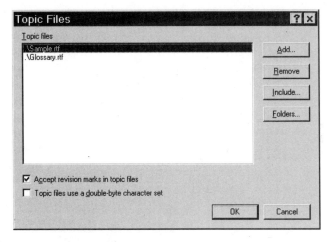

This is where you add and remove topic files from the list in the FILES section of the project file. Notice the two checkboxes at the bottom of this dialog. They're important because they control how the help compiler reacts to your RTF files. The first option allows the help compiler to automatically implement any changes you make to the RTF files during the next compile. If you leave this box unchecked, the help compiler will ignore any changes. The second option is important if you use a double-byte character set (DBCS) within your help file. This option changes the way the help compiler works with your file and allows it to preserve the special characters. (This feature is mainly used by languages with complex character sets like Chinese.)

T IP: Another way to access the Topic Files dialog is to click on the Files button on the Main window shown in Figure 15-3.

There are a couple of other options on the Files page of the Options menu. One of them is the Contents File field. If you're creating a project from scratch, Help Workshop will fill this in for you automatically when you create the contents page. The reason for including this entry is if you already have a contents page that you want to use with the current project. The TMP

15

Folder field only comes into play when your help file gets over 8MB in size. It allows you to specify something other than the current directory for the temporary files that Help Workshop creates when it compiles your help file. In most cases, you won't need to change this entry unless the current drive is short on disk space. The final field, Substitute Path Prefix, comes into play if you move the files used to create the help file and don't want to change all the path information in the project file.

Windows 95/98 help files offer something that you won't find in those of its predecessors: full text search. That's the database created when you select the Find page of the Help Topics dialog. It allows you to search an entire help file word by word. The FTS page of the Options dialog contains an option to generate this file when you compile the help file. Since Windows 95/98 generates this file anyway, I normally leave this option blank. The GID file that the help compiler creates takes up a lot of room on the distribution disks and increases compile time by a considerable margin for large files.

You'll want to spend some time learning to use the Macros page shown here.

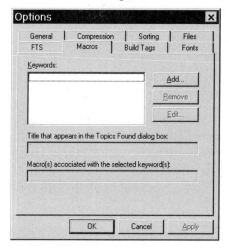

This is where you can define keyword macros to use on a file-wide basis. Not only that, but these macros appear on the Index page of the Help Topics dialog when the user tries to search for a particular topic.

Clicking the Add button on the Macros page displays a Keyword Macros dialog containing three fields. The first field contains the name of the macro. The second field contains the macro itself. The third field contains a string that tells Help Workshop how to display the macro on the Index page. I use this particular entry when I have more than one help file but want to display

Remember that the Macros page on the Options dialog is for macros that affect the entire help file—not just one window.

a particular keyword file-wide. For example, I often place the glossary and list of acronyms in a separate file and then use the JI macro to create a file-wide jump to them. The keyword macro is the method I use to do this. The user never even realizes that he or she has loaded another file—it's that transparent.

I previously talked about the * footnote with regard to build tags. The Build Tags page of the Options dialog is where you make use of this feature. I've covered this topic pretty thoroughly in an earlier section, so I won't go into detail again here. The main idea is to provide Help Workshop with a list of build tags that you want to include in a help file. Even if an RTF file contains other topics, it won't include them in the help file if you don't include that topic's build tag. If you leave this page blank, Help Workshop assumes that you want to include all of the topics in all of the RTF files you've included as part of the final help file.

The Fonts page of the Options dialog is your first chance to customize the look and feel of your help file. I normally don't use this page to control the appearance of the help file, preferring instead to rely on the formatting capabilities of my word processor. However, if you're creating an RTF file using a text editor, this particular feature can save you some time. The Character Set field allows you to select a particular character set for your help file; the default is ANSI. You can also choose from several different language types, like Arabic. The Font in WinHelp Dialog Boxes field is where you define a default font type. Click on the Change button and you'll see a Font dialog with three fields. The first defines the font name, the second the font point size. The third field defines the character set you'll use with dialogs. The list box below the Font in WinHelp Dialog Boxes field allows you to change the general fonts used within the Windows help file. It lets you substitute one font for another. The Add button displays an Add/Edit Font Mapping dialog that contains two groups of three fields. The three fields are precisely the same as the ones used in the Font dialog that I just described. The only problem with using this particular page is that it doesn't work if your word processor overrides the settings—something that generally happens if you use a product like Word for Windows.

Defining Windows

Defining options is only the first phase of creating a project file. Once you have the options in place, you need to define some windows to display your data in. I always create one window called Main. It's the main window that my application will use.

Creating a window is fairly simple. All you need to do is click on the Windows button in the Main window (Figure 15-3) to display the Window Properties dialog shown here.

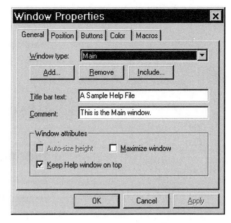

The first page you'll need to look at is the General page, shown in the illustration. Click on the Add button and you'll see an Add a New Window dialog with two fields. One field contains the name of the window. The other field contains the window type. There are three window types that Help Workshop can create: procedural, reference, and error message. There is very little difference between the procedural and reference windows. They're both autosizing and contain the three system buttons. The big difference between the two is their placement onscreen—which you can override with the settings I'll show you next. The error message window differs from the other two in that it doesn't include the three system buttons. It looks somewhat like a dialog.

Back on the General page, the Title Bar Text field determines what Windows Help places on the title bar. This entry doesn't affect the appearance of the topic title area of the help window. The Comment field allows you to place a comment next to the entry in the project file—something that I always take advantage of. There are also three attribute checkboxes. Help Workshop may disable one or more of these checkboxes, depending on the situation. For example, you can't make the main help window autosizing. If you do make an ancillary window autosizing, you can't choose to maximize it when it opens. Most procedural windows default to staying on top. This is a handy feature if you want to keep help available to a user who is trying to work with an application.

TIP: I normally turn the Auto-Size Height feature off to provide better control over the appearance of a window onscreen. The options on the Position page that we'll look at next allow you full control over the appearance of your help window onscreen.

You'll almost always want to spend some time working with the Position page of the Window Properties dialog, shown here.

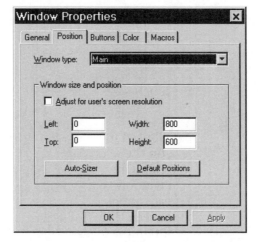

The name of this page is a bit deceiving because it provides a little more functionality than you might initially expect. While it does control the actual starting position and size of the various help windows you create, this dialog provides some easily used features that you'll really find handy.

There are four fields on the Position page: Left, Top, Width, and Height. These control the size and position of your window. I normally position my first help window in the upper-left corner and use a size of either 640×480 or 800×600, depending on the capabilities of the target machine for my application. This may seem a bit small, but the user can always resize the window as needed. Trying to find a help window on an older display when the programmer positions it near one of the edges is frustrating to say the least. I really like the Adjust for User's Screen Resolution option on this page because it prevents the help window from becoming totally hidden when the user has a low-resolution display.

There's one very special feature on this page, and you may not notice it at first. Look at the Auto-Sizer button. Clicking on this button displays the example window shown here.

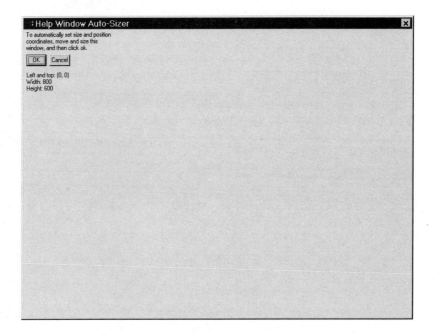

If you change the window's position, the Left and Top field values also change. Resizing the window changes the value of the Width and Height fields. This graphic method of changing the window size will definitely reduce the number of times you have to recompile the help file to take care of aesthetic needs.

Windows 95/98 defines a lot of default buttons that you can add to your help file. There are situations where you may not want to add all of them. For example, the Browser buttons aren't all that important if you don't define a browse (+ footnote) in one of your RTF files. The Buttons page shown here allows you to define the buttons used with your help window.

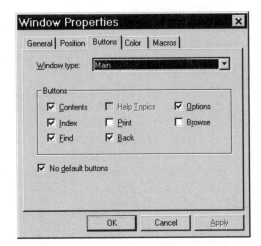

All ancillary procedure and reference windows lack both the Contents and Index buttons. Main windows contain both of these buttons as a default as well as the Print and Back buttons. On the other hand, a Main window won't allow you to select the Help Topics button. Unlike all the other window types, an error message window has no restrictions. You can include any of the default buttons that you like on it.

T IP: You can get around the Help Workshop-imposed limitations on buttons for the main help window by clicking the No Default Buttons checkbox. This checkbox only appears for the Main window, which means that you can't override the restrictions for ancillary procedure and reference windows.

The next page that you'll want to look at is the Color page. This contains two fields: Nonscrolling Area Color and Topic Area Color. Each has a Change button. All you need to do is click on the Change button to display a color palette. Selecting a different color from the palette changes the appearance of the help window.

The final page is the Macros page shown here.

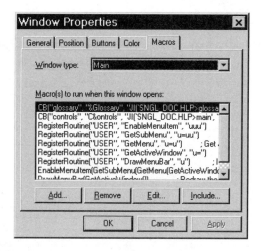

The Main window always uses the macros in the CONFIG section of the project file as a default. All of the macros you see in this section are self-executing—that's why the macros in the CONFIG section are added to the Main window. You want those macros to execute when the Main window opens. Adding a new macro to the Main window always adds it to the CONFIG section of the help project file. Adding macros to other windows changes the way those windows appear in comparison to the Main window. For example, if you add a browse to one of the ancillary windows, you might need to add a macro or two here to set up any conditions not taken care of by the default Browse button selection on the Buttons page. Each of these ancillary windows will have their own special CONFIG-<window name> section in the help project.

TIP: Another way to access the Macros dialog for the Main window is to click on the Config button on the Main window shown in Figure 15-2.

Mapping Help Topics

I've already expressed the importance of this particular part of creating a help project file. If you don't map the topic identifiers in your help file to a help context number, you can't attach context-sensitive help to the controls in your application. You'll see how this works in the section that follows on adding context-sensitive help to your application.

Clicking on the Map button displays a Map dialog like the one shown here.

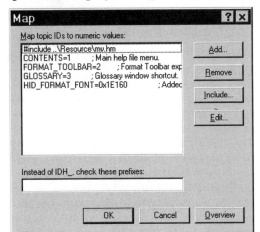

This is where you define the relationship between a topic identifier and a particular context number. Notice that I've already defined a few in this case. The topic identifier is set equal to a help context number. It's followed by a comment that describes the entry.

There are a lot of ways to keep the context numbers straight. I usually start at 1 and count up from there until I reach the last topic identifier for small help files. Large help files require something a bit more complex, though, or you'll find yourself reusing numbers. I normally use a three- or four-digit number in this case. The first two numbers are the position of the control or menu item described by the help context within the application. For example, the File menu is normally 01 and the Edit menu is 02. A description of the File | New command would receive a help context number of 0101, since the New option is usually the first one on the File menu. I assign a value of 0001 to the first non-application topic. For example, the glossary would fall into this category. The first two numbers for a control on the form of an application would be one greater than the last menu item. I use the tab order for the last two numbers since it's unlikely that a label or other nonactive component would ever appear in the help file.

It's easy to add a new map entry. Simply click on Add and you'll see the Add Map Entry dialog shown here.

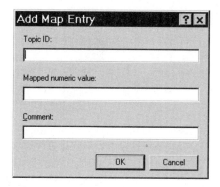

This dialog contains three fields: the topic identifier, the mapped numeric value (help context number), and a comment. Fill out the three fields and click on OK to add a new map to the project.

As I previously mentioned, you'll normally want to include an HM file with your help file to reduce the amount of work you need to do and to provide a quick and easy method for checking your work. Nothing is more frustrating than to release a help file that you thought was complete at the time of testing but turns out to be missing one or more crucial entries after you release it. All you need to do to include a file is click on the Include button. You'll see an Include File dialog like the one shown here.

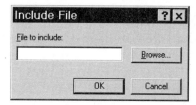

Notice that this dialog provides a Browse button so that you can simply search for your include file on the hard drive. The Browse button opens a standard Open dialog, just like the ones you've used with other applications.

Compiling Your Help File

Once you get a help project file put together, it's time to try to compile it. All you need to do is click on the Save and Compile button at the bottom of the Main window shown in Figure 15-3. The Help Workshop window will minimize while it compiles the help file. This allows you to work on something else (compiling a large help file can take a very long time). Once the compilation is complete, you'll see a dialog similar to the one shown in Figure 15-4.

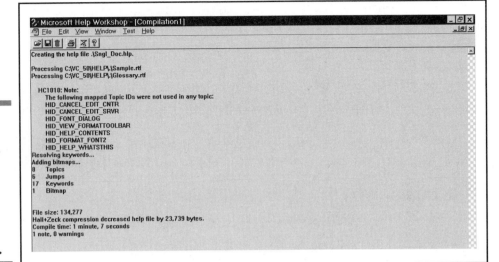

This compilation screen shows the current status of the help file and any error messages.

Figure 15-4.

You should notice something almost immediately about this dialog—it shows that there are errors in the help file (actually they're notes, but you'll still want to count them as errors in most cases). We didn't define help file entries for every entry in the HM file. What that means is that there are holes in the coverage provided by the help file that need to be filled. As you can see, using the HM file is a great help because it at least reduces the chance that you'll miss an important topic.

Is the HM file perfect? Not by a long shot. Take another look at Listing 15-2 and you'll see I had to add a Map entry for ID_FORMAT_FONT. This is a standard identifier for MFC that appears in the AFXRES.H file, not the RESOURCE.H file that contains the IDs for your custom controls. As a result, you'll need to remember to add support for standard controls—the HM file can't help you in this case.

Adding Standard Help to Your Application

It's time to add help support to our application. I chose the Resources version (see Chapter 3) of the Single Document project we started in Chapter 2 since it's the most complete. I also chose it because we didn't do anything to add help support to this program. It's important to realize that most of the work required to add help support to your application is in the help file itself. We'll add help support to the Single Document example program without using much code at all.

15

We'll actually look at two methods for adding support. One is totally automatic. All you'll really need to do is add a menu entry and one manual entry to the beginning of the MainFrm.CPP file. You'll use this method in most cases because it's simply the most efficient way to do things and you won't gain much by using the second method. The second method requires a little more work but offers more flexibility as well. In this case you'll hand-code the help access into your program. However, you'll find that there still isn't all that much to do.

The first thing we need to do is add some menu entries. Figure 15-5 shows the two menu entries you'll need to add to the IDR_MAINFRAME menu. Table 15-3 contains the parameters you'll need for the two entries.

Notice that the ID for the What's This? menu entry doesn't use the normal convention. You'll see why in a few moments. For right now, just remember that we're not using the standard ID—it's important if you want to implement the MFC help features automatically.

You'll also want to change the Help button on the IDR_MAINFRAME toolbar. Right now it displays the About dialog, which is fine if you don't have help added to your application. Since we're adding help, open the IDR_MAINFRAME toolbar, double-click on the Help button, and change its ID to ID_HELP_CONTENTS.

Our two menu entries also have accelerators associated with them, so we'll need to open the IDR_MAINFRAME accelerator shown in Figure 15-6. Notice that I've highlighted one of the entries. You'll need to add a new accelerator

You'll need to add two new menu entries to test the help file we created in the previous section of the chapter.

Figure 15-5.

ID	Caption	Prompt
ID_HELP_CONTENTS	&Contents\tF1	Display the Main Help File\nHelp
ID_CONTEXT_HELP	&What's This?\tShift-F1	Click here for context sensitive help.\nContext Help

Help Menu
Parameters
Table 15-3.

for the ID_HELP_CONTENTS menu entry and another for the
ID_CONTEXT_HELP menu entry as shown in the figure and in the
following table.

ID	Key	Type
ID_HELP_CONTENTS	VK_F1	VIRTKEY
ID_CONTEXT_HELP	SHIFT + VK_F1	VIRTKEY

Adding the accelerators is easy. Just double-click on the last blank entry and
you'll see an Accel Properties dialog like the one shown here.

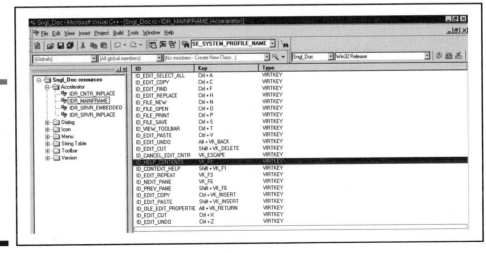

You'll need
to add
accelerators
for our two
help menu
entries to
make them
user-friendly.
Figure 15-6.

15

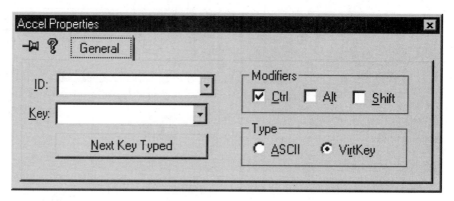

Choose the ID you want from the drop-down ID list box. Click the Next Key Typed button, and then press the key you want to assign to the ID. In our case we'll assign F1 to ID_HELP_CONTENTS and SHIFT-F1 to ID_CONTEXT_HELP. Make sure you check the appropriate checkboxes, and then close the Accel Properties dialog.

Remember that we'll be implementing one of these help options without writing an actual function. MFC supports four default help actions without any programming at all: contents, find, index, and context sensitive. We'll be implementing the context-sensitive option using the built-in MFC features. All you need to do is add a line of code like the bold code shown in Listing 15-3. Adding this one line of code activates a built-in MFC function for context-sensitive help.

Listing 15-3:

```
BEGIN_MESSAGE_MAP(CMainFrame, CFrameWnd)
    //{{AFX_MSG_MAP(CMainFrame)
    ON_WM_CREATE()
    ON_COMMAND(ID_BOLD, OnBold)
    ON_COMMAND(ID_ITALIC, OnItalic)
    ON_COMMAND(ID_STRIKETHROUGH, OnStrikethrough)
    ON_COMMAND(ID_UNDERLINE, OnUnderline)
    ON_COMMAND(ID_VIEW_FORMATTOOLBAR, OnViewFormattoolbar)
    ON_COMMAND(ID_HELP_CONTENTS, OnHelpContents)
    ON_COMMAND(ID_CONTEXT_HELP, OnContextHelp)
    //}}AFX_MSG_MAP
END_MESSAGE_MAP()
```

Now it's time to take care of the Contents menu option. The first thing we'll need to do is add a function. Use the View | ClassWizard command to display the MFC ClassWizard dialog. Choose the Message Maps tab and select CMainFrame in the Class Name field. Look for ID_HELP_CONTEXT in the

Object IDs list, and then highlight the COMMAND entry in the Messages list. Click on Add Function. Your MFC ClassWizard dialog should look like the one shown here.

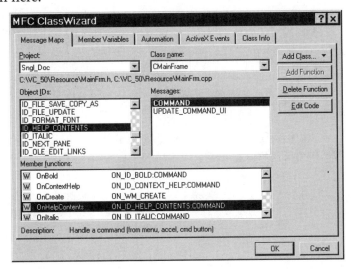

Click on the Edit Code button and you'll see a function skeleton. Listing 15-4 shows the code you'll need to add to make the Contents menu option work.

Listing 15-4:
```
void CMainFrame::OnHelpContents()
{
    // Call WinHelp to display the main help window.
    WinHelp(0, HELP_CONTENTS);
}
```

As you can see, the code for implementing the required level of help isn't all that impressive. In fact, this is probably the shortest function so far in the book. All you needed to do was call WinHelp() with the required define: HELP_CONTENTS. We didn't need to provide any supplementary information, so the first parameter is set to 0.

Creating an HTML-Based Help Package

We discuss in Chapter 8 many of the things you'll need to know to create an HTML-based help package. The basic element of HTML help is the Web page, and it's constructed the same as its counterpart on the Internet. However, HTML help doesn't end with a simple Web page; there are other considerations to take into account. For example, you need to consider the organization of the help file from an access perspective. The following sections are designed to help you create a help file setup that's both efficient and practical.

Multiple or Single-Page Files?

HTML-based help always uses multiple files to hold the help information; the layout of these files can greatly affect users' ability to find what they need.

One of the more important considerations is how you want to put your help file together. When you use Windows Help, you create a single file containing many pages of information. This kind of approach won't work with HTML-based help because it doesn't use a master file approach like Windows Help does. In sum, you have to figure out how you want to put multiple pages of information into one package, but be assured that the package you create will almost certainly contain multiple files.

Remember that your help file uses an outline and is laid out similar to a book. What you need to decide is where to block for placement in a file. There are several ways you can do this depending on how your application will get used. Table 15-4 describes the various file layout options and their benefits/detractions.

Layout Method	Description	Pluses	Minuses
Large Menu/ Dialog Control	All controls in a dialog or entries for a menu tree appear in one file. Uses anchors to allow the user to move from topic to topic. Includes a table of contents that allows a user to go directly to a topic.	First-time users will find it easy to explore the application. In addition, the layout makes the help file read more like the manual it's designed to replace. The use of a table of contents makes information easy to find.	The large file size will cause some users to think twice before incurring the cost of another file download. In addition, some longtime users will find it cumbersome wading through all the menu entries contained in one file. Updates are harder because you may have to make the same change to multiple files.

Layout Method	Description	Pluses	Minuses
Large Task	Each file contains a complete description and procedure for performing a specific task. For example, you may create a file for creating a new document.	New users will find that they can perform tasks easier. In addition, each task can be tested as a separate entity, reducing the possibility of mistakes after making changes to an application. The use of large task files will allow the writer to include specific screen shots and enhanced graphic information. Finally, this is the only layout that will work for simple tutorial help files, though the bandwidth and reliability limitations of the Internet do reduce the level of training you can provide.	Advanced users will find it hard to wade through entire procedures to find the one piece of information they need. The lack of common sub-procedures will actually increase user learning curve overall since they won't associate the common subtasks involved in performing a specific task. Help files will be harder to update and will require more space on the server due to redundant information. Remote downloads will take a long time due to increased file size.

15

Layout Method	Description	Pluses	Minuses
Small Menu/ Dialog Control	Each menu item or dialog box control appears in a separate file.	Short download times will allow users to use help even when connected through a dial-up line. Users will find information fast since they'll only see one screen. Updates are faster and more reliable since the information only appears in one file. The overall size of help on the server is reduced.	First-time users will find the constant download of information for each menu item or dialog control frustrating, especially when a dial-up connection is used. A table of contents won't be an automatic feature and will require separate maintenance time.
Small Task	A list of tasks is created and a hierarchical table of contents generated. Each task is broken up into a series of easily performed common subtasks. Any special events are covered in the overview page for the task.	The use of a table of contents makes information easy to find, especially for advanced users. In addition, the hierarchical format allows users to drill down to just the information they need. Reduced download time encourages everyone to use help rather than call the help desk for information. Updates consist of changing the information in a single subtask folder.	There is a possibility of introducing subtle errors into the task procedures. For example, a menu entry may change in one part of the application but not in another. Some novice users will find the subtask orientation difficult to understand.

HTML File Layout Methods (*continued*)

Table 15-4.

Layout Method	Description	Pluses	Minuses
Topic	Each file contains one help file topic. For example, you might have a file on data entry methods.	Users who want to find out a lot of information about a specific topic will get fast access since all of the information will arrive in one download.	Remote users who require information menu-related items will end up waiting for each item to download. Information is difficult to update since you'll need to look through several files for one menu change.

HTML File Layout Methods (*continued*)

Table 15-4.

Connection Type

It's interesting to note that some vendors who use HTML-based help assume that everyone has a T1 connection to the Internet. The truth is that many users rely on a dial-up connection to download their files. In Chapter 8 we discuss some of the realities of a dial-up connection, most notably that you must limit the size of an individual file so that a user will actually want to download it.

Even HTML-based help files must take the limitations of a dial-up connection into account when providing information to the user.

Unlike a browser, your application may not include a stop button. What this means to users is that they have a choice between not getting help, waiting eons for each page to download from an Internet server, or calling the help desk (clogging lines) when help files exceed a specific size. In most cases I can guarantee that you'll be beefing up your support staff to support an application with large HTML help files long before the user sits and waits for those pages to download.

Considering the size of the HTML files you use means that you also have to consider the use of bells and whistles to enhance the HTML-based help files. For example, most of my Windows help files use full-color screen shots to help the user get the most from the information I'm trying to provide. On the other hand, any HTML-based help files I create use black-and-white images so that I can reduce the graphics file size to a manageable level.

Use graphics in HTML-based help files with care since they can greatly increase the time required to download information.

You'll also want to limit the number of graphics images in your HTML-based help files. A reduction in color and/or resolution can only go so far in reducing the cost of downloading a file from your Web server. If the image isn't easy to see, then there really isn't any reason for the user to download it in the first place. In other words, you must maintain a certain level of image quality, regardless of the kind of help file you're trying to create.

One of the ways to combat this frustrating exercise of deciding between information quality and download speed is to ask the user up front. Some users may want just the text. You could provide this option as a link in your opening help screen. Other users may be willing to contend with low-quality black-and-white graphics, while still others may require high-quality color images. It doesn't hurt to provide two or three quality choices so users can get what they want. Providing two or three choices will also allow you to take the user's dial-in speed into account. There are, after all, some users who do have T1 connections and may be able to take advantage of everything you have to offer in the way of help.

Search Capability

Searching a help file for valuable information is what most users are going to do once they get past the novice level. What they'll be looking for is some tidbit of knowledge that they need to accomplish a task or an explanation for some control on a dialog box. Unfortunately, HTML files aren't all that searchable, a problem that many vendors have yet to deal with.

There are a few ways that you can mimic the search capability of Windows help without a lot of additional effort. In most cases you won't be able to completely replicate the search capability provided by Windows help, but you can come close. The following list provides a few ideas you can use.

◆ Create an index
◆ Define additional links
◆ Add a table of contents
◆ Produce a hot topics list

HTML-based help files normally lack word-by-word search capabilities.

The one thing that you won't be able to do with your HTML-based help file (at least not without a lot of work) is create a word-for-word index like the one provided with Windows help. This means that the user will always have some question that you didn't anticipate and that the various search features of your HTML-based help file won't be able to answer. It always pays to provide some kind of feedback mechanism with your HTML-based help files so that users can request additional links. In addition, make sure your HTML-based help file search capabilities are flexible enough that creating additional links won't be a chore.

TIP: You can get around part of the search capability problem for your HTML-based help files by using a Windows NT server with IIS version 4.0 or above installed. This version of IIS allows you to create search indexes to the files located in your Web directories. Adding a search page to your HTML-based help file isn't a major undertaking, especially if you use the generic search pages provided by Microsoft as an example.

Adding HTML-Based Help to Your Application

There are several phases to adding HTML-based help to your application. We discussed the first step in the previous section: deciding on an HTML file design and layout. The next step is to create the HTML file itself, and finally, to add the required links to your application.

Since I've already covered the basics of creating your own HTML file in Chapter 8, I won't include that information here again. However, one of the things you'll probably want to do is invest in a good HTML editor like FrontPage or Visual InterDev if you intend to create your help files from scratch. Exporting your paper documentation from Word for Windows also works well, though you'll need an add-on product like Map This to create links between your graphics and the various help topics that they address. This process is similar to the one that we performed for the previous example in this chapter using the Hotspot Editor.

For this example we'll use the same help file that we used for the Windows help example earlier in the chapter. The only difference is that I've converted it to HTML format using Word for Windows. Theoretically, you can use any tool you like to create the help file, but I find that using Word for Windows allows me to create one master document for both paper and electronic documentation. We'll also use the same example program that we used in that section, but I've copied the original resource project files to another directory to keep the help examples separate (so directory names shown in screen shots may not match those on your computer).

NOTE: You can find a complete copy of all the projects in this book, including the help files, in HTML format for this project at **http://www.osborne.com**. These project files will give you a better idea of what you'll need to do to prepare your help files.

Unlike the Windows help example in this chapter, there isn't any automated method for adding HTML-based help to your application. You must hand-code the required access for every main access point in your help file. What this means is that our example will look more like the second form of Windows help access in the first section of this chapter, than the second.

This example begins by adding two menu entries to the application Help menu. You'll find the precise procedure for doing this in the earlier section on adding standard help to your application. Look at Figure 15-4 for an example of what the menu entries will look like. Table 15-3 provides a list of parameters you'll need when creating the menu entries. Once the menu entries are in place, add a new accelerator for the ID_HELP_CONTENTS menu entry and another for the ID_CONTEXT_HELP menu entry as shown in Figure 15-5 (I've also covered this process in the earlier section on adding standard help).

NOTE: This chapter is showing one of the methods you could use to add a more traditional form of general help to your application using HTML-based help. (We won't cover context-sensitive help, but adding it is similar to adding the HTML-based help.) There are other ways of adding HTML-based help to your application. We cover one of those methods in Chapter 12. That's right, you could use the techniques in Chapter 12 to access a help desk page on your Web sight instead of the main page shown in the example.

The first thing you'll need to do is add a new dialog box to your application. All you need to do is right-click on the Dialog folder in ResourceView and choose Insert Dialog from the context menu. What you'll see is a standard dialog box. Right-click the dialog box, and choose Properties from the context menu to display the Dialog Properties dialog. Change the ID field to IDD_HELP_DLG (or whatever name you'd like to use for your help dialog) and the Caption field to Main Help (or whatever you'd like displayed on the dialog title bar). For the purposes of this example, you'll also need to change a few of the dialog box properties. Check the Minimize box and Maximize box options on the Styles page. You'll also want to choose the Resizing option in the Border field. This will allow users to resize the resulting dialog box to fit their display. Close the Dialog Properties dialog.

Now that we have a new dialog box to use as display window, we have to add a Web Browser control to display the HTML pages for our help files. Use the Project | Add to Project | Components and Controls command to display the Components and Controls Gallery dialog. Double-click the Registered ActiveX Controls folder, then highlight the Microsoft Web Browser entry. Click Insert to add the control to your project, then click OK when asked if you want to add the Web Browser control to your project. Close the Components and Controls Gallery dialog once you've added the Web Browser control to your project.

We need five command buttons and one Web Browser control for this example. Sometimes a picture is worth a hundred words, so Figure 15-7 shows how I configured my help dialog. This is the minimum you should

Make sure you configure your help dialog for ease of use.

Figure 15-7.

15

provide in the way of an HTML-based help dialog since the user will normally require some means of navigating through the help screens. Table 15-5 provides a complete list of properties for the various controls on this dialog.

Creating a dialog box doesn't make it accessible to any other part of the application. You need to create a class for it. That's what we'll do next. CTRL-double-click the dialog box (make sure you don't double-click on any of the controls). You'll see an Adding a Class dialog. Click OK to create a new class. Type **CHelpDlg** as the class name and choose CDialog as the base class. Click OK to create the new class. Close the MFC ClassWizard dialog.

While the dialog box is accessible at this point, none of the controls are. The first control that we need to do something with is the Web Browser. Double-click IDC_EXPLORER1 and you'll see an Add Member Variable dialog box. Type **m_WebBrowser** in the Member Variable Name field, choose Control in the Category field, and choose CwebBrowser2 in the Variable type field. Click OK to create the variable. What this process allows us to do is work with the Web Browser control within the application.

There are two things we need to do with the Web Browser control before we do anything else with the dialog. First, we need to initialize the Web Browser to display the main help file when the user opens the dialog box. Second, we need to resize the Web Browser so that it changes size with the dialog box. This will help users to see as much or as little of the help file as their screen will allow. It turns out that there are two messages that our dialog box provides that work perfectly for performing this task. One is WM_INITDIALOG, and the other is WM_SIZE. Open the MFC ClassWizard

Control	Property	Value
IDD_HELP_DLG	Size	350×200
IDC_EXPLORER1	Size	336×168
IDC_FORWARD	Caption	Forward
IDC_BACKWARD	Caption	Backward
IDC_GLOSSARY	Caption	Glossary
IDC_CONTROLS	Caption	Controls
IDC_HOME	Caption	Home

HTML-Based
Help Dialog
Controls

Table 15-5.

using the View | ClassWizard command. Select the Message Maps tab, then highlight CHelpDlg in the Object IDs field. Scroll through the list of Messages until you find WM_INITDIALOG. Click Add Function to add the default initialization function to your code. Do the same thing for the WM_SIZE message. Close the MFC ClassWizard dialog (we'll add the required code after a few more setup steps).

The user will also want the five pushbuttons that we added to the dialog box to perform some task. Adding a function to interact with each of the five buttons is relatively easy. All you need to do is right-click on the button (say, Forward), and choose Events from the context menu. What you'll see is a New Windows Message and Event Handlers dialog box. Highlight the BN_CLICKED message, and then click the Add Handler button. Close the New Windows Message and Event Handlers dialog box. Repeat this procedure for each of the five buttons. Here's what your dialog should look like.

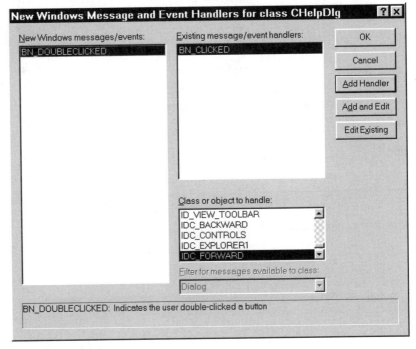

Let's make one more check of the MFC ClassWizard dialog. Here's what your dialog should look like at this point. Note that there are two functions for the Web Browser control and one for each of the command buttons.

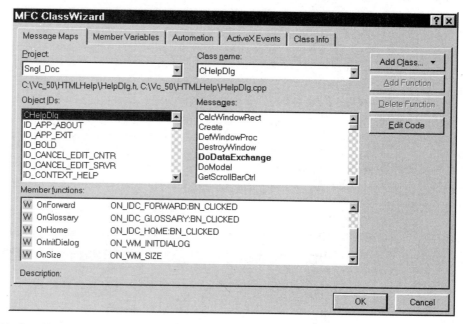

It's finally time to add some code to our project. Listing 15-5 shows the code that you'll need to add for this example. I'll explain it after you get a chance to see the code.

Listing 15-5:

```
///////////////////////////////////////////////////////////////////////////
// CHelpDlg message handlers

BOOL CHelpDlg::OnInitDialog()
{
    CDialog::OnInitDialog();

    // Navigate to the main help screen.
    m_WebBrowser.Navigate("http://nt_server/help2/sample.htm", NULL, NULL, NULL, NULL);

    return TRUE;  // return TRUE unless you set the focus to a control
                  // EXCEPTION: OCX Property Pages should return FALSE
}

void CHelpDlg::OnSize(UINT nType, int cx, int cy)
{
    CDialog::OnSize(nType, cx, cy);
```

```
        // Change the WebBrowser control size to match the dialog.
        m_Webbrowser.SetHeight(cy - 64);
        m_WebBrowser.SetWidth(cx - 28);
}

void CHelpDlg::OnForward()
{
        // Go to the next site in the history list.
        m_WebBrowser.GoForward();

}

void CHelpDlg::OnBackward()
{
        // Go to the previous site in the history list.
        m_WebBrowser.GoBack();

}

void CHelpDlg::OnGlossary()
{
        // Go to the Glossary Web page.
        m_WebBrowser.Navigate("http://nt_server/help2/glossary.htm", NULL, NULL, NULL, NULL);

}

void CHelpDlg::OnControls()
{
        // Go to the Controls (Format) Web page.
        m_WebBrowser.Navigate("http://nt_server/help2/format.htm", NULL, NULL, NULL, NULL);

}

void CHelpDlg::OnHome()
{
        // Navigate to the main help screen.
        m_WebBrowser.Navigate("http://nt_server/help2/sample.htm", NULL, NULL, NULL, NULL);

}
```

As you can see, there isn't anything too mysterious about this code, especially if you work through the examples in Chapter 12. All of the functions interact with the Web Browser memory variable we created (m_WebBrowser). What we do in the OnInitDialog() function and the OnHome() function is use the Navigate()

function to tell the browser to display the main help file (SAMPLE.HTM). Likewise, the OnGlossary() and OnControls() functions use the Navigate() function to display these specialty pages. The OnForward() and OnBackward() functions work much as you might expect. They use the GoForward() and GoBack() functions to allow the user to navigate between Web pages. The final function, OnSize(), uses the Web Browser control's SetHeight and SetWidth properties to match the Web Browser control size to the size of the dialog box. As the user changes the dialog size, the Web Browser control size will change as well.

What we have at this point is a fully functional help dialog, but no way to access it. Adding the required support to our application is easy. The first thing you'll need to do is include the help dialog in the MainFrm.CPP file as shown here in bold text.

```
// MainFrm.cpp : implementation of the CMainFrame class
//

#include "stdafx.h"
#include "Sngl_Doc.h"

#include "MainFrm.h"

// Include our help dialog.
#include "HelpDlg.h"

#ifdef _DEBUG
#define new DEBUG_NEW
#undef THIS_FILE
static char THIS_FILE[] = __FILE__;
#endif
```

We'll also need to add some code to the OnHelpContents() function as shown here.

```
void CMainFrame::OnHelpContents()
{
    CHelpDlg    oHelpDlg;      // Create a help dialog instance.

    // Display our help dialog.
    oHelpDlg.DoModal();
}
```

If you compile and run the application now, you'll be able to access the HTML-based help using the Help | Contents command. Here's an example of what your help dialog will look like in action.

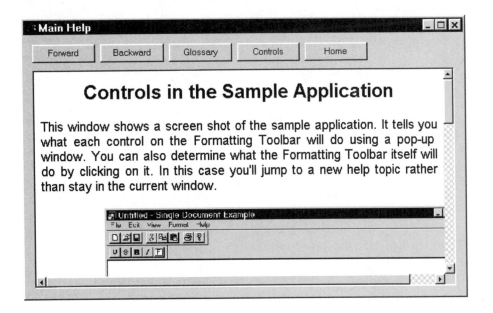

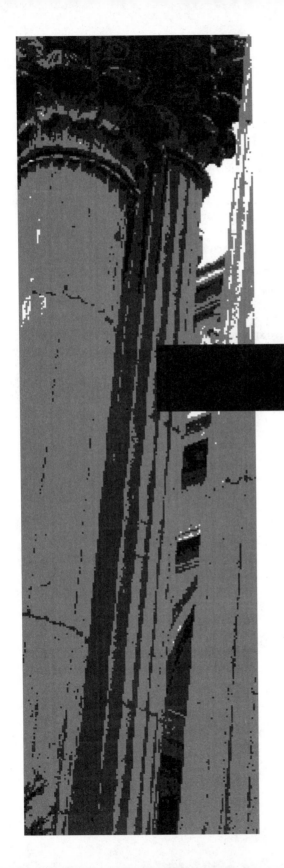

CHAPTER 16

Packaging Your Application

Packaging an application: sounds like you're going to shrink-wrap it and send it off to the store. From a programmer's perspective, packaging has nothing to do with stores, but it does have everything to do with how well an application is received by the user. When you look at something in a store, it's the package that grabs your attention. What's inside gains your attention only after you pick up the package. If users install your application and see that the setup program provides everything they need, they'll be a lot more likely to start using your application with a good attitude—something I consider crucial to the success of an application.

Packaging also has a lot to do with an application's ease of use and the user's ability to install it quickly. Imagine for a moment a car that wasn't packaged correctly. Sure, it comes with directional signals, but there isn't any light on the dash to tell drivers which way they're going. The engineer knows which way they work, so why bother to install the dash lights? You wouldn't buy a car like this and neither would anyone else. That's what an application without a good help file is like to users. You may as well just tell them to guess about how to use the application, because they'll never think to look at the README or other file you placed on the disk with a modicum of instructions.

NOTE: We cover the requirements for creating a good help file in Chapter 15. If you haven't yet created one for your application, you may want to consider doing so before you read this chapter. I'm a big believer in good help files—they save both you and the user a lot of time and effort. This chapter will assume that you're a believer in good help files, too.

Obviously, there are other packaging concerns that everyone doesn't have to deal with. For example, an in-house programmer probably wouldn't worry as much about really neat graphics—unlike someone distributing an application commercially or as shareware. However, everyone should make their application look aesthetically pleasing because appearance affects the user's attitude toward the application. I've found that attitude is about half the battle in getting a user up and running with a program. Anything you can do to improve the user's attitude also benefits you by reducing service calls and complaints. In short, bells and whistles are nice, but a good interface is required. Even your installation program has to have a great interface; after all, it's the first part of your program that the user will see. First impressions are very long lasting—especially if you're with users who didn't particularly want to use an application in the first place.

Make sure your program (including the installation program) has a very usable and very consistent interface.

A complete application always includes an install program that you can use to test the setup as a whole. Here's another scenario to think about. One programmer I know of decided to simply send out a batch file and a disk full of application files as a package. He never even bothered to test the application since it was only going to be used in-house. It didn't take too long before the programmer started getting a rash of calls from disgruntled users. It seems that he forgot to add a crucial file to the disk, and the users who were actually able to figure out the batch file couldn't get the program to work. No one ever liked that application—even after the programmer added a nice-looking interface and an install program and fixed the bugs. The problem wasn't with the program; the problem was with the user's attitude toward the program. First impressions are crucial to a program's success.

As far as I'm concerned, it doesn't matter who'll use your application; you have to package it correctly before you send it out the door. Anything less is going to be an exercise in frustration to both you and the user alike. No one wants to buy half a car—likewise, no one wants half an application. Take the time to package it correctly, even if you're designing the application for other programmers or advanced users. Everyone deserves the benefits of an application that's completely functional.

I'd be remiss in my duties to you, then, if I didn't at least take a few minutes to tell you about packaging an application. That's what this chapter is all about. We'll take a look at what I consider the two most important factors in the first impression that a user develops for the application you write: understanding the various package types and creating an installation program to get the package delivered. I'll also take a look at some of the special factors that programmers should look at in various environments. For example, an in-house programmer will probably have a few concerns not shared by someone developing shareware.

 WEB LINK: We'll be using InstallShield 6 (the Free Edition provided with Visual C++ 6.0) in this chapter. You can find out about InstallShield 6 and a lot of other useful packaging products at **http://www.installshield.com/**. Unfortunately (at least as of this writing), you can't download the Free Edition of InstallShield 6 from its Web site. However, you can call (800) 374-4353 or (847) 240-9111 to find out about the Free Edition and obtain a copy of it.

Understanding Various Packaging Types

There are a lot of different considerations when it comes to creating a package to deliver your application in. The most important consideration for most developers is the environment you plan to use the application in. An in-house developer won't have the same concerns as someone who plans to deliver an application for use by someone else. For one thing, the in-house developer probably won't have much time to get an installation program together—time becomes a factor in most in-house situations.

In this section, we're going to look at the three most common types of installation environments: corporate, shareware, and shrink-wrap. You'll likely fall into one of the three categories, but you may want to look at the other categories as well since they contain a lot of helpful tips and hints. Some of you won't fall into a distinct category. For example, if you're a consultant, you are partly an in-house (corporate) developer since most of the applications you create are customized for a particular company. On the other hand, your clients are going to want a little more out of a consultant than something that works. They're going to want something around the level of a shareware package as a minimum (some clients will expect a shrink-wrap version of your product, but that's a little on the unreasonable side).

There are three basic levels of application packaging: corporate, shareware, and shrink-wrap.

Suffice it to say that figuring out what kind of packaging to provide can be a little tricky, but it's not impossible. All you really need to do is assess the needs of the people you're writing the application for. If all they're looking for is something that works well and doesn't include a lot of hype, then using the corporate packaging style is going to work just fine.

Corporate

Corporate programmers will have the least to do with the beautification of their packaging and the most to do with customizing it. Let's face it, the corporate programmer really doesn't have to impress anyone with fancy graphics or impressive sound effects. The fact that the interface is both functional and user-friendly is enough. Frankly, your boss may not look very favorably on any time spent making an installation program look beautiful, especially if you have a stack of other programming projects awaiting your attention.

On the other hand, the corporate program is most often engaged in creating a custom application. It's not all that uncommon for custom applications, especially database applications, to require the use of specialized files. You'll likely need custom registry entries and a wealth of other custom settings as well. Creating a custom installation program that is guaranteed to work on all the workstations in a corporate environment with little help from the programmer is quite an undertaking. Plan on spending a lot of time hand-tuning the standard installation program you can create with products like InstallShield.

Media is another place where most corporate installation programs will differ from the other two categories. It's still not unusual (though it's becoming more so) for a shareware or shrink-wrap application to come on floppies. Unless the company you're working for is living in the dark ages, you'll probably have a LAN at your disposal for distribution purposes. You can use this feature to your benefit when creating an application package. Simply select the most efficient storage method possible: a CD. You'll find that you can create and test your installation program a lot faster if you rely on a CD version of the package and use a LAN to distribute it.

TIP: InstallShield 6 Professional Edition comes with the capability to install an application over an intranet. Companies that occupy more than one building can simply extend the LAN distribution principle we're talking about here to distribute the application as widely as needed. Make sure you spend some time looking at the various distribution methods that InstallShield and other packaging applications provide before making the decision to commit your application to floppy or CD and distribute it manually. Using a LAN or intranet to distribute your application is almost always more efficient in the corporate setting than any other technique.

Once you've packaged your application on the LAN, simply add an instruction to the main logon batch file for your server to install the program. The next time the user logs on, your logon batch file will check to see if the application is installed. If not, it'll call the installation program that you've placed on the LAN.

TIP: The corporate setting is one place where using UNC paths in place of standard drive identifiers comes in very handy. Using a UNC path for the source directory ensures that everyone will be able to access all the required source files for your application without too much effort.

There are some other packaging issue suggestions you may want to consider for the corporate environment, though it's by no means certain that you'll actually be able to use all of them. The following list of ideas is meant simply to provide you with some things to think about when customizing your installation program. Whether they'll work in your particular situation depends on how your corporate structure is set up and on environmental factors like the availability of network connections for the user.

◆   *Centralized common file storage*   The standard procedure for distributing applications is to place all of the files on the user's machine. When you think about it, this is the only way to do things with shareware or shrink-wrap software. As a corporate programmer, though, you can choose to keep specific common files like DLLs on the file server instead of the user's machine. There are two benefits to this approach. First, you reduce the amount of space the application requires on the user machine. Second, you reduce the time required to update custom DLLs should the user find an error in it. All you have to replace is one copy of the DLL on the server. There are also two downsides to this approach. First, the user has to have a network connection to make the technique work at all. Second, you could end up increasing network traffic substantially if the DLL gets loaded and unloaded on a frequent basis.

◆   *Absolute preferences*   A shareware or shrink-wrap application author can't assume anything about the application environment—not a source or a destination for the various application files. The machine is a total mystery as well. In fact, even the operating system is a mystery in some cases. You don't have that problem. All you really need to do is worry about the differences between the machines on your network. If you set up all the machines about the same way, you could assume a default destination. Using UNC paths means that you can always assume an absolute source since the server path name won't change from installation to installation. You may even be able to assume a certain amount about the workstation itself if your network is small and all the machines have similar capabilities. In sum, all this means that you don't have to present the user with as many installation choices and can substantially reduce the complexity of the installation program. All it takes is a little preplanning on your part.

◆   *No configuration choices needed*   Just about every shrink-wrap program out there will offer you a choice between three installation configurations: Custom, Typical, and Compact. The Custom choice allows you to choose specific program elements; the Typical configuration is designed for desktop users; the Compact configuration is intended for people who own laptops. In most cases you can limit your configuration options to two choices: Laptop and Desktop. In fact, you may want to simply use those terms to keep user confusion to a minimum.

Shareware

Shareware programmers probably have the most challenging job when it comes to packaging their application. Consider one of the main problems for a shareware programmer: installation size. Unlike the corporate developer who has a high-speed network connection to use or a shrink-wrap developer who can distribute an application on CD, the shareware developer usually has to make do with a low-speed modem connection to a BBS, online service, or the Internet. Suffice it to say that if your application exceeds 1MB, the number of people downloading it is probably going to drop drastically.

NOTE: The file sizes in this section are meant as guidelines only. The amount of disk space or time that a potential user is willing to invest in your product depends on a good many factors like perceived value and the current level of exposure you have. For example, one of my favorite shareware graphics packages takes up a whopping 7MB of hard disk space and is well over 1MB in size when compressed. People still download it and set aside the space it requires because this program is well worth the investment. Since it has been around for a while, word of mouth tends to give people a reason to download this file as well. What you need to consider is whether most people would be willing to pay the price to use your application—it's something you'll have to learn by experience if you're serious about participating in the shareware market.

OK, so you're a little limited on space. How do you get around this problem? The key is in how you market your product. Most of the successful shareware products I've seen use the same key graphics and sounds over and over again. In other words, instead of coming up with one really fancy graphic for the installation program and a totally different graphic for the application itself, the shareware programmer is content to use the same graphic for both the installation program and the application. In fact, using subtle programming techniques could allow you to get away with using the application's icon (as we discuss in Chapter 3) in several places.

Can a shareware developer get by without fancy graphics or sounds like the corporate programmer does? Not likely. If you really want someone to pay for the application you've created, you'll need to add a little polish to it. No one will pay for something that looks drab, even if it does provide much-needed functionality. Obviously, trying to weight the space needed by a feature and the amount of pizzazz it provides will be difficult.

Another problem that a shareware developer is going to run into is one of resources. I know of many shareware developers who started out as one- or two-person shops. Many of these shops also deal with consulting jobs and other money-making ventures as they wait for a shareware product to hopefully take off. Suffice it to say that time isn't on your side, and it's unlikely you'll have a professional artist or sound person at your disposal to create the multimedia presentations provided by larger companies who create shrink-wrap applications. Most people are normally satisfied if they see a shareware product that's well designed, space conscious (consumes 5MB or less of hard disk space), and provides at least a modicum of polish.

We haven't yet discussed the biggest problem for shareware developers, and the installation program is the first place you have to deal with it. Corporate programmers have the most control over their environment by virtue of the fact that they have personal access to every machine that will use the program they create. Corporate developers can get by with a minimum of machine checks and configuration options. Shrink-wrap developers come next. At least they can print a set of requirements on the box to ensure no one will use their application without sufficient hardware. The fact that users are paying for the application tends to increase their awareness of the hardware requirements for installing it. The shareware developer has no such guarantees. A user of your program could have just about any kind of machine ever made—even an old 8088 PC.

Corporate programmers have the most control over the application environment; shareware developers have the least.

What does this lack of control mean? First, you'll have to build extra detection routines in your installation program to ensure that minimum hardware requirements are met. Users will rarely read the README file you provide (the one stating the minimum requirements for using the application), and they are even less likely to pay attention to them if they do. When the installation fails, you can be sure the user is going to blame you, not his or her own lack of attention span. As a result, you've got to build in some type of detection. You'll also need to build flexibility into your application with regard to configuration. For example, you may decide to allow the user to configure the application for text mode only and forgo those fancy graphics or sounds on an older-technology machine.

T IP: The installation program is a good place to sell your shareware product if you have the time and resources to design it properly. Make sure users understand what they'll get in return for buying your product. In other words, since you have a captive audience during the installation process, you may as well use the time to sell your program.

Just like anyone else, the shareware developer does have a few tricks up his or her sleeve to make setting up the installation program easier. While the following list isn't inclusive of everything you could try, it does provide some

16

ideas on what could work. You'll need to try out a variety of packaging techniques with your application before you finally come up with something that works all of the time.

◆ *Granular packaging*   One of the ways to get around the hard disk space and download-time problems for a shareware developer is to package your application in several pieces. For example, you could place the main program in one package, the graphics in another, and the sounds in a third package. The result is that users can choose what level of support they're willing to pay for with regard to download time and hard disk space. This concept doesn't come without a price, though. You have to write your application so that it can work without the graphics and sounds (or whatever elements you decide to place in a separate package). Your installation program has to provide similar flexibility. It has to know what do to if a user decides to download one packaging element but not another.

◆ *Amplified help*   We discuss the idea of creating separate packages for help files in Chapter 15. One of the ways you can do this is to make a main and an amplifying help file. The main help file would contain explanations for basic commands, while the amplifying help file could contain user tutorials, macro language descriptions, and detailed command descriptions. Again, the user could decide what level of help to pay for in the form of download time and disk space. You could also use this feature to your benefit. A shareware package is never guaranteed to sell. Making such a large investment in time without any guarantee of a payback is difficult, to say the least. Using this approach would allow you to make a smaller initial investment until you could see whether a particular shareware product is worth fleshing out.

TIP: There are more than a few shareware companies that have used modularized programs to enhance sales. For example, ButtonWare usually provided a simple help file and most of the features for a shareware application when a user downloaded it. Buying the application entitled the user to download the full-featured program and complete program documentation. Many people are upset by what they call "crippleware" because it doesn't allow them to fully test the application before they buy. Unfortunately, unless a shareware developer provides the user with a good reason to buy its product, most people won't. (You can test the veracity of this statement anytime by looking at the number of shareware companies that die due to a lack of sales even if downloads for their products are brisk.)

Shrink-Wrap

I'm not going to pretend to tell a company like Microsoft how to market or package its product—the effects of its sales force are already legendary and I doubt that I can do much to help out. One of the things that usually sets a shrink-wrap product apart from shareware is the size of the company producing the application. Larger software companies usually concentrate on one or more products, and they have a large professional group of people to help put the packaging together. However, there are a few things that the average programmer can learn by looking at these shrink-wrap packages.

During the past few months, I have taken notes whenever I installed a shrink-wrap or shareware product. After installing about 30 products, I decided to take a look over my notes. The results were surprising in some cases. For example, the previous section mentions using the installation program as a means to sell your product if you're a shareware vendor, since you have a captive audience and fewer sales resources at your disposal. It may surprise you to find that shrink-wrap software commonly uses the installation program for this very purpose but in a different way than a shareware vendor would use it. The user has already purchased the product he or she is installing, but how about add-on products? Shrink-wrap vendors commonly use the installation program to sell some add-on product that relates to the application the user is installing (one example is an extended dictionary for a word processor).

Another thing I noticed is that shrink-wrap software commonly tells the user what's new about the program during the installation process. It doesn't surprise me too much, since the shrink-wrap companies must have figured out long ago that most users don't read the README file and the installation program is usually the last part of the product to get finished. Again, the shrink-wrap vendor has a captive audience, so it uses the installation program to give users an overview of what they would learn if they'd actually read the README file.

It should come as no surprise that the shrink-wrap installation programs are usually packed with all kinds of multimedia presentation materials. After all, the shrink-wrap vendor has the resources required to produce such a display. Even if you don't have the resources to duplicate the presentation provided by a shrink-wrap vendor, you can make notes as I have to figure out what works and what doesn't. Providing a smaller version of the same type of presentation in your installation program is a sure way to make it look more polished. Remember that you want to give users the best possible impression of your product from the outset to ensure they enjoy working with it. Creating a nice-looking installation program won't do a single thing to make your application work better, but it'll affect the user's perception of your application, which is a very important part of getting the user up and running with a minimum of support.

There are some negative lessons you can learn from shrink-wrap vendors as well. One of the best things I learned was that you can make your installation program too complex to test thoroughly. I recently tried installing one product and found that the help screens for the program were for the previous version. The vendor had forgotten to update the screens as needed for the new version of its product. The result? Since the product didn't come with any printed documentation either, I didn't have a clue as to whether I should install certain product features. If the vendor had taken a few minutes to fully test the installation program, I would have had all the information needed to make an informed decision about which product features to install.

Another very strange problem occurred when the product failed to install at all. It seems that the installation program used special graphics that relied on a product feature that was incompatible with the machine I was using. Moving the product to another machine where the installation program worked just fine showed that the product would work, even though the installation program wouldn't. Again, the vendor decided to add some really neat special effects to the detriment of the program as a whole.

As you can see from this section, looking at what other people are doing in the way of packaging a product can save you time and effort when it comes to packaging your own product. I find that taking notes and then reading them right before I write my installation program keeps me from making as many mistakes. (Very few people get an installation program right the first time around.)

Gathering the Files

Never get the idea that you can just slap an installation program together in a few seconds without doing any research. Any program that runs in the Windows environment is a lot more complicated than even the programmer realizes in most cases. For example, all of the examples in this book have relied on the C run-time files. Yet I've never mentioned adding these files to your application code, nor have you seen them referenced in any of the source code. That's because these files are automatically added to your SYSTEM folder when you install Visual C++ in the first place. You don't need to know about them while you design your application because their inclusion is automatic. The same can be said of the MFC file and those required for database applications. In most cases Visual C++ takes care of these file additions for you without much, if any, thought on your part.

However, now you're trying to put everything needed to run your application into a package for the user. At this point in the product development cycle you no longer have the luxury of ignoring those other files—they're part of your application and must be included with the package you send to the user. The problem is figuring out which files to include with your program.

Figuring out which DLLs you need to ship with your application can be a time-consuming task, especially if you resort to using trial and error to figure things out. However, there are three methods you can use to take some of the trial and error out of the process.

◆   *Method 1*   You could use the Windows QuickView utility to view the Import Table entries for your application. The Import Table list tells you which DLLs your application relies on. Here's an example of a QuickView list for the Sngl_Doc example that we looked at in Chapters 2, 3, and 15. Notice that it shows not only which files your application uses but the function within those files as well.

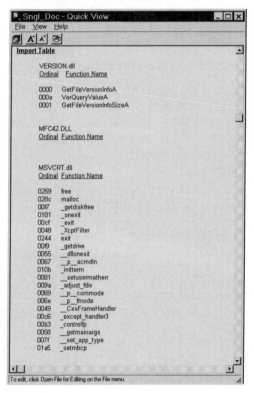

◆ *Method 2* The DumpBin utility can give you a DOS command line view of the requirements of your application. I've found that DumpBin is a little more trouble to use, but it often finds information hidden from the QuickView utility. You'll also find that it offers more options when it comes to the kinds of information you want to find. All you need to type at the command line to use this program is DUMPBIN /IMPORTS SNGL_DOC.EXE. Here's what the output of this program looks like (it's a command line utility).

```
MS-DOS Prompt - MORE                                          _ □ ×
Microsoft (R) COFF Binary File Dumper Version 6.00.8047
Copyright (C) Microsoft Corp 1992-1998. All rights reserved.

Dump of file sngl_doc.exe

File Type: EXECUTABLE IMAGE

  Section contains the following imports:

    VERSION.dll
               41C248 Import Address Table
               41B944 Import Name Table
                    0 time date stamp
                    0 Index of first-forwarder reference

                 1  GetFileVersionInfoSizeA
                 0  GetFileVersionInfoA
                 A  VerQueryValueA

    MFC42D.DLL
               41B9B4 Import Address Table
               41B0B0 Import Name Table
                    0 time date stamp
-- More --
```

TIP: You may get a missing-file message when using the DumpBin utility. Both the MSDIS100.DLL and MSPDB50.DLL files are located in the Program Files/DevStudio/SharedIDE/bin directory on your machine (assuming you've used the default settings during installation). You need both of these files along with the LINK.EXE found in the VC/bin directory to make the DumpBin program work.

◆ *Method 3* If you have the latest version of the Windows SDK, you'll find the Depends utility, which you can use to get the DLL requirements for your program.

Getting a list of files that your executable uses directly isn't the end of the process. You'll also need to check the DLLs it uses for any dependencies they may have as well. Obviously, you can ignore files like USER.EXE since the user will have them installed as part of Windows itself, but you'll need to watch for files that may not have been installed. In short, you'll manually check each file for its dependencies and then include those files with your application.

TIP: Check a clean machine for a list of files that Windows provides by default. You may want to maintain a list of these files for later reference if you plan on creating more than one installation program.

Once you have a complete list of the files you need for your application, gather them all into one place. Copy this set of files to a newly installed version of Windows (whichever version your application is targeting). Test your application to make sure it works. You'll get messages if either you're missing a file or it needs to go into the SYSTEM folder. Make sure you keep track of the files you place in the SYSTEM folder because you'll have to place them there on the user's machine as well.

NOTE: Always try to keep all of the DLLs for your application in the application folder instead of automatically placing them in the SYSTEM folder. Keeping everything in one place will help you uninstall the program later should the user want to remove it from his or her machine. You'll also find that you have fewer problems with corruption from other programs that the user installs—for example, when a DLL you need to run your application gets overwritten by an older version of the same DLL used by another application.

Creating an Installation Program

At this point, you should have figured out how you want to package your application, which includes deciding on a packaging model like corporate, shareware, or shrink-wrap. You should also have a complete list of the files needed to run your application. Make sure your file list includes specific installation areas for each file. For example, you'll want to note which files you have to install in the SYSTEM folder. Finally, you should have tested your application and associated files on a clean machine—one that has had only Windows installed. It doesn't pay to start writing an installation program until you're certain you have included all of the files it requires and that the setup works as anticipated on a clean machine.

NOTE: This section relies on the version of InstallShield provided with Visual C++ 6.0. Earlier versions of Visual C++ may not have this version of InstallShield, which means you'll probably need to modify the procedures in this section to meet your needs. Even if you are using the same version of InstallShield outlined in the book, you may see slightly different screens or have a few different options depending on the application you're trying to package. In short, it's not going to be too unusual to see a few variations from what I'm presenting here when you're using InstallShield. You will need to install the InstallShield product—it's located in the IShield directory on your Visual C++ 6.0 CD. The procedures in this section assume you've already installed the InstallShield product on your hard drive.

So far, we've added resources (Chapter 3) and a help file (Chapter 15) to the Sngl_Doc application we created in Chapter 2. Now it's time to package this application to send to someone else—well, at least for example purposes. The following procedure is going to show you how to put a typical installation program together. We won't do anything really fancy; the whole idea is to get the application ready to send to someone else. If you were to pick a specific packaging model for this example, it's very close to the corporate packaging technique that we talked about earlier.

We'll cover a generic installation program in this section; you'll need to modify it to meet the needs of your particular application and installation environment.

1. Start the InstallShield 6 Free Edition program. You'll see a window similar to the one shown in Figure 16-1. Notice that we don't have any project defined but there is an Installation Wizard entry in the Projects window. This window doesn't look precisely like the one in Visual C++, but as the procedure goes on you'll notice certain similarities that tend to ease the installation program creation process. Notice also the InstallShield link in the lower-right corner. Clicking it will open your browser and take you to the InstallShield online help site on the Internet.

2. Double-click on the Project Wizard icon in the Projects window. You'll see a Project Wizard - Welcome dialog similar to the one shown here.

The Professional Edition of InstallShield offers advanced features on the Welcome (and other) page—make sure you read about the enhancements in the help file.

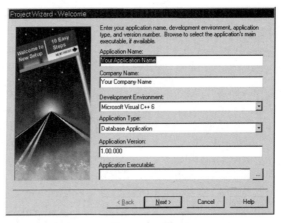

3. Type the name of your application. The example program uses Single Document Application Example.

The Free Edition of InstallShield provides only one Development Environment field entry: Microsoft Visual C++ 6.

4. Type your company name. The example program uses A Sample Company.

5. Choose one of the entries in the Application Type field. The example program uses Software Development Application—there isn't a standard utility program type, and the Software Development Application type does allow for utility programs.

InstallShield allows you to create an installation program using techniques similar to those you've already used in Visual C++ to create your application.

Figure 16-1.

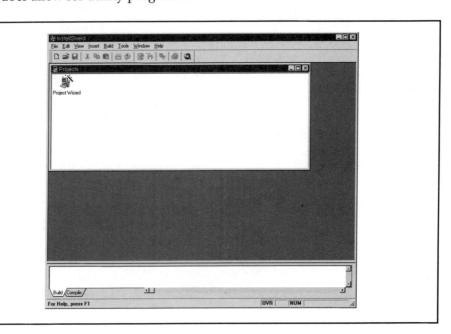

6. Type the application version number in the Application Version field. Our example program uses 1.0, but you can use any numbering scheme consistent with your company policies.

7. Click the ... (ellipsis) button next to the Application Executable field. You'll see a standard Open dialog that you can use to find the application you want to package on your hard drive. The sample application uses SNGL_DOC.EXE (the one in the Resource folder that we created in Chapter 3 and modified in Chapter 15).

8. Click Next. You'll see a Project Wizard - Choose Dialogs dialog like the one shown here.

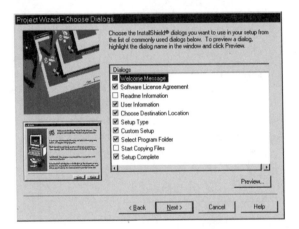

This is where you'll choose the series of dialogs that the user will see when installing your application. Since we're using the corporate model for our installation program, I unchecked the Software License Agreement, Setup Type, and Custom Setup dialogs. You'd choose some or all of these dialogs for the other packaging models we discussed earlier in this chapter. There are a few things you should notice about this particular dialog. First, look in the lower-left corner as you move from one dialog entry to the next. You'll see that the Project Wizard gives you a thumbnail view of the dialog in question to make it easier to determine whether you actually want it. Highlighting a dialog and then clicking the Preview button will display a dialog that looks exactly like the one the user will see. Obviously, you'll be able to modify this dialog later, but it helps to know what you're starting with.

9. Choose which dialogs you want to add to the installation program, and then click Next. You'll see a Project Wizard - Choose Target Platforms dialog like the one shown here.

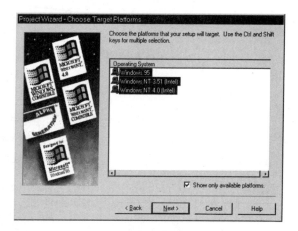

It's educational
to uncheck the
Show Only
Available
platforms
checkbox to see
all of the
choices offered
by the
Professional
Edition of
InstallShield.

Since we want to be able to install our program on any of the supported programs, we won't have to make any changes. However, there may be situations where you'll want to be a little more selective. Reducing the number of supported platforms accomplishes two things. First, it reduces the size of the installation program you create—a real plus for shareware developers who are short on space to begin with. Second, it reduces the chance that someone will try to use your program under the wrong version of Windows—a real plus for any developer.

10. Select one or more platforms as needed (but at least one), and then click Next. You'll see a Project Wizard - Specify Languages dialog like the one shown here.

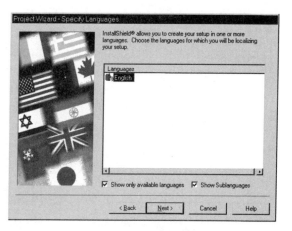

Since the Free Edition only supports one language, we don't have to make any changes here. Like other selections you've had to make so far, more is not necessarily better. Adding languages will increase the size of the installation program and could add user confusion as well; choose only the languages you need.

11. Highlight one or more languages (but at least one), and then click Next. You'll see a Project Wizard - Specify Setup Types dialog like the one shown here.

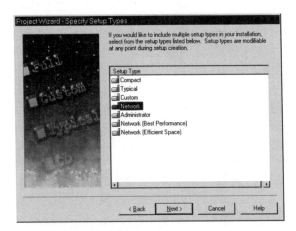

Since we're using the corporate packaging model, I've already chosen the Network setup type. Other packaging models will require you to make other selections, including the most common of all: Custom, Typical, and Compact. It's interesting to note that InstallShield does offer a wealth of other choices, though.

12. Choose one or more setup types, and then click Next. You'll see a Project Wizard - Specify Components dialog like the one shown here.

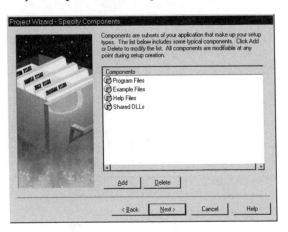

The Project Wizard doesn't assume anything about the components you want to install. The example program uses Program Files, Shared DLLs, and Help Files. You'll need to choose each of these options one at a time to define the files that go under each component type. A component type is a definition of a major program area. For example, the user may want to include all of the sample files but none of the help files. A component type doesn't necessarily define which files you'll need to perform the task, simply that the task is a separate entity that the user could either choose to install or perhaps that needs to be installed in a different directory from the rest of the files.

TIP: You can add new component types as needed to your installation program. For example, you might need to add a Database File component if you've written a database application. All you have to do is click the Add button, and the Project Wizard will add the new entry for you. Type the name of the component, and press ENTER to complete the addition process.

13. Highlight Example Files, and then click Delete. Project Wizard will remove this component type from our installation program.

14. Add or delete component types as needed, and then click Next. You'll see a Project Wizard - Specify File Groups dialog like the one shown here.

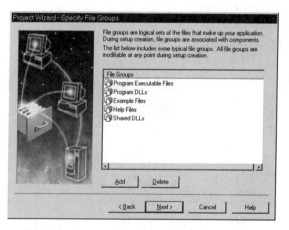

Our example program uses Program Executable Files, Help Files, and Shared DLLs. Normally you'll create file groups so that all of the files needed for a specific task are copied at one time. File groups can cross component-type boundaries. For example, say the spell checker and the grammar checker both rely on the same set of DLLs but require different

rule files. You could define a common file group for the DLLs and two
other file groups for the rule files. If the user selected the spell checker
but not the grammar checker, InstallShield would copy the spell checker
file group and the common DLL file group but not the grammar
checker file group.

15. Highlight Program DLLs, and then click Delete. Highlight Example Files,
and then click Delete. We've just eliminated the two file groups that we
won't need for the example program. Obviously, the selection of file
groups will depend on how your application is put together and where
you need to copy the files. Remember that all the files in one file group
will go to the same directory on the hard drive.

16. Add or delete file groups as needed, and then click on Next. You'll see a
Project Wizard - Summary dialog like the one shown here. At this point
you should check the list of options to make sure everything is correct
before you ask the Project Wizard to build the installation program
for you.

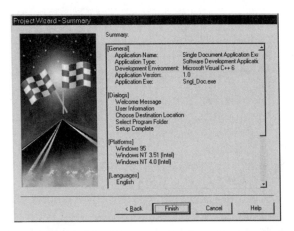

17. Click Finish. InstallShield will create the installation program using the
parameters you've just specified. At this point the InstallShield interface
will change as shown in Figure 16-2. Notice that you can now see the
C++ code required to create the installation program and that you can
modify it just like you would any other project.

NOTE: Don't get the idea that InstallShield generates source files that
are precisely like the ones used in a general project. There are some ancillary
files that you haven't seen in the past like the setup rule (SETUP.RUL) file
shown in Figure 16-2.

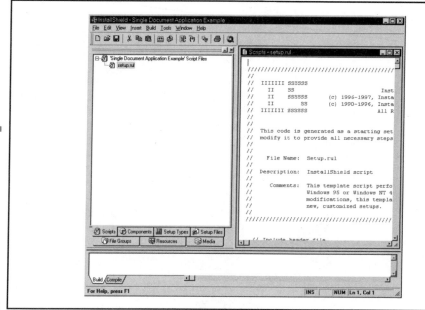

Once you've
created a
project,
InstallShield
will generate it
for you and
then display
the resulting
source code.

Figure 16-2.

At this point you should have a barely usable installation program shell.
There's still quite a bit of configuration to do, though, and we'll look at all of
it in the sections that follow. The important thing to realize is that you'll
write very little code during this process—InstallShield will do most of the
work for you as you define the various program elements.

WEB LINK: If you've still got questions about how to use InstallShield
after reading this section, there are a couple of ways to find out more
information. This is one of those times where it really pays to look in the
product README file, because it contains links to a lot of places you need to
know about on the Internet. For example, you'll find a link to the newsgroups
site at **http://support.installshield.com/newsgroups/default.asp**.
This site contains links to several InstallShield-specific newsgroups. Just
clicking one of the links will create a new folder in your newsreader containing
the newsgroup you wanted to look at. There's even a special newsgroup for the
Free Edition at **installshield.is5.free-edition**. You'll also find links for
newsgroups covering things like the IDE, scripting, and the use of multimedia.
In short, these newsgroups provide you with the contacts you need with other
developers interested in finding solutions to packaging their applications
successfully.

Setting Up the Components

16

The first task we'll need to accomplish is setting up the various components. Remember that a component is a selection that appears during the installation. If you've ever used the custom install feature of an installation program, then you know what a component is. It's the series of checkboxes that allow you to choose whether you want to install a particular program feature like the help files.

Configuring the components for your installation program is fairly easy. Click on the Components tab and you'll see a Components - Program Files dialog like the one shown here.

The components dialog contains a complete list of all the values for the selected component. Remember that we have three components in this case: Program Files, Help Files, and Shared DLLs. It's important to set up all three before you go to the next section. Double-click on the Description property and you'll see a Properties dialog like the one shown here.

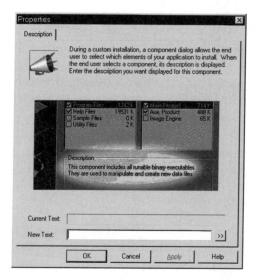

All of the other properties will show similar dialogs. Each Properties dialog will describe what you're supposed to do with this particular property. It will also allow you to type in a value for the property. In this case, type **All the files required to run the application.** and then click OK. The Description property will now contain the text you just typed.

You don't need to change all of the component properties—what you do need to change depends on the kind of application package you're creating. For example, in our corporate model installation, we don't ever allow the user to choose the components that get installed, so providing a component description is pointless. The user won't ever see it anyway. There are some properties that you should consider changing regardless of the packaging model you're using, and the following list looks at each one.

◆ *Status Text*   This is the text that the user will see while the installation program copies the files from the source to the destination. The Progress dialog will say something like "Copying program files...", which works fine for default components. You may want to define something special for custom components.

◆ *Installation*   If you've ever been annoyed by the fact that some program came along and copied over the new DLLs you just installed with really old ones that don't work, then you'll know why this property is important. It tells InstallShield whether you want to look at the time and date stamp on the component files first before you overwrite them. I always choose NEWERVERSION/NEWERDATE or SAMEORNEWERVERSION/SAMEORNEWERDATE instead of the default ALWAYSOVERWRITE. In essence, these options tell InstallShield to only overwrite a file if the source has both a newer (or same) date and a newer (or same) version than the one on the user's hard drive.

◆ *Destination* The standard destination for all of your application files is the target directory, the one the user chose for the program. However, there are some circumstances where using the target directory won't work like it should or could waste space on the user's machine. For example, most Visual C++ applications require the C run-time files and the MFC files. What if every application you installed added these files to a program directory instead of a centralized place? It wouldn't take very long to fill a hard drive with useless files. In most cases you'll probably want to copy your Shared DLLs component files to the Windows SYSTEM folder. All you need to do is change this property. (When you open the Property dialog, you'll see a map of the various locations you can use for copying the file; just choose the one you want.)

◆ *Required Components* This is where you'll set up dependencies between components as shown here. What I'm telling InstallShield in this case is that if the user installs the Program Files component, he or she must install the Shared DLLs component as well (which only makes sense since without the Shared DLLs, the program won't run).

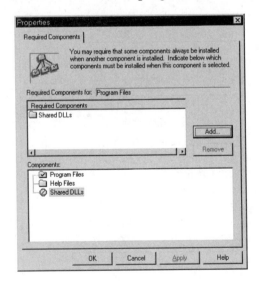

TIP: Pay special attention to the FTP Location and HTTP Location properties if you plan to install your application from an Internet or intranet site. These properties will allow a user to start the installation from a Web site link and then copy the needed files from your Web server. You would normally choose the FTP Location property if the files were under the control of the FTP server.

There's one last item that you absolutely must take care of to configure the components. Look at the Included File Groups property. Right now we haven't assigned any to the Program Files (or any other) component. Double-click on this property and you'll see a Properties dialog like the one shown here.

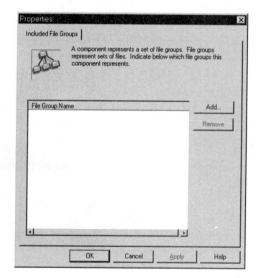

This Properties dialog contains a complete list of the file groups assigned to a particular component. Remember that I previously talked about an example where you might want to make the spell checker and grammar checker optional components of your installation. They both use the same DLLs but require different rule files. I mentioned setting up three file groups: one with the spelling rule file, another with the grammar rule file, and a third with the common DLLs needed by both. This is the property where you set up that relationship. Click on the Add button and you'll see an Add File Group dialog like the one shown here.

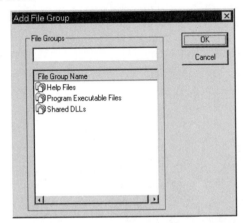

As you can see, the Add File Group dialog contains the three file groups we defined using the Project Wizard. You'll need to make the following assignments between components and file groups before going on in the chapter. Table 16-1 shows the settings I used for the example program.

Component	Property	Value
Program Files	Description	All the files required to run the application.
	Status Text	Copying Program Files...
	Overwrite	SAMEORNEWERVERSION/ SAMEORNEWERDATE
	Required Components	Shared DLLs
	Included File Groups	Program Executable Files
Help Files	Description	Files that show you how to use the program.
	Status Text	Copying Help Files...
	Overwrite	SAMEORNEWERDATE
	Included File Groups	Help Files

Component Settings for the Sngl_Doc Installation Program

Table 16-1.

Component
Settings for the
Sngl_Doc
Installation
Program
(*continued*)

Table 16-1.

Component	Property	Value
Shared DLLs	Description	Common files used by the program.
	Status Text	Copying Shared DLLs...
	Overwrite	SAMEORNEWERVERSION/ SAMEORNEWERDATE
	Destination	<WINSYSDIR>
	Included File Groups	Shared DLLs

Setting Up File Groups

Creating a set of components doesn't help the installation program very
much. You've told the user what components can be copied to the hard
drive, but you still haven't told the installation program what those files are.
This is the step where you do that. We'll define a set of files for each of the
file groups that we defined previously.

The first thing you'll need to do is click on the File Groups tab. What you'll
see is a list of the file groups and the File Groups dialog shown in Figure 16-3.
Choosing which file group you want to configure is easy. Just click on its
entry in the File Groups window on the left side of the display.

Click on the plus sign (+) next to the Help Files folder in the File Groups
window. Click on the Links entry under the Help Files folder and you'll see
the File Groups - Help Files\Links dialog shown here. This is where you'll
define a list of one or more files to include for this file group.

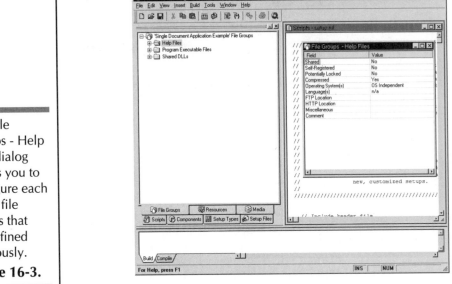

The File Groups - Help Files dialog allows you to configure each of the file groups that we defined previously.

Figure 16-3.

Right-click on the File Groups - Help Files\Links dialog and choose Insert Files from the context menu. You'll see a standard File Open-type dialog. Find the Sngl_Doc.HLP file that we created in Chapter 15. Click OK to add this file to the Help Files file group. You'll need to add the Sngl_Doc.EXE file to the Program Executable Files file group. The last file group, Shared DLLs, requires that you add the following list of files: MFC42.DLL and MSVCRT.DLL. You'll find these files in the Windows SYSTEM folder.

Defining Resources

By this time you should have the components and the file groups set up. What we need to do now is provide some identification information for the users. After all, they'll want to know a little something about the program they're installing. Click on the Resources tab and you'll see the Resources window shown in Figure 16-4. This same window contains two dialogs: Resources - String Table and Resources - String Table\English. The resources we want to change are in the Resources - String Table\English dialog.

Most of the changes we'll make in the Resources - String Table\English dialog won't affect the program at all. We're making them for identification

InstallShield uses resources in about the same way as Visual C++ does.

Figure 16-4.

purposes or to help the user in some way. Changing one of the resource values is much the same as changing a property in one of the other dialogs. All you need to do is double-click on the Identifier you want to change, and InstallShield will display a dialog that allows you to make the required change. Here's an example of the COMPANY_NAME identifier.

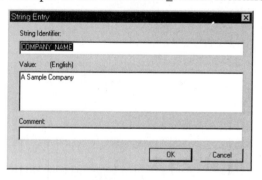

Table 16-2 shows the changes I made for the example program—obviously, many of the strings will be different for your installation program.

16

Identifier	Value
COMPANY_NAME	A Sample Company
PRODUCT_KEY	Sngl_Doc.EXE
PRODUCT_NAME	Single Document Application Example
UNINST_DISPLAY_NAME	Single Document Application Example
UNINST_KEY	Sngl_Doc.EXE

Determining a Media Type

We've come to the very last thing you must do from a configuration perspective: simply tell InstallShield what type of media you want to use for distributing your application. In most cases you'll use CD as the main distribution method and may decide to use floppies as a secondary method if the application is small enough. If your only distribution method is going to be CD, you're done. Otherwise, choose the Media tab. You'll see a Media dialog and window like the ones shown in Figure 16-5.

The Media tab allows you to define something other than CD as your distribution media.

Figure 16-5.

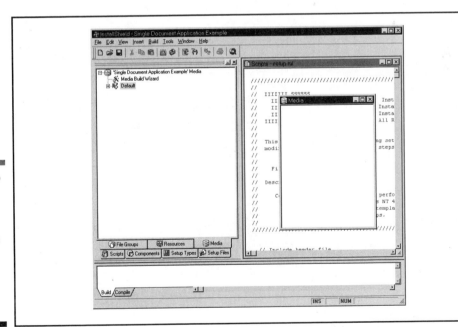

As you can see, the CD media is already in place (as shown by the CD folder in Figure 16-5). You'll need to use the Media Build Wizard to add another media to your installation program. The following procedure will take you through the steps required to add a floppy media type.

1. Click on this entry and you'll see the Media Build Wizard - Media Name dialog shown here.

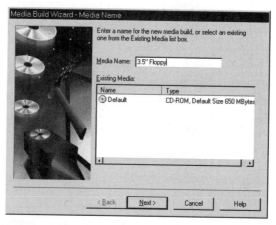

2. Type **3.5" Floppy**, and then click Next. You'll see the Media Build Wizard - Disk Type dialog shown here. Notice that InstallShield supports a wide variety of media types including 2.88MB floppies.

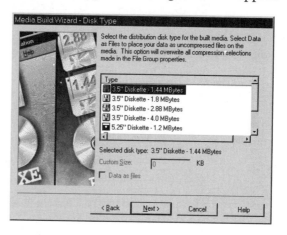

3. Highlight the 3.5" Diskette - 1.44 MBytes option, and then click Next. You'll see the Media Build Wizard - Build Type dialog shown here.

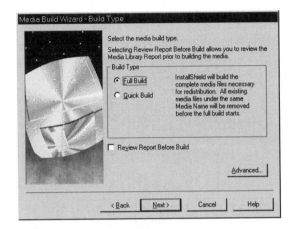

A full build will compress all the files for your application, create the required CAB files, and create the full-fledged installation program. The Quick Build option is designed for testing purposes. It allows you to see if your installation program works as anticipated.

4. Choose the Full Build option, and then click Next. You'll see the Media Build Wizard - Tag File dialog shown here. All this dialog does is allow you to enter your company name and associated application information.

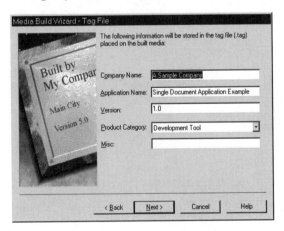

5. Type all the required information into the dialog. The example program uses ABC Corporation in the Company Name field, Single Document Application Example in the Application Name field, Word Processor in the Product Category field and Utility Style Text Editor in the Misc. field.

6. Click Next. You'll see a Media Build Wizard - Platforms dialog like the one shown here.

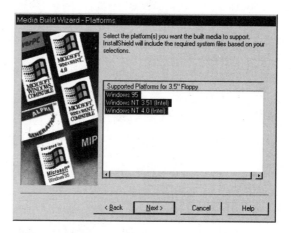

7. Click Next. You'll see a Media Build Wizard Summary dialog like the one shown here. This is your last chance to verify the settings you've used.

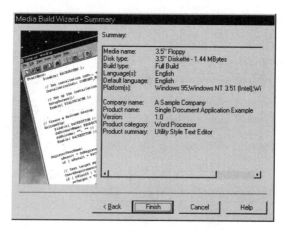

8. Verify your settings, and then click Finish. InstallShield will create the new build that you requested.

NOTE: The Free Edition of InstallShield may present an error message at this point saying that it doesn't have enough memory to create the requested build. Ignore the problem and try setting up the build again. If you still can't get it to work, complete the rest of the chapter using the default build setting. What you'll need to do is right-click on the Default folder and choose Media Build Wizard from the context menu. Choose the Default option on the first screen of the Media Build Wizard dialog, and then click Next until you get to the final screen where you got the error before. Click Finish and InstallShield will create the media for you.

16

At this point you'll see a Building Media dialog. InstallShield is actually creating your installation program for you. When the process is complete, your Building Media dialog should look like the one shown here. Just click the Finish button and you're finished!

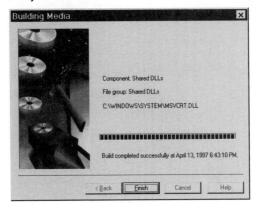

PART V

Appendixes

APPENDIX A

ActiveX and OCX Component Resources

ActiveX components fulfill a variety of purposes. In fact, that's the underlying purpose for Part 3 of this book. It shows you how to create your own components to perform just about any kind of work that you can think of, both on the Internet and within applications. (Obviously, we had to explore some related areas like scripting as well for Internet use of components.) Some people are under the mistaken impression that most components help you manage graphics better, provide file support, or act as some kind of utility. Nothing could be further from the truth. You can buy third-party components as varied as the kinds of applications that you write. Without a doubt, you'll find a component somewhere that does just about anything you need it to—in some cases, you might be surprised at just how varied those components actually are.

This appendix tells you how to find just the right component and looks at some of the third-party components available on the market. You'll probably find most of these products in the Visual Basic section of your favorite computer store or programmer's catalog, though many companies are beginning to realize that ActiveX components are for C programmers, too. This appendix isn't complete by any means—it merely shows a selection of ActiveX components from a variety of vendors. That way, if you don't see what you need, you can always contact one of the vendors listed here to see if they can provide the component you need.

 NOTE: Some of the products in this appendix are from other countries, such as England and Canada. In some cases developers in the United States may want to try to purchase the products locally instead of relying on an overseas vendor. Pinnacle Publishing, Inc. also markets many of these products. You can contact them at the following locations (the Web site is fairly new and may not provide information on every product the company handles—if you don't see what you want, give them a call):

Pinnacle Publishing, Inc.
P.O. Box 888
Kent, WA 98035-0888
Voice: (800) 231-1293
Fax: (206) 251-5057
Internet: http://www.pinpub.com

A

How to Get the Best Deal

Choosing a component can be a difficult task. How do you know one component is better than another when the descriptions provided by the vendors that produce them are almost identical? In addition, other features such as royalty rates could make a big difference in the way you view a component. Let's look at some of the criteria you should use when selecting a component. The following sections provide a list of things you might want to look for in addition to functionality. This list isn't all-inclusive (some people may have criteria that are unique to their situation), but you'll find that these kinds of considerations will help you make an informed buying decision. The important point is that this list will help you choose between a component that provides a lot of really nice features and one that is best suited to your needs.

WEB LINK: There are a lot of places to look for ActiveX components that'll meet your needs; some of them allow you to download a demo version of the product. The first place you'll want to check out is a site showing the ActiveX components offered by Microsoft and its partners: **http:/www.microsoft.com/com/gallery/default.htm**. You'll need Internet Explorer to use this site, since Microsoft doesn't include the tags required for using the NCompass plug-in with Netscape Navigator. One of the nice things about the Microsoft site is that the vendors will usually tell you in advance where a control will work. You'll also want to check out **http://www.davecentral.com**. Dave Central provides a list of VRML (Virtual Reality Modeling Language) controls—among others, like the more mundane video controls. The site provides a description of the controls plus links to a home page that shows it in use and a link to the control download site. The TegoSoft Home Page at **http://www.activex3d.com/** has quite a few interesting links, including one for 3-D ActiveX components.

Royalties

Some companies charge a royalty when you use their product for commercial purposes. If you plan to use their product in your application and then sell your application to other people, you may have to pay the company royalties to maintain the licensing arrangement. Always look first for products that don't charge a royalty. That way you don't have to worry about licensing the product at all. If you don't find one in this category, start looking for an OEM licensing arrangement. Sometimes you can get by with an annual fee or other "one-shot" licensing scheme. Obviously, using a product that requires a royalty will also increase the price of your product, so looking around for a royalty-free product is always a good idea.

Source Code

There is that rare breed of components you can buy with some level of source code support. Some of them will require an additional purchase to get the source. If you're a professional consultant or someone who distributes applications commercially, the cost of buying that source is minimal compared to what you'll gain by having it. Not only will having the source allow you to learn new programming techniques, but you can use it to enhance the component you've purchased. Needless to say, source code is a rarity when buying an ActiveX component, but you do see it offered. Normally, you'll need to know C to use the source code.

Recommendations from Other Programmers

Most of you have probably been bitten by a piece of software that was so buggy and ill conceived it was unusable. Unfortunately, the companies that produce this kind of software are usually good at marketing and offer just about everything you can imagine without delivering anything of the sort. It doesn't take most programmers very long to figure out that they should have gotten a few recommendations from other people before they bought the product. You should, too. Someone has usually purchased a product that you're thinking about buying. See if you can get a few opinions before you buy.

Demo or Shareware Versions

There are times when you can't get a recommendation from another programmer. Perhaps no one has used the product in the same way that you intend to use it. In this case, finding a demo or shareware version of the product that you want to use can save you a lot of grief later. Sure, it won't be full-featured, and some vendors actually make the shareware or demo version hide flaws in the full-featured product, but it's better than buying the product without even viewing it first. If you do try a shareware or demo version, see if other programmers have tried both the demo and final product. The feedback they provide will help you understand how the shareware or demo version of the product varies from what you'll actually buy.

TIP: Just about every product listed in this appendix includes the address of an online service. You'll find that most vendors place press releases and demonstration copies of their product on their Web site or forum. Make sure you spend the money to visit these sites before you buy a product. The visit may not only net a demo version of a product for you but also give you insights into the kind of support you can expect from the vendor.

Money-Back Guarantee

Vendors are getting smarter as the software industry matures. It's surprising to see how many offer a 30- to 60-day money-back guarantee with their product these days. (At least one of the vendors in this appendix offers a whopping 90-day money-back guarantee.) What you'll need to find out first, though, are the terms of that money-back guarantee. Make sure you can try the product out on a small project or two and return it if it doesn't work as advertised. You'll also need to check the return policy of the third-party vendor you buy a product through. In a few cases, vendors haven't honored their money-back guarantee because a programmer bought the product through a third party. Since the third-party seller didn't have a money-back guarantee either, the programmer ended up eating the cost of the purchase.

Company Stability and Support

Programmers rely on vendors to provide them with good updates on a fairly regular basis to remain competitive. If the one-man shop you buy your component from goes out of business tomorrow, how will you support the product you build with it? The problem doesn't only extend to practical matters like new technology; you'll need that support when a customer calls in with a bug that isn't in your code. You'll find that interactions between your program and a third-party product happen more often than you'd like. If the company you're working with goes out of business or charges by the minute for support, you may be out of luck when it comes time to fix that bug the user reported.

Cost-per-Component Versus Quality

Some vendors in this appendix offer a grab bag of all kinds of components at a very low cost. Be aware that those components may or may not be the best quality. Think about your own business. Could you afford to offer a lot of product for a low cost if it took a lot of time to put the application together?

In most cases, you'll agree that a vendor who offers a lot of product at a low cost must have cut corners somewhere. (Of course, some people just charge too much—the opposite side of the coin.) If someone's willing to offer you something for close to nothing, make sure you take a hard look at the product before you buy. You may find that you're simply getting an extra good buy, but more often than not, you're buying a box of trouble. The component you get won't be worth the time and effort to install it, much less use in a project.

Flexibility

One of the products in this appendix, Graphics Server, offers no less than six levels of platform support: DLL, VBX, VCL (Delphi component), OCX, FLL, and C++ class (it'll supposedly have an ActiveX component ready by the time you read this). This is a real plus because you never know when you'll need to use a component you bought for Delphi or Visual C++, for example, on some other platform, such as Visual Basic. This is especially true for consultants because the job or the client often dictate which language you'll use for a particular project. Flexibility takes other forms as well. What about a communications package that lets you use nine or ten different protocols, or a network package that works with NetWare 3.x and 4.x? Products that allow you to do more than the minimum needed are always a better deal than those that don't.

Efficiency

There's a wealth of components you probably wouldn't use to build an application, much less add to a Web site, because they require too many resources. Some vendors try to stick every bit of functionality known to programmers into one component. Sure, it'll allow you to write any kind of program in just ten minutes; but the fact that it requires 16MB of memory to run should tell you something—no one is going to be able to run the application you build. In addition, even Microsoft is emphasizing the value of small modules when it comes to writing ActiveX components. Obviously there aren't any components, OCX or otherwise, that require 16MB of memory to run, but there's an important reason to emphasize this point. You're going to run into situations when you think you just have to add one more bell or whistle to a Web page, only to find that users complain it's slow or won't run well on their machine. Look for the small and efficient component. Get the job done with the least number of resources possible, and you'll find that the people using your program are a lot happier.

Another form of efficiency when it comes to the Internet is the way a control is designed for downloading purposes. You might find that the control consumes very little space or resources by itself but requires help from a variety of support modules. A large component broken into a lot of small pieces isn't much better than a single large component. In fact, you'll find yourself spending time gathering all of the files together to ensure that a visitor to your Web site gets a complete copy of the control. An efficient ActiveX component will usually contain one, or maybe two, components. Look for vendors who have taken the time to create small controls that are actually the size they say they are. This is especially important when you know the vendor has converted an OCX to an ActiveX component. Make sure the conversion doesn't consist only of a name change.

NOTE: All prices in this appendix are current list prices as of the time of writing. They may change without notice.

Components You May Want for Your Toolbox

Finding the right component for your application can save you a lot of programming time, especially if the component is highly customizable. This section contains a listing of some of the more popular components available on the market today. The list is intended not to replace all of those catalogs you receive in the mail, but rather to acquaint you with some of the components available on the market today. After all, you have to have some idea that a component exists before you'll know to look for it in a larger catalog. This list also acquaints you with some of the more popular vendors, many of whom provide a much larger array of components than I've provided here. You can always call one of these vendors to see if it makes a component you need before attempting to write one by hand.

TIP: If you see a control in a catalog that only comes in VBX format, take time to call the vendor. You'll probably find that the catalog is out of date and that the vendor has already made the move from the 16-bit to the 32-bit world. Even if this hasn't happened yet, your call may convince the vendor to make the change. Some vendors make business decisions based (at least in part) on input from people buying their products. A phone call at the right time could mean the difference between getting the control you need and programming it by hand.

NOTE: Some of the controls listed in this section are so new that prices were not available. Be sure to contact the vendor for this information. You can also download sample copies of many of these controls from the ActiveX Component Gallery at **http://www.microsoft.com/com/gallery/**.

Graphics Server

Graphics Server SDK ($349)

Bits Per Second, Ltd.
14 Regent Hill, Brighton BN1 3ED, U.K.
Telephone: 01273-727119
Fax: 01273-731925
CompuServe: >MHS:rflowers@bits
Internet: rflowers@bits.mhs.compuserve.com
Internet: http://www.pinpub.com/gserver/home.htm

This is the full-fledged version of the run-time product included with products such as Visual Basic and Delphi. It comes with DLL, VBX, VCL (Delphi component), OCX, FLL, and C++ class support, making it just about the most versatile tool in this appendix. Like the run-time version, the server runs as an independent application outside of your Delphi or Visual Basic application. However, this product provides a lot more than the run-time version does.

TIP: Bits Per Second offers a special update deal for programmers who own Visual Basic or another product that comes with the run-time version of Graphics Server. Contact the company for the current price of this special deal.

Graphics Server is an OLE 2 graphics primitive engine. It supports commands that draw circles or squares. You can use it to perform a variety of complex drawing tasks with products other than Delphi or Visual Basic—even those that don't support OLE directly (CA-Visual Objects for one). This feature makes Graphics Server more than just an application programming tool; you could potentially use it with a variety of products in a lot of different environments.

If you don't want to work with graphics primitives, and a graph or chart is your goal, you can use the included ChartBuilder product. This is the full-featured version of the Graph control included with Visual Basic. (The latest version of Graphics Server incorporates all of these capabilities into a single product.) Just tell ChartBuilder what data points you want to display and what type of graph or chart to display them on. It takes care of all the details.

WEB LINK: Go to: **http://www.pinpub.com/gserver/gallery/ gallery.htm** to see a complete list, with examples of graph types that Graphics Server supports.

There isn't room in this appendix to talk about all of the features of this product, but here are a few more:

◆   You can use Graphics Server SDK with Microsoft Excel and Word for Windows.

◆   Versions 4.5 and above fully support VBA.

◆   It includes support for spline graphs, floating bar graphs, and error bars on all log graphs.

◆   Bits Per Second plans to release an ActiveX component that will be free for anyone to download—you'll need the graphics server on your Web server to stream data to the ActiveX component once it's installed.

About the only thing that you won't find here is source code. Bits Per Second wants to protect its investment, so you'll have to be satisfied with the compiled code. Graphics Server currently comes with a 30-day money-back guarantee, and you don't have to pay a penny in royalties when using it in a commercial application.

ALLText/TList

ALLText HT/Pro ($350)
TList Enhanced Outline ($199)

Bennet-Tec Information Systems
50 Jericho Turnpike
Jericho, NY 11753
Voice: (516) 997-5596
Fax: (516) 997-5597
CompuServe: GO BENNET-TEC
Internet: controls@bennet-tec.com
Internet: http://www.bennet-tec.com/

NOTE: Bennet-Tec Information Systems market a wealth of VBXs, OCXs, and Java applets, only two of which are mentioned here. Make sure you visit its Web site to see all of the controls it has to offer. Many of them are now 32-bit OCXs, which makes them a better choice for Internet use. Don't worry if you need a VBX or 16-bit OCX—Bennet-Tec still provides support for both in many of its products.

ALLText HT/Pro is essentially a word processor with a little extra oomph. It includes hypertext support, embedded OLE objects for graphics or other document embedding, RTF (Rich Text Format) input and output, and data-aware support. The PEN edition provides support for pen-based computing—a nice feature if you have to provide this kind of support.

RTF is the word processing format used by the Windows help compiler. Many word processors use this format as a means for exchanging data with other word processors. The data-aware support means that ALLText includes the name of the application that created an object as part of the object. You could theoretically provide a small text processor in your application and then allow the user to export the file to a full-fledged word processor such as Microsoft Word without too many problems.

TList is an enhanced outlining control. It provides more features than your typical word processor, making it more like the professional outlining tools that you see on the market. One of its special features is the ability to customize items displayed in the outline. For example, you could give an item a special color or use a different icon to display it. This product also supports advanced features such as item hiding, bookmarks, category images, and drag-and-drop.

Communications Library/Fax Plus

Communications Library 3 ($149)
Fax Plus ($249)

MicroHelp
4211 JVL Industrial Park Drive, NE
Marietta, GA 30066
Voice: (800) 922-3383 or (404) 516-0899
Fax: (404) 516-1099
Internet: http://www.microhelp.com

A

Communications Library 3 is a general communications library, which means that it provides a lot of generic capabilities that will allow you to build a specific type of communications program. It supports five terminal emulations: ANSI, TTY, VT52, VT100, and VT220. In addition, it provides support for eight file transfer protocols, including Kermit, CompuServe B+, X, Y, and Z modem. Unlike some packages, the Z modem support also provides autorecovery support. You can use Communications Library 3 up to speeds of 25.6 Kbps.

Trying to support the wide variety of modems is one of the big problems in writing a communications program. Communications Library 3 comes with over 150 initialization strings to support the most common modems. You'll also find a selection of Pascal subprograms and forms. The forms include those required for serial port and parameter selection, phone dialing, and many other functions.

MicroHelp includes VBXs, DLLs, and 16/32-bit OCXs with Communications Library 3. It provides OLE 2 support for all of your file transfer needs. The library will support multiple communication ports (eight is the practical limit).

Fax Plus is another communications product from MicroHelp. You can use it with any class 1, 2, or 2.0 fax modem. Fortunately, the product also includes some components you can use to detect the type of modem—a requirement if you plan to distribute your application commercially.

One of the more interesting features of Fax Plus is that it supports faxes through printed output. In other words, you can build an application in such a way that it can take the printed output from another application and send it as a fax. You can also import BMP, PCX, DCX, or TIFF files to send as faxes. The standard fax format is ASCII text.

Unlike Communications Library 3, Fax Plus automatically handles the fax modem initialization for you. Of course, this is limited to the set of modems it supports, so you'll need to check whether the fax modem you want to use with Fax Plus is supported before you try to use it. The package also contains a variety of sample programs and other documentation to show you how to use the product. Both Fax Plus and Communications Library 3 are royalty free.

MediaKnife/ImageKnife

MediaKnife ($399, OCX version)
ImageKnife ($549, OCX version)

OLYMPUS Software Europe GmbH
Wendenstraße 14-16

Hamburg, Germany
Voice: +49-40-23773-411
Fax: +49-40-23773-644
Internet: http://www.olympus-software.com/

NOTE: MediaKnife was originally marketed by Media Architects, so you may associate these products with that company. The new owner, OLYMPUS, provides the same list of features and level of support that Media Architects did. OLYMPUS also has a special upgrade price for owners of previous product versions—as low as $99 in some cases. Make sure you check out its Web site for special offers before paying full price. You'll also want to check out its Digital Camera Control product. This product will allow you to embed digital camera capabilities into your application.

MediaKnife allows you to create all kinds of media presentations using a variety of file formats such as AVI. You can use its WinG-based display technology to create transition effects, background buffering of images and sound, irregular hotspots, and custom cursors. This product also provides animated sprite capabilities. The best part is that you can see all of these capabilities at design time—meaning you won't spend as much time compiling an application or setting up a Web site to test a particular design.

Some of the special MediaKnife capabilities include the ability to decompress Iterated Systems' resolution-independent fractal files. The product includes editors that allow you to perform a variety of tasks, including hotspot definition, batch palette editing, and animated sprite assembly.

ImageKnife is a very complex graphics OCX that supports the Microsoft Access Paintbrush Picture OLE Object format. It helps you acquire images using the TWAIN scanner interface. That's the same interface used by CorelDRAW! and other similar products. Once you acquire an image, you can change its appearance and store it in either a file or database. You could use this library to provide an added level of support for graphics databases using the Access database format. Of course, you aren't limited to Access databases; you can also use this product with other DBMSs that support this graphics format.

Don't get the idea that you can't use ImageKnife for some of the more mundane graphics chores in your application. It also supports a variety of other file formats, including BMP, DIB, JPEG, GIF, PCX, TIFF, and Targa. You can display those files as true color (24-bit), Super VGA (8-bit), VGA (8-bit), or monochrome images. This versatility makes ImageKnife a good graphics library selection for most applications.

Both MediaKnife and ImageKnife come with a 90-day money-back guarantee. You can also include these products in your applications royalty free.

Aditi UI Widgets

Multi Shape Button, Date Select, Masked Edit, and SysInfo
(free for the price of a download)

A

Aditi Inc.
10940 NE 33rd Place, Suite 204
Bellevue, WA 98004
Voice: (206) 828-9646
Fax: (206) 828 9587
Internet: http://www.aditi.com/activex/

NOTE: While you can download these controls (collectively known as Aditi UI Widgets for ActiveX) for free as of this writing, there is no guarantee they will remain so. In addition, you'll need to contact the vendor regarding licensing and any legal requirements before using these controls on an Internet site.

Multi Shape Button is a button that can adjust its shape in a number of ways, including ellipse, triangle, pentagon, and rhombus. If the control doesn't come with a shape to suit your needs, you can always draw your own. Like a lot of other controls of this type, Multi Shape Button allows you to use custom icons and captions for each button state.

Date Select provides a selection box for picking a date. Instead of entering a date by hand, the user simply clicks a speed button. Highlighting a particular date element (month, day, or year) changes that element when the speed button is clicked. Clicking on another part of the control displays a calendar that the user can use to set the date as well.

You can never be certain of what a user will enter at a particular prompt. The results can be disastrous unless you include a lot of error-trapping code. Masked Edit takes all of the work out of doing this for you. It restricts user entries to specific, predefined input. Database applications have had this capability for years—it's nice to see it available for the Internet as well. Aditi provides a number of predefined masks for you but allows you to add any custom masks that you need.

If you haven't noticed yet, trying to write an application for the Internet is a shot in the dark. At least if you write an application for general distribution in shrink-wrap, you can include some system requirements on the box. The same isn't true for an ActiveX component. It could encounter any kind of machine ever made. That's where SysInfo comes into play. This control allows you to scan the client machine and learn some basic parameters about it, such as what operating system it's using and the size of its hard drive. You can also detect the processor type and whether a math coprocessor is present. Detecting this kind of information frees you to provide users with a specific feedback message when they can't use your site due to equipment problems.

SmartHelp

SmartHelp (price not available)

Blue Sky Software
7777 Fay Avenue, Suite 201
La Jolla, CA 92037
Voice: (800) 677-4946 or (619) 459-6365
Fax: (619) 459-6366
Internet: http://www.blue-sky.com

NOTE: This section doesn't even begin to cover all of the tools offered by Blue Sky Software—all of which are Internet oriented. Make sure you visit its Web site to learn about other tools that you can use to increase your productivity.

While Microsoft seems bent on moving you away from the Windows help format, Blue Sky seems equally determined to move you toward it. SmartHelp allows you to display a Windows help file from the user's browser. You might ask yourself why this particular control is even needed. HTML doesn't currently provide the same search capabilities that the Windows help file format does. In addition, using a help file format that the user is familiar with is one sure way to decrease support calls. Special features of this control include the ability to change the button bitmap (48 come with the product) and the type of help displayed (Windows 3.*x* or 95 style).

Light Lib

Light Lib Business ($249 Standard; $449 Professional)
Light Lib Images ($249 Standard; $449 Professional)
Light Lib Multimedia ($249 Standard; $449 Professional)
Light Lib Magic Menus ($99 Standard; $139 Professional)
Light Lib /400 (priced by the server—contact the vendor for details)

Luxent Software, Inc.
55 Eglinton Avenue E., Suite 208
Toronto, ON M4P 1G8
Voice: (416) 487-2660
Internet: http://www.dfl.com

A

There are five different versions of Light Lib that are ActiveX enabled (with more to come in all likelihood): Light Lib Business, Light Lib Images, Light Lib Multimedia, Light Lib Magic Menus, and Light Lib /400. Various versions of this product have appeared in programming languages. For example, you'll find it included with CA-Visual Objects.

Light Lib Business allows you to create charts and graphs. The actual number of charts and graphs wasn't available as of this writing, but you can be sure it will include the basic 2-D and 3-D chart types: bar, line, pie, gantt complex ribbon, stacked, and percent. The context menu displayed when you right-click on the control is pretty special, too. It allows the user to either save the current image as a file or place it on the desktop as wallpaper. The context menu contains the usual entries such as Copy and Properties as well.

Luxent bills Light Lib Images as a complete document and image management library. It certainly provides a variety of controls for adjusting an image. For example, you can adjust the brightness and contrast of an image. The preliminary control also appeared to provide gamma-correction capabilities. As with most libraries of this type, you can perform a variety of image manipulations, such as rotating. This control also includes the special context menu entries of the Light Lib Business control.

The Light Lib Multimedia controls are designed to make your animated presentations better. Luxent used to sell the sound and video controls as separate packages but found that most customers ended up getting both packages anyway. The sound-related controls provide a complete set of adjustments for a typical sound board that looks very much like the Volume Control dialog provided by Windows 95. In addition to the volume controls, you'll find a media player and set of file controls. The video-related controls look much like the AVI player provided by Windows 95. The difference is that the Light Lib player also provides volume controls. This control provides a speed setting as well that allows you to control the rate at which the video plays back.

Are you tired of looking at the same old gray Windows menus? Even if you add icons to them, there isn't a lot you can do to make using a menu fun. The Light Lib Magic Menus control can change all that. Now you can have menus that use an image as a background. You can also add some really interesting-looking bitmaps for menu entries instead of relying on simple icons to get the job done. Best of all, programming for these new menus is very minimal.

Bridging the gap between today's modern LAN and that old mainframe is a concern for more than one programmer. Light Lib /400 is a special product designed to make bridging that gap easier than ever before. For the most part you won't use this product on the Internet; it's designed for client/server application support.

MicroHelp

Various products

MicroHelp
4211 JVL Industrial Park Drive, NE
Marietta, GA 30066
Voice: (800) 922-3383 or (404) 516-0899
Fax: (404) 516-1099
Internet: http://www.microhelp.com

MicroHelp has a huge list of products—more than I can tell you about in this appendix. A recent catalog containing the wares of many different vendors included 11 pages of MicroHelp products, while some vendors were having trouble filling one page.

You'll find that MicroHelp has fully embraced ActiveX technology. You can visit its Web site or the ActiveX Component Gallery to see what's available right now. What you'll see is a variety of 3-D control types, an alarm or two, some sliders and marquees, and even some game pieces such as cards and dice. Even Microsoft couldn't match this company's output of small but useful controls ("widgets" would be a better term) on the ActiveX Component Gallery at the time of this writing.

Browser Plug-ins Based on ActiveX Components

Plug-ins are part of the reason that your browser won't stay plain for very long. They allow you to add custom capabilities to your setup. In most cases you'll find that the plug-in is free but the server for the plug-in is fairly expensive. What does this mean to you as a programmer? It means that if you decide to add a specific capability to your Web site, you'll need to pay server fees for it. In some cases, there's a price for buying the server initially and an annual maintenance fee after that. From a user's perspective it means that you can usually enhance your browser for free and gain the added features offered by a specific Internet site.

This section lists four of the more intriguing ActiveX plug-ins that you'll see now or in the near future. Always assume that there's a cost associated with buying the server required to use the plug-in at an Internet site. Contact the vendor at the address shown to get pricing information.

A

NOTE: Some of these plug-ins have been such a big success that they're actually shipped as part of Internet Explorer 4.*x* or will be shipped with Windows 98.

VDOLive/VDOLive Tools/VDOPhone

VDOLive (priced by the server—contact the vendor for details)
VDOLive Tools (priced by the server—contact the vendor for details)
VDOPhone ($79 Professional; other options available)

VDOnet Corp.
4009 Miranda Avenue, Suite 250
Palo Alto, CA 94304
Voice: (415) 846-7700
Fax: (415) 846-7900
Internet: http://www.clubvdo.net/clubvdo/Default.asp

The basic purpose of VDOLive is to let you play real-time audio and video located on a Web site within your browser. It includes the capability for playing movies and other kinds of animated media presentations. The new 2.0 version promises better video quality (10 to 15 frames per second) and image size (352×288). It'll also include an intriguing idea: storybook mode. In this mode, still images are synchronized with audio. In essence, you'll see the presentation unfold much like you would in a storybook.

You'll want to get VDOLive Tools if you plan on creating a large or complex Web site. It contains everything you need to compress video and make it Web-friendly. VDOLive Tools uses the same AVI format you've employed for just about everything in the past. This means that you could potentially use it with other kinds of programming endeavors—literally anywhere you can use an AVI file.

VDOPhone is a two-way conferencing product designed to work through your browser instead of as a separate product. This flexibility means that you can design a Web page that incorporates a lot of different features, including custom ActiveX components. Even though VDOPhone isn't as full featured as some products on the market, it is designed to work with Microsoft's NetMeeting. You can actually start NetMeeting to provide features like a whiteboard when needed during a meeting. VDOPhone does rely on streaming technology, which means that you'll need robust hardware to use it but the quality of the image you receive will be high. You can also use VDOPhone in a voice-only mode when other parties don't have a video capture board installed in their machine.

Acrobat

Acrobat ActiveX for Windows 95 (free for the price of a download)

Adobe Systems Inc.
1585 Charleston Road
P.O. Box 7900
Mountain View, CA 94039-7900
Voice: (415) 961-4400
Fax: (415) 961-3769
Internet: http://www.adobe.com/ and
http://www.adobe.com/supportservice/custsupport/LIBRARY/44ae.htm

Adobe's Acrobat reader has already appeared in several places. If you're a programmer, you have probably used it to read help files in book form on your machine at one time or another. Acrobat uses PDF (Portable Document Format) to display information in a way that makes allowances for the display device. This new ActiveX version lets you view PDF files using your browser instead of downloading the file and loading the entire Acrobat reader.

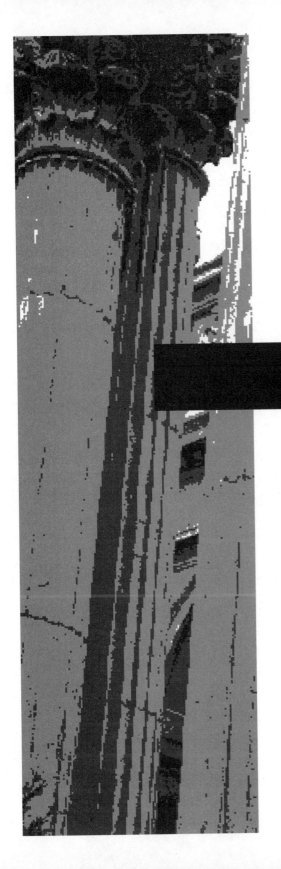

APPENDIX B

Online Resource Guide

As a programmer, you know the value of getting help when you need it rather than trying to solve a problem on your own. After all, it's very likely that someone else has already seen the problem you're working on and has just the solution you need. On the other hand, if you're anything like me, you also know about information overload. Just think of that pile of unread technical journals sitting on your desk. Getting a solution to your problem can involve wading through a lot of "solutions" that won't work. In other words, you may have to fight through an excess of information to find the answer to your question. The problem isn't so much not knowing what information you need or where to find it but how to track down the right source.

NOTE: I've provided quite a few figures and illustrations in this appendix that are typical of what you'll see on the Internet. However, by the time you actually read this appendix, those Web pages will have changed at least a little. Since the Internet is such a fluid resource, you need to consider most of the figures as examples only; your display will likely look different than mine did as I wrote this.

Unless you're hiding in a dark corner somewhere, you'll know that the Internet has become the number one source of information for most people. Most programmers I know have had at least a little experience with the Internet. CompuServe and other online services also provide an enormous range of resources for the typical programmer. The types of information that each online service provides vary, but in the long run you'll find that most of them provide some level of help you can use to solve a problem. More important, you'll expose yourself to a wealth of new ideas by tuning into discussions of the latest industry trends or programming techniques. The problem with many programmers is that they stop there. You can get a lot more from an online service or the Internet if you want to. The following list should give you a few ideas.

◆ *World view rather than local view* If you talk with your buddy down the hall, you're getting the local view of Visual C++ programming techniques. On the other hand, talking with someone on an online service, such as CompuServe or the Internet, might give you the English, Australian, or Japanese view of Visual C++ programming techniques. This international flavor will give you a better appreciation of features you might not have considered important before. In addition, the cultural differences actually work together to help you see ways that you might not have seen before of using features.

◆ *Access to vendor representatives* This is probably one of the reasons you started visiting the Internet in the first place, but most people don't realize what they're really getting. Aside from all the talking you'll do with other users, an online service also gives you access to at least one, but probably several, vendor representatives. There have been times when I've started a conversation with three, or even four, people who work for the company whose product I'm using. You'll find that the expert knowledge that the vendor representative provides often gets mixed in with the real-world view of the other users. The result is that you actually get better information from the online service than you could have gotten from the vendor's technical support line.

◆ *Vendor BBS is alive and well* If you've been programming for any length of time, you probably remember using a vendor BBS to get the information you needed in the not-too-distant past. Online services provide many of the features you once got from a vendor BBS. For example, you can go online to CompuServe, the Internet, or MSN (Microsoft Network) and download the latest patches for just about any Microsoft product. The same holds true for other vendors as well (though many of them provide only CompuServe or Internet access, so you'll have to check to make sure you'll find the vendor you need on the service you subscribe to). I've often found a needed NetWare patch on the NetWire forum on CompuServe. (Anyone writing an application that requires access to Novell's NetWare knows the significance of being able to get a required patch quickly.)

◆ *Hardware vendor access* How many times have you started working on a device driver or other low-level code only to find that the driver you have doesn't work or that you need additional information from the vendor? If you think CompuServe or any other online forum is all software, think again. Practical Peripherals, AST, Hewlett-Packard, IBM, and other hardware vendors provide valuable services here too. I think you'll find this hardware presence useful each time you need to download a new driver or ask a configuration question. (Don't feel alone if you didn't think to ask your hardware-related question online—I've actually seen a few programmers who know everything about the software forum but forget all about the hardware forums that also exist.) You'll find the same level of expertise in these areas that you find in the software areas.

B

NOTE: Don't get the idea that the Internet is an inexhaustible source of proven answers to your problems. Even though the information on the Internet (or any other online service for that matter) is free, it doesn't come with a guarantee of accuracy—not every person you run into when using an online service will be an expert. Most of them are just average users like you. However, I've had the pleasure of running into some truly remarkable people from time to time while browsing through the messages. In fact, some people are constantly looking for ways to improve their Visual C++ programming techniques in their spare time. You'll usually find them in a forum somewhere, just waiting to share this information with you. Fortunately, you'll also find more than a few experts on these newsgroups as well. Some people just hang around looking for good ideas or good questions. By asking a question, you're actually providing them some food for thought.

Let's talk a little more about the Internet as an information resource in general. In the minds of some people, the Internet has become the singles bar of the '90s—a place to meet new people and exchange ideas. The media has certainly done nothing to discourage this idea; if anything, they promote this idea by publishing the names of Internet sites helter-skelter. Just look at your television set. During one evening, a friend and I saw that no less than 80 percent of the new television shows include an Internet address as part of their programming. A few shows even depend on the Internet as a primary source of entertainment information. Of course, television isn't the only entertainment industry making use of the Internet. Many games and other products now include Internet capabilities of one sort or another as standard fare. Advertisements and just about every other form of media make use of the Internet as well.

So what do sites filled with entertainment information mean for the typical programmer? They mean that you're going to find yet another type of information overload if you're not careful. Consider the RealAudio Web site that I mention in Chapter 10. The same site that you'll visit to download an ActiveX control or plug-in is just packed with links to Web sites that have nothing to do with programmer issues. (You'll quickly find that the Internet isn't a resource for any one group—it's a source of information for just about every concern there is.) In short, you'll have to wade through a lot of extraneous information to get the control you wanted to download in the first place.

An equally interesting idea is that the Internet's some kind of remote communications magic carpet. The trade press has recently filled its pages

B

with the word "intranet"—a viable term when used in the right way. The problem is that if you read any three people's opinion on what it means, you'll come away with three equally different definitions. The true meaning of intranet is not what most people expect. I normally reserve this term for an extended form of wide area network (WAN), a business tool that allows employees to share information, even when they're on the road.

The Internet certainly fulfills some part of all these ideas. You can use it as an extremely valuable research tool. Exchanging ideas with other people has always been a part of the Internet. The idea that you can create a Web site for your employees at remote sites to check into is a possibility, too. However, none of these uses for the Internet really tells you what it's all about and how you can use it to your best advantage. That's what this appendix is all about. I'm going to spend some time telling you about the foundations of the Internet and the tools you can use to explore it.

What you should come away with is a new appreciation for what the Internet's really all about. I think you'll find that it's a lot more than what you've been told. Surfing the net should be an experience that helps you meet specific goals and broadens your horizons. The problem is, with such a large number of items on the menu, you could easily get lost.

Finding What You're Looking For

If you do a lot of research on the Internet like I do, you'll realize the benefit of finding what you need quickly. In most cases this means finding a search engine like Lycos. There are specialty search engines like Deja News (a place to find information contained in newsgroups) as well. Even though these search sites can provide radically different results when you make a request, they use similar mechanisms to allow you to make the request in the first place.

Let's talk about keyword searches for a second. All you need to do to perform a keyword search is enter one or more keywords into the blank, select a search engine, and then click the Search button. Internet Explorer or Navigator will take you to the appropriate search Web site and start the search for you.

It's time to try out a search. Select Lycos as your search engine (you'll find it at **http://www.lycos.com**), type **ActiveX** in the blank, and then click Search (this will work with either browser). Depending on the security level you've selected, you may see a security dialog before either browser does anything. Click on Yes to clear it. You'll end up on a Web page like the one shown in Figure B-1. There are a few things you should notice about this page. The first feature is that you can refine your search. Maybe a single

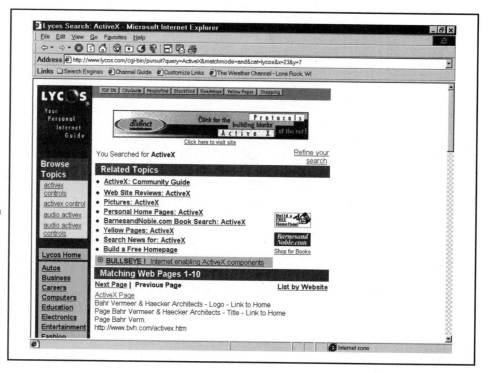

A search Web page like Lycos allows you to find specific information on the Internet.

Figure B-1.

keyword really didn't refine the search enough, and you need to find something more specific. I haven't found a single search Web page that doesn't provide this ability in some form. In fact, many of them do provide very detailed search mechanisms.

There's something else you should notice. Each one of the result entries (also called a "hit") contains a confidence level, expressed numerically (some Web sites provide this feature only as an option, so you may not see it all the time). This tells you how confident the search engine is about the results it found. Normally, the search engine uses a variety of criteria to determine this, like the number of times the keyword appears in an article or other source of information. Obviously, a Boolean search starts to make a confidence calculation more difficult. The method of determining a confidence factor is one of the things that will determine which search engines you use. I use a variety of search engines for different purposes (more on that in a bit).

Some search engines, like Lycos, also provide special features. For example, Figure B-1 shows that Lycos provides a list of related topics (this figure doesn't show confidence levels). You can use this list to find related information quickly. Unfortunately, these specialty features often don't work as well as advertised. Always take the specialty feature information with a grain of salt, since it doesn't provide a confidence factor and you have no way of knowing what the search engine used as a basis for finding these additional links for you.

Web search pages normally don't list every site that the search engine finds. Notice that Lycos lists only ten of them (other services will allow you to change the number of entries listed as part of the search criteria). You have to click the Next Documents button to see the next group of ten on the list. The order in which you list the various hits determines which sites get listed first. Lycos defaults to listing the sites it finds by confidence level. This makes sense because you want to find the best sites first. You can click the List by Website link if you want an alphabetical listing. Some search engines provide other sorting criteria. For example, the Deja News site (I'll talk about it shortly) allows you to sort by author as well.

You might think that one search engine would be enough to fulfill your needs, but that simply isn't true. The problem with trying to come up with a "best fit" answer for any of these search engines is that each one works differently. A search engine that works fine for my needs may not work at all for you. I thought it important, therefore, to provide a list of some of the more common search engines and a quick overview of how they work. I'd encourage you to try them all to see what works best for you and in what situations. The following list talks about the search engines I use; fortunately, most of them are accessed through the Search the Internet button on Internet Explorer or Navigator. I've provided URLs for those that you may have to access directly. Just click the Open button on the toolbar and enter the URL shown to access the search engine page.

Search Engine	Location on Internet	Description
AltaVista	http://www.altavista.digital.com/	You'll find that one of the benefits of using this search engine is a lack of information overload. It returns the amount of information you want about each hit. The service tends to focus on a combination of Web pages and sites, meaning that you'll get some pretty narrow hits when using it. AltaVista uses excerpts from the articles or other sources of information that it provides access to. This service uses a somewhat esoteric Boolean search engine, making it difficult to narrow your search criteria with any level of ease.
Deja News	http://www.dejanews.com/	I've used this particular search engine when I needed to find a lot of information fast. You'll notice a Power Search button on the page when you arrive. Power search may be something of an understatement; you'll have to test it out to see all that it can do. This is one of the easier sites to use as well, despite its flexibility. It uses a lot of graphics, including radio buttons and other familiar controls. The only problem with Deja News is that you may find yourself doing a search more than once to get everything it provides. There are so many search options that you'll find yourself thinking of new ways to search for a particularly tough-to-find bit of information. You can get two levels of detail—neither of which tell you much.

B

Search Engine	Location on Internet	Description
		All you can count on getting for each hit is an article title. This service doesn't provide either excerpts or summaries. It does yield a very broad base of information, meaning that you'll find just about anything you search for. You'll just spend some time weeding out the entries that really don't fit.
Excite	http://www.excite.com/	This service tends to focus on actual Web sites rather than pages on a particular site. In other words, you get to a general area of interest, and then Excite leaves it to you to find the specific information you're looking for. I find that this is an advantage when I'm not really sure about the specifics of a search. A wide view, in this case, helps me see everything that's available and make some refinements from there. Excite does provide a summary of what you'll find at a particular site. It tends to concentrate on discussion groups and vendor-specific information.
FTP Search v3.3	http://ftpsearch.ntnu.no/ftpsearch	This is a very special search engine. Instead of finding information you need on a Web site or within a newsgroup, it focuses on FTP sites. You use it to find a particular file. For example, you could use it to look for a utility that you desperately need to finish a program you're working on. You could also use it to search for device drivers, patches, or any other file you needed.

Search Engine	Location on Internet	Description
Infoseek	http://guide-p.infoseek.com/	The strength of this particular service is that it provides just the facts. It uses excerpts from the articles or other sources of information that it provides access to. The hits are a lot narrower than some search engines provide because Infoseek concentrates on Web pages rather than sites. The only problem with it is that your ability to narrow the search criteria is severely limited.
Lycos	http://www-msn.lycos.com/	Of all of the search engines I've used, Lycos tends to provide the most diverse information. It catalogs both Web sites and pages (but concentrates on pages whenever possible). Lycos provides a combination of summaries and excerpts to describe the content of a particular hit. The ability to narrow your search is superior to most of the search engines available right now. One of the down sides to using this particular search engine is that there is almost too much detail. You'll quickly find yourself searching false leads and ending up with totally unusable information if you aren't sure what you're looking for.
Magellan	http://magellan.mckinley.com:8080/	You'll tend to find esoteric sources of information with this search engine. It doesn't appear to provide a very broad base of information, but it usually yields interesting facts about what you're searching for. Magellan concentrates on Web sites rather than pages, so the view you get is rather broad. You'll also find

Search Engine	Location on Internet	Description
		that it provides few methods for narrowing the search criteria. This search engine relies on summaries rather than extracts to convey the content of a particular hit. One of the more interesting features is the method used to rate a particular site: clicking a Review button gives you a full-page summary of how the information relates to similar information on other sites.
MSJ Tools for Windows Search Page	http://www.microsoft.com/msj	This is a must-visit site for Visual C++ programmers. It's a special site supported by *Microsoft Systems Journal* that allows you to look for Windows tools of any type. The interesting thing about this search engine is that you can actually differentiate between platforms. For example, you could tell it that you were only interested in Windows 95 tools. You can also specify a product category, which includes esoteric topics like ActiveX controls or the more common database development tools. The search engine even allows you to specify a company name if you want to really narrow your search down.
Open Text	http://search.opentext.com/	Extremely comprehensive and flexible describe this particular search engine. I find that this is one of the easier sites to use, and it provides a moderately broad base of information to choose from. Open Text relies on extremely short excerpts in most cases. It does concentrate on Web pages rather than sites, meaning that you'll get a fairly narrow result.

B

Search Engine	Location on Internet	Description
SHARE WARE.COM	http://www.shareware.com/	Programmers tend to rely on a lot of shareware utilities for certain tasks, like drawing icons. This search engine specializes in helping you find that special piece of shareware you need to get a job done. Unfortunately, it appears to concentrate more on HTTP sites than FTP sites. (Use FTP Search if you need to look at FTP sites extensively.)
WebCrawler	http://www.webcrawler.com/	You'll find that this search engine requires a bit more work to use than most, because it doesn't provide much in the way of excerpts or summaries. On the other hand, it provides a full Boolean search engine and an extremely broad base of information. The only search engine that provides a broader base in this list is Lycos.
Yahoo	http://www.yahoo.com/	Yahoo provides the best organization of all those listed. It categorizes every hit in a variety of ways, making your chances of finding information contained in the search engine very high. It doesn't provide the broad range of information you'll find with other search engines, though. It also relies on very short summaries to tell you the content of a particular hit. In most cases, I rely on Yahoo as a first-look type of search engine—something that gives me the broad perspective of a single keyword.

Microsoft's Presence on the Internet

If you haven't heard much about the Internet lately, you must live on a desert island without television. I'm constantly surprised at just how much press the Internet is getting these days. All of this press wasn't wasted on Microsoft. It started a move to the Internet quite some time ago. Now it has just about abandoned any other form of support in favor of the Internet. If you really want to know what's going on with anything Microsoft, the Internet is the way to go. Microsoft's main URL on the Internet is **http://www.microsoft.com** (its home page is actually located at **http://home.microsoft.com**). Obviously, that's only the tip of the iceberg, but it's a good place to start.

TIP: As of this writing, the best place to go for both patches and information from Microsoft is the Internet. CompuServe used to be the place to go to contact Microsoft, but Microsoft has moved from there to the Internet. Older application documentation will still list CompuServe as a source of information, and it is, but you won't get vendor-specific help there any longer. WUGNet does maintain many of the forums that you used to find staffed by Microsoft employees on CompuServe, so the CompuServe GO word in your manual may still work. In addition, Microsoft continues to maintain certain features on CompuServe like the Microsoft Knowledge Base.

Getting a Good Start

It would be difficult at best to come up with a definitive hierarchy of URLs for all the sites that Microsoft supports. One of the reasons that the Internet is such a good place to provide information is that it's totally free-form. In addition, the means for changing the structure of your site resides on your own server. Online services like CompuServe reserve this capability for themselves, which makes vendors think twice about any changes. Since Microsoft controls the format and presentation of its Web site, it can, and usually does, change it quite often. Figure B-2 shows how the main Microsoft page looked at the time of this writing (note that this page has been customized to my tastes; your page may look slightly different).

WEB LINK: You can search the Microsoft Web site quickly and easily by using its special search engine at **http://www.microsoft.com/ Search/ Default.asp**. This search engine provides special features that allow you to look at a specific kind of Microsoft product or at the entire site. You can also choose the type of search (including the traditional Boolean search) to perform.

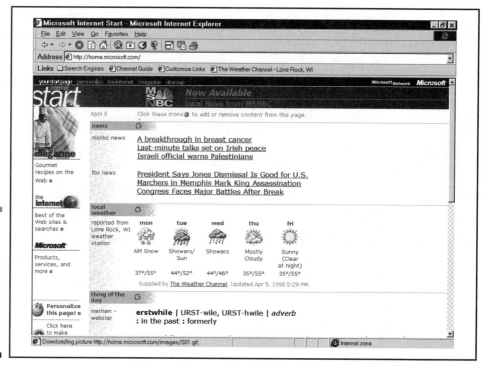

The main Microsoft Web page gives you some clues as to how to find information quickly.

Figure B-2.

So the question you need to answer is how you're going to find anything without resorting to the search techniques we discuss earlier in this appendix. Microsoft usually follows the same pattern in creating its Web pages, so coming up with a search method is pretty easy.

Look at the left side of the page and you'll see a bar. This bar usually contains a list of related topics. Clicking on one of these links will take you to another section of the Microsoft Web site—a general area in this case.

You'll also find a method of obtaining more specific information on most of Microsoft's Web pages. In this case you'll need to use the drop-down list box that contains Select a Location, and then click on Go. The sites you can select from on this page take you to areas that cater to other languages. Other Web pages will take you to places where you can find specifics about the language you're using or other topics of interest.

Finding a Newsgroup

Getting information isn't the only reason to use the Internet. A whole range of newsgroups allow you to exchange information with other people. They also let you get additional information or learn how to perform a task.

TIP: Make sure you check out all the Web Links in this book for newsgroup ideas. Just about every chapter in the book contains a Web Link that can help you find Web sites or newsgroups (in some cases, both).

B

Microsoft provides more than a few newsgroups, and finding the right one might be a little difficult if it didn't furnish some kind of menu system. Finding what you need in the way of newsgroups is a three-step process. First, go to **http://support.microsoft.com/support/news/default.asp** and you'll find a page like the one shown in Figure B-3. As you can see, the whole purpose of this page is to select a product type.

Since many of you are likely using Windows NT as a development platform, I'll go ahead and select the Windows NT entry. At the time of this writing, I also need to select a specific version of Windows NT—for the purposes of this example, I'll choose the Windows NT Server and Workstation link. Figure B-4

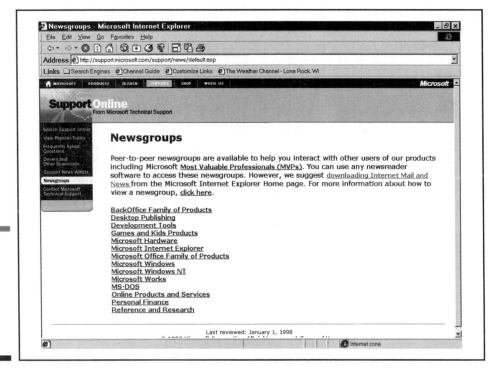

The first step in finding the right newsgroup is selecting a product type.

Figure B-3.

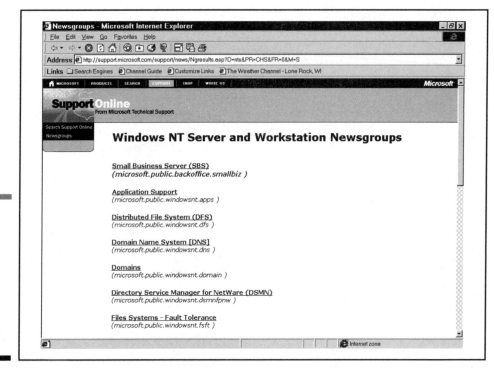

Once you select a product type, you can find out what newsgroups are available for it.

Figure B-4.

shows what you'll see next: a list of all the kinds of Windows NT information that you can find out about in a newsgroup.

Once you find the kind of information that you need, click on the link to the newsgroup. A news reader like Outlook Express will automatically pop up. Notice that the subscription checkbox in the news reader doesn't get marked automatically. You'll need to check this box if you find the information provided by the newsgroup useful and want to update your news reader automatically.

Microsoft Knowledge Base

Before I get into a full-fledged, detailed look at the Microsoft offerings on the Internet, I'd like to explore one special Microsoft URL called the Microsoft Knowledge Base. This isn't a standard Web site like the others you'll find on the Internet. Rather, it's a library of articles, white papers, and other sources of information that you'll need in order to use specific Microsoft products. We'll see later how this special forum fits into the overall scheme of things.

B

Right now, I'd like to cover why it's important and how you use it. I often look at the Microsoft Knowledge Base for information about the future direction of Microsoft products. For example, I was able to find a white paper dealing with "Program Manager Issues in Windows 95." You can also find out a lot about problems people are having—people just like you—and Microsoft's suggested solutions. One white paper told me about "Windows 95 and After Dark 2.0 Issues" that I could expect to encounter. Finally, you can find out the technical details of a product. I found a white paper that provided an "Explanation of System Resources in Windows 95" while browsing through the Knowledge Base. It's not too difficult to figure out that the Knowledge Base is more like a fax support line than anything else. However, the method you use to interact with it is a lot different.

The problem with using automated support in most cases is that unless you really know what you're looking for, you're not very likely to find it. I've been through some fax support lines that are so unfriendly you won't get any information at all unless you know a specific article name or its number. Microsoft Knowledge Base is different. It provides a search engine that you can use to actually find the information you're looking for.

So, how do you use this nifty Microsoft offering? Go to **http://support. microsoft.com/support/c.asp?M=F**. When you get there, you'll see a search page like the one shown in Figure B-5.

Notice that there are three essential questions you need to answer. The first is what product you're using. If you don't see your product in the drop-down list, then it's fairly likely that the Microsoft Knowledge Base doesn't provide the information you need. The second question asks how you want to conduct your search. In most cases you'll want to perform a keyword search because you really don't know what to look for. However, there are situations where a Microsoft support person may ask you to look at a specific article number. You can do this by selecting the Specific Article ID Number option. In other cases you may want to download a driver or other file that a Knowledge Base article refers to instead of the article itself. You can do this using the Specific Driver or Downloadable File option. The third question asks what you want to search for. This is where you'll enter the keywords, article ID number, or filename that you want to find. Once you've answered these three questions, you can click Find to search the Knowledge Base.

This page does provide two enhancements you can make to the search results. (The first option is just barely visible at the bottom of Figure B-5; make sure you spend some time with the search page online to get familiar with these options.) The first option allows you to choose between performing a full text search (takes longer, but provides more complete information) or a title search only. The second option allows you to add excerpts of the various articles to the article titles displayed on the search result page. The excerpts help you find the information you need without actually going to the article to read it. Often, the first few lines of an article will tell you whether the article is the one that you're looking for.

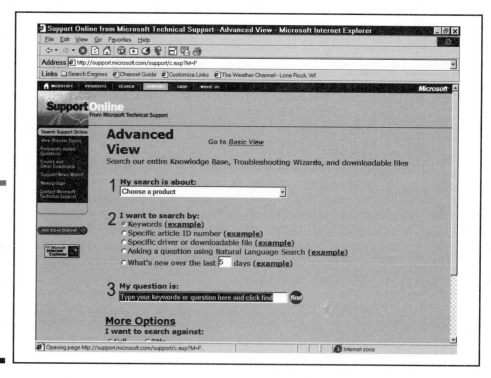

The Microsoft Knowledge Base provides an easy-to-use search engine that helps you find exactly what you need.

Figure B-5.

GLOSSARY

This glossary has several important features you need to be aware of. First, every acronym in the entire book is listed here—even if there's a better-than-even chance you already know what the acronym means. This way there isn't any doubt that you'll always find everything you need to use the book properly. The second thing you need to know is that these definitions are specific to the book. In other words, when you look through this glossary, you're seeing the words defined in the context in which they're used. This may or may not always coincide with current industry usage since the computer industry changes the meaning of words so often. Finally, the definitions here use a conversational tone in most cases. This means that they may sacrifice a bit of puritanical accuracy for the sake of better understanding.

WEB LINK: What happens if you can't find the acronym you need in the computer dictionary you just bought? Fortunately, there are two sites on the Internet that you can go to for help. The first is the Hill Associates, Inc., site at **http://mailme.hill.com/acronyms/**. This site is updated fairly often and provides only acronyms. The second site is BABEL: A Glossary of Computer Oriented Abbreviations and Acronyms. You'll find it at **http://www.access.digex.net/%7Eikind/babel.html**. While this site isn't updated as often as the first one, it does have the advantage of providing both acronyms and very brief definitions.

128-bit/40-bit encryption key	*See* Encryption level
Access control entry	*See* ACE
Access control list	*See* ACL
ACE (access control entry)	A Windows NT-specific security component. Each object (which could include anything from a file to a piece of memory) contains two access control lists (ACLs). These lists determine what type of access a user, system element, or other type of object will have to the object. Within each ACL are one or more access control entries (ACEs). There is one entry for each user, group, or other object that has access to the object. This entry defines what type of access to grant. For example, a file object can grant read and write rights.
ACL (access control list)	A Windows NT-specific security component. There are two ACLs: the security access control list (SACL), which controls Windows'

auditing feature, and the discretionary access control list (DACL), which controls who can actually use the object. The ACLs contain one or more access control entries (ACEs), which determine the actual rights for each user or object for which the ACL grants access.

ActiveX control   *See* OCX

ActiveX Data Object (ADO)   A local and remote database access technology that relies on OLE-DB to create the connection. ADO is a set of "wrapper" functions that make using OLE-DB and the underlying OLE-DB provider easier. ADO is designed as a replacement for DAO and as an adjunct to ODBC.

ActiveX Document   One of several COM-based enabling technologies used on the Internet to display documents in formats that the Internet doesn't support natively, such as the Word for Windows DOC file format. Using ActiveX Document allows the OLE server to take over the browser's frame (menu and other features such as scroll bars) and present the document within the browser window. ActiveX Document is also referred to as ActiveDocument.

ActiveX Movie   One of several COM-based enabling technologies used on the Internet to display real-time video and audio through the use of special file formats such as AVI files. ActiveX Movie may eventually allow companies to provide online presentations that don't require a person's presence at a particular site for participation.

ADO   *See* ActiveX Data Object

Animated GIF   *See* GIF

API (application programming interface)   A method of defining a standard set of function calls and other interface elements. It usually defines the interface between a high-level language and the lower-level elements used by a device driver or operating system. The ultimate goal is to provide some type of service to an application that requires access to the operating system or device feature set.

Application programming interface   *See* API

ASP Active Server Pages

ATL Active Template Library

AVI (audiovisual interface) file format A special file format that contains both audio and video in digital format. AVI is currently the most popular method for transmitting multimedia files across the Internet.

Binary values Refers to a base 2 data representation in the Windows registry. Normally used to hold status flags or other information that lends itself to a binary format.

BLOB (binary large object) A special field in a database table that accepts objects such as bitmaps, sounds, or text as input. This field is normally associated with the OLE capabilities of a DBMS, but some third-party products make it possible to add BLOB support to older database file formats such as Xbase DBF file format. BLOB fields always imply OLE client support by the DBMS.

BMP files Windows' standard bitmap graphics data format. This is a raster graphic data format that doesn't include any form of compression. It's normally used by Windows, but OS/2 (and various other operating systems) can also use this data format to hold graphics of various types.

Browse A special application interface element designed to show the user an overview of a database or other storage media (for example, the thumbnail sketches presented by some graphics applications). Think of a browse as the table of contents for the rest of the storage area. A browse normally contains partial views of several data storage elements (records or picture thumbnails in most cases) that a user can then zoom to see their entirety. A browse form normally contains scroll bars or other high-speed interface elements to make it easier for the user to move from one section of the overall storage media to the next.

Browser A special application normally used to display data downloaded from the Internet. The most common form of Internet data is the HTML (Hypertext Markup Language) page. However, modern browsers can also display various types of graphics and even standard desktop application files such as Word for Windows documents directly. The actual capabilities provided by a browser vary widely depending on the software vendor and platform.

CAB (cabinet) file A compressed format file similar to the ZIP files used to transfer code and data from one location to another. The CAB format is normally used only by developers.

CCITT (Consultative Committee for International Telegraph and Telephony) This group is now the ITU. Please see ITU for details.

CGI (common gateway interface) One of the more common methods of transferring data from a client machine to a Web server on the Internet. CGI relies on scripts to define how the data should be interpreted. There are two basic data transfer types. The user can send new information to the server or can query data already existing on the server. For example, a data entry form asking for the user's name and address would be an example of the first type of transaction. A search engine page on the Internet (a page that helps the user find information on other sites) is an example of the second type of transaction. The Web server normally provides some type of feedback for the user by transmitting a new page of information once the CGI script is complete. This could be as simple as an acknowledgment for data entry or a list of Internet sites for a data query.

Class ID *See* CLSID

Client The recipient of data, services, or resources from a file or other server. This term can refer to a workstation or an application. The server can be another PC or an application.

CLSID (class ID or identifier) A method of assigning a unique identifier to each object in the registry. Also refers to various high-level language constructs. Every object must provide a unique CLSID. The identifier is generated locally on the machine where the object is created, using some type of special software. (For example, the Microsoft OLE 2 SDK provides a utility for generating CLSIDs.) High-level languages such as Visual Basic and most C compilers normally perform the CLSID generation sequence automatically for the programmer.

COM (Component Object Model) A Microsoft specification for an object-oriented code and data encapsulation method and transference technique. It's the basis for technologies such as OLE (object linking and embedding) and ActiveX (the replacement name for OCXs, an object-oriented code library technology). COM is limited to local connections. DCOM (Distributed Component Object Model) is the technology used to allow data transfers and the use of OCXs within the Internet environment. The newest technology in Microsoft's bag of tricks is COM+. This technology should first appear in Windows NT 5. Its main purpose is to extend the current functionality provided by COM into new areas like remote execution of code.

Common gateway interface *See* CGI

Component Object Model *See* COM

Container Part of the object-oriented terminology that has become part of OLE. A container is a drive, file, or other resource used to hold objects. The container is normally referenced as an object itself.

Cookie One or more special files used by an Internet browser to store site-specific settings or other information specific to Web pages. The purpose of this file is to store the value of one or more variables so that the Web page can restore them the next time the user visits a site. A webmaster always saves and restores the cookie as part of some Web page programming task using a programming language such as JavaScript, Java, VBScript, or CGI. In most cases this is the only file that a webmaster can access on the client site's hard drive. The cookie could appear in one or more files anywhere on the hard drive, depending on the browser currently in use. Microsoft Internet Explorer uses one file for each site storing a cookie and places them in the Cookies folder that normally appears under the main Windows directory. Netscape Navigator uses a single file named COOKIE.TXT to store all of the cookies from all sites. This file normally appears in the main Navigator folder.

CryptoAPI *See* Cryptographic Application Programming Interface

Cryptographic Application Programming Interface (CryptoAPI)	The specification provided by Microsoft that enables software developers to add encryption technology to their applications. It uses a 128-bit encryption technology, which means that the developer can't export such applications outside the United States or Canada.
Cryptographic Service Provider	*See* CSP
CSP (Cryptographic Service Provider)	A specialty company that deals in certifying the identity of companies, developers, or individuals on the Internet. This identification check allows the company to issue an electronic certificate, which can then be used to conduct transactions securely. Several levels of certification are normally provided within a specific group. For example, there are three levels of individual certification. The lowest merely verifies the individual's identity through an Internet mail address; the highest requires the individual to provide written proof along with a notarized statement. When you access a certified site or try to download a certified document such as an ActiveX control, the browser will display the electronic certificate onscreen, allowing you to make a security determination based on fact.
CSS	Cascading Style Sheets
DACL (discretionary access control list)	A Windows NT-specific security component. The DACL controls who can actually use the object. You can assign both groups and individual users to a specific object.
DAO	*See* Data Access Object
DASS	Distributed Authentication Security Service
Data Access Object (DAO)	An older data access technology introduced by Microsoft that relies on the Microsoft Access JET engine for local data access. DAO does not provide remote access features, though some programmers have been able to establish unreliable connections with it. ADO and OLE-DB have largely replaced this technology.

Database management system *See* DBMS

DBCS Double-byte character set

DBMS (database management system) A collection of tables, forms, queries, reports, and other data elements. It acts as a central processing point for data accessed by one or more users. Most DBMSs (except those that are free-form or text-based) rely on a system of tables for storing information. Each table contains records (rows) consisting of separate data fields (columns). Common DBMSs include Access, Paradox, dBASE, and FileMaker Pro.

DCOM (Distributed Component Object Model) The advanced form of the Component Object Model (COM) used by the Internet. This particular format enables data transfers across the Internet or other nonlocal sources. It adds the capability to perform asynchronous as well as synchronous data transfers—which prevents the client application from becoming blocked as it waits for the server to respond. See COM for more details.

DDE (dynamic data exchange) The ability to cut data from one application and paste it into another application. For example, you could cut a graphic image created with a paint program and paste it into a word processing document. Once pasted, the data doesn't reflect the changes made to it by the originating application. DDE also provides a method for communicating with an application that supports it and for requesting data. For example, you could use an Excel macro to call Microsoft Word and request the contents of a document file. Some applications also use DDE to implement file association strategies. For example, Microsoft Word uses DDE in place of command line switches to gain added flexibility when a user needs to open or print a file.

DDF (Diamond Directive File) Similar to an INF (information) or BAT (batch) file, the DDF provides instructions to a CAB (cabinet) creation utility such as DIANTZ for compressing one or more files into a single storage file. CAB files are normally used to distribute data locally, using a CD-ROM or other similar type of media, or remotely, through an

Internet or other server connection. The DDF can also list files needed for a complete installation but are stored in other locations. Normally, these missing files will already appear on the user's computer, so downloading them again would waste time. The DDF makes it possible to download them only as needed.

DDK   Device driver development kit

Diamond Directive File   *See* DDF

Digital Signatures Initiative   *See* DSI

Discretionary access control list   *See* DACL

Distributed Component Object Model   *See* DCOM

DLL (dynamic link library)   A specific form of application code loaded into memory by request. It's not executable by itself. A DLL does contain one or more discrete routines that an application may use to provide specific features. For example, a DLL could provide a common set of file dialogs used to access information on the hard drive. More than one application can use the functions provided by a DLL, reducing overall memory requirements when more than one application is running.

DNA   Distributed interNet Applications

Drag and drop   A technique used in object-oriented operating systems to access data without actually opening the file using conventional methods. For example, this system allows the user to pick up a document file, drag it to the printer, and drop it. The printer will print the document using its default settings.

DSI (Digital Signatures Initiative)   A standard originated by the W3C (World Wide Web Consortium) to overcome some limitations of channel-level security. For example, channel-level security can't deal with documents and application semantics. A channel also doesn't use the Internet's bandwidth very efficiently because all the processing takes place on the Internet rather than the client or server. This standard defines a mathematical method for transferring signatures—essentially a unique representation of a specific individual or company. DSI also provides a new method for labeling security properties (PICS2) and a new format for assertions (PEP). This standard is also built on the PKCS #7 and X509.v3 standards.

Dynamic data exchange   *See* DDE

Dynamic link library   *See* DLL

EIT SHTTP   Extended Internet Tag Secure Hypertext Transfer Protocol

Encryption   *See* Cryptographic Application Programming Interface

Encryption level   The amount of encryption a file receives. Normally, the size of the encryption key is the determining factor in the strength and level of encryption. Most Internet browsers and local applications use two sizes: 40-bit and 128-bit. A 40-bit key can provide up to 240 key combinations and is considered moderately difficult to break. A 128-bit key can provide up to 2,128 key combinations and is considered very difficult to break. Only the 40-bit key technology is currently approved by the United States government for transport outside the United States or Canada. See Cryptographic Application Programming Interface for additional information.

File Transfer Management System   *See* FTMS

File transfer protocol   *See* FTP

FTMS (File Transfer Management System)   The Proginet Corporation introduced this ActiveX technology, which brings mainframe data to the desktop. Its Fusion FTMS will work with any development language that supports OLE containers such as Delphi, Visual C++, and PowerBuilder. Essentially, you'll place an ActiveX control on a form, define where to find the data, and then rely on the control to make the connection. Using this control reduces the amount of labor required to implement and maintain a mainframe connection. A special transfer server on the mainframe completes the package by automating all transfer requests. No longer does an operator have to manually download a needed file to the company's Web site before a client can access it. Users can directly access the data on the mainframe and download it to their local hard drive.

FTP (file transfer protocol) One of several common data transfer protocols for the Internet. This particular protocol specializes in data transfer in the form of a file download. The user is presented with a list of available files in a directory list format. An FTP site may choose DOS or Unix formatting for the file listing, though the DOS format is extremely rare. Unlike HTTP sites, an FTP site provides a definite information hierarchy through the use of directories and subdirectories, much like the file directory structure used on most workstation hard drives.

GDI Graphics Device Interface

GIF (graphics interchange format) The standard file format used to transfer data over the Internet. There are several different standards for this file format—the latest of which is the GIF89a standard you'll find used on most Internet sites. The GIF standard was originally introduced by CompuServe as a method for reducing the time required to download a graphic and the impact of any single-bit errors that might occur. A secondary form of the GIF is the animated GIF. It allows the developer to store several images within one file. Between each file are one or more control blocks that determine block boundaries, the display location of the next image in relation to the display area, and other display features. A browser or other specially designed application will display the graphic images one at a time in the order in which they appear within the file to create animation effects.

Gopher One of several common Internet data transfer protocols. Like FTP, Gopher specializes in file transfers. However, the two protocols differ in that Gopher always uses the Unix file-naming convention, and it provides a friendlier interface than FTP. Even though Gopher transfers tend to be more reliable than those provided by FTP, FTP sites are far more common.

Graphics interchange format	*See* GIF
GSS-API	Generic Security Service Application Program Interface
GUID	Globally unique identifier

HTML (Hypertext Markup Language) A scripting language for the Internet that depends on the use of tags (keywords within angle brackets <>) to display formatted information onscreen in a non-platform-specific manner. The non-platform-specific nature of this scripting language makes it difficult to perform some basic tasks such as placement of a screen element at a specific location. However, the language does provide for the use of fonts, color, and various other enhancements onscreen. There are also tags for displaying graphic images. Scripting tags for using more complex scripting languages such as VBScript and JavaScript were recently added, though not all browsers support this addition. The latest tag addition allows the use of ActiveX controls.

HTTP (Hypertext Transfer Protocol) One of several common data transfer protocols for the Internet. This particular protocol specializes in the display of onscreen information such as data entry forms or informational displays. HTTP relies on HTML as a scripting language for describing special screen display elements, though you can also use HTTP to display nonformatted text.

Hypertext Markup Language *See* HTML

Hypertext Transfer Protocol *See* HTTP

IDAPI (Independent Database Application Programming Interface) A set of Windows function calls and other interface elements introduced by companies led by Borland. IDAPI is designed to improve access to information contained in database files through the use of a common interface and data-independent access methods.

IETF (Internet Engineering Task Force) The standards group tasked with finding solutions to pressing technology problems on the Internet. This group can approve standards created both within the organization itself and outside the organization as part of other group efforts. For example, Microsoft has requested the approval of several new Internet technologies through this group. If approved, the technologies would become an Internet-wide standard for performing data transfer and other specific kinds of tasks.

IIS Internet Information Server

IMTF (Internet Management Task Force) The standards group responsible for implementing new technologies on the Internet. The problem is that it is composed mainly of volunteers. The wheels of progress grind slowly for the IMTF, just like any other standards organization. It's so slow, in fact, that many companies have come up with their own solutions for making the Internet a friendlier place to work. For example, Microsoft has developed ActiveX in response to specific Internet-related problems, while Netscape has developed Netscape ONE (Open Network Environment).

Independent Database Application Programming Interface *See* IDAPI

INF (information) file A special form of device or application configuration. It contains all the parameters that Windows requires to install or configure the device or application. For example, an application INF file might contain the location of data files and the interdependencies of DLLs. Both application and device INF files contain the registry and INF file entries required to make Windows recognize the application or device.

International Telephony Union *See* ITU

Internet Engineering Task Force *See* IETF

Internet Management Task Force *See* IMTF

Internet protocol *See* IP

Internet Server *See* ISAPI
Application
Programming Interface

IP (Internet protocol) The information exchange portion of the TCP/IP protocol used by the Internet. IP is an actual data transfer protocol that defines how the information is placed into packets and sent from one place to another. TCP (transmission control protocol) is the protocol that defines how the actual data transfer takes place. One of the problems with IP that standards groups are addressing right now is that it doesn't encrypt the data packets—anyone can read a packet traveling on the Internet. Future versions of IP will address this need by using some form of encryption technology. In the meantime, some companies have coupled TCP with other technologies to provide encryption technology for the short term.

IPSec Internet Protocol Security Protocol

ISA *See* ISAPI server application

ISAPI (Internet Server A set of function calls and interface elements designed to make
Application using Microsoft's Internet Information Server (IIS) and associated
Programming Interface) products such as Peer Web Server easier. Essentially, this set of API calls provides the programmer with access to the server itself. Such access makes it easier to provide full server access to the Internet server through a series of ActiveX controls without the use of a scripting language.

ISAPI server A special form of ActiveX control in DLL form that's placed on a
application (ISA) Web server. The DLL gets called in one of several ways like a request from a client or when a particular event takes place. There are two forms of ISA: filter and extension. A filter allows you to keep something out or in by monitoring events on your server. For example, you could create an ISA filter that keeps people out of your Web site unless they enter the right password. Another type of filter could prevent files larger than a certain size from getting uploaded to the FTP server on your Web site. Extensions are more like applications or background processes. For example,

you could create an extension that allows the user to interact with a database without resorting to using scripts. The same extension could create Web pages dynamically based on the user input and the contents of the database on your server.

ITU (International Telephony Union)   Formerly the CCITT. This group is most famous for its standards concerning modem communications. However, in recent years, it has also begun work with both fax and Internet standards (among other concerns). All of the older ITU standards still use the CCITT moniker. Newer standards use the ITU moniker. Unlike many other standards groups, the ITU is multinational and is staffed by representatives from many different countries.

JEPI   Joint Electronic Payment Initiative

Joint Pictures Entertainment Group file format   *See* JPEG file format

JPEG file   *See* JPEG file format

JPEG (Joint Pictures Entertainment Group) file format   One of two graphics file formats used on the Internet. This is a vector file format normally used to render high-resolution images or pictures.

LAN (local area network)   A combination of hardware and software used to connect a group of PCs to each other and/or to a mini or mainframe computer. Two main networking models are in use: peer-to-peer and client/server. The peer-to-peer model doesn't require a dedicated server. In addition, all the workstations in the group can share resources. The client/server model uses a central server for resource sharing, but some special methods are provided for using local resources in a limited way.

Local area network   *See* LAN

Locally unique identifier   *See* LUID

LUID (locally unique identifier)   Essentially a pointer to an object, the LUID identifies each process and resource for security purposes. In other words, even if a user has two copies of precisely the same resource option (like a document), both copies would have a unique LUID. This method of identification prevents some types of security access violation under Windows NT.

Macro   A form of programming that records keystrokes and other programming-related tasks to a file on disk or within the current document. Most applications provide a macro recorder that records the keystrokes and mouse clicks you make. This means that you don't even have to write them, in most cases. Macros are especially popular in spreadsheets. Most macros use some form of DDE to complete OLE-related tasks.

Mail Handling Service   *See* MHS

Mail Transfer System   *See* MTS

MCI   media control interface

MFC (Microsoft Foundation Classes) files   The set of DLLs required to make many Microsoft applications work. These files contain the shared classes used as a basis for creating the application. For example, a pushbutton is a separate class within these files. Normally, you'll find the MFC files in the Windows SYSTEM folder—they use MFC as the starting letters of the filename.

MHS (Mail Handling Service)   A method for encrypting and decrypting user mail and performing other mail management services. Most NOSs provide some type of MHS as part of the base system. Several standards are available on the Internet for providing MHS as part of a Web site. The two most notable specifications are IETF RFC1421 from the IETF and X.400 from the ITU (formerly CCITT).

Microsoft Foundation Classes files   *See* MFC files

MTA   message transfer agent

MTS (Mail Transfer System)   A method of transferring mail from one location to another. In most cases this requires some form of encryption along with other transport-specific issues. Most NOSs provide some type of MTS as part of their base services. However, the Internet requires special transport mechanisms. Several standards are available on the Internet for providing MTS as part of a Web site. The two most notable specifications are IETF RFC1421 from the IETF and X.400 from the ITU (formerly CCITT).

MTS Microsoft Transaction Server

Nested objects Two or more objects that are coupled in some way. The objects normally appear within the confines of a container object. Object nesting allows multiple objects to define the properties of a higher-level object. It also allows the user to associate different types of objects with each other.

Netscape ONE (Open Network Environment) A set of specialized application programming interfaces (APIs) and class libraries based on the Internet Inter-ORB Protocol (IIOP) and Common Object Request Broker Architecture (CORBA) specifications that enable a programmer to create customized Internet applications. One of the benefits of this customization is that the programmer could get by without using CGI or other scripting languages to access data on the server, a requirement using standard HTTP. ONE currently includes five Java-based foundation class libraries: User Interface Controls, User Interface Services, Security, Messaging, and Distributed Objects. Future plans include foundation classes for databases, and file server directory library access for Novell's NetWare Directory Services (NDS) and other products. This new technology also requires a JavaScript upgrade that Microsoft may or may not support.

Network interface card *See* NIC

Network operating system *See* NOS

NIC (network interface card) The device responsible for allowing a workstation to communicate with a file server and other workstations. It provides the physical means of creating the connection. The card plugs into an expansion slot in the computer. A cable that attaches to the back of the card completes the communication path.

NOS (network operating system) The operating system that runs on the file server or other centralized file- and print-sharing devices. This operating system normally provides multiuser access capability and user accounting software in addition to other network-specific utilities.

Object conversion   A method of changing the format and properties of an object created by one application to the format and properties used by another. Conversion moves the data from one application to another, usually without a loss in formatting, but always without a loss of content.

Object linking and embedding   *See* OLE

Object linking and embedding database (OLE-DB)   A low-level database access technology that relies on COM and a vendor supplied OLE-DB provider rather than the SQL used by ODBC. OLE-DB is designed to work with both remote and local databases. In addition, it can access database managers that don't rely on SQL like those found on mainframe computers. OLE-DB and ODBC are cooperative, rather than competing data access technologies. OLE-DB, when coupled with ADO, is designed to replace older database technologies like RDO and DAO.

OCX (OLE Control eXtension)   A special form of VBX designed to make adding OLE capabilities to an application easier for the programmer. Essentially, an OCX is a DLL with an added programmer and OLE interface.

ODBC (Open Database Connectivity)   A set of Windows function calls and other interface elements introduced by Microsoft. ODBC is designed to improve access to information contained in database files through the use of a common interface and data-independent access methods. Normally, ODBC relies on SQL to translate DBMS-specific commands from the client into a generic language. The ODBC agents on the server translate these SQL requests into server-specific commands.

OLE Control eXtension   *See* OCX

OLE-DB   See Object linking and embedding database

OLE (object linking and embedding)   The process of packaging a filename and any required parameters into an object and then pasting this object into the file created by another application. For example, you could place a graphic object within a word processing document or spreadsheet. When you look at the object, it appears as if you simply pasted the data from the originating application into the current application (similar to DDE). When linked, the data provided by the object automatically changes as you change the data in the original object. When embedded, the data doesn't change unless you specifically edit it, but the data retains the original format and you still use the original application to edit the data. Often you can start the originating application and automatically load the required data by double-clicking on the object. The newer OLE 2 specification allows for in-place data editing as well as editing in a separate application window.

ONE   *See* Netscape ONE (Open Network Environment)

Open Database Connectivity   *See* ODBC

PCT (Private Communication Technology)   A protocol being worked on by the IETF and Microsoft. Like SSL, PCT is designed to provide a secure method of communication between a client and server at the low protocol level. It can work with any high-level protocol such as HTTP, FTP, or TELNET. PCT is designed to prevent hackers from eavesdropping on communications between a client and server through the use of encryption, authentication, and digital signatures. As with SSL, client authentication is optional. PCT also assumes that you have TCP or another reliable transport protocol in place. It corrects some inherent weaknesses in SSL by providing extended cryptographic negotiation and other added features.

PDF   Portable Document Format

PEM (Privacy Enhanced Mail)   A set of four approved IETF specifications (IETF RFC1421 through IETF RFC1424) that define the methods for sending and receiving mail on the Internet. Of prime importance are techniques for encrypting and decrypting mail in such a way that optimal privacy is assured with a minimal amount of user interaction. The specification also covers topics related to mail encryption, including the certification of vendors to perform the service and the use of CSPs.

Privacy Enhanced Mail   *See* PEM

Private Communication Technology *See* PCT

Private key file *See* PVK

PVK (private key file) A file contained on either the client or server machine that allows full data encryption to take place. When the key in this file is combined with the public key provided with a file, the file becomes accessible. Since the PVK file never gets transmitted from one place to another, the level of data communication security is greatly increased. PVK files are used with all kinds of certificate-based communications. For example, getting a personal certificate from VeriSign or another organization involves creating a PVK on your computer. Developers also create a PVK for use with various types of Internet technologies such as ActiveX. The process of creating the private and public keys and assigning them to the actual component is called *signing*. In the same way, signed mail or other communications can greatly enhance security by making the author of the document known.

PWS Peer Web Services

RAD (rapid application development) A tool that allows you to design your program's interface and then write the commands to make that user interface do something useful. Visual Basic and Delphi are both examples of RAD programs.

Rapid application development *See* RAD

RDO Remote Data Objects

RDS Remote Data Services

Remote access The ability to use a remote resource as you would a local resource. In some cases, this also means downloading the remote resource to use as a local resource.

Remote procedure call *See* RPC

Rich Text Format	*See* RTF
RPC (remote procedure call)	The ability to use code or data on a machine as if it were local. This is an advanced capability that will eventually pave the way for decentralized applications.
RTF (Rich Text Format)	A file format originally introduced by Microsoft that allows an application to store formatting information in plain ASCII text. All commands begin with a backslash. For example, the \cf command tells an RTF-capable editor which color to use from the color table when displaying a particular section of text.
SACL (security access control list)	The SACL controls Windows' auditing feature. Every time a user or group accesses an object and the auditing feature for that object is turned on, Windows makes an entry in the audit log.
SDK	Software development kit
Secure Sockets Layer	*See* SSL
Security access control list	*See* SACL
Security identifier	*See* SID
ShellX (Shell extension)	A special application that gives some type of added values to the operating system interface. In most cases, the application must register itself with the registry before the operating system will recognize it.
SID (security identifier)	The part of a user's access token that identifies the user throughout the network—it's like having an account number. The user token that the SID identifies tells what groups the user belongs to and what privileges the user has. Each group also has a SID, so the user's SID contains references to the various group SIDs that he or she belongs to, not a complete set of group access rights. You would normally use the User Manager utility under Windows NT to change the contents of this access token.
S/MIME	Secure/Multipurpose Internet Mail Extensions

SQL (Structured Query Language) Most DBMSs use this language to exchange information. Some also use it as a native language. SQL provides a method for requesting information from the DBMS. It defines which table or tables to use, what information to get from the table, and how to sort that information.

SSL (Secure Sockets Layer) A W3C standard originally proposed by Netscape for transferring encrypted information from the client to the server at the protocol layer. Sockets allow low-level encryption of transactions in higher-level protocols such as HTTP, NNTP, and FTP. The standard also specifies methods for server and client authentication (though client site authentication is optional).

Stickey Keys One of several special features provided by Microsoft to help the physically challenged use computers better. This feature is provided as part of the Accessibility applet in Windows 95 and Windows NT 4.0.

Stream object An encapsulated data container used to transfer information from one object to another. For example, a stream object could move data from application memory to a file on disk.

Structured Query Language *See* SQL

S/WAN Secure/Wide Area Network

TCP/IP (transmission control protocol/Internet protocol) A standard communication line protocol developed by the U.S. Department of Defense. The protocol defines how two devices talk to each other. Think of the protocol as a type of language used by the two devices.

Token calls Part of the Windows NT security API that deals with user access to a particular object. To gain access to an object, the requesting object must provide a token. In essence, a token is a ticket to gain entrance to the secured object. The security API compares the rights provided by the requesting object's token with those required to gain entry to the secured object. If the requesting object's rights are equal to or greater than those required to gain entry, then the operating system grants access. Tokens are a universal form of entry under Windows NT and aren't restricted to the user or external applications. Even the operating system must use them.

UNC (universal naming convention) A method for identifying network resources without using specific locations. In most cases this convention is used with drives and printers, but it can also be used with other types of resources. A UNC normally uses a device name in place of an identifier. For example, a disk drive on a remote machine might be referred to as "\\AUX\DRIVE-C." The advantage of using a UNC is that the resource name won't change even if the resource location does (as would happen if users changed drive mappings on their machine).

Uniform resource locator *See* URL

Universal naming convention *See* UNC

Uri Universal Resource Identifier

URL (uniform resource locator) The basic method of identifying a location on the Internet. A resource could be a file, a Web site, or anything else you can access through this media. The URL always contains three essential parts. The first part identifies the protocol used to access the resource. For example, the letters "http" at the beginning of a URL always signify that the site uses the Hypertext Transfer Protocol and will present some type of visual information. The second part of the URL is the name of a host. For example, the most popular host name is www, which stands for World Wide Web. The third part of the URL is a domain. This is normally the name of the site machine and the kind of site you plan to access. (For example, MyCompany.com would tell you that the domain is a machine named MyCompany and that it's some kind of commercial site.) After the site information are directories, just like you have on your hard drive. So a URL like http://www. mycompany.com/mysite.html would point to a Web page that uses HTTP on the World Wide Web at mycompany.com.

VBA (Visual Basic for Applications) A form of Microsoft Visual Basic used by applications. It provides more capabilities than VBScript yet less than the full-fledged Visual Basic programming language. The basic tenet of this language is full machine access without a high learning curve. VBA was originally designed to allow users to create script-type macros and provide interapplication communication. It's been extended since that time to provide a higher-level programming language for times when VBScript doesn't provide enough capabilities to perform a specific task.

VBX (Visual Basic eXtension) A special form of DLL that contains functions as well as a programmer interface. The DLL part of VBX accepts requests from an application for specific services, such as opening a file. The programmer interface portion appears on the toolbar of a program, such as Visual Basic, as a button. Clicking the button creates one instance of that particular type of control.

Virtual Reality Modeling Language *See* VRML

Visual Basic eXtension *See* VBX

Visual Basic for Applications *See* VBA

VPN Virtual private network

VRML (Virtual Reality Modeling Language) A special scripting (scene description) language that allows a Web site to transfer vector graphic imaging information with a minimum of overhead. The value of this language is that it uses very little actual data to transfer the coordinate information required. VRML is still very much in the experimental stage—transaction speeds are a major concern due to the relatively narrow bandwidth of current dial-up connections and the multitude of changes that take place during a VRML session. Even using minimized data transfer doesn't make VRML a fast performer with the current state of technology.

W3C (World Wide Web Consortium) A standards organization essentially devoted to Internet security issues but also involved in other issues such as the special <OBJECT> tag required by Microsoft to implement ActiveX technology. The W3C first appeared on the scene in December 1994 when it endorsed SSL (Secure Sockets Layer). In February 1995 it also endorsed application-level security for the Internet. Its current project is the Digital Signatures Initiative—W3C presented it in May 1996 in Paris.

WAN (wide area network)   A grouping of two or more LANs in more than one physical location.

Wide area network   *See* WAN

World Wide Web Consortium   *See* W3C

WTS   Web Transaction Security

Index

NOTE: Page numbers in italics refer to illustrations or charts.